To my mother, who has sustained a natural goodness through all she has done and endured.

THE POLITICS OF EDUCATIONAL INNOVATION

Ernest R. House

University of Illinois
at Urbana-Champaign

McCutchan Publishing Corporation
2526 Grove Street
Berkeley, California 94704

ISBN: 0-8211-0754-2
Library of Congress Catalog Card Number: 74-12824

©1974 by McCutchan Publishing Corporation

Printed in the United States of America

Acknowledgments

Of the many who have helped me in thinking and writing these thoughts, I wish to express special thanks to Steve Lapan for invaluable assistance in reacting to most of the material; to Tom Hastings and the CIRCE group for providing the shield behind which I could covertly develop ideas; to Dave Harvey for serving as a fine abrasive to my thinking over the years; to those many of the Illinois Gifted Program who aroused my interest in this area and provided me with the opportunities; and to Lois Williamson, Mary Reiss, and Mary Brockett, who managed the indispensable task of deciphering my handwriting. Finally I must pay tribute to my family—Donna, Kristin, and Colby—without whose loving therapy much would not be possible.

Ernest R. House
Urbana, Illinois
May 5, 1974

Contents

Contents

Prologue

The Frozen Institution

In the winter in Chicago the wind is very cold. Light smoky clouds lie low to the ground, moving quickly against the black sky above them. Driven from the lake, they slide their way past building tops, drawn like a gauze cover over the chilled body of the city. Along the lake front, the wind dominates. Waves crash into the shore with only a thin frothy lip marking the tip from the opaque turbulence that is its force.

Over weeks as the waves pound the beach they freeze, creating huge and grotesque shapes. A great mass of ice ten feet high extends along the shore, not white, but dirty, like washwater, unrecognizable as ice except after puzzled thought. As each new wave crashes onto the shore, it leaves an accretion, a remembrance of its passage, but does not radically alter the structure.

Each day the wind shifts, but never ceases, so its effect seems erratic and bizarre. In the winter in Chicago when you walk along the lake shore you will see peculiar forms you will not recognize. You will not know the brackish substance of which they are composed, nor how they got that way.

The public schools are composed of substances so common that their study is a bore. Each feature etched on the mind of the child becomes a tiresome peculiarity to the adult. Only when we try to change them do we realize that we really do not understand their structure. Suddenly we encounter complexities we never envisioned. It scares us. It offends our sense of propriety.

I began investigating the substance of the schools as a new

teacher fourteen years ago, trying to introduce different teaching methods. I quickly learned that survival takes precedence over innovation, but I did retain enough spirit to become a demonstration teacher in one of the first demonstration centers for teaching gifted youth in Illinois. These centers, launched with federal assistance in 1963, represented one of the first large-scale change efforts in education. I later had the opportunity to become a state consultant for this program, flying the four dialect zones of Illinois and visiting incredibly diverse classrooms from Chicago to Cairo.

At that point I became involved in intensive teacher-training activities that utilized inductive teaching materials, videotaping, T-grouping, role playing, and self assessment techniques before these procedures became widely used in education. I was left to puzzle the effects, or lack of effects, of these extensive activities in the change literature I discovered in graduate school. I realized that any serious conceptualization of educational innovation must face an enormous conundrum: how can so much effort directed toward changing the schools produce so little change?

In 1967 an unparalleled opportunity was afforded me. The state decided to conduct a large-scale, four-year independent evaluation of the Illinois Gifted Program, and I was asked to direct it. In this study it was possible to assess the effects of various change activities, to understand in some detail why change had or had not occurred, and to do so in a scope that extended from the state level to the classroom. In short, the Illinois Gifted Program became the crucible of my understanding.

Since the conclusion of that evaluation I have had the opportunity to examine scores of projects as evaluator and consultant and to consider these insights in a wide variety of settings, and this has made me increasingly dissatisfied with prevailing conceptualizations of educational innovation. A few years ago I deliberately decided to organize my own insights and intuitions into a coherent framework. The search for explanations of concrete phenomena led me across many social science disciplines and into their eclectic application since no single disciplinary framework sufficed to bring my perceptions to bay.

The result, a unique and provocative view of educational innovation, is based on empirical research. It deals with the total sweep of innovation—where it originates, how it spreads among practitioners, and what its consequences are for the internal workings of the school. Particular emphasis is placed on how the internal political and social structures of the school respond to innovations and on how the school relates to larger social and institutional networks.

The book is developed on the theme that most innovation is dependent on face-to-face personal contacts and that these contacts condition the occurrence and frequency of innovation. The first chapter presents the substance, basis, and implications of this reasoning. The second chapter shows the influence of personal contacts (in the form of population centers) on the spread of educational innovations by outlining a model that describes how this occurs and applies it to education.

The third and fourth chapters address the major issue of the book—how the internal political structure of the school reacts to innovation. The basic argument is that the political and economic structure of the school allows only certain types of activities and prohibits others. Entrepreneurship (an advocate working within the system) is required to overcome the rigid internal structure if an innovation is to succeed. This results in other problems, particularly stemming from those excluded. The fourth chapter details the isolated and economically deprived environment that teachers work in, which forces them into a passive and sometimes resistant role regarding innovation. Essentially, a teacher receives few tangible rewards for adopting an innovation.

The fifth chapter embodies these ideas in a lively case study of the actual introduction of an innovation (PLATO) into school settings. PLATO is recognized as the most advanced computer-assisted instructional system in the world, and it is certain to receive wide attention in the coming decade. Here, however, the emphasis is on the internal politics and reactions of the school faculties and administration in five quite different junior colleges to the introduction of PLATO. The sixth chapter examines the painful path the teacher must tread in learning new vocational skills.

In relating educational innovation to the wider social setting, the seventh chapter confronts the matter of where innovations originate. The argument is that the conditions necessary to produce innovations do not exist within the schools and that most innovations originate outside, putting the schools in what is essentially a passive and defensive posture—at least the way the system now operates. This has serious implications for the development and promotion of innovation. The importance of belief systems for innovation is explored in the later half of the same chapter.

The eighth chapter describes not the legislation but the basic premises on which government policy has been based for the last decade, assumptions that are judged to be incorrect. What I have labeled the doctrine of transferability has misled government policy for at least ten years and has resulted in a massive failure of research and development efforts, yet the basic policies persist. Arguments presented earlier in the book are used to suggest change.

In the final chapter I take a global view of educational innovation in the total society and suggest why certain government policies persist in spite of repeated failure. Looking at the role of innovation in a technocratic society, I would suggest that the vertical division of labor implicit in the modern system creates a hierarchy of control with those at the top making the innovations and benefiting most from them while those at the bottom are robbed of initiative and not equally benefited.

The societal and governmental push on education is generally seen as an attempt to modernize the traditional educational structure so that it can be more fully integrated into the political economy of an industrialized society. Possible consequences for both education and society are outlined in considerable detail, with emphasis on education as an instrument for economic development and questions raised about the effectiveness and morality of the system.

Overall the book presents what I would call a political economy of educational innovation. I conceive of political economy as dealing with the interrelationships between political policies and economic processes and their mutual influence on social institutions. The political economy of educational innovation examines the political and economic processes of the school and illustrates how these social processes relate to government policies and to society generally. Politics as used here refers to the interaction, interests, and rivalry of factional groups whether they exist in the school, the region, the state, or the nation, especially as the groups compete for resources and attempt to influence and control each other and their own members.

Where certain features of the conceptual scheme could be modeled, I have attempted to do so. The whole process is too complex to be represented by a "model" of innovation. Although there are several schematizations, the nontechnical reader should not be misled. They are only shorthand notations for representing certain phenomena, and the verbal arguments are neither dependent on the schemes nor more valid because of them.

It is unfortunate that much of the book had to be written in research jargon, a tribute to the socializing power of vocational endeavor, for I am not easily socialized. Broad sections, however, are more readable—more so in the latter part of the book. I have also tried to provide ample concrete illustrations throughout, drawing examples from two major innovations in order to enhance the continuity of the arguments.

So, on a warm, beautiful day in May, I end this book begun sometime before with a winter metaphor. The ice has long since melted along the lake shore, and the scent of new-cut grass drifts through the window. Even though the seasons have changed, it is more evident to me now than before that the schools are as pounded as a windward shore, and that they take their shape from the social winds and waters.

It is also clearer to me now than in the beginning where these forces originate and how they are converted into the substance of the schools. There is an implicit order in American society basic to all else—the order of the institutions. The schools do not exist freely outside that order; they are an integral part of it. Education can deviate only in the direction and to the extent that society allows. To understand the substance of the schools and their peculiar forms, you must understand these basic elements. Whatever the season, education is a frozen institution.

Chapter 1

The Primacy of Personal Contact

PERSONAL CONTACT AS CONVEYER OF INNOVATIONS

To control the flow of personal contact is to control innovation. As the flow of blood is essential to human life, so direct personal contact is essential to the propagation of innovation, and, by tracing the flow of personal contact and personal influence, one can chart the likely course of innovation. Who knows whom and who talks to whom are powerful indicators of where and when an innovation is accepted, or if it is accepted at all. Just as a medical researcher might study the action of a hormone through knowing the circulatory system of the body, so might a researcher study innovation by tracing the map of personal contact. Perhaps no group has perfected the tracing of innovation (though not its politics or economics) as the geographers have.

In his studies of a small geographical area in Sweden, the Swedish geographer Torsten Hagerstrand (1953) found that diffusion of innovations, such as radios and new agricultural practices, occurred in a very regular manner. When he mapped the acceptance of the innovations over space and over time, three distinct stages became apparent. First, local concentrations of acceptances of innovations occurred, which Hagerstrand called "initial agglomerations." The locations of the initial agglomerations tended to be the same regardless of the innovation. In stage two the innovations disseminated radially from initial agglomerations in a regular manner, with acceptance decreasing as distance from the center increased. Simultaneously new secondary agglomerations developed, which grew in the same fashion and developed their own concentrations of accept-ances. Meanwhile, initial centers would "condense," that is, fill in their immediate area with ever-greater densities of acceptances. Final-ly, in the third stage, growth ceased. Saturation had occurred. The innovation had finished diffusing.

Hagerstrand was struck by the spatial regularity of the process. No matter what the innovation, the pattern was similar—like a great innovative wave had washed across the area. The only difference he noted was that general innovations, such as the radio, had more dispersed initial agglomerations and less orderly and regular dissemin-ations than agricultural innovations. (All innovations studied were externally invented and not improved upon locally during their acceptance.) Confronted with the regularity of his diffusion maps, he began seeing diffusion as a spatial distribution across social groups.

The next step taken by Hagerstrand (1967) was to build simula-tion models to duplicate the diffusion maps he had plotted. Reason-ing that innovation can be accepted by a person only if he is aware of its existence, he assumed, in simulation Model I, that distribution of information was necessary, if not sufficient, for adoption. He further differentiated between "public information," which is communicated to a majority of the population without having its meaning altered by a third party (for example, mass media), and "private information," which is given only to a single person. People responding to "public information" should lead to a random distribution of innovations, but this was apparently not the case. Empirical mapping indicated a strong "proximity" or "neighborhood" effort consistent with "private information" conveyed in face-to-face relationships. From this, Hager-strand inferred private information fields in which a person is in re-peated contact with only a limited number of other persons. Em-ploying a similar concept in his studies of Swedish emigrants to America, he reasoned that necessary information about employment and housing possibilities must be private and precede migration.

Hagerstrand's simulation Model II, assuming a private informa-tion field and face-to-face contact, much more accurately duplicated the actual diffusion maps he had constructed. Since the intensity of personal contact decreased very rapidly with distance, in fact with the square of the distance, geographic distance became the main factor in the diffusion of innovation. It was also found that the agricultural population had a more limited information field than the urban population. As in Model I, Hagerstrand used Monte Carlo techniques to simulate the actual diffusion process.

In his final model, Model III, Hagerstrand tried to account for resistance to innovation acceptance. Models I and II assumed that the stimulus for acceptance was information about the *properties* of the new phenomenon. Model III assumed that it was information about the acceptance of the innovation by certain persons that produced additional acceptances. In other words, one does not buy a radio when he hears about it; he buys it when he hears that his neighbors and friends have bought one. The focus then shifts from information about objects to information about persons.

The total diffusion process may be conceptualized as a chain reaction. Suppose that a Ping-Pong ball is released and bounces around until it hits a spring triggered to fire another ball and this process is repeated many times as each of the balls continues to bounce. Eventually hundreds of balls fill the air. To this Hagerstrand added levels of resistance to change, arbitrarily assuming that some springs might require more hits than one to fire a ball. Adding resistance in effect slows the initial rise of the traditional "S" curve associated with a chain reaction and also produces more spatial concentration. In other words, one must build up a greater critical mass to overcome resistance.

Hence, Hagerstrand (1968) saw innovation diffusion occurring through a network of social contacts. These face-to-face networks exist at the local, regional, national, and international levels. Since the communication links of the average individual rapidly decrease in number with the square of the increasing distance, proximity is a prime factor. According to Hagerstrand, adoption of an innovation is the outcome of an individual learning process so that only factors related to the effective flow of information need be considered (Brown, n.d.).

The destination of personal messages depends on the sender's network of interpersonal contacts, and the configuration of this network is dependent on the presence of such barriers as distance. Resistance may also be social, resulting from values inconsistent with adoption, or economic, responding to the pressure of practicalities. Hagerstrand does not further characterize resistance. There is, therefore, a hierarchy of networks of social communication through which innovation filters from a few innovation centers to the general population.

Hagerstrand's work has provided a powerful stimulus in the

field of geography, both in the study of innovation diffusion, which is considered a part of spatial analysis, and in the application of Monte Carlo simulation methods. Brown (1968) has surveyed various fields for potentially useful innovation diffusion models. He has examined Rappaport's study of networks, which recognizes social distance bias, island model bias, and acquaintance circle bias, as well as geographic distance bias in information flow, thereby extending the idea of distortion in information flow to social structures. Rappaport's work is theoretical rather than empirical.

One useful idea that Hagerstrand did not incorporate into his model is the differentiation between active adopters, who pass on word of the innovation, and passive adopters, who do not. Innovation diffusion essentially ends with the passive adopter. This distinction comes from epidemiology where those who may get a disease are classified as "susceptibles"; those who can communicate it to others, as "infectives"; and those who have the disease but cannot communicate it, as "removals."

A full-scale epidemic (innovation diffusion) occurs only when the relative removal rate (the ratio of the absolute removal rate to the absolute infective rate) is less than the number of susceptibles or if the population density exceeds the relative removal rate. This idea is interesting because it indicates a threshold level below which the disease (innovation) cannot spread to the whole population. Also, the most passive areas are those in which earlier adoption occurred. In his migration work, Hagerstrand distinguished between an "active migrant," one who seeks a new place because of his values, and a "passive migrant," one who seeks a new place because he has acquaintances there. Presumably the "active migrant" moves to a place where characteristics of place utility compare more favorably to his values.

In this book personal contact is seen as a basic element of educational change. Inducing change in the behavior of a number of persons requires, in effect, establishing a new social system. The number of face-to-face contacts required to maintain a social system is high indeed, and, if we choose to induce such a system directly, the great number of necessary personal contacts requires astronomical sums of money and personal involvement. It is not surprising that large-scale change programs have been resplendent failures. Financial and interpersonal costs are so high that sponsors usually resort to impersonal communications modes like the dissemination of materials. Newsletters and conference methods are relatively ineffective. Anything that impedes personal contact impedes the diffusion of innovation and, as we will argue later, impedes invention.

Why face-to-face contact is so important becomes obvious after short reflection. Indirect contact suffices to spread simple, well-structured, routine information; direct contact is much more effective where there is an element of uncertainty or when results are unpredictable. These are likely to be encountered in problem-solving situations, planning, or negotiation, any of which might involve innovation.

Tornquist (1970) has studied contact systems in government and business organizations. In some organizations direct personal contacts may represent less than 10 percent of total contacts. Among new contacts, however, the number is overwhelming. The most critical contacts are face-to-face. Nor have technical advances like the telephone reduced the need for such contacts. Managing directors spend 75 to 95 percent of their time in contacts, of which one-third are direct.

External direct contacts, those outside the organization, are confined primarily to the highest decision levels in organizations. Lower levels make their contacts primarily via the telephone or by mail, if at all. Tornquist contends that it is direct personal contacts alone that have a perceptible influence on the location of activities of organizations. To the geographer, decisions as to where to locate a plant, a town, a road, or some other facility are big decisions. Furthermore, such decisions always involve the movement of people.

In organizations the greatest number of contacts by far are made by personnel at the higher levels. Directors and high-level administrators spend forty to fifty hours each week in face-to-face information exchanges (Gould and Tornquist, 1971) while, at a secondary level, administrators spend about twenty hours a week in such exchanges. Further down there are hardly any direct external contacts at all, and information must flow up one system, be transmitted at the highest levels, and then return to the lowest levels. Direct contacts and information flow have a strong hierarchic structure, as does innovation diffusion within organizations.

Such contacts are also structured geographically. The overwhelming number of such contacts are between and within key cities, generally the capitals and the largest cities. For example, an analysis of air travel in Sweden reveals that Stockholm, Göteborg, and

Malmö account for two-thirds of all direct decision making, and they contain almost all higher-level job opportunities. Personal contacts—and hence, innovation diffusion—depend heavily on the transportation system, which is, itself, closely linked to urbanization. Once an urban hierarchy of the type discussed here emerges, extremely stable structures exist that give the course of new innovations a high degree of predictability. New innovations follow the same course as old ones. Only changes in the urbanization pattern bring about changes in the total pattern. The spread of urbanization increases direct contacts and promotes innovation.

In summary, direct personal contacts are the medium through which innovations must flow. Innovation diffusion is directly proportional to the number, frequency, depth, and duration of such contacts. Networks of personal contacts are not random. They are highly predictable and stable, strongly structured by the hierarchial nature of organizations and the nature of urbanization. The influence of these forces on innovation diffusion in education is profound.

PERSONAL CONTACT NETWORKS IN EDUCATION

Abbot (1965) has accused H. Thelen of sardonically suggesting that educational diffusion has three stages: enthusiasm, vulgarization or spread, and institutionalization. Thelen may have been closer to the truth than even he realized. It is not difficult to see educational innovations proceeding in a Hagerstrandian fashion along the social networks in education. I see a friend at a meeting and tell him about the latest thing we have done in evaluation. He goes home and tries it. One of our graduate students goes to Michigan to see a football game. While there he talks to some of his old teacher-colleagues and tells them what he has been doing, and they want to see some of the materials. Neither of these particular incidents could have been predicted, yet it can be predicted that each individual will continue to interact in his social groups. (Hagerstrand handled the unpredictability with Monte Carlo techniques.) Ideas move along the social networks of personal acquaintance.

If one could define the social networks in education, he could presumably trace the course of an innovation. We are not yet able to do that, but we do know a considerable amount about the educational systems. In the United States the system is highly decentralized, both geographically and governmentally. This means that, as in Hagerstrand's diffusion maps, distance plays an important role. In a rural, homogeneous, evenly distributed population, an innovation developed in one place should diffuse radially from its point of origin. Through regular but unpredictable contacts, secondary agglomeration centers spring up and begin diffusing the innovation. For a country as large as the United States, many secondary agglomerations are needed for the innovation to spread to a large proportion of school districts (for the moment referred to as single units). Urbanization greatly warps the entire process.

There is another important impediment: each school district is a separate governmental unit. This kind of barrier significantly impedes the flow of information and, hence, diffusion. In light of these difficulties, no innovation is likely to be accepted in a majority of school districts. It is this decentralization that federal officers lament when they talk of the lack of a system.

Education is also characterized by considerable fragmentation. The research community is an entity all its own, having little communication with, or relevance for, practitioners. Ideas travel relatively quickly within the research community itself, but scarcely creep from there to schools because the social networks simply are not there. An example of information transfer among researchers has been described by Paisely (1972). Invisible colleges consist of an informal communication network that trades preprints and other informal messages on a particular topic. The group maintains contact through the mail and a continuous circuit of meetings. These invisible colleges are limited to less than a hundred members, and they transfer information that is timely, relevant, and authoritative. Since they are exclusive and insular, however, they may miss an important idea that is at the periphery of their field. Invisible colleges greatly facilitate horizontal transfer of knowledge, but do little for vertical transfer.

Practitioners are normally divided into administrators and teachers. Administrators are further divided into superintendents and principals; teachers, into their areas of specialization. There was a rapid diffusion of the concept of team teaching through administrative ranks, which probably resulted from ready access to the administrative network. Even though such programs were established and teachers taught in them, however, teacher behavior remained relatively unchanged. Many administrative innovations do not become teaching innovations since the teacher's world is not that of the administrator. Professionalization, which enhances innovation diffusion within professional groups by promoting social interaction, inhibits diffusion across professional boundaries.

Since the basic diffusion process is the transport of innovations across social networks, interactions are complex. (How many networks must there be in a professional population of over two million people, crisscrossed by geographic, social, professional, and organizational barriers?) Teachers, however, remain isolated in classrooms within schools, which does not enhance the diffusion of new ideas within the profession. In terms of epidemiology, if a teacher were "infected" with an innovation, it would be difficult for him to pass it on except to teachers in his school who would, in turn, be isolated from other professionals. The teacher is, in effect, a removal or passive adopter with little chance of infecting anyone else. The relative removal rate is much higher than the population density (teachers being dispersed through the general population), and the innovation cannot reach the threshold rate where it can be diffused to the whole population. The very structure of the school system prevents an innovation pandemic.

There are two more complications. When geographers talk about innovations, they are talking about an externally invented innovation like a radio that is not improved upon locally during acceptance. However rarely teachers may adopt an innovation, they almost never adopt it as a whole (Gallagher, 1970; House, Steele, and Kerins, 1972). Rather, they adopt only bits and pieces, worrying about how even these will fit into the local setting. As always, they are concerned about their social group, and this has profound implications for educational change. The innovations themselves undergo transformation.

A second complication is that, just as spatial analysts have little to say about the reception of an idea, they also have little to say about its origin other than that the emission of an innovation from a primary node is likely to be a function of some form of "stress," such as density of information or congestion. Where, then, does an innovation originate?

Educational change might be conceived like wave motion (an analogy not to be taken too literally). Innovations generated or broadcast under certain organizational conditions—by certain organizations at certain times—are diffused through social networks previously described. They are picked up by receptors yet to be defined but roughly synonymous with schools. During transmission the innovation is transformed and, if received, is again transformed in accord with the structure of the receiver. A receiver is not a blank slate on which innovation may be writ, but is itself active, actually seeking some messages and forcefully rejecting others.

There are many sources of messages, as there are many broadcasting stations. The messages are sometimes similar, sometimes disparate. As they traverse the social networks, however, the waves intermingle, sometimes in phase, reinforcing one another, and sometimes out of phase, conflicting with one another. The receiver picks up garbled messages, usually because several messages have been transmitted simultaneously, which must somehow be diciphered. Only under rare circumstances—a "lab" school having direct contacts with inventors—are there any laser-pure messages.

If one compares the original innovation with its implementation, it looks impure, more like a mongrelization of noise, because of the perversity of the receiver. But that is only because the sender sees just the pure light of his own message. The receiver, the teacher, sees a melange of messages traveling to him over his own personal social networks. He integrates them, as he understands them, based on his own reference groups. In those rare cases where innovator and teachers work closely together, the teacher's view may be very close to the inventor's, blocking other messages. As the teacher moves away from this closed situation, however, the demands of other social groups become increasingly strong in proportion to distance, both geographic and social.

SUMMARY

Innovation diffusion may be conceived as being dependent on personal contact, although the two are not synonymous. Personal contacts can impede the spread of an innovation under certain circumstances. Normally, however, if an innovation is to diffuse at all, it must follow the social paths blazed by repeated personal contact. Geographers have discovered this phenomenon in tracing innovations across spatial distances and have been able to replicate their empirical maps by making a few simple assumptions. Other quantitative formulations, such as the spread of diseases in epidemiology, have also been suggested as models of the innovation diffusion process.

Personal contact is critical for innovation diffusion because it allows a full-fledged information exchange and the full exercise of personal and social influence, as every door-to-door salesman knows. It is the "private" information, defined by the person's "information field" that is most influential. Anything that structures the flow of face-to-face contacts is likely to have a profound effect on innovation diffusion. While geographers have explored the effects of geographic distance, social distance may be even more important in an urbanized society.

Formal organizations, in particular, structure face-to-face contacts in a strongly hierarchic manner, thus ultimately regulating the flow of innovations. Contact systems, both within and between organizations, are critical. Personnel at the upper levels of the organization spend a much larger proportion of their time in direct personal contact, and contact with external groups is almost exclusively handled by top administrators. This gives them a regulatory power over incoming information and, consequently, over which innovations will diffuse among organizations. In a highly urbanized society the geography and hierarchy become merged into what has been called the "urban hierarchy" of modern society, such as the Stockholm-Götegorg-Malmö triangle of Sweden. Such cities have become the innovation centers of the country.

What impact do these phenomena have on educational innovation? Schools and teachers are fragmented and decentralized and exist within the same societal structures. The flow of direct personal contact within and between educational structures has much to do with the diffusion of educational innovation, which can be analyzed by studying the social structure of education and the diffusion of innovation through different social groups.

Chapter 2

The Spread of Innovations

TEACHER AND ADMINISTRATOR INNOVATIONS

Innovations may be distinguished by the level of the adopting unit. Household innovations spread through private households or from individual to individual. Refrigerators, televisions, and classroom innovations adopted by individual teachers (we contend) are household innovations. An entrepreneurial innovation, on the other hand, has direct consequences for people other than the adopter and his family or the teacher and his classroom. Buying a refrigerator for the first time is an example of a household innovation, but locating a Sears store where people might purchase a refrigerator is an entrepreneurial innovation that directly affects many other people.

Obviously, household and entrepreneurial innovations are not independent of each other. One cannot buy a refrigerator unless there is a store in which to buy one; nor can the store be successful unless individuals purchase refrigerators. Neither can a teacher adopt an innovation for his classroom unless it is made available through the actions of an administrator. Availability is particularly important because of the relative isolation of the teacher. Teachers are associated with household innovations; administrators, with entrepreneurial ones.

Household and entrepreneurial innovations follow somewhat different rules. Several differences are worth mentioning:

1. Entrepreneurial innovation often involves a higher social, economic, or political risk.

2. For household innovation, each new adoption increases the speed of diffusion. People often adopt because they see acquaintances

16

adopting. The snowball effect is powerful. One teacher using new materials increases the chances that other teachers in the school may do so, some of which also occurs in entrepreneurial innovation. Some firms may adopt because others have done so, yet entrepreneurial innovation is also competitive in the sense that a first adoption may block rather than facilitate further adoptions. How many Sears stores does a town need? Entrepreneurial innovation entails a threshold level that allows repetition only in larger towns. Chicago has many Sears stores. In a sense, the adopting unit is the town rather than the individual. Likewise, how many innovations does a school need?

3. With household innovation there is a larger random element in determining when an individual may adopt. For idiosyncratic reasons an individual may import a refrigerator from a hundred miles away, thus getting around the fact that there is no outlet nearby. The certainty that there is a Sears store increases in larger communities, depending on the town's place in the urban hierarchy. Likewise, one teacher may use novel teaching techniques long before one would expect, considering his place in the communications network. Most, however, will not.

It is interesting that most diffusion research has been conducted on rural populations (Hagerstrand, 1967; Rogers, 1962) and has been concerned with the diffusion of new agricultural innovations. The rural population is homogeneously spread out so that "contagious" diffusion (one person talking to another person equal and similar in social status) is the rule. In such cases the major factor limiting personal contact and, hence, innovation spread is distance. How far can one go to see his neighbor? On a map the spread of such innovations appears to consist of regular waves undulating from fixed sources.

As urbanization increases, population density shifts and becomes more heterogeneous; barriers such as social status become more significant than distance in impeding personal communication. In such a situation innovations leap from one concentration of population to the next in size, creating an urban hierarchy. Innovations may also spread to the nearest concentration of population, but size predominates over distance as the key to dispersal.

Hence, household innovations have the individual as the adopting unit and are associated with rural population dispersals where the major dissemination mode is "contagious." Entrepreneurial innovations have organizations, towns, and groups as the adopting units, with dissemination proceeding from larger to smaller, and might properly be called "urban" innovations.

THE POWER OF POPULATION CENTERS

The first innovation in a region is usually introduced through the largest city or the city that has the highest exchange of ideas and people with other regions. In Illinois this would almost always be Chicago.

From the first adopting agency the innovation follows a combination of two routes: one leads from town to town along the physical transportation networks; the other leads from the largest to smaller and smaller towns down the urban hierarchy. The first is most important in less developed regions; the second dominates in more developed (urbanized) regions.

Pedersen (1970) has proposed a model to explain the empirical regularities of the diffusion process. Four subprocesses presented in the model are:

1. exposure to the innovation;
2. a general willingness to adopt innovation;
3. the economic and technical feasibility of an innovation; and
4. the presence of a potential entrepreneur.

Exposure to an innovation is a function of the information about the innovation flowing between towns. Spread of information T between two towns i and j can be described by the "gravity" model where P_i and P_j are the populations of the towns, r_{ij} is the distance between them, and X is a parameter that has larger values in under-

$$T_{ij} = \frac{k P_i P_j}{\left(r_{ij} X \right)}$$

developed regions and is small in developed areas. This says simply that information flow between towns (or schools) is proportional to the product of the populations, but inversely proportional to the distance between them. In less developed regions, X will be squared or cubed, and distance will be relatively more important than the size of the town. In urbanized areas, X will be smaller, probably "1," and the population element will be more important. Hence, this formulation captures both contagious and hierarchical diffusion.

The above formulation assumes, however, that populations are homogeneous and that all citizens participate equally in communication flow. This clearly is not the case, as indicated by Tornquist's studies (1970) of hierarchy in organizations. Innovation diffusion may be influenced through differences in per capita participation in the communication flow and through differences in the level of information necessary before innovation is adopted. Inhabitants with different characteristics participate to different degrees in information flows, even in relatively loosely organized entities like towns.

The social structure is the dominating force. In organizations, only top-level administrators, a very small proportion of the organizational population, have numerous external direct contacts. In schools only a few administrators participate freely in such information flows. Teachers are greatly restricted in their professional contacts, and the effect of such restrictions on the gravity formulation is to reduce greatly the population figures and, hence, the information flow and innovation diffusion between towns, organizations, and schools. In gravity formulation, the participating population would be more the size of the administrator population. The inhibiting effect of organizational stratification on organizational change is recognized (Hage and Aiken, 1970).

Innovation diffusion is also limited by the economic and technical feasibility of an innovation for a given town. Problems of scale are particularly important. Many products can be produced economically only on a certain scale, and some innovations can be adopted only by units of a certain size. For many innovations there will be a threshold unit size below which an innovation cannot be adopted or sustained. Below this point further diffusion is possible only with increased growth. Generally the threshold level necessary to support innovation increases during industrialization and urbanization, and, as the threshold level increases, the smallest units will be the last to adopt and the first to discontinue the innovation.

Cast in these terms, what does the model of entrepreneurial innovation diffusion mean? Part of the answer is given by a series of simulations carried out by Pedersen (1970, pages 224-226):

The stronger the distance decay (undeveloped, rural areas), the closer diffusion will follow physical distance; the weaker the distance decay, the closer the diffusion will follow the urban hierarchy. In less economically developed regions there should be a spatially defined innovation wave.

The weaker the distance decay (urbanized regions), the more rapid the diffusion process. Diffusion time should decrease as economic development increases.

High threshold innovations should terminate sooner because they reach a smaller number of units. As scale of innovation increases, diffusion over time decreases. Fewer units are involved and diffusion is faster.

If the rate of population participation decreases with unit size, the diffusion process will be retarded and diffusion down the urban hierarchy will be stronger.

The low frequency of entrepreneurs will slow down diffusion more in smaller units and the more so for spatial diffusion rather than for hierarchical diffusion. Intervening nonadopters will retard the diffusion of all stages of the spatial "contagious" process but only in the later stages of the hierarchical one since entrepreneurial talent will be sufficiently available in larger units.

THE EFFECT OF URBANIZATION—AN EXAMPLE

How relevant are these concepts to the diffusion of educational innovations? In 1963 the state of Illinois initiated a program for gifted students that provided state funds to school districts to support local activities for such students. Participation in the program was voluntary, and a school district had to submit a plan and a tentative budget to receive money, which was awarded automatically, on what was essentially a per student basis. Each school district was plotted on a map of Illinois according to the year it entered the program (requested state money), which shows the pattern of diffusion among districts. (Note that this is an entrepreneurial innovation indicating administrative action to receive extra funds, and it does not indicate what was done with the funds—an important qualification.) Figure 2-1 shows the total spread of gifted programs after five years. No trend is immediately apparent. The story is quite different, however, if the spread is shown year by year.

No data were available before the 1963-64 academic year, shown in Figure 2-2. During the first year of operation the gifted programs were located almost exclusively in the standard metropolitan areas of the state, most with populations above forty thousand. The Chicago area was not plotted on this map because of the high density

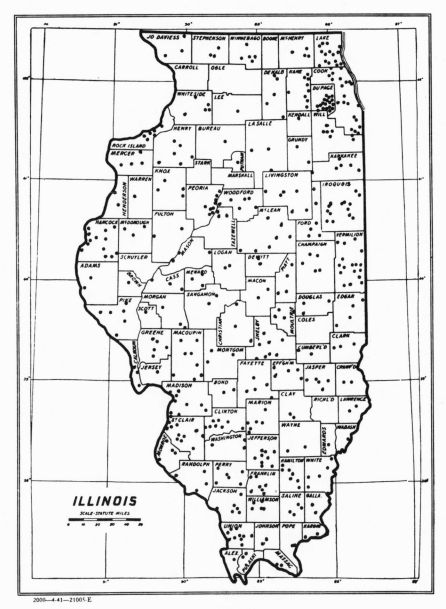

FIGURE 2-1

Total spread of gifted programs in Illinois after five years

FIGURE 2-2
Spread of gifted programs in Illinois for the year 1963-64

of towns on this scale. First-year adoption was predominantly in the Chicago area, the East St. Louis area in the southwest, the Carbondale-Marion area in the south, the Champaign-Urbana area to the east, and the larger cities of Danville, Decatur, Springfield, Quincy, and Peoria stretched across the state and having an average population of about eighty thousand. In the north, the Chicago area spills over into suburban DuPage and Lake Counties. The initial dominance of the metropolitan areas is clear, establishing the urban hierarchy for educational as well as noneducational innovations in Illinois.

Figure 2-3 shows the districts entering the second year, 1964-65. They follow very closely along U.S. Route 66, running between Chicago and St. Louis, and U.S. Route 40, moving across the state northeast from St. Louis. In the mid-1960's these were the two major roads in the state. In the northern part, several of the adopting districts lie along U.S. Route 20, the major northwest route across the state from the Chicago area. A small amount of contagious diffusion out of the Carbondale-Marion area appears in the south. The influence of the major transportation routes linking the urban hierarchy is apparent.

Figure 2-4 shows the districts joining the program in the third academic year, 1965-66. Very heavy contagious diffusion occurred out of the Carbondale-Marion area in the south and the East St. Louis area in the southwest. Both of the regions of contagious diffusion are rural and lie beyond the cities themselves. Possible contagious diffusion is seen in both the east central and the Chicago areas. Part of the sudden jump in numbers of programs is due to the fact that state agents in the metropolitan areas were deliberately visiting districts to persuade them to apply for state funds. A deliberate change strategy was in progress, but it had to work within the overall pattern.

The fourth year, 1966-67, is mapped in Figure 2-5. Heavy concentrations in Vermilion, Shelby, and Moultrie Counties in eastern Illinois represent the fact that the state education agency for the first time approved awarding funds to consortia of school districts. In each of these counties individuals from an enterprising district organized the school districts under one proposal and handled the funds. Many small districts that were not formerly involved entered the program, an interesting example of the threshold effect and entrepreneurialism. The districts had seen themselves as too small to

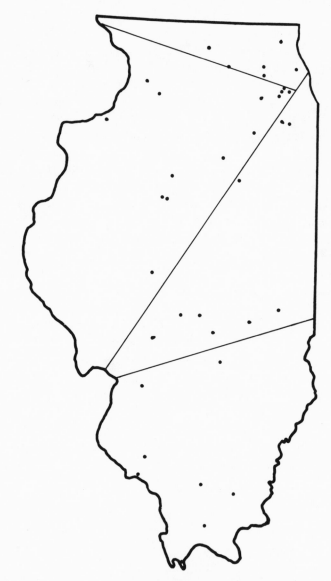

FIGURE 2-3
Spread of gifted programs in Illinois for the year 1964-65

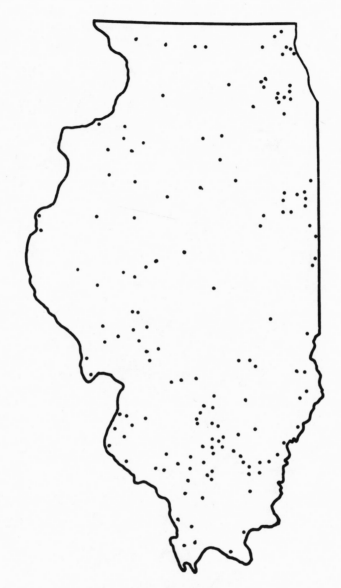

FIGURE 2-4
Spread of gifted programs in Illinois for the year 1965-66

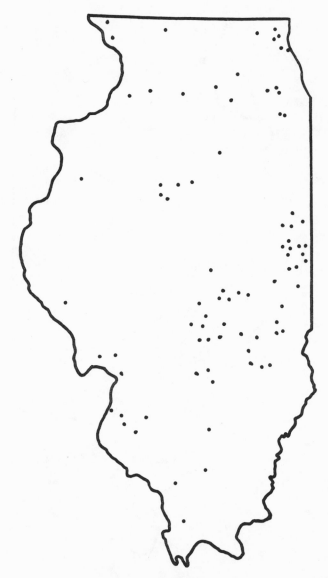

FIGURE 2-5
Spread of gifted programs in Illinois for the year 1966-67

participate. More contagious diffusion radiated into less developed areas. The centers in a line in the northern part of the state lie along another major east-west route, U.S. Route 6, connecting Joliet and southern Chicago in the east to Rock Island-Davenport in the west. Again, the explanation is simple: it is easier to travel on a major road—thus the spread of gifted programs.

The fifth year, 1967-68, is mapped in Figure 2-6. The major concentrations in central Illinois represent the organizing influence of several Title III projects promoted under the Elementary and Secondary Education Act (ESEA). These federally funded projects were regional and organized small school districts to get state funds in Hancock, McLean, Champaign, and other counties across the central part of the state. Contagious diffusion continued from the metropolitan areas to the southern part of the state, a rural area.

Again, Figure 2-1 shows all the districts receiving funds in 1967-68. Two areas of the state, the northwest and the southeast, show relatively few gifted programs. These areas were also the slowest to adopt them. There are no major urban centers and no major roads in either of these regions. Nor were there federal Title III funds to organize the districts in the northwest. In addition, the state disallowed cooperatives and consortia soon thereafter, thus prohibiting joint efforts.

Next slowest to adopt the programs were certain regions of central Illinois and regions in the south furthest removed from the Carbondale-Marion area. The most orderly contagious diffusion pattern, showing regular waves, appears far to the south, the most economically underdeveloped region in the state.

Thus, Pedersen's model explains a considerable part of the diffusion of gifted programs in Illinois. Most of the findings derived from his simulations are also supported. The urban hierarchy dominates, yet contagious diffusion is most apparent in small-town, less economically developed areas. Low entrepreneurial frequency retarded diffusion most in the less developed regions.

It is important to recognize that there is also a personal element involved in the explanation of this diffusion pattern. A participant in the program, Gordon Hoke, briefly explained the pattern in terms of events and personalities. Initially "demonstration centers" (public schools demonstrating model programs) were located in the metropolitan areas. During the first few years only a few programs were

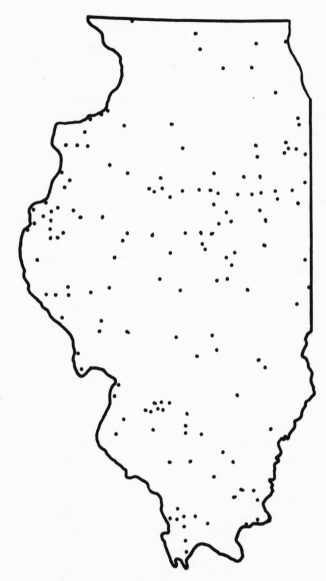

FIGURE 2-6
Spread of gifted programs in Illinois for the year 1967-68

generated by those who visited these centers. The third year, two summer institutes to train cadres of teachers and pressure from the state coordinator to get directors of local demonstration centers to move out of their centers and become "extension agents" selling programs and providing some in-service training to school personnel increased the number of participating districts. Special one-day workshops for school administrators, which outlined in eight basic steps how to obtain state funds for the gifted, were held around the state. These trends continued during the fourth year, and consortia were approved and organized in various counties. Regional training institutes were then held around the state. By the fifth year the special training institutes were losing strength. The key activist in the state agency left, and in certain counties the impact of federal Title III organizing activities was felt. Growth became spotty.

A few areas never developed beyond the third year because the original Office of Education seed money for the demonstration centers ran out; the powerful demonstration center coordinator left; and the demonstration directors themselves became more "elitist," refusing to work as much in the field. Such a history captures the personal encounters and events that shape diffusion on a day-by-day basis. Such events are no doubt accurate. Yet it is remarkable how such personal encounters were shaped over a five-year period by urbanization patterns, transportation routes, and administrative activities. Even though the major figures were acting deliberately and willfully, the innovation diffusion pattern still followed Pedersen's model.

After the fifth year of operation, the diffusion of gifted programs in Illinois reached its zenith and began an actual decline. The spread of programs is represented in Figure 2-7. Even at its peak in 1967-68, the 452 participating school districts were only 34 percent of the 1,315 districts in Illinois at that time. Figure 2-7 also indicates the decay of innovation diffusion over time. The number of participating districts declined from 452 to 365 between 1967 and 1970. Yet consolidation of school districts reduced the total number of districts in the state from 1,315 to 1,175 so that the percentage of participating districts stabilized at around one-third.

Which districts participated and which did not? Very simply, the larger ones participated, and the very small ones did not. The third of the districts participating contained over 80 percent of the student population in the state. The first participating districts were

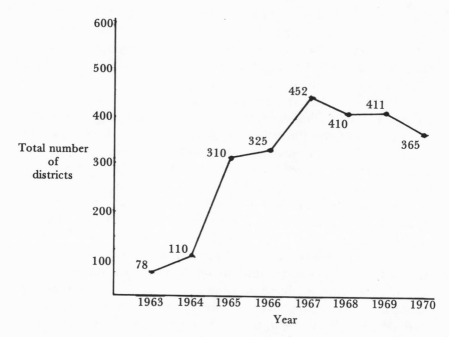

FIGURE 2-7
Number of districts participating in the Illinois plan

the large ones in urban areas. Not only were the very small, non-urban districts the last to adopt; most of them never adopted a program at all, a threshold limitation. When school districts are plotted by size and frequency, the distribution looks much like a chi-square distribution with one or two degrees of freedom. There are very few school districts with a great number of students and, even with extensive consolidation, there are hundreds of districts with just a few students. For the state as a whole this represented a high degree of urbanization and a low diffusion time. The total gifted program diffusion peaked in only five years, a remarkably short time compared to usual fifty-year estimates for most educational innovations. This speed resulted from urbanization and the high threshold level required to support such a program.

It is interesting that the states leading in gifted education in the 1960's were Illinois, California, New York, and, later, Connecticut, Florida, and Pennsylvania. The affluent, urbanized nature of these states is apparent. Why Illinois was a leader is related to entrepreneurship growing out of the University of Illinois laboratory school for the gifted and the fact that the leading scholar on gifted youth, James Gallagher, was at the university. This entrepreneurship was stimulated by a grant from the Office of Education to establish model "demonstration centers" to disseminate new educational materials. The laboratory school, University High, had just developed "new math" materials under Max Beberman. It needed a market for its new curriculum materials, and the director of the school, David Jackson, orchestrated a vast undertaking that even included the governor of the state. The leading state-wide gifted program in the United States resulted. Interstate diffusion of gifted programs would also make an interesting study. An extensive analysis of entrepreneurship appears later in this book under intraschool diffusion, but it is operative at all levels. It is important to remember that the receipt of state funds to begin a gifted program was an administrative innovation. It did not necessarily affect the performance of teachers.

The face of innovation diffusion within Illinois has been substantially changed by two main forces: the interstate highway system and school district consolidation. New interstate highways run north and south, east and west across the state. These will determine new population centers and new innovation routes. For example, Route I-57, which runs from Chicago to Cairo through the east central part of the state should greatly enhance innovation diffusion along that corridor. The town of Effingham, which lies at the juncture of this route and a major east-west route, I-70, and has never been known as a hotbed for innovation, may well become the focus and the source of educational innovation for that entire region. Hoke (1971) has recorded the effects of the highway system upon this community. While most people see the impact of the transportation system upon business and government, few realize what it will mean in terms of educational innovation.

Forced consolidation of school districts into larger units also raises the threshold level of districts that can support innovations such as special programs for gifted children. Innovation diffusion time becomes shorter in such a system both because the urban hierarchy facilitates rapid change and because the innovations have a shorter distance to travel along a network where districts are larger and fewer. It also means that there is an increasing segregation between districts that receive innovations and those that do not—between the haves and have-nots.

As a town like Effingham develops, it enters a boom period of economic growth. It attracts more people from greater distances. A relatively homogeneous population becomes increasingly heterogeneous. People come in from the farms and from the rural south looking for jobs. Larger businesses bring in corporate executives from all parts of the country and even the world. The town becomes increasingly stratified socially, and older residents graduate to upper social groups as their businesses grow. Unskilled immigrants, who make up the lower class, feel that they are not understood by the townspeople. New executives combine with the old establishment to become the new influentials.

All of these events create problems for the schools. With an increasingly heterogeneous school population there is a need for gifted programs, a need for remedial programs for the rural disadvantaged, a need for vocational programs suited to flourishing industry. As the tax base broadens, there is also more money to finance these programs. Increasing contact with the outside world via the transportation system also brings ideas for new programs from other districts, which means that location can determine the status of a school district in its region.

Still more problems arise. There is increased conflict among student groups in the schools, resulting from the introduction of new populations. The increased number of students requires an ambitious building program that must begin with attendant bond issues. Teachers, many of them new to the district, become increasingly alienated and militant. They do not understand or get along with the older teachers or new students as well. The price of housing and the general cost of living go up, and teachers want a larger piece of the prosperity they see around them. There is conflict over the demands of the teachers, the new programs, and the needed buildings.

The superintendent is not quite up to all of this. His paternalistic style is resented by both teachers and students, and he comes into increasing conflict with them and with various community groups. He does not entirely understand the new demands, and he has never had to float such a large bond issue. Sooner or later he retires or resigns. The school board, where some of the new business and professional elements are represented, wants change. The new superintendent will almost certainly be a new man from the outside who has built a reputation for innovation in previous jobs—a career-bound superintendent who plans to stay several years and move on. He may be a specialist in bond issues and new programs, and he will draw new people and new ideas.

So a new transportation system brings not only new prosperity and new ideas but new problems. As the town becomes further integrated into the urban hierarchy, it becomes more dependent on the larger centers of innovation, just as the smaller towns around it look to it as a center for innovation. Being a part of this urban hierarchy means giving up a considerable amount of autonomy and independence. One has only limited control over future innovations that will cascade down the network, whether they involve transportation or education. Whatever the governmental structure, a considerable amount of the locus of control resides elsewhere.

POLICIES TO INDUCE INNOVATION DIFFUSION

What constitutes an innovation for an administrator is not necessarily an innovation for a teacher. Administrators are linked to adopting innovations that affect other people; teachers, to innovations that primarily affect themselves and their students. The two types of innovations diffuse differently, and it is administrative innovation that is discussed here. Teacher innovation is discussed later.

Pedersen has proposed a model to explain entrepreneurial (administrative) innovation diffusion. Such diffusion is dependent on information flow; willingness to adopt, including the tightness of the social structure; economic and technical feasibility; and the presence of an entrepreneur to engineer the innovation. These variables are related to the "urban hierarchy," which forms the major corridors of innovation routes among major metropolitan areas. Pedersen uses his model as it interacts with urbanization patterns to make some predictions concerning innovation diffusion.

The diffusion of an educational innovation across the state of Illinois was mapped for the years 1963-1968. The innovation, programs for gifted children, was seen to originate in standard metropolitan areas with a population of about eighty thousand people and to diffuse, first, along the three major highways in the state at that time. "Contagious" diffusion based on face-to-face contact radiated waves of innovation from the metropolitan centers, particularly in less developed rural areas. In later years entrepreneurs organized many of the smaller districts that had apparently been beneath the "threshold" level for this innovation into cooperatives that were legalized by state policy. The districts that never adopted gifted programs or that were the last to adopt and the first to drop out were the very small districts. The areas where adoption was slowest and most sparse contained no major urban centers or transportation routes.

Connected with this educational diffusion along the urban hierarchy of Illinois was a vast, complex, well-financed, and sophisticated change mechanism operated by the state government. It included change agents, demonstration centers, experimental funds, special institute training, and other forms of deliberate propagation, but these change mechanisms and procedures still worked, perhaps effectively, within the processes defined by the geographic diffusion model. The total time required for gifted programs to diffuse to all districts that wanted them was about five years, a relatively short period. This adoption reflects only a request for state monies to support local programs for the gifted; it does not reflect what teachers did in classrooms, which is quite a different topic.

Since the diffusion of these programs in Illinois, the urban hierarchy has undergone a significant transformation because of the impact of the interstate highway system. New metropolitan areas will emerge to propagate innovation, which will then travel the new routes between centers. Some areas not previously considered innovative will become so, while others formerly but no longer on major transport networks will decline in innovative importance. Larger areas will retain their positions as leaders in the urban hierarchy and in the national and international systems of which they are a part. Chicago will continue to be the fountainhead for innovation in the Midwest. Educational innovation diffusion and adoption are highly dependent on the urbanization and transportation networks of the region.

If faster diffusion is desirable, how can this be achieved? First, it must be recognized that there are some pre-existent "natural" phenomena at work. Rather than trying to build a new diffusion system or to "force" the old, it might be possible to help the present system work faster, particularly if one's resources are relatively meager compared to the size of the system. Unfortunately, government agencies and other change agents have often attempted to build new diffusion mechanisms without any appreciation of social systems already in operation. Almost always operating with limited funds, they try to build cheap per capita systems like the Educational Research Information Center (ERIC) information retrieval system or simply publish new materials. Most of these efforts have failed.

Generally speaking, increasing personal contact will speed up the diffusion process. Pedersen suggests that the process will be slow where distance decay is strong and information diffusion is slow, where the rate of population participation is low, where innovators and entrepreneurs are scarce, where threshold levels are high, and where the urban growth process is slow. One way of speeding up the process is to improve the means of transportation and communication. While the routing of major roads and communications networks is beyond the control of educators, they can take advantage of the networks that exist. While there is no doubt considerable expense and waste involved in travel, such money is well spent in the service of diffusing innovations. Communications networks involving many professionals can be established. What is totally lacking are networks that bridge different types of educational personnel.

Perhaps the most effective way to use the urban hierarchy is to promote rapid adoption in larger regional centers. This will create diffusion down the urban hierarchy where spatial diffusion would have been the normal course. Increasing the frequency of entrepreneurs and innovators can be facilitated by improving financial rewards, reducing risks, and making resources more readily available, particularly in more remote places.

As can be seen from the Illinois Gifted Program, reducing the threshold level is an important strategy. Much of the impetus for school district consolidation has been based on the rationale that larger districts can provide better and more varied services. Pedersen suggests subsidies in order to reduce the threshold levels. Consortia and other multidistrict cooperatives have also served this purpose in Illinois, as, for example, in special education cooperatives. Reducing the threshold level is both critical and difficult since innovations continually demand economies of scale. Only the larger districts can handle the newer innovations. For example, a certain size is required before computers become economically feasible.

Perhaps the single most dramatic step for increasing diffusion is to increase the population rate of participation. According to Pedersen, this can be facilitated by increasing or redistributing income since higher income is positively associated with participation, by increasing education and propaganda activities, and by improving communication and transportation. To this list must be added reducing political, social, and organizational barriers to contact with the outside world. It is in the nature of organizations to limit such involvement. Giving teachers access to the outside personal contacts that administrators now have would tremendously increase innovation diffusion in education. General urban development will also assist in the process.

Chapter 3

The Educational Entrepreneur

THE SUPERINTENDENT AS CARRIER AND STIMULANT

In interdistrict innovation diffusion the chief executives must play a critical role. If face-to-face contact is the medium of exchange, and only top-level executives have extensive contacts outside the organization, most innovations must be transmitted into the organization through them, and this must be reflected in their communication patterns. Carlson's study (1965) of the friendship group of superintendents in Allegheny County, Pennsylvania, shows that the new math clearly followed the friendship itinerary of that group, for the central friendship group played a major role in dissemination. One of the social isolates was the first to adopt, but the innovation did not diffuse until it reached the central friendship group (see Figure 3-1). The earlier adopters were those of higher status who were more intimately involved in the social structure. The higher the superintendents were in the status structure, the more they were influenced by those identified as opinion leaders. In seeking advice, the tendency was to ask up the status ladder among the superintendents.

In Figure 3-1 the superintendents represented are those who received the most nominations in answer to the question: "Among the superintendents in Allegheny County, which three do you consider to be among your best friends?" The ones who received the most nominations were also the ones who developed the new math in the earlier years. Distance from the center of this friendship group meant that the new math materials were adopted later. Allegheny

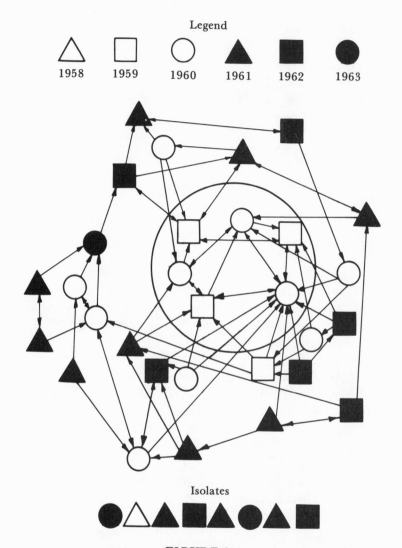

Legend

FIGURE 3-1
Friendship choices and rate of adoption
(from Carlson, 1965)

County includes the city of Pittsburgh and its environs, a highly urbanized area. Clearly innovation diffusion related to the social hierarchy exists among superintendents.

In West Virginia, a rural mountainous region, the communication structure was somewhat different. West Virginia superintendents asked advice from their fellow superintendents less frequently than did superintendents in Allegheny County, and opinion leaders were drawn from all status levels, not just the top one. Advice seeking, strongly influenced by distance in the rural area, was not related to distance in the urban area. Perhaps it was the distance factor that caused urban superintendents to seek advice from each other while rural superintendents relied more on state education personnel. Such an innovation pattern gave rural areas a regular wave-like diffusion pattern and urban areas an irregular "hopscotching" one, with superintendents tending to seek advice from those on the same "innovativeness" level.

Characteristics of the superintendents in Allegheny County were related to the rate of adoption of several innovations. The most important variables were origin of the superintendent (outside the district), conflict in performance standards (one group was most accurate judge of his work, but another group was most important to him), enrollment in his district, how recently he received his education, how well known he was among his peers, how well he knew others among his peers. In West Virginia all the superintendents were from within the district, and a similar analysis could not be done.

An attempt to establish a relationship between rates of innovation and characteristics of innovation was not successful. An important feature of this study is that acceptance of innovation was measured by simply asking the superintendent in an interview whether he had adopted the innovation. There is evidence that a superintendent's response is not an accurate indicator of what teachers are doing in the school district. Even assuming an accuracy that may not exist, superintendents', principals', and teachers' perceptions of innovation differ, and what a superintendent considers to be an innovation may have no effect on a classroom. Carlson's study documents the travel of innovative ideas among social networks of superintendents, but without any necessary relationship to classroom behavior.

Equating a chief administrator's response with the behavior

of an organization rests on a dubious assumption. It is commonplace in education to assume that school is a coordinated, integrated, problem-solving mechanism that, confronted with an innovation, assesses its merits and, if it proves worthwhile, incorporates it. Such is not the case. The organization is, in fact, a combination of various departments and interest groups, all competing for scarce resources (J. G. March, 1966). Organizational decisions are based on which coalitions of groups are in ascendancy at the moment—a political process. The effects of such a process are dealt with in the section concerned with intraschool innovation processes.

What kind of person is a school superintendent? Most are male, from white, rural, or small-town, Protestant (mostly Methodist) backgrounds (Carlson, 1972). They come from the lower-middle or upper-lower social classes, attend less prestigious colleges, and score slightly below the mean of college graduates on intelligence tests. True to their backgrounds, they are politically conservative. They invariably rise through the ranks, first as teacher and then as principal, to become a superintendent, perseverance being an important characteristic.

The prestige structure among superintendents is determined primarily by salary, which is strongly related to school size. The most prestigious positions are held by those who have occupied a number of superintendencies and have moved to the top ones. Superintendents move from place to place but usually within a limited geographic area. More than 90 percent of such moves occur within state boundaries. As a group, superintendents are rather conservative, and the school boards that select them are even more so.

Why does one superintendent adopt innovations while another does not? The best overall analysis is contained in Carlson's (1972) distinction between career-bound and place-bound superintendents.

Having examined differences between career- and place-bound superintendents it is possible, by way of summary, to speak of their different career styles. Once in public education, the typical career-bound superintendent aims from the beginning for the top of the hierarchy—the superintendency. He sets his sights high and early and views positions below his goal as steps toward the superintendency. Preparing for the career, he is active and acquires his graduate training early, to the fullest extent, and from the better institutions of higher education.

The place-bound superintendent, on the other hand, gradually escalates his occupational aspirations. His desire for the superintendency develops late and frequently appears only when the opportunity does. He sees positions below the superintendency as ends in themselves. As he fills positions of increasing responsibility and finds success, he gradually escalates his aspirations and one day finds himself in the superintendency. In pursuit of preparation he is less active than his counterpart, tends to drag out his preparation period, and secure his preparation on a part-time basis. Further he tends to acquire less than the maximum preparation and is not very particular about the prestige of the place offering the formal graduate school preparation.

The career-bound superintendent holds a more progressive view about education and aspires to greater prominence among superintendents than does his counterpart. In viewing his job he tends to be less satisfied. Regarding his career, the career-bound superintendent finds it slightly more satisfying; he sees mobility, to a greater extent, as a desired or natural element of the career; he feels more strongly that one must take an active part in the pursuit of career objectives—one must confront the environment if one is to get ahead; and he tends to hold less limited success criteria of career judgment than his counterpart [page 65].

The distinction between career-bound and place-bound is based simply on whether the superintendent comes from outside or inside the school district. In Allegheny County over 50 percent of the career-bound superintendents adopted modern math between 1958 and 1960, compared to only 20 percent of the place-bound ones. One-fifth of the career-bound superintendents adopted the innovation before a single place-bound one. The median number of innovations adopted was four for the career-bound to two for the place-bound. By far the greatest number of innovations took place in the first three years of the career-bound man's tenure. No similar distinction has been drawn for outside and inside principals.

The superintendent of a district is succeeded by a place-bound successor only about a quarter of the time, when the school board is happy with the original superintendent and does not want change. This succession seems to occur primarily when a conservative political faction, often affiliated with party politics, dominates the school board for many years. Having two place-bound superintendents in a row means about twenty years of the status quo, and a place-bound man succeeds another place-bound man only about 5 percent of the time. The longer the original superintendent is in office, however, the more likely it is that he will be replaced by someone from outside. If the administration of a school system is perceived as unsatisfactory by a school board or if change is considered desirable, a career-bound man will be chosen. Should the administration be perceived as satisfactory, either type might be chosen. In short, a successor to the superintendent chosen from within the district tends to stabilize what already exists; one chosen from outside tends to alter what exists, at least to some degree.

Career-bound and place-bound superintendents do not differ on personality measures except that the career-bound one holds more liberal views. Rather, it is mutual expectations and external forces that govern the situation: the external man changes; the internal man stabilizes. It is the mobility expectation of the superintendent that has a strong effect on innovation within the school district, as well as the social peer group in which he finds himself. Since career-bound superintendents are more involved in the interaction network of the social structure and have higher status among school superintendents, they are central to information flow, acting as information vehicles. They seek more information, attend 50 percent more meetings, seek three times more advice, and are sought three times as much for advice than place-bound ones.

When an outside superintendent enters a district, several factors merge to facilitate change. First, the career-bound superintendent's future depends on establishing a reputation among his peers, so he is inclined to change something. Also, having been hired because the school board was dissatisfied with the previous administration, he often has a mandate for change. And, being new, the career-bound man's limitations are not yet evident, while those of the place-bound man are already known.

Once the career-bound superintendent takes office, he can often "unfreeze" the social structure for a period of time, allowing some internal changes. The place-bound man, on the other hand, is tied to social groupings already existing within the district, and the new coalitions necessary for change are unlikely to be formed. Old friends and old enemies can hamper the place-bound superintendent's ability to make changes.

The social structure tends to respond differently to the two types of superintendents. Because a new man is unknown, his entrance results in horizontal cohort grouping, that is, principals associate with principals. Other school administrators, particularly the central office staff, are vulnerable under a new superintendent. In order to ensure loyalty, the career-bound superintendent is also likely to bring colleagues into the central staff with him. These people usually find it necessary to make their presence felt, and those within the organization who have the most to lose—other administrators—resent this. Hierarchical units, for example, principals that group together when a new successor comes, can either facilitate or impede change, and vertical cliques gradually reassert themselves. By far the largest number of innovations (by administrative count) are adopted in the first three years of a career-bound superintendent's tenure. His innovation adoption ratio levels off considerably after that.

Teachers, on the other hand, are essentially beyond the control of the superintendent. He cannot see what they are doing; nor can he do much about directly controlling their behavior. If he wishes to influence them more than superficially, he must resort to personal or charismatic authority. Being new and unknown, the career-bound superintendent is in a better position to gain the initial support of the teachers. When a man already known is promoted, this strengthens the vertical clique formation since old factions are perpetuated. The place-bound superintendent, less inclined or able to rock the boat, is more likely to leave professional improvement up to the teachers and not to initiate such activities.

The importance of personal aspiration for innovation diffusion has been demonstrated outside education. In a study of chief administrators of local health departments in three states, Becker (1972) found a stable communication network over the same spatial area. He contended that the time of adoption of the innovation was likely to be a cause of centrality in the informal information networks rather than a result. In other words, administrators achieved social centrality by innovating and accomplished innovation by seeking outside information sources. They were driven by a desire to maintain or increase prestige, and adopting many new programs was associated with greater prestige and higher status than using the same resources in greater depth for fewer innovative programs. Those health officers who devoted resources to existing innovative programs did not acquire higher relative centrality. The most mobile of the officers supported easy-to-adopt innovations and were oriented toward their professional group (career-bound). Difficult-to-adopt innovations were supported by locally oriented officers (place-bound) who were marginal to the communication network. Put another way, the railroad track of innovation diffusion may be the interpersonal contact network, with the train representing outside information and the engine fueled by ambition.

In summary, the school superintendent's migration, mobility, and career pattern are an important vehicle in the diffusion and adoption of educational innovations. They help tie the school district to the overall urbanization pattern. New innovations within urban areas seem to diffuse within the friendship patterns of the superintendent. Those superintendents most central to the friendship network adopt innovations first (at least easy-to-adopt innovations) and are higher in social status than the others. Whether the centrality comes from adopting innovations or vice versa is unclear. It is clear that status among superintendents is related to the salary of the district they command and that, to get to the high-prestige, high-paying districts, they must show a career pattern of innovation.

Career-bound superintendents are those superintendents who move from district to district carrying new ideas and innovations with them. Although they ordinarily move only short distances within state boundaries, their very entry into a school district unfreezes the district social structure for a period of time thus allowing new coalitions to form and some change to occur. It is also in the career interest of superintendents to promote change in order to build their reputations.

The degree of change a superintendent instigates is mitigated by his personal background and socialization pattern, by the tenuousness of his position, and by his ability to control the district he commands. As the chief executive, only he and a few of his staff members have extensive contacts with agencies outside the school district. Often only he has an opportunity to come in contact with new ideas and innovations, which can hardly be adopted or even advocated unless they become known and available. Naturally the superintendent's most credible information source, in terms of what he can expect from an innovation, is his fellow superintendents, which emphasizes the importance of the superintendent's personal friendship group. Thus, operating within the overall context of innovation diffusion, the superintendent acts as carrier, catalyst, and gatekeeper for new innovations. These functions are performed by him, sometimes deliberately and sometimes unconsciously, but always within the framework of advancing his own career.

THE POLITICS OF THE CENTRAL OFFICE STAFF

Between the superintendent and the teachers lies the central office staff, that group of men the superintendent gathers around himself to help him run the school district. Like the superintendent's role in the adoption of innovation, theirs is also critical. They have frequent contacts with the outside world, but it is as propagator or inhibitor of innovations within the district that they exert the most influence. Most studies portray the central office staff as inhibitors of change, but they have the capacity to facilitate as well as to inhibit.

The central office staff (COS) needs to perceive itself as being in control of the situation. McGivney and Haught (1973), in an excellent political analysis of the central office staff, saw this need arising from an attempt to reconcile two conflicting perspectives: one view was that COS members are professionals who know what is educationally correct; the other was that the school is fundamentally vulnerable to outside influence. When, for example, most groups seeking outside change were viewed as troublemakers and as unrepresentative of the public, the COS tried to control communications among various groups in an attempt to maintain control.

Another control technique identified by McGivney and Haught is known as "stacking the deck," and it is used in recruiting new teachers. The COS would always send two of its own members on hiring trips with a department head known for recruiting teachers who were too intellectual. Another technique is known as "lining up the ducks," where new administrative posts are only advertised publicly after the COS has already lined up a candidate.

In studying a particular school district, McGivney and Haught found that the COS could be broken into two major subgroups. The first interacted on a daily basis and in staff meetings led by the superintendent. It included two "gatekeepers"—often administrators for finance and personnel—to control information flow to the superintendent and the board of education. This major subgroup could be further divided into minor subgroups that interacted frequently on both functional and social bases, facilitated by the proximity of their offices and linked by informal social ties. The "significant others" for the minor subgroups were the superintendent and the school board.

The second major subgroup of the COS interacted daily and at monthly supervisory meetings. It was oriented more toward building principals and teachers than toward the board of education, and it was identified with the former superintendent. The second major group was also comprised of three minor subgroups held together by office proximity and social interaction. Others in the COS not belonging to the subgroups were listed as isolates.

The subgrouping pattern of the COS affected district decision making in a very important way—the groups served as forums in which group members tested beliefs and proposals before asserting them in larger groups. Virtually every idea had to achieve consensus in a minor subgroup and a major subgroup before it could be introduced into the Administrative Council Meeting, the full COS. Only then could it be advanced to the school board. Ideas which achieved COS consensus were presented at the Board Study Session, a closed meeting in which consensus could be attempted with board members. If consensus was not achieved, it could at least be predicted how each board member would react to the proposal. The fruits of this decision-making process became public at the official board meeting.

The school board almost always accepted COS proposals. If an outside group presented ideas contrary to those of the COS at the public board meeting, these ideas were always referred to the COS for consideration, and, unless they were able to run the COS consensus gauntlet, they were doomed. Usually proposals by outside groups were intercepted by the COS before they ever got to the board. The COS would impugn the credibility of such groups, if necessary, by questioning their information base and their sincerity. No action by school staff other than the COS was ever initiated at board meetings.

This appearance of unanimity was maintained before the board and the public at all costs. Even when the COS was unable to control events, such as cutbacks in state funds, it gave the appearance of controlling such events. According to McGivney and Haught's study of a medium-sized city school system, bureaucratic theory could not explain the behavior of the COS, which was far from impersonal when applying rules and procedures. Informal social considerations were extremely important within the small sociopolitical system of the COS, and much of the initiatory power of the school system resided in the COS rather than in the superintendent, the board, the teachers, or other administrators.

Innovative programs could be mounted but only if they could secure the blessing of the COS and did not threaten the established power wielders. The district studied by McGivney and Haught was instituting modular scheduling, team teaching, and other innovations. It is clear that someone pushing such innovations had to build relationships with COS members, particularly those governing powerful subgroups. The strategy also had to take into consideration the COS's need to be perceived to be in control. The perspectives of the groups, graphically illustrated in Figure 3-2, proved more important than those of individuals in effecting change.

If McGivney and Haught are correct, both the COS and the superintendent act as gatekeepers through which innovations must pass. By controlling information, the COS manages initiative. Hence, in the gifted programs mentioned earlier, one-third of the teachers did not know that they were listed as teachers of the gifted in the proposal to the state, a fact kept from them by the COS. Nor did the teachers receive any information from the state office that passed through the hands of the COS unless the COS actively supported the program. When a member of the COS chooses to promote an innovation, it is more likely to flourish. If, for example, a staff administrator or a teacher were to be given authority for the district's gifted program, the program would be much more likely to flourish than if a line administrator (either superintendent or principal) were placed in command. (A poll showed that line administrators considering ten major groups associated with schools gave lowest priority to the need for gifted programs.)

Of course, the support of the COS must be viewed in light of its desire to maintain control. For example, energetic, charismatic leaders considered too unmanageable by the COS might not be selected to head projects, even though such people are critical to successful implementation of innovations, a topic discussed below. The need for control of the COS reduces innovative behavior, especially when the COS assumes all initiatory power and is loath to establish projects or select strong project leaders.

It is not difficult to see why a new superintendent entering the school district upsets the school structure. The new superintendent is most likely to effect changes in the COS, wherein lies most of the initiatory power for new programs. Besides bringing in new people and new ideas to advance his own career, the superintendent must

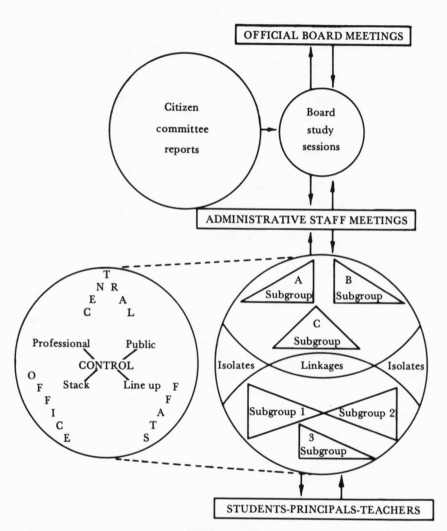

FIGURE 3-2
Decision-making model of the COS
(from McGivney and Haught, 1973)

disturb informal social relationships around which so much of the dynamics of the COS revolves. From subsequent adjustments and realignments issue forth new programs. As discussed earlier, the superintendent has direct influence over his own staff but little over the teachers themselves in their classrooms.

What about the relative influence of the superintendent vis-a-vis the COS as both affect the entire school system? Which is more influential? There is no direct evidence on this, but the COS, particularly the "ingroups," might be considered a special, elite governing group such as might be found in any type of organization. Hage and Dewar (1973) compared elite values toward change versus organizational structure in predicting innovation within an organization.

The structural variables of complexity, centralization, and formalization are often most closely associated with innovation or lack of it. Complexity—a diverse task structure, many occupational specialities, amount of professional activity, and contact with outside sources—is usually the best predictor. It is reasoned that a complex organization has more diverse inputs and, hence, more ideas. Centralization is usually negatively associated with innovation since it is assumed that ideas of the less influential will be vetoed because they may threaten the power structure and because there is less opportunity for circulation of ideas. Formalization is also negatively associated with innovation since individual initiative is stifled by rules and regulations. Structural flexibility and lack of specificity are more conducive to innovation.

Hage and Dewar compared these variables with the values of the leader, the values of the elite, and the values of the membership toward change to see which would best predict actual innovation in health and welfare organizations. The leader was defined as the director of the organization; the elite, as those who always participated in key decisions, including the executive director; and the membership, as all full-time staff members. The values of the inner circle elite turned out to be more important than those of the executive director by himself or of the entire staff in predicting innovation (as defined by the study, innovation is administrative adoption of new programs). The values of the leader were important but not quite as important as those of the elite as a group. The values of the staff were much less important in predicting change.

This finding suggests that it is indeed the organizational elite, including the leader, that makes policy and determines innovation. The "formal elite," those who hold titles and formal positions, are not nearly as influential as the informal elite of the organization. This is reflected in the COS, the power of the minor subgroups, in contrast to the "isolates," those excluded from the major subgroups.

Elite values are also slightly better predictors of change than complexity, the strongest structural indicator. But structural variables exert a strong influence independent of elite values. Hence, change is facilitated by diversity of occupational perspectives, contact with professional societies, and an elite that values change. It is interesting that, in these particular organizations, decentralization is not important. For change, as defined by Hage and Dewar, the elite do not have to allow participative decision making so it is not necessary to say anything about whether innovations are actually implemented by members lower in the organization. There is considerable evidence from other studies to indicate that innovations are not always implemented.

Hage and Dewar reemphasize that organizations are controlled at the top by an informal elite. And, in the school district, this elite consists of elements of the central office staff. The initiatory power for innovation adoption resides there, though not necessarily the power to implement the innovation. One must deal with this organizational elite in some way in order to effect educational innovation.

ADVOCACY IN A NONRATIONAL SYSTEM

When a career-bound superintendent, through his personal contacts, decides to introduce an innovation into his school district, that is only the first step. Then comes the hurdle of the central office staff, which is followed by efforts to persuade teachers to utilize the innovation. Persuading teachers is by far the most difficult task, for, over the short and medium term, the success of the innovation will depend on whether an enthusiastic "advocacy" develops around it. Advocacy requires a small group of people who protect and propagate the project in face-to-face contact. This is entrepreneurialism in its fundamental form—the organization of goals and people. If advocacy does not develop, the chances of the innovation being utilized at all are very slim, for reasons discussed in Chapter 4. Essentially, few rewards are available for teachers except those attained through group experience.

The contingencies necessary for advocacy to develop are complex and varied. For example, in an intensive evaluation of Illinois's gifted programs, it was found that 17 percent of the school districts accepting state funds had no program at all. Another 39 percent had programs rated as being of low or limited quality. Only 34 percent of the districts receiving funds had programs considered fair or good. Hence, "adoption" by no means guarantees "implementation."

A comparison of the programs indicates that quality, and existence, is dependent on a small number of variables (House, Steele, and Kerins, 1972). Two of the most important variables—size of the school district and size of the program budget—cannot be separated. Two more—norms of the unit toward the innovation and opinion leadership exercised by the program director—are also important.

Two other variables—status of the program director (*not* being a line administrator) and visits from outside consultants—have a slight influence. The number of years a district receives state funds to operate a program has almost no effect, and, since larger districts adopt gifted programs first, time variance can be extracted with size (the urban hierarchy at work).

From these data an "advocacy" model of innovation can be postulated. The school district is seen as a set of programs contending for scarce resources, and the success of the innovation depends on the ability to establish a program in a competitive field, which requires a group of advocates who see developing the program to be in their own interest. Advocates defend the integrity of the special program, recruit members, infuse them with values, and secure adequate resources. The requirements for filling such a role have been set forth by Selznick (1957) and expanded by Schumacher (1972) in a study of the utilization of materials for aesthetic education in Pennsylvania. Schumacher differentiates between cosmopolitan advocates, who see advantages in terms of the total school district or of the entire state and justify local costs on a more global basis, and local advocates, who expect a more immediate return for the local school. For the local advocate, costs often seem to outweigh benefits, making the innovation seem less worthwhile.

It is important that the school not be seen as a collection of individuals passively waiting for and weighing the merit of innovations that diffuse through. The school is, rather, a collection of cohesive active groups, coalitions that sometimes cooperate and sometimes compete with one another. Most groups actively search for new means of advancing their own interests and new ways of defending what they have. They may actively seize upon new innovations in order to advance. Outside consultants or outside monies serve as information sources and as legitimation for the new program, but, at most, they act only as a "trigger." The real energy must be released from within the organization.

Other groups resent such changes. A new program, while it may be an improvement, most certainly means some encroachment upon old prerogatives. When program change is significant, it requires reallocation of resources, and conflict is inevitable if the school district is seen as coalitions of people pursuing divergent and conflicting goals. Only small-scale changes elude such conflict. The process of change is essentially a social and political one involving competition for resources among groups within a district, and conflict is inevitable and necessary. This view is quite different than that of the school district as a unified, rational, problem-solving entity.

If the atmosphere is such that there is an opportunity for involvement in developmental projects and motivation for doing so, advocacy may develop, assuming that the teacher or administrator has sufficient entrepreneurial skills. Often the central office staff, with its penchant for control, will choose someone who can be controlled to head a project. Such a person is unlikely to let the project move at its own speed. Funds and resources are committed to the project, and additional funds are provided to keep it going, but the innovation eventually withers away unnoticed and unmourned. Only powerful sponsorship from external sources can perpetuate an innovation that lacks internal advocacy.

If the atmosphere is free and the entrepreneur is more skillful, the course of the innovation is more complex. The entrepreneur builds an advocacy as indicated above, and the innovation flourishes. Many people are involved, and the advocacy group becomes a power within the school. Either the advocate's career is advanced, or he leaves. In most such cases the advocacy group and innovation gradually fade since any program, after all, requires relationships among people.

One example would be a situation where an ambitious young

principal, taken with the idea of the "open classroom," selects teachers to work with him, organizes them, and sets the whole school off on a path toward open education. He solicits extra funds from the central office, brings in outside consultants, and begins in-service training. There is talk in the lounge. An ideology develops—the school's own version of "open" education. There is a new excitement. Teachers try different things, and younger teachers who are involved go to special conferences. Older teachers are, however, suspicious. As the ingroup feeling increases, certain hostilities surface, but the advocacy dominates. Other teachers who visit the school can see the excitement! Newspaper articles are written, the principal becomes a central figure among other principals, and other schools try open education. Then the principal, who planned to install open education in the whole district, is promoted to assistant superintendent, and he leaves the school. When his assistant is promoted to principal, things level off. It is just not the same. As enthusiasm diminishes, some people go to graduate school, and some get married. The innovation wave has passed; advocacy is over.

One may contend that real change is generated by excitement. Because the teachers are involved, because they believe in something, they are willing to change, to do something different. The support they get from their group makes change possible. In some schools excitement abates only to await the next innovation wave. On the other hand, there is always the possibility that, as in epidemiology, once a susceptible becomes infected, he becomes immune.

While advocacy flourishes, it constitutes a force within the school. Some people are, however, excluded from it, and they become either hostile or apathetic toward innovation. An advocate group spawns a counter group within the school. The counter group promotes isolation of the innovation within the school and confinement to the advocacy group itself. The formation of groups and counter groups produces new cliques within the school and new communication patterns based on the innovation (see Figure 3-3).

These dynamics suggest that most innovations are short-lived or severely contained within the social structure like a bacillus. Such is the case. Those who invent and develop innovations often expect a new innovation to be recognized on its technical merits and to sweep through a school. Actually, any innovation has meaning only within a particular social structure, and the social structure of schools is such that an innovation pandemic is unlikely.

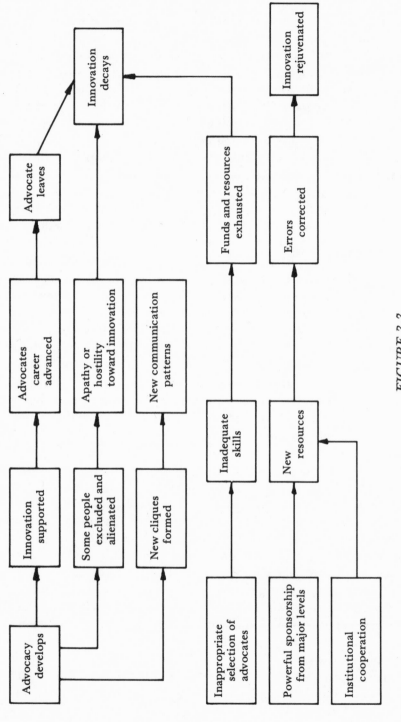

FIGURE 3-3
Progress of the advocacy

In evaluating the teacher corps, Corwin (1972) found that a split developed between established leaders of the schools and new interns who entered the structure to institute liberal reforms. The latter stood to gain from new roles that promised to open new channels of success and circumvent traditionalists within the school. The result was that the traditionalists overwhelmed the change agents, and there was little change.

One powerful factor promotes and rejuvenates innovation—sponsorship. Corwin found that the most fundamental variable may be the way a local organization is insulated or integrated into a larger network. If the innovation is supported by a powerful sponsor, more resources can always be found, and previous errors can be corrected. If the innovation is not sponsored by a powerful agency, it gets only one chance. When it runs into difficulties or exhausts its resources, it is finished. Like the son of a rich man, the well-endowed innovation gets many chances. Its deficiencies are remedial. Schumacher (1972) found that projects that successfully disseminated materials for aesthetic education were those in which the district intervened with new resources and remedial procedures. The success of the total project depended heavily on the interorganizational cooperation of the three major institutions and on the willingness of those institutions to provide remedial help where needed.

If the advocacy endures and maintains itself, eventually an "organizational saga"—a collective understanding of the unique accomplishment of the group—must develop. In his study of Reed, Antioch, and Swarthmore Colleges, Clark (1972) found that the history of a group is enhanced by mythical elements and contains powerful group sentiments. The saga, which helps the individual rationalize his commitment to the organization, begins as a strong purpose supported by a single man or a small cadre. It has a chance to grow in an open setting, such as a new organization or an established organization in crisis. The final stage of development is fulfillment, when changes become institutionalized. This process also involves fighting against newer changes that might threaten the original idea.

In most educational change there is a strong decay factor. Evans, in his study of instructional television in universities (1969), found that the use of ITV was usually inspired by a crisis, most often too many students. At all of the colleges its use would be championed by an internal advocate. When the advocate left the college and the crisis was over, the instructional television equipment would go into a storage room, apparently, as in the case of instructional television, never to be used again. A new innovation finds fertile ground in some colleges that drop ITV; traditional ones return to their previous ways. In neither case does instructional television itself come back once it has burned over an area. Innovations inspired by crisis or sponsored by highly concentrated power bases often do not induce value changes necessary to sustain them over a long period of time.

A PORTRAIT OF THE ENTREPRENEUR

At the center of advocacy is a single person who initiates, organizes, and provides direction—the entrepreneur. He may be a teacher, or even a parent, but, within the limits of school structure, he is ordinarily an administrator. Perhaps the primary motivation of the administrative entrepreneur is to advance his own career, while that of the private entrepreneur is increasing profit. It is interesting that the modern corporation is more like the former than the latter, however. According to Dresong (1973), the administrative entrepreneur is distinguished by the following qualifications:

He has access to resources that can be used to promote development.
He is self-confident about being able to influence his own future.
He believes that opportunities exist for rapid upward mobility.
He can concentrate on one project or program to maximize his success and his identification with it.

The administrative entrepreneur can operate best where there is a fragmented or loose bureaucratic structure. He pressures and persuades a small group of people to orchestrate various components needed for development, and he believes that merit and achievement, or the appearance of them, are criteria for promotion. Dresong's study of Zambian bureaucracy reveals three types of administrators: entrepreneurs, who are under thirty-five and have already experienced rapid upward mobility, see their employment as an opportunity to establish positive records that will enhance their job chances. The others are nonentrepreneurs. Cautious careerists do not believe they can do much to affect their futures so they do not jeopardize their jobs, seek visibility, or display aggressiveness; they rely on systematic opportunities for job advancement. Clock watchers do no more than necessary and do not regard their promotion prospects as bright.

The emergence of entrepreneurialism depends heavily on a setting conducive to exercising individual initiative. This means an absence of tight hierarchical control, some reward for achievement, and the opportunity for upward mobility other than through tenure. The more precise the definition of roles and the fewer the opportunities for career advancement, the less incentive there is for individuals to take risks and act dramatically in order to achieve visibility. Hence, innovation declines.

The same pattern is found in business organizations. In a study of organizational innovativeness, Normann (1971) found that all innovative projects are established as a consequence of the strong involvement of individuals (entrepreneurs). Development projects are seen as important tools for individuals seeking status and power. Hence, motivation to engage in development projects (develop an advocacy) is a function of the incentive system. But opportunity for involvement is also necessary. Often individuals who promote such projects are new, and they are entering a structure already in the process of change. (Note the similarity to the career-bound superintendent.) The structure, since it has already been unfrozen for a brief period, allows for some change.

The organization must not use failure as a basis for punishment or to create a scapegoat if it is to encourage entrepreneurship. Schools do not provide a very loose structure or opportunities in which to operate compared to other organizations. Superintendents themselves are in no position to take great risks without suffering severe punishment in the form of dismissal or stagnation in their careers. They are likely to be cautious; superintendents are indeed very cautious men. They must show some innovation but without taking too great a risk. The innovation can only be conceived within carefully controlled limits.

Normann (1971) distinguishes between two types of innovations: "variations" and "reorientations." Variations are minor changes that do not require drastic shifts within existing policies and power structures. Existing cognitions, rules, and heuristics are sufficient for dealing with minor innovation. Reorientations, on the other hand, require new types of specialized knowledge and task systems for implementation. Reorientations require new goals, new values, new, as well as realigned, power structures, and shifts in cognitive structure. These are drastic changes.

The more an innovation is a major reorientation, the more

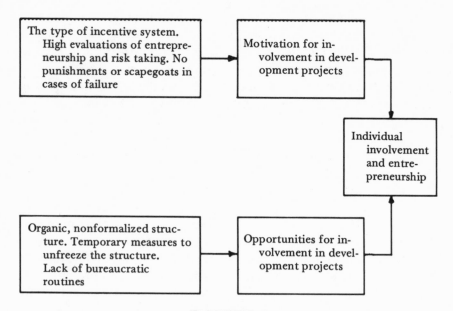

FIGURE 3-4
Factors contributing to individual involvement
and entrepreneurship in development projects
(from Normann, 1971)

necessary it is to gain resources politically, support skills technically, propagate new values emotionally, and teach new cognitions intellectually. These difficult chores must be initiated through close personal contacts; they cannot be forced. Advocacy groups, which in turn require the development of entrepreneurship, at least the way the system is currently constructed, are the major means of effecting such changes. Generally the school system does not encourage such initiative, which is why school innovations are overwhelmingly variations that do not require major changes, an observation made by many critics. There are many changes, but few are basic or carry much import. Reorientations bring organizational politics to the fore both in advocating innovation and in defending against it.

CHARISMA—HOW IT IS DONE

How does the entrepreneur operate? What does he do? Contrary to popular belief, the charismatic leader is not rare; nor is his behavior mystical. The ability to exercise charisma, a talent like any other, can be found in varying degrees. Essentially, entrepreneurial charisma is the orchestration of diverse personal needs. The entrepreneur recognizes these needs and is able to satisfy them within the scope or movement he is building, which unites an assortment of people pursuing different and personal goals into a more or less cohesive movement. Naturally it is very helpful if the entrepreneur has available an abundance of resources with which to fill needs.

Few causes are more difficult to champion in America than that of the gifted child, and efforts to build such a movement have been feeble. The dominant American ethic of equality mitigates against providing help to those already "intellectually advantaged." That such help is lavishly available to the athletically or financially advantaged child does not diminish the attitude toward the intellectually gifted.

Yet in one state an entrepreneur has successfully built a reasonably strong state movement, including special funds and legislative support for gifted programs. How can such an unpopular cause be parlayed into a successful statewide movement? Some of the dynamics of this process involve ritual—the annual gifted banquet in a populous area of the state. In this case the entrepreneur-advocate-charismatic leader is a handsome, attractive woman in her mid-thirties who has a need to achieve, to excel, and to dominate. Much of her career is centered on the organization of this constituency group, which also requires a significant element of showmanship in order to stage such events. She has a very intelligent girl Friday who attends to details and trouble-shoots. The girl Friday is not glamorous, but she derives a considerable amount of surrogate satisfaction from her role.

A key member of the loosely knit group is a Jewish physician who sees himself as intellectually gifted, which is confirmed in this account, and as having had a lonely childhood because of his abilities. The doctor is now a state legislator. He champions the gifted cause within the state legislature and provides access to other legislators and power figures in the local and state area. At this banquet the doctor-legislator is the key speaker. He admits the gifted cause is not popular in the halls of the legislature, but he keeps pushing. He is an essential figure in the group because the audience must believe that such an impressive figure is interested in the "cause." The doctor-legislator is in turn gratified by the number of people who listen to his opinion on gifted children. (On one occasion the entrepreneur was very worried because so many people arrived late since she had promised the legislator at least a hundred would show up.)

The chief administrator for special education in the state also attends. He needs to·impress the legislator to reinforce his status in the state capitol and to gain support for his special education programs in the state legislature. Although, like many former teachers of the retarded, he is skeptical about the need for special assistance for the gifted although the aid is administered through his office, he is certain about his own need for legislative support. He sits at the banquet table and gives a brief speech. The chief administrative officer for special education in the local area, a large urban complex, is also skeptical about special provisions for the gifted. He does not care so much about the state legislator (although the legislator is also a powerful local figure); he is more concerned with the local school board president in the audience, and he asks her to stand and take a bow for the accomplishments of the local area program.

The president of the local school board, a shy, retiring woman, is very wealthy and influential among the local elite, which is largely Jewish. Public service is high on her priority list, and she takes her duties seriously. Her daughter, a major assistant to the entrepreneur, has also received a fellowship for the education of the gifted from the entrepreneur.

The prominence of the local Jewish subculture plays an important role in the success of the advocacy. The subculture values intellectual attainment and provides a substantial base of wealth, ability, and influence on which to draw. The head of the supporting local citizens group married into a wealthy Jewish family, and this office provides him with respectability and status in the community as well as an opportunity to provide for his own children. The entrepreneur herself, while she is not Jewish, is cultured and sophisticated. She adapts easily to the subculture.

The state consultant for the gifted is unpolished, direct, earthy, and less than persuaded by the entrepreneur's charm. Her job is

actually enhanced by the entrepreneur's activities, yet she is also up-
staged and personally offended by the entrepreneur's manipulations.
In private conversation she aggressively picks away at the entrepreneur's manipulation of the various actors. Her remarks are felt by the
entrepreneur, but they are never broadcast beyond a safe audience.
Whatever her personal feelings, the state consultant cannot afford to
slay the source of the golden egg.

Also featured in the annual conference and seated at the banquet
table are two out-of-state authorities who lend the legitimacy of
expertise to the local proceedings. One, a representative of a national
organization for the gifted, feels honored at being invited to such
occasions; the other, an academic expert, is seeking relief from his
natural clime. Both are paid modest consultant fees. The head of the
state professional association is a displaced physics Ph.D. seeking
intellectual respectability in a new way.

Here, arrayed before the assembly to demonstrate that this is an
important event, are all kinds of authority: state and local; legal and
administrative; national, state, and local professional authorities;
technical experts; the local wealthy; and so forth. In many such movements sex and charm are an important cohesive force within a
group. Certainly the entrepreneur's job is made easier because she is
an attractive, flirtatious woman.

The leader's charisma is to recognize the personal interests and
needs of each individual and to direct them toward group activity.
Hence, a diverse group with no common interests is welded into an
effective action group effectively controlled by the entrepreneur. To
rationalize his behavior, each person embraces, to a greater or lesser
degree, the ideology of acting for the greater good, in this case doing
something worthwhile for gifted students. Each person could just as
easily be involved in something else. What brings them together is the
entrepreneur's *social organization.*

The entrepreneur's talent is her ability to recognize personal
needs—a fine talent—and to deliver on those needs, which requires
access to substantial resources. Within a school or other organization
the person who heads up a project is appointed by the administrator
and is often appointed for compliance rather than for entrepreneurial
ability. Although administrative appointments often supply necessary
resources, the entrepreneur's talent for social organization is lacking,
and the project ordinarily goes nowhere.

In this particular case, the communication structure of advocacy would consist of several loosely structured groups connected to and *only* through the entrepreneur. The groups would communicate very little among themselves. In fact, different groups and actors can, when necessary, even be deliberately housed at different motels to minimize communication. This control factor is not dissimilar to the fashion in which the central office staff controls communication within school districts. Of course, within schools advocacy would be less dramatic and less spectacular than this articulation of a state-wide movement.

Entrepreneurship is an orchestration of diverse personal needs directed toward a common goal. It is easy to be cynical about the manipulations and motivations of the actors. Yet it is difficult to see how any advocacy, however large or small, could be built in any other fashion if it is to work effectively. Whether belief in the common cause comes before or after an individual sees that his needs are being met is a moot point. What is clear is that there must be an ideology or common cause in which to believe and that individuals must satisfy certain needs if the organization is to survive. Only a cynic could survive without belief in a common cause, and only a mystic could survive without satisfying his own needs.

Most of the people in this anecdote have no awareness of the machinations or manipulations around them. They see their own motivations as being of the highest order, as indeed they are. The entrepreneur supplies social organization in its most quintessential form. From this emerges social direction and social change. It may also be that the more important the belief supplied by the entrepreneur, the more intense the charisma. Certainly in cases of high charisma the elements of mysticism and transcendence exceed personal needs.

THE SPAWNING OF ENTREPRENEURS

Innovations are initiated and flourish where an entrepreneur exists and where social conditions are proper. But when are such conditions likely to obtain? Young (1971) has proposed a macrosociological interpretation of entrepreneurship as a group phenomenon. Entrepreneurial groups display a high degree of "solidarity," which is defined as the degree to which members create, maintain, and project a coherent definition of their situation. The entrepreneur himself is only the most visible member of the group. It is clear that advocacy groups within schools also develop such a solidarity, a sense of "mission."

Drawing upon the fact that entrepreneurial groups are often minority groups in the larger society, Young contends that they lack "relative centrality" with respect to the dominant social system of which they are a part. The social identity of the group is in question. Not all groups with low relative centrality, however, develop solidarity. Only those groups with "high differentiation," defined as the range of occupations and diversity, have the capacity to do so. Solidarity is generated by a high differentiation-relative centrality ratio. When the group has high institutional and occupational diversity relative to its acceptance in the larger society, it intensifies its internal communication, and a unified definition of situation emerges. The group attempts to improve its position in the larger society. It generates common rationales and languages. Members of the group constantly search for ways to improve their situation. The group exercises tighter social control internally. Resources and help are more easily available because of the mutual trust of the group, and the network of free communication helps with problem solving.

How do groups come to be in this marginal situation? The two major ways are through migration, which lowers the relative centrality, and through regional expansion, which is a form of group migration. Young also suggests a series of "nesting" solidarity structures. As the highest-level system is subject to strain (for example, the nation), the strain is passed to smaller groups through a shifting of internal structure. Subgroups are subsequently dislocated in a chain reaction. Successive solidarity formation and entrepreneurship result. The subgroup's world view must have high focus. The formation of some calculus of group progress is an intrinsic component of solidarity. For the businessman, the group's measure is "profit." The group's perception of its efficiency and status, however, is dependent on consensual validation, and the measure of progress may be prestige, professional recognition, or some other factor. Everyone pursues "profit," but this is socially defined by the group.

How does this apply to education? It would seem that educators are not a highly differentiated group. They tend to be recruited from the same social classes, to perform the same jobs in very similar structures. In spite of the great number of schools and teachers, there is little institutional or occupational diversity. On the other hand, teachers are perceived and perceive themselves as quite central to the social order. Although not of high status, educators are seen as being within the social mainstream. This is true even within the local community. As a group, then, educators would have a very low differentiation-relative centrality ratio. According to this theory, entrepreneurism would be at a low level and so would innovation if it is indeed dependent on entrepreneurialism.

Such activities could be increased by increasing the differentiation, but this would not be easy to do. Perhaps mixing together teachers of different disciplines would have some effect. Nor would reduction in the relative centrality to the system be easy to achieve. Although some contend that education is marginal to society, educators do not see themselves that way. Whether pressures for "accountability" will have the effect of producing internal strains and, hence, reactive group formation remains to be seen. Over the last decade or so teachers have been organizing themselves for collective bargaining activities, but any student of the movement knows that they are far from a cohesive viewpoint, the sine qua non of entrepreneurship. It would appear that, among educators as a social group, entrepreneurism is mostly carried on by businessmen and others somewhat marginal to education, as, for example, private consulting firms.

What about the relative amount of entrepreneurism within educational institutions? Groups with low centrality might be those areas outside basic subjects and established departments. The areas trying to "make it" educationally and academically would be the most active. In universities this might be the applied fields. Evans (1970) found that applied departments, such as agriculture and education, were more likely to use instructional television. In public schools this might mean the more recently established programs such as counseling or pupil personnel services. In areas still striving for legitimacy, there is a considerable amount of what is labeled "empire building." Special education is a good example.

Relatively higher differentiation would be found where interdisciplinary teams work together. Again, relatively speaking, areas like pupil personnel services or special education are likely seedbeds for entrepreneurial activities. Otherwise, migration and regional expansion fuel entrepreneurial activity. It is no accident that much innovation activity occurs in the suburbs of large cities. Several of the factors mentioned here work together: migration as a factor in spreading interpersonal communication through areas of high urbanization, a loose organizational structure in which entrepreneurial behavior is rewarded, and regional expansion and migration increasing the differentiation-centrality ratio. Not only are these schools the most innovative, but many experience a surfeit of innovation. The innovations succeed each other so rapidly that a reaction sets in. Crises develop when one innovation shoves the next one out, and suburban communities have been known to develop innovation weariness. Innovations come and go so quickly that they are labeled "fads." Schools in newly developing suburbs around large cities are at the mercy of such forces, and, for ambitious school administrators, such schools are "plums."

How else might one increase entrepreneurism and innovation within the structure as it now exists? According to the dynamics outlined in this chapter, innovation could be increased by recruiting superintendents from different groups of people, by promoting superintendent interaction, and by increasing the frequency of career-bound superintendents. Increasing superintendent mobility might accomplish this, but possibly at the expense of continually starting new programs rather than improving those that exist.

Innovation must also either gain access to the inner circles of the central office staff or circumvent the staff. Circumventing the COS with a small program is possible; it is not likely with a larger one or with one requiring specific board approval or resources. Innovation must also be consistent with the values of the informal organizational elite. The way the system is now structured, initiative for innovation rests with the central control groups.

Some initiatory power can be gained by deformalizing and decentralizing the organization. More structural flexibility, lack of specificity, and less rigorous role definition would allow more room for initiative and entrepreneurial activities in the lower hierarchy. Diverse task structure, occupational specialization, and professionalism would produce more varied inputs. These factors seem to work independently of the values of the elite.

The formation of advocacy groups is enhanced by the size of the district, the budget and available resources, and the presence of an entrepreneurial leader able to provide the social cement. Formation of an advocaty group, a loose organizational structure, and an incentive system that rewards rather than punishes entrepreneurial behavior is essential to any widespread or long-lasting innovation. Opportunity for upward mobility and sponsorship of innovation by powerful outside agencies are also critical. Outside agencies provide extra resources to overcome unanticipated problems that inevitably arise. Entrepreneurial behavior is likely to be most intense in groups somewhat marginal to the main social system, but they must have enough occupational diversity and resources to mount an effective group movement.

The portrait of the school that emerges here is that of a relatively static social structure in which the power to initiate innovations resides in the central group. Occasionally this social structure is unfrozen and readjusted by a new chief executive, thus allowing some change. Otherwise, innovation on any scale requires entrepreneurial activities necessary to social reorganization. An advocacy group can form either with or without the help of the central office staff, but chances of successfully implementing an innovation are greatly enhanced if the COS or an external sponsor supplies abundant resources. These groups are led by certain types of people often ambitiously pursuing their own careers. All of these internal factors—size, looseness of structure, ambition, wealth, and so on—combine with the high central position in the urban hierarchy occupied by suburban school districts, particularly those experiencing considerable growth and, therefore, expansion often produces a surfeit of innovation and a panorama wherein one innovation rapidly and ruthlessly succeeds another.

Chapter 4

The Teacher's Predicament

ACCESS TO INNOVATIONS

The diffusion of educational innovations among schools, described earlier, was termed "entrepreneurial" because it required adoption by a unit like a town or a school district rather than by individuals. The focus was on the larger unit. This chapter deals with innovation from the individual viewpoint, previously termed "household" innovation.

The administrator deals primarily with the entrepreneurial process; the teacher, with the household one—making decisions for his classroom alone. The teacher does not usually initiate an innovation, but he almost always decides whether he will implement it or, more precisely, the degree to which he will use it. The teacher's power in educational innovation is that he can veto for himself. He is the ultimate consumer. (For the moment this ignores an important element—the teacher acting in a group.)

For household innovation, each new adoption potentially increases the chances of diffusion. If my neighbor buys a refrigerator, it is more likely that I shall also. In entrepreneurial innovation diffusion there is a competitive element; only towns of a certain size can support two stores. The unpredictable element is greater in household innovation. Time and location of adoption are subject to whim. It may be that I buy a refrigerator because of a chance contact two hundred miles away. It is because of this random element that studies of household innovation diffusion generally deal with the proportion of individual adoptions in a given area. Household innovation is less risky than entrepreneurial innovation. Less depends on my buying a refrigerator than on Sears establishing an outlet, simply because there are fewer people involved.

Diffusion among teachers resembles household innovation diffusion. There is neither much risk nor much profit involved when a teacher adopts an innovation. If one teacher adopts an innovation, there is more chance than another will do so. It is difficult, however, to predict precisely which teacher will adopt it.

Most of the previous innovation diffusion studies, such as those reported by Rogers (1962) and Hagerstrand (1967), have dealt with household innovations, and they have been based on homogeneous rural populations. Among rural populations of individuals, Hagerstrand saw innovation diffusion proceeding in a wave-like fashion as innovation was communicated from neighbor to neighbor in interpersonal, face-to-face relationships, and he saw adoption as a learning-and-persuasion process. Only information flow was considered in determining the innovation diffusion pattern. Brown (1968a) modified Hagerstrand's description of the household innovation process to include "market factors" as well as "information factors." An individual must not only have knowledge about the innovation; he must also have contact with it in order to acquire it. It is not enough that I hear about the refrigerator; I must also be able to purchase it someplace. A teacher must not only hear about an innovation; it must be accessible to him.

In Brown's model, the probability that an individual resident would adopt an innovation is equal to the probability that adoption did not occur before, plus the probability that he received sufficient information about the innovation, plus the probability that he accepted the information because he was not socially or economically resistant, plus the probability that he had sufficient contact with a distributor of the innovation.

Information can be gained through a resident of the community, mass media, or the market place. An individual may have contact with a distributor through regular shopping trips or through special distribution policies. The market factor is the likelihood that some potential adopter will convince a particular market to acquire the innovation, and the relevance of the market factor varies with different innovations. It is high in the adoption of manufactured goods, medium for acceptance of ideological innovation, and low when considering cultural change. The relevance of the market for a particular innovation depends on the presence of a distributor who is vitally concerned with propagation and who will operate impatiently through the distribution center, not on the nature of the innovation itself.

Running simulations with his model, Brown hypothesized that:

The average number of acquaintances contacted within a single time interval exerts most control over the saturation level of the adoption.

The tendency for new adopters to seek contacts outside their immediate acquaintance circle during the initial stages exerts most control over the rate of adoption during early stages of diffusion.

The strength of nondirected information exerts most control over the rate of adoption in the latter stages.

Teachers must hear about an innovation and have access to it through some market mechanism by which it might be "purchased," but this does not often occur in the teacher's world. Administrators, who normally hear about an innovation, often carefully control all information relating to it. And, if the teacher should hear about it through other sources, the resources and rewards necessary to "purchase" it are ordinarily beyond the teacher's control.

THE TEACHER'S INFORMATION FIELD

The teacher's professional information field is relatively restricted. High-level business administrators may spend over forty hours a week making external personal contacts (Tornquist, 1970), but teachers spend hardly any. Their heavy teaching load confines them to the classroom, which greatly restricts access to new ideas and innovations. If they are lucky, they get to go to an annual convention. School administrators and central office staff spend considerably more time making external personal contacts. They operate as a prime contact for teachers, but this means that they also closely control the information accessible to teachers. For example, fully 30 percent of those designated by administrators as teachers of the gifted, for which the district was receiving state funds, did not know they were teachers of the gifted. Such control facilitates an administrator's problem of deciding how much innovation he wants and who is to undertake it. Totally free information exchange between teachers and external contacts often leads to "runaway" projects, the wrong people handling the innovation, or internal conflict. Innovative ideas are often pursued by those marginal in status, particularly radical or troublesome ideas the administrator is likely to oppose. The teacher's position is isolated, information is controlled, selection for projects is dictated, and resources are allocated by others. Much of the initiative in a school is in the hands of the administrative staff. For good or ill, the overall effect is to inhibit innovation.

Even within the school itself the teacher does not have a great deal of face-to-face contact with other adults. In a survey of gifted teachers in Illinois, Hotvedt (1973) found that 80 percent had less than an hour a day, including lunch, to talk to other teachers. When asked to list sources of new information, "other teachers" received 24 percent; "periodicals," 21 percent; and "college courses," 12 percent of first choices. They did not select "administrators." It was clear that outside professional contacts were severely limited.

Teachers were also asked to list their three closest friends at school, the three people they worked closest with, and the three people from whom they got the greatest number of new ideas. The overlap among these people is shown in Figure 4-1. Of the people named, 34 percent fit all three categories, that is, friends, work associates, and sources of new ideas were the same. There was also an overlap of 8 percent between sources of new ideas and friends and of 12 percent between sources of new ideas and those with whom the teacher worked most closely. Fully 54 percent of the teacher's personal sources of information were among their closest friends and closest work associates at school. In a comparison study on a different sample, Wolf (1973) found a 74 percent overlap among the three categories within a cadre of teachers specially trained in teams during a summer institute.

In the study of an actual innovation diffusing through three Michigan high schools (Lin, Len, Rogers, and Schwartz, 1966), 73 percent of the respondents first heard about the innovation through interpersonal sources; only 25 percent heard through mass media. Because an actual innovation in the school forces some kind of personal evaluation, it is reasonable that interpersonal communication plays a stronger role.

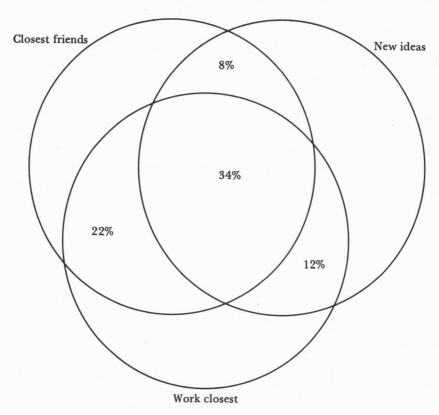

FIGURE 4-1
Overlap among friends, work associates, and personal
sources of new ideas

The same study also dramatizes the fact that what is an innovation for the administrator is not necessarily an innovation for the teacher. Although the innovation was a scheduling arrangement for the school, from 54 to 81 percent of the school faculty indicated that they did not adopt the innovation until from 4 to 18 months after the actual adoption of scheduling by the school. The field of information available to the teacher through personal contact seems to be restricted to contact with fellow teachers; it is particularly lacking in professional external contacts.

The internal teacher acquaintance structure appears to be

relatively close, despite isolation in the classroom and relatively little free time. House and Long (1974) applied directed graph theory to analyzing the complex sociograms of forty-eight elementary schools. They found that within schools with a mean faculty of twenty-eight, the faculty structure was 96 percent "reachable." Nearly every teacher could communicate with every other teacher through some-one they both knew well. The average social distance to reach some-one or to be reached by someone required an average of only 1.5 intermediaries. The average maximum distance to reach everyone was only 2.2 people.

Fully one-third of the contacts were reciprocal. If everyone did not know everyone else, he knew someone who did. The faculty acquaintance structure in this sample and this analysis was highly integrated, and ideas would presumably travel very rapidly through it if closeness of acquaintance were the criterion. The schools were reachable regardless of faculty size. Since there was so much overlap, there was also a minimum of distortion in the information, assuming that the information was worthy of being passed along at all.

House and Long also found that certain characteristics of the acquaintance structure were weakly related to a change variable. Teacher perceptions of change are positively related to the size of the schools, the percent of the faculty "reachable" in the school, and the percent of reciprocal relationships, and such perceptions negative-ly relate to average distances between people. In other words, both the larger the size of the school and the closer and more integrated the social structure, the more change is perceived as possible. Ac-quaintanceship is not necessarily the same as frequency of contact, however. Teachers could be closely acquainted and still not com-municate new ideas to each other. Perhaps one must also distinguish between professional and personal contact. In any case, there seems to be little contact with outside ideas.

In studying how computer-assisted instruction was communi-cated among faculty members in community colleges, House and Gjerde (1973) found that the source of first hearing varied from college to college (see Chapter 5). In some colleges it was first learned through a fellow teacher; in some, through an administrator; in some, through a newsletter; and, in one, through external contact. The source of first hearing had little effect on the teachers' attitude toward the innovation.

The first serious discussion about the innovation was, however, always with fellow teachers, usually one who was "well acquainted," and this was important. The teachers listed as their most important source of influence about an innovation their fellow teachers and those teachers already directly engaged in working with it. Whether they actually used the innovation, however, depended on whether they were given released time to work on it. This access, directly controlled by administrators, was limited to a few people.

TEACHER INCENTIVES–AN ECONOMY OF SCARCITY

One of the fundamental characteristics of public schools is the flatness of the reward structure (Cohen, 1973). There are few opportunities for professional advancement. Tenure and salary are tied to years of service. Ambitious teachers are forced to leave the classroom or education itself to advance professionally. Rewards for innovation in the classroom are also limited. One of the few tangible rewards for working on an innovative project is the increased chance of promotion. Otherwise, the only rewards are released time, better classes, more classroom materials, or minor classroom improvements.

Surveys of community college faculties adopting a computer-assisted instruction program revealed that they saw little or no risk in adopting the new device. The great majority of faculty members saw no tangible rewards for doing so, either. Only those granted released time by the administration indicated any substantial incentive for becoming involved with the project. People are often shocked that teachers should require tangible incentives to try a new innovation. Some teachers did indeed list "student enthusiasm" and less tangible rewards as incentives. The personal costs of trying new innovations are often high, however, and seldom is there any indication that innovations are worth the investment. Innovations are acts of faith. They require that one believe that they will ultimately bear fruit and be worth the personal investment, often without the hope of an immediate return. Costs are also high. The amount of energy and time required to learn the new skills or roles associated with the new innovation is a useful index to the magnitude of resistance. The necessity of relearning acts as a deterrent. New skills make old skills obsolete, and there comes a time when it is no longer worth the effort of learning new skills to master the innovation. Large-scale change usually requires replacing older teachers with younger ones who see the expenditure of effort as being worth the cost or using some other form of incentive to stimulate relearning and change.

Stephens (1974) found that the crucial variable associated with innovative classroom behavior was the reward system as perceived by the teacher. This factor is more closely related to teacher behavior than perceived norms of colleagues toward innovation or even the teacher's own attitude toward norms and rewards. Teachers in innovative schools see promotion depending on factors supporting innovation, while those in traditional schools see rewards as restrictive of innovation.

A teacher's classroom behavior is not a shared experience closely monitored by well-understood colleague norms. For innovations requiring a minimum of teacher-teacher interaction, behavior is unaffected by all but the most general building norms, leaving the teacher relatively isolated within the classroom itself. This isolation from fellow teachers enhances the relative power of the principal, who dispenses rewards at the building level and has direct access to classrooms. According to Stephens, any innovation must be mediated through the principal. He is in a position to control rewards to those below him. Stephens sees, in view of the isolation of the teacher, that increases in lateral communication would be an important element in changing teacher behavior.

In examining high school reward structures, though not those directly related to innovation, Spock (1974) found that the "extrinsic" rewards available to teachers were few and not greatly varied. Intrinsic rewards—"pride of workmanship," positive social interaction with peers, and ability to influence school policy—are relatively more important in the overall reward structure. Whether the greater importance of intrinsic work and peer-related rewards is because of the preferences of teachers or because of the absence of variation in extrinsic rewards could not be determined. It is clear, however, that intrinsic rewards are important and that the more material extrinsic rewards are scarce.

In some ways the teacher experiences an "economy of scarcity" and must conserve his energies carefully (Harvey, 1969). A teacher, like others living in a scarce economy, might resist new ideas in an attempt to deal with an environment that he does not control. Along with lower-class groups, the teacher must cope with a paucity of resources, variable input in the form of students with which he must deal, and the low esteem of others in the society, certainly other professionals. A feeling of powerlessness makes him tend to limit encounters to low-risk situations, especially where social and economic costs are involved. Trust is limited primarily to his own kind, and he limits his personal commitments, nurturing affective relationships with carefully chosen students and fellow teachers. He is vulnerable to attack from other professionals, other institutions, and other groups in the society. Uncontrolled variability of environment requires a simple social structure, for a complex one could not be maintained. Such conditions greatly inhibit innovation. Yet a teacher is, after all, a professional; unlike the lower classes, he has both a career and a stable job.

In most schools social rewards from peers are not very strong, either. Because teachers are isolated from each other, criticizing each other's work is impossible. Even though the communication structure is close, it communicates personal rather than professional concerns. Comparing teachers in "open space" schools (no room partitions) with those in conventional schools, Cohen (1973) found that the formal rewards available to teachers do not change, but the opportunity of seeing each other teach results in new interaction patterns. When interaction is increased, the teachers provide rewards and support to each other. Schools do not differ in chances for formal rewards or upward mobility.

Cohen found two types of ambition: professional—desire for reward and recognition within the classroom; and vertical—desire for promotion. One person might be high or low on both. Both types are positively related to the philosophy of the child-centered school approach. The vertically ambitious teacher is relatively dissatisfied in both school settings since neither provides much opportunity for upward mobility. Conventional schools discourage both ambitions, but the open-school setting proves more satisfying to the professionally ambitious because of the opportunity to work in teams and receive rewards from their peers.

Interaction in a team of equal-status workers makes teachers feel more influential, provides more chances for reward from peers, and increases job satisfaction. Cohen felt that this work environment actually increased professional ambition. She concluded that the elementary teacher was characterized not only by low social prestige but by lack of power within the school, lack of rewards for competence, and lack of professional opportunity.

The lack of opportunity for upward mobility proves very frustrating to ambitious teachers, often driving them from the profession. Changing the informal reward structure causes a growth in ambition among the teachers involved and also apparently allows teachers more power and influence within the school, thereby increasing morale and job satisfaction.

Ambitious teachers are generally important for innovation because they see the investment in relearning as worthwhile for their future. In community colleges those teachers who expected to advance in rank and who expected supervisory positions were most enthusiastic toward innovation. The more ambitious they were, the more enthusiastic they were. In a relatively scarce economy those who envision future rewards through better jobs are the ones willing to invest extra effort. In the economy of the school there are few immediately tangible rewards, which is why control of such elements as job slots and job titles is so important to the future of an innovation. In such a tight money situation, small amounts of discretionary funds, almost always controlled by an administrator, assume great importance for innovation. Only unprogrammed funds can buy the new materials, pay for the special trip, and provide necessary support to new initiatives.

Besides the prospects of future promotions and other formal rewards, there is another major avenue for involving people in innovation—informal rewards. The one mechanism that brings all these rewards together and maximizes the traditional intraschool structure for innovation is the entrepreneurial group. As indicated above, the satisfactions of working with such a group are often worth the pain and effort of learning a new innovation.

The entrepreneurial group, or "team," provides informal rewards and bargains more effectively for formal rewards. Within the flat reward structure of the schools, it is not worthwhile for a teacher, unless he is exceptionally ambitious, to labor through the introduction of an innovation. The ambitious person sees his rewards as lying in the future rather than in the immediate present, and he may follow the bureaucratic career route. The other way to break through the bureaucratic low-reward structure is through entrepreneurial activity. The entrepreneurial group can bargain for increased formal rewards, thus shifting the reward structure within the organization.

NEGATIVE INCENTIVES AND TRANSFORMATION
OF THE INNOVATION

Another critical but not well-understood phenomenon involves the concepts of "variation" and "reorientation" (Normann, 1971) discussed earlier. Variations, or small-scale changes, can be accommodated within the existing political system. The existing cognitive framework, rules, and perceptions are sufficient for variation, requiring no change of cognitive domain. Reorientations, or more fundamental changes, occasion shifts in the internal power structure. Large-scale change cannot occur without some realignment, and not only are few goals, values, and power structures necessary, but the cognitive structure must also be changed. People must "see" things differently.

Whether an innovation represents a variation on existing programs or a complete reorientation, all changes are initiated and established within the organization as a consequence of the strong involvement of individuals. New developmental projects are important vehicles for individuals seeking status and power, and individuals may ride to popularity on them.

There is a strong tendency for group values to turn reorientations into variations and variations into regular practice. For example, when Carlson (1965) interviewed teachers and principals about their use of programmed instruction, he found interesting deviations from the intentions of the program designers. Programmed instruction was designed to let each student work at his own rate, which meant that there would be wide differences in the amount of material covered. Yet teachers would not let this happen. Through various means they actually restricted the output of the fastest students. Fast students were given additional "enrichment" material to do. Slow students were encouraged to work on materials at home, but fast students could not.

In addition, teachers felt compelled to hold group meetings in order to "perform"—to capture the attention of a number of students and serve as mediator between student and information. In fact, this is what teachers defined as teaching and, to them, the new role required of them was not teaching at all. Hence, they worked through some materials as a class and stretched many programs out in order to get "performing" time in. The principals themselves, uncertain as to how to supervise teachers without lesson plans or group work, were at a loss as to how to supervise and ceased observing classes at all. The net effect was to transform programmed instruction into regular classroom instruction. The rationale given by teachers was that students miss and need personal interaction. This is precisely the same reason given by college professors for rejecting instructional television (Evans, 1969).

In similar fashion, House, Steele, and Kerins (1971) found that teachers often "transform" program intents in independent study. In one program where grades were not given, the teacher covertly introduced a system of "black marks" that were assigned to students who did not complete their homework on time. Also, incensed at students who would spend time on other things and then finish up their work shortly before it was due, the teacher developed subtle ways of pacing the students.

In a study of BSCS (Biological Studies Curriculum Study), Gallagher (1970) found that even teachers who were identified as good teachers by BSCS and who had each spent at least two summers in special training institutes varied widely in their use of the same materials. Within the same unit of study on photosynthesis, one teacher might devote as much as 30 percent of the course to "skill" topics while another teacher might ignore them. Only in that there was complete teacher dominance over the classroom were the methods similar. Schumacher (1972) found that teachers using aesthetic education materials justified them in terms of teaching "basic skills," although the materials were clearly intended for appreciation. The attempt to rationalize them in terms of local mores easily led to using them as basic skill materials.

All this is not by way of demonstrating that teachers are perverted or incompetent but, rather, of indicating that the forces impinging on the teacher in the classroom are different from those on the inventor of materials and the teacher trainer on the campus. There is no doubt that teachers can be trained to teach in a certain way under strongly reinforcing circumstances, such as proximity to campus or special consultant help in the school district. There is also little doubt that the teacher will alter that behavior considerably in the direction of the everyday environment once those supports are withdrawn, as would anyone else.

To understand the adoption and transformation of innovative ideas in the classroom, one must also understand the phenomenology of the teacher's world, particularly the relationship with students and the subculture of peers. Although relatively isolated from outside professional contacts, the teacher is within the social networks of several groups—teaching peers, supervisors, professional contacts, family, church, and especially students. For any innovation one can name, teachers muster a variety of opinions from the groups to which they belong. "Programmed instruction" and "open education" may eventually be adopted, but, when they are, they will be transformed from the philosophical purity in which they were born into something easier for the social network to absorb. The teacher will reject or adopt a piece of it, depending on who sponsors it, what is said about it, personal values, and the existential situation. Almost never will it be adopted in its entirety. Most likely, if innovative and flexible, the teacher will negotiate the differences among ideas and groups, doing a little here, a little there, but always modifying rather than revolutionizing the teacher's role. Programmed instruction may be combined with the open classroom. Innovation waves blend, reinforce, and cancel each other. The innovation is always transformed.

Just as there are incentives for innovation, there are also incentives for keeping classroom instruction much as it is—in other words, *negative* incentives. Perhaps as important as the opinions of various reference groups is the existential situation the teacher faces in the classroom. Lecture and recitation have survived for so long as instructional strategies in the face of numerous efforts to change them that there must be positive benefits from their employment.

Westbury (1973), among others, contends that teachers must perform three essential tasks: present what they wish to teach, give students opportunities to practice what is to be learned, and allow for lapses of interest and readiness. While a tutor may discover where a student is and lead him through a series of personally designed strategies, a classroom of pupils greatly complicates these tasks. Differing levels of readiness, enthusiasm, or the many other factors that influence individual learning make it difficult for the teacher to determine where each student is.

One way of handling such a situation and also managing a group of individuals whom he has not recruited and who are attending class involuntarily is to present and cover a fixed body of material, engender mastery of the material, and generate affect among students so that they will comply with the learning situation. To accomplish this, there is a teacher, a text, a blackboard, and little else. Because teachers must meet the demands of coverage, mastery, affect, and management with limited resources, they resort to lecture and recitation.

The pacing of students is a component of the management demand. Externally paced activities are easier to manage than self-paced ones. Other studies indicate that teachers pace the entire class by monitoring a criterion group of students who fall between the 10th and the 25th percentile ability group (Dahllof, 1971), one way of managing the distribution of instruction to a group of students with differing abilities. The teacher must weigh coverage versus mastery, finally electing to teach most students rather than all students. Again, these are limits imposed upon the teacher by the conventional classroom. Changes in teaching behavior must be impeded by such constraints, but significant resources would be required to overcome them. There must be more positive benefits to be derived from traditional instruction other than simply not having to change.

Variation innovations like the introduction of a new textbook do not require changes in teacher behavior. They meet the demands placed upon the teacher by the conventional classroom. Reorientations that do require great new shifts in teacher behavior and violate conventional classroom demands do not ordinarily specify how to meet the new demands or provide resources for doing so. Westbury (1973) points to the "open classroom" as an example of a major reorientation that presents such problems. Student-initiated learning disturbs the teacher's management of a class. Advocates of the "open classroom" seldom provide any concrete strategies for maintaining student involvement, attaining mastery through various activities, or managing students. Even when the teacher can be motivated in some fashion to attempt open classroom teaching, there is little concrete guidance. The problems of managing a decentralized classroom are left unsolved.

Provided with little guidance, few resources, and little time, even the most highly motivated teacher must resort to personal experience to resolve inherent classroom dilemmas. Under such circumstances, one must expect to see teacher-initiated activities, various subtle devices for pacing the class, a hidden curriculum planned by the teacher, and other ways of converting the reorientation into a variation of the conventional classroom with the innovation being transformed into something conforming to the exigencies of the teacher's world. At best, the open classroom would be manifested in idiosyncratic programs worked out within specific sets of circumstances. Innovations that conformed to classroom demands, often the least innovative, would be most likely to be adopted. Only tremendously creative teachers would invent new tactics of implementation (there would be some) and implement the innovation in conformance with the original ideology. Those who did not agree with the basic concept of the open classroom or who saw neither extrinsic nor intrinsic rewards in it would not even attempt it.

The major point is that traditional instruction is a positively organized strategy to deal with the classroom situation, and it is perceived as having strong positive benefits. Innovation, of course, offers benefits, but these must compete with the benefits offered by traditional instruction.

THE TEACHER AS CONSUMER OF INNOVATIONS

Through innovation diffusion, the innovation has now become available within the school. Should the teacher participate? His position is similar to that of the potential consumer who asks himself whether he should buy a refrigerator now that there is a Sears store in his town. One of the models used in microeconomics to analyze consumer behavior is the indifference curve.

The models presented here are only *illustrations* of verbal reasoning; they do not stand by themselves.* Like other simplifications, the assumptions on which the models are based are questionable, as indeed are the assumptions of classical economics. I distinguish between legitimate indifference curves and these modest analogies, referred to as "preference" curves. The assumptions become even more questionable in Chapter 6, where I try to measure these concepts, measurement being the triumph of expediency over truth. I have chosen the quick, dirty, easy way of data collection.

---

*The hurried reader with no stomach for abstract and obtuse speculation should move past this section and the next, which take some rather indecent liberties with models of microeconomics. The circumspect reader can glean the results of this scuffling by skimming the verbal parts of the chapter, assured that he has missed only the brutalities of a conceptual mismatch. Those who enjoy such spectacles should read on.

These models are presented in a spirit of exploration rather than rigor, in the hope that the reader will find them informative. In spite of the limitations, they provide interesting insights into the nature of innovation benefits and the teacher's involvement in innovation. These insights will be substantiated by other information in Chapters 5 and 6. The fact that valuable conclusions can be derived from shaky assumptions suggests that there are alternative arguments for arriving at the findings. So with some misgivings I present these models in the belief that a model must finally be judged by its utility rather than its purity.

Suppose that a consumer wishes to buy so much bread and butter. He has various preferences, represented in Figure 4-2. As he buys more butter, it becomes relatively less valuable to him. After all, what would he do with all butter and no bread; likewise, with all bread and no butter? So the consumer's preference for bread and

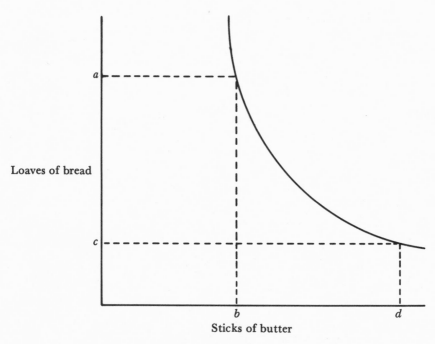

FIGURE 4-2
Indifference or "preference" curve

butter is represented by the number of loaves of bread he would trade for so many sticks of butter. As he gets more bread, he would trade more bread for butter. The more butter he gets, the more butter he would trade for bread. He wants a balance of the two. The "indifference curve" in the figure above represents the ratios of bread and butter he finds acceptable. Any ratio along the curve would be equally acceptable to him. Hence, he would be "indifferent" to any ratio as represented by a point on the curve. The consumer would just as soon trade a loaves of bread for b sticks of butter as trade d sticks of butter for c loaves of bread. Curves represent the consumer's preferences. They are referred to here as "preference" curves.

Actually, there is a whole family of preference curves rather than just one. Another curve might represent the ratio for many more sticks of butter and loaves of bread. It would be farther out from the origin. Another might be closer even to the origin, expressing the exchange ratio between a few sticks and loaves. So the consumer has a whole set of preferences depending on how much he has to spend. In reality, though, he has only so much to spend for bread and butter. This budget restriction is represented by the straight line in Figure 4-3 known as the line of "attainable combinations" or "the budget line."

This line represents how much the consumer has to spend. It represents not what he *prefers* to buy, but what he *can* buy. If he were to put all of his money into bread, he could buy the number of loaves indicated when the budget line intersects with the vertical axis. If he were to put all of his money into butter, he could buy the number of sticks indicated when the budget line intersects with the horizontal axis. He can also split his purchases, buying any of the combinations lying along the line, the "attainable combination" of a loaves and b sticks.

How much *will* the consumer buy? If he is economically rational, he will buy the most that he can afford. His satisfaction is maximized the farther the line is from the origin (more goods are better than fewer) so he will choose the combination indicated by the point of tangency between the budget line and the preference curve—in this case, a loaves of bread and b sticks of butter. The consumer's satisfaction will be maximized by this purchase.

Educational innovations rarely come in discrete units like loaves

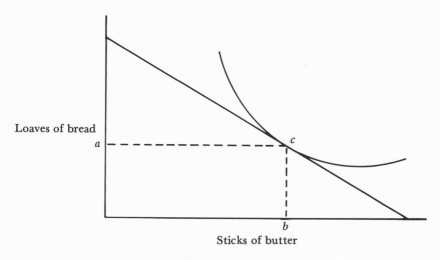

FIGURE 4-3
Line of attainable combinations

of bread or sticks of butter. But the teacher still has the problem of deciding how much of the innovation to "purchase." Presumably the teacher must give up some part of his traditional instruction in order to accommodate the innovation. He must also pay a price for the innovation. Teachers recognize differing kinds of benefits: good students in classes, enthusiastic students, a good teaching schedule, orderly classes, professional advancement, released time, promotion. Participation in the innovation may offer career advancement, released time, and more enthusiastic students. Conventional instruction may offer more orderly classes, a better fit with the existing schedule, or some other benefits suggested in the previous section. These preferences will be reflected in the preference curve (see Figure 4-4).

Here the benefits of the innovation are plotted against the benefits of conventional instruction. The preference curve represents the individual teacher's preference for the types of benefits available in the two situations. The budget line represents total teacher involvement or effort, roughly approximated by work time. The ends of the budget line indicate what benefits he could purchase if he spent all his time on one or the other, benefits which he sees as being available to him. Naturally, the preference curve reflecting teacher preference

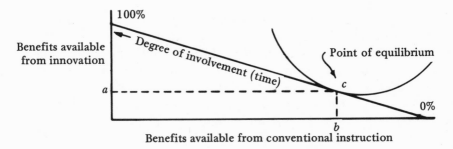

FIGURE 4-4
Teacher's preference curve

will vary with each individual. The one drawn here reflects a decided preference for the benefits of traditional instruction. The ends of the budget line are anchored in the "objective" context of what benefits are actually available to the teacher. The slope of the budget line drawn here indicates that the tangible benefits associated with the innovation are rather low, which is normally believed to be the case. The teacher derives few tangible benefits from participating in innovations. Hence, the degree of participation is low.

The teacher's participation can be increased substantially by increasing the tangible benefits associated with the innovation, such as providing released time, even without changing the teacher's subjective preference ratios. Thus, there are examples of teachers doubting the merits of the innovation but willing to devote 100 percent of their available time to it, if released to do so. The benefits available from the innovation would have to be increased considerably, however, in order to increase significantly the teacher's use of the innovation, assuming this particular preference curve.

The teacher's preference curve might be changed, but this would require a reordering of the value he sees in the different benefits. It might be simpler to choose a person who already has a different preference curve more favorable to the innovation. For example, people with ambition seem to respond more favorably to innovations. One might expect their preference curves to be tipped toward the innovation. The same increase in available benefits would elicit a much larger participation on their part. (These concepts are put to use with actual data in Chapter 6, "The Teacher as Consumer of PLATO.")

The administrator faces a somewhat different problem vis-a-vis innovation. He is concerned about cumulative benefits to the organization, not those accruing to different individuals. The administrator also wants a mix between innovation and conventional instruction, a mix determined in large part by how he conceives his constituency. He maintains innovative programs to show that the school is progressive and up to date. He maintains conventional programs so that students acquire the basic skills. Few communities want all innovation or all conventional instruction.

Whereas the teacher maintains a balance by his degree of participation, the administrator can mix people as well as percentages of time (see Figure 4-5). To maximize cumulative benefits, he may have N people at a or W people at b. He distributes his faculty between innovation and noninnovation. This means he does not want all his teachers to embrace a new innovation, contrary to the desires of reformers. Often the administrator wants only a part, often a small

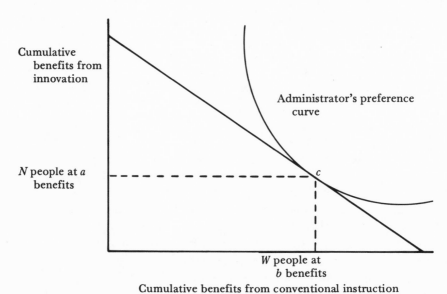

FIGURE 4-5
Administrator's preference curve

part, of his faculty to work on innovative projects. From conventional instruction he gets traditional achievement and order. From innovation he gets publicity and progress. Both are necessary.

For the administrator, group satisfaction (distance from the origin of the graph) is maintained by *some,* not all, of the people shifting to the innovation. To a considerable degree an administrator controls the rewards in an organization, making tangible benefits differentially available to members of the faculty. Thus, he can include the teachers he wants to participate in the innovative program by offering them rather high rewards, such as released time, while offering no such rewards to others for participation. It is more efficient internally to do so. The same reward to a person whose preference curve is tilted toward the innovation (who places a high value on "getting ahead") will induce a higher degree of participation than one tilted the other way. This is balanced by the administrator's need for control, however. He does not pull out all stops.

As has been mentioned, one of the most powerful inducements for participating in innovative projects is the prospect for career advancements. Teachers often want to be principals, and principals want to be superintendents. Yet such major inducements are relatively rare in education, as is demonstrated in Figure 4-6. Within the school structure teachers compete for a limited number of administrative jobs. If utilizing an innovation increases job opportunities for innovative teachers, it may lower job opportunities for conventional ones. The same is true for any other benefits that require a redistribution of internal funds.

There are two major effects when there is a shift in benefits

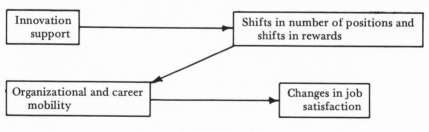

FIGURE 4-6
Innovation and career mobility

within the school: the number of individuals working on innovative and conventional instruction changes, and group satisfaction changes. The administrator wants to arrange benefits so that some people become innovative without lowering overall group satisfaction. Different situations are illustrated in Figure 4-7. The shift in benefits from a_1, b_1 to a_2, b_2 indicates a shift in benefits from conventional to innovative instruction. This would predict a shift of personnel from conventional instruction on preference curve U to innovation instruction at preference curve V. However, since indifference curve U is farther from the origin, there is a decrease in satisfaction within the organization. If an administrator took benefits away from the traditional group to give to the innovative group, it is easy to see how this could occur.

In fact, unless there is an increase in total benefits available to support the innovation, it would seem certain that total group

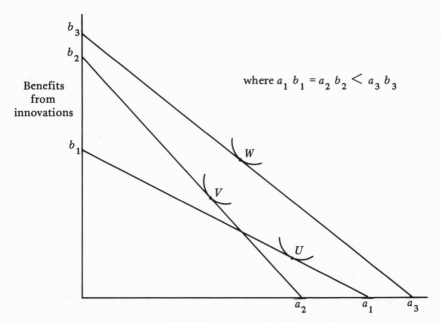

Benefits from conventional instruction

FIGURE 4-7
Shifts in benefits

satisfaction would be lower. Perhaps this is why innovations are normally supported by outside funds. Outside funds are a bonus that can be used to induce innovation with increased funds without lowering overall morale. For example, the shift from a_1, b_1 to a_3, b_3 would predict a shift in personnel toward the innovation as well as an increase in total group satisfaction. The traditional group also receives a slight increase in benefits. The latter shift might seem to promote better organizational functioning.

This consumer behavior model would seem to support the common sense notion that a general tightening of money or external resources hampers innovation efforts. Money is not available to "float" the innovation. The only way to induce innovation would be to lower benefits in other parts of the organization, which would lead to a lowering of job satisfaction and could produce a decline in overall performance. At the very least, certain internal strains appear in the organization. In effect, cutting off increased and manipulatable funding seriously dampens organizational innovativeness, for then innovation must feed on other parts of the organization.

Of course, these predictions are derivable from the model of consumer behavior. Roos (1972) found that the model does predict job satisfaction among bureaucrats and shifts in personnel between organizations, although not to the degree anticipated. The model assumes a free market in which individuals better themselves economically. Factors that limit mobility are political selection of personnel and the rewards often operative, plus the fact that benefits and costs are not known equally to all. People do, however, tend to move toward where there are jobs and higher salaries.

Other predictions about innovations are also discernible from the model. There is an optimum size for the innovative group. If people are attracted to the group by the prospect of jobs, the larger the group, the more competition there is for rewards and the less attractive the innovation is to individuals. (This ignores noneconomic rewards available from the group itself.) As more people join the innovative group, the more attractive the traditional group relatively becomes. Over time, job satisfaction evens out between innovative and traditional instruction, and the two groups stabilize. Hence, the internal growth of innovation is self-limiting. It becomes encapsulated within the organization. This effect is contrary to the common opinion that, if teachers like an innovation, if it is "good," all teachers will use it. On the other hand, if innovations are attractive because of the benefits associated with them, teachers cease shifting to the innovative group as soon as the benefits are equalized. Empirical data support the model's prediction over, in this case, that of common sense.

Given an equalization of benefits to personnel, there would be no reason to expect job satisfaction to be higher in the innovative group than in the traditional one. Once the innovative situation had stabilized, it would seem advantageous for the ambitious teacher to migrate to another organization where his particular skills could again command a premium. Imbalance in per capita benefits is remedied by interorganizational mobility. This presumes that mobility between organizations is readily possible. Again, it would seem that a scarcity of jobs would hamper interorganizational mobility and diffusion of innovation. Hence, lack of money dampens innovation diffusion among organizations, as well as limiting growth within. Career-bound superintendents have a more difficult time during times of tight money.

According to this model, to convert an entire organization to an innovation and maintain it for any given period of time, the benefits for the innovation would have to be tremendously high. First, benefits have to be high to induce naturally recalcitrant members. Second, they have to be high, perhaps constantly increasing, in order to sustain the increasing competition of having everyone involved. Huge sums of money have to be constantly available and participants have to be constantly and rapidly promoted to new jobs outside the school, or the innovation must have unbelievable intrinsic merits. What most reformers take as the norm of innovation—complete conversion—is probably impossible to sustain economically. Growth of innovation, the goal of most reformers, has strong natural limits.

In this section the teacher has been perceived as a consumer of innovation and a model of consumer behavior has been used to describe his behavior. Once the innovation is introduced to the school, usually by an administrator, the teacher has the option of participating. The model relates political, economic, and organizational change to the teacher's individual behavior mainly through the incentive structure. Social incentives, an important element, are another matter and may be achieved through the entrepreneurial group.

COSTS AND REWARDS

Economists have found that the probability of adoption of innovation in industry is a decreasing function of the amount of required investment and that expected profitability is an important factor in the rate of diffusion. Both costs and rewards have been important in decisions to try something new. Slevin (1971, 1973) constructed a speculative mathematical model of certain conditions under which individuals try new things. The model says that an individual will try new things if the probability of success of the new thing (Pn) minus the probability of success of the current strategy (Ps) is greater than the ratio of costs (C) to rewards (R).

$$Pn - Ps > C/R$$

Both probabilities of success are defined by the individual as functions of current success (S) and target (T) or future success aspiration. Costs and rewards once located in S and T space form an innovation "boundary," on one side of which the individual will innovate and on the other side of which he will not (see Figure 4-8).

The innovation boundary graphically displays relationships among costs, rewards, success level, and target. If an individual is on the left side of the boundary, he will not innovate. If he is on the right side, he will. His position relative to the boundary can be changed by changing either his location (S, T) or the position of the boundary (C/R). A person may be moved into an innovation zone by increasing his aspiration level (T) or decreasing his success. Or he may be moved into a noninnovation zone by sufficiently increasing his success level but not increasing his aspiration level.

On the other hand, the boundary itself could be changed. By decreasing costs or by increasing rewards, the innovation boundary could be moved to the left, thus bringing individuals into the innovation zone even though the target and success level did not change. When time is introduced as a factor, some interesting results appear (see Figure 4-9).

Rewards grow smaller with time and boundary moves from left to right. In order to keep the individual in the innovation zone, aspiration level (T) must be gradually increased, or success must be gradually decreased, or a combination of the two. Hence, in order to keep people innovating, rewards would have to be constantly increased

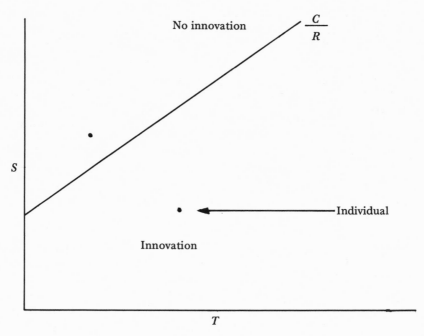

FIGURE 4-8
Innovation boundary (after Slevin)

or individuals would have to experience increasing failure. Both are difficult to maintain practically. Costs are more easily handled. In order to hold the innovation boundary in the same location, costs need only be decreased at a constant rate. This indicates a tremendous efficiency in decreasing costs as a strategy for inducing innovation.

How might such a model apply to school innovation? Suppose that a school is performing at a success level and target level indicated by *A* and will not attempt new things if the cost/reward ratio is .25. What can the school administrator do to increase the likelihood of his staff attempting new things?

Four variables can be manipulated separately or simultaneously to move the school staff into the innovation space. The aspiration level of the group could be raised by demonstrating a new innovation or by providing information about the superior performance of another group or by some form of in-service training—the "inspirational" approach to change. If the change in *T* were accomplished, it would move the staff members from *A* to *B* (see Figure 4-10).

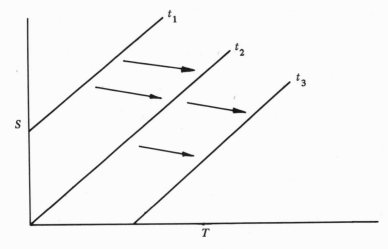

FIGURE 4-9
Change of innovation boundary with time (after Slevin)

Another strategy would be to lower the perceived success level of the staff, moving them from A to C. This could be done by making them aware of test scores, dropout rates, or other negative information. However, lowering the current success level often has negative ramifications, such as a lowering of morale, as well as being personally unpopular. According to the model, an increased feeling of success does not lead to innovative activity unless it is accompanied by an increase in aspiration level. This relationship remains to be demonstrated empirically.

Another approach is to leave the staff where they are and try to move the innovation boundary. This would eschew the personnel development strategies of the first approach. The most efficient strategy would be to reduce the costs of the innovation. In Figure 4-10, if costs were reduced to 0, the C/R ratio would move up and the innovation boundary would move past the group. The costs may be psychological as well as physical. A rigid bureaucratic organization would seem to exact more costs for change than a looser type. The type of organization that encourages entrepreneurial groups is also the type in which costs of innovation are relatively low. In fact, a major function of the entrepreneurial group is that it lowers the cost of innovation to the individual and increases his rewards.

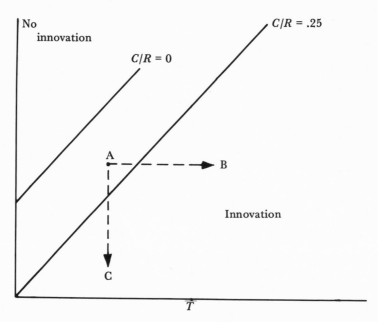

FIGURE 4-10
Hypothetical school situation (after Slevin)

Even with a C/R of 0, however, a school that feels itself to be very successful is unlikely to innovate. Increasing rewards is another way of moving the boundary up, although it is not nearly as efficient as lowering costs. Not even a very large reward would lower the C/R ratio to 0 if it were .25. In a practical strategy the administrator could lower C, lower S, and increase T and R simultaneously.

If the administrator's goal is to have all groups innovating, he would most efficiently use his resources by giving to each group or individual the minimum necessary to get it across the line. If he wants a balance of innovative and conventional instruction, as illustrated by the indifference curve analysis, however, he would be highly differential in allocating resources to individuals and groups. He might use his resources more efficiently by having a wide variation in innovative activities among groups rather than having all groups at the same level of innovative activity.

RESTRUCTURING TEACHER INCENTIVES AND INFORMATION

The basic predicament of teachers is that they are treated as passive consumers within their own organizational structure. Professional contacts with the outside world are extremely limited and mediated through the administrative structure. The information that reaches teachers is highly selective. Often they are introduced to innovations as a salesman would try to sell a new car to a customer who has little money with which to make a new purchase. The power and resources to initiate innovation usually lie elsewhere, but teachers do have one important power, that of refusing to participate in the innovation made accessible.

Faced with limited outside professional contacts, teachers turn to fellow teachers as prime sources of opinion and information. School faculties as a whole are largely isolated from external professional contact except through the administrators, yet administrators are not identified as an important source of new ideas. The internal acquaintance structure is highly integrated, at least in smaller schools. Presumably ideas would travel rapidly through such a structure, though where ideas would come from is a problem. Communication seems to be on private rather than personal matters. The teacher's professional behavior is isolated and hidden away from his peers by the traditional classroom organization.

The reward structure is quite flat. There are few opportunities for rewards or promotions, no matter what one's performance. More ambitious teachers tend to abandon the classroom. On the other hand, classroom behavior does seem to be affected by the reward system, which, insofar as it exists, is under the control of the principal. The principal seems to relate to each teacher and exercise his rewards on a private, one-to-one basis.

All in all, one might compare this social predicament to that of members of the lower social class, who must also cope with variable input, a paucity of resources, and a range of other events beyond their control. They are acted upon rather than acting. The reaction to such environments has been to evolve a relatively simple internal structure, to dwell upon affective relationships and meanings, and to avoid taking social risks. This is a defense against external manipulation. Like the lower classes, teachers are also denigrated by other professionals.

Within such an economy of scarcity, certain dynamics tend to result. One is that it is more rational for an administrator with tight resources to choose a teacher who already exhibits strong ambitions and preferences for innovation than to attempt to make available the range of benefits to everyone or to increase them to the point where they might tempt many teachers to participate in the innovation. Furthermore, the administrator wants a combination of innovative and traditional programs that is rational to his own career. He selects a few people to engage in the innovation and makes the innovation's benefits differentially available to them. This may look like favoritism to the other teachers and, in fact, it is.

In such a tight economy, rewards and job slots are in scarce supply. If participation in the innovation increases promotion opportunities for innovative teachers, it reduces opportunities for those excluded. Excluded teachers are in a position where it is rational to attack the innovation. Unless the always necessary resources for the innovation come from outside the system, they must be taken from traditional programs within. This can result in an overall decrease in group satisfaction and morale. Few innovations are "floated" without externally supplied funds.

These dynamics mean that the growth of the innovation group is self-limiting. It often becomes encapsulated within the school because to grow means to feed on others' opportunities. Hence, unlike the reformer's vision of reform sweeping through a school like a forest fire, the more likely course of events is such that it reaches a limit. When this equilibrium of benefits is achieved within the school, it might then become advantageous for the innovator to migrate to another organization. Lack of job opportunities and money also severely limit interorganizational mobility and the spread of innovation. Constant innovation requires a constant influx of new resources.

Besides increasing rewards, other tactics to promote innovation include decreasing costs, decreasing current success levels, and increasing aspirations. Many personnel development strategies try to increase aspiration or to lower feelings of success by persuasion or by providing new information, but lowering perceptions of success also causes demoralization. Reducing the costs of the innovation may be one of the most efficient ways of promoting innovation. Costs include the personal time and difficulty involved in learning new skills. Adopting innovations in industry has been shown to be inversely related to the size of the investment costs required to implement them. This may hold for individuals as well as for companies.

Constantly reducing personal costs may be a more viable strategy to maintain innovation than constantly increasing rewards.

Adequate resources either to increase rewards or decrease costs are seldom available to teachers expected to implement an innovation. They are expected to do so at their own personal expense, but it is not logical for them to do so and most do not. Innovation is left to the ambitious and to those reaping rewards from participation in an entrepreneurial group. The group can increase rewards, reduce costs, and raise aspirations, particularly the more intrinsic rewards resulting from participating in a larger cause. In such fashion does the economy of school innovation work. How could such a system be changed?

There are at least two generic strategies to radical restructuring of the incentive and information structure of the school. One would require increased differentiation among the faculty within the school itself. Much stronger differential rewards, such as merit pay or ranks among teachers, would increase the control of the school administrator, assuming he could control the necessary resources. Administrators would choose among teachers as to who would receive differential access to information and rewards. The administrator's power would be enhanced although he in turn would be highly dependent on outside funding sources to float innovations.

The other strategy would be to increase the relative power and influence of the teachers. A very mild form of this strategy is to encourage teachers within a school to interact professionally and actually examine each other's professional behavior as in the school without walls. This feeds professional ambition without changing vertical ambition and substitutes intrinsic rewards for more material ones.

A more virulent form of this strategy would be to promote professional contact and interaction outside the school if only to the extent now practiced by administrators. Much freer contact would greatly increase the flow of innovative ideas into the school. Of course, the administrative structure of the school would have a difficult time controlling these innovations. Such free access would be like unloosing a small army of entrepreneurs, and the flow, counter-flow, and combinations of ideas would be great indeed.

The most powerful embodiment of this strategy would be for the teachers as a group to bargain collectively for innovations, resources, and rewards to implement them. Initiative within the system would then move considerably lower in the hierarchy, greatly increasing the possibility of innovation. In a sense, this is what the educational entrepreneur already does on a smaller, idiosyncratic scale. So far, formal organizations representing teachers have not been inclined to bargain on innovation issues. Such organizations, like most American unions, have been content to negotiate for salaries and fringe benefits, leaving issues of policy and substance to management.

Both strategies—moving toward a more complex, differentiated structure or moving toward a less hierarchial structure in which initiative is more evenly distributed—would require more money. It is difficult to see how innovation can occur without an increase in resources to increase contact, reduce the costs, and so on. But the money must be tied to innovation activities. Simply pumping money into a system does not increase innovation (though it would do a number of other worthwhile things), since funds are distributed within existing power relationships.

Of the two strategies, the differentiating one is likely to result in more frequent, though more limited, innovation, where information and rewards would reflect the stratification of the organization. The distributive, equalizing strategy would result in less frequent, but more varied, pluralistic innovation that would be more widely and deeply embraced by all organizational members. Both strategies, of course, assume that innovation is to be desired.

Of the two pure types, I much prefer the equalizing strategy because it would give the teachers more power and influence. Although neither labor nor professional organizations have established an outstanding record of social change in America, I can envision teachers bargaining for innovations that would benefit the whole system. For reasons discussed in the latter part of this book, the distributive strategy seems closer to an ideal that, while it has suffered hard times, has remained persistent and deeply embedded within the American value system—equality. Apart from more elaborate and pragmatic arguments, the equalizing strategy is simply more just.

Chapter 5

An Illustrative Case of
Internal Politics–PLATO Comes
to the Community College

PLATO is a computer-assisted teaching system, perhaps the most advanced in the world, which has been under development by the University of Illinois since 1960. The teacher puts instructional material into the system through the "author mode" on a terminal, and the computer presents the material to the student upon command through any other terminal. The terminals, which are located all over the world, are hooked to the computer in Urbana through telephone lines.

The most recent version, the fourth generation, is known as PLATO IV. The system includes terminal equipment (hardware), a specially developed programming language called TUTOR, and various programmed lessons in many subject areas that have been developed mainly for use on campus. The instructional material can be written and edited from any terminal while sharing time with other authors and students.

The hardware is indeed impressive, a product of technological ingenuity. The PLATO IV terminal consists of a key set, like a typewriter keyset, that transmits the user's input to a large central computer and a square display panel, which can simultaneously show computer-generated graphic information and computer-selected photographic color slides to the user. The basic terminal sells for around $6,500 (1973 figure). Optional equipment, such as touch panels, random access audio, and film projectors, can be added at extra cost. The glass plasma display panel has over 250,000 individual digitally addressable points under computer control, which gives it considerably finer resolution than a television set. The response time to the student is .2 seconds. The screen can display over 2,000 characters, with 256 characters immediately available. The plasma display panel has inherent memory, which means it need not be replenished many times every second like a television screen. This frees the computer to run more terminals.

The keyset has standard typewriter characters plus special function keys. The slide projector holds 256 colored slides, which it projects through the back, allowing superimposed slide images. The touch panel has 256 addressable positions which control the computer, and one can touch the screen and have a response. This allows a child to match a word and a picture simply by touching the screen. The audio equipment has 4,000 random access messages totaling 21 minutes in length. The optional equipment—slide selector, touch panel, audio equipment—was, at the time of this study, available only for use on demonstration terminals; it was not used in the study. The estimated costs for the operational system under very optimal assumptions was fifty to seventy-five cents a student hour, but costs had not yet approached that low figure.

Lesson writing for PLATO uses a programming language called TUTOR based on English grammar and syntax presumably designed for teachers ignorant of computers. A knowledgeable teacher could write his own lesson or use materials already written. The prime lesson used to demonstrate the system has been the "fruit fly experiment." Diagrams of different kinds of fruit flies would appear on the screen, and the student could breed one with another of similar or different features as in a genetics lab. The progeny would appear on the screen randomly generated in accord with the laws of genetics. The student could then select two more to breed, and so on. The laboratory work of one semester could be reduced to a few hours using this simulation technique.

The system itself was no doubt the most technologically developed in the world. Hammond (1972) contends, in *Science* magazine, that the terminals are the most sophisticated devices ever developed for communicating with a computer. No one who saw a demonstration could fail to be impressed. Naturally the system attracted much attention from powerful groups within the society, as is demonstrated by the following excerpt from an editorial in *Science* (Abelson, 1972).

The public has begun to resist further increases in the support of education. If improvement is to occur in teaching it must come from new approaches rather than from more of the same. It is ironic that there has been so little real progress in education and that the research and development efforts needed to improve it have not been commensurate with the large total expenditure for education.

Nevertheless, we seem on the threshold of profound changes. Some of these have been discussed in a recent report of the Carnegie Commission on Higher Education [1972].

The report begins, "Higher education (and education generally) now faces the first great technological revolution in five centuries in the impact of the new electronics." The authors point to the growing use of electronic technology (computers, cable television, video cassettes) in many facets of education, including research, administration, the library, and instruction. The report predicts that by 1980 computers will have been generally introduced in libraries and that by 1990 they will have been generally introduced for instruction.

The report outlines some of the advantages for use of expanded technology in instruction. "It increases the opportunities for independent study and provides students with a richer variety of courses and methods of instruction . . . additionally it is infinitely tolerant and infinitely patient toward the slow learner." The new technology also seems to have good potential for off-campus instruction of adults. In view of these advantages and others cited in the report, the delay predicted in the introduction of the new technology seems long. Perhaps the authors have been influenced by two factors—their estimate of the inertia of higher education and their past experience with the deflation of over-optimistic claims for computer-assisted instruction (CAI).

Two systems of CAI are now under development and they are being backed on a scale sufficient to permit a realistic evaluation of its potential [Science 176, 1110 (1972)]. The most ambitious and versatile of these is the PLATO system at the University of Illinois. This project has had strong support in the engineering and development of new hardware and has drawn on talents of some 200 instructors of varying backgrounds who have designed courses for use with the computer. Ultimately, it is contemplated that one computer would serve 4000 terminals, some located hundreds of miles away. In the fall of 1973 a 2-year demonstration of the system, involving 500 to 1000 terminals, will begin.

The potentials of CAI seem to warrant more intensive effort in exploiting them. At the same time there should be critical and imaginative thinking about the likely impacts of the new technology so that possible adverse effects may be identified and avoided [Abelson, 1972].

Among other grants, the National Science Foundation gave PLATO $5 million to demonstrate the efficacy of the system in an operational setting over a three-year period. Educational Testing Service was given a million dollar contract to evaluate the system.

A major component of the demonstration was to install PLATO in several community colleges, most of which were in Chicago. A study was undertaken to provide formative feedback on the installation effort during the start-up year so that many mistakes could be corrected before the demonstration began (House and Gjerde, 1973). PLATO personnel tried to correct many of the problems discovered during this year.

The following case study, which is based on the formative study, in no way purports to be a final, complete evaluation of the project itself, or of PLATO in general. Educational Testing Service has that chore. The following study concentrates, instead, on internal organizational difficulties, particularly political, that must beset even the most highly developed innovation as it is introduced into a foreign organizational setting and on the impact such an innovation has on an organization. This study illustrates many of the dynamics revealed in the preceding chapters.

The ultimate meaning of an innovation comes from the context and social system in which it appears. As the innovation leaves the sheltered nest of its birth and development, it must inevitably contend with the "natural hazards" of the world. The names and locations of people and events have been changed to avoid recognition in the following account of a struggle for survival.* It is the struggle that concerns us.

THE NATURAL HAZARDS

Summer of 1972

By July 1972 the attitude of top community college administrators toward PLATO could best be described as one of cautious commitment. Irving Christopher, a central administrator of the Chicago Community Colleges (CCC), was enthusiastic about his new partnership with the University of Illinois. He saw PLATO being used around the clock to achieve literacy and for occupational training. Using it for the remediation of disadvantaged students, the targeted use within CCC, he saw as only a justification for introducing it to the whole system, where its eventual impact would be much wider.

---

*Only PLATO and the university are "real."

Christopher was especially proud of his relationship with the university, represented originally by Ron McCormick and more recently by Arden Mott, which he characterized as a "handshake" agreement. The written contract was then being drawn up. As evidence of CCC's good faith, Christopher could point to the increase in telephone rates. Because of agreements with the phone company and fewer terminals than indicated, the cost for use of telephone lines between the computer in Urbana and the consoles in Chicago was raised to $150,000. In spite of a tight budget, CCC was ready to absorb the unanticipated increase. The tight budget was attributed to a higher union salary settlement by the courts and less state money than anticipated. In what was perhaps a foreshadowing of future events, my interview with Christopher was cut short because he had to go to court with James Garvey, the president of Muslem Community College, to file suit against the teachers' union for harassing Garvey.

The man in operational charge of the PLATO operation was another member of the central administration, Alexander Dumas. Hearing that the university was looking for cooperating institutions for the Natural Science Foundation grant, Dumas had called Alvin Edison, the inventor of PLATO, whom he had heard speak several years before. Like Christopher, Dumas emphasized that CCC had demonstrated good faith by scraping together $150,000 to support six "authors," that is, people who write material for the system, who were living in Champaign-Urbana for a year. Six community college instructors had been chosen by the college administrators to spend a year at the university and learn to "author," that is, prepare instructional materials, for the system. This was in a fiscal year when CCC had released 42 teachers and 27 clerks. The actual agreement was worked out between Christopher and McCormick and, it was emphasized, sealed by a handshake.

The Chicago administration was pleased to work with the university faculty, and the good relationship that existed was attributed to the fact that the people from the university did not use a "hard sell" or "oversell" approach. Instead, they frankly admitted that the approach was "experimental" and might or might not work. It was a cautious approach based on "trust and frankness." "There are going to be problems," said Dumas, but they are "solvable because the commitment is there." CCC did expect special funding for PLATO from the

State Board of Higher Education and had informal indications they would get it. (This did eventually materialize.)

The top CCC management wanted PLATO as part of their Learning Center operation, which was the newest thing going. The Learning Centers, installed on each of the several campuses, would contain several media modes. The six teachers CCC had sent to the University of Illinois campus in Urbana to spend the year learning PLATO sent reports to Dumas, who said the reports were "fantastic." He heard no negative feedback.

The development and diffusion approach within CCC would be modeled after that used for "TV College," the ten-year-old instructional television operation of CCC. Teachers would be freed to produce materials that would then belong to CCC. In-service training would be held for the teachers, but progress would be cautious and experimental, in an attempt not to oversell the system. Only a limited number of places in the training sessions would be provided, encouraging teachers to fight to get in. This technique had proven to be highly successful in recruiting people in the past.

An interesting footnote was the appearance of the "Anecdote" in conversations with the Chicago administrators. The anecdote is a story, attributed to Edison, that Downstate College had not had any failures on the state licensing examination for nurses since it had begun using PLATO III many years before in its nursing program. This story was circulated several times in many different forms among PLATO personnel. The anecdote seemed to function as evidence and was passed around freely.

What was not revealed to the top administrators was some of the historical background for CCC. James Garvey, the highly publicized and controversial president of Muslem College, had drastically reorganized the college, abolishing the English department and other traditional units, and had introduced several widely publicized innovations. In the reorganization, several dozen teachers at Muslem lost their jobs. At one time Garvey claimed that eight faculty members in the Learning Resources Center were teaching 3,000 students. The dissident teachers claimed that the "teaching" consisted of passing out dittoed exercises from old grammar books. All of these cost-cutting measures were presented as "innovations."

A strong opposition group of teachers sprang up, centered in the powerful teachers' union at Muslem. This group began publishing an underground newspaper called *The Factory* and circulating it to the CCC teachers at the other eight campuses. Against this background, PLATO was introduced to Muslem. *The Factory* publicized PLATO as one more of the many innovations that had already failed, and machines were characterized as being a direct threat to teachers' jobs. The whole innovation movement at Muslem, of which PLATO was a part, was interpreted as a plot to get rid of teachers like those that had recently been fired. This underground group eventually became an opposition group within the teachers' union itself.

When the six PLATO fellows were selected to spend the 1972-73 school year learning PLATO, only two regular faculty members were chosen. The other four were from the "noncontract" people brought in by Garvey. They worked at very low salaries, had no formal contracts, and were not tenured. Most had worked in the Learning Resources Center at Muslem. The PLATO fellows were selected very quickly, without faculty knowledge according to some teachers. Within CCC, then, PLATO was interpreted by some teachers as one more "educational rip-off." The faculty saw it as being the same as other innovations. Rather than risk the open hostility of the regular faculty, "noncontract" people were chosen to introduce PLATO. These noncontract people later became, at least to some degree, social pariahs, outside the main communication stream of the school. From the beginning PLATO was fighting an uphill battle, especially at Muslem.

The situation was quite different at the one downstate community college than it was at the colleges in Chicago. Downstate College drew from an entirely different population. Serving a region perhaps thirty miles in radius, Downstate drew primarily rural, nonfarm students from small towns and a few medium-sized cities. The students were distinctly white and middle class as opposed to those in most of the Chicago schools. Their achievement tests scores were substantially higher than those of students in all but one of the Chicago schools.

Alone among the community colleges involved with PLATO, Downstate college was unique in not being a part of the CCC system, in having been involved with PLATO for many years, and in being so close to the university. Downstate started using PLATO III, the previous system, in 1969, for a course in maternity nursing developed by the wife of the PLATO inventor. At first, Gary Hinton, then

Dean of Students, and later Vice-President, thought PLATO III was great. After a while, however, students began complaining. If they misspelled a word, for example, their response would not be accepted by the system. Frustration mounted. Often the system functioned improperly or not at all. Hinton began to feel that PLATO was simply hardware development without educational implications and that Downstate was being used as a testing ground by the university without any real concern for the students. Downstate thought about dropping out of the program.

In spring of 1972, two university people, Mott and Blackman, began working to restore confidence. They gave firm commitments on the new equipment, offered some in-service training, and provided a written agreement. By the summer of 1972, Hinton commented, "You can trust what's going to happen." There was also the lure of extra money from the State Board of Higher Education. (This finally materialized, also.)

Unlike the Chicago administrators, Hinton saw considerable risk in the project. Several people released part-time represented a sizable financial investment, and, if things did not work out, there could be both a financial and a morale problem. Future difficulties were seen in the enormous cost of the system, not affordable by Downstate, and in copyrighting the material. PLATO might eventually reduce costs by increasing the number of students a teacher could handle, but, so far, costs had increased. By the summer of 1972, Hinton was forced to brand PLATO a failure. He was glad to have the help of some educational consultants.

The man originally in charge of the PLATO operation at Downstate, Paul Kelly, confirmed Hinton's feelings. He saw no way PLATO could succeed without released time for faculty and sharing programs with other community colleges. It was simply too expensive. Not in his wildest dreams could he see PLATO replacing teachers or other media forms. Originally, Downstate became involved with PLATO in order to maintain a good relationship with the university. The Downstate experience prior to the summer of 1972 had not been a good one, which Kelly attributed to engineers running the project and being concerned only with developing hardware. Inaccessibility to the machine (a few hours a week) and constant changes in TUTOR (programming language) also had Downstate on the verge of dropping out. Kelly repeated a form of the anecdote attributed to Edison, that Downstate nursing students scored higher in the maternity and pharmacology exams and that PLATO might enhance long-range retention. Although this was supposed to have happened at his college, he did not know whether it was true.

During the academic year 1971-72, CCC sent six full-time people to the University of Illinois at Urbana. They were treated the way students at a university are often treated; they were ignored. They were provided with no office space or facilities, they had difficulty in getting time on the machines, they received little formal instruction in TUTOR, and no one seemed to be responsible for helping them. They did receive some help from Blackman and others involved with PLATO when they asked for it. Blackman was assigned liaison duty the last few months of academic 1971-72, and his presence helped.

Because the authors had been led to believe that their activity was extremely important, this complete lack of interest in their progress was a shock to them. They were, however, pleased with their own progress and felt that they had learned a great deal through trial and error. They did not lose faith in PLATO as a teaching device.

The authors did express some concern for the future. First, the amount of time required to prepare PLATO materials was tremendous. During the year spent on the university campus, they had prepared little material that could be used for classes, and they questioned the willingness of their colleges to support such an activity. Second, they wondered about their colleagues' reactions, particularly the attitude of the teachers' union, the animosity between the Learning Resources Center and the academic departments at Muslem, and the willingness of students to trust themselves to an "impersonal teacher" like PLATO. Finally, they worried about the desire of the university staff to continually improve the system and the opposing need for stability.

Most of the authors, but not all, were "noncontract" people selected by administrators. Some had had previous computer experience. Others had not. Motivation ranged from professional ambition, to "a good opportunity," to idealism, to indifference. Some wanted to reduce the dropout rate of their classes, which ran as high as 70 percent. The ability to learn the TUTOR language and program competently was in question. In the fall of 1972 the authors returned to their respective campuses to await the arrival of the PLATO terminals.

The Year of the Terminals—Downstate College

Downstate College is a new school that, during the past few years, has been building a beautiful and expensive new campus. It was previously located in buildings scattered throughout the town, and much energy and money were expended to pull things together. A new physical plant offered considerable advantages for installing PLATO terminals, and at least four of the six colleges involved with PLATO were constructing new buildings in which space was specially set aside. The one older college experienced considerable renovation difficulties. Although the PLATO terminals and other hardware were paid for as part of an NSF-funded demonstration project, the costs of renovation and released time had to be absorbed by the colleges themselves.

Downstate College began the 1972-73 academic year with two major obstacles to the implementation of PLATO. One was the past history of its engagement in PLATO III. In some ways it had to overcome the feeling that it had been "used" by the university in previous years. The second obstacle was financial. Where would it get money to support released time for its teacher-authors? Where would it be when it had to support terminals and computers on its own, costs currently borne by the NSF project funds?

Confidence was restored through the work of the university's liaison people. A small grant from the Illinois Board of Higher Education later in the year helped alleviate the immediate financial problem, but costs continued to plague Downstate College more than they did the city colleges of Chicago. Whether costs were easier to absorb in the much larger CCC system or whether costs were more visible at Downstate because of the skepticism of the administration is difficult to say. Based on previous experience, the Downstate administration believed that ultimate PLATO costs would increase the per student cost of instruction, although costs might be held down by assigning more students per teacher. PLATO could be economical only by sharing it with other colleges.

A dominant fact of Downstate College's existence was its proximity to the university. That fact tended to color much of its activity. In the case of PLATO, almost all the instructors involved with PLATO worked on it at the university or became part of the informal social structure emerging around the university project.

This close association enabled Downstate instructors to receive excellent informal training and help from university personnel and to develop a higher degree of enthusiasm. It also threatened Downstate administrators with a "runaway" project. According to both administrators and instructors, the involved instructors were much more enthusiastic about PLATO than the administrators, and they wanted to move ahead much more rapidly. This presented the administrators with a control problem, particularly in light of their concern about costs. In Chicago the opposite problem obtained, with administrators introducing PLATO and trying to stimulate interest among the faculty.

During the summer of 1972, the teacher-authors from Downstate were among the most sophisticated in the colleges. Joan Veech and Peg Thomas had been working on the original nursing program and had found it unsatisfactory for two reasons: the approach was much like a textbook, and students did not like it. They also felt that they did not receive much administrative support before April 1972. By December they emphasized that, if their outside proposal were not funded, the nursing program would have to be sacrificed. "System downtime" was a major difficulty. More help was needed.

While still believing in the utility of PLATO for handling simulations and other problems in clinical nursing, both instructors complained about the system's lack of "accessibility" and felt that they had to have outside funds to support their program development efforts. Sufficient funds were not available internally to give them all the time they needed.

By December the Downstate administration felt that the university liaison people had been doing an outstanding job. Things had improved. Even though Downstate was running a $140,000 deficit, $40,000 was going into released teacher time for PLATO. One continuing area of misunderstanding involved costs. The touch panels and audio channels would cost $1,000 to $4,500 more per terminal than the original estimate. What would the final cost be? They could not help wondering.

In the fall survey of teacher attitudes toward PLATO, Downstate ranked high in optimism among the colleges and was most aware of the program's existence. There was some feeling that "too much fuss" was being made over the whole thing. There was considerable knowledge and interest among the faculty over the fact that released time was available for working on PLATO, and Downstate was high in the number of hours the faculty was willing to invest to learn it. Most teachers saw themselves continuing as teachers five years from that time, as opposed to becoming administrators, which differed from the attitude that prevailed in other colleges.

By winter the faculty attitude was still high. Most of the respondents had heard about PLATO outside the school, namely through university contacts. By the following spring Downstate had become the most optimistic faculty among the six colleges.

Besides the nursing group, at least two other strong groups were operating at Downstate. Richard Morefield headed the chemistry group. He was teaching a PLATO chemistry course at the university before he joined the Downstate faculty and, in a sense, he brought the course with him. Charles Hassell and Lila Dietz, who had also learned about PLATO through courses at the university, worked with Morefield. Morefield actually produced the programs and was concerned that the system had been oversold and oversubscribed. He felt that the higher administrators should establish better communication with the authors and make more honest projections of PLATO's capabilities so that the authors did not oversell the availability. Otherwise, the faculty could become involved, frustrated, and indifferent.

Another very strong group was the biology group. Dean Waggoner became involved through Winston Major; Lynn Hatch through her husband, a physics instructor at the university; Arthur Crawford, through a former roommate who had worked for Edison; Robert Bell through Creg Phillips, a university biology instructor; and Carolyn Mctane through Neil Jensen who was in her university class. As is evident, the downstate faculty operated through informal contacts with university personnel. In a very real sense, they were part of the engrossing social system revolving around PLATO. They came out of the university, maintained personal ties with the university, and looked to the university for guidance. The biology group itself was very innovative. Generally the Downstate authors felt that the administration was supportive but not wholeheartedly committed to PLATO.

By June 1973 the administration itself felt that it was "permanently" committed. Vice-President Hinton said that the many problems in the college had been somewhat alleviated by the receipt of a small $18,000 grant for PLATO from the State Board of Higher Education. He hoped more would be forthcoming. Some federal proposals for money had been submitted, but he was not too encouraged. As long as PLATO was "successful and financially feasible," Downstate would continue.

The administration still saw the main difficulties as being technical and financial. Increased use had led to the extended core space being too small to accommodate individual students. Students might have to be scheduled in blocks of time rather than at their own convenience, which would greatly reduce PLATO's flexibility. University engineers promised to solve the problem during 1973-74, and that year, Hinton felt, would tell the story. The other problem was that the terminals in mass production were going to cost more than had been estimated.

On the positive side, the college no longer felt it was a testing ground for the university. Credit for this was given to the work of Mott and Blackman, university education personnel. Hinton felt that the teacher-authors were making good progress. Good courseware was being developed. The number of teacher-authors would not, however, be increased beyond the current number. Some might be shifted out of nursing because of personnel difficulties. Also, in contrast to PLATO III, students who had worked in the system were still excited and interested. All in all, the Downstate administration was more optimistic and looked forward to what it thought might be a critical year ahead.

Of the six colleges involved, Downstate was most ready to meet the test of the Educational Testing Service evaluation. In spite of financial difficulties and an earlier unsatisfactory relationship with the university, physical and social closeness to the university had permitted a transfusion of technical competence not available to the other colleges despite great effort in Chicago. Some university-developed programs were immediately usable since Downstate students resembled university students more closely than those of the Chicago colleges did. Downstate instructors were often trained at the university. This association created some severe problems for the Downstate administration and made Downstate the most sheltered and successful of the colleges.

The Year of the Terminals—City Colleges of Chicago (CCC)

Muslem College

Muslem College lies along the Truman Expressway; it is a sleek black building two blocks long in the middle of the West Side ghetto. Across the expressway it faces off against County Hospital and the massive medical complex. The area, one of the roughest in the city, was the worst hit part of Chicago during the King riots. No nurse can travel the underway passage to her quarters without a guard.

Sitting in the midst of this decay is the beautiful black building of Muslem College designed by Mies Van der Roh. In front, three enormous sixty-foot flag poles fly the American flag, the white Illinois flag, and the Black Liberation flag, the latter strikingly dissonant with its thick black, green, and red bars. When the building was dedicated, James Garvey, the President, explained for television why the Black Liberation flag flies there: "At one time you couldn't fly the American flag in this neighborhood. Now you can."

Both at the parking lot and at the doors one must stop for security guards wearing black uniforms with orange Muslem insignias on the sleeve. All are reportedly former convicts. Inside, the building is handsomely furnished with heavy oak furniture and African art. In the lobby sits a black Oldsmobile dating back to the 1950's—an assassinated martyr's car.

At the time the terminals were introduced, President Garvey was a powerful political force in Chicago. The student body was nearly 100 percent black; the faculty, 95 percent. The school was run on a tight authoritarian basis. Garvey and the faculty were engaged in a tremendous protracted conflict over firings and reorganization. The President placed his own people in all the top slots in the college, and they exercised tight control. Teachers were afraid to be interviewed for fear the rooms were bugged. Distrust gripped the school.

Garvey claimed that people were out to get him. Others claimed that he had strong paranoid tendencies. In December 1972, a month after the arrival of the first PLATO terminals, irregularities in the financial accounts forced Garvey's resignation. His views on PLATO were never recorded, and attempts to reach him were unsuccessful. The day of one interview visit, someone fired three shots in his office window early in the morning. In spite of these difficulties, Garvey's actions had a strong effect, not only on Muslem, but on the rest of CCC. PLATO was one of many innovations that he tried to implement at Muslem, extracting maximum publicity for them.

Internally, he disbanded the English department and established the Learning Resources Center. The task of the Center was to teach basic reading and math skills. Learning skill instructors were ordered to have thirty contact hours per week with students. Garvey fired many instructors and hired much lower-paid "noncontract" people who could be fired without cause since they had no contracts to staff the center. Externally, Garvey claimed they were individualizing instruction. Internally, the teachers claimed it was all publicity.

PLATO was introduced into Muslem as part of the Learning Resources Center. At least three distinct groups could be identified vis-a-vis PLATO. Most directly affected were the "noncontract" people who comprised the bulk of personnel involved with the Learning Resources Center. Students unable to do regular college work were sent to the center to learn elementary reading and math skills. Ability levels varied tremendously, ranging as low as fifth grade. Any student was accepted, true to the philosophy of the school, and noncontract people were hired to "tutor" these students. The faculty work load was exceedingly heavy—thirty contact hours per week and hundreds of students. Students were supposedly handled on an individual basis, but much group work went on. The noncontract people, lacking proper teaching credentials, had no job security.

In the fall of 1972, the noncontract people were most enthusiastic about PLATO. They could see PLATO helping them with their heavy work load. They would not have to take five or six students aside every class to tutor them. They were somewhat concerned about how their students would respond to an impersonal machine, but they were hopeful. They saw student response as being the critical element, yet they knew little about PLATO. Their own major problem, they said, was not learning to use the machine, but time. They attended many meetings and performed other duties in addition to their thirty contact hours per week.

A smaller, older (around thirty), and more experienced group within the Learning Resources Center was the tenured, contract faculty. They had been around Muslem a little longer (3-5 years) and could best be described as cynical, wary, and weary. They had seen the "innovations" come and go and, as one put it, "Muslem blew the groundwork for PLATO." Like everything else in the school, in their view, PLATO had been crammed down teachers' throats and would not receive a fair trial. Instead of being soft-pedaled as a supplement, which it might be good for, it was being forced on everybody.

According to the tenured faculty, the noncontract people were enthusiastic because they had no choice. They had to reflect the administration line or be fired. The least secure people were the most enthusiastic, and the most secure were the least enthusiastic. Although PLATO would be used in the Learning Resource Center because the faculty would be ordered to do so, it would be viewed negatively by teachers. The Learning Resource Center was the lowest-status group in the college. According to the faculty, PLATO should have begun in the science group with Dean Dodd's division. They were the highest-status group in Muslem and, if that group used it, others would follow. The reverse effect was achieved by installing it in the Learning Resources Center.

As early as the summer, the authors from Muslem had identified the teachers' union and the science division as the center of resistance to PLATO. One could have predicted in advance that the science faculty would be most likely to use a technological innovation like PLATO while the noncontract people would feel the greatest job threat and resist it. In many ways, the science division (including math) was most secure and best informed about PLATO. The faculty, almost all tenured professors with technical backgrounds, enjoyed the highest prestige in the school. They taught small seminars, which made them distinctly unenthusiastic about PLATO.

Dean Dodd and his department chairmen were able to present a virtual litany of objections to PLATO. They contended that the PLATO materials were no different than what they taught their classes. The trained PLATO authors were from the Learning Resource Center and not from the chemistry and math departments. Instructors should have control over the content of their own classes. PLATO content had received minimal input from bona fide science instructors, which made it very weak.

The students needed real lab experiences, not simulated ones. Many had never had a chance to handle lab equipment in high school because of the danger of breakage. Students who were to be nurses and technicians needed concrete experiences, and such students might not respond to impersonal teaching. Some students, for example, even stayed around an extra year to take a regular class rather than take the televised classes then being offered.

Underlying these objections was a deep-seated suspicion that a technology like PLATO was used only for blacks and other minority groups; it was not used in top universities: "What do the professors at Harvard and Yale think about this operation? Are they using PLATO? No, of course they do not use it. Technology like this is used to cheapen education and provide a poor education for black and minority students as opposed to providing a good, small-group kind of education for students as at top universities."

They saw the motivation behind PLATO as mainly a matter of financing, a way of providing cheaper education now that minorities had insisted on their rights. To provide a good education at Muslem would require doubling the cost. It was simply a matter of time until PLATO would become a union problem. Yet they also expressed a willingness to give the thing a try, to be convinced. Some insisted on judging the device on currently available materials, not on potential.

A senior author, Mike Hamilton, explained that PLATO did not unduly threaten the noncontract people's jobs; these had always been insecure. On the other hand, it did threaten the science faculty because they had an easy course load. PLATO promised to make a difficult job easier for the Learning Resource personnel and an easy job easier for the tenured faculty. On returning to Muslem College after his year at Urbana, Hamilton was named PLATO coordinator for Muslem. He worked in an office very close to that of Carl Ellos.

Dumas named Ellos, formerly Director of Research at Muslem, as city-wide coordinator for PLATO. He retained his office at Muslem College, although he spent much time downtown at the central office. Physically, Ellos' office was located in the Learning Center, adjacent to the noncontract personnel. Yet he and his group were somewhat outside the Muslem social structure. They were predominantly nonblack in an almost totally black faculty and student body, and they seemed to keep to themselves, reporting to Dumas.

Hamilton, acknowledged without question as the most proficient and imaginative of the authors, was not perceived as being entirely legitimate within the Muslem structure. He helped Ellos with proposals for outside funding and, when asked, provided technical assistance for fellow authors at Muslem and elsewhere. According to some teachers, Ellos did not display very forceful leadership. Because he worked well with university personnel, he exhibited diffuse leadership within the college system, but he had a difficult time keeping things together and meeting deadlines. Teachers and others had a hard time gaining access to him, and things always seemed out of hand. The administrative situation remained confused during the entire year, according to these teachers.

The actual head of the Learning and the Instructional Resource Division was Dean Wilma Osborne. In the authoritarian structure of Muslem, she was perceived by the teachers as the most authoritarian of all the administrators. She ruled by edict and threatened to dock personnel for not attending meetings, of which there were many, they said. In November she felt the PLATO project was in a state of disarray. Since Hamilton was paid by the central office, she did not consider him to be working for Muslem. Therefore, she did not ask him to do anything internally. The installation of the terminals was confused, roles were ill defined, and there was nothing in writing. Although she considered the management of PLATO within CCC to be a complete mess, she considered the ultimate criterion of success to be how much the terminals were used. She had thought the university personnel to be enthusiastic and competent, but, since the mismanagement of the project, she had begun to wonder. There were no job descriptions for either Ellos or Hamilton, and she did not know what they were supposed to be doing, so she appointed Bonnie Glenn, who was at the university preparing to be an author, to assume the duties of on-campus coordinator.

When Bonnie Glenn returned from Urbana, she was appointed Director of Tutorials and Self-Instruction. Although she had expressed the least interest of all of the authors in advancing her career, she had become an administrator, and she spent most of her time coordinating and orienting faculty to PLATO, leaving no time to author. Although less technically proficient than the other authors, Bonnie seemed to be better liked and became more a part of the social structure than the others.

When the terminals finally arrived in November, Bonnie found more enthusiasm among the faculty than she had anticipated. Most teachers expressed an interest in writing their own programs rather than in utilizing present courses. (Even Dean Dodd became interested during his orientation and spent forty-five minutes checking out the system). The terminals were months late in arriving, but, as far as Bonnie could see, this did not dim the enthusiasm.

A survey of teacher attitudes toward PLATO was conducted in the fall. As might have been expected from the high publicity, the Muslem instructors were more aware of PLATO than the other CCC schools. Although inclined to believe that PLATO should be limited only to drill work and not extended to regular instruction, Muslem faculty was more optimistic about it than most of the other schools.

The PLATO terminals, promised in August, did not arrive until November. Authors with released time could not write lessons without the terminals. Shortly before Christmas, the Chicago newspapers began running headlines about Garvey's misuse of funds. The newspaper campaign continued for about three weeks, finally forcing Garvey to resign.

During the year or so of the troubles at Muslem College that culminated in Garvey's resignation, enrollment declined from 6,200 students to approximately 4,700. Samuel Harrison, former Vice-President of Ralph Bunche College, was appointed Acting President of Muslem. The atmosphere around the school relaxed considerably. Although the security guards were still at their posts, they no longer wore uniforms. The faculty seemed relieved that the long siege with Garvey had ended.

By spring there was much uncertainty. Many administrators, including Wilma Osborne, had been relieved of their jobs, although when they would leave was unclear. Harrison had also moved to eliminate the noncontract people, either by giving some contracts, as with one of the PLATO authors, or possibly by releasing them. So far, none had been fired, but many were anxious.

Interest in PLATO was at low tide. The noncontract people were too busy or too anxious to do anything. A walk through the Learning Resources Center where the ten PLATO terminals were located indicated that, at most, two would be occupied while repairmen worked on another two. Two consoles had never worked. After the long delay in receiving the terminals, system downtime and terminal breakdowns had taken a heavy toll on whatever enthusiasm had existed. Bob Rogers, another author, estimated the system was down 50 percent of the time, and it was not unusual for an author to lose material. Another major problem was the lack of educational materials available on the system.

By spring, Mike Hamilton characterized the Muslem attitude toward PLATO as at best one of indifference, and he suggested that some of the terminals be put someplace else where there was more interest. The only group working on PLATO at Muslem were the three or four people around Ellos and Hamilton, all selected by Ellos. All were released full-time to author except Bonnie Glenn, who had been reassigned to non-PLATO duties since she was the only one talking to the rest of the faculty. Nobody else seemed to be interested. One author explained the lack of interest at Muslem, by saying, "You must understand the history of the last three years here."

Dean Dodd seemed to be more positive now than before, yet no one from physical science was involved. The reasons he gave were varied: training was inconveniently located at Ralph Bunche; there were not enough terminals; terminals were inconveniently located. "We want to get involved, but we need the proper orientation, which hasn't existed." Apparently Harrison had put some pressure on Dean Dodd to utilize PLATO. Dodd's ultimate defense was that the appropriate courseware was not available. Whether Dodd was defending the science division's lack of use or whether his price for using PLATO was to have terminals under his control was unclear.

During the course of events from fall to winter, Muslem lost much of its enthusiasm for PLATO. True to Muslem's authoritarian structure, most of the faculty had originally heard about PLATO through an administrator, although this seemed to have no direct affect on attitude. As at other schools, fellow teachers mainly influenced the attitude. The small group of people who retained an interest in PLATO did not function much like a group. They worked more like individuals. Some felt that PLATO would not be given a long enough trial period in which to prove itself. All agreed that there would be no widespread use of PLATO in the foreseeable future, if ever.

In contrast to the fanfare that had once attended PLATO, the faculty seemed indifferent. Whether enthusiasm could be revived would depend on the administration. Harrison had proved himself resourceful at Ralph Bunche College. Bold new steps would be needed to resurrect Muslem's interest.

In the spring, Stokely Carmichael brought his fiery pan-African socialsim to Muslem. Although enrollment was down, some student enthusiasm remained. "America is not our home; Africa is our home," he said. "The black man is the victim of capitalism," the students shouted, but they were confused. Chicago was a seedbed for Black capitalism. Was this the right way? Without Garvey, under a new president, they were confused. Let others worry about the reliability of the PLATO terminals. For both faculty and students there were larger issues.

Ralph Bunche Community College

In the fall of 1972, Ralph Bunche Community College moved from its dilapidated quarters in the middle of the South Side ghetto to a handsome, massive, white, three-story, $30 million building that spans a major thoroughfare like an archway. The students were 95 percent black, which is where the similarity with Muslem College ended. While Muslem operated on the black militant philosophy, Ralph Bunche College chose the moderate road, retaining a substantial number of nonblack faculty. At the dedication of the new building, the president of the college exclaimed, "How do you like your Uncle Tom now, children? Your old Uncle Tom has now got you this beautiful building." While there were also some guards at the doors and parking lots, they were fewer in number and not uniformed. The whole school was more open than Muslem.

There was also a great difference in the style in which PLATO was introduced to Ralph Bunche. It was introduced with a minimum of publicity. The architect of the strategy was Samuel Harrison, a top administrator who later succeeded Garvey as President of Muslem College. In the summer before moving to the new buildings and before the arrival of the terminals, Harrison outlined his deliberate strategy. He had worked on computer-assisted instruction and was not very impressed with it since the materials tended to be simply programmed text. With PLATO, he saw the possibility of more interactive instruction. As with most administrators and teachers, Harrison saw the utility of PLATO in helping handle the great range of abilities and background found in community colleges.

Believing that one must get teachers involved while they are enthusiastic, Harrison felt that, once enthusiasm wore off, it would be impossible to revive interest. He intended to choose six or eight people from three to five disciplines, initially limiting involvement to them. If the project did not work out, then the college would quietly wash its hands of the enterprise and go to gaming and simulation as an alternative. He was determined to have some computer-assisted instruction as part of the Bunche Learning Center, where students could come and work at all times. Like others in Chicago, he saw little risk in trying out PLATO. Many things had been tried in the public schools; many had failed.

Harrison became the driving force behind PLATO at Ralph Bunche. He was happy with the university contact, although Bunche had no one training in Urbana during the 1971-72 academic year. Perhaps more than any administrator, Harrison kept track of what was happening to PLATO within his school. He personally chose the people to work on the project and periodically debriefed them.

Less enthusiastic was John Abel, Director of Planning and Development. His background in instructional technology led him to believe developing the courseware would be a major stumbling block, which later proved to be the case. Abel did not play much of a role in the development of PLATO.

Ralph Bunche was helped considerably when it was decided that Roger Hollis should teach a weekly university extension course there. Because the arrival of the terminals was delayed here, also, much of the fall course had to be conducted without them, although the course had been planned around their availability.

Harrison's selection of PLATO people was based on interest and ability. One of the main lines of development, from which the most viable group in CCC evolved, originated at Ralph Bunche. Arden Mott suggested to Dumas that the university biology materials were especially good. Acting on this knowledge, Harrison chose Lou Peters, the biology coordinator for CCC, and Frances Biona, a biology teacher, to become involved at the beginning of the academic year. Through personal contact, a strong PLATO group finally emerged at Ralph Bunche.

Peters and Biona, seeing that they would acquire credit hours very conveniently through a university extension course, worked to have Hollis offer the course at Ralph Bunche. According to one colleague, their main motivation was to acquire credit hours cheaply and conveniently in order to qualify for "lane changes" in the salary and promotion schedule. They could acquire credit hours much more cheaply than at one of the Chicago universities.

Without the terminals, the fall class did not go particularly well.

Although the Chicago administrators seemed to be happy with the course, many teachers were frustrated. Frances Biona felt that she simply was not learning to use PLATO and needed much more time on the machinery itself. The TUTOR language was more difficult to learn than anticipated. Another frustrated teacher was Alice Kaufman, a nursing instructor, who could envision in her mind exactly the type of lessons she wanted on the machine, but could not learn TUTOR well enough to implement her ideas. For the first time in her life, Alice felt stupid, an extremely frustrating experience.

The physics instructor at Ralph Bunche, Don Green, who had had considerable experience with computer languages, felt that TUTOR was about as difficult to learn as FORTRAN. He was one of the few people hoping to develop a whole course on PLATO (later he would decide authoring was too difficult and use university course materials). Most teachers, he felt, were too busy to learn to use it. They had too many outside interests to be able to devote the spare time necessary. Mary Smith, the chemistry teacher, felt that it required from sixty to seventy hours to produce one hour of instruction, close to the estimate of most people in the field, and both Don Green and Mary Smith felt that the university-developed course materials were simply too tough for their students. Both also felt that they needed more technical help from the university than they were then getting.

In summary, the teachers in the fall PLATO course were very frustrated, feeling that they were losing the battle with the machines. They estimated that they needed more time on the machine, perhaps eight to twelve hours per week; printed material on TUTOR, which university personnel were reluctant to provide since the system was always evolving; more technical help from the university, arguing that help within CCC was inadequate and more administrative than technical; and some examples of good programs.

At the same time Harrison, the administrator in charge, was pleased with the progress of the project. He saw a training cadre being developed from the people being trained in Hollis' course. In the face of the authors' frustrations he reiterated that he did not want it to be "one big fizz" and end as other innovative projects had in the past. He had still not extensively publicized PLATO around the college, wanting to see how it worked out. He wanted no more terminals and no more people working on them. He could see those most interested working on an informal basis rather than flooding the terminals with many curiosity seekers.

A survey of all college instructors at that time revealed that, true to the strategy as a whole, Ralph Bunche faculty were less aware and less optimistic than the other schools, their optimism being in the neutral range. Ralph Bunche faculty were most reserved about PLATO's ultimate potential and disagreed that PLATO should be supported with local funds if necessary.

By spring a strong PLATO group began forming, propelled by several events. In November five terminals were installed, and Harrison began a low-key publicity campaign. Posters appeared around the school announcing:

> NEW ARRIVAL
> Name: PLATO
> Birthdate: November 28, 1972
> Weight: 150 lbs.
> Size: 24"x20"x24"
> Parents: City Colleges of Chicago
> Grandparents: University of Illinois
>
> The proud parents cordially invite friends to visit this newest addition to the Ralph Bunche family in the Resource-Skills Center. Please Make an Appointment.
>
> (PLATO is the computer-assisted education system that allows teachers to individualize instruction.)

Meanwhile announcements were sent to all CCC faculty advertising Hollis' two new courses to be offered in the spring. (Muslem faculty claimed they never received the notice. No one from Muslem applied.) Rich White, a biology instructor, and his brother Tom, had been talking to Frances Biona during the fall, and they had also heard about PLATO at Northwestern University, where they were working for Ph.D. degrees in science education. Ed Peterson, Lou Peters' roommate, heard about PLATO from Peters, and heard that Peters and Biona were released to write PLATO lessons. All joined up for the spring course. Someone was needed in botony, so Frances Biona asked Flora Dupont to sign up, which she did.

The members of the biology group involved ranged from twenty-five to thirty-six years of age and were characterized, by themselves and others, as being oriented toward personal advancement, progress, and academic pursuits, as opposed to having social or political interests. Neither the oldest member in the department nor the eight members beginning teaching were involved. Ruth Little, the oldest department member, said that she was too busy with extraschool activities to get involved, while the beginners were having trouble keeping their heads above water. The involved group reviewed and criticized each other's PLATO work. They did not try to involve people outside their group since they were unsure of themselves and did not want to share the five terminals with others. The chairman of the biology department was a neutral figure who neither encouraged nor discouraged them.

The group, then, was comprised of the previously existing social group in the biology department. What gave them momentum as a PLATO work group was the spring authors' course. Since Hollis finally had terminals that he could work into his training procedures, he redesigned his course. He had been concerned that teacher-authors would throw a lot of poorly programmed text upon the system, and Mike Hamilton estimated that perhaps 95 percent of the material fit this description. During the summer and fall, while Hollis' instruction was on how to write better programs, teachers became totally preoccupied with learning TUTOR.

In the spring Hollis reversed his priorities and began the semester by bringing the whole class to Urbana for three long days on learning the system. This jelled the biology group. Many felt that they learned more in three days than the fall people had all semester. When they returned to Ralph Bunche, the terminals were available to work on (when the system was up). The group's enthusiasm revitalized Frances Biona, who felt they were all much better off than at the end of the fall semester. In the course of the three-day session, intense involvement forced people to come to grips with the machine. There were twenty-seven students and seven instructors, forcing it to relate to a variety of approaches and personalities.

Ruth Little, a department member not involved with the biology group at Bunche, said, "They all have drive for personal advancement that is greater. I am much less academically oriented. I'm spread too thin. I am about fifty, the oldest in the department. The others are between twenty-six and thirty-five. I have never been in the forefront of anything in my whole twenty-year career. I've never had much academic stimulation. I taught in a small junior college in Iowa for many years." Biology was always a more cohesive group than the other departments, in her opinion.

Flora Dupont, a member of the group, characterized the biology people as progressive, keeping up with the latest, not wanting to "stifle" themselves, wanting "something else," no matter how high their position. They wrote, served on committees, disseminated information. Ed Peterson, another group member, said the primary motivation for being involved was the convenient, cheap credit available from the extension course. This enabled them to make "lane changes" and move to a higher salary and promotion column, a point Dumas emphasized in his letter advertising the course. Peterson got involved by talking to his roommate, who suggested he write Dumas. Dumas let Peterson get involved. Peterson said his interest was only in having lessons for students, but he was very interested in the fact that Peters and Biona were released full time to work on lessons. Although he said that learning to write lessons took more time than it was worth and that PLATO primarily had a novelty and curiosity value, he was willing to spend full time on PLATO. His wife worked at the University of Illinois, Chicago Circle Campus, where there was much publicity about PLATO.

Vern Morgan, one of the original "PLATO fellows" described earlier, was not a member of the biology group. In a supervisory role related to PLATO at Ralph Bunche, he seemed not to have much influence on the group formation. Occasionally, he would help with some technical problems. Morgan seemed to identify more with the administrative group surrounding Carl Ellos, the CCC cordinator. During the year, he had several conflicts with university personnel, namely Roger Hollis. At one point, he complained, "You promised to help and ended up ordering us around."

Although the biology group was enthusiastic and hard working, by early spring they had not yet produced much material. By late spring, however, they had processed a good deal of material. No other strong groups were operating, although there were some productive individuals, such as Mary Smith, in chemistry. She was asked to work on PLATO by Carl Ellos. She felt that most of the faculty was pessimistic and that having to work more to prepare lessons was not very appealing. Other faculty rarely asked her questions.

Between fall and winter a survey of teacher attitudes revealed that Ralph Bunche College experienced a dramatic rise in optimism. Although the Ralph Bunche faculty still felt that local funds should not be used to support PLATO, it became one of the most optimistic schools. Besides the increased production of courseware from Ralph Bunche, there were other signs that PLATO interest was working its way through the faculty. Several faculty members signed up for the "users" course in the spring. One potential user, Enid Schmidt, who was having great difficulties learning to use the system, asked, "How can a disadvantaged kid use it if it's so difficult for the teachers?" She had no released time to work on it, and her difficulties ("I'm no big drinker, but that machine can drive you to drink. I needed one yesterday.") persisted in spite of previous computer work.

She saw the eventual utility of PLATO being like that of a film. Not everyone knows how to use projectors, yet films are shown in the schools. She could not see students who were dependent on the teacher using the machine very readily. She equated PLATO with *Sesame Street* and felt that it worked at a lower level for a great many people, but it was not good for intense education in small groups. She saw its purpose as educating to achieve a minimum level of functioning, not to develop higher, more complex skills. Like all automation, it would result in quantity but not in quality. When asked about her own involvement, she said, "I wanted to see how it operated and get credits. If 'they' want to introduce it, I will try to make use of it. I am basically a conformist." She saw herself as a follower, not an innovator.

The Director of Remedial English at Ralph Bunche, Sue Bezdek, felt that actual courseware in English was very poor. She did not see learning the codes and entry procedures as a significant impediment to use. She wanted to use PLATO the way she now used a workbook, but felt she would have to take the authors' class and do some of her own programming for it to be usable. All in all, Ralph Bunche College proved to be one of the success stories of the year.

Henry Miller, Vocational, and Touhy Colleges

Henry Miller Community College, the oldest community college in Chicago, is located in a building on the North Side that dates back to the 1940's. Its faculty and student body are overwhelmingly white. Before PLATO, Miller College had a CAI operation that did not work out too well. From that experience, James Doolin, a top local administrator, had no illusion that PLATO would save them money. He would simply be happy if it improved classroom instruction. Like other Chicago administrators, Doolin saw no real risk in the project. There was no massive investment of CCC funds in the operation, and, if it did not work, it would be dropped.

In the summer of 1972 Doolin saw no substantial problems except when Miller College would get the equipment and where they would put it. Miller was an old building not designed to handle such equipment. He saw the university staff as being quite competent, interested in helping, and quite open in admitting that they did not have all the answers, an attitude that impressed him. He was quite well aware of problems in developing courseware, and he felt that the courseware must be tailored to Miller students. Neither university material nor material developed by other schools would be useful.

A man who had previous CAI experience and in whom Doolin placed much confidence was Ted Lewis. Lewis was one of the six PLATO fellows from CCC who spent the year in Urbana. He had put together a great deal of material and was developing an entire accountancy course on PLATO. He was the senior staff member from CCC at Urbana and, during the academic year, he drew such assignments from the CCC central office as writing articles on PLATO for the CCC newsletter and otherwise publicizing PLATO.

By December James Doolin was feeling less happy. Although promised terminals by October, Miller College had only one, which was not working properly. During the academic year, the story of PLATO at Miller centered pretty much around Ted Lewis. His strategy, with one terminal available, was to identify a few people and work with them informally. Few people had seen Lewis' material, but they felt that, when his programs were ready, they would use them. Some control classes were scheduled for the next fall.

The administration was favorable and was intent on letting the PLATO project evolve slowly. There was no pressure on Lewis, whose role changed after the arrival of the terminal. He spent only from six to eight hours a week authoring himself and was drawn more and more into paper work, meetings, and helping other authors. Like the other five who spent the year in Urbana, Ted was drawn into administrative and training functions on his return, rather than authoring. Material production suffered in all cases.

Construction of space for more terminals was proceeding at Miller College. Lewis' own concerns were lack of accessibility to PLATO and fear of premature expectations on the part of the faculty. Miller was one of the places where there were some materials available, whatever the quality, plus someone willing to use them.

On the first survey of instructor attitudes in the fall, Miller

College was one of the schools least aware of PLATO, as might be expected from the very small number of people involved there. The faculty also appeared to be older and less ambitious than that found in the other schools, reflecting a relatively low optimism toward PLATO. In the spring survey, they were still lowest in optimism. Again, the deliberate strategy and the fact that the terminal was usually not working contributed to this attitude. Lewis was obviously the key to the whole scene. In a sense, he had a monopoly on PLATO at Miller College.

Doolin felt fairly optimistic by the end of June 1973. He had two instructors ready to go—but only one terminal. He expected six more immediately and from ten to fifteen by November, mentioning, however, that there were "so many things I have no control over." Whether the terminals would arrive and whether they would work were beyond his control.

He typified his staff as competent, reliable, and energetic. Renovation of the library to accommodate the terminals was moving ahead with good speed. At a meeting "downtown," it was recommended that there be a PLATO site manager at each campus who would take care of minimum maintenance and scheduling, but funding was not discussed. Doolin was hopeful that these conditions would all be met.

Vocational College, even in a system of contrasting campuses, was an anomaly in the CCC system. It was funded by the Department of Labor and similar government agencies to train the unemployed in skills that would enable them to find jobs. Each week it received new students from numerous government and unemployment agencies that it had no choice but to accept and train. Only recently had the CCC assumed control over it. Until May 1973 it was located in a ramshackle former army building near the stockyards on the South Side. Then it was moved to a new building, and there was hope that it would receive some PLATO terminals.

The President of Vocational College, Fred Brookings, was frank. According to him, the problem of training these people was so great that no one solution was going to pay off. There was no panacea. Why not try everything? Originally the chancellor was cool toward PLATO and did not want the new building specifications to include PLATO terminals. Brookings included them anyhow, and the chancellor later favored the idea. Brookings was a former political lobbyist.

What about the risk of PLATO failing? Federal agents had arrested Brookings' secretary for possession of narcotics. A few weeks earlier he had been forced to fire an instructor for peddling dope to students. We live in a risky world.

On any given Monday, twenty-five agencies could deliver people for training. Brookings wanted to see PLATO adapted to testing and diagnostic information. He was not sure, however, that the university could stomach ghetto problems or handle students such as he had, and he was concerned that, as long as PLATO had been around, no studies had been done to reassure him of its effectiveness. The university had already demonstrated its inflexibility in requiring that his people spend a day traveling to Urbana to register for the PLATO courses. He hoped that, when PLATO was evaluated, it would reflect the "natural hazards" that people in Vocational College faced every day.

The Vocational College staff belonged to the civil service, not the academic community. During 1972-73 there were twenty-seven faculty for two hundred students. This would be expanded in the new building to twelve hundred students and triple the number of faculty. Mostly the faculty were in their mid twenties or early thirties, considerably younger than the other faculties. The job was a twelve-month, two-week-vacation job with no semester breaks. Most of the faculty did not have academic degrees, and each teacher had a heavy work load. The students were extremely varied in both ability and entrance skills, and they were very difficult to teach. If they thought the teachers were not "involved," they gave them a "hard time." In all ways, the Vocational College faculty were much like the non-contract people at Muslem College.

The only contact they had with PLATO, during 1972-73, not having any terminals, was through Sally Morris and Lucy Paris, who had been released to work on PLATO. Sally chose to work at Ralph Bunche; Lucy, at Muslem. Sally was concerned primarily about introducing PLATO to the Vocational College faculty and in the spring was drawing up plans for in-service training of the faculty. She expected to be the PLATO coordinator at the new building so she knew the other instructors quite well and visited Vocational College once a month to report on her progress. She found the other instructors quite receptive.

On the fall survey, the Vocational College faculty was the most optimistic of all the schools, and also the most ambitious. Many had aspirations of becoming administrators. On the winter survey, no one from Vocational College returned the questionnaire. In the spring, one was returned.

The Vocational College President, Frank Brookings, was, by summer of 1973, still optimistic but he was also still waiting for the delivery of terminals to the new building. He had been promised a November delivery, but he was not too hopeful. Brookings was still firm in his belief that no one approach could make much difference because of the enormity of the problems. The courseware development he saw as progressing well. Plans were being laid for selecting people, motivation being a primary consideration. He was not quite as optimistic about the degree of PLATO utilization as those directly involved.

In December 1972 Dumas, a central administrator, reported that he was "very, very happy" with the PLATO project. The reaction to the fall graduate course had been favorable, and another course was planned for spring. PLATO had already been included in two grant applications that had been prepared. He also mentioned that Touhy Community College would have to be "let in."

Touhy Community College, located in the industrial area on the far South Side, was not included in the original PLATO plans. Someone suggested that Touhy had its "nose out of joint" because it was not invited to send people to Urbana. Muslem was in, Miller was in, Bunche was in. Why was Touhy a stepchild? (Several other campuses, also without PLATO terminals, were not unhappy about their exclusion.) In the fall, five people from Touhy signed up for Hollis' course. In December Hollis made a trip to Touhy in what turned out to be a sales session. Brown, the head of the Learning Center, was pushing for PLATO, but Fromm, the Vice-President, was skeptical: "We don't want gimmicks here. What difference would this make?" Hollis and Ellos contended that the terminals would be bought with a Title III grant, if received. It would cost Touhy nothing. (This grant was not received.) A wide variety of materials would be available in September 1973 and a demonstration was arranged for the faculty.

There was some thought of taking one terminal from the other schools and giving it to Touhy. Dumas vetoed this idea to avoid alienating the other schools. A note of pessimism was injected by one of the mid-level administrators who did not think the teachers would spend the necessary time on the terminals when they got them.

The student contact hours in CCC had been reduced from eighteen to fifteen to twelve hours a week now. Teachers used to argue that they needed this extra time to spend with their students. Now that they had the time, he said, they worked second and third jobs. Would they spend extra time learning PLATO?

The central figure at Touhy in spring of 1973 was Del James, who was greatly influenced by Ted Lewis of Miller College. James had worked on computers for over thirteen years and had spent ten to sixteen hours per week authoring at the Henry Miller terminal since no terminal was available at Touhy. The strongest interest groups at Touhy were in business and science. Two English instructors signed up for the PLATO users course in the spring, but they were unhappy with the lack of courseware in English. The material that did exist was, they felt, very dated—traditional grammar lessons—and it was oriented to middle-class interests, very inappropriate for black students. One teacher felt his students would laugh at the materials.

Both English teachers were critical of the introduction of PLATO to CCC. No one really seemed to them to be in control. In their opinion the noncontract people who had been given released time during the past year and the current year were not competent experienced instructors; nor did they fit into the social structure. As an example, they pointed to Vern Morgan, the Ralph Bunche PLATO coordinator, who was programming "lie and lay" lessons from old grammar books. In a letter sent to Dumas complaining about the handling of PLATO, one of the English teachers suggested in-service training for all staff, subject area coordinators within the system, and programmers to assist. The problem of authoring a book, being more lucrative in royalties, was a more complex issue. The letter concluded, "It is only because I was very impressed with the possibilities of PLATO that I am so appalled by the present situation."

Some faculty, by the spring of 1973, had come to see the central administration as "playing" PLATO for what it was worth but not really being committed to it. They predicted it would be declared uneconomical and not given a full chance. As evidence, they cited the fact that sixty people wanted to take the PLATO course and there were only fifteen terminals. Taking the course was made difficult. Teachers had to pay their own tuition, and they were treated as if they were improving their own skills rather than benefiting

CCC. Involvement was restricted. Some of the policies used by the CCC to induce commitment were seen by some teachers as a sign that the central administration was not committed.

By June of 1973, Dumas was still confident in a cautious way and still reasonably happy with the university's role. The discontent of the two Touhy faculty people who had sent him letters was attributed to lack of sufficient courseware in the English area and inability to use the machines. A lesson had been learned, he thought, in not trying areas without sufficient courseware. At Ellos' suggestion, Wayne Eisner and Todd Duchek from Muslem were released full time during the summer to work on English courseware. A total of ten people were released during the summer to develop courseware, and Del James and another Touhy instructor were involved. The released time, financed by a $195,000 grant from the State Board of Higher Education, was for development of courseware. Dumas was sure he could get more money, and he intended to try. Money was not a problem.

Dumas's knowledge of PLATO was in terms of how many people were doing what and at what cost. CCC was moving ahead in chemistry, accountancy, GED, and data processing. By the end of the year, Touhy, Miller, and Muslem would be ready for summative evaluation by Educational Testing Service, which had been delayed one semester. During the past year, according to Dumas, the main problem had been the delivery of the originally promised consoles. By the end of the calendar year, he expected the complete shipment of the year before.

Dumas was still cautiously optimistic, though quite ready to kill the project if it did not work. Good signs were in the air, he felt. It looked as if Vocational College alone might be able to acquire a grant of $45,000 from outside sources for courseware development. Mayor Daley of Chicago was present at the dedication of the new Vocational College building that housed the new terminals. Always very busy, he normally hurried through the halls and through the formalities of dedicating new buildings. When he saw the PLATO terminal, however, he stopped. Tremendously impressed with PLATO IV, the mayor played with the console for half an hour. By Chicago standards, PLATO had indeed arrived.

FACULTY RESPONSE AND THE IMPACT
OF SOCIAL-POLITICAL EVENTS

How did faculty members not intimately involved with PLATO view the innovation? Three questionnaires were sent to random samples of the overall faculty in the fall, winter, and spring. As early as fall, most teachers in the faculties at large had heard about PLATO. About half had seen a demonstration, and a third had been in discussions about it. By spring everyone had heard about it, and most had seen a demonstration or had been involved in a discussion. The publicity varied greatly from college to college.

The word spread among the faculties in different ways. Bunche found out about it through a newsletter since internal publicity was initially curtailed there. In the authoritarian structure of Muslem College most instructors first heard of it through their administrators. The first source of information at Henry Miller College was through a fellow teacher, no doubt Ted Lewis, who was "Mr. PLATO" at that school. Downstate College first heard about PLATO through its extensive outside ties to the university.

Regardless of the method of first hearing, there seemed to be no dramatic effect on the teachers' optimism. When they heard about PLATO from a person, they tended to be only "somewhat acquainted" with that person. This was ordinarily not the first person with whom they seriously discussed PLATO. The first serious discussion, presumably an opinion-forming one, involved someone with whom the teacher was "well acquainted." While more than two-thirds of the discussants were fellow teachers, some were spouses, university personnel, and administrators.

Half the teachers also talked to people outside the school about PLATO, but these were *also* teachers from other schools with whom they were well acquainted. The teachers most frequently talked to fellow teachers in the "well-acquainted" (as opposed to "very well-acquainted") category about PLATO. In deciding whether to use PLATO, the most important opinions were those of fellow teachers and teacher-authors (those teachers who had training and released time to author materials on the system). Clearly, fellow teachers were the overwhelming source of information, opinion, and influence about PLATO. At this time students were not a major influence, perhaps because they had not yet begun to use the system.

General faculty attitudes were somewhat less optimistic between fall, winter, and spring. Previous CAI studies had indicated that teacher enthusiasm might decline the more contact they had with the system. Overall the decline was not pronounced, but it was dramatic for individual colleges. The "optimism index" for Muslem declined precipitously from 1.64 to .67 to .50. Henry Miller College started low and tapered off from .67 to .60 to .37. However, both Downstate and Bunche remained strong. General faculty optimism seemed to reflect events taking place within each college.

The general faculty attitude toward PLATO was not negative, however. It was generally one of guarded optimism, but they were not willing to gamble local funds. Even among those most familiar with PLATO, only the most optimistic were willing to use local funds to support it. The most ambitious teachers and those with very heavy work loads and the most varied students were most interested in PLATO. There was a positive correlation between personal ambition and optimism. Teachers who saw themselves leaving teaching within fifteen years were most negative.

Most teachers saw no immediate tangible incentives for becoming involved in PLATO. One-fifth did, usually in terms of released time. One-quarter felt that the incentives as they existed were sufficient. Only those with at least 50 percent released time, however, had become seriously involved in authoring.

Half the teachers said they would be interested in using PLATO in classes in the fall; half said they would not. The median amount of time they said they would like to be involved was 20 percent. A different question on a different sample found the median time they would be willing to invest to be four to ten hours a week, confirming the above. The median maximum time tolerable was also 20 percent, while the minimum time tolerable was estimated at 10 percent.

By late spring of 1973, teacher estimates of perceived benefit of PLATO to what they were already doing was bimodal. The upper group found the ratio of PLATO benefits to be "60:40" in favor of PLATO, while the lower group found the benefits ratio to be "10:90" in favor of what they were already doing. The high PLATO benefits group was located at places like Downstate, and the low group was at Henry Miller College.

Some points in the case study are worth emphasizing. The initial contact between PLATO and the community colleges was through personal contact. A community college official heard Alvin Edison speak at a meeting a few years before and, when the letter from PLATO asking for cooperating institutions arrived, the City Colleges of Chicago responded. CCC had also had the previous "TV College" experience on which to build. Even later the top CCC administrators perceived their relationship with the university more as a personal one, exemplified by "the handshake agreement," much more in fact than did the university.

Personal contacts between Downstate College and the university were more ubiquitous, more diffuse, and more extensive. In particular, the university seemed to feed and maintain the PLATO project there through a transfusion of personnel trained at the university. Many people, particularly young people, who had used PLATO in classes and projects at the university took instructional jobs at the Downstate College. The university served as a major recruiting ground for Downstate since it was a new school hiring an entire faculty. Personal contacts at the university were maintained, and the PLATO project continued to infuse the Downstate people with enthusiasm and technical help, involving them in the intense social "course" milieu enveloping the university project. This intense personal contact could not be maintained with the Chicago schools because of the greater distance and because they had not recruited a great number of university personnel. Close personal contact accounted for a considerable portion of the success at Downstate, the most successful site.

The fervor generated by this contact also caused some problems for the central office staff at Downstate College. The PLATO project, as they perceived it, continually threatened to get out of control. They were not in full command of the control levers. Enthusiastic pressures from certain segments of the faculty pushed upward at them. There were advocacy groups in biology, chemistry, and nursing. These groups related internally to the four or so members within the subject area and to the university rather than to other groups or the administration.

Partly because of these feelings and because of the failure of equipment, Downstate administrators were on the verge of breaking off the PLATO project, although they had originally gotten involved to improve their relations with the university. They felt they were being "used" by the university as a testing ground without concern for educational merit. This feeling was alleviated with the addition of two new people from the university to the office staff. The staff adopted a wait-and-see attitude, although still retaining the power to kill the project within Downstate.

In contrast to the Downstate experience of having PLATO develop from the bottom upward, the City Colleges of Chicago initiated PLATO from the top downward. The central office staff initiated the project and remained firmly in control. The Chicago situation was complicated by the involvement of multiple central office staffs. The overall central office staff was in the chancellor's office in the loop. There were, however, eight separate colleges and campuses, each with its own on-site staff. Much of the politics of PLATO in Chicago revolved around the interaction and maneuvering of the downtown and college staffs. Conflict between the downtown office and Muslem College was most apparent.

Overall control and initiative was maintained by the chancellor's office downtown, which appointed the overall coordinator for all campuses as well as the coordinators for each campus. The downtown group became identified as the "central administration" group as opposed to indigenous groups on each campus, although the overall coordinator was located on the campus at Muslem. Not surprisingly, the overall coordinator chosen by the central office was in no way a charismatic leader. While he was intelligent in his own way, there was no danger of his taking over the project or of the project getting out of hand. Many teachers viewed him as ineffective. There was no doubt that he had little authority other than that derived from his immediate superior. Although named coordinator, his superior controlled the allocation of funds and the appointment of personnel.

Even the initial appointments to be PLATO fellows at the university for one year were made by the central office. They selected primarily noncontract personnel rather than regular teachers. The selection criteria were not clear, but loyalty seemed to be a prime concern. These people then became the PLATO coordinators at the various campuses, and they were identified as the "administrator" group. They were generally perceived as managerial types who were not of much help. The central staff also intentionally limited enrollment in the on-site classes offered by the university. It was reasoned that a limited enrollment would motivate prople to join. Some teachers perceived this limitation as lack of support and lack of serious intent—a control mechanism.

Another contrast between Chicago and Downstate was in the size and resources of the systems. CCC did not perceive PLATO to be a high risk at all. If it did not work, it would be quietly dropped. Even in a year of severe financial crisis, CCC could find money to make up the unexpected costs of the telephone lines. Downstate College continually worried about both failure and the current and future costs of the project. The large system could shift fairly sizable sums around; Downstate administrators felt comfortable only when they had received a small grant from the State Board of Higher Education to defray their costs.

Both Downstate and CCC used the PLATO project to write proposals for outside monies. Outside funding and sponsorship became a major factor. The State Board of Higher Education provided special PLATO funds to CCC and Downstate as well as granting $5 million to the university's PLATO project. Other funds for developing courseware were available through a number of other government agencies. It was also interesting that CCC officials felt the need to justify PLATO as a device for aiding the disadvantaged by increasing literacy and providing occupational training, while at the same time intending to expand into other areas. Downstate felt no such obligation.

It was not surprising that the Downstate faculty would remain relatively optimistic toward PLATO since several advocacy groups were operating. There was both general knowledge about released time available for authoring and interest in it. In fact, the major concern among the advocacy groups was that PLATO was being oversubscribed and oversold through too much publicity. Besides their continuing concern over money, Downstate administrators were somewhat worried that they were having to schedule blocks of time for PLATO use, often at inconvenient hours, because of a lack of system access.

In contrast to Downstate, Muslem College was an example of an innovation imposed from above, both from the central administration and from the administration of the college itself, which was considerably more heavy-handed. The whole history of relations between President Garvey and Muslem faculty gave meaning to PLATO as an innovation in that context. Earlier innovations had been used by Garvey to reduce costs and faculty, and PLATO was seen as a new threat. It received great publicity, as had other innovations at Muslem, and it was boycotted by the faculty. Like a big balloon, it blew up and burst. Along with other "idiosyncratic" innovations, it was imposed by a central authority and did not last too long.

Garvey also introduced the terminals into the Learning Resource Center, the lowest-status group in the college, which housed the non-contract people. Besides the general boycott, this ensured that the innovation would not diffuse within the Muslem social structure. The countergroup that opposed its use resided both in the Science Division, the high prestige group, and in the teachers' union. The only true advocacy group within Muslem was the "administrative" group headed by coordinators appointed by the central office. They were accepted as legitimate by neither the Muslem social structure nor the Muslem administration. The group was mostly white in a faculty that was 95 percent nonwhite.

In effect, the political events revolving around Garvey's forced resignation overwhelmed all other events and made PLATO merely a pawn in the overall struggles. The group expressing most interest in PLATO per se was the most marginal group in the school—the non-contract personnel. Not only were they faced with the heaviest work load and the greatest range of student abilities, but they also had to establish an identity for themselves that would fortify their insecure position within the social system.

Tenured teachers in the Learning Resource Center felt that the heavy-handed imposition of the innovation killed whatever chance it may have had: "Muslem blew the groundwork." Many perceived PLATO as a way of cheapening education for blacks. This antipathy and apathy were not helped by the late arrival of the terminals and their poor performance.

In contrast to the Muslem experience was the slow, low-profile development at Bunche. Although initiated and controlled by the central office staff led by the vice-president of the campus, an advisory group developed slowly and organically, starting with a few people and gradually adding more. The advocacy group was based on the previous social structure of the biology department. Both publicity and involvement were restricted until the group had a chance to work out its problems. Garvey's members helped each other absorb the ever-present frustration and work out technical details. The fact that the university courses were offered at Bunche had an important impact on building an interested group there. The major incentives were credit hours accumulation to allow salary increases, released time, and the social rewards of working in a group. Whereas Bunche started low in general faculty enthusiasm during the low publicity days, it became high in general faculty enthusiasm by the end of the year.

At Henry Miller College where one man had established almost a monopoly on PLATO, faculty enthusiasm was quite low. The faculty was older, less ambitious, and essentially uninterested. Miller also had great difficulty in remodeling its old building to accommodate PLATO terminals. Maintenance and scheduling were also major problems.

Vocational College was characterized by the attitude, "What is there to lose?" They were willing to try anything that might help in their difficult educational task. Both the president and the staff were unconventional. The president had included space for PLATO terminals in plans for his new buildings, even though the central office had originally rejected the suggestion. The staff was both young and ambitious, much like the noncontract personnel at Muslem, and it also carried a very heavy work load.

Touhy College had originally been left out of the PLATO enterprise, but had expressed indignation over being excluded. There was, however, a conflict over PLATO within its own central staff. The young director of the Learning Resource Center pushed for it, but the vice-president was skeptical. University personnel and the system coordinator were brought in and made some rather grand promises to elicit the vice-president's support.

PLATO was not meant to be ready as an operational system by 1973-74. It should be noted that it was indeed not ready. The hardware was expensive, slow in production, and unreliable in the natural setting. The software (TUTOR) was constantly changing, and it was difficult for teachers to learn. The courseware was limited in quantity and quality and proved to be more difficult and time consuming to write than anyone had imagined. All these deficiencies exacted a heavy toll in the enthusiasm and involvement of teachers, and, one must assume, in the eventual acceptance of PLATO. Solutions to these problems were needed before there could be widespread use.

Institutional acceptance of PLATO was hampered by conflict over short-range and long-range goals. Continuous changes in the system may have made for a better system over a long period of time, but they greatly frustrated the teacher-authors in the community colleges and discouraged other teachers from getting involved. Such

effects were damaging. There seemed to be a time when each institution and possibly each teacher was ready to attend to the innovation. If PLATO could not deliver at that time, interest waned,
and it was often difficult to revive.

Likewise, while the long-range strategy of training teachers as
authors might pay off handsomely in winning teacher acceptance of
PLATO, the strategy was slow, difficult, and laborious. The pressures
of the ETS evaluation, the short-range goal, and forced central
development of curricula might well be rejected by teachers.

Individual and institutional acceptance was also very much
organizationally dependent. Bringing PLATO into a highly charged
atmosphere like that of Muslem College necessarily imbued the innovation with the meanings of that setting. Past events were important. The whole history of the organization had a strong effect on
how PLATO was utilized. Larger events also tended to decrease the
importance of PLATO. Few teachers at Muslem could have gotten
excited about PLATO during the Muslem scandals. Larger events,
which are not as uncommon as supposed, tend to submerge an innovation. PLATO was simply not a central focus of life.

Tangible incentives for learning about and using PLATO were
few. Released time to author seemed to be a major attraction. Course
credits through extension courses represented another major motivation by enabling teachers to move up the salary and promotion
schedule. Only teachers who were very ambitious, who got released
time or credits, who had heavy work loads, or who had a great
number of students with varying abilities tended to get involved.
Most teachers would have had to expend much effort to learn
TUTOR with no clear means of recompense.

The colleges had a similar problem. On the one hand, they had
to share courseware for PLATO to make it affordable. Teachers were
not, however, amenable to using centrally developed courseware that
they considered unresponsive to their needs. The colleges did use
PLATO as a basis for writing proposals for state and federal grants.

Within this setting, the soft sell and trimming down of promises
worked best. Low-profile approaches caused less trouble, the most
notable example being Bunche College. Within Bunche, an interest
group developed based on previous social contacts. At Downstate,
several groups that were tied into the PLATO social system at the
university emerged. Enthusiasm and involvement were maintained
through formal and informal ties, and those groups were the only
ones that seemed really capable of surviving over time.

Chapter 6

The Trauma of Technical Skill Development

THE TEACHERS SPEAK

While political machinations and social events were swirling around the introduction of PLATO to the community colleges, what of the people who had to learn and make use of the system? The plight of the "teacher-authors" illustrates how difficult it is to learn new technical skills required to implement an innovation. Of course, all innovations are not as radically different as PLATO and do not require such a massive amount of relearning. PLATO may represent an extreme case, but, in so doing, it dramatizes the problems that exist even when more modest efforts are involved. The difficulty of implementing PLATO is spelled out here in painful detail and in the teachers' own words.

The first community college authors to be trained spent the academic year at the University of Illinois at Urbana-Champaign. They were selected by their administrators and were treated in a laissez-faire manner while at the university. Most of what they learned resulted from their own initiative. During the summer of 1972 a university coordinator, Roger Hollis, taught a formal course on PLATO authoring. In the fall he taught one at Ralph Bunche College in Chicago, and, the following spring, he taught an author's course and a course for users of PLATO, both at Ralph Bunche. These courses had varying degrees of success.

This section is based on the work of Craig L. Gjerde, "Introducing a Technological Innovation to the Community College." Unpublished doctoral dissertation, University of Illinois at Urbana-Champaign, 1974.

Some of the senior authors themselves best described their problems and frustrations with learning a new set of technical skills. One of the most competent of the community college authors, Mike Hamilton, spent the academic year in Urbana and later became the PLATO coordinator at Muslem College. Although he was a math instructor, which proved to be a big help in utilizing PLATO, he admitted that his first two months on PLATO were extremely frustrating. After two months he could do some programming, but only after eight more months of full-time work did he know the computer language well.

His style of authoring was to start by thinking of student goals for the lesson (not behavioral objectives). One-third of the time he made flowcharts for the lessons, that is, he sketched out the decision points before he sat down to program. Hamilton estimated that he spent about 10 percent of his time planning lessons and about 90 percent programming and reworking them at the terminal. After a year and a half of experience, Hamilton judged that in the future he could keep up with programming and teaching if he had three-quarters released time—taught one class a day and spent the rest of his time authoring lesson materials for the class.

Mary Smith attended the fall 1972 authors' course and was released half-time to write chemistry lessons during the spring semester. She was quite impressed with the chemistry lessons that university and Downstate authors had developed.

I was previewing some lessons, and I found one that would fit in right away with a beginning unit. So I took students from my class and put them on the terminals. Then I had an exam. I discovered that all of the six on PLATO passed the exam. It's a developmental lesson, and they can follow it much more easily on PLATO than they do in class.

The student response was what really sold her on PLATO—in spite of some difficulties with the terminals.

The students on PLATO were all highly enthusiastic and wanted to go on PLATO again. The feedback was good; I felt it was encouraging. I did this first before I paid much attention to authoring. If I don't get good feedback from the students, I will just sit here spinning my wheels—doing something that will not be consumed. The consumer is the important person here.

I feel personally encouraged. I don't want to believe what someone else tells me. I can write [lessons] because I know it [PLATO] will be accepted and it works. In between the lines you have to understand that the terminals do not work—sometimes I go insane and am ready to kick it in the face and all these kinds of things. We had a lot of trouble because I didn't know how to unhang the students. The lesson we were using hadn't been tested that much.

Mary thought that the fall course had been taught "backwards"— lesson design came first, and TUTOR language was introduced at the end of the course.

I really feel it was not as successful as the spring course. That time they started out by going down to the university and actually teaching [TUTOR language]. You're not successful when you talk about something; you've got to do it!

Basically you have to learn how to program. If you're a good lesson writer, you're going to have good lessons; if you're not, you can program beautifully, but it's going to be garbage. If a person is not a good lesson writer, he's not going to be a better lesson writer if you tell him about it.

I have an unalterable opinion that teachers are born and not made—that you either have it or you don't—nobody is going to teach it to you.

In planning to write a lesson, she reviewed several PLATO lessons and spoke with Bill Gross, a senior author, about an idea she had for a lesson. She saw some of the beginning authors "wasting time"—trying to write lessons that had already been done. "If people are going to get released time, there should really be somebody in that field who had enough [knowledge], from his own authoring or whatever, to help them in selecting a topic," she said.

The lesson she finally chose to work out was in an area she knew well. It had a logical development and was problem centered. She reviewed the theory and illustrated it by means of diagrams; then she led the student through a series of questions.

You have to outline the lesson first before you sit down at the terminal. You outline the introductory material and what you're planning to bring out. In putting the problems down, we have to ask the student what he is looking for, what he is asked to find, what are the data, etc. That way the student can write in words and not just numbers; when it becomes all symbolic, it becomes fatiguing.

The lesson should be very straightforward and fairly basic. The student wants to get done. It's nice to use animated diagrams, but sometimes it gets a bit childish. A lesson should be finished in an hour. Students want to get done fast.

Mary spent more time in planning than in programming—about 70 percent of her time planning and 30 percent at the terminals. She had originally heard that, for PLATO, the preparation-to-use ratio was thirty to one; her first hour required over one hundred hours of preparation, but she hoped to become more efficient. Teaching with PLATO would be different.

My course will change by getting students to put in additional time that many of them don't put in now. PLATO will not replace homework; I'll assign homework on top of it. There is no substitute for doing homework. I think that students will put in more time—at least for certain lesson units. You can't expect it throughout the course; this is not something that you can substitute for whole sections of the course. Otherwise they get fatigued and they're not going to do it either. There will be perhaps two units on which students will have an opportunity to use the terminals.

Mary wondered if the wrong community college instructors were chosen to author. Most of the PLATO authors were young and had a lot of energy, she said, but they did not know the students. "Beginning teachers can't write the very best lessons; they don't know what the students don't know, and their lessons lack understanding."

Lou Peter was an Anglo biology teacher at Bunche. He attended the fall authors' class and was released full-time in January to write biology lessons.

It's a slow process [developing materials], very slow. I'm working full time at it, but it still is rather frustrating because of the hardware problems for one thing— the machines going down so often. I'll have two, maybe three lessons done.

Lou could not identify any significant incentives or risks associated with the PLATO project.

I don't think there's much prestige associated with [PLATO authoring] at this point. There is released time, because they wouldn't get anybody to work on it if they didn't get released time; it is a full-time job. I enjoyed the work in the authors' course, and I was asked to help develop biology programs. I thought it would be useful to do this, because if lessons are developed—and they certainly can be developed—they can play an important part in our curriculum, if the hardware problems are solved.

There aren't really any risks, because the lessons could never completely, not even partially, take over teaching responsibility. Many people think there is a risk [of PLATO taking over], and our central administration may have that in the back of their minds, but the major ways I can see the materials helping in the biology curriculum are for accelerated students and for makeup. For regular materials, you can't replace teachers.

The formal training was inadequate, and Lou had to resort to using other authors as resources.

We didn't get much training [in the fall course], because the machines weren't available in Chicago for the first half of the course. We finally went down to the university and received a couple days of fairly intensive and extremely valuable introductory training, but from there it's been trial and error, self-teaching and asking. You just have to parasitize the experienced authors. There are no PLATO materials until you get fairly advanced and know where to look for them. There are a few things printed, but not very much that's useful. When I need something, the only practical thing is to ask, because reading the material again in a shotgun, random approach is not helpful. I still don't know TUTOR; some parts are pretty difficult. The people in the spring course are in a much, much more advanced state than we were at a comparable time.

Authoring PLATO lessons made Lou think about his teaching in different ways.

You try to initiate a little more creativity than in the traditional lecture way of teaching. There are more options available. I thought that the best use of PLATO was in simulation of laboratory materials, taking the place of actual laboratories or adding to laboratories, so I limited it to that, rather than putting information on the screen, which I don't consider a valid use [of] computer time. They can read a text if they're going to be doing that. I thought that something [a lesson] where data was actually generated would be a more useful aspect of the machine. I went through the various laboratories that seem to be interesting to students and evaluated how each one could possibly be put on PLATO terminals.

The materials in the lesson are based on what we have been doing, based on the text, and what the other teachers do. When I sit down (to design a lesson) I already have the basic objectives in my mind, but I'm not going to bother writing them down. And basically I outline what I want to do—a beginning and an end point. Then I go from point to point and see how each step can be programmed and what I can put into it which would make it more interesting than a typical laboratory or a typical lesson as it's normally and traditionally produced.

At the beginning, I thought out whole lessons on paper and rewrote them about four times, but the machine was down at that time. I wasn't writing any objectives as such. My basic objective was to do something in a better way than I can do in a traditional situation. I outlined the lesson in that way, adding as much as I could at the time. My competence on the machine wasn't too great at first, so I started with the hardest things first, then as I got more familiar with the language I put all the scattered parts together.

I can't say how much I'm intellectualizing; I don't write too much down. I think about my lessons. Most of my work is done sitting at the terminals. At the beginning there's more planning than writing; I'd say now it's 30 percent planning and 70 percent writing. There's certainly more sitting at the terminals than there is planning. It's different, too, depending on the experience of the author; the more experience, the less time he's going to have writing in comparison to planning.

I have just about finished one lesson about one hour long. The ratio [of authoring time to student use time] is about five hundred to one; hopefully the next lesson won't take nearly as long.

Lou animated a laboratory experiment on blood-typing. "I lead the student into giving a response, then show the response being carried out in the animation. It's a different kind of reinforcement." What were his criteria for a good lesson?

Since it's using this computer, it has to be basically doing something which can't be done as effectively by some less expensive, less time-consuming means. If it makes the material more alive and more interesting and it teaches it better, then I consider it a successful lesson.

PLATO should be used for remedial work and placement for what goes on in the class. You lose something [in using PLATO], and you gain something. You lose the actual technique of blood typing; students know every stage, but there's no replacement for the real thing. You gain from the creative aspects of the lesson itself, interest, and the number of trials possible in a short time.

Right now the system is in such a state that, until it's improved, it's virtually worthless for students. I've made that comment several times, and I'm going to stick to it because it's very difficult now for an author not to want to destroy the whole machine! There are hardware and telephone problems. Some keyboards aren't working well—either you press a key and the wrong response shows up or sometimes you have to press the key three or four times. Then the machine goes down.

They were assuming in February that the system would be in fine shape by March after a week's layoff, but it hasn't worked as well as it did back before they hooked up that second computer. The other thing is the availability of terminals and the problems when one breaks down. We have actually four people released full-time here and two released part-time, with five terminals. Wednesdays and Thursdays [days of the classes] it's impossible unless you sit down and camp there and bring your lunch to the machine.

Some of the [lessons] produced at the university are very good; others aren't as good. You have to be very selective in using your lessons. I just won't use too many lessons; at this point the only lessons I'd use will be my own—and a couple of Getz'. The rest of them are useless for me, either because of the way they're constructed or because they don't have any relevance to the course as we teach it. Everybody pretty much has to author for his own little school. I don't see there being wide adaptability of lessons.

Don Green, an Anglo physics instructor at Bunche College, enrolled as an author in the fall course. When he went to the university, he found that the lesson he was trying to write had already been done, as well as several other physics lessons. Since he was the only physics author in Chicago, he felt that there was no way he could prepare a sufficient body of lessons by himself. He also felt that he was not efficient at authoring so he refused to be released full-time to author and accepted 30 percent released time to review lessons for community college use. In this role he reviewed lessons and made notes about the suitability of the lessons and possible supplemental materials that could be developed. The most serious flaws in the lessons he reviewed were the narrowness of acceptable answers and poor explanations.

A good lesson must be extremely flexible and comprehensive. I can tell the difference between the well-honed lessons and the short-time linear ones. There is a tremendous difference in the effectiveness of lessons and their way of turning on the students. With the mechanics program [one of those he discovered] a student would even overlook the hardware problems.

About 20 percent of the physics lessons excited him; the other 80 percent needed more work.

Don's greatest fear about the success of PLATO was in the technical area. He repeatedly warned that hardware failure might be a serious problem with PLATO, as it had been with other CAI systems.

I'm overly sensitive about technical support. If we have machines, we need a technician. It is the weakest link in the chain. The real crisis will be hardware. PLATO will go or not go on the basis of hardware. So far my suspicions are borne out. If the problems are not solved, we can't test the courseware. With current time constraints, they must deliver on the merchandise.

I feel that we would be better off from the CCC point of view if the PLATO coordinator here were a technician with a knowledge of TUTOR. He would be more valuable than a supervisor. We need a technical type of person— an engineer. Vern [the Bunche coordinator] is committed to authoring; it is impossible to author and coordinate. He does not have the hardware capabilities; he can only call for help.

Don's previous experience with FORTRAN and ITRAN did not help him much in learning TUTOR.

The TUTOR language is beautiful in comparison with FORTRAN, but there is a credibility gap in efficiency. TUTOR can do things, but translating those ideas into TUTOR takes too long. I'm just used to FORTRAN. The rules were simpler, though not so powerful. My FORTRAN made me feel satisfied because I could do it so quickly; sitting at PLATO terminals appeared such slow progress to me and bruised my ego. PLATO is so ambitious and difficult; I have ideas in my mind that I can't translate. By not being an author, I can't design my instructional system.

PLATO has unlimited horizons; it will be hard to keep the developers from wanting to move on to PLATO V. The current generation of terminals, however, is only PLATO II quality and needs updating.

Another of Don's concerns was the central administration's control of PLATO in the Chicago colleges.

I'm disappointed in the CCC philosophy of how PLATO should be administered under the Learning Resource Center; thus the Central Office coordinator (Ellos) and the individuals assigned to the campuses (Vern Morgan and Mike Hamilton) are tied to the Central Office. That is bad, because we are a college, not a campus. We should deal directly with the university. If there is a coordinator here, he should be a Bunche person. It is unwise for him not to be selected by the Bunche administration. There should be a faculty committee to screen candidates with the administration. There is no real knowledge of PLATO by the front office staff, and this results in their assuming that PLATO is not worth spending time thinking about.

Don was also concerned that the CCC apparently had no plan on how to use PLATO or how PLATO might relate to Bunche's plans. Because of the way in which PLATO was being administered by the central administration, the Bunche staff saw it as a tool of the central administration and not as their own tool.

Some points made by the authors are worth reiterating. The initial contact was personal, through a demonstration. Both the most enjoyable and most profitable part of the spring training consisted of the face-to-face meeting with experienced authors in Urbana. Also, people with math and computer backgrounds adjusted best to learning PLATO. And training was very difficult when there was no "hands-on" experience with the terminals.

The difficulty of initial learning on the system was also emphasized. Even the most sophisticated author experienced a strong sense of failure for the first eight to ten weeks; the time was longer for most people. Hamilton became sophisticated, by his own estimate, only after ten months. Most teachers tried to carry their classroom style over to the machine, even to the extent of trying to replicate their discussions with multiple-choice questions. Hamilton also estimated that he would need three-quarter released time to "keep up" with the system—an enormous amount of time.

The extreme frustration elicited by the improper working of the terminals was apparent in the authors' comments. Student enthusiasm was a major hallmark for at least some of the authors. Some teachers assigned homework in addition to the PLATO work. Estimates for the number of hours to program one hour of instruction varied greatly: from 100 to 1, from 500 to 1, and so forth. All were very high. No author believed that any teachers would work on PLATO without released time.

The learning process required a prolonged and intense period of time working on the machines and interaction with more experienced authors: "You have to parasitize the experienced authors." Although the authors learned under different training circumstances and at different times, all experienced intense frustration and were slow to develop lessons.

Support was an important concern. To be successful, the authors needed to be near peers working in the major subject area, and they needed assistance from the university to learn programming and to maintain the terminals. While PLATO represented a more severe learning task than most innovations, technical skill development is always a frustrating and demanding experience for the individual. It is neither undertaken lightly nor sustained without reward and resources.

ENDEMIC FRUSTRATION

The natural frustration of the learning process was exacerbated by the deadlines under which the project worked in order to meet the deadlines set in a government grant. Fifteen months from the beginning of the project materials were supposed to be ready for evaluation. This proved to be a ridiculously optimistic estimate. Yet the community college authors did not feel that they were being forced to produce materials. The initial deadlines were simply not met.

Bunche became the center of training activities in Chicago since Hollis decided to hold his classes there and would often spend the whole day there. Fewer than 50 percent of the teachers who began the authors' class completed it. The main resource the authors had to draw upon was the experience of the other authors. Few beginners were able to develop usable lessons by the end of the course. Frustration created a stronger bond among PLATO cohorts as many teachers, fearing failure, avoided earlier associates, according to Hamilton. Failure was attributed to lack of time, lack of printed learning materials to study, and lack of terminal access.

At first the authors were very defensive about the inevitable errors. They were reluctant to admit mistakes. "I can't believe I didn't see that." After a while, they became less defensive. Very competent authors like Hamilton became competent after eight months and claimed that learning tapered off after a year. The production rate among released-time authors was about one lesson per semester of released time. Three to four months of labor were required to produce the first lesson. Later lessons took almost as long to develop, but were appreciably better.

The focus was on behavioral objectives and simulation training. Most experienced authors felt PLATO was most uniquely utilized in simulation exercises. Whatever their previous teaching styles (which most teachers felt were innate), the approach to PLATO authoring was usually the same. First, a well-known topic was selected. Then student-outcome goals were delineated. Major and minor points were organized, and a flowchart of the lesson was written. Then the lesson was translated into TUTOR commands. The author programmed the lesson on the terminal. Finally, lesson "bugs" were pursued until they were eradicated.

Few authors believed that behavioral objectives were useful in stating student goals. Many authors skipped the flowchart, and most omitted writing the lesson out in TUTOR commands. Median author behavior was to spend 30 percent of the time planning and conceptualizing the lesson and 70 percent programming and debugging it. Authors who had little facility with TUTOR wrote more linear lessons, used no animation or simulation, and spent less time at the terminals.

PLATO personnel at the university estimated it would take twenty-six hours to prepare one hour of lesson. Community college estimates ranged from 80:1 to 1000:1, with 250 hours of instruction being the median time to prepare one hour of instruction. Released-time authors produced from one to fifteen hours of instruction, having worked anywhere from one semester to two years on the system. Authoring was a much slower process for the community college instructors than had been expected.

The authors were often highly critical of the lessons their peers were writing, although they could also be tolerant. The most common paradigm was the inductive example-rule format. Traditional English lessons were criticized for their rule-example-drill format, though not all fit that mold. In general, English and accounting authors based their lessons on printed learning materials and wrote linear lessons. Some felt that teaming an experienced programmer with a subject-matter specialist would have been a better approach, and some informal teams did form.

There seemed to be a critical mass of time required to come to grips with PLATO, usually frequent blocks of two or three hours' minimum duration per sitting in order for the author to recall where he left off, to determine what to do next, and to achieve reasonable progress. Only those with released time were productive. Lessons started by those without released time were usually abandoned. Authoring also required intense concentration and individual effort. While most help was provided by fellow authors, most authors at work were reluctant to interrupt a fellow author, especially a senior one. One author spent a whole day trying to solve a programming problem. She interrupted no one and sought no help, partly to prove she could solve the problem by herself.

Released time was conceived by authors to be a necessary, but not a sufficient, condition for authoring. They could not imagine anyone wanting, or being able, to author without it. Since administrators allocated release time, they had some control over the authoring process. Authors were also motivated by a need for help in their courses, a desire for summer employment, the opportunity to gain graduate credit, and the challenge of being creative and solving problems. One author saw PLATO as a job threat and thought he would learn to use it to protect his job. Authors were also seeking better tools for teaching.

They saw little prestige connected with the project when it began, but felt it might eventually be important. Some authors were also able to identify risks. Since the central office had been identified with using PLATO to reduce costs and instructional staff, some were afraid that their colleagues might see them as "sellouts" to the administration. Some felt that their jobs might suffer before they got back to them.

Clusters of terminals effectively defined groups of authors at the various locations. Having a group of authors working on the same subject area at one location was an important condition of success. Collegial friendship influenced enrollment in courses as well as authoring itself. Personal and institutional politics were also involved in deciding which authors received released time.

Almost all the authors were reluctant to have their lessons inspected and criticized by anyone but their friends. Most felt that PLATO lessons should be better than classroom lectures, and they did not want to expose their lessons until they were polished. Only in March did the math authors agree to let others inspect their nearly completed lessons.

Another peculiarity of PLATO authoring was its public character. One of the university authors made a reference to sex in his lesson set theory: "Union is a joining together—like in sex." He also included urinals in his lesson. This generated controversy. One author forbade his ten-year-old daughter to view the lesson. Many authors seemed to agree that PLATO lessons should be more conservative than classrooms. Generally, the Chicago authors felt that motivation was a most important element in the lessons for community college students. The university author who used the urinals in his lesson had taught in a community college. In response to the controversy, he said: "No one said to be traditional; they just hired us and told us to write." University-based authors were much more academic discipline oriented.

Deadlines, delays in delivery of the terminals, and politics were general problems. Also, there were too few terminals for the released-time authors in Chicago, which increased competitiveness. Most of the frustration among the authors, however, focused on the hardware. The computer broke down, phone lines went bad, terminals malfunctioned, parts of lessons were lost, and there was no storage room for new lessons.

The technical problems began as soon as the terminals were installed. For about one day out of five, all terminals were inoperative. Some of the terminals never worked, and authors quickly learned to avoid the bad terminals. About one time in fifteen the key pressed by the author would not appear on the screen, so an author automatically had to look up at the screen to verify the message he had typed.

A more serious problem was the whole system "crashing." One Muslim author estimated the system was down 30 percent of the time in the spring, either because the computer was not operating or telephone connections were bad. At times parts of lessons would be lost. Frustration was at its highest when the system malfunctioned unexpectedly. When the system went down, authors were content to sit patiently and punch the "NEXT" key until the system response returned to normal. After a few minutes, frustration increased. Authors sometimes felt a desire to destroy the machine. After fifteen minutes authors gave up and left the terminal area. Those authors who had traveled to terminal sites from remote locations were especially disturbed to find the system inoperative. Some of these problems were mitigated when a new computer was installed late in the year; others were not.

Another major problem was learning TUTOR, the programming language. This was considerably more difficult than anyone imagined. Although the community college instructors who enrolled in the authoring classes were self-selected and presumably better than average, about 40 percent dropped out of the class. Of the 60 percent who finished the course, only half succeeded in learning the language. Within ten to fifty hours at the terminal, an author could learn ten commands that would enable him to program a simple lesson with a minimum of branching. One-sixth of the released-time authors reached only this minimal level of competence. Few authors without released time got beyond the minimum level. At this level of competence, lessons were unimaginative and barely used the PLATO potential. When a more complex level was needed, the author had to seek help from a more advanced author.

Two out of three released-time authors reached an "adequate" competency that allowed them to move beyond the programming of text and devote time to animation—a heart beating, a game of concentration. These authors who believed the potential of PLATO lay in simulation and gaming, saw programming as challenging and as requiring intense concentration and hours of painstaking attention to details.

Another sixth of the released-time authors achieved superior competency as programmers. They went beyond the simulation stage and learned to keep student records and program in more basic language. They served as informal consultants, and they were very helpful to less sophisticated authors.

Learning TUTOR was complicated by the fact that the language changed weekly. Although experienced authors did not have too many problems, beginners did. In fact, lessons developed on the PLATO III system were not transferable to PLATO IV without complete reprogramming, and many authors simply abandoned their lessons rather than try to rewrite them.

As a result, not many lessons were produced, and both the quantity and the quality were disappointing. Most authors produced only two or three lessons, and it was estimated that only one in five was very good. Most were "page-turning" lessons that made poor use of PLATO's potential. The community college authors themselves naively overestimated how many lessons they would produce and how long each would take. One author estimated she would produce about a thousand hours within a year; she produced three hours. As noted above, the production ratio was about 250 to 1.

Originally, people had talked about developing whole courses. More and more they came to talk about developing only modules, or even just lessons. Authors opposed using lessons written by university personnel. They were particularly interested in developing personalized lessons for their own use. Naturally, the more the lesson was adjusted to fit particular students, the less other teachers were interested in it. Community college instructors also felt the university-developed materials did not have the right motivation, were too difficult, were culturally unsuited, were designed for different courses, required too much reading, were "nonfunctional for our purposes," were "only narrowly applicable to inner-city students," "used an approach not commensurate with what we teach," needed more substance, and took too long to complete. Almost everyone had a reason why he would not use the lessons of others.

Chicago authors considered lessons written for their own students to be more useful than those produced for students in other Chicago colleges. Even lessons written by peers were harshly criticized. The two major criticisms were inappropriate presentation and restrictive correct answers. It did not appear that instructors would be quick to use other people's materials, even though the efficacy of the system seemed to hang on large-scale use.

The difficulty and trauma of having to relearn vocational skills was expressed both in terms of difficulty for teacher-authors and in terms of results. Only about a third of the instructors enrolled in the course were able to learn TUTOR under the conditions obtaining. Only those authors released at least half-time were able to develop any lessons at all, and they averaged only a lesson a semester. Of these lessons only a fifth were of acceptable quality as rated by fellow authors. Apparently a user with less than 75 percent released time could not design his own instructional materials.

University officials inched ever closer to centrally developed materials. The choice seemed to be to invest tremendous sums of money in training teachers or to go to centrally developed materials. Yet the instructors who would have to use them showed no enthusiasm for such materials, and there were indications they would not use them. So PLATO was faced with the dilemma encountered in innumerable curriculum development projects in the 1960's—the problem of implementation—which none had managed to solve.

THE TEACHER AS CONSUMER OF PLATO

In a section of Chapter 4 entitled "The Teacher as Consumer of Innovations," the degree of teacher participation in innovation was treated as a function of the benefits available from innovation and from traditional instruction and as a function of the teacher's personal preference for these benefits. The teacher's alternatives were projected onto the indifference curve model of consumer behavior. Considerable liberties were taken with the economic concepts. In this section, liberty becomes license as we purport to measure the concepts.

The queasy reader is once again invited to hurry through this section and consider his deduction a capital gain for good taste. Those who wish to read carefully will be rewarded with both puzzlement and consternation, but there are also some different and interesting insights into the behavior of various teacher and author groups involved with PLATO, along with some predictions for the future.

Constructing preference curves empirically is not an easy task. Apparently economists have wisely avoided this problem by constructing theoretical models, reasoning "What if . . . ," then pretending it happened. In the original preference curve model the units of measure were loaves of bread or sticks of butter, homogeneous units of measure that could ultimately be equated in terms of money. A teacher does not buy innovations with money. Time is perhaps her most valuable commodity. So in this data analysis the "budget line" represents work time. Unlike money, however, time is not indefinitely expandable. One has only so much. For ease of measurement here, the budget line is conceived as representing 100 percent of the teacher's work time. Hence, it is a unit measure that will not expand much in length. (In a sense this violates the idea of marginal utility.) Participation in the innovation is represented by the percent of line allocated to the innovation or to traditional instruction (see Figure 6-1).

TP is the total budget line that includes 100 percent of the teacher's time. If the teacher were 100 percent into the innovation, that is, bought 100 percent of the innovation's benefits, he would be at point *P*. If he bought 0 percent, he would be at point *T* and hence buying 0 percent of the innovation and participating 100 percent in traditional instruction. Lines *NT*, *CT*, and *WT* represent other degrees of participation along the line. (Among many other assumptions, this analysis assumes the budget line is straight.)

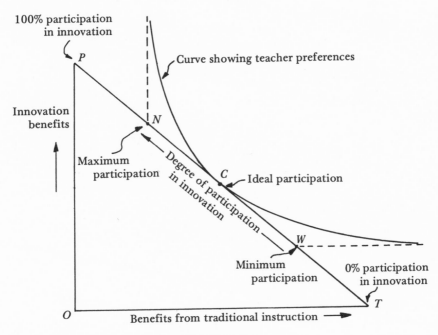

FIGURE 6-1

Preference curve relating perceived benefits of innovation to teacher's participation in innovation

The teacher's preference curve was determined by asking teachers and authors how much time they would spend on the innovation. A random sample of teachers from the community colleges were asked how much time they would *ideally* like to spend working on PLATO if they had their choice. It was reasoned that their ideal point would be the point of tangency between the preference curve and the budget line, the point of equilibrium if they were given free choice. (The terms "traditional instruction" and "conventional instruction" are used synonymously in this chapter and in Chapter 4. One could, however, distinguish between them.)

It was also reasoned that there would be a minimum amount of traditional benefits that they would not give up. Perhaps they could not bear to give up personal contact with their students entirely and hence would not give up a certain part of traditional instruction no matter how powerful other inducements for innovation—such as promotion opportunities—might be. This point was determined by asking teachers: "What is the *maximum* percent of time you could *tolerate* working on PLATO?" This is point N in Figure 6-1. A line running through this point perpendicular to the traditional benefits line forms an asymptote for the indifference curve. This line represents one boundary for the teacher's preferences.

At the other end there is also a boundary. There is a certain amount of innovation benefits that the teacher cannot do without. Teachers were asked: "What is the *minimum* percent of time you can *tolerate* working on PLATO?" Perhaps the teacher could not do without a part of the excitement that goes with a new innovation. Perhaps she could do without it all. The minimum tolerable time became the point through which a line perpendicular to innovation benefits forms an asymptote for the other side of the preference curve. Thus, the teacher's preference curve is based on estimates of her ideal, maximum, and minimum estimates of participation in the innovation. These are represented by lines CT, NT, and WT in Figure 6-1. The curve is drawn within these limits.

Establishing the ideal point of participation determines one point on the budget line, but does not determine the slope and, hence, the rest of the current line. In this conceptualization the slope of the line is determined by the benefits available if one were to participate 100 percent in either the innovation or in traditional instruction. (This threatens the independence of the measures.) As mentioned, sticks of butter or loaves of bread are homogeneous scales easy to measure concretely. "Innovation benefits" are not. Benefits comprise a heterogeneous assortment that might differ from person to person and be weighted differently from one person to the next. The measurement problems of such scales are solvable but difficult. I chose to avoid the problem by asking the teacher for the *ratio* of PLATO benefits to traditional instruction as the teacher now perceived them. Other questions might have been more appropriate, but the ratio of benefits enables us to determine the slope of the budget line without directly measuring the benefits themselves.

Teachers were asked what ratio of benefits was derivable from PLATO and what was derivable from what they were now doing. The ratio of *OP* to *OT* represents the ratio of PLATO benefits to those of traditional instruction as perceived by the teacher. Presumably these benefits are objectively available in the environment. Perhaps PLATO offers strong opportunity for promotion while traditional instruction offers affective relationships with the students. The teacher wants both, but, if 100 percent time is put into one or the other, a teacher will lose what the other has to offer. What can be done?

A teacher can buy various combinations of PLATO and traditional instruction benefits and find a combination that will be optimally satisfying under the circumstances. The preference curve indicates the teacher's preferences, which are equally receptive to any combination of benefits on that curve. Which will the teacher choose? The teacher will choose the point of tangency between the curve and the budget line, for that is where one of the preferences meets what is objectively available in the teacher's environment. The more constrained the curve, the narrower the range of choices the teacher finds acceptable regardless of what benefits are available. The broader the curve, the wider the range of choices the teacher would find acceptable and presumably the more the teacher would respond to the externally available benefits. In other words, teacher involvement would be more proportional to the perceived benefits.

Figure 6-2 represents the preference curve for sixty-five teachers drawn at random from the community-college faculties. The mean maximum time was 33 percent participation. The mean minimum time was 11 percent, and the ideal time was 20 percent. The ideal time was validated by other questionnaires drawn from random samples indicating that the average teacher would be willing to invest about eight hours a week on PLATO under ideal circumstances. From these three estimates was constructed the preference curve representing the average teacher's preferences in Figure 6-2. Presumably the teacher would be receptive to any of the combinations of benefits on that curve.

What is the actual ratio of benefits that now obtains? The mean ratio of PLATO benefits derivable to what the teacher is now doing was 35 to 65. One can see from rotating the budget line (assuming that there would be some elasticity in time expenditure and that the shape of the curve would remain stable with different ratios) that increasing the PLATO benefits would elicit extra participation only up to about 30 percent. Participation would fall off very sharply thereafter. Decreasing the benefits would result in a slight decrease down to 11 percent participation unless the decrease in PLATO benefits was extreme. The average teacher's range of participation is relatively constrained. True to predictions, all benefits are not seen as lying on one side or the other, though the preference is clear.

Figures 6-3, 6-4, 6-5, and 6-6 are the preference curves based on Downstate, Muslem, Bunche, and Miller Colleges, respectively. Notice the difference between the all-teacher situation just described

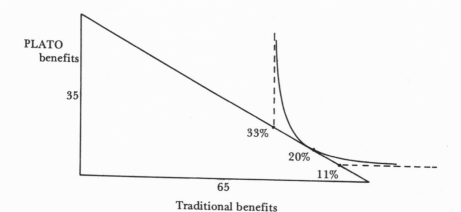

FIGURE 6-2
PLATO preference curve for all teachers

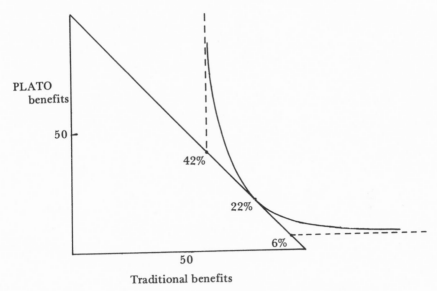

FIGURE 6-3

PLATO preference curve for Downstate College teachers

in Figure 6-2 and the situation diagramed for Downstate College teachers in Figure 6-3. The Downstate teachers present a situation where there is greater sensitivity to perceived benefits. They are receptive to much greater ranges and combinations of PLATO with traditional benefits. Participation will increase more in proportion to perceived benefits. At the same time PLATO benefits would have to be drastically reduced to cause a great reduction in participation in PLATO. Since the benefits ratio is already perceived to be fifty-fifty, there is considerable room for increased participation. All in all, this diagram indicates a favorable situation for PLATO at Downstate College, a finding congruent with other information. The teachers see more benefits, and, even though their ideal participation time is near the average, they are open to much wider participation.

Muslem College, diagramed in Figure 6-4, is quite another story. For the average Muslem teacher, the PLATO to traditional benefits ratio is perceived to be only 20 to 80, the lowest among the colleges. What is more, even though the ideal participation rate is

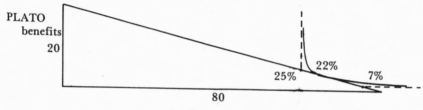

PLATO benefits
20

25%
22%
7%

80

Traditional benefits

FIGURE 6-4
PLATO preference curve for Muslem College teachers

exactly the same as at Downstate, even a tremendous increase in
PLATO benefits would not increase participation in the innovation.
On the other hand, even a slight decrease in PLATO benefits would
greatly decrease participation down to a floor of 7 percent. The
future for PLATO at Muslem College looks bleak indeed. Both the
available benefits and the teachers' actual preferences at Muslem
would have to be changed. Again this situation is quite congruent
with the case study.

The situation for Bunche College, diagramed in Figure 6-5,
is more optimistic, more like the all-teacher curve. It has a lower
ceiling and PLATO-traditional benefits ratio than at Downstate

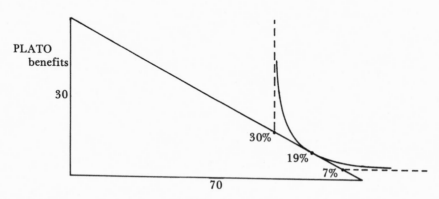

PLATO benefits

30

30%

19%
7%

70

Traditional benefits

FIGURE 6-5
PLATO preference curve for Bunche College teachers

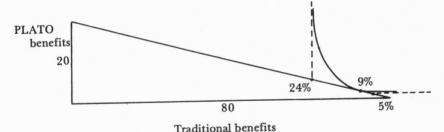

FIGURE 6-6
PLATO preference curve for Miller College teachers

College. There is less capacity for greater participation. The diagram for Miller College is similar in shape, but both the ceiling and, particularly, the ideal participation are much lower. There is little room for less participation than already exists since the ideal is close to the floor. There is some room for improvement if the low PLATO-traditional benefits ratio could be increased, but Miller's ceiling is close to the ideal of the other schools. Both the Bunche and Miller profiles conform to other facts known about these schools. On the basis of these profiles, an administrator would have to conclude that his best chances for eliciting faculty participation exist at Downstate and Bunche. Only at Touhy College, Figure 6-7, are the benefits perceived as much higher. Only a few people from Touhy responded to the questionnaire, and Touhy was the only college faculty with no experience with PLATO and no terminal.

All in all, the range of participation for teachers is severely constrained both by their preferences and by the benefits available to them.

The indifference curves for the authors present quite a different picture, as one might expect. The authors were all released either half- or full-time to work on PLATO. As revealed in Figure 6-8, the average author sees the possibility of deriving much higher benefits from PLATO. In fact, the ratio is in PLATO's favor for the first time. The diagram also reveals that the authors find acceptable a much broader range of combinations of PLATO and traditional benefits, making their participation much more contingent on the available benefits ratio. The diagram shows that the authors are

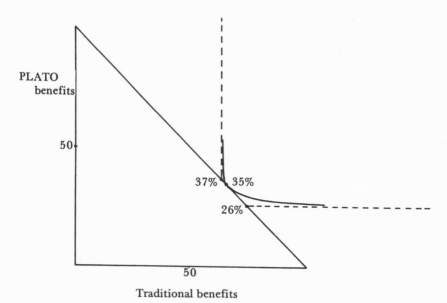

FIGURE 6-7
PLATO preference curve for Touhy College teachers

already working at the higher end of their curve. More benefits could not induce much greater participation. One is reminded of Mike Hamilton's comments that an author must retain at least one-quarter of his time in the class in order to be effective. Benefits available to the authors could actually be reduced somewhat without greatly decreasing their participation in the innovation.

Muslem College authors again present an extreme case, revealed in Figure 6-10. Their ideal and maximum are the same so they are working at their maximum participation level. Further benefits would do nothing. Their benefits ratio is also the highest of all the groups. On the other hand, the rate at which the curve drops away from the line indicates that decreases in benefits would cause substantial reductions in their participation, down to the 50 percent level.

The Bunche author curve in Figure 6-11 represents the most proportional situation among the authors. More participation could be elicited by increasing benefits, but not much more. Participation could also be lowered by decreasing benefits. The Bunche benefits

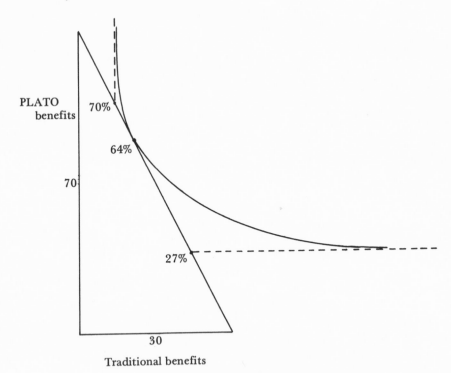

FIGURE 6-8
PLATO preference curve for all authors

ratio is the lowest among the authors and only somewhat higher than that perceived by the Downstate teachers. Generally, one could conclude that authors have more than sufficient benefits to elicit their participation and that authors are more receptive to these benefits than most teachers. Perhaps the administrators did pursue a selective-differential reward strategy.

To elicit greater participation from many more teachers would require more than increasing the perceived benefits available from the innovation. It would require changing the subjective preferences of the teachers for the innovations themselves. There are built-in reservations among the mass of teachers regarding the kind of benefits that an innovation like PLATO offers, and they are willing to invest only a limited portion of their time to gain such benefits. The much greater receptivity of the authors to much wider variations of benefits

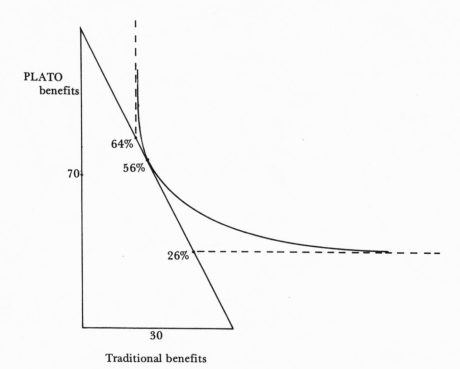

FIGURE 6-9
PLATO preference curve for Downstate College authors

indicates that they may be different types of people as reflected in their preference ordering. In fact, the author's minimum limit is about the same as the teacher's maximum. And, of course, for PLATO a different degree of benefits has been made differentially available to them. Clearly the fruit of these dynamics would be to have those who innovate and those who do not.

It is also interesting to note that the difference in perceived PLATO benefits is greatest at Muslem College—75 percent for authors to 20 percent for teachers—where morale and optimism are lowest. Morale is highest where the gap in PLATO benefits is perceived to be smallest between authors and teachers—70 percent to 50 percent at Downstate College. Morale is second best where the gap between authors and teachers is second smallest—60 percent to 30 percent at

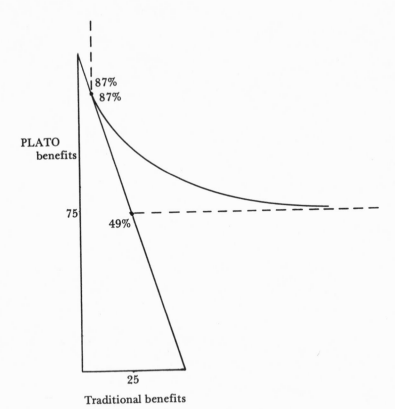

FIGURE 6-10
PLATO preference curve for Muslem College authors

Bunche. These latter two sites are the most promising and have actually produced more instructional materials.

While highly speculative, this technique of analysis offers some promise. Even though I pursued the data with a lack of rigor, the results are highly consistent with the great deal of information already available on the groups of community college teachers and authors, an acid test of validity. I also violated some of the assumptions of classic indifference curve analysis, but that is not too disturbing since models are only metaphors to be used when useful and to be discarded when they are not. In order to describe teacher behavior toward innovations as consumer behavior, it is necessary to define different units and relationships than the original model allows.

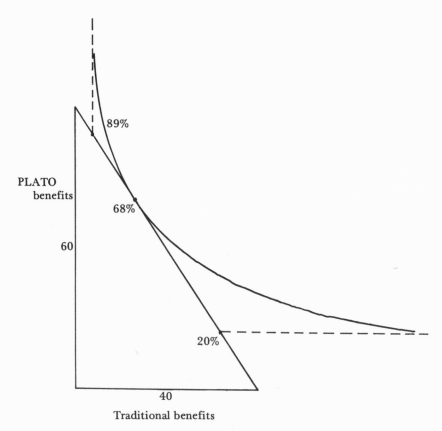

FIGURE 6-11
PLATO preference curve for Bunche College authors

It would, however, be good to eliminate some of the inconsistencies within the model. It would be better to define the budget line in terms of absolute quantities that could be increased or decreased to "purchase" more or less of both types of benefits. The budget line should be easily expandable or contractible. It should not be so completely tied to the ratio of benefits, which should also be expandable on their own. All the measures should be arrived at more independently than they were here.

Perhaps the most serious limitation is that benefits are not articulated with costs. It was originally reasoned that costs would be deducted from overall benefits, but, in thinking through the problem, costs seem to be important enough to deserve special consideration on their own. The great difficulty of learning a new form of behavior, as dramatized earlier in this chapter, is not adequately represented in the purchase of available benefits.

FIXING THE BURDEN

A line of reasoning that began in Chapter 2 distinguishes between the meaning of an innovation for a teacher and for an administrator. By now it is clear that not only is the spread of administrator and teacher innovations different, so also are the respective rewards and costs. The rewards are greater for those higher in the hierarchy, and the costs are greater for those lower. It is teachers who must struggle to learn TUTOR or to deal with the endless pains and frustrations intentionally detailed in this chapter, and they must do this in spite of very limited rewards and resources. They are also usually blamed if the innovation is not properly implemented. There are many versions of the PLATO story that has been outlined in the last few chapters, which stress the heroic efforts of several individuals to make the system work in the face of great handicaps.

Frustrations are not limited to high-technology innovations like PLATO where the innovation is manifested in concrete form and specific detail. Charters and Pellegrin (1973) outlined the course of events in attempts to develop "differentiated staffing" in four schools. They recognized two phases in the process—the "preparation-formulation" phase and the "implementation" phase. The first phase began when the school district, at the instigation of a small group of central office staff members, entered into a formal agreement with a funding agency to install an innovative program. (Probably the central office staff contacts followed the dynamics of entrepreneurial innovation diffusion. Although Charters and Pellegrin do not describe the origin of the initial contact, it is clear that schools must be tied into a larger network.)

The agreement was based on a hastily constructed proposal put together to obtain funds. The proposal described the innovation in "highly abstract, global terms," emphasizing the educational benefits rather than what was to be done. The most concrete parts were in terms of procedures: workshops, committees, travel, among others.

(The PLATO administrators' knowledge generally consisted of the same kind of information.) Since each school was unique, it was presumed that the teaching staffs would have to play the key role in development.

A district-wide project director was selected, presumably by the central office staff, and schools in the district were invited to participate. Although the schools may already have been selected, it was decreed necessary to obtain the approval of the teaching staff. In two of the schools, principals were given the choice of whether to participate, and individual members of the teaching staff were given the choice of transferring to another school. As Charters and Pellegrin note, however, from the teachers' viewpoint neither costs nor benefits of participation could be assessed at that time.

Once the schools were chosen, the staffs were expected to follow procedures specified in the new program, with lead times ranging from three months to two years. Project administrators provided teachers with reading materials, arranged visits to other schools, scheduled committee meetings, and made other arrangements. The teaching staff was beset with a number of problems, including uncertainty as to their task, regular duties competing for time, and no salient decision-making structure of their own. The teaching staff was unclear as to what the project was all about, and neither the proposal nor the administrators were much help. Although the teaching staff was supposed to be responsible for the program, it was initiated, organized, and paid for by someone else. The staff, unused to such collective responsibility, spent much time trying to decide where the responsibility really rested. Press of time for regular duties remained severe, and, though project deadlines were near, only one or two afternoons a week were available to define and organize such a complex change. There was no way to use outside help. Final plans were understandably vague and not well considered.

The implementation phase began with the opening of school. The program was "implemented" when all the appropriate administrative acts were performed: new organization chart drawn up, new titles announced, salaries set, and new personnel hired, among others. The staff, still unclear about what to do, was swamped with such additional duties as meetings with teachers and parents and altered schedules. The meetings appeared aimless. The costs of participation, mainly in terms of diversion from other teaching responsibilities, outweighed the benefits. Some absorbed the demands on their time without sacrificing other responsibilities, but disillusionment was great.

Outside visitors—educators, parents, other teachers—came, and the program had to be explained to them. This burden fell to the administrators, who developed definitions for external consumption that were couched in global language and at odds with what was going on internally. Project goals began to be redefined more in accord with what was happening. Soon outside evaluators began arriving and were themselves confused over how to evaluate such an amorphous project. The evaluation reports told the staff little that they did not know, if they were seen at all. There was no way for the staff to set the project on a different course. Administrators reviewed the reports for funding implications. Before the projects were even under way, decisions had to be made for the next year's program. After the first year of implementation, two of the four schools withdrew from the project.

Charters and Pellegrin gleaned from this project several "chronic problems" of the change process, which included:

- —gross unclarity in conceptualization of the substance of the change;
- —heavy reliance on "structural" change, such as job descriptions and title changes;
- —fallacious assumptions that general program objectives could be translated easily into appropriate behaviors;
- —unrealistic time perspectives;
- —disjunction between established administrative structure and temporary project management;
- —scant teacher experience or preparation for implementation or collective decision making;
- —conflicts in values, goals, and interests between the central office staff, project managers, and teaching staff;
- —absence of effective monitoring procedures;
- —failure to recognize severity of "role overload" among teaching staff;
- —assumptions that schools need few additional resources to cope with change.

In its formlessness and lack of specification, the differentiated staffing program described here is more akin to the innovations of

the Illinois Gifted Program than the highly tangible, concrete man-
ifestation of an innovation like PLATO. Yet nearly all the problems
mentioned above were also attendant upon the introduction of
PLATO to the community colleges. Learning TUTOR was a highly
precise task; but, no matter what the degree of specification, learning
new tasks is difficult, painful, and unavoidable. The degree of resistance to an innovation is at least partly the function of the difficulty
of learning a new mode of behavior.

In the case of PLATO, this learning was made considerably
more difficult by the poor reliability of the machinery and the
distance from the developers. As in the differentiated staffing projects,
the innovation was introduced from above. It was assumed that procedures like workshops and consultants could get the job done, and
there was much change in titles, job descriptions, and other superficial aspects. It was assumed that the global program objectives
could be handily translated into appropriate behavior. The time
necessary to accomplish things was greatly underestimated, partly
because the funding agencies' time schedules were highly unrealistic.
There was disjunction between the established administrative structure, the project management, and, it might be added, the teachers.
Authors trying to implement the project were often caught among
all three.

Although a few teachers were sent to the university to learn
the system a whole year in advance, even this time period proved
inadequate for learning the complex skills required by the new innovation. The training period set aside for other teachers was grossly
inadequate. Among the various interested groups great differences of
values and interests occasionally surfaced over how the machines
should be used. There were serious attempts to monitor the progress
of events, and the monitoring prevented larger failures from occurring
but could not correct the most basic difficulties. For the most part,
the enormous burden that fell on the teachers was underestimated,
though some recognition of the difficulty was apparent through
the granting of released time to several authors. Even so, the technical and emotional resources necessary to carry the innovation
effectively through even a first stage of implementation were grossly
inadequate. Those involved did as well as they could with what they
had.

Ultimately, where the innovation was successful, the teachers had to turn to each other or to themselves for help. Those who could latch onto experienced and competent programmers were fortunate. There was some, though not nearly enough, help from the technical personnel at the university, but there was little help available from the administrative structure itself. It was difficult to break away from old lesson routines, even under optimum conditions. Without adequate technical and emotional support, innovation became impossible.

Outside observers concluded that teachers could not or would not be able to master the system and develop their own instructional materials and began to assume that they would be justified in taking over. Teachers, for their part, felt disillusioned and frustrated at the lack of time and resources placed at their disposal. Perhaps these were the inevitable fruits of trying to innovate in an economy of scarcity.

The theme of this chapter is simple: the burden of innovation must inevitably fall on the teacher. The teacher must implement the innovation and learn the new skills that are required. Depending on how different the innovation is, the burden can be costly indeed, and benefits seldom approach costs. The teacher is expected to finance the innovation with personal effort, in effect depleting her professional skills without recompense, which represents a poor investment. Some do; some do not. In any case, innovation can be realized only through the changing work skills of the teaching work force, or it cannot be realized at all.

Chapter 7

Sources of Innovation

CONDITIONS FOR INCEPTION

Where do innovations originate? One might reason that, since innovations are borne through social networks and since the values of social reference groups transform innovations, innovative ideas are generated under special group conditions. It is significant that the study of creative conditions has taken place primarily in business organizations, the invention of economic products being more acceptable than the invention of social forms.

Invention is at least partially dependent on organizational structure (Thompson, 1969). Conditions ideal for the generation of innovative ideas are: psychological security and freedom, diversity of inputs into the organization, internal commitment to searching for solutions, a moderate amount of structure to help define the problem, and a moderate amount of benign competition.

Unfortunately, few organizations offer these conditions. Most are concerned with predictability, reliability, accountability, and control. The organization is perceived as a tool of either the owner or the government so there can be only one source of legitimacy. Since conflict generates problems and uncertainties, it implies pluralism—a dispersion of legitimate power. Conflict cannot be tolerated. Control is facilitated by narrow job definition and programmed activities. The only legitimate interest is the owner's or the manager's. A "production ideology" develops that leads to central control and overspecification of resources.

The "production ideology" specifies that management's interest is in controlling all organizational behavior. The organization is evaluated in terms of how it maximizes formal goals. Any "slack" in the organization, that is, surplus satisfaction beyond that needed to induce employee contribution, is considered inefficient. All activities must be programmed, and, where activities are entirely programmed, there can be no innovation. Production and innovation vary inversely.

Actually invention itself is a nonrational process. When there is considerable slack (the excess of objective achievement to the subjectively set aspiration level of the organization), there is a relaxed, indulgent, decision-making situation conducive to invention. For those who see the environment as largely uncertain, the development of new knowledge is important. Flexibility, pluralism, multiple approaches—even duplication—become appropriate. Freedom to exploit uncertainty is the strategy, and programmed behavior prohibits such exploitation.

If one assumes that he already knows the answers or that truth is the monopoly of some minority, then having freedom to explore makes little sense. Those who assume set and fixed goals are confounded by emergent phenomena and cannot deal with uncertainty. In the monocratic organization, invention is sacrificed to maximizing production. Organizational slack must be used to intensify goal pursuit. Conflict is not legitimate.

On the other hand, various claimants advertise, propagandize, organize coalitions, and otherwise promote partisan positions within an organization, and decisions are largely the result of the claimants' enthusiasm and success in advancing their views. Innovative organizations are "think tanks," manifesting the conditions mentioned earlier.

The conditions necessary for invention are far from those that obtain in public schools. Few operations could be more programmed than having to prepare for and meet thirty students six hours a day, five days a week. The number of contact hours minimizes any "slack" time the teacher may have. Nor does the school system as a whole value invention. Business firms often try to solve their lack of innovation by establishing segregated research and development (R&D) units. (Even then, most R&D personnel are likely to spend much of their time in such noninnovative activities as troubleshooting and testing.) Only a few tenths of a percent of school budgets are spent on research and development, as compared to 5 percent in medicine and 10 percent in defense (Elboim-Dror, 1971). State and federal education bureaucracies are as bad as local schools. Responding to daily crises, attempting to administer millions of dollars in funds, these organizations are among the most monocratic in education. While they are able to capitalize on a new idea, often to the point of obsession, one will wait a long time before the government apparatus produces a new one.

Currently, universities and some other institutions have the "slack" resources to be inventive. Arcane and esoteric though many of these ideas may be, they are made possible because the universities are relieved of the burden of being immediately practical. Only one in a thousand of the ideas may be practical. Comparison with evolution is appropriate. It takes thousands of mutations, many of which are harmful, to produce one mutation beneficial to the species. It takes a high degree of tolerance for "messing around" to progress. Immediate accountability and immediate practicality are not beneficial for invention. They are attempts to impose rationalistic constraints on nonrational processes. To program activities toward some set goal is to smother invention, though it might enhance problem solving. To impress immediate responsibility upon the inventor is to turn exploration into tradition.

The university has a "production ideology" of its own—publication. Contributing to a discipline, which operationalizes itself in publishing certain types of articles in certain journals, is far removed from improving educational practice. In fact, the most highly developed fields, called "sciences," ignore the complexities of reality at least long enough to produce abstract models (Kuhn, 1962). When enough of the contingencies are stripped away, such models enable prediction within an extremely narrow domain. But then they are not very good for dealing with practical problems since real-world contingencies are still there. For example, modern physics and engineering may specify exactly how to put a man on the moon, but they cannot specify what the social costs, benefits, and consequences are. They accomplish the former by totally ignoring the latter.

The most innovative unit is not the one with similar specialists all exploiting the same scientific paradigm; rather, it is the one with layers of people on a continuum between abstract models and everyday practice. Interaction among these people—some seeing the abstractions; others, the complex reality—results in conflict of ideas and in new perceptions. Researchers with researchers and practitioners with practitioners simply reinforce the paradigms in which each lives. Special organizations, such as regional laboratories, produce innovations, but they also have their own difficulties—mainly the type of accountability to which they are subject.

In spite of the size of the educational establishment, very few organizations provide the type of setting in which invention can occur. This is not accidental, and it does reflect the relative powerlessness of education as an institution. With economic institutions occupying the premier spot in the institutional hierarchy, perhaps only the religious institutions are less powerful than educational ones. This powerlessness is reflected in the dependence of educational institutions on economic institutions. For example, it is usually taken for granted among educational planners that the educational system should adapt to labor needs (Elboim-Dror, 1971). Seldom is the possibility that supply creates its own demands mentioned in education, although it is a prime idea in marketing. Likewise, the accountability movement in education has strong overtones of subordinating educational to economic goals. The very assumption that there is a fixed and limited goal that can be maximized by proper manipulation of inputs is the cornerstone of "economic rationality," which operates to the exclusion of political rationality and invention (House, 1972). Economic planners and systems analysis have never been able to account for the economic utility of research and development expenditures (Thompson, 1969), not because invention is mystical, but because it is nonrational. Yet the efficacy of invention is demonstrated by the huge sums of money that business and defense establishments continue to spend on it.

There can be few better ways of keeping an institution dependent than to deprive it of new ideas. The educational institutions accept outside ideas like performance contracting or PPBS (Program Planning and Budgeting Systems). Intellectually weak as these inventions are, they appear strong in a vacuum. When a new idea like economic accountability appears, schools are intellectually helpless before it. There are few better ways of emasculating an institution than to strip it of its idea-creating power and its initiating ability. It must then either be impotent to change or subject to the whims of popular sentiment as interpreted by third parties. It is an easy make.

Assuming that an invention is born, it must then find its way into the social networks of the practitioners. The isolation of the research community from practitioners in education is legend. Geographic distances, status differentials (as between researchers and practitioners), legal boundaries, and a dozen other barriers inhibit its journey. Most innovations never make it so far. Those that do, like Individually Prescribed Instruction materials, are transformed in the process. The final metamorphosis is performed by the practitioner, who blends the invention with his other messages and shapes them to his own ends, which are certain to be far removed from the vision pursued by the inventor. In addition, the very process of "overselling" the invention may damage its long-term viability.

THE IMPORTANCE OF SPONSORSHIP

In many ways the development of PLATO is a classic illustration of complex technological development.* Two hundred people and tens of millions of dollars were engaged over a thirteen-year period in order to develop PLATO IV, the fourth generation system. It is bigger, more successful, and more publicized than most other innovations. Perhaps it is for these reasons that its strengths and weaknesses are magnified, but it is nonetheless representative of the genre of educational, particularly technological, inventions.

The organization from which PLATO sprang was a university-based applied science laboratory doing classified military research. In the late 1950's the vice-president for research at the university saw that the days of classified military research on university campuses were numbered, and he suggested to the laboratory director, Ron McCormick, that the laboratory begin to investigate civilian applications technology. Both agreed that, with the rising costs of education and the consequent lowering of productivity, education was a ripe field for employing computer technology.

McCormick's first move was to establish a campus-wide committee of prominent education and computer experts, some of whom

---

*In no way are the events in this chapter a complete history of the PLATO project. They represent only one man's memory, albeit one close to the project. Here, as elsewhere, the interpretations are mine alone. I have selected events only to illustrate certain principles.

were already exploring the possibilitiҫs. The committee turned into a Tower of Babel with none of the experts being able, or perhaps not caring, to understand one another. They concluded that such a computer-based system was impossible to build. McCormick realized he had made a mistake, and he disbanded the committee.

He recognized that the problem could only be solved by an interdisciplinary approach, but he also realized that the approach must differ from a multidisciplinary approach in which each man remained faithful to his discipline. McCormick then decided to find an interdisciplinary person who could envision the total system within his own mind—hardware, software, and implementation. The man would have to know computers intimately and also know something about education. Within a few days he found a young, unknown electrical engineering professor, Alvin Edison, and Edison went to work for the laboratory. He reported only to the laboratory director who had total control, discretion, and enough money to support this high-risk venture.

For several years, most of the years of development, Edison was supported on overhead funds generated by the classified military research contracts. As McCormick was fond of saying, PLATO was a product of the military-industrial complex. For the first several years, McCormick and Edison sought funds, but they were never able to find the kind of support they wanted. There were always too many strings attached. Meanwhile Edison envisioned the system, particularly the economics of it, and built the first generation model. As he worked, the laboratory began running out of enough computer time to support both the regular projects and Edison's endeavors. The military saved them by granting the laboratory a million dollars to buy its own computer.

The next crisis arose after two years of the development work, when the engineering department of the university recommended that Edison be refused tenure in the university since he had not met normal university requirements for publishing. (Later, even after thirteen years, not many articles had been published by the PLATO staff.) The laboratory director, a powerful figure in the university, interceded on his behalf, and got him tenure. As the project developed, Edison needed more hours of prime computer time. The rest of the laboratory scientists objected to his usurpation of time, particularly since he was not working on a regularly funded project. The laboratory director met with the president of a major computer manufacturing company and obtained free use of a computer for the project. By the advent of PLATO IV that company seemed to have an inside track on marketing the system, and the project purchased this brand of computer when it could later afford to buy its own.

A whole series of inventions over a period of thirteen years was necessary to produce PLATO IV, acclaimed by many to be the most advanced computer-based system in the world. Although two hundred persons were employed on the project over that time span, many more contributed to the project. A special computer language, TUTOR, appropriate for authoring lessons, was developed to enable people with minimum training to use the system. Any terminal could be used as an authoring terminal. A major jump from PLATO III to PLATO IV involved the invention of a special plasma display panel. The PLATO III console used an oscilloscope display which, like any television, had to be replenished many times a second in order to maintain the image. This process used a great amount of the computer's capacity, thereby limiting the number of terminals that could be attached and the economic feasibility of the system.

The major inventor, Edison, envisioned a plasma display panel consisting of a thin tube filled with gas and having very thin wires crisscrossing it. He saw the panel as a matrix of neon signs with low voltage passing through to keep it lit. Once a dot from the crossed wires was "turned on" it would stay on like a neon light and not have to be replenished by the computer. The capacity of the computer would be greatly increased, and thousands of terminals could be attached. Having envisioned the plasma display panel, Edison invented it. It worked. Later, while explaining it to a group of physicists in the laboratory, he found that the display panel worked on an entirely different set of principles than he had hypothesized, principles he did not fully understand. He invented it, but the physicists had to explain it.

Over the thirteen-year development span of the project, innumerable improvements were made on the system, again often by chance. A group of high school students given an opportunity to spend some time on the system managed to break the security code that protected material in the computer. They could gain access to whatever they wanted. Having done so, they showed the PLATO people how they did it and how to fix it, providing PLATO with a very sophisticated security system. As terminals were hooked up all over the campus, the country, and finally, the world, thousands of very bright people worked on them in fascination twenty-four hours a day. One graduate student said that the genius of the system was that it was open and interactive so that it managed to "suck in" the collective ingenuity of thousands of individuals. The PLATO people were proud of the fact that, although few papers had been written about PLATO, there were fifteen patents on the system.

The conditions for the birth of PLATO matched those outlined earlier for developing an invention:

Psychological security and freedom. The inventor seemed to live in an almost entirely supportive environment. He was encouraged and protected by the laboratory director, allowing him to work at his own speed and in his own direction. He was given total control over the shape of the project. When outside research money could not be found to support the project, it was supported from the overhead funds of the laboratory and, beyond that, was backed up by the university. Edison was allowed to use unlimited computer time in an era when such time was scarce. He also was allowed to use prime daylight time, forcing others whose projects were actually paying for the computer to work at night. When that approach became untenable, he was given his own computer. He was even granted university tenure without meeting normal university requirements.

Diversity of inputs into the organization. Edison operated within one of the leading military research laboratories in the country, which was filled with competent scientists and professionals. The computer department had developed one of the first large digital computers, and the computer facilities and personnel were unparalleled. The engineering school was among the top in the nation, and the whole campus was oriented toward technology.

Internal commitment to searching for solutions. The whole purpose of the applied science laboratory was to apply technology to the solution of practical problems. Besides a computer-based education system, the laboratory also developed a navigation system and an air traffic control system. All were real-world problems.

A moderate amount of structure to help define the problem. The structure of the problem was outlined from the beginning when Edison was selected to do the job. Some structure was also supplied by knowing the nature of the school system in which PLATO would be employed. Particularly important in Edison's thinking were the economics of the situation. PLATO would have to be economically competitive with the costs of an elementary school, a goal toward which he strove.

A moderate amount of benign competition. Edison was also in mild competition with the other projects within the laboratory. Since in a sense he was living off funds generated by them, he must have been spurred somewhat to succeed. There was also competition from commercial firms. During the 1960's considerable effort and publicity were generated by computer-assisted instruction. A major system was developed at another university prior to PLATO, and a completely separate and older system existed within the psychology department of the university itself. The older system finally dissolved and the chief sponsor left. Commercial firms quickly introduced several computer-assisted instruction systems on the market. None worked very well.

McCormick, the laboratory director, felt that the poor quality of the commercial systems set computer-assisted instruction back at least a decade because of popular disillusionment after much publicity and ballyhoo. Although at that time the leading commercial firm had spent seven times the money invested in PLATO, the company did not have nearly as good a system. McCormick was adamant that top quality development takes many years, and commercial firms suffered from the "production ideology" mentioned earlier. They felt that they must turn a profit within a few years; they could not think in longer terms. PLATO IV, in development for thirteen years, still had not reached many of its goals.

Edison was removed from the normal demands of accountability and control that exist even within a university. Although university structures are normally freer than those of other organizations, as evidenced by the production of new ideas, they have, as was mentioned earlier, their own "production ideology"—publication—that forces a professor to attend to his discipline as operationally defined by journals in the field since he must publish in such journals in order to maintain his job and be promoted. He must undertake the same types of studies that usually appear in the journals. While there may be something to be said for the discipline of a discipline, it cannot be said that it is oriented toward practical problems. It does not allow the professor to search in an interdisciplinary fashion for solutions to social problems unless the area of specialization is intentionally organized around practical considerations as it is in animal husbandry. (Colleges of agriculture, which have been organized in this way, have been more successful in their search for practical solutions.)

In the case of PLATO, Edison was freed from these concerns to the point of receiving tenure in a manner antithetical to university policy. What university would wait thirteen years to see a man's work? The "organizational slack" in the laboratory, the excess of resources over what was necessary to carry out military contracts, underwrote the cost of Edison's experiments. The "excess" funds were not drained off in profits, programmed into other uses, or returned to the Department of Defense in order to increase the efficiency rating of the laboratory. Efficiency was not at issue; invention was. Perhaps it should be said also that, if Edison had not had the requisite genius and perhaps luck, the project would have failed. Others probably did; we are writing about this one because it did not. The fact is, Edison's great talents are rare, but the conditions under which such talents can develop and the willingness to suffer the ninety-nine failures for the one success are equally rare.

The laboratory director was willing to endure, tolerate, and even promote a certain amount of conflict between Edison and the rest of the laboratory workers, illustrated in the demands over computer time. He was also quick to find a way out by getting a new computer when the conflict became disruptive, when fellow workers rebelled.

The nonrational, or at least nonprogrammed, nature of invention is also well exemplified by the serendipity by which many improvements in PLATO were made. Only a few were mentioned. Edison was able to invent the most critical piece of equipment for PLATO IV, the plasma display panel, even though he misunderstood the principles that made it work. In fact, science has normally followed, rather than led, technological invention. Edison envisioned the panel through a metaphor, through seeing it as a grid of neon lights flashing on and off. Brilliant as Edison's accomplishments were, many of the necessary inventions were contributed by individuals whose names are no longer remembered. It may be, as the graduate student suggested, that the real genius of the system lay in opening it up to thousands of people, many of whom contributed a little piece through their own ingenuity. The real invention may have been the open social system that allowed such participation.

By 1972, however, there were signs that the system was closing. A graduate student in industrial design wanted to redesign the PLATO IV keyboard. The keyboard was essentially that of a typewriter, and he thought he could make it more efficient. Try as he might, he was eventually frozen out of attempting the redesign, although he wanted to do it as an individual project like many before him. Terminals were being mass produced and shipped all over the country. There were orders to fill. Industrial production lines had been set up to manufacture the equipment. Although engineers continued to work on hardware development, at least part of the system had closed.

In his reminiscence on the development of PLATO IV, the laboratory director, McCormick, stated his belief that the social invention of the laboratory itself, the type of organization it was, had to precede the technological invention. Otherwise there would have been no PLATO IV. All the support that Edison had was necessary. It was also essential that the problem be approached from an interdisciplinary framework and that at least the person in charge be interdisciplinary himself. The laboratory had to be problem oriented and, of course, a long period of time, unobstructed by demands for immediate profit or demands for results, was needed for full development.

In his writings McCormick stressed the differences between an interdisciplinary and a multidisciplinary research center. In a multidisciplinary center individual scholars from different disciplines share facilities, but the problems they attack are defined by the discipline and do not require the participation of others in reaching a solution. In an interdisciplinary center the nature of the problem determines the selection of personnel and requires interaction for a solution. The problem attacked is a complex, real-world one. The organization, function, administration, and rewards of the two centers are quite different. One is addressed to enhancing the participant's professional standing in his discipline; the other, to the successful design of solutions to a problem.

The multidisciplinary center is more compatible with traditional university structure. The director's function is that of coordinator and spokesman. The interdisciplinary mission is more delicate and unpredictable. It calls for charismatic leadership rather than coordination. It is not motivated and directed by the disciplinary reward system embedded in the academic world. Struggling with a difficult complex problem that necessitates interaction with several others for an unclear reward demands different leadership. The interdisciplinary people must relate to the problem and to each other.

The similarity between scholars breaking out of their disciplines to become problem oriented and teachers breaking out of their daily routines to embrace new innovations is marked. Both require resources; both seek less tangible rewards, although ambition is a fuel; and both are difficult. The one overriding staff requirement in an interdisciplinary effort is that there be at least one person in a leadership role who is an interdisciplinary person. A man who has spent his life's career in one discipline, however prominently, is not likely to be such a man. University professors are usually too captured by their disciplines to play such a role, and business administrators are often obsessed with the problems of productivity and distribution, according to McCormick.

Hence, universities are not inclined toward solving social problems. Nor are business organizations. Part of the reason for the cohort organization of the universities is the past research and development policies of the federal government. For the past twenty years government agencies have been pursuing "central national goals" for research and development, such as national defense or space exploration, rather than "distributed national goals" for research and development, such as rebuilding cities and environmental concerns. The latter programs are characterized by local determinants in the nature of the problems, the approach to solutions, and anticipated consequences. There are local variations in clients and in sponsors. (More will be said about these policies in Chapter 8; see also Alpert, 1970.)

Universities have organized themselves to pursue central national goals, which keeps them from pursuing others. In fact, there is a distinct lack of attention to local and regional variations. The clients are national agencies, which specify what they want. The agencies are both sponsor and client. However, when the agencies specify products which must be "purchased" by individuals, such as teachers, the products are often unacceptable, particularly when they have no sensitivity to local variations. The universities are well suited to getting grants from government agencies by meeting the agencies' criteria. Yet there are no clients for these inventions other than the agencies themselves. Hence, the university invention mechanisms are oriented away from domestic problem solving such as occurs in education. The U.S. Office of Education's policy toward federally sponsored laboratories and research and development centers is an excellent example. The government, its agencies, and the universities search ceaselessly for the Golden Fleece, those inventions which will work in all settings, and they are ceaselessly frustrated. Officials even use the moon landing as one analogy for devising educational materials. In the United States there are seventeen thousand educational governance units, two million teachers, and over sixty million students. How many moons are there?

The most critical question now facing PLATO is precisely this problem of universal application. For some time it has been promoted as a twenty-first-century blackboard, that is, every teacher is his own author and puts his own materials on the machine. The alternative is a twenty-first-century textbook in which materials are centrally developed and "piped" out to the classes, like *Sesame Street.* Pressures, particularly economic ones, push the project more and more toward the latter course. Teachers have difficulty learning TUTOR, they are slow in getting material into the system, and the material developed is unimaginative and poor. More and more funds are being put into central development teams and into the university developing the material. The long time period allowed for developing the hardware is not allowed for developing courseware. It is much more efficient to develop courseware centrally. Part of this is the push for immediate results by sponsors and evaluators of the project.

Whether teachers will use the material centrally developed is problematical. Most say they will not. As was demonstrated in the community college description, the acceptance of PLATO was institutionally dependent. Local variations made profound differences. The overwhelming rationale given by both teachers and administrators for wanting to use PLATO was to handle the immense differences among students. If PLATO decision makers continue to be pushed into centrally developed and controlled curricula, teachers will probably not be very interested in it. The National Science Foundation will become client as well as sponsor. It will pay people to use the system by purchasing terminals for them, paying for training, and so on. Many terminals will be sold, like the new math materials, but teacher behavior will not change. McCormick has contended that developing solutions to social problems requires "academic entrepreneurs" who can define and coalesce new clients into local markets so that it becomes feasible to develop solutions with local variations for local problems. Only in this way is it possible to break the monolithic monopoly on invention.

It is clear that invention has many similarities to the entrepreneurial act of implementing new innovations in the school. It requires an entrepreneur to overcome the set structure, a great deal of talent and resources, and a very long stretch of unimpeded development time. It is also clear that, while schools may possess the raw talent and the problem orientation, not one school system in the country can meet the other requirements. Within the current social-political-economic structure of the school, implementing innovations is difficult, and inventing them is impossible. This puts schools in an exceedingly passive position. They have no real initiatory power or any capability of consciously transforming themselves. Initiation of new ideas always comes from outside the system, leaving schools in a perpetually defensive position. Various agencies and groups can mount educational reforms before which the schools must either fall prostrate or defend themselves. This sullen, defensive posture befits education's position far down in the institutional pecking order of our society, which is to say the same thing in different words.

Once again, as with innovation diffusion among schools, and as with innovation implementation within schools, it is the pattern of interpersonal grouping and the organization of personal contacts that ultimately controls the invention of innovations—its location, its rate, and even its substance.

THE PROMISE AND THE PROMISES
OF INNOVATION—OVERSELLING

An extremely important innovation phenomenon revolves around the promise of and promises for an innovation, around selling and overselling. At all levels—school, project, and national—a certain amount of "selling" is necessary if the innovation is to make headway against tradition. In fact, one might say that the one indispensable attitude of those involved is faith in the future. Faith in the future of the innovation is required, as in any religion, because the innovation can never, in the present, live up to its future promises. Faith is necessary to justify putting vast amounts of resources and efforts into something that does not work well now. Innovation, particularly for the pioneers, is an act of faith.

An important source of this faith is the entrepreneurial group, which can provide strong internal support and maintain faith even in the face of great adversity. An important function of the entrepreneur is to provide his group with splendid visions of the future and to convert the uninitiated in order to gain new recruits and to obtain necessary resources to keep the project going. This function is known as "selling the innovation." As the political economy of innovation is presently constructed, this is an absolutely vital function in which successful innovation centers must engage.

One of the major difficulties is in "overselling" the innovation. When this happens, nonbelievers begin to focus on the gap between the promises made for the innovation and its performance and begin to label its propagators as medicine men or charlatans. In the worst of innovations, shoddy character may be readily perceived from the beginning. It may be apparent that the only things driving the innovation are the self-interest and salesmanship of the propagators. But good innovations can also be oversold as the necessary propagandizing gets out of hand or the success of the innovation stimulates entrepreneurs into making excessive claims. The very act of obtaining necessary support often seduces the entrepreneur into making promises impossible to fulfill. Any innovation faces a certain number of such problems, but, when the claims become too exaggerated, they often result in countermoves and disillusionment on the part of those who must use it. Of course, true believers never falter—a phenomenon that occurs at all levels.

As the PLATO project developed, it turned from the lean one-man days, picked up money and personnel, and became a movement. Tremendous sums of money began to flow in from the major technocratic institutions of society. The basic PLATO IV "demonstration" project received five million dollars from the National Science Foundation to demonstrate the feasibility of the system. Most of the money went into hardware development. Additional hundreds of thousands of dollars were granted to develop courseware. The State

Board of Higher Education granted another five million dollars to the project as well as several hundred thousand dollars to community colleges engaged in the demonstration. In effect, both terminals and released time for teachers to author were provided.

A group of generals and admirals, always interested in PLATO, were quite impressed with a demonstration of PLATO IV. Soon a grant of 1.2 million dollars arrived from the Department of Defense. The DOD decided to install terminals at four major military training bases. After the purchase of the terminals, the grant left $800,000 for the project to spend as it saw fit—no strings attached. Perhaps it needed another computer. This occurred in 1972, when the Nixon administration limited expenditures for education and for all domestic purposes. Money poured in from major funding sources—$595,000 to develop courseware for the school of basic medical sciences, $45,000 to develop courseware for Vocational College, and so. The list of funds appeared to be endless.

The university itself had invested an indeterminate amount (one administrator estimated $300,000) in the form of individual positions, time, and facilities. PLATO was powerful enough within the university to offer tenure-tract professorships to full-time personnel during an exceedingly restricted budgetary period. When the former university president was commemorated through a lecture series in his honor, Clark Kerr of the Carnegie Foundation, formerly President of the University of California, could list PLATO as one of the five most significant accomplishments of the university during the man's twenty-year tenure. The Carnegie Foundation itself, in its influential report on the use of computers in education, gave PLATO prominent mention.

Within one of the major research universities in the world PLATO had become perhaps the major project, certainly the most publicized. Political infighting among university administrators over who would control which piece of PLATO terrain became intense and ceaseless. A great entourage of followers, often full of messianic fervor, developed around the project itself. Many were graduate students who had forsaken their dissertations in order to work as research assistants on the many special projects. Some who moved away came back. Programmers would spend literally all night working out their problems on the machine and trading information and stories about PLATO. One program enabled people to talk to anyone else plugged into a console via the computer. Myths began to grow.

Among the faithful, the invention of PLATO was compared quite seriously to the invention of the printing press. Alvin Edison, the inventor, and his inventive brilliance became grist for the myth mill. Edison became head of the entire project, overshadowing his mentor, the former laboratory director. PLATO became an independent laboratory of its own within the university. So, in thirteen years the sheltered, surreptitious little project evolved from an invention into a social movement of considerable force and magnitude through the grace of technological ingenuity and the sponsorship of some of the most powerful institutions of the society. Sponsorship was exceedingly important. Not only did it assure propagation throughout the society, but it guaranteed resources to meet any problem PLATO might face. If an unexpected difficulty arose, new resources were always available to correct it. Such sponsorship was as good a guarantee against failure as was possible.

PLATO became nationally, then internationally, famous. Edison spent much of his time traveling around the world demonstrating the machine. He carried a terminal in a specially designed traveling case to demonstrate in Paris, Hong Kong, and Moscow. Even the Russians were interested. His demonstrations took priority over the other functions of the system. In order to ensure core space for the demonstration, he would "knock down" the entire system, putting it totally at his disposal.

The promises made for PLATO were great indeed. In a paper entitled "The World after PLATO IV: The Implications of Computer-based Systems on Education of the Future" prepared for the Select Subcommittee on Education, U.S. House of Representatives, two of the major developers outlined the shape of the future (Alpert and Bitzer, 1971). The key features were:

1. It would provide low-cost communication channels among several educational institutions.
2. Each institution would control its own curriculum and would establish the institutional setting for PLATO. Since each student console could function as an authoring console, each instructor could write his own material.
3. It would allow separation of the management of the computer center and the publication of lesson materials from the management of the educational program or the writing of materials.

The initial system costs would be $1.50 per hour and decrease rapidly toward $.35 per student-contact hour.

The two major problems that PLATO IV would address itself to would be declining educational productivity and the diverse educational needs of different student populations. PLATO IV was to achieve each of the major demands placed on the educational system.

Diverse background, preparations, and motivation of students. Since PLATO is highly individualized, students of great diversity could be accommodated. Slow students could proceed at a slower pace, and fast ones could be given enrichment materials. Continual testing and monitoring could indicate each student's progress.

Demands to expand options and to improve performance. Classroom lockstep is no longer necessary. Each student can have his own options. Each student's personal "objectives, background, learning patterns" could determine his instruction.

Imposition of hard financial constraints. By the late 1970's PLATO would attain a cost of $.35 per student-contact hour as compared to $.70 for public schools, $1.50 for community colleges, and $3.00 for universities. Hence, computer-based instruction could have significant importance in lowering costs of education.

At the public school level PLATO could improve the teaching of critical skills and lower the failure rate for disadvantaged pupils at less cost. At the community college level it could provide superior instruction at lower costs or meet the need for large increases in instructional staff. At the university level it could provide more options, reduce the proportion of instruction by graduate assistants, relate education to the problems of society, and reduce the years necessary to obtain degree programs.

Using their experience with PLATO III, the developers were persuaded to make the following assumptions:

1. Computer-based education will be enthusiastically accepted by teachers and students alike at all levels of education.
2. Many new educational concepts will be introduced through the capabilities of the computer.
3. Many new options will be available to the students through individualized instruction.
4. Human teachers will turn to PLATO for providing students with the acquisition of basic skills.

They concluded with a grand vision of what might happen if 5 percent of the current national annual education budget were put into PLATO. The three billion dollars annually could:

1. "provide ½ of individual instruction per day for each of 50 million pupils from age 6 to 18." Human tutors at $5 per hour to handle this function would cost $30 billion a year; PLATO, only $1.5 billion.

2. "double the total amount of currently available instruction at the community college level; increase by 35 percent the amount of undergraduate instruction at universities and four-year colleges." This increase would cost only $600 million per year for half a million terminals compared to the total cost of $20 billion per year. The baccalaureate program could be reduced from four to three years without increasing the teaching load on existing staff.

3. "provide for each of 15 million adults 100 student-contact hours of instruction annually in fields of their choices." The cost would only be $0.5 billion compared to $10 billion by conventional means.

All of the above could be achieved for three billion dollars as compared to thirty billion by conventional means. In other words, PLATO was ten times more cost-effective than the regular institution. And this was only the beginning. This assumed that computers would operate only eight hours a day. Eventually PLATO would transform the goal of instruction from peddling facts to fostering understanding. Every home and office would have its own terminal. Universal literacy would be obtained. ". . . PLATO will bring about a major change in the place of education in our style of life" making education "a continuous part of the life experience of all people. The knowledge necessary to operate our complex society, now largely in the domain of narrow specialists and 'experts,' will then become a part of the common understanding."

The paper concluded "We view the PLATO IV experiment as a test not only of cost and effectiveness, but also of acceptance by the educational community. We have approached the problem with the point of view that the failure of a new technology to be utilized is due at least as much to the limitations of the technology as to the limitations of the institutions that the technology was intended to serve. It is for this reason that the PLATO system has been designed expressly to engage students and teachers through the superior effectiveness of an interactive (rather than a passive) medium, and to appeal to educational administrators on the basis of budgetary and management advantages. Thus, we have not been oblivious to the problems of acceptance; rather we have assumed on the basis of our experience with PLATO III that PLATO IV will be enthusiastically received."

This was indeed a grand vision, particularly in light of the first large-scale tryout of the system described in the PLATO case study done later. Consumers of the innovation would take issue with how many of these promises had been achieved. Administrators were beginning to view with alarm the increasing costs of the system. The community college administration that had had the most experience was convinced that the system could never decrease costs, but hoped that it would not add prohibitively to total instructional costs. This was when the initial expense of computer and console ($6,500 each, without important options) was being paid entirely from outside funds. The $.35 per hour was nowhere in sight.

There was serious doubt about the capacity of each school to develop its own materials and control its own curriculum. It was more difficult for teachers to learn computer language than had been anticipated. A conservative estimate was that fifty hours of author-ing were required for each hour of student time, even after learning the language. Only teachers released at least half-time even attempt-ed to author materials, and the materials authored the first year tended to be poor in quality. Faced with these problems and an im-pending evaluation of materials by the Educational Testing Service, the university turned increasingly to centrally developed curricula, written on campus by graduate students.

Some teachers at schools in the field, who contended that university-developed materials could not meet the needs of their particular students, would not use them. Both teachers and admin-istrators were adamant that PLATO could only supplement the teacher's role, never supplant it. It was precisely the twin problems of declining educational productivity and dealing with diverse stu-dents that PLATO was supposed to solve, according to the develop-ers. Yet is seemed to force costs up and to lean more and more toward standardized programs and materials.

In the congressional document, exactly how PLATO would individualize and motivate students who had failed in the system before was left unclear. The suggested procedure of continual testing and monitoring, tried before in such widely publicized programs as Individually Prescribed Instruction, had been found wanting. Allowing each child to proceed at his own pace and escaping the lockstep nature of schooling, though easier to achieve, was also in doubt. Because of demands on the system, administrators at Downstate College had been asked to schedule classes within certain blocks of time.

Perhaps some of the most interesting claims were assurances that teachers and administrators would accept PLATO IV enthusiastically based on past experience with PLATO III. A few years later the school having the most experience with PLATO III was on the verge of dropping out of the project entirely because of dissatisfaction with performance of the system rather than costs. Both PLATO III and PLATO IV were greeted with what was considerably less than enthusiasm on the part of many teachers, which was not helped when, during the first year of demonstration, not even the hardware worked reliably. The system was down much of the time, and many of the terminals coming off the production line did not work at all.

In point of fact, two years after the developer's document and after thirteen years of development, few if any of the goals had been realized. But none of this mattered. The hardware would be made reliable. The teachers would learn TUTOR and would accept good centrally developed courses. The courseware would cease being poorly programmed instruction and become imaginative and interactive. Production costs would come down. Operating costs would reach the prescribed levels. All things would improve, all problems would be solved—all in the future. It was a belief in the promise of the innovation, a promise deliverable in the future, that satisifed participants.

Faith in the future made the PLATO project almost impermeable to data and evaluation. How could one have evaluated the printing press? When innovation is supported internally by a large group of believers and externally by powerful sponsors, evaluation based on immediate facts and circumstances must always yield to the belief that problems will be solved, given a little more time. In this, PLATO was no different from any other innovation. In fact, it was a tangible, magnificent piece of machinery on which to hang hopes.

The bold claim made by the developers that PLATO consoles

could be installed in every educational system in the country for no less than three billion dollars was made without benefit of any substantive, formal summative evaluation. As part of the demonstration grant for PLATO IV from the National Science Foundation, the Educational Testing Service was given a million dollars to evaluate PLATO. Even in the first year of the evaluation, however, as ETS personnel struggled to come to grips with the project, they were skeptical that any negative findings would be taken seriously by the sponsor. A project officer at NSF had said that PLATO IV was, in his opinion, an "unqualified success," even before the three-year demonstration project had begun.

In spite of essentially negative research results on computer-assisted instruction in general, dire warnings on CAI by leading computer experts, and formidable problems of its own, the project gathered momentum. How, indeed, could one conscientiously evaluate the printing press? By the quality of the first books run off? Surely handwritten books were better. By the cost? A scribe was cheap. By the fervor of its inventors and disciples? A success. By the fact that it would put a book in the hands of every man and destroy the power of the church? Evaluation questions are not simple.

There were also signs that a countermovement was emerging. Some people thought that the promises of PLATO were too great, exceeding the bounds of common sense. Those in a competitive situation, especially, were looking for information to support their case. A letter to me, dated July 20, 1973, tells the tale:

Dear Ernie,

The large and many off-shooted grapevine brings me word that you have done an in-house evaluation of the PLATO Junior College effort. The enclosed article gives a glimpse of the project we have been working on for three years. It does not have the up-to-date status, i.e., that a Burroughs B6700 has been installed at _____ College here in _____ to serve all the colleges and that 16 of the 21 colleges in _____ will be involved in some way this fall.

I am writing to ask you specifically if I could see your report, confidentially or otherwise. I'll be frank about my motives, namely that _____ and Computer Company are putting the big sell on the _____ colleges to tie in to PLATO rather than to use our system. The University of _____ has one PLATO terminal (display and microfiche, no audio or touch) on-line via a leased line, so we have spent many hours investigating the current system ourselves. We have been discouraged by the number of crashes and by the lack of space in ECS for courses supposed to be available. It is difficult to pin anyone down on future plans except that Computer Company is saying privately that they will put up a 256-terminal PLATO system on a small system for any buyer (or leasor).

To be even more frank, _____ has ceased to be a professor and has become a super salesman, extolling the many virtues of his "product" while concealing its deficiencies. He exaggerates the amount of courseware available to any one user by a factor of 10 or so, and he similarly misrepresents the number of schools, colleges, and industries "using" the system. In a climate of this kind, I think we have to try for open disclosure of as much responsible information as is available, hence my hope that your report can be made public as soon as possible. If it is favourable, so much the better; if it points out a few of the problems, even better still.

I am embarrassed to say that so far we have no objective outsider to evaluate our efforts and report accordingly. In _____ , the few evaluators are at _____, some of them working on the CAI project! Hmmm. Our own completely un-biased, objective evaluation is underway.

As with Christianity, the transformation of PLATO into a social movement occurred without benefit of any substantial evaluation of its worth or workability of the system, and in this regard was no different from other innovations, only more successful. The gap be-tween its promise and reality remained unanswered, perhaps unanswer-able. PLATO had achieved a life of its own which, like religion, operated on an exotic fuel—faith in the future.

THE UTILITY OF BELIEFS—IDEOLOGY AND SAGA

Perhaps the "World after PLATO" paper is best understood as a statement of ideology designed to appeal to those interests that best lend support, but it should not be taken too literally as the goals of the project by which it must be evaluated. An ideology is a unified, coherent, shared belief system that is often used to formally coalesce the entrepreneurial group and to appeal to powerful and important audiences. This statement can be compared to one that served a sim-ilar purpose at the inception of the Illinois Gifted Program.

The Illinois Gifted Program's public political strength was inte-grated through a series of governor's conferences throughout the state, to which were invited powerful educational figures, including school administrators and state legislators. The following excerpt was from a speech delivered by Otto Kerner in May 1962, while he was Governor of Illinois.

The educational problems facing Illinois and our nation include the alarming loss of talent from early high school drop-outs. This sets off a chain reaction which makes suitable employment opportunities in a technological world virtually non-existent and triggers the extension of delinquent patterns of behavior.

In addition, our problems include extending educational opportunities to mentally and physically handicapped youth and facing the problems, both rural and urban in character, of socially and economically underprivileged youth.

Unless the schools and society in general attend to these problems, we can expect the cost of public welfare programs, expanding law enforcement and penal operation to increase further.

We can reduce this rate of attrition in drop-outs and cut the cost of programs that treat the symptoms of these failings by a program that gives more systematic and organized attention to youngsters with above average talents in intellectual and aesthetic endeavors. There is no question that residents of Illinois recognize the great importance of this problem.

In the White House Conferences on Education, more Illinois counties reported concern for the education of gifted children than any other single problem. And a study just reported by the research division of the National Education Association indicates similar concern on the part of teachers.

A carefully selected sample of our nation's 1.4 million teachers were asked the following question: "In your opinion, does the school in which you teach tend to underemphasize appropriate education for any of three groups of children: The gifted, the average and the slow learners?" Almost half of the teachers believed the underemphasis was on the gifted.

At this point Illinois has been most fortunate in the efforts and careful study of our gifted children. Only two other states among the 50 approach us in this regard. I hope as study and planning come to an end, the action that follows will be so decisive that Illinois will be recognized as the very best state in which a gifted child may be born and raised.

The parallels between the appeal for the Illinois Gifted Program and PLATO are striking. How could aspirations for two such totally dissimilar innovations, even separated in time, be so similar? PLATO was a highly focused, highly materialized innovation residing in an elaborate computer terminal with set procedures and programmed materials. The Illinois Gifted Program was a highly diffuse granting of funds to local districts with no set materials, procedures, or methodologies other than a vague humanitarian-creative theme. One claims to serve the gifted; the other the disadvantaged.

Yet in these formal documents both innovations addressed themselves to loss of talent and the failure to provide basic skills. Both claimed to address a pressing national problem. Both were concerned about the employment capabilities of the youngsters in later society. The provision of educational opportunities, particularly for the disadvantaged student, is an important theme even for the Gifted Program. Cutting educational costs is prominent in both, although more prominent in PLATO. The investment of money in an innovation is important because it can reduce dropouts and eventually curb the public costs of welfare and other expenses of the society. Both statements also emphasized that teachers, administrators, and the general public believed that the innovation should proceed and that it would be received enthusiastically. An additional theme was that Illinois would be the very best state in that regard, whereas PLATO often referred to itself as the best computer-based system in the world.

Why are these statements so similar? The reason, of course, is that both were constructed to appeal to those audiences and to caress those themes necessary to garner support and to avoid opposition. Audiences and themes remain relatively stable, even over a ten-year span. The PLATO statement emphasizes costs considerably more, reflecting the money concerns of the seventies. The sixties climate reflected the Sputnik era in American education that emphasized academic excellence in order to beat the Russians. Yet the same themes are surprisingly present in both, in spite of profound societal changes. Both innovations promise improved societal efficiency, efficacy, opportunity, even fairness. At one point the PLATO statement even promises a turning away from expertise and. elitism, a populist theme that plagued the Gifted Program and diminished the program's vigor over time. Gifted advocates were continually fighting the elitist connotation.

Besides the orientation to technocratic values, there are also bows toward the ideology of the educator, represented in more options, opportunities, and the fact that teachers like it. Obviously the statements better reflect the themes toward which the innovations must appeal more than they reflect the intrinsic nature of the innovations themselves, if indeed there is any such thing. One might compare public ideology to dressing for a formal dinner: everyone's tuxedo looks the same. The purpose of an ideology, though it is believed by many, is to garner support.

It might be more valuable for the evaluator to evaluate what the innovation does rather than what it aspires to do in its public professions. It might do much good, yet entirely miss each of its self-ordained goals. In fact, it is difficult to see how any innovation could live up to public aspirations for it.

Clark (1972) distinguishes between an ideology and a saga. The organizational saga emphasizes the normative bonds holding the group together. If the ideology is necessary for public consumption and support, the saga is necessary for internal support and eventually for continuity of effort. The saga is a collective understanding of the unique accomplishment of the group. Originally historical, it is embellished through retelling and rewriting. The saga provides a rational explanation of certain events, but mainly it imbues the project with affect and sentiment so that participants may devote themselves to it. Clark described the saga in studying the history of three distinctive colleges—Antioch, Reed, and Swarthmore.

The basis of the saga emerges from a "thin stream of shared experience" which is elaborated into an account of group uniqueness. The saga helps rationalize the commitment of the individual to the project, even though he may receive little tangible reward from it. The saga can be so overpowering that the outside world seems like an illusion. Sagas are highly durable when they are built slowly in structured social contexts, as opposed to the ephemeral nature of sagas that spring up in the unstable atmosphere of, say, professional sports. The slow saga has a chance to "seep" into the social structure on its own, based on stable relationships among people, as opposed to inundation through the mass media. Decades, not months or even days, may be required for development.

Clark recognizes two stages of development: initiation and fulfillment. The saga begins as an advocacy—a strong purpose conceived and initiated by a man or small cadre within a setting that is relatively open. As mentioned in earlier chapters, open organizations are the best settings. Advocacies can be described as nascent sagas, most of which never develop into full-blown ones. The best setting for a saga to develop is in an established organization that is either in crisis or has a new sense of mission, often self-defined. The difficulty with the organization in crisis is that old values and habits often reassert themselves when the crisis is past, and the organization abandons the innovation. Evans (1971) has documented this effect in the case of universities adopting educational television in response to the pressure of increased enrollments during the 1950's and the 1960's. When the pressure eased, television equipment went into the storage room, apparently never to be used again.

Clark has isolated necessary elements of the fulfillment stage: personnel, program (visible practices), an external social base, a supportive student subculture, and appropriate imagery. In the case of the sagas constructed at the three colleges, the key variable was the support of senior faculty. Although a leader could initiate a new program, powerful faculty had to pick up on it and remain committed, even after the initiator was gone, for the innovation to survive. Believers replaced themselves through selective recruitment and socialization. When necessary, they prevented new innovations from developing, a critical function.

The college program itself, that is, the innovation, had to have visible practices to support claims of distinction. These unique practices often became a communal set of symbols, such as not reporting grades to the student, and the program was recognized as being distinct by both outsiders and insiders. An external social base was required to support and defend the innovation. In this case, it was the alumni. Student support was not as important, but it was necessary. The students came to see themselves as personally responsible for upholding the image of the college. Finally, the more unique and forceful the claim, the more intense was the development of imagery and other ways of sharing and symbolizing the innovation.

The saga then became a self-fulfilling belief working as "a switchman, helping to determine the tracks along which action is pushed by man's self-defined interests." Believers define themselves by affliation and often come to feel that they are the lucky few within a routine world. Personnel remain loyal, stay with the organization, and produce uncommon effort and achievement. Participants derive personal pleasure and pride, even their own identity, from the group. They thereby increase their return from organization life.

These processes are carried out in miniature within advocacy groups in schools, as indicated in earlier chapters. In order for a program to become a sweeping social movement, the processes must be writ large. Both innovations analyzed in detail in this book developed their own sagas. To be successful on a large scale, an innovation must.

The Illinois Gifted Program and PLATO began from a particular organizational base. For the Illinois Gifted Program it was University High School, the University of Illinois laboratory school, in which Max Beberman, often called the father of the "new math," was developing UICSM mathematics. Supported by millions of dollars in grants from the Carnegie Foundation and the National Science Foundation, Beberman developed a large set of materials in the late 1950's and the 1960's. University High, a wide-open organization in flux, was stimulated by ideas of "inductive" teaching and new subject matter reforms. Projects also developed in other subject areas.

The catalytic national event was Sputnik. It provided academic reformers concerned with content and conservative educational critics such as Admiral Rickover with a cause. Education became a tool in the Cold War. The new curriculum materials sprang from this concern, as did renewed concern for the education of the gifted, originally conceived as "engineers and scientists." Against this social context, an organization like University High was searching for a sense of mission. Its principal, David Jackson, was an accomplished entrepreneur. His organization was producing volumes of new materials. Where would they be used? In a masterful political campaign involving funds from the Office of Education, the governor of the state, and university personnel, a demonstration project was established which soon became the Illinois Gifted Program, funded at four million dollars a year, a large sum in 1963. The program was arranged in such a way as to introduce curriculum materials, mostly from Uni High into the public schools. The official public ideology of this program was discussed earlier.

Operational control of the program was turned over to a charismatic leader, William Rogge, a master of group dynamics. He built around him a group of twenty demonstration directors and several staff consultants, a powerful group that met once a month in some part of the state. The beginning of the saga was based on the early accomplishment of political entrepreneurship. It was the political accomplishments and early experiences of the demonstration director group that formed the thin stream of shared experience, which was consummated in two intense summer workshops held in the summers of 1964 and 1965. Much group dynamics work was undertaken, and a tightly joined cadre of advocates from all over the state emerged. This communications network was maintained by the travels of the central staff and the demonstration directors. The cadre group met together once a month to regenerate their own enthusiasm.

Since the state program was new, it provided for advancement.

The original demonstration director and state staff group were drawn mainly from classrooms around the state. A new career pattern was open. A new ideology beckoned. Over the course of ten years the directors, because of their contacts with school districts, would eventually take administrative posts and reluctantly leave the cadre. Their posts would be filled by people specially recruited to fit the philosophy of the group and quickly socialized to the norms of the group through the special institute training and the monthly meetings. The program served as a conduit to new positions and provided a career opportunity for many classroom teachers that had not existed before.

The dynamics of the program fostered much searching for self-identity among participants and strong identification through the program. Before the advent of federal legislation it was one of the few self-proclaimed "change" programs in the country. And, the saga began as a strong purpose initiated by a small cadre in an open setting. It developed slowly, but, although the saga seeped into and was maintained by the personal bonds of the participants, the core organization always remained outside the legitimate organizations. The demonstration directors were supported with external funds and were dependent on the source of the funds, the state department of education.

The major themes of the organization were set in the first years under the guidance of the original charismatic leader. The saga and attendant myths and stories were then developed. The saga exercised control over the life of the project and the behavior of project personnel for at least ten years. Through at least four generations of demonstration directors and state staff, major themes were enacted in the visible practices and imagery. The themes were such things as creativity, risk taking, personal expression, and "doing your own thing." Other themes tended to disappear. The unique characteristics of the program passed from generation to generation with fervor.

Former participants in the program provided an external source of support. Since many graduated to more influential positions via the program, they were often in a position to do favors, and they were asked to do so. There was also external support from outside the state since influential people saw the program in gifted education as being unique and outstanding. Illinois was the acknowledged leader in the field; other states followed.

The cadre perceived themselves as "annointed." From this feeling accrued great advantages. When carried to excess, however, the feeling that the rest of the world was unreal was occasionally dangerous. The main battles were fought with the state department of education, the source of funds and, supposedly, control. From the beginning the program was a runaway project, pursuing its own rather than bureaucratic goals. From the beginning the state department sought to control it, making it less boisterous and less prominent. Because program participants had many material advantages, they could break many rules normally followed in bureaucratic programs. The esprit de corps and method of operation in the field threatened four groups of state department officials. Many attempts were made, usually through rules and regulations, to domesticate the program, but the bureaucrats could not be too heavy-handed because of the program's reputation, and its external support. Many of the rules and regulations were circumvented. In fact, fighting with bureaucratic officials was a major source of pleasure and satisfaction for the type of people selected into the program, and it became part of the saga.

Eventually, though, the long war of attrition had its effects. After ten years the funds for demonstration centers were slashed in half, and experimental funds were entirely wiped out. This directly cut the cadre group's operation. Cutting experimental funds was a master stroke of bureaucratic management. The funds had been used to initiate new thrusts and, just as important, to justify the program's existence. When the program was threatened with extinction after five years of operation, it undertook a unique and extensive evaluation to justify its existence. The results were reported to the legislature and top government officials, giving the program renewed life and an extra million dollars in funds. A few years later, however, the discretionary funds were taken away. All funds were committed, and no new thrusts could be initiated. Experimental funds were easy to eliminate by using charges of inefficiency, and immediate tangible results were difficult to see. As in most bureaucracies, initiatory power was usurped at the top levels of management (control being the central concern), thereby reducing the program to a regulatory agency filing forms. The simultaneous reduction of the political cadre of demonstration directors greatly reduced the political and proselytizing power of the program. It was reduced to passivity, and, after ten years, it was approaching organizational senility. The saga of the Illinois Gifted Program was drawing to a close.

How much had the Illinois Gifted Program changed education? Its effects were measurable and probably quite successful compared to other programs, although, of course, it did not live up to its justifying materials. (For an analysis of this type of change, see House, Steele, and Kerins, 1971.) It had been mainly successful in stimulating individual teachers in local schools to adopt some vaguely humanistic practices. The stimulation resulted from special training and outreach activities that inspired the teachers and indicated certain practices they might try. A communication network was established through the demonstration directors and central staff that sometimes reached classroom teachers and sometimes did not. The frequent personal contact attempted among those in the network followed the urban hierarchy diffusion pattern mapped earlier.

A small amount of money granted to local districts legitimized a few teachers undertaking new practices. The funds supported trips to meetings. The strongest effect was felt in districts where an advocacy formed (see Chapter 3). With the decline of the central state-wide propagation cadre, only in those advocacies within local districts that had developed a strong central group of their own did the effects continue. Long-term continuation would require the construction of new sagas embedded within the social fabric of the organization, as had occurred at Antioch, Reed, and Swarthmore Colleges. With the demise of the propagation group, the culture developed within the Illinois Gifted Program would probably fragment. Even where advocacies survived, the original culture would be transformed to correspond to the local exigencies of the group.

The limits of the effects of the Illinois Gifted Program could be attributed partially to an inability to secure the sponsorship of the more powerful institutions in the society. Its humanistic theme did not correspond well with the themes of an increasingly technocratic society. Efficiency and national achievement were more likely to receive strong institutional support and, hence, resources. These themes were closer to the values of the dominant institutions of the society and, in fact, closer to the original purpose of the gifted program itself. Because of sponsorship, the PLATO innovation was much more likely to receive widespread dissemination throughout the country.

The origins of PLATO were similar. It grew from a laboratory looking for a new mission since classified military research on campuses was diminishing. It latched onto a nationally prominent theme— reducing educational costs. Computers were available (as inductive teaching materials were available in the other case). How could they be employed in education? The PLATO saga began growing from the shared experience and technological accomplishments of the early days, and was manifested in the computer-based laboratory.

The cadre of believers was socialized and replenished within the laboratory. The saga again grew from a few men with a strong purpose operating in a setting that was relatively open. Talented personnel could be recruited from the ranks of a large university. Within that setting new innovations were suppressed by the senior staff when necessary. The innovation itself was highly visible in the form of a fancy and modernistic computer terminal that could perform upon command. The computer language itself, the entry procedures, and a surfeit of esoteric knowledge produced a wealth of material for rituals and imagery. The saga developed slowly over thirteen years and embedded itself deeply into the social fabric, almost constructing a social fabric of its own.

What is perhaps most significant, the innovation received the sponsorship of powerful institutions like the National Science Foundation, the Department of Defense, and many others. Its appeal as a complex machine promising massive efficiency reforms was enormous. The saga of PLATO exercised enormous control over the lives of hundreds. Its appeal approached religious fervor. The saga had been quite soundly constructed and showed every sign of gaining momentum. Unlike the Illinois Gifted Program, there were few signs of faltering. Indeed, PLATO looked as if it could become one of the most widely distributed educational reforms of all time. The major questions seemed to be how well it would eventually perform, how it would fit into the school structure, and how willing teachers would be to use it. Would it change educational practice or would it sit unused in the corner of the school as had so many of the innovations introduced before it? Would it be useful at all, or merely imposed from above and resisted from below? And, of course, the real question: What kind of world would it create?

Chapter 8

Government Policy toward Innovation–The Doctrine of Transferability

THE DEBRIS OF FEDERAL PROGRAMS, 1962-1972

During this ten-year period, the United States Office of Education's budget increased from $477 million to $5.5 billion. The federal share of total education expenditures rose only from 4.4 percent to 7 percent, the bulk of the total expenditures being supplied by local and state taxes. Kirst (1974) deftly outlined the growth and limited influence that increased federal funding has had. He has suggested that there are six major modes of federal influence:

1. general aid with no strings attached;
2. categorical aid to earmarked areas of federal concern, such as funding of the National Defense Education Act;
3. regulation by certification, licensing, and imposed standards;
4. discovery and utilization of new knowledge as in research and development activities;
5. provision of services such as technical assistance or consultants;
6. moral suasion as exerted through speeches and publications.

For more than a hundred years the Office of Education typically provided services and a limited amount of categorical aid. The great increase in federal funds resulted in a modal shift to differential and categorical funding in the 1960's, with some emphasis on federally sponsored research and development and some moral persuasion exercised through critical speeches made by important government officials. General aid was rejected because local and state viewpoints did not accurately reflect national priorities. As Harold Howe, one of

204

the important policymakers during this period, expressed it: "The postwar period has radically altered the demands we place on our schools; a purely local or state viewpoint of education cannot produce an educational system that will serve national interest in addition to more localized concerns."

The federal government had decided to push national priorities in education. The complex categorical aid programs of the sixties were an outgrowth of political bargaining between fragmented educational interests and the new concern for the national interest. By 1972 the Office of Education had thirty-seven separate authorizations in support of low-income pupils and twenty-two separate authorizations in support of reading programs. As the Office of Education greatly expanded its staff, specialized consultants and subject matter specialists were succeeded by managers and public administrators who had no backgrounds in education. Whereas formerly state administrators had maximum discretion in interpreting and implementing federal categorical laws, new managers and new programs tended to bypass the states and exert more influence on the local districts, according to Kirst.

What has been the influence of these programs? Compensatory education was nonexistent in large cities before federal aid. Federal funds have been used to provide a wide variety of services, particularly remedial instruction in basic skills. These new programs were not, however, much different in method and content from those that existed previously. The funds bought "more of the same." Innovations, whether sponsored by government or foundations, rarely were found in classrooms. The programs had to be implemented through the local school district, a problem neither fully comprehended nor well understood by the bureaucrats in charge.

Local school administrators traditionally "divert" federal funds to items in their own budget, treating federal programs as windfall money that may soon evaporate. Hence, there is great reluctance to institute federal programs on a permanent basis since the district may be caught "holding the bag" and absorbing the costs for programs in which it is not really interested. This reluctance has been strengthened by what has happened in the past. Most innovative federal programs have disappeared after a few years, only to be replaced by new ones. The wise local administrator handles federal funds in such a way as to provide maximum help (and perhaps maximum publicity) for his district, while avoiding dependence on a federal program that he knows may soon pass or may have to be funded within a tight local budget.

The succession of federal programs in Washington is guaranteed by the bureaucratic career pattern and by ever-shifting political coalitions. Even more than the school superintendent, every new federal bureaucrat must promote and become identified with a "new innovative" program of his own in order to advance his own career. Since turnover in jobs occurs at least every few years, endless successions of bureaucrats drop old programs and publicize their own. If the jobs do not turn over, constant internecine warfare within the bureaucracy over power and control of resources ensures that jobs and programs will be redefined and relabeled. Perpetual reorganizations reflect political forces ceaselessly at work. The endless profusion of new organization charts is not a mapping of lines of authority. Rather, it is a mapping of internal political struggles.

Just as the teacher has his own phenomenological world from which it is almost impossible to escape, the Washington bureaucrat has his, and, no matter how sincere or talented, he cannot escape. He must fight for control and resources if he is to be successful and the longer he does so the less knowledgeable or concerned he becomes about the effect of the program "in the field"—except as it facilitates fighting his own bureaucratic battles. "Rat race" is perhaps a suitably descriptive term to apply, and the rigors of the race eventually lead to a feeling that the internecine battles and paper programs have real meaning for people in the rest of the country. After a few years of this struggle, more conscientious men seek some other employment.

Seeing this profusion of activities and programs without import, the local school official takes the longer view. Each new federal program brings its own cadre of young believers and proselytizers, fresh from graduate school or a liberal arts college, who take it upon themselves to persuade the local school establishment that this, the new "Quadruple X," is *the* program that will make the difference. The old school superintendent smiles. Experience has made him wiser. He makes the minimum moves to get the money he badly needs and does little more. Perceiving what he takes to be reluctance and even deceit when the spirit of the new program or "cause" is abandoned, the proselytizer becomes bitter and eventually becomes a professor, a dean, or the head of a foundation where he can vent his anger and frustration. By this time the chief has left or the program has become part of a new reorganization, and the school superintendent settles back to await the next program onslaught as the dramaturgy repeats itself.

Some of these themes were sounded by a high education official, James J. Gallagher, formerly Director of the Bureau for Education of the Handicapped in Lyndon Johnson's administration and Deputy Assistant Secretary for Planning, Research, and Evaluation in the U.S. Department of Health, Education, and Welfare in Richard Nixon's administration. In a paper entitled "Unfinished Educational Tasks (Thoughts on Leaving Government Service)," Gallagher (1970) attacked the policymaking processes that led to such instability. "The credibility of the Federal government is under serious and justified attack because of its failure to follow through on programs once they have begun. In the second or third year of their efforts— their political glamour worn off—their favored place was taken in the Administration by new, bright, and shiny programs that are polished by hope and unsullied by experience."

Many of the programs, Gallagher believed, "become victims of persons who have no sense of history or respect for programs begun before their entry upon the scene, but who are eager to push their own pet projects to 'make their own mark' in Washington." Some of the difficulty lies in the levels of bureaucracy itself (six major layers of policy review in the executive branch alone). "The multiplication of people who have authority to change programs, but who leave others to face the often negative consequences of their actions is one of the most severe morale problems in government."

In the centralization of power in the White House that occurred during Nixon's administration, the Office of Education no longer made major educational decisions by 1970. "Various administrative spokesmen, from the White House down, seemed willing to make education and educators the scapegoat for a multitude of societal problems not of their making, but at the same time were not willing to provide the high priority and necessary resources to get needed educational tasks accomplished." On what basis were decisions made? Actually, "fiscal considerations and budget technicians often determine major educational policy decisions, no matter [what] the rhetoric of the visible spokesman for the administration."

The result of such forces, according to Gallagher, was unstable and erratic policy. "Often such inconsistency is the result of the swirl of shifting alliances of power groups within government that throw up new policies like corks on the waves, and just as easily submerge those not in current favor." The dramaturgy of failure would be repeated again and again. "As we start new programs again, and paint our bright portrait of what those new programs will accomplish, is there any reason to believe that the same cycle of excitement-frustration-despair will not be repeated by the way in which we make our future decisions?"

Gallagher suggested giving the Office of Education cabinet rank in order to gain more influence within the executive branch and establishing a National Institute of Education, comparable in status and design to the National Institutes of Health, to handle research and development activities—setting aside 20 percent of the education budget every year for continuing programs instead of playing roulette with the money in annual budgeting; giving maximum flexibility to local school administrators to handle federal funds; concentrating federal funds on research, training, and communication; and greatly increasing federal spending for education. Gallagher concluded, "the federal government may well be crying out for educational reform on the outside, when the needs for reform may be greatest on the inside of the federal establishment." Frustrated, he resigned his position.

The difficulty in getting local districts to implement federal priorities is usually interpreted by most federal planners as resistance on the part of local districts: "the ability of outside forces to influence local educational organizations is hampered by a number of impediments stemming from organizational and teacher rigidities" (Kirst, 1974). Perhaps, but one might also add that a number of impediments also stem from federal and bureaucratic rigidities. Federal bureaucrats have developed a perspective that sees federal aid as being delivered from the top down.

The numerous constraints on effective and focused implementation (at each level of the political system) are indeed disconcerting. It is a long delivery chain from USOE to a classroom in Houston, Texas, with many potential sandtraps and chasms in between. When one aggregates the various structures and individuals at all three levels that must be changed or overcome by categorical aid (that asserts the primacy of federal goals over state and local objectives), it is an awesome implementation task.

Essentially, federal aid relies on a top-down strategy (operating largely through administrators wielding federal-state regulations and guidelines), but lacks necessary sanctions and incentives to insure the aid reaches the intended targets or reorients classroom practice [Kirst, 1974].

According to Kirst, policy demands at the federal level must work their way through the elaborate implementation machinery at the federal, state, and local governmental levels. Each state and each district are different, so uniform policy inputs do not result in uniform policy outputs, and it has been suggested that federal policy is extremely unstable. Federal agencies have succeeded in influencing state education agencies by financing growth in specified areas. For example, 70 percent of the Texas education agency is financed through federal funds. The USOE has been the chief influence in the growth and orientation of state agencies. On the other hand, supervising 19,000 local agencies is beyond federal control. Perhaps that is why recent federal grants to state agencies have emphasized state planning, information processing, and evaluation. For example, most of the "accountability systems" development underway in varying stages in all fifty states (consisting almost exclusively of state-wide testing programs), were funded by federal money. The complexity of these relationships is illustrated by the fact that the funds used to promote tighter control measures over teachers were originally secured with considerable lobbying help from the national teachers' organizations, although they were apparently unaware of how the funds would be used or administered.

In spite of OE influence, state agencies have not been particularly successful in implementing federal legislation. Congressional involvement, traditionally the bastion of local interests, has been limited to seeing that the legislator's district gets a fair share. Since local districts behave as described above, categorical aid programs become a nightmare of administration and paper work when they are faced with as many as a hundred separate funding sources. In practice, though not on paper, funds tend to be lumped together at the local level, and local officials are not inclined to worry too much about whether distant, vaguely defined, ill-administered federal priorities are being met. Federal agencies have exerted considerably more influence on institutions almost totally dependent on federal funds, such as the research and development laboratories—not, it might be added, to any good effect. With those research agencies the federal government has also pursued a top-down strategy that will be discussed later. The research and development agencies are expected to produce federally approved innovations that can be implemented in the categorical programs.

NATIONAL GOALS FOR RESEARCH AND DEVELOPMENT

A critical distinction in understanding governmental policy toward innovation is understanding the difference between central national goals and distributed national goals. The National Academy of Sciences distinguishes among national goals for research and development as follows:

Central National Goals for R&D—such as leadership in the important fields of science, nuclear power, space exploration, and national defense—in which the program is national in focus, sponsorship, funding, and overall direction.

Distributed National Goals for R&D—such as the development of human resources, the rebuilding of our cities, water resources, and regional environments for living—in which the programs are characterized *by local determinants in nature of the problems, in the approach to solutions, and in their anticipated consequences* [Alpert, 1970; emphasis added].

Education is one of society's major distributed national goals. As I have tried to indicate, it serves a multiplicity of interests. It is influenced locally by school boards, administrators, teachers, students, parents, and a host of others. As the nature of educational problems is locally determined, so should the solutions be. Yet the policies pursued by the federal government to influence education are invariably central national goals that usually lead to failure and frustration.

Most past educational programs have been in pursuit of central goals. For example, the National Defense Education Act (NDEA) was specifically motivated by fear of an external enemy, as were most of the federal monies flushed out in the wake of Sputnik. Whether the NDEA monies resulted in a stronger defense posture vis-a-vis the Russians is questionable. But it was directed and funded on that basis.

Central national goals are mission oriented and addressed to central national problems like defense or space exploration—questions of national leadership. The prototypical mission-oriented project is the National Aeronautics and Space Administration's (NASA) man-on-the-moon program. One of the Nixon administration's first educational moves was to launch a right-to-read program that would enable every child in the country to learn to read. The space program was used as the explicit model for the program. Somehow proper research and development would produce techniques, even a single technique, that would unlock the door to reading for each child, just as American technology and know-how had enabled the first man, an American, to set foot on the virgin moon.

The right-to-read program, unable to be conceived as a single act in time and space by a single or a few individuals under clearly defined and constant conditions, did not fare so well. It did not have twenty-one billion dollars to spend, but that was not the only difficulty. Not all children learn to read the same way. Children are quite different, even difficult at times. They learn to read in widely different sets of circumstances impossible to control. Not much is heard about the right-to-read program anymore.

The former director of a major research laboratory contends that the major universities have been shaped in the post-World War II period primarily by the pursuit of central national goals (Alpert, 1970). The principal rationale for federal support of universities was to enable universities to pursue central national goals. It was believed that societal problems could be solved by the dissemination of knowledge and the generation of new knowledge. Mission-oriented agencies such as the Department of Defense, the National Science Foundation, and the National Institutes of Health stimulated growth in the physical sciences and in other fields. Universities, when they became national rather than regional in character, also became aware of the problems of the federal government.

Alpert, a former director of a leading military research laboratory, claims that the reward system, the research objectives, and the departmental organization of a university are directed toward central goals when it is organized for problem solving at all. Ordinarily it is organized to garner disciplinary rewards. Not all federal programs have been oriented toward the pursuit of central goals, and not all university departments have been so organized. The founding of land grant colleges eventually led to the development of better agricultural products, essentially a distributed national goal. Furthermore, colleges of agriculture organized themselves into interdisciplinary problem-oriented units, such as animal husbandry and horticulture.

There is a critical difference in the problem approach to both goals. For central national goals, the federal agency must relate research and development products to the mission of the agency and of society itself. The agency not only sponsors research and development, but *it is also the client*. In agriculture the client was the individual farmer. He had to be persuaded to plant a new type of seed corn. Successful development demands an understanding of the client, particularly of the political and social constraints within which he operates. In departments of agriculture the professors, often having been raised on farms themselves, know their clients well. As is true in agriculture, distributed problems are often regional, even local problems, but the benefits may ultimately be more far-reaching. Much of the criticism of modern agricultural research and development is directed toward the belief that modern clients of research are the agribusinesses and not individual farmers. In fact, research often harms the small farmers.

It is precisely in attention to the consequences for individuals that the two types of goals differ. Those who pursue central national goals, like national defense or the space program, are essentially oblivious to the consequences of their activities upon individuals. They pursue impersonal ends and propagate impersonal products. Those who pursue distributed goals, like pollution control or education, are relatively concerned with consequences for individuals. They must allow for personal considerations. Education obviously has quite a pluralistic and multifarious clientele in its many governing units, its total student body, and its teachers. Yet federal policy has been directed to the pursuit of central goals—bolster national defense, cure racism, alleviate poverty (racism and poverty were handled as central goals to eliminate conflict).

The mechanisms suited to pursuing these central goals become so elaborate that they are good for little else. Writing in the *New Republic* about the aerospace corporations, Peter Barnes (1971) contends that these corporations have become so technologically well developed that, like a muscle-bound strong man, they have lost all flexibility. The talent of such corporations is that they are able to focus on an enormous technological challenge in a systematic way, first attacking it with great quantities of scientific brainpower and then surmounting it by building a few extremely sophisticated and expensive pieces of equipment. In order for such corporations to flourish, certain peculiar conditions are necessary.

One of the conditions is that the technological challenge be unequivocally defined by the federal government or by a major industry with uniform needs. A second condition is that the market for the hardware be concentrated in a single government agency or a single industry. When these conditions are met, they permit research, development, management, and delivery to flow according to carefully scheduled plans. Such a market mechanism is easily programmed, concentrated in the hands of a few high-level bureaucrats, and set apart from the fluctuating desires, pressures, and vested interests of people and local government. Aerospace executives have pleaded with the federal government, according to Barnes, to give them a social national goal, to allow them to set up a federal agency, to appropriate money on a massive scale, and to let them develop the appropriate technology and hardware. Social problems do not, however, readily lend themselves to such closed solutions.

Unfortunately, educational policy at the federal level has pursued this technocratic dream. It has sought not so much to stimulate innovation in the field as to control the types of innovations that are invented. Even though the educational challenge cannot be unequivocally defined by the federal government, attempts to do so—headstart, right-to-read, career education—continue. Nor can the education market be concentrated in a single government agency. It is spread out over thousands of school districts and involves many teachers. Nonetheless, federal education agencies continue to behave as if they were the market and to request materials and programs that please them. Such materials are not often valued by teachers in the field; nor are they used. The federal agencies remain in control of the programs, but the programs are ineffective in promoting innovations. The agencies are in control of empty vessels. Such behavior is the result of pursuing the technocratic paradigm of innovation.

In order to mass produce a solution, one must be able to distribute it universally, or at least on a very large scale. Most federal policy has been directed toward finding these few magic solutions and disseminating them throughout the educational populace. One must assume that the innovation or product will be widely accepted and have highly generalizable results in different local situations. This search for a generalizable solution, an innovation that will transfer from one setting to another, I call the *doctrine of transferability*.

This doctrine exists as part of the creed of an industrialized technocratic society. It says that everything can be "fixed," whether physical or social. When the problem becomes acute enough, like the "energy crisis," one can always fix it by the application of resources and technological know-how. The means of fixing it is often technological—a package that can be mass produced and widely disseminated, like automobiles. Being mass produced, such solutions are relatively inexpensive per unit and highly profitable for those who produce them. This system is obviously disposed to produce goods rather than services, and, where it does produce services, they are impersonal (for example, bureaucratic, rather than personal). The producers control the process and the type of innovation. This doctrine underlies most federal policy. In educational policy it is embodied in what has become known as the "research, development, diffusion" approach to innovation.

THE FAILURE OF FEDERAL R&D POLICY

The programs and monies most closely associated with change and innovation in education are commonly referred to as "research and development" to distinguish them as "targeted" for innovation as opposed to more general financial aid. The general conceptual model of change, known as the "research, development, diffusion" paradigm of educational change, emerged from the confident liberalism of the Kennedy era. The federal education establishment may have inherited it from personal contacts with the National Science Foundation and have been infected with the pursuit of central goals.

The National Science Foundation was formed to deal with central national goals in science, and it naturally employed a strong technological orientation in solving problems. NSF also fell heir to educational funds to improve science and math teaching in the public schools. When the Office of Education came into its majority, it turned to the experience of the more prestigious and experienced National Science Foundation.

In the heady optimism and supreme confidence of the postwar era, especially during the Kennedy administration, it was believed that research for new knowledge and the proper technologizing and dissemination of that knowledge could solve technical, societal, indeed, *any* problems that might be encountered. It was primarily a matter of attention, application, and money—of engineering. Whether it was the rebellion in Vietnam or the low quality of public education, all problems could be solved with the mustering and management of appropriate resources. In both Vietnam and in education, problems could be solved by the application of technology generated by the research and development process. It is important to note, although painful to remember, that this confidence was sustained by nearly everyone, the more so for the improvement of education than for "winning the peace" in Vietnam, and not by just a few miscreants in the federal bureaucracy.

One of the earliest and most important formulations of the research, development, diffusion paradigm was in a paper entitled "The Function of the United States Office of Education and the State Departments of Education in the Dissemination and Implementation of Education Research" (Clark, 1962). This paper was delivered in an important forum—Phi Delta Kappa's Third Annual Symposium on Educational Research. The author was even more impressive—David Clark, the Director of the Cooperative Research Program in the U.S. Office of Education. That program would later become the progenitor of the Bureau of Research, the regional laboratory, and the research and development center program, as well as most innovation efforts of the Office of Education. The paper itself would later be expanded into the best-known and most respected of the educational change paradigms of the sixties, the so-called "Clark-Guba" model.

In that paper Clark began his argument by stating his assumptions:

1. Educational research should be subdivided into a "quasi-linear" sequence.

2. The educational practitioner had assumed and would continue to assume a relatively passive role, "and in most cases a resistant role" in the processes of implementation and dissemination.

3. "The existing programs of the United States Office of Education and the state departments of education in the process of disseminating and implementing educational research findings are so inadequate and ineffective as to be nearly useless for discussion purposes except as examples of what should not be done."

4. "The present efforts of all educational agencies concerned with dissemination and implementation are so inadequate

that thoughts of minor adaptations and new emphases should be abandoned and the big problem should be faced with a big solution."

After this rousing introduction, Clark then analyzed the six basic steps in research:

1. basic scientific investigation (content indifferent);
2. basic scientific investigation (content relevant);
3. the investigation of education-oriented programs;
4. classroom experimentation prior to field testing;
5. field testing; and
6. demonstration and dissemination.

Clark gave as an example the development of standardized tests, from step 1 "psychometric theory" to step 6 "marketing." Dissatisfaction in the field, he asserted, was due not to step 6, but to deficiencies in steps 1 and 2. Failure to make these differentiations in the past had led to not being able to identify the reasons for failure of the total process. Note two of Clark's assumptions: the practitioner has and will continue to have a passive role in the innovation process; and out of the fractionated "research" paradigm would emerge a finished product capable of solving problems and capable of being used in many, if not all, contexts. The paradigm assumed that research was the starting place for innovation, and the unquestioned purpose was to get research findings into use.

At that time Office of Education and state department efforts consisted of sending out subject-matter specialists or bulletins, neither of which practitioners saw as credible sources of information. What would work? Clark saw increased assistance in terms of translating and engineering the innovation in practice and demonstrations of new programs in real settings as the answer to the credibility problem. The program should also be decentralized. President Kennedy even called for an educational extension service.

In the discussion immediately following his paper, Clark emphasized that the key to an effective program was decentralization "so that the local school district, the administrators, and teachers, have some control over the program and actually participate in it." Clark later emphasized that the practitioner should be involved only when the educational program was being field-tested, not before. Another discussant pointed out that there was a basic difference between farmers and teachers. Adopting new procedures meant little in terms of material reward for teachers; nor were results very visible. Most discussants, while chary, seemed to feel that teachers could be persuaded ultimately. Clark concluded, "I think we have vastly over-estimated the difficulty that confronts an administrator so far as teacher resistance to the process of change is concerned." The administrator was the key practitioner, Clark emphasized, and demonstration was the best method of persuasion. One of the first sizable federal grants for demonstration centers went to the Illinois Gifted Program.

By 1965 Clark had joined with Egon Guba to refine the model (Clark and Guba, 1965). Known as the Clark-Guba model (see Figure 8-1), it was widely circulated and discussed. The model analyzed four aspects of educational change: research, development, diffusion, and adoption. The purpose of "research" was to advance knowledge that might serve as a basis for development; the purpose of "development" was to invent and build a solution to an operating problem; the purpose of "diffusion" was to introduce the innovation to practitioners; and the purpose of "adoption" was to incorporate the innovation into the target system. Each stage was further refined into substages, and each substage had criteria that it should meet. The whole schema moved an invention from knowledge to institutionalization within an ongoing operating system. As such it has been labeled a "pipeline" or "linear" view of educational change. It, or more properly one interpretation of it, became the major paradigm for thinking of educational change in the American educational research community.

Later, after five years of operation, the Illinois demonstration centers were evaluated by House, Kerins, and Steele (1972) using criteria derived from the Clark-Guba schema. The evaluation tested only one link of the schema, but it was a critical one. The diffusion link presumably influences a passive consumer to implement the fruits of science through a demonstration process. Evaluators found that demonstration centers were successful on criteria for the earlier stages, but that successful demonstrations did not lead to implementations. "The fact that visitors valued the demonstration programs highly had little relationship with later adoption. Situational constraints in the adopting district seemed to be of greater importance than the intrinsic characteristics of the demonstrated program or the process of demonstration itself."

	RESEARCH	DEVELOPMENT		DIFFUSION*			ADOPTION	
		Invention	Design	Dissemination	Demonstration	Trial	Installation	Institutionalization
OBJECTIVE	To advance knowledge	To formulate a new solution to an operating problem or to a class of operating problems, i.e., *to innovate*	To order and to systematize the components of the invented solution; to construct an innovation package for institutional use, i.e., *to engineer*	To create widespread awareness of the invention among practitioners, i.e., *to inform*	To afford an opportunity to examine and assess operating qualities of the invention, i.e., *to build conviction*	To build familiarity with the invention and provide a basis for assessing the quality, value, fit, and utility of the invention in a particular institution, i.e., *to test*	To fit the characteristics of the invention to the characteristics of the adopting institutions, i.e., *to operationalize*	To assimilate the invention as an integral and accepted component of the system, i.e., *to establish*
CRITERIA	Validity (internal and external)	Face validity (appropriateness) Estimated viability Impact (relative contribution)	Institutional feasibility Generalizability Performance	Intelligibility Fidelity Pervasiveness Impact (extent to which it affects key targets)	Credibility Convenience Evidential assessment	Adaptability Feasibility Action	Effectiveness Efficiency	Continuity Valuation Support
RELATION TO CHANGE	Provides basis for invention	Produces the invention	Engineers and packages the invention	Informs about the invention	Builds conviction about the invention	Tries out the invention in the context of a particular situation	Operationalizes the invention for use in a specific institution	Establishes the invention as a part of an ongoing program; converts it to a noninnovation

*The area enclosed by a broken line represents the intended role of demonstration centers in the Illinois plan.

FIGURE 8-1

Classification schema of processes related to and
necessary for change in education
(from House, Kerins, and Steele, 1972)

Providing "follow-up" help to visitors in their home districts was the variable most related to implementation of what the visitors had seen at the demonstration center. The study concluded:

The Illinois centers must be judged successful at the immediate goals of dissemination and demonstration but not at the ultimate and most important goal of adoption. Judged entirely in terms of the Clark-Guba model the centers must be regarded a success because they met most of the criteria of that model. In short, visitors were informed and were convinced that the programs they saw operating were worth adopting. It should follow that visitors would adopt the programs—but most did not. The finding that follow-up should be more important to adoption than the nature of the demonstrated program suggests something seriously wrong with the model itself.

Research and Development models of change assume a passive user population which is shaped by the dissemination process itself. The facts belie this assumption. Of far greater importance are the variables controlling the would-be adopter's everyday world in his home district. The individual is caught in a powerful social web that determines his behavior more than do his individual impressions gleaned at a demonstration visit. The variables that influence whether he will adopt are those that shape this home environment [page 12].

Clark and Guba (1972) responded to this study in a lengthy rebuttal. Although not attacking the methodology and data of the evaluation, they contended that the data did not support the conclusions about their schema and that their schema had in fact been grossly misinterpreted by nearly everyone including the evaluators. First, they contended that the Illinois demonstration centers were not an appropriate test of the schema and that the schema was not invalidated because visitors convinced at the demonstrations did not adopt it. The substantive issue and the relevance of the test revolved around whether the model was "linear," that is, represented a necessary flow from research to diffusion to development to adoption. Clark and Guba contended that the model was not linear and that they had never intended it to be.

In the counterresponse House (1972) contended that the schema was linear. "The thing speaks for itself. Logically, can 'adoption' of an intervention precede its 'development'? Can 'institutionalization' precede its 'dissemination'? Let the reader perform his own experiment by drawing the categories of the 'schema' at random from a hat. If the schema is not sequential, the order should make no difference." In their rebuttal Clark and Guba also denied that they conceived the consumer as a tabula rasa or as passive. House cited Clark's earlier statements as counterevidence and contended that Clark and Guba had already changed their own conception of their schema on the basis of later experience and were the better for it.

In one important aspect, Clark and Guba were correct—contending that their schema had never been fully interpreted. For example, Clark's call for decentralization in the 1962 document was never emphasized, and it well may be that Clark and Guba never intended that social and political forces within the local setting be ignored. Instead, the schema was interpreted by nearly everyone as putting heavy emphasis on research and development. (Almost anyone, including myself if I had the ability, would have formulated such a paradigm. It was the temper of the times, and Clark and Guba were able to achieve a formalization of thought that was enthusiastically received.) In short, Clark and Guba contended that their schema should not be seen as an example of the research, development, diffusion paradigm. Whether this particular schema should be included is not important. What is important is that the general research, development, diffusion paradigm itself be seen as inadequate.

In his review of the literature on the dissemination and utilization of knowledge, Havelock (1971) identified three major schools of thought: the research, development, diffusion perspective; the problem-solving perspective; and the social interaction perspective. Havelock said that the RD&D school depicts the process of change as an orderly sequence in which the initiative is taken by the researchers, the developers, and the disseminators. It begins with identifying a problem, finds or produces a solution, and diffuses the solution to a target group. The major emphasis of all RD&D theorists (Clark and Guba are also the prime example for Havelock) is on the planning of change on a large scale.

The RD&D paradigm posits a user population that can be influenced through dissemination activities, provided that the dissemination is preceded by extensive research and development. Havelock identifies five features of the model:

1. There is a *rational sequence* of activities that moves from research to development to packaging *before* dissemination takes place. It includes stages such as "basic research," "applied research," "development," "production," and "packaging."

2. There is *massive planning* in order to coordinate and control all these activities.
3. There is *division of labor* and separation of roles and functions in order to carry out these activities.
4. It assumes a *passive consumer,* a defined target audience, to accept the innovation if it is delivered in the right way at the right time. "Scientific evaluation" acts as a quality control at every stage to assure this process.
5. It accepts a *high initial development cost* because it expects an ultimate payoff in terms of "efficiency, quality, and capacity to reach a mass audience."

Every state department of education and every government branch has its own version of this model. It is particularly popular with macrosystem planners because it divides knowledge (and innovation) flow into neatly functional roles. As Havelock notes, "it does appear to supply much of the rationale for current policy planning in the U.S. Office of Education."

In criticizing the model Havelock contended that the RD&D model is "over-rational, over-idealized, excessively research oriented, and inadequately user oriented . . . ." Empirically one could contend that the model simply has not resulted in much discernible educational change. Although not many studies such as the evaluation of the Illinois demonstration centers have been conducted, there is a widespread feeling that U.S.O.E. and foundation-supported programs have not been effective.

One of the most ambitious programs was the establishment of regional laboratories and research and development centers, a widespread, multimillion-dollar system designed to bridge the gap between basic research and practice by development and diffusion (regional laboratories) and by applied research and development (research and development centers). These were institutions clearly designed to fill the gap in the research, development, diffusion paradigm. The regional laboratories were particularly designed to attend to regional interests, as Clark had suggested in his decentralization schema—an absolute necessity, he thought, if the labs were to attend to practitioner differences. Nonetheless, the labs were supposed to translate research findings into practice, be a conduit as it were, adjusting to local differences.

Even this freedom to adjust within the overall scheme was

denied them, however. As with most government programs, the central office was never willing to relinquish control. Instead of attending to regional concerns and contexts and perceiving the local people as the clients, the labs were forced to attend to central national goals as defined by the Office of Education. As usual, the federal agency became the client as well as the sponsor. What was seen as a problem in Washington, D.C., was not what local school people saw as the problem in Minnesota or Texas, indeed could not have been. The refusal of the Office of Education to grant autonomy, even of a minor sort, by keeping a tight grip through extremely tight supervision from Washington and uniform annual budgeting procedures kept the labs responding to whatever winds were blowing in Washington and away from attending to the problems of local school personnel. The labs that did not conform lost their funding altogether. More than 50 percent of the resources of many labs were spent in maintaining liaison with the Office of Education.

The materials and programs that did emerge were few, often poor in quality, and not attuned to individual school structures as analyzed in this book. The products, with few exceptions, were mostly ignored by school personnel. There were other problems, such as the type of personnel attracted to the labs in the face of unstable funding, but the primary difficulty was that the labs were never given the autonomy to treat school personnel as clients. This type of control has continued to the present day since the transfer of the program to the National Institute of Education. The Regional labs have tried to mitigate the vagaries of excessive and arbitrary control by forming an association. The outcome of the program, into which many millions of dollars have been poured, is considered by most observers to be rather abysmal.

Research Millions Bear Little Fruit, Study Says. More than $200 million in education research has produced "little evidence of... significant impact in classrooms," according to a General Accounting Office (GAO) report to Congress. GAO reviewed the findings of independent consultants hired by the U.S. Office of Education (USOE) and found that the products of laboratories and research centers have not proved effective and have been sent out to schools after inadequate and ineffective evaluation of their usefulness. U.S. Comptroller Gen. Elmer B. Staats says USOE must accept some responsibility because it provided "inadequate guidance" in some areas, and "frequent changes in USOE leadership have also affected the successful operation of programs." (Since the Cooperative Research Act began funding education research centers in universities in 1963, there have been six HEW secretaries and seven education commissioners. In addition, USOE's research and development program has been under four different managers from 1968 to 1971.) [*Washington Monitor*, December 17, 1973, page 96].

No doubt the regional labs would have worked better without the heavy-handedness of the Office of Education. But, while some consider such behavior to be an anomaly, the very essence of the RD&D approach is control, and the regional lab experience was neither accidental nor uncommon. Control over the laboratories was always justified in terms of central national goals—Washington knew best. The essence of the RD&D paradigm is that it places the initiatory power to the research side of the R&D chain. There is only one source of legitimacy. For the regional labs, the client was really the Office of Education and, perhaps as not-quite-equal partners, they would decide together how practitioners or "performers," the third party, would be acted upon. The fact that the fruits of these labors had no relevance for practitioners had to come as a shock.

Why does not the RD&D paradigm work better? First, as mentioned, by stripping the practitioner of initiatory power, the paradigm treats him as passive. In fact, use of the paradigm is justified on the basis of the belief that the practitioner is passive and will not initiate innovation on his own. The teacher is seen as slightly resistant, though someone who can be induced through persuasion to accept the new innovation—perhaps a little simpleminded and not too complex. Such a depiction justifies acting upon these people.

When one does try to induce him to use a new innovation, one finds that the practitioner is not so passive. Being constrained is not the same as being passive. The practitioner operates in a context essentially foreign to the developer. As with the Illinois demonstration centers, the situational constraints existing in the practitioner's home district are more important than characteristics of the innovation. In spite of caveats delivered, usually far down the line, the developer is never able to take full cognizance of the practitioner's world since the innovation process always starts on the R&D side. The heaviest attention is paid to marketing research. The RD&D paradigm puts the practitioner immediately in the position of a consumer who is going to be sold a piece of goods which he has the option only to buy or reject. Ordinarily he uses his only remaining power—not to buy. Since the goods are often damaging to the child or himself in ways the developers cannot comprehend, this is frequently a wise decision.

The research, development, diffusion paradigm assumes that the innovation will be invented on the left, developed, and passed along the chain. But even assuming a passive consumer, such a sequence of events is unlikely. The large-scale division of labor into research, development, and other interest groups almost assures it will not. There are two conditions under which such a scheme might work (House, 1971). One is that the actors share the same values and end in sight, that is, inventing and diffusing the product. But they do not. Researchers work to publish articles. The reward system is based on disciplinary contribution and far removed from developing products. Developers have traditionally been concerned with turning out products and not with research or dissemination. The different actors can work at cross-purposes with the overall scheme.

The other condition under which the scheme might work is that someone have the power to force compliance with the overall system goals. While federal agencies might devoutly pray for such power, they do not have it; nor does anyone else. As already mentioned, while not having the power to initiate, the teacher in his classroom is beyond the power of almost anybody. Only in situations where the institution is integrated into a larger network does innovation diffusion occur.

All this is to say that the RD&D paradigm would work only if it were an integrated social system, which it is not. In fact, what is needed for change to occur is the development of a social system through extended personal contact as outlined in the first chapter of this book. The RD&D paradigm tries to lash together pieces of several separate and distinct social systems such as researchers and practitioners and to invent whole new ones, such as developers and disseminators, to link the two together. As is the wont of the federal government, there has been an attempt to do this on a massive scale. The failure of these efforts to control either the envisioned process or the actors therein led to a stronger emphasis on evaluation to discover and correct errant behavior. Disappointment in the results of several federal programs has led to the rise of an evaluation establishment, albeit one very much in the service of the federal government and one attuned to the particular demands of the RD&D paradigm.

The emphasis on research and development (under control of the federal government) as the legitimate starting point of educational innovation justifies "high initial development cost," which of course means more money for research and development. Placing money at that end of the chain is justified, as Havelock notes, by claims of great "efficiency, quality, and capacity to reach a mass audience." Research and development not so planned are considered to be unproductive or at least of low priority.

The direction and coordination of these activities require a great deal of global planning, and it is this facet that appeals most to government officials. Massive planning does not, however, impel people to implement the plans, and, when plans deviate from people's self-interest and the way they perceive the world, they are merely pieces of paper. Federal planning for educational innovation has created a great paper world of self-deceit for the planners. A virulent strain of "Potomac fever" is the belief that plans conceived in Washington are carried out by the rest of the nation when, in fact, they seldom have effect beyond the east bank of the Potomac. Washington sends out paper and receives paper in return. As one noted authority on planning says, planning cannot create the conditions for its own success (Wildavsky, 1972).

The research, development, diffusion paradigm is rational then only from the viewpoint of global government planners and perhaps from the perspective of researchers and developers. It imposes an orderly sequence of events on the innovation process and thereby directs attention to the planners, but it is not necessarily rational from the point of view of anyone else. A central theme of this book is that all people are rational in pursuing their own self-interest but that different situations define self-interest in such a way that what is rational for one man seems irrational to another. While the research and development paradigm seems perfectly reasonable to government officials, it may not seem very reasonable to teachers. Their failure to embrace it is seen by the planners as recalcitrance or resistance.

Centralizing the initiating power for innovation, of course, is ultimately rationalized as being necessary for the pursuit of central national goals, as being in "the national interest." The research, development, and diffusion paradigm justifies the concentration of power, resources, and expertise under centralized control and prescribes how problems will be solved, and, implicitly, which problems will be attacked—problems that gain the attention of the machinery of national policy. At the same time it precludes defining problems that are local or regional in character and nearly guarantees that problems distributive in nature will not be addressed.

The "solutions" generated by this process can often be worse than the problems themselves. The solutions can be so insensitive to the context of their implementation that they rend the social fabric they propose to help.

The side effects problem is a further difficulty with the engineering metaphor and in fact is a profound difficulty in the field of engineering itself. It certainly has proved vexing in all the social policy fields in which it has been used. It is becoming clearer that social policy initiatives taken during the 60's using managerial styles have failed. We hear about housing programs that destroyed a sense of community, about poverty programs that enriched exploiters of the poor, about health programs that did little more than increase the income of physicians. Yet in education many of the engineered plans are still receiving attention beyond their worth [Atkin, 1973].

In summary, the research, development, diffusion paradigm of change posits a *rational sequence* of activities—rational from the view of those who will control and benefit most from the paradigm. It posits a *division of labor*—a hierarchical division of labor in which the controlling group will do the initiating and the controlling and the groups further down the line will conform and be acted upon. Naturally, in order to coordinate all these activities the governing group must do *massive planning* and control large sums of *development* monies for the sake of efficiency. Since the initiation and control reside at the top, it is necessary to posit a *passive consumer* willing to use these innovations at the bottom.

One must also posit that the products spewing forth from this pipeline can be used and useful under varied circumstances and local conditions, and that the major problem is merely to "transfer" them to areas where they can be used. What I have labeled the doctrine of transferability has guided federal education policy in the last decade, and is, in fact, a mainstay of all liberal social policy. It is justified in the name of overwhelming national requirements, central national goals defined by the national elite.

WHAT HAS THE FEDERAL BUREAUCRACY LEARNED?

Daniel Ellsberg has said that the essence of bureaucracy is that it cannot learn. If the Vietnamese War were turned back to the first day, the U.S. State Department would repeat the same mistakes. Individuals might learn, but the bureaucracy cannot. How true is this indictment of federal education policymaking of the last decade?

One of the most intelligent and thoughtful reflections on federal policy was made by Alice Rivlin (1971), former Assistant Secretary for Planning and Evaluation in the Department of Health, Education, and Welfare during the Johnson administration and now with the Brookings Institution, an organization renowned for liberal establishment thinking on United States foreign policy. Although Rivlin's book deals with the application of systems analysis to domestic policy, it discusses the failures of federal policy and suggests what is needed for successful programs.

Surveying the wreckage, she concludes that health, education, and welfare programs did not work very well and that program planning and budgeting, which she helped install in the Department of Health, Education, and Welfare, did not contribute much to the success of these programs. She believes that the reason for the failure was that the programs themselves were not designed so that it was possible to learn what was effective and what was not. Information gleaned from the "natural experiments," such as the large-scale categorical programs, did not produce data to show what inputs are related to outputs. The two premises on which she bases an analysis of educational programs are, first, that some of the important outcomes of education are measurable (almost always test scores). Second, that fairly stable relationships exist between these outputs and the inputs, that is, that a "production function" exists between the resources used and the output.

The large-scale categorical federal education programs resulted neither in large gains in achievement test scores nor in defining what inputs are related to outputs. There were no control groups, no appropriate experimental design, or any other facets of an experimental program because the programs were not set up as experiments. The answer, she thinks, is for the federal government to organize, fund, and evaluate systematic experiments in delivering social services. In education the first step would be to identify new teaching methods and ways of delivering education services. The second step would be to systematically try out the new methods under various conditions. Finally, these methods would be evaluated so that valid conclusions about the relative effectiveness of the various methods could be drawn.

Rivlin labels the strategy of the 1960's "random innovation." People in the field were encouraged to try out their own innovative ideas. According to her, tens of thousands of innovative projects were produced, but some were wasteful or foolish. Most did not produce convincing evidence or statistics, and the random innovation strategy made no provision for the dissemination of results. No one outside the immediate community knew about the good projects. Another problem was uniqueness. Nobody could be sure how relevant a project might be in other circumstances. Perhaps it depended on a charismatic administrator or a gifted teacher. In the absence of systematic trial, how would one know what to publicize?

Rivlin contends that the innovation must be tried under a variety of circumstances—"systematic experimentation." Individual project leaders have to follow the plans and agree to use common measures of what is accomplished so that results can be compared. All this requires "strong central leadership" in the design of a coordinated series of experiments, a strategy for social reform that only the federal government is capable of managing, in her opinion.

What about the conflicting and multiple goals and criteria always implicit in the evaluation of social programs? These should not be insurmountable, Rivlin says, as long as one is not seeking a "definitive 'best' approach." Communities can select information that fits in with their own objectives. On this point, however, Rivlin's statements are equivocal if not self-contradictory. In the chapter entitled "Can we find out what works?" she says, "It would be a mistake to adopt systematic experimentation in the hope that it would 'tell us what works.' " On the next page, she says, "But random innovation does not yield knowledge of what works best for whom or under what conditions." Although there are several disclaimers, the import of her argument is that there is a best way and systematic experimentation will discover it, publicize it, and disseminate it to other places. Nor is she unsure of the method itself: "The argument for systematic experimentation is straightforward: Information necessary to improve the effectiveness of social services is impossible to obtain any other way."

If the results are to be generalizable to other situations, she argues, the same specifications must be followed. Here she explicitly draws a parallel to physical experiments in which exact specification of what is to be done and control of all factors is paramount. She recognizes that creative teachers are likely to alter the method substantially as they go, and one must expect and allow some variation from one classroom to the next—"but not too much." If there is wide variation in what is done (the bane of past field experiments), these variations might overwhelm differences between the two treatments.

In order to successfully evaluate these systematic experiments, one more thing is necessary: better performance measures to evaluate their effectiveness. What about decentralization, community control, and more of a market system for education, all of which have been suggested as counterpolicies to replace heavy government control? Rivlin says, "In particular, the success of all three depends on two conditions: (1) the development and use of better measures of the effectiveness of social services; and (2) vigorous and systematic attempts to find and test more effective methods and to publicize the results."

Responding to the criticism that the federal government has not been able to manage social action programs effectively, Rivlin agrees that tighter management from Washington did not work in the 1960's. The belief then was that more could be learned and transmitted to the local level through federal guidelines regulations and technical assistance. As knowledge accumulated, guidelines could be tightened, and programs would become more effective. Although in favor of this approach at the time, Rivlin concedes that it was naive and unrealistic. The country was too big and diversified to be run by universal rules. They did more harm than good. It was impossible to write detailed rules to fit every case.

The "new realists" are not yet ready to decentralize operations, however. One reason is the inequality of resources among state and local agencies. Another is that the federal government has the lien on income tax as a source of revenue. Also, "a deep-seated fear that the money will be misused and misdirected has always made the liberals—and, indeed, most of the Congress—leary of turning over federal tax money to lower levels of government without strict guidelines." In addition, "in practice state and local governments have hardly been models of efficiency, effectiveness, or even honesty. Moreover, not sharing national objectives, state and local governments may underfund such programs . . . ." While tight management procedures did not work before, why not hold the lower governmental levels accountable in terms of output rather than input?

"Hence a new approach is in order: state the accountability in terms of outputs and reward those who produce more efficiently." This new form of accountability requires the development of "performance measures" to use as incentives. Otherwise, without incentives, why should decentralized units produce any better? Furthermore, there is no hope at all for decentralizing research and development activities. "Moreover, for any hope of success, some problems demand a critical mass of talent and resources that only the federal government can mobilize," for example, the atomic and hydrogen bombs, the lunar landings, and breakthroughs in biomedical research. "Breakthroughs in social service delivery seem likely to require similar concentrations of effort."

If community control of schools becomes a reality in big cities, the community will have to "search for proven models of effective education" and to evaluate them by performance measures, according to Rivlin. In fact, perhaps only on this condition should higher levels of government be willing to relinquish control. Even a voucher system must depend on the development and employment of performance measures; otherwise, how could a voucher system lead to "intelligent consumer choice?" In fact, Rivlin becomes more and more adamant: "No matter who makes the decisions, effective functioning of the system depends on measures of achievement."

She concludes her book with some caveats about the performance measures but with no diminution of enthusiasm. "We are unlikely to get improved social services (or, indeed, to know if we have them) until we make a sustained effort to develop performance measures suitable for judging and rewarding effectiveness." Current efforts to publish test scores are the first steps to better education, but eventually we will be able to collect experience and delineate performance. "All the strategies for finding better methods in these pages, especially social experimentation, depend for their success on improving performance measures."

What are we to make of Rivlin's analysis? It is an intelligent and thoughtful discussion of the problems of government administration in the 1960's. Failures are dealt with frankly, and discussions of the difficulties of evaluating social programs are handled well. When she suggests alternative policies, however, we see not only what she has left behind but what she has carried forth with her. Undressed, her policies are kin to the research, development, diffusion paradigm, but they have been given a new set of clothes. It is information to solve our problems, but it is information provided only to the bureaucracy and generated by certain methods and techniques. Instead of allowing "random innovation," which often resulted in foolish projects, the government would control projects more fully by running them as controlled experiments.

The doctrine of transferability lives. There are universal solutions which can be found (through systematic experiments) and which can be generalized and disseminated via distribution of research results to local districts. Engineered solutions are of course controlled and funded by the federal government. Analogies to national defense and lunar landing problems are drawn explicitly. These processes demand concentration of resources, as opposed to distribution.

There is also a lack of description of what local school districts are like or what the unanticipated consequences of these innovations may be for them. There is, in fact, a fear and distrust of what state and local authorities might do with the money and resources. They might misuse them, or they might not address national problems. The dynamics of policy are explained almost entirely in terms of the planner and the bureaucrat, not in terms of the teacher. One must provide practitioners with incentives in the form of "performance measures" which they must strive to increase. Curiously missing in her analysis are political considerations of how policies are formulated, how they will be implemented, and other matters, although her examples testify to the importance of such forces.

Perhaps one of the most basic ideas in this liberal technocratic view of the world is that there is a common measure of "payoff," or, at the very least, a few, represented in this case by performance measures. The effectiveness of educational programs can be registered in performance measures. No one, whether in a decentralized voucher system or in any system, can determine good or bad, or even better or worse, without reference to performance measures. One can always define and use a single index of effectiveness to compare two programs in a comparative experiment. These measures will, of course, be determined by further information gleaned from the research process. There is no reference to the possibility that different people might legitimately apply different criteria to an educational program and derive a significantly different index of effectiveness, or to the possibility that the official measures of effectiveness, necessarily few in number, may be entirely removed from what a local person might want.

Rivlin's whole scheme depends on the establishment of performance measures. Innovations are to be tested in field experiments, and performance measures must be used to control flow through the research, development, diffusion paradigm. Perhaps one of the most curious characteristics of the recommendations is the absolute certainty with which they are delivered. Systematic experimentation and the development of performance measures to monitor success and provide incentives are the only way to improve social services—a curious attitude considering the record of the sixties. Many procedures are questioned, but never the assumptions and goals on which the policies are based. In many ways Rivlin's argument, which contains many good insights, is a defense of federal control of social reform initiative and the liberal policies and assumptions that govern it. In somewhat disguised form it is brother to the research, development, diffusion paradigm, which is not a policy for innovation so much as a policy for control of innovation.

Reviewing Rivlin's book in the *Wall Street Journal* (Bartley, 1971), an editorial staff writer questions man's ability to draw up rational presumptions for changing society. As he notes, correctly, Rivlin's belief that such procedures will turn up answers is a matter of faith not of science, and it is this faith that keeps her liberal credentials intact. Buried beneath the cloak of technical processes and technical rationality lie implicit judgments and assumptions that are ultimately political in nature.

Drawing upon the classic conservatism of Tocqueville and Burke, as well as the more simplistic political philosophy of the *Wall Street Journal* itself, the reviewer suggests that meddling with the complexities of a social system that no one understands is in fact more foolish than taking apart a clock without knowing how to put it together again, and it is a considerably more damaging and immoral action. It is the rational prescription delivered from confident ignorance and an American tradition of activism that leads to mischief. While not agreeing with the *Journal* editor's argument for not interfering with the status quo, one of the nonliberal themes of this book is that one should tamper with a social system, whether it be Vietnam or a school, only after more than a superficial understanding of the system itself and even then only with considerable trepidation. Otherwise, one is likely to propagate not only unproductive but counterproductive, even harmful policies. It seems to be an abiding feature of American political liberalism that it has neither understanding nor trepidations, at least as practiced in the sixties. If, as Ellsberg suggests, behavior is recorded in a bureaucracy's genotype, bureaucracy may indeed be incapable of learning anything significantly new.

PIROUETTES OF THE NATIONAL INSTITUTE OF EDUCATION

Faced with intense criticism from almost all quarters, the research and development function of the Office of Education was split off into the National Institute of Education. The NIE was to be a "visible indication of our commitment to systematic improvement of educational programs . . ." (Gallagher, 1970). The new agency was established by legislation in 1972. Two years of lead planning gave the agency the time and autonomy to rethink its innovation policies, especially in the face of widespread dissatisfaction with past policies.

As it often does when looking for new directions, the federal government turned to the Rand Corporation to do its thinking. One of the major planning documents was written by John Pincus (1974) of the Rand Corporation. Pincus emphasized the market structure and incentive systems of the school as they affected adoption and implementation of innovations. He argued that the school is a self-perpetuating bureaucracy that is not market oriented. It is the captive servant of a captive clientele. It is open to public scrutiny. It cannot unambiguously define its goals of methodology. It makes a modest and uncertain contribution to learning. And it is decentralized in governance. He concluded that this type of "market structure" led schools, more than private firms, to adopt innovations that do not require complex changes in management structure or organizational relations. Such innovations could satisfy staff and client demands for change without changing the basic structure.

Pincus concludes that schools will voluntarily adopt innovations that enhance their self-image, prove it is "up-to-date," "efficient," "professional," and "responsive," but cause no major changes. If research and development products are to be accepted by practitioners (an unstated assumption on Pincus' part), the R&D organizations had better work closely with school administrators because social pressure for adoption is important. External pressure, subsidy, or incentives can also help. State and federal R&D policy should be directed at innovations the schools are otherwise reluctant to attempt, for the government will also have to pay for such reforms. He suggests large-scale, well-planned efforts and collaboration with school administrators and teacher organizations.

The most common complaint of the R&D community, Pincus says, is that innovations are not implemented as prescribed. The reasons are: R&D organizations do not provide sufficient guidance, teachers and administrators do not accept the "obligation to change their behavior pattern," schools may not know how to implement, and "verbal adoption" may be sufficient. The only control the federal government has is the unlikely one of withdrawing funds. Federal policies have discouraged implementation by subsidizing R&D without reference to the effects on school outcome, ignoring evaluation reports, frequent shifts in funding, viewing federal contribution as only seed money, and inconsistent innovation policies.

After this assessment, Pincus suggests that R&D policy be based on trying out systematic innovations and assessing their consequences rather than the rationalist approach of first defining goals and then seeking to achieve them efficiently. This suggests policies that appeal to existing bureaucratic incentives, as well as policies to modify these incentives; policies that permit more public access; and policies that introduce changes in the market structure of the school. Pincus suggests five emphases for R&D policy in encouraging adoption and implementation of innovations: large-scale experimentation, collaboration between R&D agencies and educational leadership networks, case studies of successful innovation, research on the existing pattern of school incentives, and trying out methods of restructuring the incentive structure.

A major difference between Pincus and Rivlin in their advocacy of large-scale experiment is that Pincus wants to study the long-range, unintended effects on the school system rather than look at performance measures. This includes looking for reasons for success or failure. Like Rivlin, he prefers large-scale experiments because of their visibility. For closer collaboration with practitioners he recommends that R&D organizations be interdisciplinary and problem oriented, that R&D organizations work with administrators and teachers during development, that R&D organizations conduct more training, that R&D organizations understand regional and national influence networks, and that R&D personnel work closely with school staff during implementation. Overall he suggests that R&D institutions turn toward a more clinical model of change that adapts general findings to specific circumstances of the client, not to the engineering model.

Like Rivlin, Pincus concludes by making a plea for accountability and for providing information to policymakers and the public. Rather than proceeding from a priori objectives, however, he suggests that experimentation might determine what people want. He concludes that the target of such policy should be a diversity of approaches to schooling rather than the "most effective" approach. Diversity should be offered within the framework of a public market place, and this can be brought about by more sophisticated and enlightened R&D management.

As represented in the Pincus paper, the National Institute of Education recognizes the complex nature of the school as a social system. If the NIE were to affect educational practice, it would have to understand something about how the system operated, particularly its personnel and institutional incentives. In developing products for schools, R&D agencies would have to work closely with practitioners and understand their framework. Many of Pincus' arguments are obviously supported here. The understanding of the school as a social system with its own rewards is a shared perspective. Pincus moved quite a long way from the original R&D perspective, the most remarkable difference being the disregard of central national goals.

At the end of the paper Pincus even makes a plea for diversity in the school structure. Different innovations may work in different places under different specific circumstances. Experiments and case studies should look at the unintended effects of the innovations in terms of specific people over time. This is a long way from the doctrine of transferability underlying most government thinking. Pincus did not abandon the RD&D model; he did, however, stretch it pretty far toward the consumer. In his schema, innovation will still be fueled by centrally developed products, though these products will differ somewhat and be more attuned to the characteristics of the consumers. Although diversity is to be promoted, it is the government's task to provide such diversity. Ultimately there is a common measure of success and payoff. There must be an accountability scheme to collect such monitoring information and feed it to that ever-brooding, ever-deciding group of men—government decision-makers. Diversity will result as a product of more sophisticated R&D management. While Pincus' position does not indicate a break with the RD&D paradigm, it does represent a substantial and well-considered deviation.

Could it be true that the government is learning something and, in the embodiment of a newly born agency, about to set out on an enlightened policy? As of this writing, it is too early to tell. But there are abundant signs that NIE is being pulled back into the old habits and thought patterns of government agencies. The chairman of the advisory panel that was to set policy for the National Institute of Education was Patrick Haggerty, chairman of Texas Instruments Incorporated and a strong proponent of "accountability" in education.

In an article entitled "Research and Development, Educational Productivity and the American Economy," Haggerty (1973) set forth his views on American education and its lack of "productivity." He argued that the rapid increase in research and development expenditures have "stretched the resources of the entire nation and, as a consequence, produced sharp inflationary pressures." As evidence of the lack of productivity in education, Haggerty pointed out that costs of public elementary and secondary education have increased two and a third times since 1950. Higher education costs have increased two and a half times, thus proving that productivity has not kept pace. If it had, costs would not have increased. In areas like education "we have not learned how to use technology, capital, and management to increase productivity per person on a regular basis. . . . Further, research and development efforts aimed at more effective organizational structures, better understanding, and markedly improved productivities per person . . . would have higher payoffs than in industry."

Haggerty said that the threefold increase in spending over the last twenty-five years has not improved the effectiveness of the system or the quality of the end product. Industry can maintain its productivity because "culture" demands it: "we improve productivity or die." As for education, "our goals must change so as to find ways that maintain the quality of education with fewer adult hours per student hour." He sets a goal of 2 to 5 percent productivity increase per year. Not only does Haggerty set the specific goal, he suggests exactly how to accomplish it. Why not let fifteen- and sixteen-year-old students go to work four to six hours a day? They could be educated via television at work. "I am convinced that the development of such a television-based educational system can produce both a quality of education and a productivity per educator far above that accepted as the norm in the high school or university; and, further, that the system can be self-supporting."

For most students, in-school classes could be terminated after the tenth year. Schooling could be completed in close connection with their jobs. "The course content quite properly should be set to augment the career being pursued and with the collaboration of the organization at which the individual is working . . . ." All vocational-oriented courses, even college-level training such as tax law and cost accounting, could be better taught on the job. In fact, preparation for a career in today's society is a process that must continue throughout one's life.

I am confident that whatever the complexity, so long as the system is designed to predetermined student-instructional-hour costs and is based on an adequate and improving level of productivity per instructional and overhead person involved, the end result will be a lower cost per student-instructional-hour and a superior education, and we will have less difficulty financing it than we do our present system.

Educational research and development once again gets its marching orders. This time it is not to produce scientific personnel to compete with the Russians nor to redress inequities and conflicts in the social system. This time it is to reduce the cost (improving the productivity is exactly the same thing to Haggerty) of American education as a whole. Even before Haggerty assumed the chairmanship of the first National Institute of Education, he had decided that the goal of educational research and development was to find ways to reduce costs to balance off salary gains. In that way, education would not require a larger share of the gross national product.

Once again the problem was a central national one, and it would be addressed by the production of technologies and management systems that could be applied to reduce costs to a previously determined level. The costs would be reduced by reducing the number of adult hours per child and substituting the capital-intensive methods used in high technology. Research and development would develop the necessary high technology systems and career education programs located on the job. Apparently ignorant of the large-scale introduction of television many years before, Haggerty was confident that such approaches would work.

It is not difficult to imagine the projects that would be funded under the guidance of such a policy: studies of cost-effectiveness and how to reduce costs; studies of school and teacher efficiency; large-scale technological development of presumed cost-cutting devices such as television and CAI (PLATO is a certainty for massive support); packaged courses on cassettes, videotape, or other such mediums; career education programs; programs that would eventually give large sums of money to industries. To what extent this viewpoint was instituted as formal policy remains to be seen. Haggerty was in a powerful position to influence future policies, and many key positions within NIE were staffed by economists brought in from other agencies, who might prove a receptive audience.

One could imagine that captive and satellite agencies like the regional labs would be quick to respond to the new direction, at least if they wished to survive. By 1974 NIE influence in the internal workings of these supposedly autonomous agencies extended to deciding the placement of key personnel. In some labs, major personnel could not be hired or assigned new duties without specific approval from Washington. One can imagine the flood of new products issuing forth from these agencies over the next five years. It would seem that such products might be even less enthusiastically received, given their content, than previous ones. Then there will be new articles on the resistance of the schools to change and new attempts by federal and stage governments to force compliance.

Research and development agencies would once again be responding to problems formulated outside education altogether. The clients would not be the schools or school personnel. In fact, the import of these policies would be to reduce the number of educational personnel. Schools would once again be "acted upon." Research and development would produce a set of products to reduce costs. The search for universal solutions (always technological ones) was on again; the doctrine of transferability was reincarnated.

After the initial draft of this chapter had been written, the National Institute of Education released a report compiled by the special "task force" studying the problem of educational innovation (National Institute of Education, 1973). In the introduction, the authors summarized past federal policy decisions as:

—The apparent choice not to support development of local school-system R&D capacity.
—The growth of targeted R&D towards nationally-defined problems, and the resulting rapid increase of money flowing to non-university, non-profit organizations equipped to respond quickly to new possibilities.
—The concomitant decline of basic research funding . . . and the resulting decrease of university faculty involved in the R&D system.
—Few resources remaining to be used in relating the R&D system to its ultimate clients in the operating system.

The report continues: "The result of past choices seems to have created a system of external agents, new institutions for the most part, anchored neither in any well-tested scholarly understanding of a domain of practice, nor in any intimate knowledge of operational problems. . . . It may have been enormously important politically . . . to have specific targets being worked on by contractors who could be held to performance standards spelled out by the government. . . . However, the result in relation to the reform of education, seems to have been weak; an R&D system with growing resources flowing to it, does not seem to have articulated well with the operating school and school districts of the nation." It is, the report contends, the R&D paradigms that need rethinking and the report's intent is to review the past and provide redirection.

The report is unequivocal in its interpretations of past practice:

We wish to stress again that despite the unstable achievements of the past decade of research, product development, evaluation, and dissemination, the schools are much as they have always been, and not always by choice. We attribute this in part to the whole way R&D has been thought about—as an external activity whose results will inevitably be found useful by operating agencies.

The report goes on to trace the growth of federal support for education "in fields considered vital to the nation's military and technological strength," and notes that the responsiveness of the nonprofit agencies to governmental direction may have been achieved at the expense of responsiveness to the ultimate clients. In addition, federally directed R&D has significantly increased the amount of contract work going to private business. For example, in 1971 45 percent of the evaluation research funds went to profit organizations. Another 29 percent went to nonprofit organizations, mostly satellite organizations like the regional labs. Only 21 percent went to colleges or universities.

The section on the current R&D system concludes: "Whoever presumes to participate in the improvement of public education must understand the nature of the current system." The analysis of the current operational system continues by asserting that "the primary source of energy for reform and renewal must be found within the operating system and in the lay community served by that system."

Halfway through the report it appears that the NIE staff may be on a collision course with the conservative chairman of the NIE advisory panel over his concern for educational productivity. Reform from inside the system is quite different from imposing externally invented capital-intensive innovations. Could it be that at last the NIE staff had renounced the doctrine of transferability in its denunciation of past policy? Not quite. "Yet it is not clear that local innovation is organized and supported in a way that leads to sustained improvement. Most local innovations are limited in scope and tend not to generalize to other populations." Nonetheless, following Pincus' analysis, the report contends that schools and teachers have few resources or little incentive either to adopt or to implement innovations. Schools lack the capacity for "renewal."

As a result of its analysis, the report proposes an "interactive model" of change. Rejecting the "linear" model of change as deficient in projecting a passive or compliant consumer, past thinking has emphasized external research and development too much and internal research and development, internal linkage and support, and external linkage and support too little. (Internal refers to activities carried out inside the operating systems.) To the report writers, "research and development" means the production of generalizable knowledge and material. They lament the lack of rigorous "development-field testing-evaluation" in state and local education agencies and the fact that "There is little to guide us in determining how, and in what domains, SEA's and LEA's can play more effective roles in the production of generalizable knowledge and materials."

After devoting half the report to lamenting the past results of the linear change paradigm which treats the practitioners as passive or compliant, the last half outlines recommendations for new directions. This is where the imagination of the NIE task force largely fails them. There are four major directions:

> *To develop a monitoring system within NIE* to gather and and analyze data on the "knowledge production and utilization system."
>
> *To strengthen the extenal R&D system.*
>
> *To build a linkage and support system* between the R&D system and the school.
>
> *To build problem-solving capacity into the operating system.*

Upon close examination, every one of the details of the "new directions" would serve to strengthen rather than change the basic RD&D paradigm. All serve to enhance the ties between researchers, developers, and practitioners without shifting any initiatory power from the planner's to the practitioner's side of the spectrum. The federal government would still retain control, in fact increased control, of the total innovation process. The effect of the new directions would be to increase the vulnerability of the practitioners if they worked at all. Giant data banks, model building, studies, information dissemination, and dissemination of NIE "products" would all operate under complete federal control.

At the very end of the document we get to the fourth of the new directions. Although the document takes its title from this topic and the first half of the document is devoted to documenting lack of attention to this area, only 18 of the 112 pages are devoted to the exegesis of the new policy, which essentially is *to conduct surveys, do case studies, and hold conferences.*

Such activities will show how to build a capability for "problem-solving behavior," which in turn will lead to the objectives of:

> —more effective use of the products of the external R&D resource system;
>
> —increased and better articulated demand from the schools for more appropriate R&D products; and
>
> —increased ability at the local level to utilize local resources effectively.

The circle is complete. If one cannot get districts to accept the products of government R&D, then conduct studies to determine how "problem-solving capabilities" can be built in that will cause practitioners to use the products of the external R&D system. "Our major strategy is a program of directed experimental studies to develop, test, and disseminate approaches for building problem-solving capacities in schools." After new interventions were tried in selected districts, the "most promising components" could be integrated at "assembly districts." The purpose of the studies would, of course, be to provide information for consumers and decisionmakers.

Thus will the National Institute of Education build capacity for reform and escape the linear model. All the strategies require dissemination of information or products produced under NIE control. In spite of strong disclaimers in the first half of the document, they are all directed toward schools absorbing the products of external R&D, most of which have been tried before. The most novel strategies are to increase communication between external R&D and practitioners. Practitioners are allowed "feedback" about the products, but there is no question about their status as consumers. Whatever the causes, there seem to be few ideas that would allow abandoning the RD&D model and the doctrine of transferability. Even alternatives to the model are conceived in terms of the model.

To be fair to the task force, thinking beyond the assumptions of the paradigm is a most formidable problem. Given the lack of new assumptions and strong pressure from above, federal policy may well retreat to the past.

CRITERIA FOR NEW FEDERAL POLICIES

In this section I would like to advance some suggestions for new directions for federal policy. I do so tentatively, realizing that new policies usually turn out to be old policies in disguise, even when conceived with the best of intent. The first stipulation is that government policy be directed toward working with the educational system as it exists rather than trying to overcome it or to impose various kinds of external standards and processes from above. This requires an in-depth understanding of the educational system and a commitment to its evolutionary development over time. A commitment to organic rather than mechanical development means that good parts of the current system are not destroyed under the guise of improvement and damage to the people who inhabit the system is avoided.

It means working with, rather than operating on, the school system. Directions and energies must be mobilized from within the system itself.

As all policy makers know from experience, policy does not consist in prescribing one goal or even one series of goals; but in regulating a system over time in such a way as to optimize the realization of many conflicting relations without wrecking the system in the process. Thus the dominance of technology has infected policy-making with three bogus simplifications, just admissible in the workshop but lethal in the council chamber. One of these is the habit of accepting goals—states to be attained once for all—rather than norms to be held through time, as the typical object of policy. The second is the further reduction of multiple objectives to a single goal, yielding a single criterion of success. The third is the acceptance of effectiveness as the sole criterion by which to choose between alternative operations which can be regarded as means to one desired end. The combined effect of these three has been to dehumanize and distort beyond measure the high human function of government—that is, regulation—at all levels [Vickers, 1970].

The function of government should be to regulate educational innovation with some ecological gentleness. Regulation is not simple-minded prescription. One of the most difficult tasks is to avoid the heavy-handedness of impersonal and unintelligent bureaucratic action.

Within the educational system as I have portrayed it, there are several routes to increasing innovation, and I have made specific suggestions toward the end of most chapters. Briefly, one can increase interschool communication among administrators, increase intraschool communications among teachers, increase entrepreneurism, increase rewards to teachers for innovation, decrease the personal costs of innovation, and facilitate conditions necessary to invention in the public schools. One can also mitigate the effects of various dysfunctions like overselling.

These all represent general substantive directions in which government policy might move and any number of specific policies would be necessary to pursue each direction. In fact, such goals could never be attained, only approached. The more these conditions are increased, the more innovation could be increased, but obviously there would be a limit beyond which one would not want any more innovation. There would be too much. From the government perspective, innovation would need to be slowed down.

Government control would consist of stimulation and regulation.

The image is more of a man withdrawing or inserting a lead rod in an atomic stockpile, thereby regulating activity. This is quite different from manufacturing a part and installing it on a machine. For example, in stimulating innovation diffusion the government might provide travel funds to increase communication among teachers without specifying the meeting to be attended or the type of innovation to be adopted. Or the government might provide a great number of small grants for invention to many people without determining the kind of innovation to be worked on.

In both cases innovation diffusion and invention of innovation would be increased or decreased with the flow of funds, but the government would not try to control the types of innovations produced and disseminated as it does now. The quality and effects of such innovative efforts could be assessed through evaluations of specific local efforts whenever the project was large enough to warrant it. The intent of the project would not, however, be to produce highly transferable innovations. Rather, the intent would be to produce innovations useful in a specific local situation. If they could be adapted to another local situation, fine. That would be up to the local people.

The main object of new policies would be to get the government away from the vertical division of labor and the hierarchical control implicit in the RD&D paradigm. There are any number of policies that might accomplish this, but they should be evaluated against a set of criteria. Generally new research and development policies should:

Avoid a hierarchical division of labor. This makes some people active and some passive, some autonomous and some dependent; some the actor, some the spectator. A small group doing all the research, development, and inventing means less diversity, and, I shall contend in the next chapter, great inequities. Inventing, research, and development activities should be spread around.

Result in a distribution rather than concentration of resources. It is highly unlikely that one R&D center with $800,000 would be as productive as eight centers with $100,000. Even if it were, the gain in pluralism and autonomy would be very great with more centers. Generally, decreasing the gap between those who have the resources and those who have not is a good idea and also has practical payoff. Only hierarchical control is facilitated the other way.

Pursue distributed rather than central goals. The individual child should be seen as the recipient of educational services. Goals for education to bolster the national defense or alleviate poverty distort the focus of the educational process and are impossible to accomplish if not suspicious in intent. Distributed goals depend on local determinants and have consequences for local personnel. Distributed goals such as teaching a particular child to read can only be achieved within specific contexts. There are no ulterior purposes.

Feature the individual child, parent, and teacher as the client rather than the government agency. The client is not standardized so that all will be well served by a single innovation. The clients should be seen as extremely diverse and having many different needs. When the agency becomes the client for the innovation, as well as the sponsor, a predictable set of standardized values emerge. They are not the values of a pluralistic clientele.

Avoid the primary pursuit of transferable innovations. Distributed problems cannot be solved by a single solution or a single innovation. There is no single innovation that will work in all local settings, for those settings are not only different and unpredictable in specifics, but they are also constantly changing. There is no doubt that some innovations, like textbooks or the chalkboard, are useful in many settings (given the knowledgeable actors and the social situations in which they are used) and that an innovation like PLATO will combine some of the good features of both of these. PLATO will not, however, solve reading problems any better than the chalkboard or the textbook. Different innovations will be more or less useful under widely different specific circumstances of their application. There is no Golden Fleece.

Avoid establishing or relying on common measures of payoff. One of the most ingrained notions in liberal social policy is the belief that there is a single measure of value. In education this is often assumed to be achievement scores. In economics it is the gross national product. If there are distributed goals and diverse clientele, there can be no single measure of worth, for what is good for one group may not be good for another. Increases in the GNP do not necessarily benefit all. Aggregate value increases cannot be assumed to benefit all. There can be many measures of value but not even the value of distribution itself is an adequate measure by itself. Policy that tries to maximize one aggregate value is policy pursued in the interest of one faction at the expense of others.

Determine the success of government policies by independent, diverse, and honest evaluations of specific projects. Sooner or later social science must move away from abstract and predictive theories to specific explanations of concrete social phenomena. Rather than try to predict success a priori based on a hopelessly inadequate experimental research design, a more practical and theoretically sound procedure is to look at the actual manifestations of the project. Of course, the criteria for success will vary from group to group and time to time.

Share control of the entire innovation process with those engaged in it and most affected by it. Although almost always contained in the program's ideology, this safeguard is almost never carried out. Most policies are controlled by the few people running the program, and only symbolic participation is allowed. In fact, the prime consideration of past policies seems to be that the government group retain complete control whatever the consequences.

Generally new policies should be aimed at increasing personal contact and providing adequate resources, particularly time, to those close to the problems. I am not suggesting turning over the money entirely to local agencies. That would simply mean that the money would be spent by the local establishment on current demands, probably to lower property taxes. Money should be ear-marked for innovation, used for innovative projects, and monitored as such, though the monitoring should be less strict than it is now.

One way of meeting most of the criteria presented here is to undertake smaller projects. Relieving the projects of having to produce transferable results or materials means more effort can be used to attack specific local problems. Of course, this means that there must be very large numbers of such projects if they are to have significant impact. The grandiose projects on which federal bureaucrats have built their careers, and which inevitably collapse under their own weight after a few years, should be relics of the past. There might be need for some large projects, but such projects should grow out of specific and smaller circumstances and be closely examined before expansion.

Many small grants ranging from ten to fifty thousand dollars could produce much more in the way of innovations and ideas than the heavy concentration of funds that now exists. That even limited resources cannot be abundantly sprinkled over the landscape of the country in smaller amounts simply indicates the current low level of government funding for research, development, and innovation. Smaller amounts of money given for longer, multiyear time periods would enable one to come to grips with a problem rather than having to scurry to spend funds in an annual potlatch. The smaller amounts should be more productive, even at current funding levels. Any stability in the project's life would be helpful, though that is not likely to be assured.

It is also imperative that the innovations not be dictated from above or approved by committees far removed from the actual problems, as in the NIE "field-initiated" research program. In spite of the advertising, such programs are always trimmed, pushed, and selected for the "national interest." There is no reason for projects devoted to solving local educational problems or inventing local innovations to be so shaped. What might be appropriate would be the stimulus of experts acting in certain areas or communication among people working on similar problems. Existing institutions like the regional laboratories should be given much more freedom in defining problems in terms of their clientele, rather than in terms of Washington. The larger projects should still be extensively evaluated, of course.

Such policies would produce more, and more diverse, innovation that would be better adjusted to the local situation. Concentration of innovation resources has meant that only certain kinds of standardized innovations are produced under government control. The parallel with economic development in foreign countries may be an apt one.

In economic development there has been little emphasis on small-scale entrepreneurism, although, according to a report from the 12th World Conference of the Society for International Development (1971), there is little evidence that small-scale agricultural operations are less productive than large ones, although they are much less capital-intensive. It has been assumed that "big" is good, and few resources are channeled to new entrepreneurs.

Policies have continually separated production from distribution. Less than 2 percent of R&D expenditures are in developing countries; new technologies are imported. The focus in economic development has been on gross national products, and the result has been increased poverty. According to the report, there are two major false steps in such development. The first step involves the focus on per capita income as the aggregate measure of wealth, worrying about how much is produced and how fast it is produced rather than what is produced and how it is distributed.

The second mistake is to assume that income distribution policies can be divorced from growth policies. Once production is organized to exclude large numbers of people and support a technological elite, which is the pattern in most countries, it becomes impossible to redistribute income to those not participating. According to some observers, the first badly needed paved roads in developing countries are usually built from the capital to the airport so that the elite will have some place to drive a Mercedes. It becomes impossible to convert luxury cars and houses to low-cost housing and buses. The pattern of consumption and distribution of goods is built into the pattern of production.

According to the report, economic development should be defined as a selective attack on poverty rather than an increase in the gross national product with the assumption that the benefits will be for everyone. Developing countries should define threshold consumption standards and get away from the "demand" concept, which distorts consumption in favor of the "haves." Mainly production and distribution must be combined. One country has shown the fallacy of the belief that poverty and unemployment can be eliminated only by high growth rates over many decades—China.

Educational and economic development are not precisely parallel, but there is considerable merit in the idea that the production and distribution of new technologies should be much more closely interconnected than is now the case. The creation of context-specific innovations is likely to be more relevant and much more deeply implemented and accepted than externally invented innovations. Small-scale entrepreneurism would be one way of attacking the problem.

No doubt other policies would also meet the criteria that I have outlined, probably better ones. This policy direction does break away from past federal efforts in supporting development of local R&D capacity, drawing R&D away from nationally defined problems, and relating R&D to the ultimate clients.

I have citied these examples to indicate that it is possible, though not easy, to break away somewhat from the old conceptual sterotypes. But I do not really expect such bold departures to be taken by the federal bureaucracy. They are dominated by powerful societal forces.

Chapter 9

The Political Economy of Innovation

MODERNIZING EDUCATION

What is the political import of the educational innovations that are being developed and disseminated today? Travers, a noted educational psychologist and editor of the *Second Handbook of Research on Teaching* (1973), has assessed the impact of modern educational technology, especially that emanating from the sponsorship of the federal government. He traces the idea of an educational technology back to the writings of Pressey, who in 1932 envisioned an industrial revolution in education that would parallel the significance of the industrial revolution that occurred in manufacturing. Pressey saw the revolution to be a mechanical one involving the introduction of machinery into the teaching process, just as machinery had been introduced into manufacturing.

Pressey also saw the technology as being based on scientific knowledge, a theme later amplified by B. F. Skinner, who thought the science of learning had advanced to the point where it could be used as a guide in the development of such technology. He saw a body of psychological knowledge waiting to be applied, and he did not view the "technical" problem of providing the instruments as being particularly difficult. Pressey viewed the schools as needing the efficiency of a factory; Skinner saw the school as needing more effective control over behavior. Travers, for his part, saw the development of technology until modern times as independent of scientific knowledge.

Travers feels that government sponsorship of educational research and development has been based on the approaches of Pressey and Skinner. As far back as 1954, the Cooperative Research Act implied that, with the development of knowledge and demonstrations of that knowledge, there could be an industrial revolution in education. The Elementary and Secondary Education Act of 1965 indicated that much more was needed—a network of laboratories and centers that would build and disseminate the new technology. The R&D laboratories were set up with little thought about the best conditions for development and no thought for the possibility that the new technology might have detrimental side effects.

The research and development centers were seen as the sources of packaged technology, and the regional laboratories were viewed as dissemination centers for the technology. (See the discussion of the research, development, diffusion paradigm in Chapter 8.) These organizations quickly turned to operant psychology as the basis for development. The blue ribbon committees that established such programs lived in an age when it was believed that the development of a technology was necessarily beneficial.

Travers, in reviewing the histories of technology, concludes as a general principle that the development of any technology is closely related to the ruling class by whom it is sponsored. For example, innovations related to the horse enhanced the power of European nobility in the Middle Ages. The horseshoe protected the animal in damp soil, and the stirrup enabled a warrior to swing a sword from his horse without falling off so that cavalry became a major source of power for many years. Technological developments that benefited the peasants developed apart from those that benefited the nobility. In fact, breeding horses for warfare made them useless for farming. Only centuries later did the use of the horse become widespread in agriculture. The barbarians invented the harness, and that, in combination with the iron plow, revolutionized food production.

Travers concludes that, when technology is sponsored by the government or group in power, it tends to develop only those ideas that are of particular value to the power group. Printing was seized upon by the church to consolidate its power by exercising control over ideas disseminated. The church's power, which eventually paralleled that of the nobility, was, in turn, eroded through use of the printing press. Power groups have always exploited technology as a source of political power.

Turning to government-sponsored educational technology, Travers sees its purpose as achieving the traditional goals of education more efficiently in educating more people at less cost. Government agencies saw the problems of society as produced by the inability of certain groups to fit the cultural pattern approved by the majority-elected government. Schools had failed to produce the uniform pattern of behavior that would lead minority groups to the majority's concept of the civilized life. The new technology was expected to provide more effective education for the same expenditure, or the same quality of education for less expenditure. (Note the emphasis on increasing per capita productivity.) Educational technology was focused on what the power structure viewed as threats to the status quo, as earlier technologies had been. The goal was to maintain the status quo.

The machinery of education reform modeled itself after industrial enterprises and sought to change the school by delivering packaged products. Machinery already existed for delivering such materials. Travers believes that there are political messages implicit in the materials themselves. For example, reviewing *The Alaskan Readers* (Portland, Oregon: Northwest Regional Educational Laboratory, 1970), Travers looks at the materials teaching traditional academic skills to minority groups. While technically competent, they are much like the "Dick and Jane"-type readers. "The materials are developed upon the assumption that if minority groups can be trained to fit into the system all will be well." This contrasts with developing materials that might help a child grapple actively with his own environment.

The materials developed are usually escapist, recreational, and based on a step-by-step analysis of so-called "basic skills." It is assumed that the basic skills will always be basic, and the only problem is how to teach such skills effectively. Improvement is in terms of time and cost. Travers sees technology as promoting the skills needed by workers to run an industrialized society. The materials concentrate on stimulus control of behavior similar to that in an assembly line. He defines government-sponsored technology as "inevitably conservative, cost-conscious, blind to the social issues of the day, and creative only within very narrow limits."

Travers sees the trend of current technology as bringing the student under identifiable stimulus control and inducing a passive acceptance of control such as is needed in the industrial system. Curricula like Individually Prescribed Instruction allow pupils to make only trivial decisions, stifling autonomy. School programs are designed to teach children to become passively controlled by their circumstances, and the effects of treating a child as a manipulatable object go unexamined. The choice of operant psychology as a set of guiding principles was not, Travers thinks, accidental. Operant psychology is very close to the assumptions of a capitalistic society. The scientists have formed an alliance with government powers. Even so, the connections between new materials and research are often difficult to discern. Most educational products of the regional laboratories result from a systematic analysis of the problem rather than being a product of scientific analysis.

Travers concludes that knowledge is not there waiting to be used: "Uses of knowledge have to be invented by persons of genius." Government agencies have chosen materials that reflect their own concern and bias and then tried to find applications for them, choices that have little to recommend them. "The formula involving discovery, then application, and finally dissemination has little rationale to it."

If anything, pressures toward industrialization of education have intensified since Travers' analysis. As noted, Patrick E. Haggerty, Chairman of the Advisory Board of the National Institute of Education and head of a highly technological industrial empire, has called for increases in educational productivity in the strongest terms. This productivity can be accomplished by the use of complex technology, by shifting part of the educative function to corporations, and by making training much more job related. This would do away with many unnecessary, nonjob-oriented frills. The federal bureaucracy has put heavy emphasis on "career education" and such efficiency-oriented reforms as competency-based education, which divides education into component parts so it can be achieved more efficiently. A high priority of the research program of the National Institute of Education is to find new ways of reducing educational costs and to support the development of new educational technologies.

One such scheme has been suggested by a former deputy assistant secretary at the Department of Health, Education, and Welfare, now director of research for the National Center for Resource Recovery, Inc. Abert (1974) directly calls for the industrialization of education.

There are some lessons to be learned from industry here. In fact, it is clearly time that educators look at education as an industry and start to speak of the effects of shifting such ratios as capital to labor and output to labor. These are important variables in industrial planning. The proposals advanced here call for capitalizing the education system—that is, "putting tools in their hands"—and for radically shifting the structure of the labor force.

Abert calls for the funding of experimental school programs to vary the costs of education in order to determine the effects of various kinds of arrangements. Education as an enterprise must compete with other industries for a share of the gross national product. In fact, education must learn to live within its share of the national income.

Being more labor-intensive than manufacturing, education must constantly exert a claim for a proportionately larger share of national income to maintain wage parity with manufacturing. To improve its position relative to manufacturing requires an even larger diversion of resources from the rest of society to education.

Abert suggests two classic strategies for reducing costs. The first is to follow the lead of manufacturing industries by substituting capital for labor. Of course, the substitution of machines and tools for labor means that there will be fewer laborers, as Abert points out. The savings come because capital for financing the machines is cheaper than labor.

The second alternative is to vary the "labor mix," putting large numbers of employees at the low end of the wage scale and hence holding down the average wage. This could be done by hiring students, retirees, and housewives to teach. As Abert notes, the "cheaper" people cannot receive compensation on the scale of certified teachers for that would be self-defeating. Pay should be determined by supply and demand.

Varying the labor force mix, the second strategy suggested, is also designed to live within education's means, when those means are defined as being roughly proportional to education's traditional share of the available national income, and when it is assumed that this share of the pie, while likely to rise absolutely, will not rise relative to the share of other claimants.

For Abert, the question is whether the substitution of capital and hence the substitution of innovations in the form of machines "coupled with the potential to continue to upgrade and increase the financial returns for the managers of the educational enterprise, detracts, holds even, or perhaps even enhances educational outcomes."

Abert's proposal is only one of the more recent and explicit ones for transforming education into a "modern" enterprise. In a society dominated by industrialism, technology, and bureaucracy—a technocratic society—the pressures for "modernizing" education are bound to be powerful, particularly from the technocratic national elite who govern the society (whether American, Russian, or European) and consequently from the federal government itself, as suggested by Travers.

In the United States, in particular, the additional powerful force of private capitalism must be added. Private profit is still potent as motivation and symbol in American society. It is significant that both the chairman of the NIE and Abert, as well as many other modernization advocates, come from private rather than public institutions. Nor is it unusual for them to circulate back and forth between the federal government and private enterprises.

Most of the pressures to make schools adopt innovations (not to invent themselves) are intended to transform the school into a "modern" structure and integrate it more fully and effectively within the larger technocratic society. In fact, the school itself is a relatively "traditional" structure. In spite of many bureaucratic trappings, it has strong nonbureaucratic elements, particularly manifested in the work behavior of the teacher (Dreeben, 1973; Lortie, 1973). The teacher's behavior is learned by imitation and tradition and, in spite of a large hierarchy of administrators, it is not effectively controlled by hierarchic decisions.

Teachers do not teach in accord with system-wide rules; nor is the "quality control" over teacher behavior strong. The lack of susceptibility to higher influence contrasts vividly with that most modern of work places—the assembly line. Neither, on the other hand, are teachers autonomous professionals who manage their own affairs. As indicated in this book, teachers lack the power of initiation and the conditions necessary for invention and innovation on their own.

Resistance to innovations (more accurately to the adoption of certain types of innovations) as portrayed here is characteristic of a "traditional" society as opposed to a "modernistic" one. In fact, the distinction between "modernistic" and "traditional" societies is drawn between those societies that will accept innovations propagated by a third (more modern) party and those that will not. As one of the leading scholars of innovation diffusion defines it,

Modernization is defined as the process by which individuals change from a traditional way of life to a more complex, technologically advanced, and rapidly changing style of life. This is best indicated by an individual's use of new ideas in agriculture, health, family living, and other fields [Rogers and Shoemaker, 1971].

Some demands for educational reforms are for "demodernizing" schools, for "humanizing" them, especially the demands of the so-called educational romantics like Holt and those in the alternative-school movement who believe schools are already too bureaucratized and inhumane. Some advocates of alternative schooling are not in the counterculture movement, and it is easy to tell the difference, for the latter are well funded and supported by powerful sponsors while the romantics are not. Innovations like desegregation (or the appearance of it) are relatively well sponsored for reasons to be discussed later in this chapter. Overall public demands for change have not been given much coverage here. Part of the reason is the observation that general public demands do not have much lasting impact unless manifested in powerful institutional sponsors. Where are student demands for decision power in the university now, and where will they be five years hence? In fact, powerful institutional sponsors normally precede public demand and work to foment it, as in the "accountability" movement.

Only innovations that are persistently and aggressively sponsored by powerful institutional forces have much chance of long-range effects. In the United States the powerful institutions are obviously technocratic, particularly economic and industrial ones. Innovations that have been aggressively pursued are those that offer solutions to threats posed to the national interest, which should perhaps be read as national elite. As I indicated in the chapter on government policy, over the last decade these have included threats to national technological supremacy, the reduction of internal racial conflict, and now increased educational productivity. The first threat was posed by the Russians and resulted in the National Defense Education Act; the second, by the racial minorities, resulted in Title I and other compensatory programs; the third, by the organization of teachers to obtain their expanding share of the gross national product, resulted in a growing concern for accountability and productivity. True to the nature of the dominant institutions, the innovative solutions have been technological.

The overall societal import and pressure is far more profound, however. It is the conversion of education from a semitraditional to a modernistic structure. In a traditional structure the status quo is maintained by the static nature of custom and history. *The basic fact about a technocratic structure is that the status quo is maintained by constant innovation.* Of course, changes must be of a very particular kind, externally invented and propagated by the major technocratic institutions themselves. Otherwise, the societal order could be disrupted. While it is easy to preceive the status quo in a traditional structure, the status quo of modernistic society is not so easy to discern because constant innovation holds a strange fascination. But for society as a whole these are changes of content, not of structure. Innovations allowable within that structure have very definite limits.

What does a technocratic order gain by transforming education into a more modern institution receptive to externally produced innovations? Travers (1973) mentions two benefits. One is to make education more efficient and more productive so that it will cost less. Reduction in overall costs can be accomplished by packaged technology. A second benefit is that the materials and equipment of such a technology can carry conservative political messages, either explicitly or implicitly, that favor those in power. According to Travers, such innovations have tried to fit minorities into the system. The innovations can help train students to run an industrialized society, which Travers believes they do. The effect is to bring the student under control and to induce passive acceptance of such control.

Two other benefits should be mentioned in addition to those cited by Travers. If the school becomes receptive to a constant stream of innovations, each replacing the last and each an "improvement," one has created an eternal market for innovative products. To a certain extent this market already exists for textbooks, and, indeed, most innovations have consisted of new packages of materials the school must buy. But textbooks and materials represent a small portion of the educational budget. More then 80 percent of educational costs are for personnel. One can no longer buy and sell new people. In a labor intensive enterprise like education, therefore, one must convert the funding to materials, equipment, and machines if one is to realize that vast potential.

A textbook may cost only five dollars, but a PLATO terminal costs a thousand times as much. The market opened up by conversion from a labor-intensive to a capital-intensive enterprise staggers the imagination, as the president of IBM has said. So far, no industry has been able to take full advantage of the potential because of the way the money is now spent. But modernization of the schools will make them receptive to successive waves of capital-intensive innovation. Of course, the industrial machinery is well suited to exploit such a market. If one buys PLATO IV, can PLATO V be far behind?

The fourth advantage to modernizing education is less obvious, but it is at least as important as the first three. Modernization makes education as an institution dependent on those who can supply the innovations. Innovation becomes necessary for success and even for survival. The institution, unable to create its own innovations, must purchase them from external sources, whatever the price and whatever the content. Education thus becomes much more dependent on external controls—on those who control the flow of innovations. As of now, some traditional school defense postures resist external influence.

The sum total of pursuing innovation in this manner is that education becomes far more efficiently and effectively (and dependently) integrated into the technocratic structures of the society. The dominant institutions, industrial and economic, can contain rapidly increasing educational expenditures within the current education share of the gross national product. These institutions can make a great deal of money by inventing, manufacturing, and selling capital-intensive innovation to the schools. This is not only highly profitable in and of itself, but it provides a huge market for which much larger-scale technological innovations can be produced. The latter means maintaining a technological advantage over international competition in high-technology areas like computers.

In addition, the materials produced are designed to teach job skills, attitudes, and beliefs necessary to work in an industrial society without either the cost or the threat of teaching extraneous knowledge. As an institution, education would be much more dependent and under control. During the 1960's there was some restiveness within education on the part of both students and teachers. Colleges were the first to break the solid institutional facade, although reluctantly, over the issue of the Vietnamese War. As harbingers of some traditional values, they are sometimes archaic and out of step with modern society although they remain vital to it. Modernization will remedy that.

To the extent that this analysis of the political economy of educational innovation at the societal level is correct, innovations propagated strongly by major societal sponsors will have a distinctive set of features. To the extent that government policies reflect the goals of the national elite, so will government-sponsored innovations.

INNOVATION IN A TECHNOCRATIC SOCIETY

What is the overall function of innovation in a modernized industrial system? To increase productivity. Some economists believe that innovation is the lifeblood of industrialized society, whether it be capitalist or communist. One interesting analysis is provided by Janossy (1971). Observing that the "productivity trend line" rises at a constant rate within each industrialized country, except for the duration of major disruptions like wars, Janossy argues that increases in labor productivity depend on the rate at which innovations can be absorbed by the working population.

Increased labor productivity can be accomplished only by a qualitative transformation in the concrete labor activity itself. For example, the increase in labor productivity gained from using horses in agriculture to using tractors necessarily entails a qualitative change in methods of working. Driving a tractor is quite different from driving a team of horses. While driving a tractor may be no more difficult, in fact not as difficult, it requires that the worker learn new skills. "Progress," then, the base of the industrial society, depends on the invention of new innovations and on diffusing them widely before productivity gains can be realized.

In a capitalist society analyzing the cost of producing the innovation is often subsumed under the investment of capital. The utility of the innovation for the entrepreneur is that it gives him a temporary edge in obtaining extra profit. By being the first to employ the innovation, he can increase his productivity over that of his competitors, an advantage that exists, however, only until the competitors also employ the labor-saving technique. Then everyone is on an equal footing, and, if the entrepreneur is to maintain an advantage, he must find another innovation. Overall, then, productivity is increased as an unintentional side effect of trying to maximize profit derived from investment.

Janossy notes that it is easy to believe that economic development depends on the availability of appropriate research findings, but this is only partially true. Productivity depends on the realization of these research findings in production—quite a different proposition. Accordingly, the tempo of economic development depends on the speed of the innovation's diffusion and implementation. Diffusion of innovations depends on many factors I have discussed earlier.

Innovation, then, requires the qualitative transformation of saving labor. The "saving" of human labor, according to Janossy, is both the purpose for, and the result of, the diffusion of innovations and, hence, the driving force of the process. Resistance to the innovation resides in the fact that concrete activity must be transformed, and the amount of energy and time required for this individual relearning process is a measure of the resistance. It is, in fact, resistance to the transformation of labor that regulates the rate of diffusion and, consequently, the rate of economic development. The more different the activities of the traditional work mode and that of the innovation, the greater the resistance.

In this view, then, economic development depends on the qualitative transformation of concrete activity. The knowledge generated in the research and development process reaches the worker in the form of formal education, training manuals, on-the-job training, and operation of the innovation itself. The collective knowledge of society grows enormously, but individual knowledge merely changes. The worker may actually be performing a simpler job than that performed by a serf many years ago although the total knowledge of the society has been increased. Much of the worker's skill is "taught" to him by the means of production itself.

The eventual result of such processes is the structural transformation of knowledge and the structural transformation of the labor force, a result of the division of labor. In a more primitive division of labor, the craftsman or peasant had a holistic picture of the production process, and an important part of technical knowledge is transferred through the means of production. No matter what the preparation, one learns to drive a car by driving it. The critical lack of the means of production leads to the mistaken impression that perfecting machinery is the primary factor of economic development instead of only one important link, according to Janossy.

During the industrial revolution the most immediate effect of a radical division of labor was to degrade unskilled labor to tending machines, a level far below that of earlier manufacture so that the tasks could be, and were, performed by children. Even at that time, however, the control and repair of the machines depended on highly skilled workers. Early workers were tied to their vocations for life, locked in by their accumulated skills. Only with the entry of the machine did training reach such a low level that there arose a vocationless, unskilled stratum of workers who could be employed anywhere because they had no vocational skills. They did not need to be retrained and never hampered productive capacity. It was this aspect of industrial development that contributed to the misconception that progress was independent of workers and their skills. The more that job skill demands complex activity, the more it requires true vocations, and the more economic development depends on the labor force.

Changes in vocational structure and skills can be achieved only when new workers replace those leaving the labor force or when those who remain must be reeducated and retrained. In either case, the vocational structure itself becomes a major impediment to innovation and, hence, to economic development. Janossy defines *vocation as the totality of all the innate and acquired abilities required for the performance of a certain activity*, not simply what a man happens to be doing at the moment. Vocation is the concrete activity for which he is best qualified by knowledge and skill. One who "possesses" a vocation has something to lose. Whoever loses the possibility of using some of his capabilities by being forced to perform some activity other than that for which he is best qualified is losing something real. The "vocational structure" is the composition of a country's total labor force defined by vocations and the number in them.

The crux of Janossy's argument is that economic development can occur only to the extent that the vocational structure changes; hence, *vocational structure is the prime determiner of productivity increases, although these may be mediated by changes in the means of production*. As mentioned, the vocational structure changes by the training or retraining of those already in the vocation or by entry of newcomers into it. Retraining is the more difficult process. Not only does relearning require "unlearning" old habits and techniques, but the older work force is likely to be less interested in new techniques. This is partly because learning becomes more difficult at a later age and partly because older workers have less to gain by learning new techniques. How long will a sixty-year-old have to use a new technique? It is not profitable for him to invest much time in learning one. Certainly some sixty-year-olds will feel that it is worthwhile, but most will be less enthusiastic than thirty-year-olds.

The process of innovation and economic development, then, makes the worker's skills increasingly obsolescent. The faster the pace of innovation and development, the faster the obsolescence. *The process of innovation requires that workers not use acquired knowledge and skills, but continually learn new ones.* This becomes less profitable for the individual as time goes on, as well as more difficult. Even highly developed skills become obsolescent. While the handloom may be thrown away, the handweaver cannot be. The handweaver retains his knowledge and skill, but, if the value of it decreases, he may have to perform simple, unskilled labor. This is not a happy prospect for any rational person concerned about his own welfare.

Only by acquiring a new vocation or new skills can the worker raise the value of his labor, but this becomes more difficult with advancing age. The total of one's accumulated knowledge is lost in such a change, and the labor required to learn increases with age (as anyone knows who has played memory games with his young children). The number of years one may apply the new knowledge also declines, making the learning investment less worthwhile for economic reasons. These forces intensify vocational bondage and make the given labor supply the primary regulator in economic development. The labor supply keeps changes in the vocational structure within narrow limits.

An interesting sidelight on this is reflected in the transformation of the research findings themselves into a commodity value. Increased research continually makes earlier research and those who know the old research obsolescent. For example, in educational research multivariate statistics are slowly replacing analyses employing fewer variables. Whatever their merits, multivariate techniques tend to make obsolescent those who harbor older knowledge, primarily older researchers. Most researchers, unless they are young or ambitious, do not find it worthwhile to master multivariate statistics.

Only a few senior professors grapple with the relearning, although it is not too demanding. The complaint against multivariate techniques—no one understands them—is defensive as well as accurate.

Yet statistics is conveyed through formal coursework, with the older generation teaching the younger one. Most statistics courses teach the older body of knowledge, with perhaps a few multivariate courses tacked on at the end of the sequence. One or a few professors, propagators of the techniques, teach multivariate statistics to a few advanced graduate students. Other researchers must learn the techniques by working on a specific problem related to their work, perhaps with a knowledgeable colleague or graduate student, or not learn them at all. Even the most brilliant older researchers usually do not find the relearning worthwhile. They have more pressing things to do.

Even in branches of labor which specialize in research and learning, people become obsolescent, and the vocational structure changes very slowly. Sometimes whole vocations are affected. Janossy estimates that, calculating entries and exits, most vocations can only change at a maximum rate of about 10 percent a year. Assuming that employees in a given vocational branch are distributed in a normal age distribution at the beginning of a vocation's decline, its complete demise could still take forty years. The existing age distribution in a vocation has much to do with capacity for change. Age distribution and entry into a vocation are determined by many factors over a great period of time. The continual obsolescence of the individual in modern society is tempered by the inertia of the vocational structure itself.

In precapitalist society technical knowledge and the means of production were both harmonious and stagnant. Improvement in production was hampered by traditional work methods, and change in work methods was hampered because the means of production passed from father to son. With the beginnings of wage labor, the self-contained circle was opened up by separating the means of production from the worker. The owner of the means of production, the capitalist, changed and perfected it in his own competitive drive for profit. At the same time he "robbed" the worker of his sole possession of value—his knowledge and skill—forcing the worker not only to work more, as the feudal lord did, but also to work differently. In so doing, some contend the worker was robbed of his dignity.

The structure of the means of production was several steps ahead of the structure of labor power, forcing individuals to learn and relearn. People are forced to run to expand their outdated knowledge to change their activity, to create better production equipment, and to perpetuate the compulsion for learning. It is this tension that provides the atmosphere for modern industrial society, whether capitalist or communist. While increasing labor productivity, it also produces personal tension. As Brecht notes in *Threepenny Opera,* "Everyone runs after happiness, but happiness runs behind."

The actual accumulation of the means of production, the totality of all available means of production that makes possible the performance of only certain concrete activities. Janossy calls the "workplace structure." The tension between the workplace structure (the jobs available) and the vocational structure (the skills of the workers) promotes the tension that forces workers to change. Shifts between these structures are reflected in the supply and demand of different types of workers and wages that fluctuate accordingly. As long as the production processes run smoothly, it appears that all depends on the machines themselves. When machines break down, however, it is clear that vocations are required.

In a capitalist society the process is motivated by the drive for surplus profit. The entrepreneur is interested only in increasing his productivity vis-a-vis his competitor. To the entrepreneur it appears that his means of production are the controlling force, while the vocational structure is only a labor pool upon which he can draw without limit. Only when the workplace structure gets too far ahead of the vocation structure does the binding relationship become apparent. The entrepreneur concentrates on replacing and perfecting his equipment. When tension becomes too great and rate of change is too rapid, the vocational structure offers not only inertia but positive and increasing resistance.

Janossy contends that, because of the regulation of the tempo of economic development by the vocational structure, an intensified rate of investment cannot accelerate development except in an extreme case. Only when investments serve to train the labor force can increased investment accelerate development. Plant and equipment put to use by untrained workers leads to inefficient utilization and premature obsolescence of the machinery, an unprofitable investment. Only "unprofitable" investment in the training of workers pays off.

In a capitalist system this avenue is generally closed to the entrepreneur. He owns the equipment, but not the workers, so improving their skills does not pay off unless he can tie the improvement to his enterprise. In Japan this is done by establishing a lifelong relationship with the workers. Otherwise, the government must pay for the training. For example, the Soviet Union forced the mechanization of agriculture by turning over tractors and farm equipment to unskilled workers. The workers wore them out prematurely, but learned in the process. In this case, investment becomes education. This investment accelerates change in the vocational structure. Often the individual must bear the brunt of his increased obsolescence without retraining. At best there is a limit to which even "unprofitable" investment in education and retraining pays off and, hence, a limit to the rate of economic development. Outlay for "unprofitable" investment must eventually affect the standard of living.

The country at the pinnacle of industrial development, the United States, must create its own innovations, but developing countries can profit from those already invented. The less developed the country, however, the greater the inertia of the vocational structure. The "center" of development diffuses its innovations to lower levels of development. In a country with the highest level of development *the state of the means of production is determined both by the ability of the workers to master the new processes and by their ability to create new materials.* In developing countries the second bond can be loosened by importing innovations. If the tie to the vocational structure is overlooked or underemphasized, it appears falsely that in highly developed countries economic development depends solely on research and development, and in developing countries it depends solely on importing the means of production.

To what extent does educational innovation fit the general pattern of industrial innovation? It would seem that educational innovation also requires a qualitative transformation in concrete behavior. Programming a PLATO terminal is quite different from delivering a lecture before a class. Some people also see an innovation like PLATO as reducing costs. Certainly many observers would see innovations as reducing costs by replacing teachers, by reducing the labor-intensive nature of education. Interestingly, most teachers are reluctant to reduce the human contact nature of education. Even those concerned with PLATO see it as a supplement to regular instruction, not a replacement for it. As a supplement to regular teaching, while it might enhance effectiveness, PLATO would cost more rather than less. Only as a replacement is it cheaper.

Although we have noted that entrepreneurism plays a critical role in educational innovation, the competitive element is not quite as strong as in the industrial world—a lack that some people lament. Neither, of course, does the entrepreneur own the means of production. It is clear that there is quite a distinction between developing innovations and realizing their implementation. The vocational structure of education is a powerful force in determining the rate of innovation. One might regard federal efforts at establishing the research, development, diffusion paradigms as an attempt to force innovation upon the schools, separating the development of innovations from the hands of the teachers and putting the teachers into the position of workers forced to relearn or to become obsolescent.

That relearning may be painful is eloquently expressed by teachers involved in learning TUTOR. Both the expense and pain of this relearning were greatly underestimated by the sponsors. As Janossy suggests, the sponsors of innovations often forget the link to the vocational structure and believe that the only impediment to innovation is the availability of innovations made accessible through development or diffusion. All innovations from the new math to PLATO seem to follow the same path of introducing materials or equipment, being surprised by misuse or nonuse, and then resorting to retraining as a frantic effort.

With PLATO even those teachers previously trained in computer languages and mathematics, although most successful, experienced considerable difficulty. The training proved to be inadequate, even the more intensive training. Estimates by the most competent author that it took him eight or nine months to become truly proficient suggests the magnitude of the task. If resistance in innovation is proportional to change in the traditional work mode, resistance to PLATO will be strong indeed. There are several ways around this problem. One is to provide better and much more extensive training, with appropriate rewards for undertaking it. Another is to train people in the simpler techniques of using preprogrammed materials. This would reduce the flexibility and attractiveness of the machine, but it would greatly simplify the amount of training necessary. The PLATO project had already moved in this direction. A third alternative would be to train young people, probably at the undergraduate level. Not only do they learn more easily, but it is a better economic investment for them, particularly as it gives them an edge in the job market in future years. It was the younger, more ambitious members of the faculty who were most enthusiastic about PLATO in the community colleges. For successful diffusion PLATO terminals would have to be set up in workplace structures to provide incentive and on-the-job training.

Like other workers, teachers face the problem of becoming obsolescent with increased innovation, although not to the same extent. It would also seem that piecemeal analysis of their jobs, as in competency-based instruction, could lead to breaking a relatively complex job into component parts that could result in a downgrading of skills similar to what occurs on the assembly line in the industrial process. This line of development results from overemphasizing materials and machines and underemphasizing vocational skills. There does seem to be an expectation on the part of many developers, and one expressed in the RD&D paradigm, that teachers are very pliable and plastic and should adjust to any teaching mode. Only a few years ago there was talk of "teacher-proof" materials. As those developers found out, however, this resulted in an overemphasis on the means of production.

Janossy also implies that there is a limit as to how fast the vocational structure of education can change. As a whole, a 10 percent change per year would be a maximum estimate. Change depends, however, on the age distribution of the vocational structure. Since education experienced a growth boom in the 1950's and 1960's, many new people were added; now teaching jobs are hard to find. Over the next several years few new people will be entering the vocation, and the total group will grow older. This portends less innovation in education. The fight for availability of jobs at the beginning level may make beginning teachers more receptive to new techniques, but there will be fewer of them in the total structure.

The modern teacher, like the modern worker, does not control the "means of production" nor the means of improving production. Like his worker counterpart, he is committed to working a full week without the time or resources to invent his own innovations. Whether he could develop his own innovations has never been answered, for it has not been tried. There are some indications that he could. In any case the decision has been made for him. He finds himself in his classroom with his textbook or other materials, and he is treated like and perceived as a possible consumer. His position is quite analogous to that of the worker. As demonstrated repeatedly in this book, the teacher is perceived as being at the bottom or next to the bottom of his own chain of being—the research, development, diffusion paradigm, usually administered through the offices of the federal government. Innovations flow down the chain to him, and he is expected to implement them. To do so requires a great deal of sacrifice and effort on his part, with little chance of reward. The flow of innovations makes him obsolescent or tries to. To the extent that he implements them, it is usually through the services of an educational entrepreneur.

As in the industrial setting, the vocational structure is treated as a passive, elastic labor pool that is noticed only when it refuses to cooperate. An intensified rate of investment in new innovations has resulted in many untested innovations, that have not been implemented. Only the "unprofitable" investment of extensive retraining seems to accelerate change. But putting emphasis on the R&D end of the paradigm neglects training. Like the worker, the teacher is often expected to bear the brunt of obsolescence on his own. As one PLATO teacher said, "'They' act as if we are improving ourselves rather than the educational system, and we are expected to pay for it." One difference between workers and teachers is that teachers have not faced the same coercive situation faced by the workers who have no choice but to implement. As professionals, teachers have more control over their workplace, the classroom. Yet there is much activity, such as accountability schemes, performance contracting, and educational vouchers, that would bring more coercive instruments to bear.

In summary, then, an innovation is a change in concrete activity in a technocratic society. Such change increases productivity either by increasing effectiveness or by reducing cost. It is a major engine of economic development, the major focus of an industrialized society. Education is subject to forces similar to those that promote innovation in the industrial sector.

ECONOMIC DEVELOPMENT AND HIERARCHY

What are the effects of increasing the economic productivity of education by diffusing successive sets of innovations? I noted some effects of the urban hierarchy on educational innovation diffusion earlier (see Chapter 2). There are other reverse effects, however, that are somewhat more subtle. Consider, for example, a cost-effectiveness study of an "individualized instruction" program at Florida State University. Doughty and Stakenas (1973) attempted a thorough cost analysis of the new program. The difficulty of this task is greatly underestimated.

The Division of Instructional Research and Service at the university was established in hopes of improving instruction through the increased use of instructional technology. According to Doughty and Stakenas, the administration hoped such use would calm student unrest and reduce costs. The division became involved in a project to revamp the basic earth sciences course by using the "audio-tutorial" method. In their cost analysis, four alternatives were examined:
1. traditional small-group instruction with one instructor and thirty students;
2. conventional large-group lecture-laboratory;
3. the individualized course with locally developed materials;
4. the individualized course with commercially prepared materials.

The innovative program was analyzed in two forms (3 and 4), since it was believed that considerable savings could be realized if materials could be purchased rather than developed locally. Although one might argue with the cost estimates for the four alternatives (I think they are somewhat biased in favor of the innovation, for example, estimating project life as a rather long ten years and thus amortizing the costs), the results are interesting.

Unit costs are heavily dependent upon the number of students being taught. In other words, cost savings are primarily *economies of scale*. For example, if there were only fifty students in the class, the cheapest instructional mode would be traditional small-group instruction. For as many as two hundred students, the cheapest mode of instruction is the conventional large-group lecture-laboratory. Only when student enrollment is at the four hundred-student level do individualized instruction options become cheaper. Even at this very large course size, conventional large-group instruction is at only a modest cost disadvantage.

These startling findings illustrate two things: one is that traditional instruction is already organized on an extremely cheap per capita basis. The second point is that innovations can mainly increase productivity by using fewer people to teach more students. In other words, innovations primarily achieve economies of scale.

Economy of scale is also registered at another level. Buying commercially developed materials would be substantially cheaper than producing locally developed ones, although no such materials were available at the time of the study. Producing one set for the whole market would save Florida State University its research and development and materials costs. The same cost logic applies to PLATO and its materials development, and to most innovations that lay any claim to cost-effectiveness.

Of course, analysts do not calculate losses. Although they admit that most instructors would not be very happy with the new mode of instruction, true unexamined costs lie deeper. If the courses consisted of only thirty-people sections (still most efficient for up to fifty students or so) there could be eight different courses offered instead of one huge one. Or one could have eight varieties of the basic course offered by eight different types of instructors.

Instead of this variety, one has an enormous class of four hundred or more. One of the ironies of modern instructional technology is that "individualized instruction" means that a great mass of people will plow through exactly the same material. Fewer alternatives are available. Presumably the "individualization" lies along one dimension—that the materials can be self-paced. While this may be possible in an environment that favors the innovation, it does not follow that the innovation will be implemented faithfully even on this one dimension.

For example, when similar materials like those of Individually Prescribed Instruction are used in the competitive environment of the elementary school classroom, the effect is to intensify competition so that the materials are paced by the fastest students. Since every child proceeds through the same workbooks, individualized instruction amounts to putting the children on a racetrack with clearly demarcated lanes so that every child knows what book every other child is in, even in the first grade. Naturally these considerations are very difficult to include in the effectiveness calculations.

If Florida State University loses instructional pluralism and flexibility, what does it gain by this economy? Obviously it saves money. In order to realize the economy, however, classes must number four hundred or more, which means that the student body and the university itself must be of a certain size. This increases the overhead, the administrative staff, and many other things associated with large organizations. It is ironic that one of the reasons given by administrators for attempting reform was to alleviate student unrest, which, it was claimed, resulted from large classes and impersonal treatment. Of course, the innovation would result in larger classes and even more impersonal treatment. "Individualizing" in this sense is quite different from "personalizing."

Florida State University does elicit real gains, mainly of a competitive economic sort, from the innovation. Some contend that such savings can be passed along in the form of smaller classes and more personal attention in other areas. That they can be, ideally, is perhaps true, although the dysfunctions of such savings are not well analyzed, and the savings are less than one might think. Whether the savings will be passed along is a greater question. If one maximizes productivity, the savings certainly will not be, for that will not reduce the overall costs of instruction. As Abert (1974) noted above, costs are reduced only by reducing the amount of labor. I suspect that these savings seldom remain within the educational arena.

Another advantage the university gains is to advertise its cost saving and its "individualization" to its sponsors and its prospective students, respectively. However real the savings, their appearance enhances a competitive position by attracting more external funds and more students. There is also payoff for the administrators' careers as the innovation is advertised to other universities. For other universities to economically utilize the innovation, they will have to be large enough to have four hundred students in the beginning geology class. The innovation is of little use to a small college (although it can be used). Thus, large schools reap a competitive advantage.

If the productivity theme is pursued to maximum advantage, other colleges adopting the innovation will purchase materials from an outside source rather than developing their own. As such a market builds, universities become increasingly dependent on commercially developed material. The more intense the economic pressures on other schools, the more interested they may be in such adoption. The more profit in commercially and externally developing such materials, the more aggressively agents propagate the materials. Market linkages are established between the producer and the universities, and universities become progressively involved in an overall network of material dissemination and marketing. This network can be used for the next innovation.

Of course, the larger the market the cheaper materials can be produced, but it is also less likely that the materials will satisfy a particular set of students. The materials must be transferable. So, economies of scale underlie the doctrine of transferability. Eventually a mass market production and distribution system will have been established. As the competitive advantage of the innovation fades, it will be profitable for the producer to develop a new innovation, a new set of materials (more profitable if the innovation is a "variation" rather than a "reorientation" since the latter would be far more disruptive to the established set of relationships). Already having the market linkages established greatly facilitates this step and gives the marketing-communication network a high degree of permanency.

Not all parts of the system grow at the same rate, however. In the next round of innovation, the larger schools and those in certain positions will be in a situation to take advantage of the new innovation, particularly if it should offer economy of scale. Earlier I noted the powerful effects of the urban hierarchy on the diffusion of innovations. The effect of innovation diffusion itself is to create such hierarchies and to intensify their effects. Those units which are larger and have the innovations get more innovations, while other units fall behind. The gap between the "haves" and the "have-nots" increases. A steeper hierarchy is created, and it has a polarizing effect. Thus, economic development is differential, with those at the bottom of the hierarchy getting less and never being able to catch up.

In order to understand educational innovation in its larger context, it is helpful to understand differential economic development. Lasuen (1972) has proposed a theory that relates the economic development of geographic regions to the diffusion of new innovations. Regions seem to grow economically in such a way that their hierarchical size-order relative to each other is not altered. Although the hierarchical orderings are stable over time, the larger ones tend to widen the economic gap between themselves and the smaller ones, creating "have" and "have-not" regions. This regional structural change can be explained in the same way that one explains how firms adopt successive innovations.

Technological and organizational changes result in several successive innovations to achieve greater efficiency. The time lapses between sets of innovations grow shorter, changing in industry from an average of fifty years at the beginning of the nineteenth century to seven years today. The scale of operations grows progressively larger with each set of innovations. Even though small-and medium-sized firms invent as much or more than larger ones, new innovations are adopted faster by larger firms because of the increasing scale of successive innovations. This also results in an increase in per capita productivity.

Economic development thus conceived is a process of structural change that comes about when a country adopts successive sets of innovations. A "developed" country is one utilizing the latest set available, while an "underdeveloped" country is one utilizing earlier sets. If an underdeveloped country wants to catch up to developed countries, it must adopt each set of innovations in less time than the advanced countries adopt newer ones. The differential adoption rates cause underdeveloped countries to fall progressively farther behind. How to accelerate the adoption of successive sets of innovations becomes the key issue in determining policies of economic development, usually addressed through policies aimed at increased savings and investment (see the end of this chapter).

Lasuen contends that conventional investment theory has failed to recognize the critical importance of factors controlling the subprocesses determining the adoption rate of innovation. He breaks the diffusion process into three familiar subprocesses: the generation of new innovations, the diffusion of knowledge of new innovations, and the spread of adoptions. Most innovations are generated in a small number of regions of only a few countries so that what usually matters is how innovations are diffused to their firms and how the firms adapt to the new knowledge. The salient feature of the second and third processes is the stability of adoption patterns among both firms and regions, a phenomenon noted earlier. Diffusion and adoption of innovations progress significantly unchanged throughout the hierarchical paths going from earlier to later adopting firms and regions.

This stability Lasuen attributes to market linkages between firms. The adopters of later innovations are either the manufacturers of earlier products serving a similar need (for example, the producers of bicycles in the case of motorcycles, the middlemen who previously imported the product, or the people who serviced and repaired the products) or those universities or schools that adopted earlier innovation. Whether fast or slow, innovation diffusion follows the diffusion of specific knowledge directed through people in the trade. The sensitivity to specific information depends on the intensity of the firm's market linkages to the product to which the information refers. Since the firms are the adopting units and the firms themselves are very stable in geographic space, the diffusion of successive innovations results in the geographic stability of the successive diffusion patterns among regions.

Lasuen views adoption as a learning process. The firm is the learning unit. Learning is a way of solving stress (overcoming competition problems); it is sequential and only takes place if it has proved to solve the stress; it proceeds from the concrete to the abstract and is generalized slowly (the more specialized and fewer the vested interests, the more likely the adoption); and it is Socratic, even if tutored. The individual must determine the pattern himself.

Changes in geographic adoption patterns are explained by changes in factors controlling the feasibility and desirability of applying new knowledge: the transportation revolutions, the increasing scale of successive sets of innovations, and the reorganization of business firms. *The transportation revolution and increasing scale have pushed toward the concentration of economic development in the urban hierarchy.* Faster and cheaper modes of transportation have favored the reduction in the number of adopters and increased their location in central places. Increasing scale of operations has progressively reduced the number of adopters, even though would-be adopters have access to new knowledge. Changes further accelerate geographic polarizations.

Another change has been the internal reorganization of firms from the one-product, one-plant, one-city type to the multiproduct, multiplant, multicity firm. The "holding corporation" of the United States became the prototype of the industrial corporation. The leading firm became a loose organization that tries to deliver to the market the most profitable mix of changing products and services rather than one that tries to make a better and cheaper product. What matters is to be able to move in and out of a line, to mix lines in the most profitable manner at any time, and to avoid attachment to a particular line. This leads to much subcontracting of activities and to a coordinating function over production. The result is to intensify market linkages among firms and channels of specific information. Linkages are intensified so that the spread of adoptions is increased. This organizational change tends to spread adoptions rather than concentrate them, although the spread is tied to being part of an ever-larger network of communication and innovation controlled by the larger firms. Smaller firms are tied by market linkages to larger ones.

Hence, the units of a territorial system grow in an orderly hierarchical manner determined by the stability of the diffusion patterns (which maintain stability in the order of regions) and at different rates because adoptions are more feasible in larger towns or regions. The increasing scale of operations with each successive innovation set and the shorter time lapses between sets further concentrate adoptions in firms and in geographical space. Successive diffusions reach down to a shorter number of units before new sets of innovations become superimposed. The result of those forces means increasing differences between the units, and over time the system hierarchy is stabilized and the hierarchy of territorial units exhibits successively larger differences in size between units.

According to Lasuen, the stability of the communication network between firms, which is controlled by market linkage intensities, is the central explanation for the geographical stability of diffusion patterns. If the communication network among firms was altered by changes in the market linkages between firms, geographical patterns of diffusion would change. The alternative would be to change the location of the firms themselves. For example, Lasuen would contend that the fastest and cheapest way to accelerate agricultural development in a backward region would be to bring in competent farmers skilled in advanced techniques. Land reclamation, agricultural extension, and vocational training are slow and inefficient ("unprofitable investments," in Janossy's terms). Moving the farmers is tantamount to changing the location of firms already plugged into the overall network. A second solution would be to induce the location of firms, such as canning plants, which would establish stable and intense market linkages with the backward farmers through long-term contracts, thus "forcefully" exposing them to innovations.

Current changes in firms, such as product diversification and geographical branching, are not likely to alter diffusion patterns of the past. Concentration of more products in fewer firms will probably make each diffusion pattern resemble previous ones. Geographical branching will shorten diffusion rates from the center to the periphery. Diffusions will, in essence, go through the central nucleus of the firms, which will remain in older locations and be controlled from the center.

Lasuen's reasoning may be applied to the development of regions within countries, to differential development between countries, and, as we shall soon claim, to differential development of institutions within a society. For example, Pedersen (1970) has tried to explain innovation diffusion between national urban systems as well as within them. In comparing the innovation diffusion times within Chile to the diffusion time between all Latin American countries, Pedersen concludes that the international diffusion time has not decreased as much over the past 150 years as has the innovation diffusion time within the country. He offers the explanation that the introduction of a new innovation in a country is due to its national elite, which has had few economic limits to its communication with other countries.

The Latin American elite has been in frequent and continuing contact with Europe, the United States, and, to a lesser extent, other Latin American countries. In Chile the economic constraints to diffusion from the national elite in the main cities to the peripheral population were more serious, and the decrease in communication costs over the last 150 years has made a bigger difference at the national level than at the international.

In studying innovation diffusion among eighteen Latin American countries over the past 150 years, Pedersen found three critical factors. The first was related to the Spanish colonial administrative structure. The second was concerned with the total economic national product of the countries. Pedersen notes that the present-day national product is dependent on the old colonial administrative system.

The third factor was the influence of North America and Europe. The northern half of the continent trades relatively more with the

United States; the southern half, with Europe. These three factors probably were of differential importance over the last 150 years according to Pedersen. The colonial administrative hierarchy is important in explaining the spread of universities, the only innovation, according to the study, that actually spread in colonial times.

After liberation from Spanish rule, European-North American dominance became more important. Initially the orientation was toward Europe, but, as the world invention center moved from London to New York, United States dominance grew. In the future Pedersen sees the influence of the colonial administrative hierarchy fading, and bias toward the United States increasing. Limited accessibility to the United States economically disadvantages the southern part of the continent. The main point is that innovation diffusion and economic development in Latin America over the last 150 years have been dependent on external domination patterns.

The effect of the urban hierarchy on education has already been illustrated. Comparing relationships among schools is parallel to comparing innovation diffusion and economic development among Latin American countries. The adoption of gifted programs within Illinois exhibited concentration of innovation adoption in fewer adopters and the effects of scale, the transport system, and organization. Because of these factors, the innovation diffused in a relatively short time span.

Comparing innovation adoption within schools, however, is like talking of economic development in Latin American countries without mentioning the hegemony of the United States. Education as an institution is strongly affected by the dominance of economic institutions. There is a societal hierarchy among institutions, and this relationship may ultimately prove more important in determining economic development and innovation than the within-school order. In a sense education vis-a-vis the economic institutions of the society is like an "undeveloped" country facing a "developed" country. In the nonterritorial situation, economic development consists of the more advanced country inventing and passing along older innovations. If the analogy holds, the gap between institutions higher and those lower in the hierarchy widens.

INSTITUTIONAL IMPERIALISM

Who benefits from the hierarchic innovation diffusion process? The hard fact about the innovation diffusion process itself is that it is central to economic development and that the process lends itself to, in fact promotes, great inequality among developed and developing nations, among regions, and, I contend, among institutions. The process increases the difference in living conditions for first users and later adopters. The tremendous inequality on an international level between "Center" and "Periphery" nations has led Galtung (1971, 1973) to postulate a structural theory of imperialism that may be applicable to the societal order as well as to the international order.

Galtung defines imperialism as a precise dominance relation between collectivities. The system splits up collectivities and relates the parts to each other in harmony and disharmony of interests. Conflict of interest occurs when two parties are coupled in such a way that the gap between their "living conditions" (income, standard of living, quality of life) is increasing. There is no conflict or disharmony of interest if the parties are coupled together in such a way that the gap between them decreases to zero. In order for this dominance to obtain, of course, the parties have to be coupled together, to interact. There was neither harmony nor disharmony of interest between Africa and Europe before the white settlers came. The coupling implies a social causation resulting from interaction as it relates to their inequality.

Imperialism is defined as one way in which the Center nation dominates the Periphery nation in such a fashion as to cause disharmony of interest between them. The imperialistic relationship is such that there is a harmony of interest between the elite of the Center nation (what Galtung calls the center of the Center) and the elite of the Periphery nation (the center of the Periphery). There is more disharmony of interest within the Periphery nation than within the Center nation. There is disharmony of interest between the periphery in the Center nation and the periphery of the Periphery nation.

Inside both nations there is a disharmony of interest. Both nations are vertical societies that can be divided into a ruling elite (the center) and the rest (the periphery). The gap between center and periphery is not decreasing but is at best constant. There is, however, more disharmony of interest in the Periphery nations than in the Center nation, which means there is more inequality in the Periphery. This allows the Center nation to dominate. In the Center nation there may be more redistribution of goods and less disharmony.

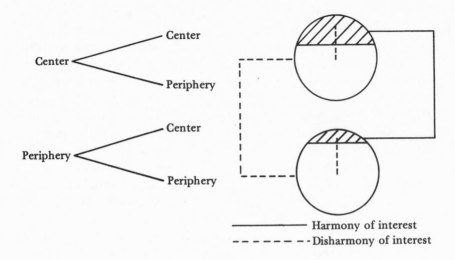

FIGURE 9-1
Structure of imperialism
(from Galtung, 1971)

In the Periphery nation the center grows economically faster than the periphery—in fact, at its expense. Much of the value extracted from the periphery of the Periphery nation is passed through its center to the center of the Center nation where some of it dribbles down to the periphery of the Center nation. The total arrangement is in the interest of the periphery in the Center although it is in some disharmony with its own center. It gets a piece of an increasing pie. The whole process is controlled by the center of the Center nation, which of course profits most. Both centers are tied together in mutual interest and the periphery of the Center is tied to the center of the Center. This prevents an alliance between the two peripheries. The most severely exploited group is the periphery of the Periphery. The imperialism relationship is not simply one between nations; it is also one between internal parts of the nations. All this is to say that the ruling elites of both nations exploit the periphery of the weaker one, having bought the quiescence of the periphery of the Center nation. Explicit physical force is not necessary to the exploitation system.

Galtung describes two mechanisms by which imperialism is exercised and maintained. One is the principle of *vertical interaction relation* and the other the principle of *feudal interaction structure*.

The Center nation exacts a value exchange between nations that is highly asymmetric and beneficial to the Center nation. In economic trade this means that the Center nation receives raw materials from the periphery nation and sends it manufactured goods. The manufacturing of goods leads to many side benefits in spin-off industries, which results in increased developed and enrichment inside the Center country. The export of a raw material produces no such derivative side benefit for the Periphery country. Higher-level processing leads to increased knowledge as a result of the need for more research, new skills, and better education, further increasing the living condition gap.

Galtung sees such vertical interaction as the major source of inequality, whether it takes the form of looting, highly unequal exchange, or highly differential spin-off effects. He does not mention the innovation diffusion process, but it can be seen as a form of unequal vertical interaction of a very sophisticated nature. It does not require developed and undeveloped countries trading raw materials for manufactured goods, but it does require differing levels of industrial development and an urban hierarchy to disseminate the older innovations down the line. Those at the bottom must trade old innovations for new ones, but must always remain behind and, according to some calculations, must fall ever farther behind. The Center nations are the centers of innovation, the heads of the hierarchical system.

If vertical interaction is the major mechanism behind inequality, the feudal interaction structure is the factor that maintains and reinforces the inequality. Interaction between the Center and the Periphery is vertical. Interaction between the Periphery and the other Peripheries is nonexistent. Multilateral interaction involving all three is missing. Interaction of the Periphery with the outside world is monopolized by the Center. Periphery interaction with other Centers is also missing. Hence, the Peripheries do not have the communication interactions by which to get themselves together in any kind of concerted action. The shape of the domination has a structural form.

If the units are nations, there are international economic implications. First, there would be a concentration on trade partners. There would be heavy import concentration and export concentration in the Periphery as opposed to the Center nation. Second, there would be a commodity concentration. The Periphery is likely to have only a few primary products to export. Whatever the resources of the Periphery nation, to begin exploiting new raw materials in a region might upset the local power balances. The effect of those conditions is to make the Periphery heavily dependent on the Center. The Periphery becomes vulnerable to demands and prices. The center in the Periphery depends on the Center for consumer goods. In terms of Lasuen's regional economics, through intensified market linkages the Periphery country becomes increasingly sensitive to innovations, dependent on the Center, and tied into the overall hierarchic network.

As Galtung notes, how could a tiny foggy island in the North Sea rule a quarter of the world? It could be done by isolating the Peripheries from each other, by keeping them far enough apart to impede alliance formation, by making separate deals to tie them to the Center in particularistic ways, by reducing multilateralism to a minimum with all levels of graded membership, and by having the Center serve as the window to the world.

The same mechanisms work within nations as work between them. There is a vertical division of labor within as well as between nations. It is the operation of the mechanisms at two levels that stabilizes the system. The periphery of the Periphery is generally impoverished as the result of the vertical division of labor within the Periphery nation and the heavy inequality and disharmony of interest. Interaction, mobilization, and organization of the periphery of the Periphery are impeded by the fedual structure within Periphery units. In addition the whole Periphery nation is impoverished by the vertical division of labor between nations. The feudal interaction structure between nations makes it difficult to interact with other Periphery units. The center in the Periphery has the monopoly on international interactions of all kinds. Neither can the periphery of the Periphery appeal to the periphery of the Center or to the center of the Center because of the disharmony of interest.

Galtung also enumerates five types of imperialism—economic, political, military, communications, and cultural. Although most of his examples are phrased in economic terms, he claims that no type of imperialism is more basic than another. Economic imperialism consists of the Center nation supplying processing and the means of production while the Periphery nation supplies raw materials and markets. In political imperialism the Center supplies decisions and models for the Periphery to imitate while the Periphery provides obedience and imitation of the models. Center nations usually possess a superior structure for others to imitate as long as the Center's position is not challenged. Models originating from the Center automatically have a legitimacy by virtue of their origin, not their substance. Militarily, only the Center has the industrial capacity to produce the technological hardware or the social structure compatible with a modern army. The Center produces the decisions; the Periphery implements them.

Communications imperialism rests on the feudal interaction structure and on the ability of the Center to produce means of communication and transportation. The preceding generation of means can always be sold to the Periphery in a general vertical trade interaction, as can the obsolescent means of production, the means of destruction, and the means of creation. Since the Center holds the reins of innovation, the Periphery cannot catch up. The Center even dominates the news of the Periphery. In cultural imperialism the Center provides teaching and means of creation—autonomy and initiative. The Periphery provides learning and cultural validation—dependence. The Center provides the teachers and the definition of what is worth learning. The Periphery provides the learners. In accepting cultural transmission, the Periphery implicitly validates the Center's culture. This reinforces the Center, stimulating it to continue to develop culture as well as transmit it, creating lasting demand for the latest innovations.

Galtung contends that science also has its vertical division of labor by which scientific teams from the Center collect data from the Periphery in order to sell the product back to the center of the Periphery. The research may also provide valuable information to the Center about the Periphery.

Galtung also identifies periods of imperialism in history. In the past imperialism has consisted of physical occupation. The center in the Center establishes a bridgehead in the Periphery by transplanting settlers to the Periphery nation. This is known as colonialism. With improved means of transportation, particularly the steam engine, such heavy-handed control was unnecessary. The two centers were linked by rapid transportation, and the link was provided by international organizations. The harmony of interest between centers can be translated into equality within the international organization, which is neocolonialism.

Galtung traces five phases in the development of an imperial organization, whether it is General Motors or the International Communist movement. The first phase of the organization is the national phase, when the organization resides in its home country. In the second phase the organization goes abroad by establishing subsidiary or subversive organizations run by agents. The agents establish a bridgehead in the Periphery country, but this is a preimperialist phase since the bridgehead is not in the center of the Periphery. Even so, agents may be highly successful in effecting change.

The third phase is the true imperialist one. Elites who identify with the elites of the Center emerge in the Periphery. The organizations have become multinational, but the Center company dominates in an asymmetric relationship. The Periphery is concerned with making raw materials and workers available to the Center company. The top leadership of the international organization is always the leadership of the Center nation, and there is a vertical division of labor between them. Of course, the general interaction structure becomes feudal. This is the present state of most international organizations, and such organizations are used by the Center nation to proselytize and disseminate its culture.

In the fourth phase the Peripheries begin to demand more equality within organizations. Still operating through the multinational organization, the Peripheries begin to question the division of labor. Why not distribute research contracts and strategic planning activities more equitably? Why not build interaction among the Peripheries? Overall the total network becomes more symmetric. This is still, however, an equality essentially among the elites rather than among the Peripheries. According to Galtung the fourth phase is just beginning. In the fifth and final phase the nation-states fade out to be replaced by a global organization. In the current period of international organization the center of the Center interacts with the center of the Periphery through organizations. In the future period the interaction will be via improved communications networks.

Galtung also insists on the convertibility of one type of imperialism into another. Political imperialism can be converted into economic imperialism by dictating favorable trade agreements. (One difference between liberal and structural peace theory, of which Galtung represents the latter, is that liberals believe in sheer volume of trade while structuralists are concerned about equality and composition.) Military imperialism can be converted into communications imperialism by involving the military necessity for centralized command over communication and transportation facilities. The more connected the economy of a country, the more a demand proliferates. Of course, traditional societies are less connected.

Communication imperialism can be converted into cultural imperialism by regulating the flow of information. Cultural imperialism is convertible into economic imperialism in ways such as technical assistance. Technical assistance stimulates a demand in the poor country for the goods of the rich. A technical assistance expert writes the "standard operating procedure," and it is up to his counterpart to follow it.

In an imperialistic state economic, political, military, communications, and cultural inequality should be distributed in an inegalitarian way. The Center nation should not be equal, but should be less unequal than the Periphery. This gives the Center a more cohesive structure and makes the periphery of the Center nation feel it has a stake in the system. Relative equality of access exists in the liberal democracies—the Center nations. Instead of seeing democracy as a consequence or condition for economic development within certain nations, Galtung contends, it can also be seen as a condition for exercising effective control over Periphery nations.

Throughout his analysis Galtung talks of the Center and Periphery as a dyad. However, there is nothing to prevent other parties from intervening between the top and the bottom of the hierarchy. One can easily and more realistically have a continuum of social classes within each nation or have the government serve as an intervening force. Likewise, a third nation could also serve as a go-between for the Center and Periphery. Of course, within the international structure as a whole, Galtung sees the United States as the Center, with Japan and the Soviet Union as competing Centers.

The analysis can also be applied to nonterritorial actors like organizations. They are collectivities that have a vertical division of labor within and could share a division of labor. They could also be chained together with imperialistic relationships. In applying the center-periphery theory of imperialism to nonterritorial actors, Galtung suggests that the emphasis be on whether the Center has established bridgeheads in other actors and whether they are able to organize systematically some vertical division of labor.

Although Galtung does not include the innovation diffusion process as a part of his theory, it is clear that it would qualify as an important part of the critical vertical interaction relationship. The vertical division of labor is divided so that inventors and developers reap the benefits by selling the innovations down the diffusion hierarchy. Perhaps this is clearest in the American hegemony, where the United States sells its old secondhand warplanes and computers to the rest of the world. Thus, the United States maintains its position as the center of invention, development, and production and reaps the spin-off effects that Galtung considers so important.

Actually the world order would appear more complex, like the urban hierarchy magnified on a global scale. If European countries are somewhat dependent on the United States in this structural system, less developed countries are in turn dependent on them, and even less developed countries dependent on the third tier, and so on. The result is a set of countries in a finely gradated vertical exchange system. The exchange between any two may not be overpoweringly unequal, but the difference between the top and the bottom is great, indeed. This difference is dramatized by trade between the United States and Latin America where the exchange balance is tremendously unequal.

The vertical division of labor permits the less developed countries to produce only raw materials and less complex manufactured goods, which are then traded at a price very favorable to developed countries. The recent oil boycott of the industrial countries by the Arab producers and the multiplication of the basic price for oil indicates that industrial countries need oil much more than undeveloped countries need manufactured goods. Yet the price ratio benefit has always been in the other direction. The oil boycott disrupted the entire industrial system and indicated that "supply and demand" were not the impersonal determiners of the price of oil except as they could be manipulated by external political forces.

The oil producers had always traded at prices far lower than they could have gotten, partly because the ruling elites of the countries were able to amass enormous wealth even from such low exchange rates and partly because they never realized that they could organize a successful price control effort. As Galtung indicates, considerable fragmentation kept them from making such an effort. Only confrontation with a formidable political enemy enabled them to overcome this fragmentation.

The central issue of this section, however, is the degree to which education as an institution suffers the type of "imperialism" that Galtung sees between international territorial collectivities. In the case of institutional imperialism the protagonists would be the stronger institutions in the society, particularly the economic institutions. Do the economic institutions control education in such a way that the gap in "living conditions" between the two is not decreasing toward zero?

Galtung does not deal in any detail with the relationships between nonterritorial collectivities, but suggests that such an analysis focus more on whether the center is able to establish bridgeheads in other nonterritorial actors and whether they are able to organize systematically some vertical division of labor. It seems to me that the answer for education to both questions is a highly qualified "yes." Economic institutions have been able to establish a "bridgehead" in the educational system through the use of school boards. It is well known that business interests are most heavily represented on school boards.

Studies going back many years indicate that real estate men and their relatives alone comprise a substantial portion of school board members, not to mention other businessmen. This book did not explore these important relationships since proving the thesis that education is dominated by business interests was not my main concern. Businessmen also dominate state and national education boards, as well as large city boards where corporate headquarters are located. Some state boards do not allow educators to serve on educational boards at all. It is true that occasionally university presidents sit on corporate boards, but such reverse controls are rare.

Local school boards themselves date back to an agrarian economy, when land was the major form of wealth and the boards tended to keep down the property tax, still the major source of income for the schools. As the source of wealth shifted more and more to corporate industrial income, land became less important as wealth. Fewer important financial decisions involved the local school board. Although "buying" the tax assessor in order to hold down property taxes on branch plants is a common practice, larger school financial decisions are related to the tax structure at the state and federal levels. Large corporate interests are very active there. Local school boards increasingly operate within the resources made available to them by the higher powers.

As I have indicated in an early part of the book, the conservative nature of school superintendents is partly a product of local school boards whose conservatism matches that of the superintendent. Generally, though, local school boards represent the local, older, more traditional social structure of small- and medium-sized towns. These small businessmen have been interested in keeping down educational costs while at the same time attaining special educational advantages - for their own children. Local elites have perpetuated their own forms of control and inequality, but they have been on the defensive economically against national elites who control the technocratic corporate structure into which small businessmen have been progressively integrated, thereby creating dependence on national mass markets. It is not the local elites who have promoted innovations (like desegregation)—quite the contrary. As reflected in government policy, the concern of the national elites for "national issues" is of relatively recent origin. Although the schools may always have been attuned to the existing economic order, it is the modern corporate industrial order that now clearly dominates and that seeks to shape the school in its own image.

As indicated in the chapter on government policy, the purpose of federal policy itself has been to assert national priorities against local concerns. Federal policy has been directed in part at circumventing local control. In Galtung's terms, though, the control exercised by local school boards over school functions is not very subtle nor entirely convincing to school personnel. While teachers and administrators recognize and accept school boards as legitimate, school board members are essentially perceived as "outsiders." In Galtung's terms, their legitimacy is akin to that of white colonial settlers. Neither do most school boards have the desire or the ability to change traditional, labor-intensive school practices with which they grew up. They represent more of a traditional rather than a reform force in education, while at the same time representing the interests of middle-class businessmen.

A more subtle and substantive thrust into the structure of the school itself is the influence on school administrators. Callahan (1962) has documented the strong influence of business and industrial values on education between 1910 and 1929. This influence was exercised through vulnerable school administrators who adopted the practices of "scientific management," and it continues today. Callahan notes that he was not surprised to find business ideas and practices being used in education. "What was unexpected was the extent, not only of the power of the business-industrial groups, but of the strength of the business ideology in the American culture on the one hand, and the extreme weakness and vulnerability of schoolmen, especially school administrators on the other." It is probably through the school administrator's emulation of business executives that industrialism had its greatest impact on education.

In Galtung's model the administrators are in a position to become the elite of the dominated (the center of the Periphery) and to lead the schools into more of an imperialistic and exploited relationship with economic institutions. Both by identification with the economic elite and by dependency in the form of vested economic interests, administrators are vulnerable to becoming the local elite that leads the way to modernization. It is fair and accurate to say that this has happened only partially thus far. Because of recruitment patterns administrators still identify with traditional schooling and teachers to a considerable extent, and they have resisted many of the modernizing practices. Many still harbor humanistic values, and they are reinforced in this traditionalism by feedback from parents. Neither have they achieved equality with the economic elites. On the other hand, many pressures are exerted in the other direction, particularly by the state and federal governments.

Galtung (1973) suggests that there are three aspects to what he calls "structural power": *exploitation, fragmentation,* and *penetration.* In exploring whether an "imperialistic" relationship exists between the economic and educational institutions of the society, I have been examining the latter—penetration—the degree to which the elite of the dominating collectivity penetrates the elite of the dominated collectivity. While there is clear evidence of some penetration, I do not think it is deep enough to be a complete imperialistic relationship in Galtung's scheme. While all the elements of control are one-sidedly with the economic institutions, I would label the relationship a dominant rather than a completely imperial one.

What about the other two aspects? A considerable portion of this book has been devoted to showing the considerable fragmentation of the educational community. In its great geographic and specialized diversity, it speaks with many tongues. Contact between schools, particularly among teachers, is severely limited. There is little external professional contact and what little does occur is usually with school boards or governmental organizations. Again, however, although communication is severely fragmented in terms of little horizontal contact with cohorts, particularly in the trade of of ideas, and although the contact that exists is vertical toward networks controlled from above, contact is not extensively or exclusively with economic institutions. Rather, the pattern is more one of traditional organization—not much contact at all. The contact would appear to be fragmented horizontally, not tightly integrated into a vertical network, though government pressures would make it so. Current orientations are up the administrative hierarchy.

According to Galtung, the essence of the fragmentation strategy is "to divide and rule." The Center prevents horizontal contacts between Peripheries, especially trying to prevent any organization from developing around a pattern of interaction. The Center deals with Periphery collectivities one at a time and not in the presence of the others. By having multilateral relationships and restricting the Periphery to only one, the Center can dominate many Peripheries.

The most fundamental aspect of the imperialistic relationship is the exploitation that results from the vertical interaction relationship. There is exploitation if one collectivity gets much more out of the exchange than another. The vertical division of labor gives the power to initiate an "economic cycle" to the stronger party. Labor-intensive production and consumption are the lot of the poor, while administration, finance, and research are functions of the rich.

Disregarding for the moment what education and the economic institutions "exchange," which will be discussed next, the exchange rate highly favors economic institutions, I believe. In Galtung's more formal definition of imperialism as a gap in "living conditions" that is not decreasing to zero, the "living conditions" in economic institutions are clearly superior to those in the public schools. While education's share of the gross national product has increased somewhat over the last ten years, owing as much to the organization of teachers as anything, it is precisely this phenomenon that has created the general alarm that education costs will not be contained within the current share—thus, the cry for productivity. That economic institutions should garner a much larger part of the gross national product than education seems perfectly natural, a testimony to the power of the system to legitimize itself.

I indicated earlier the dominance of economic institutions over educational ones in political terms. Economic institutions supply decisions and models, like PPBS, while education supplies obedience and imitation of the models. Business models have legitimacy by virtue of their origin, however weak their substance. Economically the Center supplies the processing and the means of production while the Periphery supplies raw materials and obedience. According to Galtung, the difference is between challenge, exploration, and new discoveries, on the one hand, and standardization and routine, on the other. As I have shown, schools are pressed more and more toward standardization and routine.

As a global judgment now it would be fair to say that education is not fully integrated into a total imperialistic relationship with economic institutions, though it is subservient and dominated by them. In part, the lack of full integration is because of education's traditional character. What would fully integrate education into the modern system would be to make it fully dependent on innovations produced by private capital. Being part of a modern innovation diffusion hierarchy, it would constantly exchange newly produced innovations in uneven trades.

In such a system the Center provides the investment and the Periphery provides the market. The Center provides the research and know-how and the Periphery provides unskilled labor. In such a vertical interaction system the Center retains control and initiative. A production system that emphasizes capital-intensive, research-intensive, and elite-oriented production ties the Periphery to the Center both economically and intellectually. The Center supplies what the Periphery needs and feels it cannot attain elsewhere. Exploitation is achieved through a vertical division of labor that creates dependency.

By interacting through marketing forces only, schools will be continuing their fragmentation, interacting only through propagators of innovations. There will be little opportunity to form strong alliances. Finally, the Center achieves penetration by the schools' dependence on the market. Administrators see it as being in their interest, particularly their career pattern, to promulgate new innovations as best they can. They become more like corporate executives. Earlier and more obvious forms of penetration like school boards become less important and less effective in controlling the schools. The dependency bonds become much more invisible.

Earlier I suggested four ways a technocratic society might gain by modernizing education. Education is made more efficient and less costly through mass production. The new innovations convey messages favorable to the ruling political and economic structure. Education itself becomes an enormous market for mass-produced materials. And, as I have emphasized here in particular, education as an institution becomes more dependent on the ruling institutions of the society.

Fully modernizing and totally integrating the somewhat anachronistic and traditional structure of education into the overall technocratic society draws all the wires of society into a more coherent entity. It substantially strengthens the total technocratic control of society and presents a more unified, agressive, powerful countenance toward the rest of the world. Such internal social coherence enhances external domination, and this has been the direction of federal policy.

THE INSTITUTIONAL FUNCTION OF EDUCATION

What role does education serve in society, or, more important, what role will it come to serve in the future? Certainly it acts as a socializing force within society as a whole, but to what values should students be socialized? Thomas Green (1969) thinks one can determine the social consequences of schooling and ask what values are reflected in those consequences. The predominant values that shape the schools, in his opinion, are managerial, traditional, humanistic, or religious.

Managerial education is that system in which schools are "assessed primarily by the utility of their 'product' to other institutions of society—most notably the economic and military institutions." Schools are viewed as productive enterprises that prepare people to take a functional role in an "increasingly orderly, rational, and productive society." The schools are evaluated by their ability to accomplish the tasks involved when managerial values are predominant.

Effectiveness and efficiency in meeting society's demands for educated manpower are the underlying criteria, and the school is measured against aggregate rather than distributive values. Aggregate values are values aimed at maximizing a good for society, even though it may not be maximized for each individual within the society. A distributive value is one maximized for each individual, but not necessarily for society as a whole. Managerial education is a system in which policy is shaped by aggregate values. The function of the school is to provide human resources for other institutions.

Almost the opposite type of education identified by Green is humanistic education, which strives to cultivate the independence of each individual and "develop each person to his fullest." This is the official ideology of most educators, and it is based primarily on distributive values. The needs of the individual are placed above those of society. Green notes that although this is often articulated, it can seldom be implemented in the school, for, among other reasons, it is not a fully attainable ideal.

Traditional education is education to preserve a collective memory, to build a group identity, and to create a sense of community. Finally, the function of religious education is to focus on the holy, to nurture a consciousness in which relationships with others are theologically mediated.

Of the four types of education, Green believes that managerial education dominates today and will increase its predominance in the future, even though educators will continue to express humanistic goals. Green questions whether any society has ever succeeded in assessing the educational system except in relation to other institutions. Is not the minimum condition of a successful education system that it provide for the preparation of people to assume positions within economic institutions? Is it possible, as in humanistic education, to assess the results of an educational system apart from its contribution to other institutions? This would require assessment entirely in terms of what it does for persons.

For example, most demands for ghetto education, according to Green, are demands that education provide the skills necessary for employment. This is managerial education although it is often expressed in humanistic and traditional terms. Not the least of the demands on lower education is that it prepare students to enter the upper levels of the educational system. This demand imposes managerial values on any type of education.

Green believes that the use of educational credentials to place people in jobs and social roles ensures that people take them seriously, even though the skills required in school might be different from those required in a job. The function of the schools is to train manpower for other institutions in society, and such education is based on aggregate values.

The managerial function of schools seems to be widely accepted in American society, particularly as it facilitates equality of opportunity. Whereas in older days the function of education was to establish a common heritage, modern education is to supply the cognitive and job skills essential for employment, especially for "getting ahead." Much in education is justified as necessary for future advancement.

Such justifications are central to American society, for education is seen as the road to upper social mobility—the avenue of opportunity—for most people. Even though most workers feel they are trapped within unrewarding jobs, by hard work they can enable their children to "get an education" and climb in the social hierarchy. What the school must do is teach the necessary cognitive knowledge and skills that will enable the child to do this. Jobs are presumed to depend on certain knowledges and skills associated with schooling or, at the very least, with "the degree" itself.

This is why parents in black and other minority groups become so upset when schools do not teach the "basic skills." An inability to obtain good schooling is seen as robbing minorities of the opportunity to rise out of the ghettos, presumably a result of their educational deficiency. Liberal social policy has focused on providing good educational opportunities to those groups at the bottom of the social hierarchy. Liberal policy assumes that educational deficiencies are caused by poor education and that, once these deficiencies are corrected and the proper skills are provided, the disadvantaged child can learn the basic skills and advance up the hierarchy.

The function of innovation is to provide the means of teaching these populations the basic skills. As Travers (1973) has suggested, once they have learned the skills, all will be well. Equality means equality of opportunity to learn the basic skills and advance up the social hierarchy—the basis of liberal policy.

A somewhat more radical critique is presented by two economists who contend that the primary purpose of the school system is to legitimize the hierarchical division of labor and, hence, the class structure of an industrial, capitalistic society. They see the raging controversy between liberals and conservatives over the genetic basis of "IQ" as essentially irrelevant. Conservatives say that the poor are poor because they are intellectually incompetent, an incompetency rooted in biology and, hence, part of the natural order of things. Liberals contend that the poor are intellectually incompetent because of environmental influences and that remediation programs should be undertaken to ensure equal opportunity.

Bowles and Gintis (1973) contend that this debate is irrelevant to understanding poverty, wealth, and inequality of opportunity because intellectual competence is not a major determinant of occupational success or income. Rather, the emphasis on intelligence as a basis for economic success serves to legitimate the "authoritarian, hierarchial, stratified, and unequal economic system of production and to reconcile the individual to his or her objective position within this system." Legitimation is enhanced when people believe in intellectual competence as the determiner of success. Strong associations among IQ, social class, education, cognitive skills, occupational status, and income facilitate this belief.

Actually, according to Bowles and Gintis, access to occupational status is contingent upon noncognitive traits, such as motivation, orientation to authority, discipline, and internalization of work norms, as well as a set of personal attributes such as sex, race, age, and educational credentials. The school promotes these traits and plays a central economic role in legitimating the structure of authority in modern society. The generation of cognitive skills becomes a spin-off of the stratification mechanism grounded in the supply, demand, production, and certification of noncognitive attributes.

The liberal's doctrine is that progressive social welfare measures can gradually reduce and eliminate class and race differences, which means acceptance of the societal hierarchy as it stands, with everyone being given an equal opportunity to rise in it. After bias is eliminated and intellectual competence or the ability to cope becomes the major determiner of success, everyone should find his own level within the hierarchy. In other words, a meritocracy would result. Bowles and Gintis counter this doctrine by presenting evidence to show that IQ is not really an important criterion for economic success.

The technical relations of production in an advanced technological economy are not really the basis for stratification, they contend. The "social relations" of production—the rights, responsibilities, duties, and rewards that govern individual interaction in organized productive activity—are considered more critical. In advanced capitalistic society the stratification system is based on the hierarchical division of labor, "characterized by power and control emanating from the top downward through a finely graduated bureaucratic order." The distribution of reward and privilege is an expression of the hierarchical division of labor within the enterprise.

Legitimation is extremely important within a society like the U.S. because the production system is "totalitarian" in a way not totally carried through in family, political, and other institutions. Acceptance of the hierarchical division of labor is always problematic. The "IQ ideology" is conducive to a technocratic and meritocratic view of the stratification system that tends to legitimate these social relations. The IQ ideology operates to reconcile workers to their eventual economic positions via the schooling experience and its supposed objectivity and efficiency in supplying the cognitive needs of the labor force.

"If one takes for granted the basic economic organization of society, its members need only be equipped with adequate cognitive and operational skills to fulfill work requirements, and provided with a reward structure motivating individuals to acquire and supply these skills." The first task is accomplished through family, school, and on-the-job training; the second, through a wage structure patterned after the job hierarchy. "The bedrock of the capitalist economy is the legally sanctioned power of the directors of an enterprise to organize production, to determine the rules that regulate workers' productive activities, and to hire and fire accordingly, with only moderate restriction by workers' organizations and government regulations." But this hierarchical division must constantly be legitimized since the economic enterprise exists as both political dictatorship and social caste system. Radical thrusts against the hierarchical division of labor have been deflected into more manageable wage and status demands without altering the overall system.

The individual must come to accept the overall characteristics of work in such a system: bureaucratic organization, hierarchical authority, job fragmentation, and unequal reward. Allocating individuals to positions within the system involves intense competition in the educational system and individual assessment and choice by employers. The total process must appear egalitarian. The individual must see his position as being a just one.

The hierarchical division of labor is justified by the necessity for and the efficiency of industrial organization which is corroborated by similarities in the Soviet Union. Large-scale production is a requirement of advanced technology, and hierarchical division of labor is the only way of coordinating the interdependent parts. Technological efficacy is the primary justification. Naturally individuals should be matched to jobs in a meritocratic fashion, and it is presumed that strict economic criteria are important. The hierarchical division of labor is seen as "technically necessary" (although politically totalitarian), and job allocation as egalitarian (although severely unequal).

Bowles and Gintis argue that popular acceptance of these "myths" is the unique contribution of the educational system. The "IQ ideology" does not conform to the experience of most workers on the job. They do not see intellectual competence as determining success. Distribution of rewards within the school is seen as being based on objectively measured cognitive achievement, and schools are seen being oriented toward the production of cognitive skills. The higher levels of schooling are seen as a major determiner of success. Thus, it appears that high achievement is acquired in fair and open competition in school, and that is what consequently determines economic success.

Day-to-day contact with the school heightens parents' perceptions of the connection between cognitive attainment and economic success. Those who do not succeed drop out and take jobs lower in the hierarchy, convinced that their positions are just because of their inability to handle cognitive material. Those with undesirable personality traits do the same, convinced that lack of schooling determines their fate. Actually allocating workers to job slots on the basis of cognitive abilities would seriously inhibit allocation of workers to occupational slots.

In Bowles and Gintis' view, common schooling was sparked by the need for a stable work force reconciled to the wage-labor system. Individual attributes of order, discipline, sobriety, and humility were required. Rationalistic efficiency in the classroom meant competition, hierarchy, uniformity, and individual accountability through testing. While the Progressives strove in vain for a more humanistic, more egalitarian education, a bureaucratized, test-oriented school system evolved. "Only a strong labor movement dedicated to construction of a qualitatively different social order could have prevented this, or a functionally equivalent, outcome."

The hierarchical division of labor is reproduced by an inter-action of social class and schooling. To get a job, one must meet two tests: one must be able and willing to work, and one must be of the appropriate race, sex, age, education, and demeanor so that his or her assignment to the job will contribute to the sense that the social order of the firm is just. The worker must be "acquiescent to the employer's monopolization of power." The ability to operate at different levels in the job hierarchy is based on one's experiences at home and at school. In capitalist society personal attributes such as skills, motivation, attitudes, personality, and credentials become important in jobs.

Work roles are characterized by hierarchy, job fragmentation, bureaucracy, and control from the top. They are organized in such a way as to reproduce the social relations of production and secure long-term profit. Three objectives that the directors of an enterprise try to meet in order to perpetuate their class standing are *technical efficiency, control,* and *legitimacy.* Technical efficiency requires that work roles be organized in such a way that maximum output be produced. Control requires the retention of decisionmaking power at the top and maintenance of labor costs in line with those in the whole economy. Both are problematic. Workers continually contest control over working conditions. Hierarchically organized production and fragmented tasks divide workers against one another, weaken their solidarity, and convince them of their incapacity to control. Control sometimes conflicts with technical efficiency as exemplified in studies showing greater productivity when workers participate in decisionmaking, have greater job breadth, and work in teams.

The third objective is that work roles be organized so as to legitimate the authority relations in the firm—the right of the superior to direct and the duty of the subordinate to submit. The superior must always possess a higher salary and other attributes of superior status; women or blacks are not placed above men or whites; the young do not boss the old; educational credentials, regardless of competence, legitimate superior position in the hierarchy. The author-ity structure must conform to that of social values.

Corresponding to this organization of the work roles are five sets of worker attributes which employers demand. The first set is grouped around cognitive attributes and technical skills. The second set is concerned with personality traits such as motivation, persever-ance, docility, and dominance. The third set depends on modes of self-presentation such as manner of speech and dress and peer identification that help legitimate the system. The fourth set concerns ascriptive characteristics such as race, age, and sex. The fifth set concentrates on credentials such as level of education. Bowles and Gintis contend that all of the sets of attributes are integral to the stratification process except for the cognitive one, which is a by-product of the process. Cognitive achievement is only a minor criterion of job placement. The hierarchical division of labor is attributable, therefore, not to technical efficiency but to the struggle of a small group to control economic activity.

According to Bowles and Gintis, efficient workers must fit into the bureaucratic order, which has four characteristics: the duties and privileges of individuals are determined by preset rules that limit actions; relations among individuals are determined by hierarchical authority and interdependence; while control is from the top, workers have circumscribed areas of decision and choice; workers cannot be motivated by intrinsic rewards from the work process.

These conditions of work require some general traits from all workers. All must be dependable, be subordinate to authority, internalize the values of the organization (particularly if they have areas of personal initiative), and respond appropriately to the external incentives of the organization. All must work equally efficiently no matter how they feel about the task at hand. There are also important qualitative differences among workers. The lower levels must obey the rules; the middle levels must be dependable and predictable; the higher levels must internalize values in order to initiate activity. Qualitatively different modes of self-presentation are also associated with different levels of the job hierarchy.

How do workers acquire their appropriate characteristics? Ascriptive ones are acquired at birth. Credentials require survival in the school system. Work-related personality characteristics and modes of self-presentation are acquired through the combined influence of schools and family. Bowles and Gintis contend that the social relations of schooling are much like those in production—bureaucratic order, hierarchical authority, rule orientation, stratification by ability and age, sex role differentiation, and external incentives. Since the system is so similar, they contend, it is likely to develop the same traits required for work. Students are graded for being subordinate, disciplined, and orderly, independent of cognitive achievement. There are studies showing that teacher evaluation of conduct is a better predictor of work adequacy as perceived by the supervisor than grade point average. And so the educational system both selects and generates appropriate attributes for the industrial system.

The process must replicate the job hierarchy, however, with those at the bottom obeying rules and those at the top making decisions. Comparisons in schooling between college and high school, between junior colleges and elite liberal arts colleges, or between a working-class and a wealthy suburban high school illustrate differences in programs. These differences also exist within schools through devices such as tracking. Social-class differences are reflected in educational patterns. In fact, working-class parents prefer more authoritarian educational practices, perhaps reflecting their own work experiences.

Generally, social-class inequalities are reinforced by inequalities in financial resources. The schools at the top receive more lavish financial support. Poor support forces upon teachers and school administrators in working-class schools a type of social relation that mirrors the regimentation of the factory. They must work with large classes, use strict disciplinary measures, limit the curriculum, and so forth. Poor financial support mitigates against small, intimate classes, electives, free time for teachers (see arguments against PLATO by the blacks of Muslem College). Lack of financial support requires production line education with an emphasis on obedience, dullness, and routine. Those that do not drop out to take the lowest jobs must conform. Meanwhile the rich suburban schools, while maintaining low tax rates, offer much creative, independent work that is not only more entertaining, but that also prepares the students for performance in the upper job levels. (In the Illinois Gifted Program noted above, it was not the rich suburban districts that supported the state program. They already had small humanistically oriented classes. The medium-sized industrial cities, which had many gifted students but not particularly appropriate classes, were the main beneficiaries.)

Family background also has an important influence. Middle-class families are likely to emphasize self-direction; working-class parents, conformity to external authority. Of course, styles of self-presentation are also determined by family background.

Finally, Bowles and Gintis assail liberal social reform policies. Liberal reform is based upon accepting the hierarchical division of labor and inequality of economic outcome as they stand, but trying to guarantee that everyone has equal access to the hierarchy. Equality means only equality of opportunity and not of outcome. Bias and bigotry should be eliminated, but the hierarchy and inequality are necessitated by technical development. By making everyone, particularly those excluded from the system, able and willing to work, the problem will be solved insofar as possible. Social ills can be ameliorated, but not eliminated.

Bowles and Gintis contend that such liberal reform policies have failed and must continue to fail since inequality of opportunity is a by-product of the organization of production and cannot be attributed to dysfunctional attributes of those lower in the hierarchy or to conservative and unfeeling social policy. Individuals develop according to their relationship to the social division of labor, as do social subcultures. "In addition to performance-related individual capacities normally developed on a class basis, beneath the surface of rationality, meritocracy, and performance-oriented efficiency, the capitalist economic system operates on a subtle network of ascriptions and symbolic differentiations. . . ."

To the extent that Bowles and Gintis are correct in their analysis, educational innovations that are powerfully sponsored within society (a major condition of success) will be the type that prepares workers for job roles by emphasizing subordination, discipline, observance of rules, dependency, reliance on external incentives, and orientation to social stratification. According to Travers, these are the types that have emerged under federal sponsorship. Generally workers must be prepared to accept change imposed from above.

But there must also be differential education for different social classes in order to reproduce social stratification. Generally the upper groups will be provided with smaller, more humanitarian classes that promote some autonomy and internalization of norms. The lower groups will be presented with mass education that promulgates strict discipline and subordination. The difference between these two types of education is vividly described by the blacks who resented PLATO at Muslem. ("Will the classes at Harvard and Yale be conducted through PLATO terminals?")

Again, to the extent that Bowles and Gintis are correct, in a modernized political economy, educational work roles will be characterized by technical efficiency, control, and legitimacy. Work roles will be organized for maximum productivity, decision power will be at the top, and the total hierarchical authority will be legitimized. As I have described it, the innovation diffusion hierarchy of the research, development, diffusion paradigm would meet these criteria. The paradigm serves to legitimize the hierarchical and fragmented work structure within educational innovation, and liberal policy would contend that such a hierarchy is necessary for innovation to occur at all.

Thus, the political economy of educational innovation fits well with the political economy of modernized society as a whole, and it fits particularly well with the role that education plays within the institutional order.

Epilogue

The Morality of Innovation

What judgments can we make about the morality of the innovation system as it operates? Innovation is almost always assumed to be good in the abstract, but that is an unreflective judgment born of the particular parochialism of a modernistic society. In portraying how the system works, I have featured some of the personal and social costs of perpetual innovation, rather than simply extolling its virtues. Of course, the balance of good and bad is a complex one.

In analyzing the school and the school district I intentionally neglected most considerations of the content of the proposed innovations and their consequences for children in order to emphasize the political and social dynamics of the system. There is no question that estimates of the quality of an innovation and its presumed consequences for students have an important effect—at least I hope so.

On the other hand, major mechanisms of innovation, like the intensive pursuit of the career pattern and entrepreneurism, are essentially amoral. They can be used to promote either good or bad innovations. If the school moves from a semitraditional, semibureaucratized society to a fully bureaucratized and modernized institution, one would expect the amorality as well as the innovation to increase. For example, the much-decorated and highest-ranking dissenter of the Vietnamese War attributes the atrocities of that war to careerism in the American officer corps:

Reporter: *Surely it wasn't Army policy to kill indiscriminately just for the sake of the count.*

Herbart: To hell it wasn't. Every commander knew what the boss wanted. You
    don't have to give direct orders. The only question that was ever asked on
    operations was how many bodies did you get. Divisions were rated strictly
    according to their body counts.
Reporter: *According to you, careerism rather than racism is the ultimate expla-
    nation of events like My Lai.*
Herbart: Careerism was responsible for the atrocities, but racism made them a
    little easier to swallow in the lower ranks [Lieutenant Colonel Anthony
    Herbart, in *Midwest Magazine*, March 18, 1973].

While such an example is extreme, it is a reminder of the extreme immorality to which such a system can lend itself. The propagation of poor, even harmful, innovations in education is a relatively
simple matter. Nor is it difficult to envision the promotion of harmful innovations by entrepreneurs, especially when it benefits them
and when their sensibilities are entangled in the webs of their own
ideologies and sagas.

Unquestionably the benefits of a liberal, modernistic society
are great—unsurpassed material prosperity for most people, increased
life span, labor-saving devices, political and religious freedom, and a
host of other benefits too long and too familiar to list. Much of this
can be attributed to the innovation system that has developed over
the past few hundred years. The modern system of innovation has
been a mechanism for systematic improvement when it has worked
well. Traditional societies, while they can supply the very important
benefits of stability and the sense of community essential to personal
well-being, often have no mechanisms for improving themselves.

Unfortunately, modern society improves only certain facets of
life, mainly economic productivity, through only one means, technological innovation. Other facets are either ignored, or they are
devastated by the impact of technological and economic development. Total disregard for ecology, both natural and social, has marked the onslaught of "progress." There is little reason to believe that
such destructiveness will not engulf education as it converts from a
traditional to a modern social system or that the harms engendered
by the process will not be visited upon the persons at the bottom of
the social order—teachers and children.

Within the innovation process itself the worker at the bottom of
the hierarchy is expected to learn new modes of behavior and to
make the innovation work primarily at his own personal expense.

The rigors and frustrations of such an experience have been clearly set forth. In a fully modernized system, which education is not, the individual is coerced by the constant fear of vocational obsolescence, which grows stronger with age. The burdens on the student, though not expounded here, are equally heavy. The system runs in constant flux, and the stability and community of the individual's world can be seriously and constantly damaged. Like a hamster on an electric exercise wheel, the individual must run ever faster and simultaneously try to construct a cognitive map of the world and his situation in it. There are some signs that the entire modern system may be racing beyond control, like an engine without a governor (Vickers, 1970).

One of the features of the modern system is that those who must most forcefully bear the burden of perpetual innovation receive the fewest tangible rewards from the process, while those higher in the vertical division of labor benefit most. Built into the operation of the modern innovation system as a whole is integral inequality of benefits—between individuals within a workplace, between urban centers, between institutions within a society, between regions of a country, and between countries of the world. Those farther up the hierarchy benefit more than those farther down.

When the innovation hierarchy reaches the point where those at the head fully exploit those at the bottom for their own interests, then I believe the system has achieved a state of structural imperialism. Inequality becomes exploitation. The condition is not yet fully realized in the relationship between education and the dominant economic institutions of this society. However, pressures for modernizing education and fully integrating it within a totally industrialized, technocratic economy are strong. I have enumerated the advantages of this for the technocratic elite: education would cost less, students would be more efficiently trained for industry, the conservative message could be conveyed, there would be an enormous perpetual market for technological innovations, and dependency on external suppliers of innovations would grow.

Such a transformation would substantially enhance the power of the American ruling elite, both internally and externally. It would make society more cohesive, for, in building common values, supplying technical skills, and enhancing the legitimacy of authority, education is critical to the social order, despite contrary criticisms. It would strengthen American power, the goal of which, at home and abroad, would be the further pursuit of economic development.

But there is great immorality in such a system of inequality and exploitation, and every American who reads this knows intuitively that this is so. For, although cohesive institutional integration in the pursuit of economic development may seem peculiarly American (in the sense that the United States is the most advanced industrial society in the world with a history of materialistic opportunism), such a system of inequality violates the most basic value of American society—the principle of equality.

Although this principle is commonly compromised through the competing principles of freedom and opportunism until it is transformed into equality of opportunity rather than equality of results, it runs deep. Ultimately, however long the suspension of judgment in the face of immediate pragmatic benefits, an innovation system built on inequality and exploitation must be declared immoral, as was slavery and the Vietnamese War. That the modernistic system results in no more inequality than the traditional one is probably true, but this does not invalidate the judgment.

In addition to the inequalities visited upon the participants, there is at least one other way in which the morality of the modernistic innovation system is suspect: in its insensitivity to people as persons, and to groups as communities. Inherent in the process is the production of standardized materials for a mass market, which the logic of large-scale economics demands. It is difficult to see how education can be personalized or how the pluralism and diversity of culturally different groups can be respected under such conditions. To the extent to which the system predominates, all differences are smothered.

Unwittingly, perhaps, but necessarily, the innovation system exerts a cultural totalitarianism that is unremitting in its pressure. There can be no appeal to the participants, for, to the extent that they have bought into the system, they must follow the logic of their self-interest. I have noted deeds done for career. To the degree that such a machine is exclusively in the service of a purpose like economic development, its effect can be merciless.

Yet I cannot discount the benefits the system is able to provide, however inequitably, for many (although often at the expense of others). I am reluctant to leave education as a changeless traditional society and loathe to convert it into a modernistic industry. There must be a state that transcends both alternatives, preserving some of the major benefits of each. Rather than being totally dominated by economic institutions and totally dependent on them, education might try to assume a position of institutional equality.

The opposites of dominance and dependency are equality and autonomy. Education as an institution should strive to assert its equality and autonomy in order to protect and defend the human values it nurtured long before the hegemony of economic institutions. If education does not do that, then it violates its own institutional integrity.

For those who say that education must always be judged by its service to other institutions, the value placed on managerial education remains high, and the degree to which education serves economic purposes is of paramount importance. Autonomy would suggest that education primarily pursue its own humanistic values, even though it is subject to some economic criteria. To abandon humanistic values would be an immoral act for education itself. A state of equality would demand that businesses and economic institutions in turn be subject to educational and humanitarian criteria.

How education can be converted to an innovative institution without subjecting itself to a state of perpetual dominance is a most formidable problem, akin to how developing countries can develop economically without becoming satellites of the powerful. Part of the answer may lie in the metamorphoses of the vertical division of labor, as prescribed in the research, development, diffusion paradigm of change.

A horizontal division of labor would bring the invention, production, and distribution of innovations closer to the people who must use them so that they will be more useful in conception, better implemented, and produce fewer inequities. The features of such a horizontal division of labor might mean shorter, less alienating development cycles where participants can see and understand what is going on and have immediate control. This would mean more self-reliance and the utilization of the local, indigenous expertise and resources at hand (Galtung, 1973).

It might also mean more "intermediate," "soft" technology, which would be cheaper and more labor-intensive than the high, capital-intensive kind. It might mean more job rotation and less specialization. The theory of a horizontal division of labor as opposed to the highly developed vertical division of labor lies entirely open. Presumably it would lead to greater equity in production and equality in distribution (Galtung, 1973). Its development will have to rely on visions greater than mine. Fortunately, among the two million people in education, there are those capable of such thought.

Although in the previous chapter I suggested a government policy that might promote such development (there are much better policies), I have little hope the government will initiate such reforms. Government officials see the world through a fully developed bureaucratic prism which, whatever the angle of refraction, cannot pass the light of anything that appears a diminution in control. The bureaucracy naturally serves the national elite, which is fixed on economic development. To turn control back to local government is to return to the local business elite—a journey to no change.

One group capable of catalyzing such a metamorphosis is the two-million-member teacher force, which is only now beginning to organize itself as a political force. Serious observers have recognized the organization of teachers and other professionals as one of the most significant social transformations in America today. According to Bell (1973), the growth of such professional classes represents the "sociologizing" forces of society as opposed to the older "economizing" forces. Critical to the future of educational innovation will be whether the organized teachers decide to "buy in" to the system, in the way that American labor unions have tended to do, or whether they will decide to defend and promote the humanistic values of their institution.

I do not know which way they will go. History suggests that they will accept the industrial metaphor and, for a price, become a highly bureaucratized, technologized segment of a fully integrated economy. But emerging leaders are egalitarian, humanistically oriented, and tough. It could be that the teachers will draw the line at the industrial corporation dominating not only our adulthood but our childhood as well.

REFERENCES

Abbott, Max G., 1967. "Hierarchical Impediments to Innovation in Educational Organizations," in Max G. Abbott and John J. Lowell (eds.), *Change Perspectives in Educational Administration.* Auburn, Ala.: Auburn University School of Education.

Abelson, Philip H., 1972. "The Fourth Revolution." *Science,* 177.4044(July 14).

Abert, James G., 1974. "Wanted: Experiments in Reducing the Cost of Education." *Phi Delta Kappan,* 15.7(March):444-445.

Alpert, Daniel, 1970. "University Research on Problems Posed by Society." Speech to Illinois Chapter of Sigma Xi on February 19.

———, and Bitzer, Donald L., 1971. "The World after PLATO IV: The Implications of Computer-Based Systems in Education of the Future." Paper prepared for the Select Subcommittee on Education, U.S. House of Representatives, June.

Atkin, J. Myron, 1973. "The Rhetoric and the Reality of Educational Change." *Educational Technology,* 13.11(November).

Barnes, Peter, 1971. "Aerospace Dinosaurs." *The New Republic,* 164.13(March 27):12-19.

Bartley, Robert L., 1971. "On the Limits of Rationality." *The Wall Street Journal,* September 10.

Becker, Marshall H., 1972. "Sociometric Location and Innovativeness: Reformulation and Extension of the Diffusion Model." *American Sociological Review,* 35.2(April):267-282.

Bell, Daniel, 1973. *The Coming of the Post-Industrial Society.* New York: Basic Books.

Bowles, Samuel, and Gintis, Herbert, 1973, 1974. "I.Q. in the U.S. Class Structure." *Social Policy,* 3.4 and 5(November/December and January/February):65-96.

Brown, Lawrence A., 1968a. *Diffusion Dynamics: A Review and Revision of the Quantitative Theory of the Spatial Diffusion of Innovations.* Lund, Sweden: Royal University of Lund.

———, 1968b. *Diffusion Processes and Location: A Conceptual Framework and Bibliography.* Regional Science Research Institute.

———, and Moore, Eric G., no date. "Diffusion Research in Geography: A Perspective." Department of Geography Discussion Paper, No. 9-11. Iowa City: University of Iowa.

Callahan, Raymond E., 1962. *Education and the Cult of Efficiency.* Chicago: University of Chicago Press.

Carlson, Richard O., 1965. *Adoption of Educational Innovations.* Eugene, Ore.: Center for the Advanced Study of Educational Administration, University of Oregon.

———, 1972, *School Superintendents: Careers and Performance.* Columbus, Ohio: Charles E. Merrill.

Carnegie Commission on Higher Education, 1972. *The Fourth Revolution: Instructional Technology in Higher Education.* New York: McGraw-Hill.

Charters, W. W., Jr., and Pellegrin, Roland J., 1973. "Barriers to the Innovation Process: Four Case Studies of Differentiated Staffing." *Educational Administration Quarterly,* 9.1(Winter):3-14.

Clark, Burton R., 1972. "The Organizational Saga in Higher Education." *Administrative Science Quarterly,* 17.2(June):178-184.

Clark, David L., 1962. "The Function of the United States Office of Education and the State Department of Education in the Dissemination and Implementation of Educational Research," in *Third Annual Phi Delta Kappa Symposium on Educational Research.*

———, and Guba, Egon G., 1965. "An Examination of Potential Change Roles in Education." Seminar on Innovation in Planning School Curriculum, October.

———, and Guba, Egon G., 1972. "A Re-Examination of a Test of the Research and Development Model of Change." *Educational Administration Quarterly,* 8.3(Autumn): 93-103.

Cohen, Elizabeth G., 1973. "Open-Space Schools: The Opportunity to Become Ambitious." *Sociology of Education,* 46.2(Spring):143-161.

Corwin, Ronald G., 1972. "Strategies for Organizational Innovation: An Empirical Comparison." *American Sociological Review,* 37.4(August):441-454.

Dahllof, Urban S., 1971. *Ability Grouping, Content Validity, and Curriculum Process Analysis.* New York: Teachers' College Press.

Doughty, Philip L., and Stakenas, Robert G., 1973. "An Analysis of Costs and Effectiveness of an Individualized Subject Offering," in Creta D. Sabine (ed.), *Accountability: Systems Planning in Education.* Homewood, Ill.: ETC Publication, pp. 165-191.

Dreeben, Robert, 1973. "The School as a Workplace," in Robert M. W. Travers (ed.), *Second Handbook of Research on Teaching.* Chicago: Rand McNally, pp. 450-473.

Dresang, Dennis L., 1973. "Entrepreneurialism and Development Administration." *Administrative Science Quarterly,* 18.1(March):76-85.

Elboim-Dror, Rachel, 1971. "The Resistance to Change of Educational Administration." *Future,* 3.3(September):201-214.

Evans, Richard I., 1970. *Resistance to Innovation in Higher Education.* San Francisco: Jossey-Bass.

Gallagher, James J., 1970. "Unfinished Educational Tasks (Thoughts on Leaving Government Service)." *Exceptional Children,* 36.10(Summer):709-716.

———, Nuthall, Graham A., and Rosenshine, Barak, 1970. *Classroom Observation.* AERA Monograph Series on Curriculum Evaluation, No. 6. Chicago: Rand McNally.

Galtung, Johan, 1971. "A Structural Theory of Imperialism." *Journal of Peace Research,* 8.2:81-117.

———, 1973. *The European Community: A Superpower in the Making.* London: George Allen and Unwin, Ltd.

Gjerde, Craig L., 1974. *Introducing a Technological Innovation to the Community College.* Unpublished doctoral dissertation, University of Illinois at Urbana-Champaign.

Gould, Peter, and Tornquist, Gunnar, 1971. "Information, Innovation, and Acceptance," in Torsten Hagerstrand and Antoni R. Kuklinski (eds.), *Information Systems for Regional Development—A Seminar.* Lund Studies in Geography, Series B, No. 37. Lund, Sweden: Royal University of Lund.

Green, Thomas F., 1969. "Schools and Communities: A Look Forward." *Harvard Educational Review,* Reprint Serial No. 3:111-142.

Hage, Jerald, and Aiken, Michael, 1970. *Social Change in Complex Organizations.* New York: Random House.

———, and Dewar, Robert, 1973. "Elite Values versus Organizational Structure in Predicting Innovation." *Administrative Science Quarterly,* 18.3(September):279-290.

Hagerstrand, Torsten, 1953. *The Propagation of Innovation Waves.* Lund, Sweden: Royal University of Lund.

———, 1967. *Innovation Diffusion as a Spatial Process.* Chicago: University of Chicago Press.

———, 1968. "A Monte Carlo Approach to Diffusion," in Brian J. L. Berry and Duane F. Marble (eds.), *Spatial Analysis: A Reader in Statistical Geography.* Englewood Cliffs, N.J.: Prentice-Hall.

Haggerty, Patrick E., 1973. "Research and Development, Educational Productivity, and the American Economy." *Educational Researcher,* 2.9(September): 4-10.

Hammond, Allen C., 1972. "Computer-Assisted Instruction: Two Demonstrations." *Science,* 176.4039(June 9).

Harvey, David L., 1969. "An Ethnography of a White Workingclass Community," in *Research and Development Program on Preschool Disadvantaged Children,* Volume III. U.S. Department of Health, Education, and Welfare, Project No. 5-1187, Contract No. OE 6-10-235.

Havelock, Ronald G., 1971. *Planning for Innovation.* Ann Arbor: Center for Research on Utilization of Scientific Knowledge, Institute for Social Research, University of Michigan.

Hoke, Gordon, 1971. *Goodbye to Yesterday.* Urbana-Champaign: Center for Instructional Research and Curriculum Evaluation, University of Illinois.

Hotvedt, Martyn O., 1973. "Communication Patterns within the Gifted Program." Center for Instructional Research and Curriculum Evaluation, University of Illinois at Urbana-Champaign, July 1973 (mimeo).

House, Ernest R., 1971. "A Critique of Linear Change Models in Education." *Educational Technology,* 11.10(October):35.

———, 1972a. "The Dominion of Economic Accountability." *Educational Forum,* 37.1(November):13-24.

———, 1972b. "A Response to Clark and Guba: The Logic of Revisionism." *Educational Administration Quarterly,* 8.3(Autumn):104-106.

———, and Gjerde, Craig L., 1973. *PLATO Comes to the Community College.* Urbana-Champaign: Center for Instructional Research and Curriculum Evaluation, University of Illinois.

———, Kerins, Thomas, and Steele, Joe M., 1972. "A Test of the Research and Development Model of Change." *Educational Administration Quarterly,* 8.1(Winter):1-14.

———, and Long, John M., 1974. "Applying Directed Graph Theory to Faculty Contact Structure." Paper presented at Annual Meeting of the American Educational Research Association, Chicago, April 19.

———, Steele, Joe M. and Kerins, Thomas, 1971. *The Gifted Classroom.* Urbana-Champaign: Center for Instructional Research and Curriculum Evaluation, University of Illinois.

———, Steele, Joe M., and Kerins, Thomas, 1972. "A Conflict Model of Change: The Advocate." Paper presented at Annual Meeting of the American Educational Research Association, Chicago, April 4.

International Development, 1971. Twelfth World Conference of the Society for International Development, Ottawa.

Janossy, Fernenc, 1966. *The End of the Economic Miracle.* White Plains, N.Y.: International Arts and Sciences Press.

Kirst, Michael W., 1974. "The Growth of Federal Influence in Education," in *Uses of the Sociology of Education,* Seventy-Third Yearbook of the National Society for the Study of Education, Part II. Chicago: the Society.

Kuhn, Thomas S., 1962. *The Structure of Scientific Revolutions.* Chicago: University of Chicago Press.

Lasuen, J. R., 1971. "Multi-Regional Economic Development: An Open-System Approach," in Torsten Hagerstrand and Antoni R. Kuklinski (eds.), *Information Systems for Regional Development—A Seminar.* Lund Series in Geography, Series B, No. 37. Lund, Sweden: Royal University of Lund.

Lortie, Dan C., 1973. "Observations on Teaching as Work," in Robert M. W. Travers (ed.), *Second Handbook of Research on Teaching.* Chicago: Rand McNally, pp. 474-497.

McGivney, Joseph H., and Haught, James M., 1972. "The Politics of Education: A View from the Perspective of the Central Office Staff." *Educational Administration Quarterly,* 8.3(Autumn):18-38.

March, James G., 1966. "Organization Factors in Supervision," in *The Supervisor: Agent for Change in Teaching.* Washington, D.C.: Association for Supervision and Curriculum Development, National Education Association.

Nan Lin, and Len, Donald J., Rogers, Everett M., and Schwartz, Donald F., 1966. "The Diffusion of an Innovation in Three Michigan High Schools: Institution Building through Change." Michigan State University, East Lansing (mimeo).

National Institute of Education, 1973. *Building Capacity for Renewal and Reform.* Washington, D.C.: the Institute.

Nobile, Philip, 1973. "The American Army: An Exercise in Distorted Values." *Midwest Magazine* (March 18):33- .

Normann, Richard, 1971. "Organizational Innovativeness: Product Variation and Reorientation." *Administrative Science Quarterly*, 16.2(June):203-215.

Paisley, William, 1972. "The Role of Invisible Colleges in Scientific Information Transfer." *Educational Researcher*, 1.4(April):5-19.

Pedersen, Poul Ove, 1970. "Innovation Diffusion within and between National Urban Systems." *Geographical Analysis*, 2.3(July):203-254.

———, 1971. "Innovation Diffusion in Urban Systems," in Torsten Hagerstrand and Antoni R. Kuklinski (eds.), *Information Systems for Regional Development—A Seminar.* Lund Studies in Geography, Series B, No. 37. Lund, Sweden: Royal University of Lund.

Pincus, John, 1974. "Incentives for Innovation in the Public Schools." *Review of Educational Research*, 44.1(Winter):113-144.

Rivlin, Alice M., 1971. *Systematic Thinking for Social Action.* Washington, D.C.: Brookings Institution.

Rogers, Everett M., 1962. *Diffusion of Innovations.* New York: Free Press.

———, and F. Floyd Shoemaker, 1971. *Communication of Innovations.* New York: Free Press.

Roos, Leslie L., Jr., 1972. "Politics, Organizations, and Choice: Applications of an Equilibrium Model." *Administrative Science Quarterly*, 17.4(December): 529-543.

Schumacher, Sally, 1972. "Limitations of a Research, Development, and Diffusion (RD&D) Strategy in Diffusion: A Case Study of Nine Local Implementations of a State-Adopted Curriculum." Paper presented at the National Council for the Social Studies, Boston, November.

Selznick, Philip, 1957. *Leadership in Administration.* Evanston, Ill.: Row, Peterson.

Slevin, Dennis P., 1971. "The Innovation Boundary: A Specific Model and Some Empirical Results." *Administrative Science Quarterly*, 16.4(December): 515-531.

———, 1973. "The Innovation Boundary: A Replication with Increased Costs." *Administrative Science Quarterly*, 18.1(March):71-75.

Spuck, Dennis W., 1974. "Reward Structures in the Public High School." *Educational Administration Quarterly*, 10.1(Winter):18-34.

Stephens, Thomas, 1974. "Innovative Teaching Practices: Their Relation to System Norms and Rewards." *Educational Administration Quarterly*, 10.1 (Winter):35-43.

Thompson, Victor A., 1969. *Bureaucracy and Innovation*. Tuscaloosa, Ala.: University of Alabama Press.

Tornquist, Gunnar, 1970. *Contact Systems and Regional Development*. Lund, Sweden: Royal University of Lund.

Travers, Robert M. W., 1973. "Educational Technology and Related Research Viewed as a Political Force," in Robert M. W. Travers (ed.), *Second Handbook of Research on Teaching*. Chicago: Rand McNally, pp. 979-996.

Vickers, Geoffrey, 1970. *Freedom in a Rocking Boat*. Baltimore: Penguin Books.

Washington Monitor, 1973. "Research Millions Bear Little Fruit, Study Says." National School Public Relations Association, Arlington, Virginia, December 17.

Westbury, Ian, 1973. "Conventional Classrooms, Open Classrooms, and the Technology of Teaching." *Journal of Curriculum Studies*, 5(November): 99-121.

Wildavsky, Aaron, 1972. "Why Planning Fails in Nepal." *Administrative Science Quarterly*, 17.4(December):508-528.

Wolf, Robert L., 1973. "A Case Study of Change in the Illinois Gifted Program." Center for Instructional Research and Curriculum Evaluation, University of Illinois at Urbana-Champaign, July (mimeo).

Young, Frank W., 1971. "A Macrosociological Interpretation of Entrepreneurship," in Peter Kilby (ed.), *Entrepreneurship and Economic Development*. New York: Free Press.

ORGANIZATIONS

rational, natural, and open systems

ORGANIZATIONS

rational,
natural,
and

SECOND
EDITION open systems

W. RICHARD SCOTT

Stanford University

Prentice/Hall International, Inc.

Library of Congress Cataloging-in-Publication Data

SCOTT, W. RICHARD.
    Organizations : rational, natural, and open systems.

    Bibliography: p. 339.
    Includes indexes.
    1. Organization.   I. Title.
HM131.S335 1987   302.3'5   86-9368
ISBN 0-13-640665-3

The author wishes to thank the copyright owners for permission to reprint in the text the following figures, tables and quotations:

Fig. 1-1. From Harold J. Leavitt, Applied organizational change in industry: structural, technological and humanistic approaches, in J. G. March (ed.), *Handbook of Organizations*, p. 1145. Copyright © 1965 by Rand McNally College Publishing Company, Chicago, Illinois. Reprinted by permission.

Figs. 4-1 and 4-2. Adapted from Robert L. Swinth, *Organizational Systems for Management*, pp. 18 and 23. Grid, Inc., Columbus, Ohio, 1974. Reprinted by permission.

continued, page 362

Printed in the United States of America

10   9   8   7   6   5   4   3   2

Manufacturing buyer: Carol Bystrom

ISBN 0-13-640665-3   01

Prentice-Hall International (UK) Limited, *London*
Prentice-Hall of Australia Pty. Limited, *Sydney*
Prentice-Hall Canada Inc., *Toronto*
Prentice-Hall Hispanoamericana, S.A., *Mexico*
Prentice-Hall of India Private Limited, *New Delhi*
Prentice-Hall of Japan, Inc., *Tokyo*
Prentice-Hall of Southeast Asia Pte. Ltd., *Singapore*
Editora Prentice-Hall do Brasil, Ltda., *Rio de Janeiro*
Prentice-Hall, *Englewood Cliffs, New Jersey*

again for
Jennifer, Elliot, and Sydney

contents

7   CREATING ORGANIZATIONS   143

8   BOUNDARY SETTING AND BOUNDARY SPANNING   170

preface

When I was invited by a European colleague earlier this year to describe the effects of the current "crisis" in sociology on the state of organization theory, I conjured up this picture of the contemporary scene:

> The dominant cathedral of Rational Structure has been partially dismantled and, although portions are still standing, many of its building blocks have been carted off to be reconfigured into alternative and challenging contructions. More fragile shelters and colorful but perhaps temporary tents have been thrust up in vacant lots. The scene is one of much animation and energy: raw materials and scaffolding are strewn about; lamps in windows and camp fires burn far into the night. The image I wish to convey of the present situation . . . is partly that of crisis and confusion but more that of vigorous controversy and an enriching profusion of competing models and methods. (Scott, 1986)

Though I perhaps became somewhat carried away in the poetry of the moment, I do believe that the overall portrait is substantially correct. The field of organizations has undergone enormous change in the past few decades. It is currently, I believe, the most lively and vigorous area of study within sociology, and perhaps within all of the social sciences. This is a source of both excitement and confusion. Much is happening in the field, and developments are occurring faster than our ability to assimilate them into coherent patterns.

In the first edition of this book, published in 1981, the dominant transformation described was the shift from closed to open system models of organizations. Prior to the 1960s, most of the theorizing and research on organizations looked inside the organization not only for topics of study but also for bases of explanation. Organizations were assumed to be relatively autonomous and complete systems, and understanding was to be found in examining factors and processes within their fixed boundaries. Beginning about 1960, all this changed. The openness of organizations to their environments was recognized, and the linkages among "internal" and "external" objects and events was more likely to be taken into account. Organizations came to be viewed as less internally coherent and more externally connected than formerly assumed.

The first edition also described the revitalization—as well as the renewed criticism—of rational system models and the developing interest in natural system models. Rational system models have continued to grow and flourish, especially the transactions costs version pursued by the new institutional economists. The newer, challenging natural system conceptions could only be sketched or incompletely described six years ago. Now it is possible to present a much fuller account of them. The ecological, resource dependence, Marxist, and institutional approaches are more fully elaborated, and increasingly constitute full-fledged alternatives to rational system arguments. Views emphasizing cultural explanations have also gained much currency in recent years, and we consider these insights as well. Attention is also given in this edition to the recently developing ethnomethodological and interactionist approaches. There is much new work to review.

There was a time, approximately in the mid 1960s, when it appeared as if organizational sociology was in danger of being submerged under administrative science, which addresses the important but narrow issues of rational design and technical efficiency. That danger now appears quite remote. Organizational sociologists have rediscovered their intellectual roots and are enthusiastically addressing the old, central issues of the discipline—the distribution and use of power, the determinants and consequences of inequality, the creation of commitments and of meaning—within a set of new theoretical frameworks. It is a time of great excitement and ferment. This revised edition attempts to reflect this creative agitation. As before, we propose to deal with some of the complexity by showing that it can be understood as reflecting continuing controversies among three theoretical perspectives: the rational, natural, and open systems approaches. This framework is severely tested by the multiplicity of new ideas and concerns, but its seams appear to have held against the onslaught.

In the preface to the first edition, I attempted to acknowledge the help I have received from my former teachers and students and my current colleagues. This list is now too long to enumerate. I know who they are and they know. I hope they also know how grateful I am for all they have taught me.

Among my immediate circle at Stanford, I rely ever more heavily on the wisdom and virtue of Jim March, Jeff Pfeffer, and John Meyer. They are smarter and more productive than I, but gracious enough to treat me as an equal. In the stimulating intellectual community of organizations students on this campus, these three are a major resource for us all.

My wife Joy and our children continue to indulge and support my scholarly activities, even though they cut deeply into our evenings and weekends. The children will settle only for some tangible evidence of my guilt, and have again claimed their place on the dedication page. Joy knows the value of intangibles.

W. Richard Scott

Stanford, California

ORGANIZATIONS
rational, natural, and open systems

PART ONE

AN INTRODUCTION TO ORGANIZATIONS

Organizations play a leading role in our modern world. Their presence affects—some would insist that the proper term is *infects*—virtually every sector of contemporary social life. Peter Drucker thus observes, "Young people today will have to learn organizations the way their forefathers learned farming." Chapter 1 endeavors to amplify and justify this advice by examining both the practical and theoretical benefits to be gained from a better understanding of organizations.

Part One pursues the two major themes of *commonality* and *diversity*. Organizations share certain features, which serve to differentiate them from other social forms. Students of this field believe that we can understand much about a specific organization from knowing about other organizations. Understanding how a factory functions can illuminate the workings of a hospital; and knowledge of a governmental bureau can help us understand the workings of a union.

Diversity appears in many guises. While organizations may possess common, generic characteristics, they exhibit staggering variety—in size, in structure, and in operating processes. Just as organizations vary, so do those who study them. Students of organizations bring to their task varying interests, tools, and intellectual preconceptions. Of particular importance are differences in the level of analysis employed and in the theoretical perspectives utilized.

Three influential perspectives are introduced in Chapter 1 as competing definitions of organizations. Part Two is devoted to an intensive examination of these perspectives, which have shaped and continue to govern our understanding of organizations.

1 the subject is organizations

The recurrent problem in sociology is to conceive of corporate organization, and to study it, in ways that do not anthropomorphize it and do not reduce it to the behavior of individuals or of human aggregates.

Guy E. Swanson (1976)

The philosopher Alfred North Whitehead once suggested that, properly organized, education should proceed through three stages. In the first stage, that of *romance,* the student's interest is aroused: he or she is brought face to face with the object of study in all its power and mystery. If the subject is mechanical engineering, for example, the student could be taken to see a steam locomotive or a steel mill in operation. In the second stage, labeled *discipline,* the student acquires the concepts and methods required to analyze the subject and its parts and processes. And in the third stage, that of *fruition,* the methods and concepts are applied to the subject so that its structure and functioning may be understood and, perhaps, improved (Whitehead, 1929).

Our subject is organizations. We do not need to plan a field trip for students to observe this phenomenon in action: organizations are all around us. Because of their ubiquity, however, they fade into the background, and we need to be reminded of their impact. This chapter begins with a discussion of the practical and the theoretical importance of organizations: we attempt to arouse your interest so that an intellectual courtship can begin. We also begin the task of developing concepts for analyzing organizations; this work will continue throughout the volume. We do not intend to postpone the phase of fruition until the final chapters but will attempt early and often to demonstrate how the use of the concepts and methods can improve our understanding of the structure and functioning of organizations and, in some cases, contribute to their betterment.

THE IMPORTANCE OF ORGANIZATIONS

There is no need to belabor the assertion that ours is an organizational society—that organizations are a prominent, if not the dominant, characteristic of modern societies. Organizations were present in older civilizations—

Chinese, Greek, Indian—but only in modern industrialized societies do we find large numbers of organizations engaged in performing many highly diverse tasks. To the ancient organizational assignments of soldiering, public administration, and tax collection have been added such varied tasks as discovery (research organizations), child and adult socialization (schools and universities), resocialization (mental hospitals and prisons), production and distribution of goods (industrial firms, wholesale and retail establishments), provision of services (organizations dispensing assistance ranging from laundry and shoe repair to medical care and investment counseling), protection of personal and financial security (police departments, insurance firms, banking and trust companies), preservation of culture (museums, art galleries, universities, libraries), communication (radio and television studios, telephone companies, the post office), and recreation (bowling alleys, pool halls, the National Park Service, professional football teams). Even such a partial listing testifies to the truth of Parsons's statement that "the development of organizations is the principal mechanism by which, in a highly differentiated society, it is possible to 'get things done,' to achieve goals beyond the reach of the individual" (1960:41).

Even though organizations are now ubiquitous, their development has been sufficiently gradual and uncontroversial that they have emerged during the past few centuries almost unnoticed. The spread of public bureaucracies into every sector and the displacement of the family business by the corporation "constitutes a revolution" in social structure, but one little remarked until recently.

> Never much agitated, never even much resisted, a revolution for which no flags were raised, it transformed our lives during those very decades in which, unmindful of what was happening, Americans and Europeans debated instead such issues as socialism, populism, free silver, clericalism, chartism, and colonialism. It now stands as a monument to discrepancy between what men think they are designing and the world they are in fact building. (Lindblom, 1977: 95)

The prevalence of organizations in every arena of social life is one indicator of their importance. Another, rather different index of their significance is the increasing frequency with which organizations are singled out as the source of many of the ills besetting contemporary society. Thus, writing in 1956, C. Wright Mills pointed with alarm to the emergence of a "power elite" whose members occupied the top positions in three overlapping organizational hierarchies: the state bureaucracy, the military, and the larger corporations. At about the same time, Ralf Dahrendorf (1959 trans.) in Germany was engaged in revising and updating Marxist doctrine by insisting that the basis of the class structure was no longer the ownership of the means of production but the occupancy of positions that allowed the wielding of organizational authority. Such views, which remain controversial, focus on the effects of organizations on societal stratification systems, taking account of the changing bases of power and prestige occasioned by the growth in number and size of organizations.

A related criticism concerns the seemingly inexorable growth in public-sector organizations. The two great German sociologists Max Weber (1947 trans.) and Robert Michels (1949 trans.) were among the first to insist that the central political issue for all modern societies was no longer the type of economic structure that prevailed—whether capitalist, socialist, or communist—but the increasing dominance by the public bureaucracy of the ostensible political leaders.

Other criticisms point to the negative consequences of the growth of organizations in virtually *every* area of social existence. Borrowing from and enlarging on a theme pervading the thought of Weber, these critics decry the rationalization of modern life—in Weber's phrase, the "disenchantment of the world" (1946 trans.:51). The essence of this view is graphically captured by Norman Mailer: "Civilization extracts its thousand fees from the best nights of man, but none so cruel as the replacement of the good fairy by the expert, the demon by the rational crisis, and the witch by the neurotic female" (1968:83). Organizations are viewed as the primary vehicle by which, systematically, the areas of our lives are rationalized—planned, articulated, scientized, made more efficient and orderly, and managed by "experts." (See, for example, Mannheim, 1950 trans.; Ellul, 1964 trans.; Goodman, 1968; and Galbraith, 1967.) The dark side of such progress is depicted by Roszak, who defines the technocracy as "that social form in which an industrial society reaches the peak of its organizational integration." He writes, "Under the technocracy we become the most scientific of societies; yet, like Kafka's K., men throughout the 'developed world' become more and more the bewildered dependents of inaccessible castles wherein inscrutable technicians conjure with their fate" (1969: 5, 13).

A new generation of feminist critics reminds us that it is not just "men" who are trapped in organizational cages. Like Roszak, Glennon (1979) decries the growth of technocracy, but on the feminist grounds that it feeds the "dualism of private-expressive and public-instrumental selves and worlds" and engenders a bureaucratic rationality that extends instrumental and administrative orientations into everyday— including private—life. Ferguson (1984: 203) is even more direct in her criticism:

> The organizational forms and discourse of bureaucratic capitalism institutionalize modes of domination that recreate the very patterns of oppression that feminism arose to combat.

These critics thus add their voices to others who have called attention to the ways in which organizational structures damage the personalities and psyches of their participants. Alienation, overconformity, and stunting of normal personality development are among the consequences attributed, not to such special cases as prisons and concentration camps, but to everyday, garden-variety organizations (see Argyris, 1957; Maslow, 1954; Whyte, 1956).

We attempt to evaluate such criticisms of organizations at appropriate points throughout this volume. Here we simply note that these negative views towards organizations provide further testimony to their importance in the modern world.

In addition to their being mechanisms for accomplishing a great variety of objectives and, perhaps as a necessary consequence, the source of many of our current difficulties, organizations have yet another important effect on our collective lives. This effect is more subtle and less widely recognized, but it may be quite profound in its implications. It is, perhaps best introduced by an analogy: "The medium is the message." This twentieth-century aphorism was coined by Marshall McLuhan (1964) to focus attention on the characteristics of the mass media themselves—print, radio, movies, television—in contrast with the content transmitted by these media. McLuhan defines media very broadly as "any extension of ourselves"; elaborating his thesis, he notes, "The message of any medium is the change in scale or pace or pattern that it introduces into human affairs" (1964: 23, 24).

McLuhan's thesis appears to be more clearly applicable to our subject—organizations—than to any specific media of communication. First, like media, organizations represent extensions of ourselves. Organizations can achieve goals that are quite beyond the reach of any individual—from building skyscrapers and dams to putting a person on the moon. But to focus on what organizations *do* may conceal from us the more basic and far-reaching effects that occur because organizations are the *mechanisms*—the media—by which those goals are pursued. A few examples may suggest some of these unanticipated organizational effects:

- In his crucial decision on how to react to the installation of Russian missiles in Cuba, President Kennedy had to select from among a naval blockade, a "surgical" air strike, and a massive land invasion, not because these were the only conceivable responses, but because these were the principal organizational routines that had been worked out by the Pentagon (see Allison, 1971).
- Although we seek "health" when we visit the clinic or the hospital, what we get is "medical care." Clients are encouraged to view these outputs as synonymous although there may be no relation between them. In some cases, the relation can even be negative: more care can result in poorer health (see Illich, 1976).
- Products manufactured by organizations reflect the manufacturing process. They often reflect the need to subdivide work and to simplify tasks, and the manufacturing pressures toward standardization of parts and personnel (Veblen, 1904). Customization—in the genuine sense, not in the Detroit sense—becomes prohibitively expensive. Metal replaces wood and plastic replaces metal in many products to satisfy organizational, not consumer, needs.

To suggest that our organizational tools shape in unanticipated ways the products and services they produce would appear to be a relatively sweeping and unsettling generalization on which we might be content to rest our case. However, our arguments concerning the importance of organizations are not quite finished: we give the screw one final turn.

We will fail to perceive the importance of organizations for our own lives if we view them merely as tools for achieving goals. Organizations must also be viewed as actors in their own right, as *corporate persons*, to use Coleman's phrase (1974). They can take actions, utilize resources, enter into contracts, and own property. Coleman describes how these rights have gradually developed since the Middle Ages to the point where now it is accurate to speak of two kinds of persons—*natural* persons (such as you and me) and corporate or *juristic* persons (such as the Red Cross and

General Motors). The social structure of the modern society can no longer be described accurately as consisting only of relations among natural persons: our understanding must be stretched to include as well those relations between natural and corporate persons, and between corporate and corporate persons. In short, we must come to "the recognition that the society has changed over the past few centuries in the very structural elements of which it is composed" (Coleman, 1974: 13).

A different kind of rationale for justifying the study of organizations as a basic social science pursuit is suggested by the following statement of Homans: "The fact is that the organization of the large formal enterprises, governmental or private, in modern society is modeled on, is a rationalization of, tendencies that exist in all human groups" (1950: 186–87). To say that organizations exhibit "tendencies that exist in all human groups" is to suggest that organizations provide the setting for a wide variety of basic social processes, such as socialization, communication, ranking, the formation of norms, the exercise of power, and goal setting and attainment. If these generic social processes operate in organizations, then we can add as much to our knowledge of the principles that govern their behavior by studying organizations as by studying any other specific type of social system. But Homans asserts something more.

To say that we can perceive in organizations "a rationalization of tendencies that exist in all human groups" is to suggest that organizations are characterized by somewhat distinctive structural arrangements that affect the operation of the processes occurring within them. For example, social-control processes occur within all social groups, but there are some forms or mechanisms of control—for instance, a hierarchical authority structure—that are best studied in organizations, since it is within these systems that they appear in their most highly developed form.[1] The processes of interest can occur at various levels of analysis, as will be discussed in the following section. Also, decidedly, one of the important tasks is to spell out clearly what is meant by *distinctive structural arrangements*. We will begin this task in the present chapter but will find it sufficiently challenging that we will need to keep it before us throughout this volume.

At this point, however, we assert our belief that the study of organizations can contribute to basic sociological knowledge by increasing our understanding of how generic social processes operate within distinctive social structures.

ORGANIZATIONS AS AN AREA OF STUDY

Emergence of the Area

The study of organizations is both a specialized field of inquiry within the discipline of sociology and an increasingly recognized focus of

---

[1]This general argument has been elaborated elsewhere (Scott, 1970). The basic premise is that a set of generic social processes—such as socialization, integration, status, power, adaptation—may be identified in all social structures. However, each of these processes operates differently depending on the structural context in which it is acting so that, for example, the process of integration is effected in a small group differently than in an organization, and both differ from the same process occurring within a community, and so on.

multidisciplinary research and training. It is impossible to determine with precision the moment of its appearance, but it is safe to conclude that until the late 1940s, organizations did not exist as a distinct field of sociological inquiry. Precursors may be indentified, but each lacked some critical feature. Thus, there was some empirical research on organizations by, for example, criminologists who studied prisons (for example, Clemmer, 1940), political analysts who examined party structures (for example, Gosnell, 1937), and industrial sociologists who studied factories and labor unions (for example, Whyte, 1946). But these investigators rarely attempted to generalize beyond the specific organizational form they were studying. The subject was prisons or parties or factories or unions—not organizations. Similarly, in the neighboring disciplines, political scientists were examining the functioning of legislative bodies or public agencies, and economists were developing their theory of the firm, but they were not attempting to generalize beyond these specific forms.

Industrial psychologists did pursue such general problems as low morale, fatigue, and turnover within several types of organizational settings, but they did not attempt to determine systematically how the varying characteristics of different organizational contexts influenced these worker reactions. And although, from early in this century, administrative and management theorists such as Fayol (1949 trans.) and Gulick and Urwick (1937) did concentrate on the development of general principles concerning administrative arrangements, their approach was more often prescriptive than empirical. That is, they were interested in determining what "should be" in the interests of maximizing efficiency and effectiveness rather than in examining and explaining organizational arrangements as they existed.

Within sociology, the emergence of the field of organizations may be roughly dated from the translation into English of Weber's (1946 trans., 1947 trans.) and, to a lesser extent, Michels's (1949 trans.) analyses of bureaucracy. Shortly after these classic statements became accessible to American sociologists, Robert K. Merton and his students at Columbia University attempted to outline the boundaries of this new field of inquiry by compiling theoretical and empirical materials dealing with various aspects of organizations (Merton et al., 1952). Equally important, a series of pathbreaking and influential case studies of diverse types of organizations was launched under Merton's influence, including an examination of the Tennessee Valley Authority (Selznick, 1949), a gypsum mine and factory (Gouldner, 1954), a state employment agency and a federal law-enforcement agency (Blau, 1955), and a union (Lipset, Trow, and Coleman, 1956). For the first time, sociologists were engaged in the development and empirical testing of generalizations dealing with the structure and functioning of organizations viewed as organizations.

In a similar fashion, analysts working in other social science traditions focused increasingly on general organizational issues. After World War II, students of industrial psychology, public administration, social anthropology, and institutional economics began to pay less attention to divergent backgrounds and more to common interests. Intellectual ancestors, such as Machiavelli, St. Simon, Weber, and Frederick Winslow Taylor, were uncovered, and more recent academic forbears, such as Elton Mayo (1945) and Chester Barnard (1938; 1948), were rediscovered and reprinted. Even a couple of token women contributors were identified, in the persons of Lillian M. Gilbreth—who collaborated with her husband in finding ways to improve work efficiency in factories but also applied the techniques at home and whose feats are celebrated in the book and movie *Cheaper by the Dozen* (see Gilbreth and Gilbreth, 1917)—and Mary Parker Follett (1942), an early student of management and change working in the human relations tradition. After about a decade of empirical research and theory development, three textbook-treatises—March and Simon (1958), Likert (1961), and Blau and Scott (1962)—provided needed integration and heightened interest in the field. Also, a new journal, *Administrative Science Quarterly*, founded in 1956, emphasized the interdisciplinary character of the field.[2]

Common and Divergent Interests

What features do all organizations exhibit in common? What are the general organizational issues analysts began to perceive among the great diversity of specific goals and structural arrangements? Most analysts have conceived of organizations as social structures created by individuals to support the collaborative pursuit of specified goals. Given this conception, all organizations confront a number of common problems. All must define (and redefine) their objectives; all must induce participants to contribute services; all must control and coordinate these contributions; resources must be garnered from the environment and products or services dispensed; participants must be selected, trained, and replaced; and some sort of working accommodation with the neighbors must be achieved.

In addition to these common operational requirements, some analysts have also emphasized that all organizations are beset by a common curse. A high proportion of the resources utilized by any organization is expended in maintaining the organization itself rather than in achieving the specified goals. Although organizations are viewed as means to accomplish ends, the means themselves absorb much energy, and in the extreme (but perhaps not rare) case become ends in themselves.

There is a convergence of interest around these common features, but we must not overlook the many bases of divergence. Most obvious, organizations come in a bewildering variety of sizes and shapes. The largest of them are very large: General Motors employed 690,000 persons in 1985; American Telephone and Telegraph, before divestiture, counted more than 3 million stockholders. Most workers in this country are employees of someone else: only about 8 percent of the work force is self-employed. And more workers are employed by fewer and larger companies: by 1975, 3 percent of the employing organizations accounted for 55 percent of the employed, and about one quarter of the total work force was employed by firms with more than 1000 employees. Still, small organizations remain the most common type: 51 percent of all employing organizations in 1975 employed 3 or fewer individuals. (U.S. Department of Labor, 1979) And the predominant ownership form remains the sole proprietorship, with

---

[2]Other brief histories of the development of organizations as an identifiable field of inquiry are provided by March (1965: ix–xvi) and Pfeffer (1982: 23–33). An entertaining, if jaundiced, view of the evolution of organization theory can be found in Perrow (1973).

more than 12 million establishments, compared with about 2.8 million corporations and about 1.5 million partnerships. Of course, the corporation far outstrips the other forms in assets, employees, and earnings. (U.S. Bureau of the Census, 1984) These employment organizations also vary greatly in the types of goods and services provided: from coal mining to computers, from fortune-telling to futures forecasting.

Large and growing numbers of people are employed in the public sector. In 1984, over 16 million individuals—about one fifth of the number working in the private sector—were employed in federal, state, and local governments. The number of units or agencies involved is difficult to determine because of the nested character of governmental forms. *The United States Government Manual* (U.S. Office of the Federal Register, 1984) provides organizational charts and brief descriptions of the principal agencies. It currently numbers almost 1000 pages! It is well to recognize that federal employees make up only about 20 percent of all governmental officials, the vast majority of whom are employed at the state (3.8 million) and local levels (9.3 million), where there is great variation in organizational arrangements.

Employing organizations do not exhaust the list of organizational forms. Verba and Nie (1972) estimate that about two thirds of adult Americans belong to one or more voluntary associations, not counting churches. The number and variety of such forms is large, and includes labor unions, political parties, professional societies, business and trade associations, fraternities and sororities, civic service associations, reform and activist groups, and neighborhood organizations. Two "slices" into this world suggest how diverse it is. A vertical slice, extracting only one occupational group, doctors of medicine, reveals over 380 specialty associations listed in the *Directory of Medical Specialists*. A horizontal slice, an attempt to compile a detailed list of all voluntary associations in Birmingham, England, reported 4264 such organizations. (Newman, 1975)

In addition to size and sector, organizations vary greatly in structural characteristics. The relatively flat authority and control structure found in many voluntary associations stands in sharp contrast with the multilayer hierarchy of a military unit or a civil service bureaucracy. And both seem relatively clean and simple in comparison with the project team or matrix structures (discussed in Chapter 9) found in an advanced research and development unit of a space exploration company. Some organizations are capital-intensive, placing most of their resources in machinery and automated equipment. Others invest heavily in the "human capital" of their work force, selecting highly qualified personnel, underwriting their further specialized training, and then struggling to keep them from taking their expertise to some other company. Organizations vary in these but also in many other important ways, as we will see.

Another basis for divergence resides not in the organizations themselves but in the interests, training, and employment setting of those who investigate them. As implied earlier, researchers from different disciplines vary to some extent in the kinds of organizations they choose to study. Political scientists continue to focus on political parties and state administrative structures, economists on business firms, sociologists on voluntary associations and on agencies engaged in social welfare and social control functions, and anthropologists on comparative administration in primitive, colonial, and developing societies. Disciplinary differences remain even when a single type of organization is selected for study: specialists tend to look not only at different objects but also at different aspects of the same object. Thus, the political scientist will be likely to emphasize power processes and decision making within the organization; the economist will examine the acquisition and allocation of scarce resources within the organization and will attend to such issues as productivity and efficiency; the sociologist has quite varied interests but if there is a focus it will likely be on status orderings and on the effect of norms and sentiments on behavior; the psychologist will be interested in variations in perception, learning, and motivation among participants; and the anthropologist will call attention to the effects of diverse cultural values on the functioning of the system and its members. The study of organizations embraces all these interests, and students of organizations work to develop conceptual frameworks within which all of these topics and their interrelations may be examined. And, increasingly, organizational analysts attempt to specify what is distinctive about power, or status, or motivation, because that process is carried on within the context of organizations.

Cutting across these disciplinary divisions is another, more general basis of divergence among those who study organizations: the adoption of a *basic* versus an *applied* research orientation. Some studies are aimed primarily at accurately describing existing features and relations of organizations in order simply to better understand their nature and operation. Others seek knowledge in order to solve specific problems or to bring about desired changes in these sytems. Of course, there is not a hard-and-fast line between these interests. Basic research, particularly in the long run, can lead to practical applications and applied research often contributes importantly to our general knowledge. Both rest on interests and values: neither is value-free and the same investigators often conduct both basic and applied studies.

Still, there are important differences in these orientations. Basic research is driven more by theory—in its choice both of problems and of variables. Particular concepts—authority, legitimacy, institutionalization—are of interest because of their place in theoretical arguments, not because of their practical significance. Basic research is more likely to focus on the independent variables—on understanding the effects of certain concepts of interest—than on the dependent variables. Conversely, applied research is driven by an interest in solving some identified problem—low morale or productivity, high turnover—and is willing to incorporate any factors, whether economic, psychological, or technical, that may shed light on it. Thus, applied studies are much more likely to be interdisciplinary: practical problems do not respect disciplinary boundaries.

Although there are many exceptions, applied research is more likely to be conducted by researchers located in nonacademic settings: in governmental bureaus, research units of corporations, consulting firms, or policy-research organizations. The results of these studies are less likely to be published in scholarly journals; often they result in no publications at all, only a report to the client group and/or chief executive officer. Basic research is conducted largely within the academic departments of colleges and universities. This work is either unfunded—and hence subsidized by the academic institution (which may, for example, permit low teaching loads and reward faculty for their research productivity)—or is funded largely through research grants from government sources or private foundations.[3] These organizations support research primarily because of "public interest" arguments: it is better to know than not to know, and all benefit from the discovery of new knowledge.

An intermediate group of scholars "swing" both ways. These scholars are faculty members in professional schools: business, educational administration, public administration, public health, engineering management, social-work administration, and so forth. These faculty are more likely to engage in consulting work for private companies or public organizations than those located in academic departments, and they are generally more likely to carry out applied studies, in part because of pressures from their students—past (alumni) and present—who are interested in usable practical information and in skills that will affect the "bottom line," e.g., profits. At the same time, these faculty are confronted by demands from their school and university to contribute to basic knowledge—that is, to publish in scholarly journals. As faculty members of a university, they are subject to the academic culture and its requirements, although these pressures vary from campus to campus and school to school.

Both the basic and the applied-science orientations have made and may be expected to continue to make important contributions to our knowledge of organizations—what they are and how they work. In the long run, each orientation depends on and complements the other, and a healthy scientific enterprise requires that both types of research receive attention and support.

Levels of Analysis

Although organizations furnish a common locus of research for many social scientists, by no means are all investigators interested in finding answers to the same questions. Even apart from the variety of conceptual schemes and orientations that guide inquiry and the differences in methodological tools, investigators differ in the level of analysis at which they choose to work (see Blau, 1957). For present purposes, the level of analysis is determined by the nature of the dependent variable—that is, by whether the phenomenon to be explained is (1) the behavior or attributes of individual participants within organizations, (2) the functioning or characteristics of some aspect or segment of organizational structure, or (3) the characteristics or actions of the organization viewed as a collective entity. We will briefly discuss each of these levels.

Some investigators are interested in explaining individual behavior within an organization. At this level, organizational characteristics are viewed as context or environment, and the investigator attempts to explore their impact on the attitudes or behavior of individuals. Such a perspective is labeled *social psychological* and is exemplified by the work of March and Simon (1958) and Porter, Lawler, and Hackman (1975).

[3]Increasingly, however, scholars within academic departments are also affiliating with other organizational units—laboratories, centers, institutes—both within the university and outside. These organizations serve as a research base for studies that are often applied in character.

At the second level, the major concern is to explain the structural features and social processes that characterize organizations and their subdivisions. The investigator working at this level may focus on the various subunits that make up the organization (for example, work groups, departments, authority ranks) or may examine various analytical components (for example, specialization, communication networks, hierarchy), attempting in both cases to account for their characteristics and to explore their interrelations. This level of analysis is labeled the *structural,* and examples of its use are found in the works of Udy (1959*b*) and Blau and Schoenherr (1971).

At the third level of analysis, the focus is on the organization as a collective actor functioning in a larger system of relations. Within this approach, the analyst may choose either to examine the relation between a specific organization or class of organizations and the environment (for example, Selznick, 1949; Pugh et al., 1969) or to examine the relations that develop among a number of organizations viewed as an interdependent system (for example, Aiken and Hage, 1968; Warren, 1967). This level of analysis is labeled *ecological.*

Admittedly, distinguishing among these three levels of analysis is somewhat arbitrary and ambiguous. Many levels of analytical complexity can be identified as one moves from organizational-individual to societal-organizational relations.[4] Nevertheless, if only to remind us of the complexity of the subject matter and the variety of aims and interests with which analysts approach it, the three types can prove useful as a rough gauge for distinguishing among broad categories of studies.

Of course, the level of analysis at which we choose to examine organizational behavior also affects somewhat the types of data gathered and how they are treated. We cannot provide in this volume a detailed discussion of research methods used in the study of organizations,[5] but one set of methodological distinctions is of particular significance to this discussion of levels of analysis. Lazarsfeld and his colleagues (Lazarsfeld, 1959; Lazarsfeld and Menzel, 1961) have developed a typology of measures that usefully illustrates ways in which information gathered at one level may be employed in analyses at a different level. They begin by distinguishing between two generalized units: *members* and *collectives*—units at different levels in the sense that members are defined as parts of collectives. The subjects of interest may vary. For example, for one type of analysis, the members may be persons and the collectives, departments; for another, the members may be departments and the collectives, organizations.

Members may be characterized by a number of different types of properties:

---

[4]In Chapter 6 we introduce and define several additional levels of analysis, all of which are distinctions made within the ecological level.

[5]Survey chapters discussing simulation techniques, field methods, and laboratory methods applied to the study of organizations are contained in March (1965). Research techniques and instruments appropriate for analyzing individual jobs, the structure of subunits, and the structure and performance of entire organizations are described in Van de Ven and Ferry (1980). And a review of methods and instruments for assessing interorganizational relations, with an emphasis on professional service organizations, is provided by Morrissey, Hall, and Lindsey (1982).

1. *Absolute:* properties based solely on information concerning the member—for example, the age or sex of an individual.
2. *Relational:* properties obtained from information about relationships among the members—for example, sociometric (preference) choices given or received by an individual.
3. *Comparative:* properties based on information obtained from comparing the member's value on some property with the distribution of values on that property over the collective—for example, the relative seniority of an individual worker.
4. *Contextual:* properties based on information about the collective to which the member belongs—for example, an individual being characterized as an employee of a large versus a small department. (Lazarsfeld and Menzel, 1961: 431–33)

Note that the fourth measure differs from the first three in that it is based on information gathered at a different level: a property of a collective is used to characterize its members. In reverse fashion, information based on members can be combined and used to characterize a collective. The first two of the following three measures of *collectives* are of this type:

1. *Analytical:* properties based on a summary measure of some property of each member of the collective—for example, the average age of the members of a department.
2. *Structural:* properties based on a summary measure of the relationships among members—for example a measure of cohesion based on the relative number of sociometric choices directed by members to others within the collective as compared with those directed outside.
3. *Global:* properties of collectives not based on information concerning individual members or their relationships—for example, the assets of a company. (Lazarsfeld and Menzel, 1961: 426–29)

Although the formal definitions of the various properties are based on the source of the data, the full schema reflects the important fact that level of analysis is determined not by the *source* of the information but by the *use* to which that information is put. An analytical property of a collective, for example, is based on information obtained from members but is used to characterize the collective.

Perhaps it is apparent that these measures were spawned in the effort by survey analysts to find ways to utilize survey data obtained from individual respondents to characterize structural features of groups (see Kendall and Lazarsfeld, 1950). These innovations, and their codification in the typology proposed by Lazarsfeld and Menzel, were instrumental in shifting the attention of analysts from the social psychological characteristics of participants to the structural properties of collectives such as organizations. They ushered in a wave of studies that examined the impact of the properties of organizations (collectives) on individual (member) behavior (for example, Lazarsfeld and Thielens, 1958; Lipset, Trow, and Coleman, 1956; Blau, 1960), and they paved the way for later work that focused on the interrelations of structural features within organizations (collectives).

Early research on organizations was conducted almost exclusively at the social psychological level. The structural level of analysis became prominent in the early 1960s and continues to be heavily utilized by sociologists. The ecological level was the last to develop, emerging in the late 1960s, and continues to acquire adherents.

THE ELEMENTS OF ORGANIZATIONS

Organizations are highly varied and often highly complex, so it may be helpful to begin with a simplifying model allowing us to focus on basic characteristics. The proposed model shown in Figure 1–1 is adapted from Leavitt (1965).[6] Let us briefly consider each element.

Social Structure

Social structure refers to the patterned or regularized aspects of the relationships existing among participants in an organization. The social structure of any human grouping can be analytically separated into two components. As Kingsley Davis (1949: 52) suggests,

> . . . always in human society there is what may be called a double reality—on the one hand a normative sytem embodying what *ought* to be, and on the other a factual order embodying what is. . . . these two orders cannot be completely identical, nor can they be completely disparate.

We shall refer to Davis's first component as the *normative structure;* this component includes values, norms, and role expectations. Briefly, *values* are the criteria employed in selecting the goals of behavior; *norms* are the generalized rules governing behavior that specify, in particular, appropriate means for pursuing goals; and *roles* are expectations for or evaluative standards employed in assessing the behavior of occupants of specific social positions. A social position is simply a location in a system of

[6]Leavitt identifies the four "internal" elements but does not include the environment as a separate factor. As will be obvious from our discussion, we regard the environment as an indispensable ingredient in any organizational model.

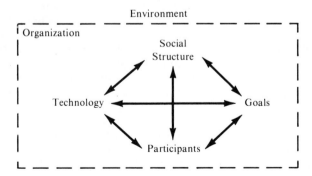

FIGURE 1–1   Leavitt's Diamond: A Model ot an Organization. *Source:* Adapted from Leavitt (1965), Figure I, p. 1145.

social relationships. (For a basic formulation of positions and roles, see Gross, Mason, and McEachern, 1958.) In any social grouping, values, norms, and roles are not randomly arranged, but are organized so as to constitute a relatively coherent and consistent set of beliefs and prescriptions governing the behavior of participants. It is for this reason that we speak of a normative *structure*.

The second component, which Davis refers to as "a factual order," we will call the *behavioral structure*. This component focuses on actual behavior rather than on prescriptions for behavior. Homans's (1950: 33–40) well-known classification of social behavior into activities, interactions, and sentiments suggests the types of elements that constitute the behavioral structure. Because our concern is with the analysis of behavioral *structure*, rather than simply behavior, we focus on those activities, interactions, and sentiments that exhibit some degree of regularity—the recurrent behavior of a given individual or similarities in the behavior of a class of individuals. Such actions, exhibiting some consistency and constancy in their general characteristics, are themselves arranged into larger patterns or networks of behavior. For example, we may observe in a group over a period of time which individuals attempt to influence others and with what degree of success, and in this way obtain a description of the power structure within that group. Or by observing the patterning of sentiments among group members—who is attracted to or rejected by whom—we can describe the sociometric structure of the group. Both the power structure and the sociometric structure are specific instances of behavioral structures.

As the passage from Davis reminds us, the normative structure and the behavioral structure of a social group are neither independent nor identical, but are to varying degrees interrelated. The normative structure imposes an important set of constraints on the behavioral structure, shaping and channeling behavior and helping to account for much of the regularity and patterning that exist. On the other hand, much behavior departs from the normative structure and is an important source of additions to and changes in that structure. Behavior shapes norms just as norms shape behavior. Groups vary in the extent to which their normative and behavioral structures are aligned. In some situations precept corresponds closely to practice: this appears to be the case in many utopian communities or communes—at least in their early stages of development (see Kanter, 1972). In other situations a sizable gulf appears between professed beliefs and behavior. Reports suggest that Victorian England might represent an instance of this situation with respect to sexual morality versus practice. In any case, the normative and behavioral structures are always in a state of dynamic tension—each existing and changing somewhat independently of the other at the same time each exerts continuing force on the other.

All social groups—or *collectivities*, to use the more general term—are characterized by a normative structure applicable to the participants and by a behavioral structure linking participants in a common network or pattern of activities, interactions, and sentiments. These two interrelated structures constitute the *social structure* of a collectivity.[7]

Organizational participants are likely to emphasize the amount of

[7]For a more extensive discussion of normative, behavioral, and social structures, see Scott, 1970:102–10.

confusion, the indeterminacy, and the unpredictability of the actions of their co-workers, in part because such matters draw their attention and require their energies. However, to focus on the social structure of organizations is to emphasize the impressive amount of order exhibited by the behavior of participants in organizations. Every day hundreds or thousands of persons in organizations perform millions of individual acts, yet the outcome is not bedlam, not total confusion or chaos, but a reasonable approximation of order. This phenomenon deserves our attention.

Emphasizing the importance of the social structure of organizations does not commit us to the view that relations among participants are all sweetness and light: social structure does not connote social harmony. Conflict is always possible and usually present among participants in any social structure. An emphasis on social structure should enable us to see that much of whatever conflict is present in the organization is patterned, in the sense that it is built into the structure of relations between individuals and groups and is not due to innately aggressive individual participants. Not only stability and order but tension and stress, deviance and change can often be attributed to structural factors. (See Merton, 1957: 131–60)

The social structure of an organization varies in the extent to which it is formalized. A *formal* social structure is one in which the social positions and the relationships among them have been explicitly specified and are defined independently of the personal characteristics of the participants occupying these positions. By contrast, in an *informal* social structure, it is impossible to distinguish between the characteristics of the positions and the characteristics of the participants. In an informal structure, when specific participants leave or enter the system, their roles and relationships develop and change as a function of their personal characteristics and the interactions that occur among them.[8]

Participants

Organizational participants are those individuals who, in return for a variety of inducements, make contributions to the organization (Barnard, 1938; Simon, 1957). All individuals participate in more than one organization, and the extent and intensiveness of their involvement may vary greatly; the decision as to who is to be regarded as a participant is thus often a difficult one and may legitimately vary with the issue at hand. For example, a single individual may simultaneously be an employee of an industrial firm, a member of a union, a church member, a member of a fraternal lodge or sorority; a "member" of a political party, a citizen of the state, a client of a group medical practice, a stockholder in one or more companies, and a customer in numerous retail and service organiza-

---

[8]Of course, at any given point in the history of a particular structure, new jobs are being created around the particular skills and interests of specific individuals. Miner (1985) has labeled these positions *idiosyncratic jobs* and notes two subtypes: *evolved jobs*, created around current organizational members, and *opportunistic hires*, created around people outside the organization. The number of such positions appears to vary considerably by type of organization, as does the extent to which such informal positions become codified and formalized. Informal job redefinition followed by codification appears to be a significant form of mobility in some organizations. (See also Miner and Estler, 1985.)

tions. Analysts disagree, as we shall see, on the extent to which organizations do and should incorporate facets of participants. How much of the personality and personal characteristics of individual participants is relevant to the functioning of the organization also varies from one type of organization and role to another: consider the situation of a novice in a religious order versus that of an occasional customer in a supermarket.

The demographic characteristics of participants—for example, their age, gender, ethnic distributions—have important consequences for many aspects of organizational structure and functioning; we will explore those implications in Chapter 7. And the structural features of organizations—the opportunities they create and the sorting rules they use for selection and retention and promotion—have equally fateful consequences for participants, as we discuss in Chapter 8.

Goals

The concept of organizational goals is among the most important—and most controversial—concepts to be confronted in the study of organizations. Some analysts insist that goals are indispensable to the understanding of organizations; others question whether goals perform any function other than to justify past actions. Then, too, behaviorialists are fond of pointing out that only individuals have goals; collectivities, such as organizations, do not. We will not attempt to tackle these prickly issues here but promise not to duck them indefinitely.

For most analysts, goals constitute a central point of reference in the analysis of organizations. Goals are tentatively defined as *conceptions of desired ends*—conditions that participants attempt to effect through their performance of task activities.

Since goals figure prominently in some definitions of organizations, we will consider them further in the following section, and we will discuss the major issues and problems bearing on their analysis in Chapter 11.

Technology

To focus on the technology of an organization is to view the organization as a place where some type of work is done, as a location where energy is applied to the transformation of materials, as a mechanism for transforming inputs into outputs. The connotations of the term *technology* are narrow and hard, but we will insist that every organization does work and possesses a technology for doing that work. Some organizations process material inputs and fabricate new equipment and hardware. Others "process" people, their products consisting of more knowledgeable individuals, in the case of effective school systems, or healthier individuals, in the case of effective medical clinics. Still others process primarily symbolic materials, such as information or music. Technologies consist in part of machines and mechanical equipment but also comprise the technical knowledge and skills of participants.

All organizations possess technologies, but organizations vary in the extent to which these techniques are understood, or routinized, or efficacious. Some of the most interesting theoretical and empirical work in recent years has focused on the relation between the characteristics of technology and the structural features of organizations. This work is described and evaluated in Chapter 9.

Environment

Every organization exists in a specific physical, technological, cultural, and social environment to which it must adapt. No organization is self-sufficient; all depend for survival on the types of relations they establish with the larger systems of which they are a part. Early analysts of organizations, as we will see, tended to overlook or underestimate the importance of organization-environmental linkages, but recent work places great emphasis on these connections. And, indeed, the number and variety of these connections are impressive. Let us briefly reconsider each of the four organizational components in this light.

Very few organizations assume full responsibility for the socialization and training of their participants. Employees come to the organization with heavy cultural and social baggage obtained from interactions in other social contexts. With very few exceptions—such as inmates in "total institutions" (Goffman, 1961)—participants are involved in more than one organization at any given time. These outside interests and commitments inevitably constrain the behavior of participants in any given organization and, in some instances, strongly influence it. To regard participants as completely contained by the organization is to misperceive one of the fundamental characteristics of organizations: that they are systems built on the *partial involvement* of their members.

Similarly, few organizations create their own technologies; rather, they import them from the environment in the form of mechanical equipment, packaged programs and sets of instructions, and trained workers. Any specific organization must also adapt to the larger occupational structure—e.g., union rules or professional norms—in the selection and deployment of workers within the organization. Moreover, the environment is the source of the inputs to be processed by the organization, just as it is the "sink" to which all outputs are delivered—as products to be sold, clients restored to function, or waste materials to be eliminated.

Parsons (1960) has called attention to the important relation between an organization's goals and the larger societal environment. What is termed a goal or objective by a specific organization is, from the point of view of the larger society, its specialized function. An organization may thus expect societal support for its activities to reflect the relative value society places on those functions: if health represents a strong positive value for a society, for example, then those organizations that supply health care may expect to receive a disproportional share of resources supporting their work.

Last, the social structure of the organization will reflect important features borrowed from or impressed upon it by the environment. Structural forms, no less than technologies, are rarely invented and are usually borrowed from the environment. Part Three of this volume explores the thesis that environmental complexity tends to be incorporated within and reflected by the structural features of organizations. These incorporations may give rise to formal components such as rules or offices or departments, or they may form the basis for informal cliques or for work patterns not sanctioned by the formal structure. Both formal and informal structures can have their roots in the environment.

While insisting on the pervasive and critical importance of environmental influences on organizational forms and operations, we must not assume that the causal processes work in only one direction. Organizations not only are influenced by but also affect their environments. Although modern theorists differ in their views of the relative importance of these casual connections, as we will discuss in later chapters, they generally agree that the relations between organizations and environments are vital, complex, and interdependent.

Each of these organizational elements—social structure, participants, goals, technology, environment—represents an important component of all organizations. Indeed, each element has been regarded as of surpassing importance by one or more analysts of organizations. However, the chief value of Leavitt's diamond is as a graphic reminder that no one element is so dominant as to be safely considered in isolation from the others. Organizations are, first and foremost, *systems* of elements, each of which affects and is affected by the others. Goals are not *the* key to understanding the nature and functioning of organizations, no more than are the participants, the technology, or the social structure. And no organization can be understood in isolation from the larger environment. We will miss the essence of organization if we insist on focusing on any single feature to the exclusion of all others.

DEFINING THE CONCEPT OF ORGANIZATION

Consistent with the objectives of this volume, not one but three definitions of organizations will be presented. These definitions pave the way for our description and evaluation in Part Two of three major perspectives employed in the analysis of organizations. Thus, we leave to later chapters the considerable task of spelling out the implications of these differing definitions. We give special attention here to the first definition—actually, several related definitions will be discussed—both because it has tended until recently to dominate the field and because it has served to establish organizations as a distinctive field of study. This definition is most consistent with a *rational system* perspective on organization. Two other definitions—one associated with the *natural system* perspective and the other with the *open systems* perspective—will be briefly described here and examined more fully in later chapters.

A Rational System Definition

Since a primary function of a definition is to help us to distinguish one phenomenon from another, most definitions of organizations emphasize the distinctive features of organizations—those that help to distinguish them from related social forms. Many analysts have attempted to formulate such definitions, and their views appear similar, as illustrated by the following four influential definitions.

According to Barnard (1938: 4),

formal organization is that kind of coöperation among men that is conscious, deliberate, purposeful.

According to March and Simon (1958: 4)

> organizations are assemblages of interacting human beings and they are the largest assemblages in our society that have anything resembling a central coordinative system. . . . The high specificity of structure and coordination within organizations—as contrasted with the diffuse and variable relations *among* organizations and among unorganized individuals—marks off the individual organization as a sociological unit comparable in significance to the individual organism in biology.

According to Blau and Scott (1962: 5),

> since the distinctive characteristic of . . . organizations is that they have been formally established for the explicit purpose of achieving certain goals, the term "formal organizations" is used to designate them (Blau and Scott, 1962: 5).[9]

And, according to Etzioni (1964: 3),

> organizations are social units (or human groupings) deliberately constructed and reconstructed to seek specific goals.

All of these definitions point to the existence of two structural features that distinguish organizations from other types of collectivities.

•Organizations are collectivities oriented to the pursuit of relatively specific goals. They are "purposeful" in the sense that the activities and interactions of participants are centrally coordinated to achieve specified goals. Goals are *specific* to the extent that they are explicit, are clearly defined, and provide unambiguous criteria for selecting among alternative activities.

•Organizations are collectivities that exhibit a relatively high degree of formalization. The cooperation among participants is "conscious" and "deliberate"; the structure of relations is made explicit and can be "deliberately constructed and reconstructed." As previously defined, a structure is *formalized* to the extent that the rules governing behavior are precisely and explicitly formulated and to the extent that roles and role relations are prescribed independently of the personal attributes of individuals occupying positions in the structure.

It is the combination of relatively high goal specificity and relatively high formalization that distinguishes organizations from other types of collectivities. Note that both goal specificity and formalization are viewed as variables: organizations may be characterized by higher or lower levels

[9]This definition, which I developed with Blau a good many years ago, now strikes me as somewhat misleading. Emphasis is placed on the conditions present at the founding of the organization: on whether the unit was "formally established for the explicit purpose of achieving certain goals." The wording suggests that factors associated with the founding of the unit—in particular, the intent of the founders—are of critical importance. Such historical considerations seem much less important to me now than the current state of the system—that is, the extent of goal specificity and of formalization.

of each. Nevertheless, as a structural type, organizations are expected to exhibit higher levels of formalization and goal specificity than other types of collectivities, such as primary groups, families, communities, and social movements. In general—there certainly are exceptions—families and kinship structures tend to rank relatively high on formalization but low on goal specificity (Litwak, 1968; Litwak and Meyer, 1966); social movements tend to exhibit low levels of formalization combined with higher levels of goal specificity,[10] although the specificity of goals varies greatly from movement to movement and from time to time (Gusfield, 1968); and communities are characterized by low levels of both goal specificity and formalization (Hillery, 1968: 145–52; and Moe, 1959).

We arrive, then, at the first definition: *organizations are collectivities oriented to the pursuit of relatively specific goals and exhibiting relatively highly formalized social structures.* Note that this definition focuses not only on the distinctive characteristics of organizations but also on their normative structure. It is compatible with the rational system perspective.

A Natural System Definition

Gouldner (1959) reminds us that the distinguishing features of a phenomenon are not its only characteristics and, indeed, may not be the most important ones. Although organizations often—not always—espouse specific goals, the behavior of participants is frequently not guided by them, nor can they be safely used to predict organizational actions. Similarly, formal role definitions and written rules may have been developed, but they sometimes provide few if any restrictions on the behavior of members. Thus, if the behavioral structure is attended to, rather than the normative structure, the first definition of organizations can be quite misleading.

It is of interest that although many conventional organizations, such as public schools and government mental-health services, have felt the need to develop explicit goal statements and formalized job titles and procedures, other organizations have decided to do away with such superfluous decorations and camouflage. Such appears to be the case with a set of organizational forms labeled *collectivist* organizations (Rothschild-Whitt, 1979). These organizations include many recently developed innovative forms, particularly in the service sector—for example, free medical clinics, alternative schools, rape-counseling centers, and legal collectives—as well as some earlier forms, such as food and producer cooperatives. Some of these organizations clearly are pursuing relatively broad and diffuse objectives, such as societal reform or the promotion of more open and authentic relations among their participants. Others have defined relatively specific objectives. However, virtually all of them eschew formalization as a structural characteristic. Rothschild-Whitt's (1979) survey of the structural features of collectivist organizations suggests that many go to

---

[10]In recent years, analysts of movements have placed more emphasis on their organizational features—for example, the extent to which they are guided by a full-time, paid staff and have regularized mechanisms for obtaining resources and recruits and for setting goals. (See Zald and Ash, 1966; McCarthy and Zald, 1973.) It would appear that this shift in emphasis reflects both changes in the perspectives employed by social analysts, who are increasingly sensitive to organizational features, and changes in the nature of social movements, which are more likely to adopt organizational models.

great lengths to eliminate or reduce formalization. They deny the authority of office, seek to minimize the promulgation of rules and procedures, attempt to eliminate status gradations among participants, and do away with role differentiation and specialization of function. Great stress is laid on equality in decision making, and differences in interests and preferences among individual members are deemed of great importance. The personal qualities of members do matter! Thus, if our first definition of organization is used, collectivities such as these are excluded.[11]

A natural system conception of organizations is not entirely based on what organizations are not, although this is an important ingredient in the perspective. Positive attention is devoted to examining the way in which organizations—like all collectivities—attend to the needs or requirements of their own system. Organizations are viewed as organic systems imbued with a strong drive to survive, to maintain themselves as systems. The development of informal structures and distinctive cultures is regarded as an important means to this end. These structures grow out of the natural abilities and interests of participants and enable the collectivity to benefit from the human resources of its membership.

Hence, a second definition of organizations, useful for viewing them as natural systems, is proposed: *organizations are collectivities whose participants share a common interest in the survival of the system and who engage in collective activities, informally structured, to secure this end.*

An Open System Definition

The previous definitions tend to view the organization as a closed system, separate from its environment and comprising a set of stable and easily identified participants. However, organizations are not closed systems, sealed off from their environments, but are open to and dependent on flows of personnel and resources from outside. Also, if an organization is to survive, it must induce participants to contribute resources, energy, and time to it. Individuals have different interests and value various inducements: they join and leave the organization depending on the bargains they can strike—the relative advantage to be had from staying or going. Thus, rather than viewing the organization as a coherent system of relations oriented to the pursuit of specific goals, we might view it more accurately as an opportunistic collection of divergent interest groups temporarily banded together.

We arrive, then, at a third definition, useful for viewing organizations as open systems: *organizations are coalitions of shifting interest groups that develop goals by negotiation; the structure of the coalition, its activities, and its outcomes are strongly influenced by environmental factors.*

[11]We would argue, however, that although these forms are excluded by the rational system definition, they are also illuminated by it. Collectivist forms do not simply exhibit relatively low levels of formalization; they are characterized by active hostility to formalization. They are self-consciously and energetically antiformal in practice and, more important, in their ideologies and normative systems. Indeed, much of the interest and energy they generate among their participants can be directly attributed to the ideological battle they wage against the more conventional formalized and hierarchical models. They are organized in opposition to the prevailing model of organizations—a model so widely shared that its *negation* can serve as a potent basis of organization.

It is no doubt unsettling to be confronted so early with three such diverse views of organizations. But better to know the worst at the outset! The definitions are quite different in that they not only encompass somewhat divergent types of collectivities but also emphasize different facets of a given organization. But this is precisely why they are useful. It is essential to remember that definitions are neither true nor false but are only more or less helpful in calling attention to certain aspects of the phenomenon under study. With the help of these definitions, and the more general perspectives with which they are associated, we can expect to see and learn more about organizations than would be possible were we to employ a single point of view. As we proceed, we will call attention to the stimulating vistas and profound depths charted by each of the conceptions. Each has its own charms (as well as its own blemishes), and each carries its own truth (as well as its own biases).

A Note on Bureaucracy

The term *bureaucracy* will come up again and again throughout this volume, and so we would do well to confront this concept head-on at an early stage. The term is a problem because, although frequently used by students of organizations, it is defined in many ways. The term also carries with it a great deal of emotional freight. For many the terms bureaucracy and bureaucrat are epithets—accusations connoting rule-encumbered inefficiency and mindless overconformity. (See, e.g., Mises, 1944; Parkinson, 1957.) Indeed, these are probably the most common views of bureaucracy held by the people in this society. By contrast, the foremost student of bureaucracy, Max Weber, used the term to refer to that form of administrative organization that, in his view, was capable of attaining the highest level of efficiency! (Weber, 1947 trans.: 339).

If we set aside for the moment its pejorative uses, we can see that organizational analysts employ the concept descriptively in at least three different ways. Some use the term bureaucracy as a general synonym for organization; others reserve it for public organizations or the administrative units of the nation-state; and still others, most notably Weber, use the term to designate a particular type of administrative structure. All of this can be very confusing, not only to beginning students but to all of us who attempt to study organizations. Although we cannot dispel all of the confusion, we will try to be clear about how we propose to use the concept, and we can suggest how our own usage relates to some of the other definitions.

Our definition of bureaucracy is indebted to the work of Bendix, who writes: "Seen historically, bureaucratization may be interpreted as the increasing subdivision of the functions which the owner-managers of the early enterprises had performed personally in the course of their daily routine" (1956: 211–12). Such functions include supervision, personnel selection and management, accounting and financial management, record keeping, job design, and long-range planning. In this sense, bureaucracy refers to the middle layer of the organization: the head of the organization—whether president, dictator, owner, or leader—is excluded, as are the lower levels—for example, the production workers. A useful way of thinking about a bureaucracy is that it consists of those positions (or activities) whose function is to maintain the organization itself. In short, *bureaucracy* is defined as the existence of a specialized administrative staff.

Like formalization and goal specificity, bureaucracy should be viewed as a variable: organizations vary in terms of how much of their personnel resources are devoted to administrative, as opposed to production, activities. Bendix, following Melman (1951), has proposed that for industrial organizations a crude but serviceable index of the degree of bureaucratization is the ratio of administrative (salaried) to production (wage) employees. Data compiled by Bendix (1956: 214) from several sources show that for a number of Western countries the ratio of administrative to production workers in industry steadily increased from under 1:10 in 1900 to over 1:5 by 1950. And there is evidence that the rate of bureaucratic expansion may be increasing. Edwards (1979: 135) reports that one important component of the bureaucracy, the proportion of foremen in manufacturing companies, increased at a rate of 15 percent between 1910 and 1940 but jumped to a rate of 67 percent between 1940 and 1970. The causes of increased bureaucratization will be discussed in Part Three of this volume.

Although the precise identification of bureaucratic positions or activities may often pose problems to the investigator, the conceptual distinction suggested by Bendix seems clear in the case of industrial or commercial organizations. Unfortunately, this is not the case for public organizations. Consider the Internal Revenue Service of the State Department of our federal government. In the case of these units, the entire organization is devoted to administrative activities! We believe that our conception of bureaucracy can encompass these situations, but only if we are clear about the level of analysis at which we approach such systems.

If we choose the ecological level and focus on the State Department as an organization within a larger system of organizations, as a specialized administrative arm of the executive office of the president, then it is consistent with our definition to view the entire department as a bureaucracy. These "bureaus" and their officials may appropriately be seen as working to maintain our nation. On the other hand, if we choose the structural level of analysis, concentrating on the internal structures and processes of the State Department, then we will observe that there is within this bureau a specialized administrative staff that assists the secretary of state in the administration of the department. Each bureau has its own internal bureaucracy: a group of officials who do not directly carry out the work of the agency but supervise, regulate, and support those who do (see Downs, 1967).

Weber's conception differs from our own. As noted, he defines bureaucracy as a special type of administrative structure—the structures that developed in association with a rational-legal mode of authority relation. The distinctive characteristics of these structures include a clear differentiation of responsibilities among officials, the hierarchical arrangement of offices, the use of technical criteria of recruitment, and impersonal norms governing the relations among officials. Weber argued that these bureaucratic structures—present in both private and public organizations—were gradually replacing administrative systems based on traditional authority relations. His conception of these structures and the processes leading to their ascendancy will be discussed in more detail in Chapter 2. We introduce it here merely to distinguish it from our own definition of bureaucracy.

It is of interest that from all three points of view described, the level of bureaucratization is increasing. If we define bureaucratization at the structural level as an increase in the proportion of resources devoted to administrative compared with production activities, then, as we have seen, bureaucracy is increasing. If we define bureaucratization at the ecological level as an increase in the size of the administrative machinery of the nation-state, then in virtually all contemporary societies bureaucracy is increasing. It is in this sense that Jacoby (1973 trans.) writes of *The Bureaucratization of the World*. And if we adopt Weber's definition and view bureaucracy as a special type of administrative structure, then he is clearly correct that in most modernizing societies over the past century, bureaucracies have been replacing more traditional administrative forms. It is with reference to Weber's definition of bureaucracy that some analysts, such as Bennis (Bennis and Slater, 1968), assert that the most advanced organizations are currently moving toward the development of *postbureaucratic* forms. These developments will be described and evaluated in Chapter 9.

Finally, although we will not ourselves employ the term bureaucracy as a pejorative label for stagnant, incompetent administration, we will want to consider the causes of administrative pathology and, in particular, to struggle to understand how it is that arrangements created and adopted to ensure efficient and responsive administrative performance sometimes—indeed, all too often—result in the exact opposite. These questions are addressed in Chapter 12.

SUMMARY

Organizations are important objects of study and concern for many reasons. They are vital mechanisms for pursuing collective goals in modern societies. They are not neutral tools because they affect what they produce; they function as collective actors that independently possess certain rights and powers. Both as mechanisms and as actors, organizations are alleged to be the source of some of contemporary society's most serious problems. Organizations encompass generic social processes but carry them out by means of distinctive structural arrangements.

Although an interest in organizational forms and processes may be traced far back in history, a distinctive field of sociological inquiry focusing on the creation and empirical testing of generalized knowledge concerning organizations did not develop until after 1950. This development was linked with and greatly stimulated by the translation into English of Max Weber's historical and comparative studies of administrative organizations, conducted during the first two decades of this century. The field of organizational studies is becoming increasingly interdisciplinary. Among the bases on which studies vary is the level at which analysis is carried out: some research occurs at the social psychological level and emphasizes the interaction of individuals and groups within organizations and the impact of organizational characteristics on these processes; other studies are conducted at the structural level and attempt to account for variations in the patterned features of organizations; and still other research is focused at the ecological level, viewing the organization as an actor or subunit in a more comprehensive system of relationships.

Three contrasting definitions of organizations are presented. Each is associated with one of three perspectives on organizations to be elaborated in Part Two: the rational system, the natural system, and the open system perspectives. The first definition views organizations as highly formalized collectivities oriented to the pursuit of specific goals. The second definition views organizations as collectivities seeking to survive. And the third definition views organizations as coalitions of interest groups highly influenced by their environments. Each of these definitions is viewed as opening up a useful, if partial, view of organizations.

THREE PERSPECTIVES ON ORGANIZATIONS

PART TWO

In this century, three more or less distinct perspectives have been employed in the study of organizational structure. The term *perspective* is used advisedly since we will be dealing in each case not with a single, unified model of organizational structure but rather with a number of varying approaches that bear a strong family resemblance. Thus, our concern will be with three types of approaches or three schools of thought, the notion of perspective serving as a conceptual umbrella under which we may gather the related views. To add further to the complexity, the three perspectives partially conflict, partially overlap, and partially complement one another.

An understanding of these perspectives is valuable for several reasons. It is very difficult to comprehend or to fully utilize the large literature on organizations without knowledge of the differing perspectives underlying this work. Why does one analyst concentrate on one type of problem while another completely ignores it? Why do some investigators emphasize historical materials while others deal exclusively with contemporary data? These are the sorts of questions we can begin to answer by examining the perspectives employed. Also, we should expect to receive help not only in making sense out of past studies but in examining the current efforts of organizational analysts. For although these perspectives emerged at different times, later perspectives have not succeeded in supplanting earlier ones: the three perspectives continue to coexist and to claim their share of advocates.

Although we devote some effort to describing the history of each perspective, the perspectives are not primarily of historical interest. They are analytical models intended to guide—and to interpret—empirical research. They have changed over time as one school has replaced another within each of the traditions, but to a surprising extent, the general outlines of the three perspectives have remained reasonably clear.

In their pure form, the perspectives share many of the features of *paradigms* as described by Kuhn in his influential essay on scientific revolutions. Kuhn describes paradigms as "models from which spring particular coherent traditions of scientific research" (1962: 10).

The three perspectives to be considered are the rational, the natural, and the open system perspectives. They are considered in the order of their emergence. For each, we first discuss the basic model that forms its core. Then we consider three or four representative theorists or schools within that tradition. Each discussion concludes with an evaluation of the contributions and limitations of the perspective. Chapter 2 reviews the rational system perspective, following its development from Weber to Simon. In Chapter 3, we describe the natural system perspective, beginning with Michels and ending with Parsons. And Chapter 4 reviews the open system perspective, from its origins in the general systems theory as advanced by Bertalanffy through its application to organizations by analysts ranging from Boulding to Weick. Most of the work reviewed in these introductory chapters extends only up to the 1960s. These chapters provide the first, not the last word on perspectives on organizations.

Beyond this point, matters become more complex and, we think, more interesting. There have been a number of attempts to combine the perspectives into more complex models. In Chapter 5 we review three of these efforts by other theorists and propose a fourth of our own. Combining the perspectives provides a framework that enables us to conceptually "place" a number of the more important, recent theoretical developments, including transactions costs, resource dependency, population ecology, Marxist approaches, and institutionalization theory.

2 organizations as rational systems

A well-designed machine is an instance of total organization, that is, a series of interrelated means contrived to achieve a single end. The machine consists always of particular parts that have no meaning and no function separate from the organized entity to which they contribute. A machine consists of a coherent bringing together of all parts toward the highest possible efficiency of the functioning whole, or interrelationships marshalled wholly toward a given result. In the ideal machine, there can be no extraneous part, no extraneous movement; all is set, part for part, motion for motion, toward the functioning of the whole. The machine is, then, a perfect instance of total rationalization of a field of action and of total organization. This is perhaps even more quickly evident in that larger machine, the assembly line.

John William Ward (1964)

From the rational system perspective, organizations are instruments designed to attain specified goals. How blunt or fine an instrument they are depends on many factors that are summarized by the concept of rationality of structure. The term *rationality* in this context is used in the narrow sense of *technical* or *functional* rationality (Mannheim, 1950 trans.: 53) and refers to the extent to which a series of actions is organized in such a way as to lead to predetermined goals with maximum efficiency. Thus, rationality refers not to the selection of goals but to their implementation. Indeed, it is perfectly possible to pursue irrational or foolish goals by rational means. Captain Ahab in Melville's classic *Moby Dick* chases the white whale across the seven seas musing, "All my means are sane, my motive and my object mad." Nazi Germany provides a more terrible, nonfiction example. Adolf Hitler's insane objective of eradicating Europe's Jewish population was efficiently pursued by hosts of functionaries who, like Adolph Eichmann, took the goal as given and worked faithfully to rationally bring it about. (Arendt, 1963) It is essential to keep in mind the restricted definition of *rationality* used within the rational system perspective.

THE DEFINING CHARACTERISTICS

From the standpoint of the rational system perspective, the behavior of organizations is viewed as actions performed by purposeful and coordinated agents. The language employed connotes this image of rational calculation: such terms as *information, efficiency, optimization, implementation,* and *design* occur frequently. But another somewhat different set of terms also occurs within this perspective; it indicates the cognitive limitations of the individual decision maker and the effects of the organizational context in which rational choices are made. These terms—*constraints, authority, rules, directives, jurisdiction, performance programs, coordination*—imply that the rationality of behavior within organizations takes place within (some analysts would argue, because of) clearly specified limits.

It is no accident that the key features of organizations emphasized by rational system theorists are the very characteristics that have been noted to distinguish organizations from other types of collectivities. Rational system theorists stress goal specificity and formalization because each of these elements makes an important contribution to the rationality of organizational action.

Goal Specificity

Goals are conceptions of desired ends. These conceptions vary in the precision and specificity of their criteria of desirability. Specific goals provide unambiguous criteria for selecting among alternative activities. As viewed by economists or by decision theorists, goals are translated into a set of preference or utility functions that represent the value of alternative sets of consequences. Without clear preference orderings among alternatives, rational assessment and choice are not possible.

Specific goals not only supply criteria for choosing among alternative activities; they guide decisions about how the organization structure itself is to be designed. They specify what tasks are to be performed, what kinds of personnel are to be hired, how resources are to be allocated among participants. The more general or diffuse the goals, the more difficult it is to design a structure to pursue them.

It is important to note that some organizations espouse quite vague and general goals, but in their actual daily operation are guided by relatively specific goals that do provide criteria for choosing among alternative activities and for designing the organization structure itself. Consider the case of education. Although both educators and laypeople will argue endlessly about the true function of education and about the virtues of liberal arts versus more practical types of programs, within a given school there will be considerable agreement on such matters as what disciplines should be represented among the faculty, what courses will count toward graduation, and how many units are required for a student to graduate. With agreement on such matters as these, administrators can safely allow the faculty occasionally to debate the ultimate aims of education. Similarly, although physicians cannot agree on abstract definitions of health or illness, they do successfully organize their work around such proximate outcomes as relieving pain and prolonging life.

Vague goals do not provide a solid basis for formal organizations.

Either the goals become more specific and limited over time, as often happens, or the structures developed are likely to be unstable and amorphous. Collective movements such as radical political sects or protest groups may temporarily succeed in mobilizing resources and participants around vague concepts such as liberation or ecology. Indeed, their generality may broaden their appeal and enlist the support of diverse groups. But unless more specific and delimited goals emerge, we would not expect such movements to give rise to formal organizations.

The most precise description of the manner in which specific goals support rational behavior in organizations is that developed by Herbert Simon, whose classic, *Administrative Behavior,* first appeared in 1945. His ideas on this subject will be summarized later in this chapter as an example of one of the major contributions to the rational system perspective.

Formalization

All rational system theorists assume the existence and presume the importance of a formalized structure, but few make explicit the contributions that formalization makes to rationality of behavior in organizations. Let us attempt to do so.

Recall that a structure is formalized to the extent that the rules governing behavior are precisely and explicitly formulated and to the extent that roles and role relations are prescribed independently of the personal attributes of individuals occupying positions in the structure. Formalization may be viewed as an attempt to make behavior more predictable by standardizing and regulating it. This, in turn, permits "stable expectations to be formed by each member of the group as to the behavior of the other members under specified conditions. Such stable expectations are an essential precondition to a rational consideration of the consequences of action in a social group." (Simon, 1957: 100)

Formalization may also be viewed as an attempt to make more explicit and visible the structure of relationships among a set of roles and the principles that govern behavior in the system. It becomes possible to diagram the organization's structure or work flow and then consciously to study and manipulate it—to design and redesign the division of responsibilities, the flow of information or materials, or the ways in which participants report to one another. As Gouldner (1959: 405) notes,

> fundamentally, the rational model implies a "mechanical" model, in that it views the organization as a structure of manipulable parts, each of which is separately modifiable with a view to enhancing the efficiency of the whole. Individual organizational elements are seen as subject to successful and planned modification, enactable by deliberate decision.

Thus, in a fundamental sense, the organizational structure is viewed as a means, as an instrument, which can be modified as necessary to improve performance. Organizational designers and managers draw and redraw the organizational chart; coaches attempt to improve performance by diagraming plays and giving chalk talks; and consultants are employed to recommend better arrangements for achieving business goals. In recent years, highly technical managerial systems, such as management by objectives (MBO), planning, programming, and budgeting systems (PPBS), program evaluation review techniques (PERT)—all designed to provide greater visibility and, hence, greater accountability for the critical work flows—have been developed and widely adopted to facilitate rational decision making within complex organizational systems. (See Haberstroh, 1965; Odione, 1965; Drucker, 1976; Wildavsky, 1979: 26–40.)

Formalization can contribute to rationality in other, less obvious ways. In addition to making behavior more available for conscious design, the structuring of expectations prior to interaction carries with it another distinct advantage. Laboratory research by Bales (1953) documents the strains and tensions generated when a status structure begins to emerge among individuals who entered the situation as presumed status-equals. These status battles and their associated interpersonal tensions are reduced by the prestructuring of differentiated role expectations in which an individual is assigned a role prior to his or her participation. Thus, in an experimental study, Carter and his colleagues (1953) found that group leaders who had been appointed to their position by the experimenter spent less time attempting to assert their power and defend their position and encountered less resistance to their leadership efforts than leaders who emerged on their own. (See also Verba, 1961: 161–72.)

Formalization also serves to objectify the structure—to make the definitions of roles and relationships appear to be both objective and external to the participating actors. These qualities contribute substantially to the efficacy of these systems in controlling behavior. A series of experiments conducted by Zucker (1977) demonstrates this effect. Subjects placed in an ambiguous situation were much more likely to accept influence from another when that person was defined as holding a specified organizational position (not, by the way, a position of authority but simply a named office) than when the person was described simply as "another person."

The social cement that binds and regulates activities and interactions in informal groups is the sociometric structure—the patterning of affective ties among participants. The creation of a formal structure constitutes an important functional alternative to the sociometric structure. With formalization, the smooth functioning of the organization is to some degree made independent of the feelings—negative or positive—that particular members have for one another. As Merton (1957: 195) notes, "formality facilitates the interaction of the occupants of offices despite their (possibly hostile) private attitudes toward one another." Indeed, many organizations discourage the development of positive sentiments among their members for fear that such emotional ties will undermine discipline and judgment and interfere with attempts to deploy participants rationally.

Formalization makes allowances for the finitude of humans. The process of succession—the movement of individuals into and out of offices—can be routinized and regularized so that one appropriately trained person can replace another with minimal disturbance to the functioning of the organization. In this sense, organizations can—although few actually do—achieve a kind of immortality. The Roman Catholic church may be cited as a particularly successful example.

Formalized structures are thus rendered independent of the participation of any particular individual; a related consequence is that it becomes less essential to recruit unusually gifted individuals for the key positions. The power and influence of leaders can be determined in part by the definition of their offices and not made a function of their personal qualities—their charisma. Referring to political structures, MacIver notes, "The man who commands may be no wiser, no abler, may be, in some sense no better than the average of his fellows; sometimes, by any intrinsic standard, he is inferior to them. Here is the magic of government." (1947: 13) More generally, here is the magic of formalization. To explain more clearly the alchemy of this process, Wolin (1960: 383) draws an analogy between the formalization of structure and scientific method:

> Method, like organization, is the salvation of puny men, the compensatory device for individual foibles, the gadget which allows mediocrity to transcend its limitations. . . . organization, by simplifying and routinizing procedures, eliminates the need for surpassing talent. It is predicated on "average human beings."

In the highly formalized organization, the innovating entrepreneur is supplanted by a corps of administrators and technical specialists. Leadership, even innovation, is routinized and regularized by being incorporated into the formal structure. (See Schumpeter, 1947; Galbraith, 1967.)

We have reviewed some of the major contributions that formalization of structure can make to rational functioning of the organization. We must note here, however, that we have discussed only the *form* of a formalized structure; nothing has been said about its *content.* That is, we have stated that in a formalized structure positions are specified, roles are defined, and role relationships are prescribed independently of the personal attributes of participants, and we have indicated certain advantages that stem from such arrangements. But we have not concerned ourselves with the content of these specifications, definitions, and prescriptions. The content of the formal structure has also been of great concern to certain rational system theorists, as we will see when we discuss their contributions in the next section.

SELECTED SCHOOLS

The preceding discussion represents an effort to distill the central elements characterizing the rational system perspective. This perspective does not reflect a unitary position but includes a set of somewhat varied, historically distinct approaches. Before briefly characterizing some of these major schools, we must first acknowledge that only one of them— that associated with Simon's work—explicitly emphasizes goal specificity. The rest assume its presence. And few concern themselves with formalization per se but consider specific ways in which organizations can or should be designed to attain maximum effectiveness. That is, most of the advocates of the rational system position assume the importance of formal structure and concern themselves with specifying the nature or content of that structure. Four schools will be briefly described: Taylor's scientific management; attempts by Fayol and others to formulate administrative principles; Weber's theory of bureaucracy; and Simon's discussion of administrative behavior.

Taylor's Scientific Management

The scientific management approach received its primary impetus from the work of Frederick W. Taylor (1911) in the late nineteenth and early twentieth centuries but was carried forward by the contributions of others, such as Frank and Lillian Gilbreth, Henry Gantt, and Charles Bedeaux. Taylor and his followers insisted that it was possible to scientifically analyze tasks performed by individual workers in order to discover those procedures that would produce the maximum output with the minimum input of energies and resources. Efforts were concentrated on analyzing individual tasks, but attempts to rationalize labor at the level of the individual worker inevitably led to changes in the entire structure of work arrangements. Ward (1964) describes the sequence of changes that resulted from Taylor's efforts to improve the efficiency of performing such menial tasks as shoveling coal and iron ore in a steel mill:

> First, a variety of kinds of shovels had to be designed to handle different kinds of materials. That also meant building shovel rooms in the various parts of the yard, so that a gang would have the proper tools at hand. To eliminate the waste motion of wandering about so large a yard, it meant, as Taylor said, "organizing and planning work at least a day in advance," so that when men checked in, they would be at that day's work. This meant, Taylor reported, building a labor office for a planning staff—a bureaucracy, as we would say. Large maps of the yard were then necessary to show at a glance the location of different kinds of work and the location of men. Furthermore, the installation of a telephone network was essential for more effective interior communication. Once the yard was mapped so that one could see at a glance the relationships in time and sequence between different jobs, it led, naturally enough, to the reorganization of the yard itself, so that materials could be delivered or dumped in a more logical sequence.
>
> One can see readily enough what happened. Taylor's attempt to make the crudest physical act of labor efficient led inexorably to a further organization of every aspect of the production process. (Ward, 1964: 64–65)

It was not only, or even primarily, the lot of workers that was to be altered by the introduction of scientific management: the role of management was also to be transformed. Taylor aspired to replace the arbitrary and capricious activities of managers with analytical, scientific procedures:

> Under scientific management arbitrary power, arbitrary dictation, ceases; and every single subject, large and small, becomes the question for scientific investigation, for reduction to law. . . .
> The man at the head of the business under scientific management is governed by rules and laws which have been developed through hundreds of experiments just as much as the workman is, and the standards which have been developed are equitable. (Taylor, 1947: 211, 189)

The activities of both managers and workers were to be rationalized; both were equally subject to the regimen of science.

Taylor believed that the adoption of scientific management principles by industrial concerns would usher in a new era of industrial peace. The interests of labor and management would be rendered compatible. Workers would be scientifically selected to perform those tasks for which they were best suited. Scientifically determined procedures would allow them to work at peak efficiency, in return for which they would receive top wages. "Once work was scientifically plotted, Taylor felt, there could be no disputes about how hard one should work or the pay one should receive for labor. 'As reasonably might we insist on bargaining about the time and place of the rising and setting sun,' he once said." (Bell, 1960: 228) Managers would cooperate with workers in devising appropriate work arrangements and pay scales and would enjoy the fruits of maximum profits.

The underlying spirit of Taylor's approach—an amalgam of the Protestant ethic, social Darwinism, and a view of human beings as motivated exclusively by economic incentives—found widespread acceptance among American managers at the turn of the century. However, many were disquieted by Taylor's vision of their own new role: "After all, Taylor had questioned their good judgment and superior ability which had been the subject of public celebration for many years. Hence, many employers regarded his methods as an unwarranted interference with managerial prerogatives." (Bendix, 1956: 280) Workers for their part resisted time-study procedures and attempts to standardize every aspect of their performance and rejected incentive sytems requiring them to perform continuously at a peak level of efficiency. Nevertheless scientific management has had a profound and lasting effect on industrial practice and on theoretical conceptions of work organization.[1]

Administrative Theory

A second approach, developing concurrently with scientific management, emphasized management functions and attempted to generate broad administrative principles that would serve as guidelines for the rationalization of organizational activities. Whereas Taylor and his disciples proposed to rationalize the organization from the "bottom up"— changes in the performance of individual tasks affecting the larger structure of work relations—the administrative management theorists worked to rationalize the organization from the "top down." Henri Fayol, a French industrialist writing in the early part of this century, was probably the earliest exponent of this approach, but his ideas did not become widely available in this country until 1949, when his major work was translated. Influential participants in this movement in the United States included two General Motors executives, Mooney and Reiley (1939), whose treatise on management principles gained a wide following, and

[1]Perhaps the most useful overview of Taylor's conception is contained in his testimony before the Special House Committee to Investigate the Taylor and Other Systems of Shop Management in 1912. This testimony is reprinted in Taylor (1947). Summaries of and commentaries on his contribution will be found in Bell (1960: 222–37), Bendix (1956: 274–81), and Mouzelis (1968: 78–87). A severe critique of Taylor's work from a Marxist perspective is provided by Braverman (1974: 85–138).

Gulick and Urwick, who in 1937 collaborated to edit the volume *Papers on the Science of Administration.*

The various contributors to this perspective did not reach agreement as to the number of principles required or the precise formulation of many specific principles, but there was considerable consensus on the importance of two types of activities: coordination and specialization (Massie, 1965; Tausky, 1970). The major principles developed to guide coordination activities include the scalar principle, which emphasizes the hierarchical organizational form in which all participants are linked into a single pyramidal structure of control relations; the unity-of-command principle, specifying that no organizational participants should receive orders from more than one superior; the span-of-control principle, which emphasizes that no superior should have more subordinates than can be effectively overseen (theorists were unable to agree on the precise number of subordinates who could be supervised); and the exception principle, which recommends that all routine matters be handled by subordinates and that the superior be free to deal with exceptional situations to which existing rules are inapplicable. Specialization issues include decisions both about how various activities are to be distributed among organizational positions and about how such positions can most effectively be grouped into work units or departments. Among the principles espoused to guide these types of decisions is the departmentalization principle, which maintains that activities should be grouped so as to combine homogeneous or related activities within the same organizational unit. Homogeneity might be based on similarity of purpose (activities contributing to the same subgoal—for example, marketing), process (activities requiring similar operations—for example, typing), clientele (activities performed on the same set of recipients—for example, a medical team organized around the care of a specific group of patients), or place (for example, services provided to individuals in a given regional territory). Also proposed is the line-staff principle, by which all activities directly concerned with achieving organizational goals are designated as line functions, to be distinguished from staff activities, which consist primarily of advice, service, or support. Staff units are to be segregated from the scalar organization of power and responsible and subordinate to appropriate line units.

Note the heavy emphasis on formalization implicit in these principles. Careful specification of work activities and concern for their grouping and coordination is the hallmark of the formalized structure. Mooney (1937: 92) makes explicit this call for formalization by distinguishing between jobs (positions) and the person on the job:

> In every organization there is a collective job to be done, consisting always of the sum of many individual jobs, and the task of administration, operating through management, is the co-ordination of all the human effort necessary to this end. Such co-ordination, however, always presupposes the jobs to be coordinated. The job as such is therefore antecedent to the man on the job, and the sound co-ordination of these jobs, considered simply as jobs, must be the first and necessary condition in the effective co-ordination of the human factor.

The more astute administrative theorists recognized that their managerial principles furnished at best only broad guidelines for decision making. Thus, Fayol (1949 trans.: 19) reminds practitioners,

> The soundness and good working order of the body corporate depends on a certain number of conditions termed indiscriminately principles, laws, rules. For preference I shall adopt the term principles whilst dissociating it from any suggestion of rigidity, for there is nothing rigid or absolute in management affairs, it is all a question of proportion. Seldom do we have to apply the same principle twice in identical conditions; allowance must be made for different changing cirumstances.

And Gulick (Gulick and Urwick, 1937: 31) cautions,

> Students of administration have long sought a single principle of effective departmentalization just as alchemists sought the philosopher's stone. But they have sought in vain. There is apparently no one most effective system of departmentalism.

In spite of such disclaimers, the managerial principles enunciated by the administrative theorists came under increasing attack. Three types of criticisms have been made: (1) that the principles are mere truisms or common-sense pronouncements; (2) that the principles are based on questionable premises; and (3) that the principles occur in pairs or clusters of contradictory statements with little guidance for application to a given situation. (See Massie, 1965: 406.) With respect to the first type of criticism, it is quite correct that many of the proposed administrative principles are primarily definitional, outlining the characteristics of a hierarchically structured formal organization, whereas others are sufficiently vague and imprecise to be of little help to practitioners or researchers. In regard to the second, Massie (1965: 405) has provided a lengthy listing of questionable premises, including the assumption that individuals are motivated primarily by economic interest, that they prefer the security of a definite assignment to the freedom of discretionary activity, that they prefer not to work and so must be constrained to do so, and that managers are capable of predicting work needs in advance and establishing effective arrangements for work and its coordination. The problem is not that these assumptions are inevitably false, but that they are not made explicit enough to serve as specifications for the application of the principles. The third type of criticism has been given greatest currency by Simon, whose influential text on administration commenced with "an indictment of much current writing about administrative matters" (1957: 36). Simon, examining one after another principle, concluded variously that they involved inconsistencies, lack of specification, or "a deceptive simplicity—a simplicity that conceals fundamental ambiguities" (1957: 21).

Without gainsaying any of these criticisms, we can admire what the administrative theorists attempted to do. They were pioneers in identifying the fundamental features of formal organizational structure, audaciously clinging to the view that all organizations contain certain common structural characteristics. With the improved vision of hindsight, it is now apparent that their search was confounded not so much by their inadequate theory of motivation or by the prescriptive cast of their propositions as by their failure to develop conditional generalizations—statements that specify the limits of their applicability to particular situations or types of organizations.[2]

Weber's Theory of Bureaucracy

Contemporaneous with and yet independent of the scientific management school and those who attempted to formulate administrative principles was the work of Max Weber, the influential German sociologist writing at the turn of the century. Weber's analysis of administrative structures was only a limited aspect of his much larger interest in accounting for the unique features of Western civilization. (See Bendix, 1960.) In his view, what was distinctive was the growth of rationality in the West, and his active mind roamed across legal, religious, political, and economic systems, as well as administrative structures, as he searched for materials to test and extend his notions by comparing and contrasting differing cultures and historical periods. Weber's analysis of administrative systems can be fully appreciated only if it is seen in this larger context, since his listing of the structural characteristics of bureaucracy was generated in an attempt to differentiate this more rational form from earlier forms.

In his justly famous typology, Weber (1947 trans.: 328) distinguishes three types of authority:

•*Traditional authority*—resting on an established belief in the sanctity of immemorial traditions and the legitimacy of those exercising authority under them

•*Rational-legal authority*—resting on a belief in the "legality" of patterns of normative rules and the right of those elevated to authority under such rules to issue commands

•*Charismatic authority*—resting on devotion to the specific and exceptional sanctity, heroism or exemplary character of an individual person, and of the normative patterns or order revealed or ordained by him.

Clearly, the basis for the typology is differences in the beliefs by which legitimacy is attributed to an authority relation. Associated with each authority type is a distinctive administrative structure. Traditional authority gives rise to the particularistic and diffuse structures exemplified by patrimonialism and its various manifestations, including gerontocracy, patriarchalism, and feudalism. (See Delany, 1963; Dibble, 1965.) The simplest way to visualize a *patrimonial* system is as a household writ large: an estate or production organization governed by a ruler-owner who in managing the enterprise relies for assistance on a variety of dependents, ranging from slaves to serfs to sons. Rational-legal authority provides the basis for the more specific and universalistic structures of which the most highly developed form is the bureaucracy. And charismatic authority is associated with the "strictly personal" relations linking an impressive leader with his devoted coterie of followers or disciples.

[2]This is the major insight that underlies the *contingency theory* of organizations, described in Chapter 4.

In Weber's view, only traditional and rational-legal authority relations are sufficiently stable to provide the basis for the formation of permanent administrative structures. And, during recent centuries, particularly in Western societies, traditional structures are viewed as gradually giving way to rational-legal structures, most notably in "the modern state" and in "the most advanced institutions of capitalism," due to their "purely technical superiority over any other form of organization." (Weber, 1946 trans.: 196, 214) Charismatic forms arise in periods of instability and crisis when extraordinary measures are called for and seemingly offered by individuals perceived as possessing uncommon gifts of spirit and mind. Lenin, Hitler, Gandhi, and Mao are only a few recent examples of such charismatic leaders, ilustrating their diversity and their power to inspire the fanatical devotion of others around their personal vision of "reform." However, for such movements to persist, they must move in the direction of one or the other stable forms, by establishing "new" traditional structures[3] or new bureaucratic structures. Charisma becomes routinized: the circle of adherents expands to include more but less committed participants; systematic sources of support replace voluntary and heartfelt, but irregular, contributions; personal ties between leader and followers are replaced by more orderly but impersonal arrangements; and rules of succession are developed in recognition of the truth that no one lives forever—not even a superhuman leader (Weber, 1947 trans.: 358–73).

Weber's typology of authority is of interest not only because it underlies his conception of basic changes occurring in administrative systems over time. The distinction between traditional and rational-legal forms also serves as the basis for his influential conception of the characteristics of bureaucratic structures. In many presentations of Weber's work, this model is depicted as a simple list of administrative characteristics present in bureaucratic forms, characteristics such as these:

- •a fixed division of labor among participants
- •a hierarchy of offices
- •a set of general rules that govern performance
- •a separation of personal from official property and rights
- •selection of personnel on the basis of technical qualifications
- •employment viewed as a career by participants

However, his contribution can be better appreciated if these bureaucratic elements are described in relation to the traditional features they supplanted. Thus, according to Weber (1946 trans.: 196–204; 1947 trans.: 329–36), bureaucratic systems are distinguished from traditional administrative forms by the following features:

1. Jurisdictional areas are clearly specified: the regular activities required of personnel are distributed in a fixed way as official duties (in contrast with the patrimonial arrangement, in which the division of labor is not firm or regular but depends on assignments made by the leader, which can be changed at any time).

[3]The art of "inventing" traditions is described by Hobsbawm and Ranger (1983).

2. The organization of offices follows the principle of hierarchy: each lower office is controlled and supervised by a higher one. However, the scope of authority of superiors over subordinates is circumscribed, and lower offices enjoy a right of appeal (in contrast with the patrimonial form, where authority relations are more diffuse, being based on personal loyalty, and are not ordered into clear hierarchies).

3. An intentionally established system of abstract rules governs official decisions and actions. These rules are relatively stable and exhaustive, and can be learned. Decisions are recorded in permanent files. (In patrimonial systems, general rules of administration either do not exist or are vaguely stated, ill-defined, and subject to change at the whim of the leader. No attempt is made to keep permanent records of transactions.)

4. The "means of production or administration"—for example, tools and equipment or rights and privileges—belong to the office, not the office-holder, and may not be appropriated. Personal property is clearly separated from official property, and working space from living quarters. (Such distinctions are not maintained in patrimonial administrative systems since there is no separation of the ruler's personal household business from the larger "public" business under his direction.)

5. Officials are personally free, selected on the basis of technical qualifications, appointed to office (not elected), and compensated by salary. (In more traditional administrative systems, officials are often selected from among those who are personally dependent on the leader—for example, slaves, serfs, relatives. Selection is governed by particularistic criteria, and compensation often takes the form of benefices—rights granted to individuals that for example, allow them access to the stores of the ruler or give them grants of land from which they can appropriate the fees or taxes. Benefices, like fiefs in feudalistic systems, may become hereditary and sometimes are bought and sold.)

6. Employment by the organization constitutes a career for officials. An official is a full-time employee and looks forward to a lifelong career in the agency. After a trial period he or she gains tenure of position and is protected against arbitrary dismissal. (In patrimonial systems, officials serve at the pleasure of the leader and so lack clear expectations about the future and security of tenure.)

When we thus juxtapose Weber's list of bureaucratic characteristics and the related aspects of patrimonial systems, a clearer view emerges of Weber's central message. He viewed each bureaucratic element as the *solution* to a problem or defect contained within the earlier administrative systems. Further, each element operates not in isolation but as part of a system of elements that, in combination, were expected to provide more effective and efficient administration. To capture both the notions of distinctive elements and their interrelation, Weber employed what is termed an *ideal-type* construct. This approach attempts to isolate those elements regarded as most characteristic of the phenomenon to be explored. The term "ideal-type" is somewhat misleading, since it does not refer to a normatively preferred type but rather to the construction of a simplified model that focuses attention on the most salient or distinctive features.

Even though Weber's model of administrative systems emphasized that they were composed of many, interrelated factors, in his own analysis he focused primarily on the type of authority relation between superiors and subordinates in the administrative structure. In contrasting the rational-legal with the other two (nonrational) types, he stressed two seemingly contradictory points. First, the rational-legal form provides the basis for a more stable and predictable administrative structure for both superiors and subordinates. The behavior of subordinates is rendered more reliable by the specificity of their role obligations, the clarity of hierarchical connections, and their continuing dependence on the hierarchy in the short run for income and in the longer term for career progression. And superiors are prevented from behaving arbitrarily or capriciously in their demands made on subordinates.

On the other hand, the rational-legal structure permits subordinates to exercise "relatively greater independence and discretion" than is possible in the other types of administrative systems (Smith and Ross, 1978). Because obedience is owed not to a person—whether a traditional chief or a charismatic leader—but to a set of impersonal principles, subordinates in bureaucratic systems have a stronger basis for independent action, guided by their interpretation of the principles. They also have a clear basis for questioning the directives of superiors, whose actions are presumably constrained by the same impersonal framework of rules. By supporting increased independence and discretion among lower administrative officials constrained by general administrative policies and specified procedures, bureaucratic systems are capable of handling more complex administrative tasks than traditional systems. (This general argument will be amplified in Chapter 10.)

Weber was no Pollyanna, believing in costless progress. He was quite ambivalent about the developments he charted, observing that bureaucratic forms appeared capable of growing with an inexorable logic of their own, concentrating great power in the hands of their masters, reducing individual participants to the status of "cog in an ever-moving mechanism" and imprisoning humanity in an "iron cage" (1946 trans.: 228; 1958 trans.: 181). Bureaucracy's greatest fan was at the same time one of its most severe critics. We consider these and related problems associated with the growth of bureaucracy in later chapters, particularly Chapter 12.

Weber's analysis of bureaucratic structure, while influential, has also been controversial. We briefly review two important criticisms. Since type of authority relation goes a long way toward determining the nature of administrative structures, in Weber's conception, criticisms of his views of the type of authority prevailing in bureaucratic systems take on special significance. Both Parsons and Gouldner have suggested that Weber tended to confuse two analytically distinguishable bases of authority. On the one hand, in his discussion of the administrative hierarchy of bureaucracies, Weber notes that authority rests on "incumbency in a legally defined office." On the other hand, in his discussion of criteria for recruitment and advancement, Weber appears to argue that authority is based on "technical competence." (Parsons, 1947: 58–60) Indeed, at one point Weber states, "Bureaucratic administration means fundamentally the exercise of control on the basis of knowledge" (1947 trans.: 339). Gouldner (1954: 22–23) underlines the contradiction:

> Weber, then, thought of bureaucracy as a Janus-faced organization, looking two ways at once. On the one side, it was administration based on discipline. In the first emphasis, obedience is invoked as a means to an end; an individ-

ual obeys because the rule or order is felt to be the best known method of realizing some goal.

In his second conception, Weber held that bureaucracy was a mode of administration in which obedience was an end in itself. The individual obeys the order, setting aside judgments either of its rationality or morality, primarily because of the *position* occupied by the person commanding. The content of the order is not examinable.

One might defend Weber by insisting that there is a high positive correlation between a person's position in the hierarchy and his or her degree of technical competence. Such may have been the case in Weber's day, when on-the-job experience was a major source of technical competence, but seems far off the mark in today's world of minute specialization supported by prolonged and esoteric training in institutions separated from the work setting. Thompson (1961: 47) convincingly portrays the ever-widening gap between ability and authority in modern organizations, asserting that

> authority is centralized, but ability is inherently decentralized because it comes from practice and training rather than from definition. Whereas the boss retains his full *rights* to make all decisions, he has less and less *ability* to do so because of the advance of science and technology.

Staff-line arrangements, in which the positional authority of the line administrator is distinguished from the technical expertise of the staff specialist, appear to be not so much a solution to the difficulty—see studies by Dalton (1950; 1959) and others on staff-line conflict—as a structural recognition of the distinctiveness of the two sources of authority sloughed over in Weber's analysis.

A second criticism of Weber's formulation is that his ideal-type construct of bureaucracy is "an admixture of a conceptual scheme and a set of hypotheses" (Blau and Scott, 1962: 33), the difficulty being that Weber does not clearly distinguish definitions from propositions in his model. Weber's conception not only calls attention to what he regards as the key elements of bureaucracy—a set of characteristics—but also contains numerous propositions linking the various elements. For example, it is implied that organizations having a well-developed hierarchy of authority also attempt to standardize the performance of tasks by applying rules and formalized procedures, and that these same organizations also employ technical criteria in recruiting and promoting personnel, and so on. Weber's conception contains numerous propositions about the interrelations of structural characteristics in organizations, some explicit but many implicit. For a long time sociologists following in Weber's footsteps took as given the interrelations posited in his schema.

Udy (1959a; 1959b) was among the first to suggest that Weber's model could be regarded as identifying a set of structural variables whose interrelations should not be taken as a matter of definition but as a subject for empirical exploration. His lead was quickly followed by numerous others, including Hall (1963; 1968), Pugh and colleagues (1968; 1976), and Blau and associates (1966; 1971), all of whom documented the great variety exhibited by structural systems. Perhaps of greatest interest, studies by Udy (1959*a*) questioned Weber's assertion that bureaucratic organizations (in Weber's sense) were necessarily also rational in form. Employing a sample of 150 organizations from 150 nonindustrial societies (settings that afford greater variation in structural features), Udy distinguished the "bureaucratic" attributes of these organizations, including such features as a hierarchical authority structure and a specialized administrative staff, from their "rational" attributes, including specified, limited objectives and the distribution of rewards based on performance.[4] Although structural features within each of the two clusters were positively interrelated, Udy found no association between the two sets of variables: organizations that possessed more bureaucratic features were not more likely than organizations lacking them to exhibit rational features. Similarly, studies by Hall (1963; 1968) of samples of United States organizations found that an emphasis on technical qualifications was negatively correlated with other bureaucratic features, such as a hierarchy of authority, emphasis on rules, and a division of labor. This finding not only challenges Weber's ideal-type conception of bureaucracy and supports the earlier criticism that Weber confused authority of office with authority of expertise, it raises the interesting question of when—under what conditions—bureaucratic structures are rational structures. This central query is addressed in many of the following chapters.

Although it is clearly possible to criticize and improve upon many specific aspects of Weber's formulation, he remains the acknowledged master of organization theory: the intellectual giant whose conceptions continue to shape definitions of the central elements of administrative systems, and whose historical and comparative vision continues to challenge and inform our understanding of organizational forms and their evolution.[5]

Simon's Theory of Administrative Behavior

Herbert Simon, both in his early work on administration[6] and in his later collaborative work with March, has clarified the processes by which goal specificity and formalization contribute to rational behavior in organizations. (See Simon, 1957, 1964; March and Simon, 1958.) We have already observed that Simon was critical of the platitudes developed by Fayol and others searching for management principles. He also criticized the assumptions made by Taylor and other early theorists about the actors in organizations. For the "economic man" motivated by self-interest and completely informed about all available alternatives, Simon proposed to

---

[4]Although we have no quarrel with the specific organizational features selected by Udy to represent "rational" characteristics, we are uncomfortable with the assumption that any given organizational feature can be regarded as rational irrespective of the circumstances in which it operates. In short, we believe that it is much preferable to view rationality as applicable to the *relation* between means and ends rather than to either means or ends viewed in isolation.

[5]Summaries and critical reviews of Weber's contributions to organization theory are provided by Albrow (1970), Bendix (1960), and Mouzelis (1968).

[6]Simon's basic work, *Administrative Behavior*, first appeared in 1945. However, all our references are to the second edition of this work, published in 1957, which contains an extensive new introduction.

substitute a more human "administrative man," who seeks to pursue his self-interests but does not always know what they are, is aware of only a few of all the possible alternatives, and is willing to settle for an adequate solution in contrast with an optimal one.

Following the lead of Barnard (1938), Simon distinguishes between (1) an individual's decisions to join and to continue to participate in an organization and (2) the decisions an individual is asked to make as a participant in the organization. Only the latter set of decisions is of interest in the present context.[7] A scientifically relevant description of an organization, according to Simon (1957: 37), details what decisions individuals make as organizational participants and the influences to which they are subject in making these decisions. In general, in Simon's view, organizations both simplify decisions and support participants in the decisions they need to make.

A primary way in which organizations simplify participants' decisions is to restrict the ends toward which activity is directed. Simon points out that goals affect behavior only as they enter into decisions about how to behave. Goals supply the value premises that underlie decisions. *Value premises* are assumptions about what ends are preferred or desirable. They are combined in decisions with *factual premises*—assumptions about the observable world and the way in which it operates. The more precise and specific the value premises, the greater their impact on the resulting decisions, since specific goals clearly distinguish acceptable from unacceptable (or more from less acceptable) alternatives. Typically, participants higher in the hierarchy make decisions with a large value component, whereas lower participants are more apt to make decisions having a larger factual component. Those closer to the top make decisions about what the organization is going to do; those in lower positions are more likely to be allowed to make choices as to how the organization can best carry out its tasks. Simon (1957: 45–56) insists that quite different criteria of correctness underlie these two classes of decisions: choice of ends can be validated only by fiat or consensus; choice of means can be validated empirically.

Ultimate goals served by organizations are frequently somewhat vague and imprecise. Some organizations exist to develop and transmit knowledge, others to maintain public order, and others to care for and cure patients. Such general goals in themselves provide few cues for guiding the behavior of participants. However, as March and Simon (1958: 191) argue, they can serve as the starting point for the contruction of *means-ends chains* that involve

> (1) starting with the general goal to be achieved, (2) discovering a set of means, very generally specific, for accomplishing this goal, (3) taking each of these means, in turn, as a new subgoal and discovering a set of more detailed means for achieving it, etc.

In this manner, there is established a hierarchy of goals in which each level is

---

[7]Factors affecting the first type of decision—decisions to participate—are discussed in Chapter 7 of this volume. See also March and Simon (1958: 52–111.)

considered as an end relative to the levels below it and as a means relative to the levels above it. Through the hierarchical structure of ends, behavior attains integration and consistency, for each member of a set of behavior alternatives is then weighted in terms of a comprehensive scale of values—the "ultimate" ends. (Simon,1957: 63)

For example, in a manufacturing organization, an assignment to an individual worker to constuct a specific component of a piece of equipment such as an engine provides that worker with an end toward which to direct his or her activities. This end, viewed from the level of his or her supervisor, is only a means toward the creation of the engine. The supervisor's end is to ensure that all parts are available when needed and are correctly assembled to produce the engine. However, this objective, when viewed from the next higher level, is only a means to the end of completing the final product, such as a lawn mower, containing the engine. The completion of all parts and assembly operations required to produce the lawn mower, while an end for the manufacturing division, is only a means at a higher level to the ultimate end of selling the lawn mower for profit to retail outlets. Viewed from the bottom up, the rationality of individual decisions and activities can be evaluted only as they relate to higher-order decisions; each subgoal can be assessed only in terms of its consistency or congruency with more general goals. Viewed from the top down, the factoring of general purposes into specific subgoals that can then be assigned to organizational subunits (individuals or departments) enhances the possibility of rational behavior by specifying value premises and hence simplifying the required decisions at every level. From this perspective, then, an organization's hierarchy can be viewed as a congealed set of means-ends chains promoting consistency of decisions and activities throughout the organization.

The ultimate goals—making a profit, achieving growth, prolonging life—are those that, by definition, are not viewed as means to ends but as ends in themselves. They may be determined by consensus or by decree. In either case, any challenge to these ultimate objectives is likely to be met with strong resistance. Physicians, for example, often refuse to consider the merits of euthanasia, and capitalists react with righteous indignation to any questions concerning their rights to profits. Apart from any considerations of self-interest, such emotional reactions are partly caused by the half-conscious realization that any challenge to the ultimate objectives calls into question the premises around which the entire enterprise is structured.

Organizations also support participants in the decisions they must make. A formalized structure supports rational decision making by dividing responsibilities among participants and providing them with the necessary means to handle them: resources, information, equipment. Specialized roles and rules, information channels, training programs, standard operating procedures—all may be viewed as mechanisms both for restricting the range of decisions each participant makes and for assisting the participant in making appropriate decisions within that range. As Perrow (1979: 149–53) notes, Simon's model of organizational influence stresses unobtrusive control of participants: training and channeling of information and attention play a larger role in producing dependable behavior than do commands or sanctions.

Underlying Simon's model of organizational decision making is a conception of cognitive limits on individual decision makers.[8] Simon (1957: 79) stresses that

> it is impossible for the behavior of a single, isolated individual to reach any high degree of rationality. The number of alternatives he must explore is too great, the information he would need to evaluate them so vast that even an approximation to objective rationality is hard to conceive. Individual choice takes place in an environment of "givens"—premises that are accepted by the subject as bases for his choice; and behavior is adaptive only within the limits set by these "givens."

By providing integrated subgoals, stable expectations, required information, necessary facilities, routine-performance programs, and in general a set of constraints within which required decisions can be made, organizations supply these "givens" to individual participants. This is the sense in which March and Simon (1958: 169–71) intend the concept *bounded rationality*—a concept that both summarizes and integrates the two key elements of the rational system perspective: goal specificity and formalization.[9]

The model developed by Simon also can be used to explain how the very structures developed to promote rationality can, under some conditions, have the opposite effect. These and other sources of organizational pathologies will be discussed in Chapter 12.

SUMMARY AND TENTATIVE CONCLUSIONS

Any conclusions reached at this point must be tentative; it is difficult to appraise the strengths and limitations of any one perspective in isolation from the others. Nevertheless, a few general observations on the rational system approach can be made at this time.

From the rational system perspective, structural arrangements within organizations are conceived as tools deliberately designed for the efficient realization of ends. As Gouldner (1959: 404–5) notes, "the focus is, therefore, on the legally prescribed structures—i.e., the formally 'blueprinted' patterns—since these are more largely subject to deliberate inspection and rational manipulation." All theorists utilizing this perspective focus on the normative structure of organizations: on the specificity of goals and the formalization of rules and roles. There are, however, important differences among the various schools considered in their approach to the normative structure.

[8]More recent studies by cognitive psychologists have pursued in detail the types of cognitive biases and errors that commonly afflict individual decision makers. These researchers have given primary attention to the types of *heuristics* employed by individuals when confronting uncertainty. (See Tversky and Kahneman, 1974; Nisbett and Ross, 1980; Kahneman, Slovic, and Tversky, 1982.) Simon's work should stimulate organizational researchers to examine more closely the ways in which structural arrangements within organizations overcome or amplify the biases of individual actors.

[9]A good overview of Simon's contributions to the analysis of decision making in organizations is provided by Taylor (1965). An interesting critique of Simon's work is provided by Krupp (1961), and useful applications and extensions of Simon's framework are carried out by Allison (1971) and Steinbruner (1974).

Taylor was highly pragmatic in his approach, placing his faith in a method by which, beginning with individual jobs, superior work procedures could be developed and appropriate arrangements devised for articulating the various tasks to be performed. Work planning was distinguished from work performance, the former becoming the responsibility of management. Taylor was concerned primarily with devising methods for the planning of work and working arrangements. The administrative theory group was less pragmatic and more prescriptive in its approach. They believed that general principles of management could be devised to guide managers as they designed their organizations, and so they busied themselves constructing lists of "do's and dont's" as guides to managerial decision making. Weber was less concerned with discovering ways— whether pragmatic or prescriptive—for improving organizations than with attempting to develop a parsimonious descriptive portrait of the characteristics of the newly emerging bureaucratic structures. Like Weber, Simon was also descriptive in his approach, examining the effect of structural features on individual decision makers within the organization. Simon's conception, in particular, enables us to understand better how thousands and even hundreds of thousands of individual decisions and actions can be integrated in the service of complex goals. Such rational, purposeful collective behavior requires the support of an organizational framework.

The four types of theorists also differ in the level of analysis at which they work. Taylor and Simon operate primarily at the social psychological level, focusing on individual participants as they perform tasks or make decisions; they treat structural features as contexts affecting these behaviors. By contrast, the administrative theorists and Weber work at the structural level, attempting to conceptualize and analyze the characteristics of organizational forms.

Thompson (1967: 54) provides a simple summary of the general argument underlying the rational system perspective: "structure is a fundamental vehicle by which organizations achieve bounded rationality." The specification of positions, role definitions, procedural rules and regulations, value and factual inputs that guide decision making—all function to canalize behavior in the service of predetermined goals. Individuals can behave rationally because their alternatives are limited and their choices circumscribed.

In a larger sense, however, rationality resides in the structure itself, not in the individual participants—in rules that assure participants will behave in ways calculated to achieve desired objectives, in control arrangements that evaluate performance and detect deviance, in reward systems that motivate participants to carry out prescribed tasks, and in the set of criteria by which participants are selected, replaced, and promoted. Because of its emphasis on the characteristics of structure rather than the characteristics of participants, Bennis has dubbed the rational system perspective one of "organizations without people" (1959: 263).[10]

---

[10]Consistent with this conclusion, Boguslaw (1965: 2) has pointed out that whereas the classical utopians strove to achieve their end of the perfect social system by "populating their social systems with perfect human beings," the "new utopians"—systems engineers and control-systems experts—have become impatient with human imperfections, so that "the theo-

Let us not forget, however, that the conception of rationality employed by this perspective is limited. At the top of the organization, the value premises that govern the entire structure of decision making fall outside the system: as long as they are specific enough to provide clear criteria for choice, these premises can support a "rational" structure no matter how monstrous or perverted their content. And at the bottom of the organization, "rational" behavior often consists in turning off one's mind and one's critical intellectual judgment and blindly conforming to the performance program specified by the job description (see Veblen, 1904).

We have noted the great emphasis the rational system places on control—the determination of the behavior of one subset of participants by the other. Decision making tends to be centralized, and most participants are excluded from discretion or from exercising control over their own behavior. Most rational system theorists justify these arrangements as being in the service of rationality: control is the means of channeling and coordinating behavior so as to achieve specified goals. Few perceive the possibility that interpersonal control may be an end in itself—that one function of elaborate hierarchies and extensive divisions of labor is to allow some participants to control others. The critical or Marxist perspective calls attention to these possibilities. We will examine this critique in more detail in Chapter 7.

None of these rational system theorists took much notice of the effect of the larger social, cultural, and technological context on the structure of the organization. Although Weber attempted to account for the emergence and growth of bureaucratic structures by pointing to larger societal changes (see Chapter 7), he did not examine variations in structure among bureaucratic organizations and relate these to differences in social context.

Also, by concentrating on the normative structure, rational system analysts have virtually ignored the behavioral structure of organizations. We learn much from these theorists about plans and programs and premises, about roles and rules and regulations, but very little indeed about the actual behavior of organizational participants. The implication is that if planning is good, if decisions are sound, implementation will take care of itself. Others note the need to motivate and control participants so that their actions will coincide with design, but these theorists—Taylor, for example—are criticized for holding an oversimplified view of human beings and for having inadequate knowledge of what factors will and will not prove effective in motivating behavior.

These and related criticisms gave rise to alternative perspectives on organizations. The second perspective to be considered, the natural system perspective, developed specifically in opposition to the rational system model and was designed to correct its oversimplified conception of organizational structure and its naïve conception of individual participants.

---

retical and practical solutions they seek call increasingly for decreases in the number and in the scope of responsibility of human beings within the operating structures of their new machines systems.

. . . the new utopians are concerned with non-people and with people-substitutes."

3 organizations as natural systems

> To administer a social organization according to purely
> technical criteria of rationality is irrational, because it
> ignores the nonrational aspects of social conduct.
>
> Peter M. Blau (1956)

The natural system perspective developed in large measure from critical reactions to the inadequacies of the rational system model. And in our own discussion, we shall make frequent references to these criticisms. However, the natural system perspective should not be seen as merely providing a critique of another perspective. Rather, it defines a novel and interesting view of organizations that deserves to be considered and evaluated in its own right. As with our discussion of the rational system approach, we will first attempt to isolate those more general or basic ideas common to most natural system advocates and then briefly examine selected schools within this perspective.

IMPORTANT VERSUS DISTINCTIVE CHARACTERISTICS

Whereas the rational system theorists conceive of organizations as collectivities deliberately constructed to seek specific goals, natural system advocates emphasize that organizations are, first and foremost, collectivities. Thus, the rational system perspective stresses those features of organizations that distinguish them from other types of social groups, but the natural system theorists remind us that these distinguishing characteristics are not their only characteristics (Gouldner, 1959: 406). Indeed, they may not even be the most important characteristics.

We have already seen that much is made by rational system theorists of goal specificity and formalization as characteristics differentiating organizations from other types of collectivities. Natural system theorists generally acknowledge the existence of these attributes but argue that other characteristics—characteristics shared with all social groups—are of greater significance. Take first the matter of organizational goals and goal specificity.

51

Goal Complexity

Organizational goals and their relation to the behavior of participants seem much more problematic to the natural than to the rational
system theorist. This is largely because natural system analysts pay more
attention to behavior and hence worry more about the complex interconnections between the normative and the behavioral structures of organizations. Two general themes characterize their views of organizational goals.
First, there is frequently a disparity between the stated and the "real"
goals pursued by organizations—between the professed or official goals
that are announced and the actual or operative goals that can be observed
to govern the activities of participants. Second, natural system analysts
emphasize that even when the stated goals are actually being pursued,
they are never the only goals governing participants' behavior. They point
out that all organizations must pursue *support* or "maintenance" goals in
addition to their *output* goals (Gross, 1968; Perrow, 1970: 135). No organization can devote its full resources to producing products or services;
each must expend energies maintaining itself.

These distinctions, though useful, do not go quite far enough. They
do not capture the most profound difference between these two perspectives on organizational goals. The whole thrust of the natural system view
is that organizations are more than instruments for attaining narrowly
defined goals; they are, fundamentally, social groups attempting to adapt
and survive in their particular circumstances. Thus, formal organizations,
like all other social groups, are governed by one overriding goal: survival.
Gouldner (1959: 405) emphasizes this implication of the natural system
perspective:

> The organization, according to this model, strives to survive and to maintain
> its equilibrium, and this striving may persist even after its explicitly held
> goals have been successfully attained. This strain toward survival may even
> on occasion lead to the neglect or distortion of the organization's goals.

Under many conditions, organizations have been observed to modify
their goals so as to achieve a more favorable adjustment. If their survival
is at stake, organizations will abandon the pursuit of their avowed objectives in order to save themselves. It is because of such tendencies that organizations are not to be viewed primarily as means for achieving specified ends, but as ends in themselves.

Two types of explanations have been proposed to account for the
survival instincts of organizations. The first, and more elaborate, argues
that the organizations are *social systems* characterized by a number of needs
that must be satisfied if they are to survive. This view is linked to a
broader theoretical framework known as functional analysis, which we
will briefly describe later in this chapter. Other theorists reject such assumptions as being anthropomorphic at worst and unnecessary at best.
They suggest instead that one does not have to posit a survival need for
the collectivity itself. It is sufficient to assume that some participants will
have a vested interest in the survival of the organization. Because it is a
source of power, or resources, or prestige, or pleasure, they wish to see it

preserved and will include among their own goals as participants that the organization itself be protected and, if possible, strengthened.

One of the earliest analyses, and in many ways still the best, of how some participants may seek to preserve an organization even at the sacrifice of the goals for which it was originally established is that provided by Robert Michels (1949 trans.), a contemporary of Weber's writing in pre–World War I Germany. His analysis of the changes that occurred in the largest socialist party in Europe, Germany's Social Democratic party, is rightly regarded as a classic. This work is most famous for its formulation of "the iron law of oligarchy," which equates the processes by which complex administrative work is carried out in an organization with the processes by which power shifts from the rank-and-file members to a small group of leaders. "Who says organization says oligarchy" (see Chapter 12). Of greater interest for present purposes are Michels's views on the consequences of these oligarchical tendencies for the professed goals of the organization. The leaders of the party continue to give lip service to its revolutionary objectives, but over time become increasingly conservative, reluctant to risk the gains they have achieved or to endanger the party, which is their source of strength. Michels (1949 trans.: 390) gloomily concludes,

> Thus, from a means, organization becomes an end. To the institutions and qualities which at the outset were destined simply to ensure the good working of the party machine (subordination, the harmonious cooperation of individual members, hierarchical relationships, discretion, propriety of conduct), a greater importance comes ultimately to be attached than to the productivity of the machine. Henceforward the sole preoccupation is to avoid anything which may clog the machinery.

Another way of viewing differences in the uses of goals by rational and natural system analysts is suggested by Brunsson (1985). He argues that the rational system decision-making model is in fact rational only if attention is focused on the decision as outcome. If instead we attend to actions (goal implementation) as outcome, then a more "irrational" decision process produces better results. Irrational decision processes speedily remove alternative possibilities and overestimate probabilities of success attached to the chosen alternative in order to structure participants' expectations, eliminate conflicts, and mold commitment to the selected course of action. Rational system theorists emphasize the normative structure and so focus on decisions—designs or proposals for action—as if they were the principal outcomes. Natural system theorists stress the behavioral structure and are more interested in examining what is done rather than what is decided or planned. Commitment and motivation loom as more salient variables than search and calculation if action rather than decision is the focus.

Informal Structure

If the ends that organizations are designed to serve are not pure and simple and specific in the view of the natural system analysts, neither are the structures that exist to attain them. The natural system theorists do not deny the existence of highly formalized structures within organizations, but they do question their importance, in particular their impact on the behavior of participants. Formal structures purposefully designed to regulate behavior in the service of specific goals are seen to be greatly affected—supplemented, eroded, transformed—by the emergence of *informal* structures.

While there is widespread agreement as to the importance of informal structure, there is little consensus on how it is to be defined. Indeed, the distinction between formal and informal is quite confusing since so many superficially related but different meanings have been associated with this dichotomy. Some analysts equate the formal structure with the normative system designed by management—the "blueprint" for behavior—and the informal structure with the behavioral system—the actual behavior of participants. Roethlisberger and Dickson (1939: 558–62), founders of the human relations school discussed in more detail below, come rather close to this position in their pioneering discussion of these concepts. They propose that

> the patterns of human interrelations, as defined by the systems, rules, policies, and regulations of the company, constitute the formal organization. . . . It includes the systems, policies, rules, and regulations of the plant which express what the relations of one person to another are supposed to be in order to achieve effectively the task of technical production. (1939: 558)

By contrast, the informal organization is described as follows:

> Many of the actually existing patterns of human interaction have no representation in the formal organization at all, and others are inadequately represented by the formal organization. . . . Too often it is assumed that the organization of a company corresponds to a blueprint plan or organization chart. Actually, it never does. (1939: 559)

Most analysts, however, view informal structures as encompassing both normative and behavioral dimensions, so that it is possible to speak of formal norms *and* formal patterns of behavior, and of informal norms *and* informal patterns of behavior. Still, there is disagreement about the basis for distinguishing between the two types of structures. Some analysts tend to equate this dichotomy with such earlier distinctions as primary–secondary and *gemeinschaft–gesellschaft* relations (see Dubin, 1968: 104), but Blau (1955: 143) argues that relations within organizations are "clearly distinct" from either of these polar types. Another definition of these concepts is supplied by Litterer (1963: 10), who suggests that "by formal is meant those aspects of organizations which have been, or possibly might be, consciously planned" whereas "the informal organization is conceived of as being the aspects of organization that are not formally planned but that more or less spontaneously evolve from the needs of people."

All of these conceptions of the distinction between formal and informal are different from the one we propose. As first discussed in Chapter 1, we find it useful to equate formal structures with those norms and behavior patterns that exist regardless of the characteristics of the individual actors. Informal structures are those based on the personal characteristics or resources of the specific participants. Thus, for example, formal authority refers to those control rights that are available to and exercised by all incumbents of a given position, such as supervisor or teacher; informal authority would indicate those rights that become available to a particular supervisor or teacher because of his or her special qualities or individual resources. Obviously, one of the clearest ways to distinguish empirically between the formal and the informal elements in a given situation is to observe what happens to beliefs and behaviors when there is a change in personnel.

Regardless of differences in the specific conceptions, all natural system analysts emphasize that there is more to organizational structure than the prescribed rules, the job descriptions, and the associated regularities in the behavior of participants. Individual participants are never merely "hired hands" but bring along their heads and hearts: they enter the organization with individually shaped ideas, expectations, and agendas, and they bring with them differing values, interests, and abilities.

Expressed through interaction, these factors come together to create a reasonably stable informal structure. One of the most important insights of the natural system perspective is that the social structure of an organization does not consist of the formal structure plus the idiosyncratic beliefs and behaviors of individual participants but rather of a formal structure and an informal structure: informal life is itself structured and orderly. Participants within formal organizations generate informal norms and behavior patterns: status and power systems, communication networks, sociometric structures, and working arrangements.

In the early studies exploring informal structures, it was presumed that they characterized only the lower strata of the organization: managers and executives were immune to such developments. But empirical studies by Dalton (1959) and others dispelled such notions. Also, early studies emphasized the dysfunctional consequences of the informal structures as private and "irrational" concerns that impeded the implementation of the elegant formal design. Thus, Roethlisberger and Dickson decided that the formal structure expresses the "logic of cost and efficiency" whereas the informal structure embraces the "logic of sentiments" (1939: 562–64). Increasingly, however, analysts have emphasized the positive functions performed by informal structures—in increasing the ease of communication, facilitating trust, and correcting for the inadequacies of the formal systems (see Gross, 1953).

Greater appreciation for the functions of informal systems was coupled with increasing skepticism that formalization was conducive to rationality. Natural system analysts emphasize that formalization places heavy and often intolerable burdens on those responsible for the design and management of an organization. No planners are so farseeing or omniscient as to be able to anticipate all the possible contingencies that might confront each position in the organization. Attempts to program in advance the behavior of participants are often misguided, if not foolhardy. Such programming can easily become maladaptive and lead to behaviors both ineffective and inefficient, giving rise to the "trained incapacity" that Veblen (1904) called attention to long ago and for which some organizations have become notorious. (See also Merton, 1957: 197–200.) Further, formal arrangements that curtail individual problem solving and the use of discretion undermine participants' initiative and self-confidence, causing them to become alienated and apathetic. Such restrictive arrangements not only damage participants' self-esteem and mental health but prevent them from effectively contributing their talents and energies to the larger enterprise (Argyris, 1957; McGregor, 1960). In sum, natural system analysts insist that highly centralized and formalized structures are doomed to be ineffective and irrational in that they waste the organization's most precious resource: the intelligence and initiative of its participants.

Functional Analysis

Functional analysis has served as an important underpinning for the work of some of the most influential natural system analysts. The origins of this widely used model are to be found in the work of a group of British social anthropologists, most notably Malinowski (1939) and Radcliffe-Brown (1952). Merton's essay (1957: 19–84) has become the most influential statement of this approach in sociology. The paradigm is complex, and there are many variants; nevertheless, its central features can be quickly summarized. The model assumes that the social unit, in our case the organization, has certain needs or requirements that must be met if it is to persist in its present form. As we will see when specific schools are discussed, analysts vary in how explicit they are in formulating the set of functional prerequisites. The specific structures that constitute the organization are analyzed in terms of the needs they meet, the functions they perform in ensuring the survival of the system. By analogy, if the human body is to survive, a continuing flow of oxygen must be supplied to the blood; the lungs perform this function. Similarly, if the organization is to survive, information about salient changes in its environment must be communicated to decision makers; the internal communication system performs this function. Showing that a given structure meets a functional need constitutes a functional "explanation" for that structure. The existence of an element is explained in terms of its consequences—the functions it performs—rather than by reference to its origins. "Final" causes are emphasized over "efficient" causes.[1] The model also emphasizes that the structural elements are themselves interdependent, so that variation in one causes modification in the others. Such systems are often viewed as tending toward a state of equilibrium; such views follow the work of Pareto as interpreted by Henderson (1935). (See Buckley, 1967: 11–17.)

Many aspects of the functionalist paradigm are problematic. In the case of social systems, unlike biological systems, it is difficult to specify the essential needs; indeed, it is often difficult to specify what is meant by survival of the system. It is also not easy to link a specific structure to a particular need. As Parsons (1966: 24–25) notes, social structures vary in their degree of differentiation: some are highly developed, so that each

---

[1]Blau (1955: 9–10) suggests that this theoretical postulate of the functional model can be accounted for by its distinctive historical origin: social anthropologists studying primitive societies could not test historical explanations for particular structural features since there were no historical documents. To overcome this limitation, they developed a different type of explanation, one that emphasized the contemporary contribution made by the element to the maintenance of the larger social system. Attention shifted from a focus on origins to a concern with the persistence of a particular structural feature.

structural unit performs a highly specialized function, whereas others are much less developed, each structure performing a range of functions. Further, a given function may be performed by more than one type of structure—the concept of *functional equivalents or substitutes*—so that a functional explanation may not be sufficient to account for the development of a specific structural form.[2] Finally, organizational forms are not as highly interdependent and as tightly coupled as biological systems, a point to be amplified in the next chapter.

In spite of all these problems and reservations, functionalism provided the dominant model for organizational (and, more generally, sociological) analysis from the 1930s into the 1960s. Many of our most important insights and generalizations concerning organizations are products of this tradition; despite its flaws, it remains a popular and useful perspective from which to examine organizations.

SELECTED SCHOOLS

As with the rational system perspective, the natural system perspective is an umbrella under which a number of rather diverse approaches can be gathered. While they share certain generic features, they differ in important particulars. We will be content to discuss briefly four influential variants: Mayo and the human relations school, Barnard's conception of cooperative systems, Selznick's institutional approach, and Parsons's social system model.

Mayo and the Human Relations School

We will not recount in detail the famous series of studies and experiments conducted at the Hawthorne plant of the Western Electric Company outside Chicago during the late 1920s and early 1930s. This research is meticulously described by Roethlisberger and Dickson (1939) and given its most influential interpretation by Elton Mayo (1945). Mayo, along with Roethlisberger, was a member of the Harvard Business School faculty. He was trained as an industrial psychologist, and his early work grew out of the research tradition established by Frederick W. Taylor. Like Taylor, Mayo studied individual factors such as fatigue in an attempt to determine the optimum length and spacing of rest periods for maximizing productivity. The early work in the Hawthorne plant followed the scientific management approach: the researchers set about to determine the optimal level of illumination for the assembly of telephone relay equipment. Mayo (1945: 69) summarizes the surprising results:

> The conditions of scientific experiment had apparently been fulfilled— experimental room, control room; changes introduced one at a time; all other conditions held steady. And the results were perplexing. . . . Lighting improved in the experimental room, production went up; but it rose also in the control room. The opposite of this: lighting diminished from 10 to 3

---

[2]In addition to these theoretical and empirical problems, certain logical difficulties attend the use of this model (see Nagel, 1961: 520–35). But if carefully employed, it can be of value in analyzing self-regulating systems (see Hempel, 1959).

foot-candles in the experimental room and the production again went up; simultaneously in the control room, with illumination constant, production also rose.

The researchers were in confusion. Other conditions were run with similar inexplicable results. In desperation, they asked the workers themselves what was going on and learned that the workers were so pleased to be singled out for special attention that they had tried to do the best they could for the researchers and for the company! The "Hawthorne effect" was discovered.

Additional studies carried out by the Harvard group—the second relay-assembly group, the mica-splitting test room, the bank-wiring observation room—all served to call into question the simple motivational assumptions on which the prevailing rational models rested. Individual workers did not behave as "rational" economic actors but as complex beings with multiple motives and values;[3] they were driven as much by feelings and sentiments as by facts and interests; and they did not behave as individual, isolated actors but as members of social groups exhibiting commitments and loyalties stronger than their individualistic self-interests. Thus, in the bank-wiring observation room, workers were observed to set and conform to daily work quotas—group norms restricting production—at the expense of their own higher earnings. And informal status hierarchies and leadership patterns developed that challenged the formal systems designed by managers (see Roethlisberger and Dickson, 1939: 379–447; and Homans, 1950: 48–155). At the social psychological level, the Hawthorne studies pointed to a more complex model of worker motivation based on a social psychological rather than an economic conception of man; at the structural level, the studies discovered and demonstrated the importance of informal organization.

The Hawthorne trunk has given rise to numerous research and reform offshoots, each of which has produced many individual branches. The major research issues pursued include studies of the work groups in the organizational environment, leadership behavior, and the impact of worker background and personality attributes on organizational behavior. Reform attempts include the use of personnel counselors, leadership training, job redefinition, and participation in decision making. Each of these interests merits a brief description; all of them are still flourishing.

The discovery of informal group processes in organizational settings both stimulated and received impetus from the study of small-group behavior carried on by social psychologists and sociologists. Among the former, Maier (1952) and Katz (Katz, Maccoby, and Morse, 1950; Katz et al., 1951) were particularly influential; among the latter, Homans (1950) and Whyte (1951; 1959) were effective in analyzing group processes in organizational settings. A few analysts, such as Sayles (1958), attempted to understand how organizational factors affected the number, types, and

---

[3]After inspecting the results of the bank-wiring observation room study at the Hawthorne plant, Mayo (1945: 43) concluded, "It is unfortunate for economic theory that it applies chiefly to persons of less, rather than greater, normality of social relationships. Must we conclude that economics is a study of human behavior in non-normal situations, or alternatively, a study of non-normal human behavior in ordinary situations?"

tactics of groups that emerged; most focused not on the determinants but on the consequences of group membership—for example, the impact of group cohesiveness on individual conformity to production norms (Roy, 1952; Seashore, 1954).

From the human relations perspective, leadership is conceived primarily as a mechanism for influencing the behavior of individual participants. Early studies sought a set of leadership traits or characteristics that would stimulate individual performance in the service of organizational goals. Thus, studies by White and Lippitt (1953) reported that participants in experimental task groups performed more effectively under "democratic" than "laissez-faire" or "authoritarian" leaders. Later research stressed the relational aspects of leadership. For example, a series of studies conducted at Ohio State (Stogdill and Coons, 1957) isolated two basic dimensions of leadership behavior: *consideration,* the extent to which trust, friendship, and respect mark the relation between the supervisor and his or her workers, and *initiating structure,* the degree to which the supervisor is a good organizer who can "get the work out." These dimensions were observed to vary independently, and in general, the more effective leaders—that is, the leaders whose subordinates performed better and had higher morale—were those who scored high on both dimensions.

Later efforts emphasized that leadership characteristics vary with the nature of the situation (Fiedler, 1964; 1971) and the specific needs or motivations of the individual subordinates (Cartwright, 1965). Studies by Pelz (1952) suggested that a supervisor's relation to his or her own superior—specifically, the extent of his or her influence upward—is a powerful determinant of the supervisor's influence over his or her own subordinates. Likert (1961) built on this finding to create his model of the supervisor's critical function as a "linking pin" relating lower to higher levels of the hierarchy. Most of these leadership studies ignored the effects of incumbency in a formal office on an individual's influence, either by overlooking this aspect of the situation or by deliberately holding it constant—for example, by studying differences in leadership behavior among all first-line supervisors in a given office or factory situation (see Katz and Kahn, 1952). Blau (1964: 210) has pointed out that "although managerial authority in organizations contains important leadership elements, its distinctive characteristic, which differentiates it from informal leadership, is that it is rooted in the formal powers and sanctions the organization bestows upon managers". It is in keeping with the natural system perspective to ignore this distinctive component of leadership in formal organizations. (We ourselves will focus on it in Chapter 11).

From the very beginning, human relations analysts have emphasized the great variability of individual characteristics and behaviors and have insisted on the relevance of these differences in understanding organizational behavior. Early research demonstrated that such officially irrelevant differences as race (Collins, 1946), class (Warner and Low, 1947), and cultural background (Dalton, 1950) had strong effects on allocation to work roles and organizational behavior. These studies are important forerunners of the more recent interest in the relation between stratification and organizations, which we discuss in Chapter 8.

The human relations school has also given rise to much effort directed at changing organizations—modifying and improving them as social environments. The original Hawthorne researchers were themselves interested in pursuing practical applications of their findings. Stressing the positive relation in their studies between worker satisfaction and productivity, they sought techniques to improve the adjustment and morale of individual workers. One approach involved the introduction of a set of personnel counselors, distinct from the line hierarchy, whose task it was to listen sympathetically to workers' complaints (Roethlisberger and Dickson, 1939: 189–376, 590–604). The interviewing techniques devised for this program contributed to the development of nondirective counseling techniques now in wide use.

Another change strategy devised by the human relations school stressed the importance of supervisory skills in promoting worker morale. Supervisors required special training if they were to become more sensitive to the psychological and social needs of their subordinates. Mayo (1945), influenced in part by Barnard, stressed the important role to be performed by supervisors and managers whose social function it was to elicit cooperation among workers—cooperation that could no longer be assumed to be automatic (see Bendix and Fisher, 1949). Thus, the human relations approach helped to spawn many diverse efforts in leadership training, from simple attitude-change efforts to more intensive Bethel-type sensitivity or T-group training. (See, for example, Argyris, 1962; Blake and Mouton, 1964; National Training Laboratories, 1953.)

Yet another reform approach focused on the need to redefine and enlarge the role definitions specified for workers. Contrary to the assumptions of the rational system model, the human relations group stressed the dangers of excessive formalization with its emphasis on extreme functional specialization. Job enlargement or, at least, job rotation, was advocated as a method of reducing the alienation and increasing the commitment and satisfaction of workers performing routine work (see Argyris, 1957).

Still other reformers stressed the importance of worker participation in decision making within the organization, particularly decisions directly affecting them. Although the notion of linking participation to motivation and commitment was given encouragement by the Hawthorne studies, more direct support has come from the experimental and theoretical work of Lewin (1948) and his colleagues (for example, Coch and French, 1948). Presently, participation by workers in managerial decision making is given much more emphasis in certain European countries than in the United States (see Blumberg, 1968; Tannenbaum et al., 1974; Hofstede, 1984).

Virtually all of these applications of the human relations movement have come under severe criticism on both ideological and empirical grounds. Paradoxically, the human relations movement, ostensibly developed to humanize the cold and calculating rationality of the factory and shop, rapidly came under attack on the grounds that it represented simply a more subtle and refined form of exploitation. Critics charged that workers' legitimate economic interests were being inappropriately deemphasized; that actual conflicts of interest were denied and "therapeutically" managed; and that the roles attributed to managers represented a new brand of elitism. The entire movement was branded as "cow sociology": just as contented cows were alleged to produce more milk, satisfied workers were expected to produce more output (see Bell, 1960: 238–44; Bendix, 1956: 308–40; Landsberger, 1958; Braverman, 1974: 139–51).

The ideological criticisms were the first to erupt, but reservations raised by researchers on the basis of empirical evidence may in the long run prove to be more devastating. Several decades of research have demonstrated no clear relation between worker satisfaction and productivity (see Brayfield and Crockett, 1955; Schwab and Cummings, 1970); no clear relation between supervisory behavior or leadership style and worker productivity (see Hollander and Julian, 1969); no clear relation between job enlargement and worker satisfaction or productivity (see Hulin and Blood, 1968); and no clear relation between participation in decision making and satisfaction or productivity (see Vroom, 1969: 227–39). Where positive relations among these variables have been observed, the direction may be opposite to that predicted: productivity producing satisfaction (Porter and Lawler, 1968) or productivity influencing supervisory style (Lowin and Craig, 1968), rather than vice versa. Even the original Hawthorne results have been reanalyzed and questioned (see Carey, 1967; Sykes, 1965).

Our brief survey of the human relations school cannot do justice to the variety of theoretical implications, empirical studies, and practical reform efforts it has generated. It is only a small exaggeration to suggest that the academic field of industrial sociology first saw the light of day at the Hawthorne plant, with Mayo serving as midwife. Moreover, sociological work on organizations well into the 1950s was shaped primarily by the human relations model—whether it was attempting to fill in the model's missing pieces or attacking its shortcomings and biases. And all of the thousands of studies concerned with motivation, morale, and leadership either have been directly stimulated by or are indirectly beholden to a tiny group of workers who kept increasing their output even though the lights were growing dimmer.[4]

Barnard's Cooperative System

At the same time that Mayo and his associates were conducting their studies and extrapolating from them to underline the importance of interpersonal processes and informal structures, Chester I. Barnard was expanding his own views of the nature of organizations. Barnard was not a researcher but an executive, president of New Jersey Bell Telephone company. Although Barnard's major book, *The Functions of the Executive* (1938),[5] was a very personal work reflecting his rather distinctive views and concerns, he was in regular contact with the human relations group at Harvard, including Mayo, Roethlisberger, and Henderson. Barnard's influence on the field was great, in part because his treatise was one of the first systematic attempts to outline a theory of organization available to U.S. readers, Weber's work not yet having been translated. Barnard's ideas contributed to human relations approaches and provided a basis for both Selznick's institutionalist views and for Simon's theory of decision making.

---

[4]For a more detailed summary and a highly critical assessment of the human relations school, see Perrow (1979: 90–138).

[5]Unless otherwise indicated, all references in this section are to this work.

Barnard stressed that organizations are essentially cooperative systems, integrating the contributions of their individual participants. As already reported in our review of organizational definitions in Chapter 1, Barnard defined a formal organization as "that kind of coöperation among men that is conscious, deliberate, purposeful" (p. 4).[6] Two separable ideas are embedded in this definition. First, organizations rely on the *willingness* of participants to make contributions. Participants must be induced to make contributions—a variety of incentives can be used to motivate them to do so, including material rewards, opportunities for distinction, prestige, personal power, and associational attractions—and make them in sufficient quantities, or the organization cannot survive.[7] Second, whatever the specific motives that procure cooperation in the enterprise, efforts must be directed toward a common *purpose*. "The inculcation of belief in the real existence of a common purpose is an essential executive function" (p. 87).

Thus, Barnard attempts to combine and reconcile two somewhat contradictory ideas: goals are imposed from the top down while their attainment depends on willing compliance from the bottom up. This view of accepted direction is developed most fully in Barnard's conception of authority. He argues that it is a "fiction that authority comes down from above" (p. 170), noting the many situations in which leaders claim authority but fail to win compliance. This is because authority depends ultimately on its validation from the response of those subject to it: "the decision as to whether an order has authority or not lies with the persons to whom it is addressed, and does not reside in 'persons of authority' or those who issue these orders" (p. 163). Still, some types of orders have a greater "potentiality of assent of those to whom they are sent" (p. 173). These are orders that are products of a well-ordered and integrated communications system that links all contributors in a purposeful cooperative framework.

> At first thought it may seem that the element of communication in organization is only in part related to authority; but more thorough consideration leads to the understanding that communication, authority, specialization, and purpose are all aspects comprehended in coördination. All communication relates to the formulation of purpose and the transmission of coördinating prescriptions for action and so rests upon the ability to communicate with those willing to coöperate. (p. 184)

This conception of an organization as a purposefully coordinated system of communications linking all participants in such a manner that the purposes of superordinates are accepted as the basis for the actions of subordinates became the foundation for Simon's theory of decision making, as described in Chapter 2.

Barnard's views thus contain many ideas that are consistent with a

---

[6]Like many natural system theorists, Barnard defined organizations so as to emphasize their rational system features—their distinguishing features—but then concentrated on other, more generic aspects in his analysis.

[7]Simon later adopted and elaborated upon Barnard's "contributions-inducements" theory of organizational equilibrium. We review these developments in Chapter 7.

rational system conception of organizations. What sets them apart is his insistence on the nonmaterial, informal, interpersonal, and, indeed, moral basis of cooperation. Material rewards are viewed as "weak incentives" that must be buttressed by other types of psychological and social motivations if cooperative effort is to be sustained. As for informal organization, Barnard argued that "formal organizations arise out of and are necessary to informal organization; but when formal organizations come into operation, they create and require informal organizations" (p. 120). Informal structures facilitate communication, maintain cohesiveness, and undergird "the willingness to serve and the stability of objective authority" (p. 122). Interpersonal ties at their best create a "condition of communion": "the opportunity for commandership, for mutual support" forming the "basis of informal organization that is essential to the operation of every formal organization" (p. 148).

But the most critical ingredient to successful organization is the formation of a collective purpose that becomes morally binding on participants. This is the distinctive function of the executive.

> The distinguishing mark of the executive responsibility is that it requires not merely conformance to a complex code of morals but also the creation of moral codes for others. The most generally recognized aspect of this function is called securing, creating, inspiring of "morale" in an organization. This is the process of inculcating points of view, fundamental attitudes, loyalties, to the organization or coöperative system, and to the system of objective authority, that will result in subordinating individual interest and the minor dictates of personal codes to the good of the coöperative whole. (p. 279)

On the one hand such views sound quaint and hopelessly old-fashioned; they have been subjected to scathing attack by critics such as Perrow (1979: 70–89), who scoff at Barnard's moral imperialism and point out the duplicity inherent in "willing" cooperation that is managed from above. On the other hand, many of these themes have again become highly fashionable as students of organizations rediscover the importance of organizational cultures shaped by zealous managers supplying strongly held values to their members.[8] (See, e.g., Peters and Waterman, 1982.) We discuss these neo-Barnardian views in Chapters 9 and 11.

Consistent with the natural system framework, however, Barnard recognized the existence of organizational forces even more powerful than purpose:

> Finally it should be noted that, once established, organizations change their unifying purposes. They tend to perpetuate themselves; and in the effort to survive may change the reasons for existence. (p. 89)

The necessity of survival can override the morality of purpose.

---

[8]This aspect of Barnard's work no doubt accounts for his enormous popularity among students of organizations in Japan, where many "Barnard Societies" are still active.

Selznick's Institutional Approach

Philip Selznick, a student of bureaucracy under Merton at Columbia, but an intellectual descendant of Michels and Barnard, has developed his own unique natural system model. Selznick's work has been applied and extended by several of his students, including Burton Clark, Charles Perrow, and Mayer Zald. More recently, his framework has been adapted and elaborated to constitute a major school of organizational theory and research. We restrict attention here to Selznick's seminal early contributions and to the work of his immediate intellectual followers.[9] Unlike Barnard, Selznick has not systematically presented his approach in any single source, but has scattered his ideas through several books and articles. We will attempt to provide a short but coherent sketch of his approach.

For Selznick, "the most important thing about organizations is that, though they are tools, each nevertheless has a life of its own" (1949: 10). He agrees with the rational system analyst that the distinguishing characteristic of formal organizations is that they are rationally ordered instruments designed to attain goals. However, these formal structures can "never succeed in conquering the nonrational dimensions of organizational behavior" (1948: 25). The sources of these nonrational features are (1) individuals, who participate in the organization as "wholes" and do not act merely in terms of their formal roles within the system; and (2) the fact that the formal structure is only one aspect of the concrete social structure that must adjust in various ways to the pressures of its institutional environment. In short, organizational rationality is constrained by "the recalcitrance of the tools of action": persons bring certain characteristics to the organization and develop other commitments as members that restrict their capacity for rational action; organizational procedures become valued as ends in themselves; the organization strikes bargains with its environment that compromise present objectives and limit future possibilities (1949: 253–59).

As I have noted elsewhere,

> if the organization as conceived by Weber operates like a smoothly functioning professional football team, Selznick's image corresponds more closely to Alice's efforts at croquet with equipment and competition provided by the Queen of Hearts. Alice swings her flamingo mallet but the bird may duck his head before the hedgehog-ball is struck; just so, the manager issues his directives but they may be neither understood nor followed by his subordinates. (Scott, 1964: 511)

Selznick views orgnizational structure as an adaptive organism shaped in reaction to the characteristics and commitments of participants as well as to influences from the external environment. He explicitly embraces a functional form of analysis, explaining,

> This means that a given empirical system is deemed to have basic needs, essentially related to self-maintenance; the system develops repetitive means of self-defense; and day-to-day activity is interpreted in terms of the func-

---

[9]Later contributions to the institutional approach are first discussed in Chapter 5 and reappear throughout the rest of the volume.

tion served by that activity for the maintenance and defense of the system (1948: 29).

Insisting that the overriding need of all systems "is the maintenance of the integrity and continuity of the system itself," Selznick attempts to spell out certain more specific "derived imperatives," including the security of the organization as a whole in relation to its environment, the stability of lines of authority and communication, the stability of informal relations within the organization, and a homogeneity of outlook toward the meaning and role of the organization. However, he regards the list as suggestive, not definitive. Acknowledging its vagueness, Selznick defends the concept of organizational need because it directs attention to the internal relevance of organizational behavior, including behaviors that are ostensibly directed outward (1948: 29–30).

To this point Selznick's model appears to be a rather conventional version of the more general natural system model described early in this chapter, but its development takes an unexpected turn. He proposes that we will learn more interesting things about organizations if we do not attempt to examine the satisfaction of all needs of the organism but, like Freud, focus on those needs "which cannot be fulfilled within approved avenues of expression" (1948: 32). Thus, attention is directed away from the formal structures and procedures, insofar as they are functioning smoothly and toward those features created to deal in irregular ways with unmet needs. Such mechanisms include informal structures, ideologies, and co-optation.

Selznick has described this same approach in slightly different language. He argues that rather than following the lead of experimental psychologists who study routine psychological processes, we should imitate the clinical psychologists who examine the dynamic adaptation of the organism over time. Instead of focusing on the day-to-day decisions made in organizations, we should concentrate on those critical decisions that, once made, result in a change in the structure itself. The pattern of these critical decisions, viewed over time, results in the development of a distinctive character structure for each organization, just as an individual's critical decisions and typical mode of coping with problems give rise to the development of a distinctive personality (Selznick, 1957).

Selznick refers to the process by which an organization develops a distinctive character structure as *institutionalization*. As Selznick uses the term, to become institutionalized is to become "infused with value beyond the technical requirements of the task at hand" (1957: 17). In his view

> the term "organization" thus suggests a certain bareness, a lean, no-nonsense system of consciously co-ordinated activities. It refers to an expendable tool, a rational instrument engineered to do a job. An "institution," on the other hand, is more nearly a natural product of social needs and pressures—a responsive, adaptive organism. (1957: 5)

Institutional commitments develop over time as the organization confronts external constraints and pressures from its environment as well as changes in the composition of its personnel, their interests, and their informal relations. No organization is completely immune from these external and internal pressures, although the extent of institutionalization varies from one organization to another.

Following Barnard, Selznick believes that leadership can play a critical role in this evolutionary process. Leaders must define the mission of the enterprise: it is their responsibility to choose and to protect its distinctive values and "to create a social structure which embodies them" (1957: 60). Among the critical decisions confronting any enterprise are the selection of a social base—what clientele, what market to serve; the building of an institutional core—the selection of central personnel; and the determination of the nature and timing of formalization of stucture and procedures (1957: 102–7).

Selznick thus invites us to observe the process by which organizations develop distinctive structures, capacities, and liabilities; he proposes, in sum, a natural history of organizations.

If we examine some of the empirical work stimulated by Selznick's institutional model, we will obtain a clearer picture of both the strengths and weaknesses of the proposed approach. Selznick's most famous study is of the Tennessee Valley Authority (TVA), a decentralized government agency created during the depression to improve the economic status of the entire Tennessee Valley, a chronically depressed, flood-ravaged region. Massive federal funds—at least by the standards of the 1930s—were provided to support a broad-gauged attack on the problems of the area. Flood control, hydroelectric power, and soil conservation efforts were to be provided in an integrated manner. Top agency officials were located at the site, not in far-off Washington, so that officials would not be inclined to impose solutions from above but would work with the local inhabitants in developing acceptable projects (see Lilienthal, 1944).

As we would expect, Selznick (1949) focuses on the "internal relevance"—the consequences for the agency—of these strategies. He points out that the democratic ideology not only served to recruit and motivate talented participants but also enabled the New Deal agency to gain access to a suspicious and conservative area. Agency officials employed co-optation as a strategy to gain legitimacy and political support. *Co-optation* is a mechanism by which external elements are incorporated into the decision-making structures of an organization: in the case of the TVA, local leaders were recruited to participate in the agency's decision-making and advisory bodies. This tactic ensured that the agency would enjoy local political support for its programs, but such support always comes at a price: local leaders exchanged support for a measure of influence on the agency's programs and goals. As a consequence, some public interest goals were subverted to serve private interests. For example, improved land values surrounding water projects that were supposed to benefit the public often fell into private hands, and reforested land intended as watershed was taken over by lumber interests.

Selznick's analysis set the pattern for a number of similar studies that examined the ways in which the original goals of an organization can be displaced or undermined. Thus, Clark's (1956) study of an adult education program in Los Angeles argues that its professed goals of providing cultural and intellectual programs could not be realized because of its marginal organizational and institutional status. Because the program lacked full legitimacy, only those parts of it that could attract large numbers of students were retained, with other academically valuable but less popular offerings losing out to the "enrollment economy." Messinger's (1955) analysis of the Townsend movement, a pressure group developed in the 1930s to represent the economic interests of the elderly, records how the movement attempted to survive by transforming its original radical political objectives into noncontroversial recreational programs. And Zald and Denton (1963) describe the transformation of the YMCA from a religious organization performing rehabilitative and welfare services for the urban poor into a social and recreational center for suburban and middle-class young people.

These and related studies exhibit several common features. The analyst focuses on the administrative history of the organization: the structural features and programs of the organization are viewed as changing over time in response to changing conditions. The methodology employed tends to be that of the case study, and heavy reliance is placed on the analysis of organizational documents and interviews with informants knowledgeable about the organization's history. Given this approach, most of the organizations selected for study have been relatively recently founded. Selznick (1957: 142) insists that he is interested not in recounting the history of any given organization for its own sake but in seeking "to discover the characteristic ways in which types of institutions respond to types of circumstances." However, this interest in generalization is somewhat at odds with the intensive case-study approach. As Cohen (1972: 402) notes, "As the desire to explain more and more aspects of a single study, situation, or phenomenon increases, the possibility of using this explanation outside the situation for which it was created approaches the vanishing point."

Thus, in these earlier uses of the institutional approach, a rather consistent pattern emerges. Fundamentally, analysts sought to explain changes in the goals of the organization—not the professed goals, but the ends actually pursued, the operative goals. The general mode of explanation was similar to that offered by Michels: to increase their own security, organizational participants modify controversial goals in the face of hostile environments. As Perrow notes, the literature spawned by the approach— to which Perrow himself has contributed (see Perrow, 1961)—takes on an "exposé" character: "The major message is that the organization has sold out its goals in order to survive or grow" (1979: 182). Although cynicism seems often justified, this early work stimulated by Selznick's conception appears to go out of its way to inspect the seamy side of organizational life. The studies tend to focus on the forces that undermine the organization's principles and subvert its formal ends to narrow interests. The work seems tinted by a "metaphysical pathos" (Gouldner, 1955). There is no doubt that these accounts of "friction, dilemma, doubt, and ruin" (Selznick, 1948: 25) served as a useful antidote to the paean to organizational rationality being sung during this era by some overexuberant rational system theorists. But it also is the case that Selznick and company were acting as "clinical sociologists" of organizations, and like their role models, the clinical psychologists, they chose to focus primarily on deviance and abnormality.

However, with time, this strongly negative emphasis has been tempered by more constructive concerns about how precarious values can be protected. Selznick himself, as we have noted, began to emphasize that leaders could and should act to defend and, if necessary, reinterpret and renew the mission of their organization (1957). And Clark (1970; 1972) turned his attention to how such "distinctive" and successful colleges as Antioch, Reed, and Swarthmore managed to survive and to preserve their special character. This somewhat redefined and broadened research agenda has gained many adherents. Not only is Selznick's work recognized as providing the underpinnings for the institutionalist perspective, but his concern for the role of leaders in making critical decisions and in defining institutional values has contributed to the current interest in strategic decision making and the creation of organizational cultures. We will consider these developments in later Chapters.

Parsons's Social System

More so than other analysts working within the natural system tradition, Talcott Parsons has developed a very explicit model detailing the needs that must be met if a system is to survive. Parsons's approach is the product of a lifetime devoted to perfecting a general analytic model suitable for the analysis for all types of collectivities—from small, primary groups to entire societies (see Parsons, 1951; Parsons, Bales, and Shils, 1953; Parsons, 1966). He first applied the model to formal organizations in two papers published in the late 1950s and collected in his book on societies (1960).

Parsons' model is identified by the acronym AGIL, which represents the four basic functions that all social systems must perform if they are to persist:

A*daptation:* the problem of acquiring sufficient resources.
G*oal attainment:* the problem of setting and implementing goals.
I*ntegration:* the problem of maintaining solidarity or coordination among the subunits of the system.
L*atency:* the problem of creating, preserving, and transmitting the system's distinctive culture and values.

In addition to being applicable to all types of social systems, the schema may be applied at more than one level in analyzing a given type of system. Thus, Parsons applies his model to organizations at the ecological, the structural, and the social psychological levels. Linkages across these levels are also stressed.

First, at the ecological level, Parsons relates organizations to the functioning of the larger society. Applying the AGIL at the societal level, Parsons suggests that subordinate social units such as organizations can be classified according to their societal function (see Table 3–1). For example, economic organizations such as firms are said to serve the adaptive needs of the larger society. As Parsons (1960: 19) points out,

> what from the point of view of the organization is its specified goal is, from the point of view of the larger system of which it is a differentiated part or subsystem, a specialized or differentiated function.

Because of this functional linkage, the place or role of the subsystem is legitimated, and it may expect to receive societal approval and resources

TABLE 3–1   Parsons's Typology Based on Societal Functions

SOCIETAL FUNCTION	ORGANIZATIONAL TYPE	EXAMPLES
Adaptation	Organizations oriented to economic production	Business firms
Goal attainment	Organizations oriented to political goals	Government agencies Other organizations that allocate power, such as banks
Integration	Integrative organizations	Courts and the legal profession Political parties Social-control agencies
Latency	Pattern-maintenance organizations	Cultural organizations, such as museums Educational organizations Religious organizations

in accordance with the value placed in the society on the particular functions it performs.

Shifting to the structural level of analysis, Parsons notes that each formal organization may also be analyzed as a social system in its own right, and each must develop its own differentiated subsystems to satisfy the four basic needs. Thus, each organization must develop structures that enable it to adapt to its environment and must mobilize resources needed for its continued operation. Arrangements are also needed to enable the organization to set and implement its goals. To solve its integrative problems, an organization must find ways to command the loyalties of its members, enlist their effort, and coordinate the operations of its various sectors. And mechanisms must be developed to cope with latency problems, to promote consensus on the values that define and legitimate the organization's output and system goals.

While Parsons does not insist that a specific structural unit will develop to manage each of these functional needs, he does argue that structural differentiation will tend to occur along these divisions. Functional imperatives generate the fault lines along which a social structure becomes differentiated. The explanation for this linkage between functional requirements and structural arrangements is simply that the various functional needs are somewhat in conflict, so that efforts directed at solving one functional problem interfere with efforts directed toward the others.[10] Specifically, energies devoted to adapting the organization to its

---

[10]Parsons's reasoning at this point is illuminated by knowledge of the intellectual origins of the AGIL schema. His conception of these system problems grew out of his work on the *pattern variables*—basic value dichotomies representing the dimensions along which structures are arranged. The pairs of opposing values—universalism–particularism, affectivity–affective neutrality, ascription–achievement, and specificity–diffuseness—were cross-classified, producing the four system needs. Thus, values identified as most appropriate for solving the problem of adaptation are universalism, affective neutrality, specificity, and achievement; at the opposite extreme, values appropriate for improving integration are particularism, affectivity, diffuseness, and ascription (see Parsons, 1951; Parsons, Bales, and Shils, 1953).

environment partially conflict with efforts toward goal attainment—a problem emphasized by Selznick and his colleagues—and efforts directed toward integration—a tension emphasized by Bales (1953)—and so on.

A structural "solution" to these tensions is to create roles and subsystems focused on each problem area. For example, Bales and his colleagues argue that in informal groups the inherent tensions involved in goal attainment (for example, winning the game) versus integration (for example, providing satisfaction for all participants) is partially resolved by the emergence of a "task" leader, who specializes in directing and controlling goal attainment activities, and a "socio-emotional" leader, who specializes in motivating members and reducing tensions (Bales, 1953; Slater, 1955). And in formal organizations, specialized departments and roles—supervisors, maintenance workers, personnel counselors, inspectors—emerge to carry out the multiple, and somewhat conflicting, functions.

This solution only simplifies the definitions of individual roles and subsystems and does not, of course, eliminate the incompatibilities: these are merely pushed to a higher level of the system for resolution. For example, at the level of the informal group, Bales (1953) argues that the differentiated leader roles provide a stable basis for group functioning only if the two leaders form a coalition of mutual support. At the organizational level, Lawrence and Lorsch (1967) have argued that organizations characterized by a higher level of structural differentiation are in greater need of integrative and conflict-resolution mechanisms.

In moving toward a more micro or social psychological level, Parsons again employs the AGIL schema, arguing that each subsystem within the organization itself comprises finer subdivisions that can be distinguished in terms of the functional requirements. For example, within the goal attainment (G) subsystem—that part of the organization with the power to set and mobilize resources for goal attainment—Parsons distinguishes four kinds of decisions:

> *Policy decisions:* decisions concerning what goals are to be pursued and how they are to be attained (the Gg subsector—the goal attainment subsector of the goal attainment subsystem);
>
> *Allocative decisions:* lower-level decisions regarding the allocation of responsibilities and resources among personnel (the Ga subsector);
>
> *Coordinative decisions:* decisions about how personnel are to be motivated and their contributions coordinated (the Gi subsector);
>
> *Supporting values:* values that serve to legitimate and authorize the decision-making rights within this subsystem (the Gl subsector).

Parsons outlines how each of the other subsystems is also differentiated into the appropriate subsectors. Finally, he also uses the four system problems as a means of describing the relationships—in his terms, boundary processes—between systems and subsystems (see Parsons, 1960: 22–41; see also Landsberger, 1961: 227–31).

Like many natural system models, Parsons' framework emphasizes a set of functional needs that all social systems must satisfy in order to survive. As noted, this approach emphasizes the similarities between organizations and other types of social systems. But unlike other natural system models, Parsons's formulation also provides a clear basis for distinguishing between organizations and other social systems. Parsons states, "As a formal analytical point of reference, primacy of orientation to the attainment of a specific goal is used as the defining characteristic of an organization which distinguishes it from other types of social systems" (1960: 17). Within the Parsonian framework, this definition implies more than the widely shared view that organizations tend to pursue specific goals. Parsons calls attention to the relative importance placed on the goal-attainment subsystem in organizations. That is, organizations are social systems placing greater priority on those processes by which goals are set and resources are mobilized for goal attainment than is the case in other social systems.

We cannot hope to summarize all of Parsons's ideas on organizations—his framework rapidly becomes exceedingly complex—but we will review one other useful set of distinctions. In addition to his analysis of the functional differentiation that occurs along a horizontal axis at any given level of analysis, Parsons also distinguishes three major levels of organizational structure. At the bottom layer is the *technical* system, where the actual "product" of the organization is processed. This level is exemplified by the activities of workers on assembly lines, scientists in the laboratory, and teachers in the classroom. Above the technical level is the *managerial* system, whose primary functions are to mediate between the organization and the immediate task environment, including those who consume the organization's products and supply its raw materials, and to administer the organization's internal affairs. At the top of the organization is the *institutional* system, whose function is to relate the organization to the larger society; "the source of the 'meaning,' legitimation, or higher-level support which makes the implementation of the organization's goals possible" (Parsons, 1960: 63–64). Parsons makes the interesting point that there exists a "qualitative break" in the line-authority relation at the two points where the three systems are linked (p. 65). (This distinction among levels anticipates some of the concerns of open system theorists, described in Chapter 4. The significance of the break between levels is discussed in Chapter 10.)

Parsons' theoretical model has been employed by some, but not many, researchers to guide their empirical studies of organizations. Georgopoulos (1972; Georgopoulos and Matejko, 1967) has adapted it in his analysis of hospitals, and Lyden (1975) makes use of it in his study of public organizations. Of course, Parsons's generalized social system paradigm has had considerable impact on the work of sociologists, and many of his specific concepts and ideas have influenced work in the area of organizations. We will limit ourselves to only a few general comments in assessing Parsons' contributions. On the positive side, his work attempts to develop and perfect a limited set of abstract concepts that can then be adapted for use in examining the structure and functioning of diverse social groupings. Using the same generic concepts helps us to see similarities in social structure and process across systems that appear to be quite different. Also, more than those of other natural system theorists, Parsons's framework is quite comprehensive, encompassing the formal and rational aspects of organizations as well as the informal. Further, Parsons is more explicit than others in defining the system needs that must be served for survival.

Problems with the Parsonian framework are numerous. They include the difficulty in translating his analytic concepts into operational variables. For example, although it is reasonably easy to give examples of roles designed to increase integration, it is often difficult to assign a given structural feature such as a role or subunit to any single function (Morse, 1961). Landsberger (1961: 232) is correct that we should not expect concrete social structures to match closely analytical distinctions, but we do need to have a clearer set of rules for relating one to the other than Parsons provides. Finally, as many others have noted, Parsons's formulation tends to be more of a theoretical framework than a substantive theory. We are provided with numerous concepts that help us to see interesting distinctions, but given relatively few testable propositions. The functionalist paradigm underlying the approach does provide some implicit hypotheses—such as, unless the system needs are met the organization will not survive—but as already noted, such predictions are difficult to test.[11]

SUMMARY AND TENTATIVE CONCLUSIONS

Whereas the rational system model focuses on features of organizations that distinguish them from other social groupings, the natural system model emphasizes commonalities among organizations and other systems. The natural system theorists do not deny that organizations have distinctive features, but they argue that these are overshadowed by the more generic systems and processes. Thus, the specific output goals of organizations are often undermined or distorted by energies devoted to the pursuit of system goals, chief among which is the concern to survive. And the formal aspects of organizational structure that receive so much attention from the rational system analysts are treated as faded backdrops for the "real" informal structures. More generally, whereas the rational system model stresses the normative structure of organizations, the natural system model places more emphasis on the behavioral structure. And where the rational system perspective stresses the importance of structure over the characteristics of participants, the natural system perspective reverses these priorities—so much so that Bennis (1959: 266) labels this orientation as one of "people without organizations."

Most of the early theorists who shaped the natural system perspective embrace a functional model of analysis, although they vary considerably in how explicitly and how fully they pursue its development. The human relations analysts tend to be less overt and less complete in their use of this model than is Barnard or Selznick or Parsons. All schools within the natural system framework presume the existence of certain needs that must be met if the system is to survive, and all direct attention to discovering the mechanisms by which these needs are satisfied.

Varying views of the environment appear to be associated with the natural system theorists. Most of the human relations analysts simply overlook it as a factor. Like the rational system theorists, they concentrate on

---

[11]A useful general discussion of Parsons' social system model will be found in Morse (1961). Landsberger (1961) provides an excellent description and critique of Parsons' model as it applies to organizations.

the internal organizational arrangements and their effects on participants, treating the organization as a closed system. This neglect is especially striking in the case of the Hawthorne studies, which were conducted during the 1930s, in the depths of the Great Depression. In the bank-wiring observation room study, for example, the workers' efforts to restrict production were viewed as irrational conformity to group norms. Given the larger economic situation, however, these activities may instead have been a highly rational response to the threat of being laid off (see Landsberger, 1958: 58; Blau and Scott, 1962: 92–93). Indeed, during the period of the research there were many layoffs at the Hawthorne plant; in fact, the bank-wiring room study had to be discontinued because so many workers were let go! (Roethlisberger and Dickson, 1939: 395.)

Barnard takes somewhat more account of the environment than the human relations group. He shows awareness that organizations must attract participants by providing them with inducements, indeed must compete with other organizations that are attempting to attract their services and loyalties. Moreover, he recognizes that a given individual participates in many cooperative groups simultaneously, so that his involvement in any single organization is both partial and intermittent. It is undoubtedly such insights that cause Barnard to put such emphasis on obtaining contributions and inspiring commitment. However, Barnard does not attempt to explicitly conceptualize the environment or to examine the extent to which organizations vary in their environment locations.

Selznick and his students, by contrast, do explicitly consider the environment in their analyses of organizations. However, their view is a highly selective one: the environment is perceived primarily as an enemy, as a source of pressures and problems. In most of the earlier studies in this tradition, the organization is viewed as capitulating to a tyrannical and hostile environment as the price of its survival.

In the work of Parsons we begin to have a more balanced view of the environment. Great stress is placed on the importance of the organization-environment relation, the organization being viewed as a subsystem within a more comprehensive social unit, and the environment seen more as a stabilizing element sustaining and legitimating the organization in its special mission than as a source of resistance. In these ways, Parsons anticipates the view of the open systems theorists in his treatment of the environment.

Two quite different perspectives on organizations have now been described. How could two such different viewpoints have arisen? Several explanations have been proposed. Since each sheds additional light on the subject, they will be briefly reviewed.

Lawrence and Lorsch (1967: 163–84) propose that some of the differences in perspective may have been produced by variations in the experience and background of the analysts themselves. They point out that among the rational or *classical* theorists, as they label them, Fayol, Mooney, and Urwick were all practical men with managerial experience. Taylor's training was as an industrial engineer. By contrast, among the natural systems theorists, Mayo, Roethlisberger, Selznick, McGregor, and Parsons were all from academic backgrounds with experience largely in the university. (Exceptions to this division were, on the one side, Weber, who was a university professor—however, in terms of life-style and experience he is more accurately described as a recluse scholar—and Gulick, who was also an academic. On the other side, of course, was Barnard, a company executive.) Lawrence and Lorsch argue that divergent backgrounds shaped the reactions of these analysts to organizations. Coming from the relatively unstructured arrangements of a university, the natural system analysts would be prone to react negatively to the formalism of an industrial plant, and might even be inclined to attribute their own needs for autonomy to workers in this situation.

A second explanation offered is that the analysts concentrated on different types of organizations. The rational system analysts were more likely to investigate industrial firms and state bureaucracies, while the natural system analysts tended to focus on service and professional organizations—schools, hospitals, and the YMCA. Since the degree of formalization and of goal specificity clearly varies greatly across the spectrum of organizations, it is quite possible that the rational system analysts concentrated on the relatively highly structured end of the continuum and the natural system analysts on the less structured end.

A third but related explanation for the differences between the two perspectives also comes from Lawrence and Lorsch, who suggest that organizational forms may vary as a function of their environments: "In simplified terms, the classical [rational] theory tends to hold in more stable environments, while the human relations [natural] theory is more appropriate to dynamic situations" (1967: 183). This important thesis is simply introduced at this point; it will be explored throughout the next several chapters.

Although differences in the analysts' backgrounds or in the particular organization on which they chose to focus may account for some of the variance in these two perspectives, it is our view that these points of view represent more fundamental divisions than are suggested by these explanations. Underlying the perspectives are quite basic divergences in moral and philosophical viewpoints.

The natural and the rational system theorists tend to hold differing conceptions of the actual and the proper relation of individual participants to organizations. Thus, the rational system theorists argue that only selected behaviors of participants are relevant as far as the organization is concerned and that only these "task-related" behaviors are at issue. The natural system theorists tend to expand the definition of organizationally relevant behavior to include more and more aspects of the individual's activities and attitudes. They have done so on two grounds: that such behaviors do in fact have an impact on the task behavior of participants, and thus are *empirically* relevant to an understanding of organizational behavior, and that organizations as social contexts affect the participant's well-being, a relation that has *normative* significance to anyone concerned with bettering the human condition. Many of these theorists point to the dysfunctions arising from the partial inclusion of participants and argue, partly on moral grounds, that organizations should take more responsibility for the "whole person." These arguments are not without merit, but all of the morality is not on one side. It is important to recognize that formal organizations developed in part to place limits on the demands superiors could make on their subordinates. The development of formal role definitions—definitions of the limits of a participant's obligations—was an important step in increasing the freedom of individuals. Whether the organization's purview should incorporate more or fewer facets of the lives of its participants is a basic philosophical difference separating the two perspectives.

Finally, the two approaches are characterized by quite divergent views of the fundamental nature of social systems. These differences are reflected in the contrasting imagery or metaphors employed by the two schools. For the mechanistic model of structure of the rational system perspective, the natural system substitutes an organic model. Rational systems are designed, but natural systems evolve; the former develop by conscious design, the latter by natural growth; rational systems are characterized by calculation, natural by spontaneity. Lest we regard these images of social structure as being of recent vintage, Wolin (1960: 352–434) reminds us that they have a long history in political and social thought. The view of organizations as economic, technological, efficient instruments is associated with the work of such social theorists as Hobbes, Lenin, and Saint-Simon—the precursors of Taylor, Weber, Fayol, and Simon. The view of organizations as communitarian, natural, antirational, organic systems may be traced back to the social theories of Rousseau, Proudhon, Burke, and Durkheim, the intellectual ancestors of Mayo, Barnard, and Selznick. With such lengthy and distinguished pedigrees, it is unlikely that either of these two lines of thought will soon end, or that their differences will be quickly resolved.

organizations as open systems

That a system is open means, not simply that it engages in interchanges with the environment, but that this interchange is an essential factor underlying the system's viability.

Walter Buckley (1967)

The open system perspective emerged as a part of the intellectual ferment following World War II, although its roots are much older. This general intellectual movement created new areas of study, such as cybernetics and information theory; stimulated new applications, such as systems engineering and operations research; transformed existing disciplines, including the study of organizations; and proposed closer linkages among scientific disciplines. The latter interest has been fostered especially by general systems theory. Its founder, biologist Ludwig von Bertalanffy, was concerned about the growing compartmentalization of science: "The physicist, the biologist, the psychologist and the social scientist are, so to speak, encapsulated in a private universe, and it is difficult to get word from one cocoon to another" (Bertalanffy, 1956:1). Bertalanffy and his associates argued that certain general ideas could have relevance across a broad spectrum of disciplines. In particular, they endeavored to show that many of the most important entities studied by scientists—nuclear particles, atoms, molecules, cells, organs, organisms, ecological communities, groups, organizations, societies, solar systems— are all subsumable under the general rubic of *system*.[1]

All systems are characterized by an assemblage or combination of parts whose relations make them interdependent. While these features underlie the similarities exhibited by all systems, they also suggest the bases for the differences among them. The parts of which all systems are composed vary from being quite simple in structure to very complex, from being highly stable in their state to highly variable, and from being relatively impervious to system forces to being highly reactive to the workings of the system to which they belong. As we move from mechanical through

---

[1]In his monumental book *Living Systems,* Miller (1978) identifies seven basic levels: the cell, the organ, the organism, the group, the organization, the society, and the supranational system.

organic to social systems, the parts of which systems are composed become more complex and variable. Similarly, the nature of the relations among the parts varies from one type of system to another. In this connection, Norbert Wiener, the founder of cybernetics, notes "Organization we must consider as something in which there is an interdependence between the several organized parts but in which this interdependence has degrees" (1956: 322). In mechanistic systems, the interdependence among the parts is such that their behavior is highly constrained and limited. The structure is relatively rigid and the system of relations determinant. In organic systems, the connections among the interdependent parts are somewhat less constrained, allowing for more flexibility of response. In social systems, such as groups and organizations, the connections among the interacting parts become relatively loose: less constraint is placed on the behavior of one element by the condition of the others. Social organizations, in contrast with physical or mechanical structures, are *loosely coupled* systems (see Ashby, 1968; Buckley, 1967: 82–83).

Also, as we progress from simple to complex systems, the nature and relative importance of the various flows among the system elements and between the system and its environment change. The major types of system flows are those of materials, energy, and information. And, as Buckley (1967: 47) notes;

> whereas the relations among components of mechanical systems are a function primarily of spatial and temporal considerations and the transmission of energy from one component to another, the interrelations characterizing higher levels come to depend more and more on the transmission of information.

The notion of types or levels of systems that vary both in the complexity of their parts and in the nature of the relations among the parts has been usefully elaborated by Boulding, who has proposed a classification of systems by their level of complexity. Briefly, Boulding identifies the following system types:

1. *Frameworks:* systems comprising static structures, such as the arrangements of atoms in a crystal or the anatomy of an animal.
2. *Clockworks:* simple dynamic systems with predetermined motions, such as the clock and the solar system.
3. *Cybernetic systems:* systems capable of self-regulation in terms of some externally prescribed target or criterion, such as a thermostat.
4. *Open systems:* systems capable of self-maintenance based on a throughput of resources from its environment, such as a living cell.
5. *Blueprinted-growth systems:* systems that reproduce not by duplication but by the production of seeds or eggs containing preprogrammed instructions for development, such as the acorn–oak system or the egg–chicken system.
6. *Internal-image systems:* systems capable of a detailed awareness of the environment in which information is received and organized into an image or knowledge structure of the environment as a whole, a level at which animals function.
7. *Symbol-processing systems:* systems that possess self-consciousness and so are capable of using language. Humans function at this level.

8. *Social systems:* multi-cephalous systems comprising actors functioning at level 7 who share a common social order and culture. Social organizations operate at this level.
9. *Transcendental systems:* systems composed of the "absolutes and the inescapable unknowables." (Boulding, 1956: 200–207)

Boulding's typology is illuminating in several respects. It quickly persuades us of the great range and variety of the systems present in the world. Levels 1 to 3 encompass the physical systems, levels 4 to 6 the biological systems, and levels 7 and 8 the human and social systems. From levels 1 to 8, systems become progressively more complex, more loosely coupled, more dependent on information flows, more capable of self-maintenance and renewal, more able to grow and change, and more open to the environment. Boulding adds level 9 so that his classification will not be closed but open to new possibilities not yet envisioned.

Although the nine levels can be distinctly identified and associated with specific existing systems, they are not meant to be mutually exclusive. Indeed, each higher-level system incorporates the features of those below it. For example, it is possible to analyze a social organization as a framework, a clockwork, a cybernetic system, and so on up to level 8, the level that captures the most complex, the higher-level, processes occurring in organizations. Boulding argues that because each level incorporates those below it, "much valuable information and insights can be obtained by applying low-level systems to high-level subject matter." At the same time, Boulding reminds us that "most of the theoretical schemes of the social sciences are still at level 2, just rising now to 3, although the subject matter clearly involves level 8" (1956: 208). This is an important criticism of theoretical models of organizations, one we need to keep before us as we review more recent attempts to develop open systems models.

SPECIAL EMPHASES

Broadly speaking, the contributions of the general systems perspective to organization theory up to this time have been to raise the level of our theoretical models up to level 3, where organizations are viewed as cybernetic systems, and to level 4, where they are viewed as open systems. Although Boulding's typology suggests we still have a long way to go before our models capture the complexity of organizational behavior, the insights obtained by moving to levels 3 and 4 are of great value. Along with our consideration of organizations as cybernetic and as open systems, we also take note of two other concepts emphasized by this perspective: organizations as loosely coupled systems and organizations as hierarchical systems.

Organizations as Cybernetic Systems

Systems functioning at Boulding's level 3 are capable of self-regulation. This important feat is attained through the development of specialized parts or subsystems related by certain processes or flows. Consider the mechanical example of the thermostat related to a source of heat. The

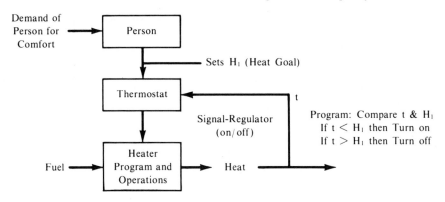

FIGURE 4-1   Illustration of a Cybernetic System: The Thermostat and the Heater. *Source:* Swinth (1974), Figure 2-1 (p. 18).

system contains three parts: (1) a mechanism for converting inputs into outputs–in this case, a heater that converts fuel into heat; (2) a mechanism for comparing the level of outputs with some desired target level and issuing instructions to the first mechanism based on any discrepancy—in our case, a thermostat that compares the temperature in the room with a desired level and switches the heater on or off accordingly; and (3) a mechanism for setting the desired target level that governs the activity of the second mechanism—in our example, a person who determines the desired temperature for the room and sets the level of the thermostat. Figure 4–1 depicts these three parts and the flows among them for the thermostat example.

Figure 4–2 diagrams the same type of system, but at a more general or abstract level. To view an organization as a cybernetic system is to emphasize the importance of the operations, the control, and the policy centers and to analyze the flows among them (Swinth, 1974). The policy center sets the goals for the system. This activity occurs in response to demands or preferences from the environment (flow 1 in figure 4–2); some of the preferences take the form of specific orders (flow 2). Note that the setting of organizational goals is based on information about preferences in the environment so that exchanges between the environment and the organization can occur. The flows out of the policy center (flow 3) are the goals of the system itself. The control center monitors the performance of the operations level, keeping its outputs in line with the goals established by the policy center. The control center also obtains information about the outputs of the operations level (flow 4). This information is compared with the standards prescribed by the goals issued by the policy center and results in a set of instructions or directives to the operations unit (flow 5). As Buckley emphasizes, such feedback-controlled arrangements result in behavior that is "goal-*directed,* and not merely goal-*oriented,* since it is the deviations from the goal-state itself that direct the behavior of the system, rather than some predetermined internal mechanism that aims blindly" (1967: 53). Further, a feedback mechanism detects departures from the established goals no matter what their cause, an important control characteristic as systems become so complex that all the

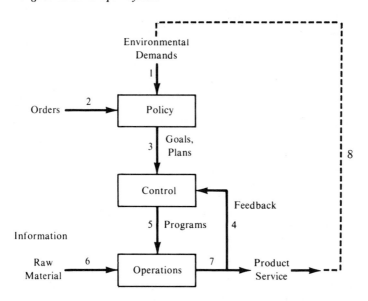

FIGURE 4–2   Abstract Model of Cybernetic System. *Source:* Swinth (1974), Figure 2–4 (p. 23).

potential sources of disturbance cannot be identified in advance (see Beer, 1964: 29–30).

The operations unit receives the raw materials (flow 6) and transforms them into products or outputs that are distributed outside the system (flow 7). The cybernetic model places great emphasis on the operational level of the organization—the level at which the production processes of the system are carried out. The analysis of these technical flows—inputs, throughouts, and outputs—is regarded as vital to an understanding of the system; indeed, the control and policy centers are examined chiefly in terms of their impact on these technical flows.

This analytic framework can be applied to the organization as a whole or to any of its subsystems. It can be used, for example, to analyze the operation of a company's personnel subsystem, which must meet the demands of other subsystems for trained employees and must control the recruitment and training of new workers and monitor their turnover (see Carzo and Yanouzas (1967: 345–47)). Or it can be used to examine the working of an entire company, which responds to demands from its marketplace and oversees the production and marketing of desired products for external customers (see Clough, 1963).

While cybernetic mechanisms involving feedback loops are readily discernible in organizations, we must be aware that our discussion of them (like others in this literature) has carried us far above Boulding's level 3 model. Level 3 is that of the thermostat that regulates temperature to a given value; our discussion has included *within* the system a mechanism for selecting the desired value: the policy center. To the extent that this center takes into account the system's past behavior, we then have a second feedback loop (flow 8). Ashby (1952) points out that in such double feedback systems the primary loop handles disturbances in "degree," applying existing decision rules, while the secondary loop handles disturbances in "kind," determining whether or not it is necessary to redefine the rules controlling the operating levels. Monitoring environmental feedback on the system's past behavior—for instance a company's keeping records on sales by product lines—is an important mechanism of adaptation for any open system.

Organizations as Loosely Coupled Systems

The cybernetic model gives the impression of a taut system—an arrangement of parts such that each is highly responsive to changes in the others. Such system elements are certainly found within organizations, but we should guard against overgeneralization. One of the main contributions of the open systems perspective is the recognition that many systems—especially social systems—contain elements that are only slightly related with other elements and that are capable of fairly autonomous actions (see Ashby, 1968; Glassman, 1973).

This insight can be applied to many different components or elements of organizations and their participants. Thus, we have seen that from the standpoint of the natural system analysts, the normative structure of an organization is only loosely coupled with its behavioral structure. Rules do not always govern actions: a rule may change without affecting behavior, and vice versa. A similar observation has been made at the social psychological level. Some analysts have noted that an individual's goals or intentions may be only weakly, linked to his or her actions (see March and Olsen, 1976; and Chapter 11). The concept of loose coupling can also be applied to the relationship among structural units such as work groups or departments. Inspection of official organizational charts may lend the impression that these units are all highly interrelated and closely coordinated, whereas observation of their actual behavior may reveal that they are slightly and occasionally connected.

A particularly important application of the loose coupling image is that proposed by Cyert and March (1963) and adopted by Pfeffer and Salancik (1978). As noted in Chapter 1 in the open system definition of the concept of organization, these theorists propose to view the key participants in organizations not as a unitary hierarchy or as an organic entity, but as a loosely linked *coalition* of shifting interest groups. According to Pfeffer and Salancik (1978: 36);

> the organization is a coalition of groups and interests, each attempting to obtain something from the collectivity by interacting with others, and each with its own preferences and objectives.

Rather than being oriented to the pursuit of consistent, common objectives, these coalitions change

> their purpose and domains to accommodate new interests, sloughing off parts of themselves to avoid some interests, and when necessary become involved in activities far afield from their stated purposes (1978: 24).

Contrary to first impressions and to rational system assumptions, open system theorists insist that loose coupling in structural arrangements can be highly adaptive for the system as a whole (see Weick, 1976; Pfeffer and Salancik, 1978; see also Chapter 10). It appears that loose coupling need not signify either low moral or low managerial standards.

The Characteristics of Open Systems

Organizations may be analyzed as cybernetic systems, but they also function at higher levels of complexity (recall Boulding's typology). They operate as open systems. Open systems are capable of self-maintenance on the basis of a throughput of resources from the environment. As Buckley (1967: 50) notes, this throughput is essential to the system's viability. Some analysts have mistakenly characterized an open system as having the capacity for self-maintenance *despite* the presence of throughput from the environment; their assumption is that because organizations are open, they must defend themselves against the environment. This view is misleading, since interaction with the environment is essential for open system functioning. As Pondy and Mitroff (1979: 7) argue, rather than suggesting that organizational systems be protected "against environmental complexity," one should realize that "it is precisely the throughput of nonuniformity that preserves the differential structure of an open system."

This is not to say that open systems do not have boundaries. They do, of course, and must expend energy in boundary maintenance. But it is of equal importance that energies be devoted to activities that span boundaries. Because of the openness of organizations, determining their boundaries is always difficult and sometimes appears to be a quite arbitrary decision. Does a university include within its boundary its students? Its alumni? Faculty during the summer? The spouses of students in university housing? Pfeffer and Salancik (1978: 30) propose to resolve this type of problem by reminding us that individual persons are not enclosed within the boundaries of organizations, only certain of their activities and behaviors. Although this interpretation helps, we all know that many actions have relevance for more than one system simultaneously. For example, a sale from the standpoint of one system is a purchase when viewed from another, and what is an act of conformity for one system can be an act of deviance for another. Moreover, as will be emphasized, all systems are made up of subsystems and are themselves subsumed in larger systems—an arrangement that creates linkages across systems and confounds the attempt to erect clear boundaries among them. Finally, our determination of whether a system is open is itself a matter of how the boundaries of the system are defined. As Hall and Fagen note, "whether a given system is open or closed depends on how much of the universe is included in the system and how much in the environment. By adjoining to the system the part of the environment with which an exchange takes place, the system becomes closed." (1956: 23)

General systems theorists elaborate the distinction between closed and open systems by employing the concept of *entropy:* energy loss or energy that cannot be turned into work. According to the second law of thermodynamics, all closed systems move toward a state of entropy—a random arrangement of their elements, a dissolution of their differentiated structures, a state of maximum disorder. By contrast, open systems, because they are capable of importing energy from their environment, can experience *negative entropy,* or negentropy. By acquiring inputs of greater complexity than their outputs, open systems restore their own energy and repair breakdowns in their own organization. Bertalanffy (1962: 7) concludes, "Hence, such systems can maintain themselves at a high level, and even evolve toward an increase of order and complexity."[2]

To emphasize these twin properties of open systems, Buckley (1967: 58–62) distinguishes between two basic sets of system processes: morphostasis and morphogenesis. The term *morphostasis* is applied to those processes that tend to preserve or maintain a system's given form, structure, or state. Morphostatic processes in biological systems would include circulation and respiration; in social systems, socialization and control activities. *Morphogenesis* is applied to those processes that elaborate or change the system—for example, growth, learning, and differentiation. In adapting to the external environment, all open systems typically become more differentiated in form, more elaborate in structure. Thus, in biological systems, organs whose sensitivities to external stimuli are coarse and broad are succeeded by more specialized receptors capable of responding to a wider range and finer gradations of stimuli. Biological organisms move toward greater complexity through the process of evolution: individual organisms are little affected, but over time, as mutations occur and are selected for their survival value, species are gradually transformed. Social organizations, more variable and loosely coupled than biological systems, can and do fundamentally change their structural characteristics over time. The General Motors of today bears little if any structural resemblance to the company of the same name of fifty years ago. Indeed, social organizations exhibit such an amazing capacity to change their basic structural features that researchers who study organizations over time have difficulty determining when the units they are studying are the same organizations with reorganized structures and when they represent the birth of new organizations.

To repeat, the source of system diversity and variety is the environment. From an open systems point of view, there is a close connection between the condition of the environment and the characteristics of the systems within it: a complex system could not maintain its complexity in a simple environment. Open systems are subject to what is termed the *law of limited variety:* "A system will exhibit no more variety than the variety to

---

[2]It is interesting to note that some information theorists posit a close relation between the concepts of organization and entropy: they are viewed, in effect, as opposite states. If entropy is a state of randomness, or zero organization, it is also the state that provides maximum variety, maximum information, to someone observing a set of elements. As organization develops, constraints and limitations grow, restricting the number of states that may be present among the elements. Miller elaborates this point:

> A well-organized system is predictable—you know what it is going to do before it happens. When a well-organized system does something, you learn little that you didn't already know—you acquire little information. A perfectly organized system is completely predictable and its behavior provides no information at all. The more disorganized and unpredictable a system is, the more information you get by watching it. (Miller, 1953: 3)

Based on such reasoning, information theorists Shannon and Weaver (1963) have proposed a measure of information, H, which assesses the amount of entropy present in a set of elements—their variation, their relative frequency of occurrence, and their interdependence. The higher the H level, the more information and the less organization is present (see also Buckley, 1967: 82–89).

which it has been exposed in its environment" (Pondy and Mitroff, 1979: 7). Although the processes by which such "laws" operate are not clearly understood, Part Three of this volume is devoted to explicating and illustrating the interdependence of organizations and environments.

Organizations as Hierarchical Systems

General systems theorists also stress that hierarchy is a fundamental feature of complex systems—not so much hierarchy in the sense of status or power differences, but hierarchy in the form of clustering and levels. Systems are composed of multiple subsystems, and systems are themselves contained within suprasystems. This is such a common feature of virtually all complex systems that it is easily overlooked. Books like this one are made of parts, chapters, sections, paragraphs, words, letters. The U.S. political system is constituted of precincts, counties, states, and regions, all contained within the nation-state. And organizations are made up of roles contained within work groups, within departments, within divisions; many organizations are themselves subsystems of larger systems: corporate structures, or associations, or the executive branch of the government. (A diagram illustrating the major clusters to be found in a modern corporate organization will be found in Figure 10–1 of this book.)

Combining the notion of hierarchy with that of loose coupling, we note a common feature of complex systems: the connections and interdependencies within a system component are likely to be tighter and greater than those between system components. In a well-written book, for example, the ideas expressed in a single paragraph should be more closely interrelated than those expressed in different paragraphs. Similarly, interactions within a given academic department within a university are likely to be more frequent and more intense than those occurring between departments. Indeed, as will be discussed in Chapter 9, this tendency provides the basis for an important principle of organizational design.

When subsystems take the form of "stable subassemblies"—units capable of retaining their form without constant attention from superior units—then hierarchical forms have an important survival advantage over other systems (Simon, 1962). Many seemingly complex organizational systems are made up of, and depend for their stability on, units that are highly similar and capable of relatively autonomous functioning—for examples, similarly organized work teams or departments; franchise units; and chain stores. From this perspective, the apparent complexity of many systems becomes simpler: everything is *not* connected to everything else; there are loose connections and missing connections; and many components of systems are identical or nearly so. (See Aldrich, 1979: 75–80.)

To this point, we have emphasized that all systems are composed of subsystems. Let us briefly comment on the significance of the fact that all systems are also subsumed by other, more encompassing systems. This suggests that to understand the operation of a system, it may be as important to look outside the system at its context as to look inside the system at its component units. Schwab (1960) has termed this perspective *rationalism,* the opposite of reductionism. Rationalism occurs when explanation comes by looking outside an entity to the environment or a higher system in which it is embedded. (See also McKelvey, 1982: 5.) In many ways, the open systems perspective points to the significance of the wider environment.

SELECTED SCHOOLS

As with the previous perspectives, we turn now to several schools that exemplify the open systems approach. We will briefly describe the systems design approach; contingency theory, which can be regarded as a school growing out of the systems design approach; and Weick's social psychological model of organizing. Although open systems approaches to organizations were the last of the three perspectives to emerge, they have spread very rapidly and have had an enormous effect on organization theory. We discuss in this section only a few early developments; in Chapter 5 and later chapters we will consider other approaches embodying open systems assumptions and insights.

Systems Design

A large and growing number of organization theorists look to general systems theory as a source of ideas to improve the design of organizations—determining proper work flows, control systems, and planning mechanisms, and their interrelations—for carrying out their designated functions (see Carzo and Yanouzas, 1967; Khandwalla, 1977; Swinth, 1974; Mintzberg, 1979). Unlike some of the schools devoted to the study of organizations, the orientation of this group is pragmatic and applied: they seek to change and improve organizations as viewed from a managerial perspective, not simply to describe and understand them.

Many of the analysts attempting to apply systems ideas to organizations are aware both of the great complexity of organizations as one type of system and of the danger of misapplying or overextending analogies based on the operation of other, less complex systems. Beer (1964) proposes a classification of systems ranging from those that are both simple and deterministic, such as the behavior of a block and tackle system, to those that are complex and probabilistic, such as the operation of an assembly line in a factory, to those that are "exceedingly complex" and probabilistic, such as an entire organization (for example, a company). Complex probabilistic systems, whose behavior can be generally described and predicted with statistical procedures, are the province of operations research; exceedingly complex probabilistic systems have given rise to the fields of cybernetics and systems design (Beer, 1964: 18). Because of their great complexity, the latter systems currently defy conventional mathematical modeling approaches. Instead, the most widely employed technique of analysis is to simulate the operation of the system. "Here, all the variables and relationships of interest are linked as understood into a model and then the manager-analyst-researcher manipulates certain ones and observes how others change as the simulation of the system plays itself out" (Swinth, 1974: 11). Note that this approach emphasizes the importance of treating the system as a system.

Complex systems cannot be understood by an analysis that attempts to decompose the system into its individual parts in order to examine each part and relationship in turn. This approach, according to Ashby (1956: 36), one of the founders of the general systems movement,

> gives us only a vast number of separate parts or items of information, the results of whose interactions no one can predict. If we take such a system to pieces, we find that we cannot reassemble it!

Simulation techniques are popular with systems analysts because they are consistent with this image of a unit whose behavior can be understood only as the resultant of complex and probabilistic interactions among its parts. They also support the systems view that to understand organizations one must focus on the operational level of the organization. Thus, a systems design analyst would be more interested in obtaining charts depicting the flows of information, energy, and materials throughout the organization than in inspecting the formal table of organization. In examining a football team as a social system, for example, such an analyst would rather inspect the play books governing the activities of the various players during the course of a game than the formal authority arrangements among the players, coaches, managers, and owners of the club.

It is consistent with the holistic emphasis of the systems analyst that the approach deals with objects or parts of systems, the detailed structure of which is unknown or regarded as irrelevant. These basic units are the so-called black boxes, the smallest elements of the system under study (Haberstroh, 1965: 1174). For the purposes of systems analysis, all the information that is required is a description of the inputs to and the outputs from each of the basic elements (or the relation between the inputs and the outputs). It is not necessary to know the internal working of these system components to understand or simulate the workings of the larger system.

An important characteristic of exceedingly complex, probabilistic systems is that the whole is more than the sum of its parts, in the pragmatic sense that given the properties of the parts and the laws of their interaction, it is not a trivial matter to infer the behavior of the larger system. As a consequence, it is virtually impossible to predict and protect against all the ways in which such systems can fail. Perrow has labeled such failures *normal accidents:* normal because the accidents emerge "from the characteristics of the systems themselves" (1982: 1; see also Perrow, 1984). From an in-depth analysis of the near disaster at the Three Mile Island nuclear plant in Pennsylvania, Perrow notes the more obvious and ever-present problems of design and equipment failures and operator error but emphasizes the role played by "negative synergy."

> "Synergy" is a buzz word in business management circles, indicating that the whole is more than the sum of its parts, or in their congenial familiarity, two plus two equals five. But minus two plus minus two can equal minus five thousand in tightly-coupled, complex, high risk military and industrial systems . . . where complex, unanticipated, unperceived and incomprehensible interactions of off-standard components (equipment, design, and operator actions) threaten disaster. (Perrow, 1982: 18)

Gall (1978: 97) identifies concisely the dilemma posed by these systems: "When a fail-safe system fails, it fails by failing to fail safe."

Among the various flows connecting system elements, the flow of information is the most critical. The gathering, transmission, storage, and retrieval of information are among the most fateful activities of organizations, and design theorists devote much attention to them. (See Sage, 1981.) We have already described in Chapter 2 Simon's views on the cognitive limits of decision makers. From the perspective of systems design, Simon is pointing out the limitations of individuals as information processors.[3] Viewing individuals in this manner, Haberstroh asserts that they exhibit "low channel capacity, lack of reliability, and poor computational ability." On the other hand, individuals possess some desirable features: "The strong points of a human element are its large memory capacity, its large repertory of responses, its flexibility in relating these responses to information inputs, and its ability to react creatively when the unexpected is encountered" (Haberstroh, 1965: 1176). The challenge facing the systems designers is how to create structures that will overcome the limitations and exploit the strengths of each system component, including the individual participants.

Of course, not all environments place the same demands on organizations and their participants for information processing. Recognition of this important point has given rise to a special perspective known as *contingency theory*, which we will briefly summarize next. More generally, a number of theorists argue that the very existence of organizations is explained by the information-processing limitations of individuals confronted by complex situations. These arguments, developed by Arrow (1974) and Williamson (1975), are reviewed in Chapter 7.

Contingency Analysis

Jay Galbraith (1973:2) states the two assumptions underlying contingency theory most succinctly:

•There is no one best way to organize.
•Any way of organizing is not equally effective.

The first assumption challenges the conventional wisdom of those administrative theorists who have sought to develop general principles applicable to organizations in all times and places. Such a quest not only overlooks the vast diversity of existing organizational forms but also fails to recognize the great variety of tasks undertaken by organizations. The second assumption challenges the "know-nothing" position that the complexity and variety of organizations are such that it is futile to search for any underlying principles to guide their design. A third assumption can be formulated to represent the position of the contingency theorist:

•The best way to organize depends on the nature of the environment to which the organization relates.

---

[3]Simon's contributions to organizations relate as closely to these concerns of systems design as to the rational model of organizations (see Simon, 1960; 1962).

As a branch of systems design, contingency theory emphasizes that design decisions depend—are contingent—on environmental conditions.

Contingency theory is guided by the general orienting hypothesis that organizations whose internal features best match the demands of their environments will achieve the best adaptation. The challenge facing those who embrace this orientation is to be clear about what is meant by "the organization's internal features," "the demands of their environments," "best adaptation," and, most difficult of all, "best match." Details of attempted answers to these questions are best postponed to Part Three, but two general approaches can be briefly described to illustrate the directions pursued within this theoretical tradition.

Lawrence and Lorsch (1967), who coined the label *contingency theory*, argue that different environments place differing requirements on organizations: specifically, environments characterized by uncertainty and rapid rates of change in market conditions or technologies present different demands—both constraints and opportunities—on organizations than do placid and stable environments. They conducted empirical studies of organizations in the plastics, food processing, and standardized container industries to assess the relation between these environments—ranging from high to low uncertainty—and the internal features of each type of organization. They also suggest that different segments of subunits within a given type of organization may confront different external demands. Thus, within plastics manufacturing companies, the research and development units face a more uncertain and more rapidly changing environment than the production departments. To cope with these varying environments, organizations and their subunits develop differentiated characteristics. For example, the normative structure may be more or less highly formalized, or the time orientation of participants may be focused on long- or short-range outcomes. The more varied the types of environments confronted by a given organization type, the more differentiated the organization structure needs to be. Moreover, the more differentiated the structure, the more effort that must be devoted to the integration of the various subunits. In sum, Lawrence and Lorsch propose that the match or coalignment of an organization with its environment occurs on at least two levels: (1) the structural features of each organizational subunit should be suited to the specific environment to which it relates; and (2) the differentiation and mode of integration characterizing the larger organization should be suited to the overall environment within which the organization must operate (see Chapter 10).

Galbraith's (1973; 1977) version of contingency theory is similar to the systems design school in its stress on information processing. As in Lawrence and Lorsch's view, the environment is characterized in terms of the amount of uncertainty it poses for the organization. Galbraith connects the concepts of environmental uncertainty and information processing in the following useful manner: uncertainty enters the organization by affecting the work or tasks that organizations perform, and "the greater the task uncertainty, the greater the amount of information that must be processed among decision makers during task execution in order to achieve a given level of performance" (1977: 36). Various structural arrangements, including rules, hierarchy, and decentralization, may be viewed as mechanisms determining the information-processing capacity of the system. The design challenge is to select a structural arrangement appropriate for the information-processing requirements of the tasks to be performed. We will consider Galbraith's specific arguments in more detail in Chapter 9.

Weick's Model of Organizing

While the design and continency theorists have developed their version of the open systems approach at the structural level of analysis, Karl Weick has attempted to pursue some of the implications of this approach at the social psychological level (1969; rev. 1979). We cannot do justice to his subtle and imaginative ideas in this overview but will note some of his lines of argument and attempt to capture the flavor of his work.

Weick cites with approval Bateson's (1972: 334) motto "stamp out nouns." He argues,

> The word, organization, is a noun and it is also a myth. If one looks for an organization one will not find it. What will be found is that there are events, linked together, that transpire within concrete walls and these sequences, their pathways, their timing, are the forms we erroneously make into substances when we talk about an organization. (Weick, 1974: 358)

Rather than talking about organizations, the focus of our attention should be "organizing." This is a very explicit example of the manner in which the systems perspective attempts to shift attention from structure to process.

Weick defines organizing as "the resolving of equivocality in an enacted environment by means of interlocked behaviors embedded in conditionally related processes" (1969: 91). We will attempt to unpack this dense definition. Weick argues that organizing is directed toward information processing generally and, in particular, toward removing its equivocality. He explains that

> the basic raw materials on which organizations operate are informational inputs that are ambiguous, uncertain, equivocal. Whether the information is embedded in tangible raw materials, recalcitrant customers, assigned tasks, or union demands, there are many possibilities, or sets of outcomes that might occur. Organizing serves to narrow the range of possibilities, to reduce the number of "might occurs." The activities of organizing are directed toward the establishment of a workable level of certainty. (Weick, 1969: 40)

This work is carried out by sets of "interlocked behaviors"—"repetitive, reciprocal, contingent behaviors that develop and are maintained between two or more actors" (1969: 91). The activities are carried on in three stages: enactment, selection, and retention. It is important to note that these three stages are Weick's translation of the three phases of natural selection or evolution as developed by Campbell (1969). (See Chapter 5.) Weick substitutes the term *enactment* for Campbell's label of *variations* for the first stage to emphasize the more active role organizational participants carry out in defining the environments they confront. Individual information processors *create* the environment to which the system then adapts (Weick, 1979: 147–69). The process of enactment introduces information (variety) into the system, which is dealt with according to organizational rules or routines: the greater the equivocality in the information introduced, the smaller the number of rules that will be activated to deal with the input. If the input is highly equivocal, only a small number of general rules are used to attempt to structure the input; however, if the input is better understood, a greater number of rules can be applied in responding to it (1969: 73). The application of the rules reduces (by selection) the equivocality of the information. The final phase of information processing determines what information is to be retained for future reference. Although the entire process operates to reduce equivocality, some equivocal features do and must remain if the organization is to be able to survive into a new and different future. In other words, "organizations continue to exist only if they maintain a balance between flexibility and stability" (Weick, 1979: 215). The information received and selected by the organization must be both credited (retained) and discredited or questioned if the organization is to safely face a future that may resemble, but must inevitably differ from, its past.

Weick's major concern is to spell out the implications of the open systems perspective when applied to the level of individual participants and the relationships among them. The semiautonomy of the individual actors is stressed: the looseness and conditionality of the relationships linking them is emphasized. Further, familiar social psychological processes become more problematic when viewed through the lens of a systems analyst. Where the conventional view would stress the use of perceptual sets that give continuity and stability to individual responses, Weick emphasizes the importance of "attention" processes that are more variable because they take into account situational factors—the "particular here and now" that determines what is selected out and what neglected from the available cues (1969: 39). Similarly, whereas conventional wisdom asserts that goals precede activities, that intention precedes action, Weick (1969: 37) insists that behavior often occurs first and then is interpreted—given meaning. The view of interpersonal processes such as coordination and control is similarly affected: such "interlocked behaviors" are viewed as loosely coupled systems allowing individual performers great latitude in interpreting and implementing directions (Weick, 1976). More generally, in his view of causation, Weick embraces and applies many of the most basic concepts of the systems analyst—for example, the concept of *equifinality*, which asserts that a given outcome may be the result of quite different processes, and the concept of *causal arc*, which insists on the likelihood of reciprocal rather than unilateral causation (Weick, 1974; see also Buckley, 1967). In these and related ways, Weick has attempted to "open up" our conception of organizational structure and behavior.

A number of other theories that draw heavily on open system insights have recently appeared, but we reserve discussion of them to later chapters.

SUMMARY AND TENTATIVE CONCLUSIONS

The open systems perspective developed later than the rational and natural system views, but it has gained adherents rapidly and has profoundly altered our conception of organizations and their central features and processes. The open systems view of organizational structure stresses the

complexity and variability of the individual parts—both individual participants and subgroups—as well as the looseness of connections among
them. Parts are viewed as capable of semiautonomous action; many parts
are viewed as, at best loosely coupled to other parts. Further, in human
organizations, as Boulding emphasizes, the system is multi-cephalous:
many heads are present to receive information, make decisions, direct
performance. Individuals and subgroups form and leave coalitions. Coordination and control become problematic. Also, system boundaries are
seen as amorphous; the assignment of actors or actions to either the
organization or the environment often seems arbitrary and varies depending on what aspect of systemic functioning is under consideration.

Open systems imagery does not simply blur the more conventional
views of the structural features of organizations: it shifts attention from
structure to process. Whether viewed at the more abstract level through
concepts such as enacting, selecting, and retaining processes, or at the
more concrete level with concepts such as input, throughput, and output
production flows and feedback-control loops, the emphasis is on organizing as against organization. Maintaining these flows and preserving these
processes are viewed as problematic. As Weick insists, "processes are repetitive only if this repetitiveness is continuously accomplished" (1969:
36). Both morphostatic and morphogenetic processes are of interest: the
former emphasize self-maintenance and stability, the latter, development
and elaboration of structure. A process view is taken not only of the
internal operations of the organization but of the organization itself as a
system persisting over time. The organization as an arrangement of roles
and relationships is not the same today as it was yesterday or will be
tomorrow: to survive is to adapt, and to adapt is to change. As Leavitt and
his colleagues conclude:

> the complex organization is more like a modern weapons system than like
> old-fashioned fixed fortifications, more like a mobile than a static sculpture,
> more like a computer than an adding machine. In short, the organization is
> a dynamic system. (Leavitt, Dill, and Eyring, 1973: 4)

The interdependence of the organization and its environment receives primary attention in the open systems perspective. Rather than
overlooking the environment, as tends to be true of the rational system
perspective, or viewing it as alien and hostile, as is characteristic of the
natural system perspective, the open systems model stresses the reciprocal
ties that bind and relate the organization with those elements that sur-
round and penetrate it. The environment is perceived to be the ultimate
source of materials, energy, and information, all of which are vital to the
continuation of the system. Indeed, the environment is even seen to be
the source of order itself.

It seems premature to attempt even a tentative assessment of the
open systems perspective at this time. The general systems approach—the
mother ship—was itself launched only about three decades ago, and although its applicability to social organizations has been underscored from
the very beginning, the working out of its specific implications is still
underway. Some problems and dangers are already apparent. There is a
strong tendency to work from analogy, applying insights from one type of

system to another—for example, from the thermostat-heater system to the control system of an organization. While insights can be generated by such analogies, so can errors and misconceptions. Also, more so than the other perspectives, the open systems approach seems to carry with it a large number of highly abstract and often abstruse new concepts and labels, such as cybernetics, morphogenesis, equifinality. New concepts appropriately understood and applied can open our eyes to new facets of reality, but sometimes open systems theorists seem bedazzled by the richness of their new vocabularies and appear to be content simply to relabel the various components of the organizational system under study.

Such problems, however, often accompany new intellectual developments. In general, it seems clear that the open systems perspective brings with it a much-needed dimension to—if not a reorientation of—previously existing viewpoints. After the emergence of the open systems perspective, the old image of a closed, self-contained, self-sufficient system will be difficult to resurrect. The doors and windows of the organization have been opened, and we are more than ever aware of the vital flows and linkages that relate the organization to other systems. Further, we see more clearly now that organizations are processes as well as structures, and that some of these processes are not recurrent cycles but forces changing the existing structures.

5 combining the perspectives

Political revolutions aim to change political institutions in ways that those institutions themselves prohibit. Their success therefore necessitates the partial relinquishment of one set of institutions in favor of another.
Like the choice between competing political institutions, that between competing paradigms proves to be a choice between incompatible modes of community life. Because it has that character, the choice is not and cannot be determined merely by the evaluative procedures characteristic of normal science, for these depend in part upon a particular paradigm, and that paradigm is at issue. When paradigms enter, as they must, into a debate about paradigm choice, their role is necessarily circular. Each group uses its own paradigm to argue in that paradigm's defense.

Thomas S. Kuhn (1962)

The three preceding chapters have described and illustrated three perspectives on organizations. We have attempted to present these perspectives succinctly but fairly, discussing examples of work from each, and assessing their strengths and limitations. We have sought to avoid treating these viewpoints as caricatures or as approaches having only historical interest. In our opinion, each is valuable: each focuses on a set of significant and enduring features of organizations.

In this chapter, we begin by reviewing three important attempts to combine and reconcile these three perspectives. Then we propose an alternative combination. The latter approach is used both to briefly review theories previously discussed as well as to introduce new conceptions developed during the past two decades. Since there has been a flurry of theoretical activity during this period, the catalog of new approaches is embarrassingly long: too many ideas are covered too quickly. But, fortunately for the sake of comprehension and utility, the objective is only to introduce the theories that will be considered in more detail in Parts Three and Four of this volume. Each theory is briefly set out in one place so that it can be more easily compared with others, and easily located for review as needed.

As noted in Chapter 1, the three perspectives operate as paradigms, as Kuhn (1962) defines this concept. Functioning as conceptual frameworks and as sets of assumptions guiding empirical investigations, paradigms are not themselves subject to verification. A paradigm is not so much disproved as it is dislodged or supplanted by a different paradigm providing a new map of the territory—indeed, not only a new map but new directions for map making. As Kuhn (1962: 108) observes,

> in learning a paradigm the scientist acquires theory, methods, and standards together, usually in an inextricable mixture. Therefore, when paradigms change, there are usually significant shifts in the criteria determining the legitimacy both of problems and of proposed solutions.

Thus in some respects the differences between competing paradigms cannot be completely resolved by scientific evidence or argumentation.

Nevertheless, noting the selectivity of the perspectives, a number of theorists have attempted to develop more encompassing formulations, combining selected portions of the earlier traditions. We will briefly review three of these synthetic frameworks: the models of Etzioni, of Lawrence and Lorsch, and of Thompson.

THREE ATTEMPTS AT INTEGRATION

Etzioni's Structuralist Model

Etzioni (1964) has proposed a "structuralist" approach as a synthesis of the classical (rational) schools and the human relations (natural) schools. (See also, Gross and Etzioni, 1985: 65–88) In contrast with our view, Etzioni does not regard Weber as a contributor to the classical approach but argues that Weber together with Marx provides the basis for the synthetic structuralist model. Marx and Weber both believed that regardless of the best efforts of managers and workers, their economic and social interests are inevitably in conflict. Marx (1972 trans.) viewed factory workers as alienated from their work since they owned neither the means of production nor the product of their labor. Weber (1946 trans.: 221–24) generalized this assertion, noting that soldiers in modern armies did not own their weapons, nor did research scientists own their equipment and supplies. Both assumed that those who owned the means of production could control their use. In this sense, all employees in large organizations can be viewed as alienated from their labor (see Chapter 12). Thus, for Etzioni, control becomes the fundamental issue in understanding organization, and both the rational and the natural system theorists have important, and different, things to say about control systems within organizations. The rational system theorists contribute to the analysis of control by focusing on the distribution of power among organizational positions; the natural system theorists make their contribution by insisting that naked power only alienates, that power must be acceptable to the subordinates in the power relation if control attempts are to be effective, as Barnard (1938) insisted.[1] Weber, according to Etzioni, combines both of these points of view in his examination of the distribution of power, on the one hand, and of the bases on which it is seen to be legitimate by participants in the system, on the other (Etzioni, 1964: 50–51; 1961; Weber, 1947 trans: 324–29).[2]

In addition to combining the rational and natural perspectives in the analysis of the central issue of power, Etzioni proposes that the structuralist model gives equal attention to formal and informal structures, and in particular to the relations between them; to the scope of informal groups and the relations between such groups both inside and outside the organization; to both social and material rewards and their interrelation; and to the interaction of the organization and its environment (Etzioni, 1964: 41–49). In approaching all of these matters, however, the structuralist point of view recognizes fully

> the organizational dilemma: the inevitable strains—which can be reduced but not eliminated—between organizational needs and personal needs; between rationality and non-rationality; between discipline and autonomy; between formal and informal relations; between management and workers, or more generically, between ranks and divisions (Etzioni, 1964: 41).

In sum, the structuralist model suggests that the rational and the natural system perspectives are complementary. Each view represents a partial truth. If the perspectives seem at times to conflict, this is because the organizational elements to which they point sometimes conflict. The recognition of such conflicts is an important part of the "whole" truth about organizations, their structural features, and their functioning.

Lawrence and Lorsch's Contingency Model

We have already reported Lawrence and Lorsch's various proposals for reconciling the rational and natural system perspectives (Chapter 3) and described their contingency model of organizations (Chapter 4). We briefly review these ideas at this point to emphasize that they suggest a basis on which all three perspectives can be reconciled.

In essence, Lawrence and Lorsch (1967) argue that if an open system perspective is taken—so that any given organization is viewed not in isolation but in relation to its specific environment—then the rational and the natural system perspectives may be seen to identify different organizational types which vary because they have adapted to different types of environments. The rational and natural system perspectives are at variance because each focuses on a different end of a single continuum representing the range of organizational forms. At one extreme, some organizations are highly formalized, are centralized, and pursue clearly specified goals; at the other extreme, some organizations are less formalized, rely greatly on the personal qualities of participants, and lack consensus on

---

[1]Hopkins (1961) has proposed a quite similar basis for reconciliation of the two points of view.

[2]These matters involving power, authority, legitimacy, and control will be more fully discussed in Chapter 11.

goals. The two extreme types depicted by the rational and the natural systems models should not be viewed as differing aspects of the same organization—as, for example, Etzioni's structuralist model would suggest—but rather as different forms of organizations. And, as emphasized by the open systems perspective, the nature of the form is determined by the type of environment to which the organization must relate. Specifically, the more homogeneous and stable the environment, the more appropriate will be the formalized and hierarchical form. And the more diverse and changing the task environment, the more appropriate will be the less formalized and more organic form.

Thus we arrive at the contingency argument: there is no one best organizational form but several, and their suitability is determined by the extent of the match between the form of the organization and the demands of the environment. The general form of this argument is ecological; the argument assumes that different systems are more or less well adapted to differing environments. Environmental conditions determine which systems survive and thrive: those best adapted are most likely to prosper.[3] By this argument, Lawrence and Lorsch attempt to account for the different forms of organizations and for the different theoretical perspectives that have developed to characterize them. Note that their views can also explain why the rational system perspective preceded in time the natural system perspective if it is assumed, as most open system analysts would contend, that the environments of organizations were more stable in the past and have become progressively more volatile.

The open systems perspective is viewed by Lawrence and Lorsch as the more comprehensive framework within which the rational and natural system perspectives may be housed, since each of the latter constitutes only a partial view depicting particular organizational adaptations to differing environmental conditions.

Thompson's Levels Model

Simultaneously with the emergence of Lawrence and Lorsch's contingency model, James D. Thompson (1967) developed a somewhat different basis for reconciling the three perspectives. In his influential work *Organizations in Action,* Thompson argues that analysts should be mentally flexible enough to admit the possibility that all three perspectives are essentially correct and applicable to all organizations. However, they do not all apply with equal force to all organizational locations. Thompson borrows the distinctions proposed by Parsons (1960: 60–65), summarized in Chapter 3, identifying three organizational levels: the technical level, that part of the organization carrying on the production functions; the managerial, comprising those activities relating to the control of the production functions and the procurement of inputs and the disposition of outputs; and the institutional level, consisting of those activities relating the organization to the larger community and institutional sectors. Thompson's argument is that the three perspectives apply differentially to the three levels of organizations.

---

[3]These arguments are most fully developed in the population ecology approach, described in more detail later in this chapter.

Thompson's model in a nutshell is that organizations strive to be rational although they are natural and open systems. It is in the interest of administrators—those who design and manage organizations—that the work of the organization be carried out as effectively and efficiently as possible. Since technical rationality presumes a closed system, Thompson (1967: 10–13) argues that organizations will attempt to seal off their technical level, protecting it from external uncertainties to the extent possible.[4] Thus, it is the level of the core technology—the assembly line in the automobile factory, the patient care wards and treatment rooms in the hospital—that we would expect the rational system perspective to apply with the most force. At the opposite extreme, the institutional level, if it is to perform its functions, must be open to the environment. It is at this level, where the environment must be enacted or adapted to, that the open systems perspective is most relevant. In the middle is the managerial level, which must mediate between the relatively open institutional and the closed technical levels. To do so effectively requires the flexibility that is associated with the less formalized and more politicized activities depicted by the natural system theorists. It is also the managers—whose power and status are most intimately linked to the fate of the organization—who have the greatest stake in the survival of the organization as a system.

There is much to be said for, and learned from, each of these efforts to reconcile the three perspectives. In a real sense, they are all true, or what may be more important, useful: Etzioni is surely correct that all organizations embody conflicting tendencies between the formal and informal, rational and nonrational aspects of their structures; Lawrence and Lorsch are correct that some types of organizations exhibit higher formalization and goal specificity than other types and that these differences are associated with environmental conditions; and Thompson is correct that some segments or levels of the organization are more closed or open than others. These combinations and applications of the three original perspectives have illuminated additional facets of organizations, and in this way, the utility of the perspectives has been reinforced for a new generation of students of organziations.

CROSS-CLASSIFYING THE PERSPECTIVES

There is yet another sense in which the three perspectives may be seen as persisting up to the present time, albeit in new combinations. Our introduction to the perspectives in earlier chapters suggested that they fell into a neat time order with the rational perspective preceding the natural system view, and the open system perspective developing most recently. We will suggest now a slightly more complex view—namely, that there have been not three but four phases, created by cross-classifying the three perspectives.

At the risk of considerable oversimplification, we suggest that theoretical models of organizations underwent a major shift about 1960, at the

---

[4]Specific mechanisms, termed *buffering strategies*, used to seal off the technical core are described in Chapter 8.

time open systems perspectives supplanted closed system models. Analyses focusing primarily on the internal characteristics of organizations gave way at approximately that date to approaches emphasizing the importance for the organization of events and processes external to it. After 1960, the environments of organizations, conceived in terms of economic, political, cultural, social, technological, and interorganizational elements, figure prominently in attempts to explain organizational structure and behavior.

On both sides of this watershed representing the transition from closed to open system models, a second trend can be identified: a shift from rational to natural system models of analysis. It appears that this shift has occurred twice! It occurred for the closed system models in the late 1930s and early 1940s, as we have already described in Chapters 2 and 3—the rational system formulations of Weber and Taylor giving way to the natural system approaches of Mayo and Barnard—and it appears to be occurring again for the open systems models at the present time, in ways to be discussed in this chapter.

That is, we suggest that the dominant theoretical model for analyzing organizations up to the late 1930s was the closed rational system model (type I). This model was succeeded by the closed natural system model (type II), which held sway through the 1950s. The open systems models came into prominence during the 1960s. However, this perspective was quickly combined in the work of several major theorists with a resurgence of the rational system model. Open rational systems models (type III) dominated the field well into the 1970s. Recently however, the most prominent theoretical contributions appear to represent a revival of the natural system perspective, but now combined with the open system model (type IV). Although it is possible to thus identify a dominant theoretical orientation for each period, that is not to say that all of the important work associated with that orientation was produced during that period or that important work associated with the alternative orientations was not taking place. The time periods identified are not absolute; and all combinations of theoretical work are active up to the present time.

In addition to varying in their dominant perspective, the approaches reviewed also differ in level of analysis, as we have noted throughout. Closed system models, whether rational or natural, restricted attention (by definition) to the internal characteristics of organizations, but did vary in focus between social psychological and structural properties of organizations. With the advent of open systems models, ecological analyses became an important new source of theorizing about the determinants of organizational behavior and structure. A great deal of the recent theoretical work in organizations has occurred at the ecological level. (Indeed, as will be discussed in Chapter 6, several varying layers of analysis have emerged within this level.)

Table 5-1 summarizes this pattern and lists representative theories and theorists associated with each type of perspective. While there are important similarities between types I and III, the rational systems models, and between types II and IV, the natural systems models, the differences generated by the transition from closed to open models are at least as important. A brief discussion of each type can highlight these similarities and differences. Before reviewing each type, however, we note the relation of these four types to the organization of the present volume. To this point, our discussions of the rational and the natural systems models have emphasized their closed-system versions, types I and II. Although we have stressed the differences between a closed and an open systems perspective, we have deliberately refrained from serious attention to the new generations of rational and natural systems models, types III and IV, which have emerged since the development of the open systems perspective. These most recent contributions receive primary attention in succeeding chapters. Hence, our discussion of types I and II will serve as a brief review of the work of major theorists prior to 1960, as described in Part Two of this volume. And our discussion of types III and IV will serve to preview the work of major theorists since 1960, to be discussed in greater detail in Part Three.

Type I: Closed Rational System Models

The representative theories and theorists listed in table 5–1 for the closed rational systems models should by this time look very familiar: Taylor, Weber, Fayol, and Gulick and Urwick are old friends. Simon represents a transitional case: his early work (Simon, 1957, first published in 1945) is more closely related to type III models. As emphasized in Chapter 2, all of these theories portray organizations as tools designed to achieve preset ends, and all of them ignore or minimize the perturbations and opportunities posed by connections to a wider environment. Thompson (1967: 5–6) stresses the closed system assumptions of these theorists. Speaking of Taylor's contributions, he says,

> Scientific management achieves conceptual closure of the organization by assuming that goals are known, tasks are repetitive, output of the production process somehow disappears, and resources in uniform qualities are available.

And of the work of Fayol, Gulick, and Urwick,

> Administrative management achieves closure by assuming that ultimately a master plan is known, against which specialization, departmentalization, and control are determined.

And of Weber's model of bureaucracy,

> Bureaucratic theory also employs the closed system of logic. Weber saw three holes through which empirical reality might penetrate the logic, but in outlining his "pure type" he quickly plugged these holes. Policymakers, somewhere above the bureaucracy, could alter the goals, but the implications of this are set aside. Human components—the expert officeholders—might be more complicated than the model describes, but bureaucratic theory handles this by divorcing the individual's private life from his life as an officeholder through the use of rules, salary, and career. Finally, bureaucratic theory takes note of outsiders—clientele—but nullifies their effects by depersonalizing and categorizing clients.

TABLE 5–1   Dominant Theoretical Models and Representative Theorists for Four Time Periods and Three Levels of Analysis

LEVELS OF ANALYSIS	CLOSED SYSTEM MODELS		OPEN SYSTEM MODELS	
	1900–1930 Rational Models Type I	1930–1960 Natural Models Type II	1960–1970 Rational Models Type III	1970– Natural Models Type IV
SOCIAL PSYCHOLOGICAL	Scientific Management Taylor (1911) Decision Making Simon (1945)	Human Relations Roy (1952) Whyte (1959)	Bounded Rationality March & Simon (1958)	Organizing Weick (1969) Negotiated Order Strauss et al. (1963) Ambiguity and Choice March and Olsen (1976)

STRUCTURAL	Bureaucratic Theory Weber (1904–5) Administrative Theory Fayol (1919)	Cooperative Systems Barnard (1938) Human Relations Mayo (1945) Dalton (1959)	Contingency Theory Lawrence & Lorsch (1967) Comparative Structure Udy (1959) Blau (1970) Pugh et al. (1969)	Socio-technical Systems Miller & Rice (1967) Strategic Contingencies Hickson et al. (1971) Pfeffer (1978)
ECOLOGICAL			Transactions Costs Williamson (1975) Ouchi (1980)	Population Ecology Hannan & Freeman (1977) Aldrich (1979) Resource Dependence Pfeffer and Salancik (1978) Marxist Theory Braverman (1974) Edwards (1979) Institutionalist Theory Selznick (1949) Meyer & Rowan (1977) DiMaggio & Powell (1983)

Thus, in all of these models, the variety and uncertainty associated with an organization's openness to its environment is stifled, curtailed, or denied.

Type II: Closed Natural System Models

Our prime candidates for natural system theorists working predominantly with a closed system conception are the human relations theorists. As described in Chapter 3, this conception originated with the empirical research of Roethlisberger and Dickson (1939) and the theoretical work of Mayo (1945) but expanded throughout the 1940s and 1950s to encompass a great deal of the sociological research on organizations (for example, Whyte, 1946; Whyte, 1948; Katz et al., 1951; Roy, 1952; Dalton, 1959). Although this work caused our view of organizational structure to become more complex and flexible, as diffuse and conflicting goals were recognized and participants were endowed with multiple interests and motives, most of the work within this tradition restricted attention to the inside of the organization. We learn a great deal about the emergence of informal structures—interpersonal systems of power, status, communication, and friendship—and their impact on formal systems, but whether the concern was with formal or informal systems or the relations between them, the focus was primarily on the organization's internal arrangements.

This criticism does not, however, apply to Selznick's (1948) institutional model or to Parsons's (1960) social system model, which we reviewed in Chapter 3. As noted, Selznick's view of the environment is a rather jaundiced one, whereas Parsons's is more balanced, but both of these versions of natural systems models represent more open system conceptions and, hence, are important precursors to type IV models.

Type III: Open Rational System Models

Beginning in the late 1950s and continuing to the present, a new generation of theories have again focused on the organization as a rational system, but with a difference: now the organization is also viewed as an open system. An important figure in this transformation was Simon, whose major early contributions have already been described. His more recent work with March illustrates the joining of rational and open systems concerns at the social psychological level of analysis. The contingency theorists, whose work we discussed to illustrate open system approaches, also combine rational with open system concerns. We briefly review this work before describing two other types of theories combining these perspectives. Indeed, all of the discussions will be brief since the intent here is merely to introduce important contemporary theories that will be considered at length in Parts Three and Four.

Bounded rationality revisited   Important changes are apparent in Simon's view of administrative behavior as developed with March in the late 1950s (March and Simon, 1958, especially chaps. 6 and 7). While there is still a concern with the cognitive limits of individual decision makers and with how structures can help to support improved decisions, there is more recognition of the variable nature of the challenges posed by tasks and environments. The organization is viewed as more open to its environment. March and Simon identify "performance programs" that guide the decisions of individuals, but whereas some of these programs can be routinized others must be problem-solving responses, requiring the decision maker to exercise more discretion in the face of greater uncertainty (p. 139). Moreover, it is recognized that some organizations face such volatile environments that they must institutionalize innovation, devising programs for "routinely" changing existing performance programs, often rapidly (p. 186).

March and Simon suggest a number of additional ways in which decision making is simplified within organizations. Organizations encourage participants to "satisfice"—to settle for acceptable as opposed to optimal solutions, to attend to problems sequentially rather than simultaneously, and to utilize existing repertories of performance programs whenever possible rather than developing novel responses for each situaiton. There is a stronger sense in this later work that organizations face environments of varying complexity, that they must adjust their internal decision-making apparatus to take these variations into account, and that some environments pose levels of complexity that organizations cannot manage unless they impose simplifying restrictions on the information processed.

Contingency theory reviewed   We have already described the central ideas of contingency theory as introduced by Lawrence and Lorsch (1967). Their realization that organizations—indeed, divisions within organizations—confront varying environments that pose differing challenges for them is a clear recognition of the open system character of organizations. Their further assumption that organizations will, or should in the interests of effectiveness, adapt their structures to these environmental requirements incorporates the rational system argument.

The combination of open and rational system assumptions also figures strongly in Thompson's (1967) approach. Thompson was among the first organization theorists to recognize the importance of the environment for the structure and performance of organizations, and, as noted, he argued that different locations or levels within structures were differentially open to environmental influences. More so than most theorists, Thompson is quite explicit about the rationalist assumptions that undergird his approach. He prefaces virtually all of his empirical predictions with the phrase "Under norms of rationality, organizations seek to . . ."

Thus, the problem that Thompson and the contingency theorists set for themselves may be stated like this: Given that an organization is open to the uncertainties of its environment, how can it function as a rational system? As hinted at in our review of Thompson's levels model, his principal answer to this question is this: It can do so by creating some closed system compartments in critical parts of its structure. How this is done, by what sealing mechanisms and buffering strategies, will be described in detail in Chapter 8. For now, we simply note the juxtaposition of rational and open systems perspectives that underlie this form of analysis.

Comparative structural analysis   Parallel to but somewhat distinct from the efforts of systems design and contingency theorists is the work conducted during the same period by analysts attempting to account for variations in organization structures. Whereas the efforts of the former group tend to be more qualitative and prescriptive, the work of the latter is more quantitative and descriptive. Among the leading figures in comparative structural analysis are Udy (1959*b*), Woodward (1965), Pugh and associates (1969), and Blau (1970) and his colleagues. These were the first analysts to collect systematic data on large samples of organizations rather than on individual participants or organizational subunits. In this work, formal structure is viewed as the dependent variable, its characteristics to be measured and explained. A large variety of explanatory (independent) variables have been examined—with most attention concentrated on size, technology, and uncertainty—but most studies have focused on characteristics of the environment in which the organization is located. In short, organizations are viewed as open systems.

At the same time, organizations are presumed to design their structures rationally. An assumption underlying most of these studies is that organizations are striving to develop effective and efficient structures. Environmental demand and organizational response are mediated by designers or managers who are concerned with cutting cost, developing adequate arrangements to cope with environmental complexity, and creating coordinative mechanisms to manage the requirements of information processing. These are the assumptions of a rational system model, and they dominate much of the empirical and theoretical work on organizations during the 1960s. The findings of these theorists are reviewed in Chapter 10.

Transactions costs analysis   An important new perspective combining open and rational systems assumptions was introduced in the mid 1970s by Oliver Williamson (1975; 1981). Based on the work of earlier institutional economists (such as Commons, 1924; Coase, 1937), Williamson has proposed that analysts focus on the costs of entering into transactions—exchanges of goods or services between persons or across boundaries of any sort.

> With a well-working interface, as with a well-working machine, these transfers occur smoothly. In mechanical systems we look for frictions: do the gears mesh, are the parts lubricated, is there needless slippage or other loss of energy? The economic counterpart of friction is transaction cost: do the parties to the exchange operate harmoniously, or are there frequent misunderstandings and conflicts that lead to delays, breakdowns, and other malfunctions? (Williamson, 1981: 552)

To focus on transactions rather than on commodities or services is to shift attention away from technical production concerns to governance structures. For individuals to be willing to enter into exchanges, they must feel certain that their interests are safeguarded. Simple economic transactions that take place "on the spot" as one good or service is exchanged for another of equal value pose no problems and can be safely conducted in the free marketplace. However, as exchanges become more complex and uncertain—because the environment is not stable or predictable and because others cannot always be trusted to abide by the terms of the agreement—various kinds of external controls and supports must be devised to aid the exchanges—that is, to reduce the transactions costs. Organizational structures are viewed as one important arrangement for establishing and safeguarding transactions.

Williamson and his colleagues argue not only that organizations develop in order to reduce transactions costs, but that organizational forms may be expected to vary with the types of exchanges to be governed. We reserve for Chapter 7 a fuller description of this approach to explaining organizations and their structural variety. Here we merely underscore yet another approach that assumes that organizations are both open—responding to the differential demands of their environments—and rational—doing so in such a manner as to economize on the costs of engaging in transactions.

Type IV: Open Natural System Models

It appears that we are currently in the midst of a major shift in the types of theoretical models that guide our investigations of the structure and operation of organizations. The open rational models that have dominated theory and research since the early 1960s are being challenged by a wide variety of approaches stressing the open but natural character of organizations. The open rational models have not been replaced but they are being joined—and at least for the time being, outnumbered—by open natural approaches. These new models place great emphasis on the importance of the environment in determining the structure, behavior, and life chances of organizations: they are clearly open system models. The assumption that organizations behave as rational systems is strongly challenged in this work. In this section, we will do no more than provide a quick sketch of the more important of these new models. We will begin with a review of Weick's model and then introducing two others developed at the social psychological level, continue with two located at the structural level, and end with several oriented to the ecological level.

Weick's social organizing again Just as it was necessary, armed with our more complex schema, to reclassify contingency theories as not only open but also rational, so it is necessary to re-view Weick's model as combining open with natural systems assumptions. As noted in Chapter 4, Weick gives great attention to the cognitive processes entailed in creating and sustaining organizations, but his view of these processes, unlike those of Simon, for example, is that they operate in an evolutionary fashion: they involve trial and error, chance, superstitious learning, and retrospective sense-making. Also, Weick rejects the notion that evolution necessarily entails improvements in the surviving forms. He points out that successful interlocking of behaviors (that is, organized patterns of action) "can occur without any necessary increase in the productivity or viability of the system" (1979: 179) and insists that we must "free ourselves from the notion that selection is for environmental advantage" (p. 127). In these and many other respects, Weick's model is that of a natural, not a rational, system. And, he combines it with his open system perspective already described to create a view that is both open and natural.

Negotiated order   Continuing the tradition begun by the human relations group, a number of more recent social psychologists have emphasized the extent to which social structure—including organizational structure—grows out of interaction processes among participants. What distinguishes some of the more recent contributions is the joining of these earlier natural system interests with an open system model. This connection is developed only haltingly and gradually and is still not firmly established, but its outlines are becoming clear.

Their roots stemming from both Weber (1947 trans.), with his concern that social action can be understood only by taking into account its meaning for those involved, and from the social philosopher George Herbert Mead (1934), who insisted that meanings arise only in the process of social interaction, a large and varied number of researchers have focused minutely on how meanings are created and maintained in organizational settings. This work has been carried on by analysts in the U.S. working in the "symbolic interaction" tradition (for example, Roy, 1952; Goffman, 1961) and by those in England who have been developing an "action approach" to the analysis of ongoing organization (such as, Silverman, 1971; Salaman and Thompson, 1980). In these accounts, such structural features as roles and rules dissolve into a much more fragile set of understandings, misunderstandings, negotiations, and gambits as individual actors struggle for control and meaning.

Especially in the work of Strauss and colleagues (Bucher and Strauss, 1961; Strauss et al., 1963), however, these negotiations are seen as transcending the boundaries of organizations. In their work on medical organizations, for example, these analysts examine the negotiations occurring both among the various segments of the medical profession—such as surgeons and internists—as well as between the profession and other societal groups in order to demonstrate that the division of labor and the control structures within this profession are subject to continuing change and negotiation. Moreover, the results of these wider contests help to shape and constrain the negotiation of order within specific organizational units such as hospitals.

A related approach is suggested by Goffman's (1974) concept of *frames*—a set of background rules that actors impose on specific situations in order to define their meaning and suggest what kinds of interaction are appropriate. (See Gonos, 1977). "Playing a game," "dining," "going to the movies"—all are examples of well-known frames that we impose on everyday situations. As Goffman (1974: 1–2) notes,

> presumably, a "definition of the situation" is almost always to be found, but those who are in the situation ordinarily do not *create* this definition, even though their society can be said to do so; ordinarily, all they do is to assess correctly what the situation ought to be for them and act accordingly.

In short, students concerned with capturing "the rich texture of everyday social life" (Gonos, 1977: 856) that is to be found in great variety within organizations and that has long been of interest to natural system theorists, increasingly recognize that these interactions are framed by meanings and structures external to these situations and organizations.

This concern with negotiated order bears a close relation at the micro (social psychological) level to the work conducted by ethnomethodologists such as Garfinkel (1967), and at the macro (ecological) level to the interests of the institutional theorists discussed later in this section.[5]

Choice under ambiguity   James March collaborated with Simon in the work that pushed decision theory toward incorporating more of the concerns of open system analysts, as we have noted. (See March and Simon, 1958). In the years since, March and a number of associates have continued to challenge one after another of the simplifying assumptions associated with the rational system model. At the level of the individual decision maker, March agrees with Weick that actions often precede rather than follow goals, that our preferences are neither very precise nor stable, and that they often need to be discovered. Indeed, one of the more important kinds of learning that occurs is that which changes our ideas about what it is we want. (See March, 1978). Another important feature of many decision situations is that the decision process is often more important than the outcome. "Decision making is, in part, a performance designed to reassure decision makers and others that things are being done appropriately" (March, 1981: 232). Further, many decision situations are fraught with ambiguity. We act and, at least sometimes, elicit a response from the environment, but whether the response is to our actions or completely independent of them is often difficult to determine. Thus, our "learning" is often superstitious.

More important for our purposes than these modifications of the model of individual decision making, however, are March's ideas about decision making in organizations. Thus, March early set aside the assumption of a single or unified decision maker, developing instead the concept of a loose and shifting "coalition" that selects organizational goals (Cyert and March, 1963). The implications of this change are quite profound:

> As long as we assume that organizations have goals and that those goals have some classical properties of stability, precision and consistency, we can treat an organization as some kind of rational actor. But organizations do not have simple, consistent preference functions. They exhibit internal conflict over preferences. Once such conflict is noted, it is natural to shift from a metaphor of problem solving to a more political vision. (March, 1981: 215)

Processes of exchange, of combat, and of compromise and alliance supplant images of a hierarchy of goals or of means-ends chains linking participants throughout the organization. And decision outcomes are seen to be strongly influenced by their contexts as it becomes important to know how the decision has been defined, who is participating, what interests—both problems and solutions—are brought to the occasion, and by what "rules" individual choices are aggregated to produce an organizational decision. (See March and Olsen, 1976.)

We shift now to the structural level of analysis, briefly describing two approaches that emphasize the open natural system perspective.

---

[5]Ethnomethodologists place primary emphasis on how people "go about the task of seeing, describing and explaining order in the world in which they live" (Zimmerman and Wieder, 1970: 289). Differences in focus and approach distinguishing ethnomethodological and symbolic interaction are reviewed in Maines (1977) and in Burrell and Morgan (1979).

Socio-technical systems   At the end of World War II, the Tavistock
Clinic, a voluntary outpatient center for psychotherapy in England, reconstituted itself as the Tavistock Institute of Human Relations. Influenced by the human relations research in the U.S., the Tavistock team of
researchers began to conduct a series of studies in differing work organizations on ways to improve productivity and morale. From the beginning,
the preferred approach was one of "action" research, the investigators
working with management and labor to introduce change into a work
setting and then attempting to learn from its results (Jaques, 1951). In
addition to this somewhat distinctive research style, the group also developed a rather particular problem focus. They proposed that the distinguishing feature of organizations is that they are both social and technical
systems: "Their core interface consists of the relation between a nonhu-
man system and a human system" (Trist, 1981: 25).

Rather than insisting that individual and social units must conform
to technical requirements, the socio-technical system approach emphasizes
that the needs of both should be served. Rather than obtaining the best
"match" between technical and social components, the goal should be one
of the "joint optimization" of the needs of both, since the two systems
follow different "laws" and their relationship represents a "coupling of
dissimilars" (Emery, 1959). The "grain of the fifties" was the celebration
of top-down, manager-controlled, technical bureaucracies, but the Tavistock group attempted to go against this grain by designing systems that
emphasized discretionary behavior, internalized regulation, and work-
group autonomy (Trist, 1981).

Although their early empirical efforts were concentrated at the individual and work-group level, the Tavistock researchers discovered that
changes made at these levels did not long survive unless there were compatible changes in larger structures. Further they became increasingly
aware that the organizations themselves were open to the wider environment. As Trist (1981: 50) recalls,

> In our action research projects at that time, we and our organizational
> clients were baffled by the extent to which the wider societal environment
> was moving in on their more immediate concerns, upsetting plans, prevent-
> ing the achievement of operational goals, and causing additional stress and
> severe internal conflict.

In addition to developing a widely influential typology of organizational
environments and speculating on their effects on organizational forms
(see Emery and Trist, 1965), to be described in the next chapter, the
research group attempted to discover ways in which the larger enterprise
is shaped by its needs to survive in a specific social and economic environment. (See Rice, 1958; Miller and Rice, 1967.) The most resilient building
blocks available to organizations as they respond to these demands are the
sets of semiautonomous groups, capable of self-regulation as cybernetic
systems, and the larger networks of groups organized into "primary work
systems," that are functionally interdependent. Interest in the creation of
these units is a common thread throughout many specific studies describing the history of change attempts in particular industrial settings, and it
is this emphasis that locates the perspective at the structural level of analysis. Throughout their work, the Tavistock group has remained strongly

committed to creating organizational forms that serve the values of human community as well as the interests of technical efficiency.[6]

Strategic contingency This approach starts from the same set of assumptions that guide the contingency theorists, such as Lawrence and Lorsch and Thompson, but by introducing a intermediate, strategic process, it arrives at a very different explanation for the structural features of organizations.

Following contingency theory, the strategic approach assumes organizations to be open systems that confront and respond to variable challenges and opportunities in their environment. Different parts of the environment pose varying challenges, and it is argued that organizations become structurally differentiated—develop specialized subunits—in order to better respond. Up to this point, the arguments are parallel. However, the strategic version, unlike the rational approach, emphasizes that participants in organizations vary in their interests: organizations are coalitions, not monolithic actors. Workers in the production unit may prefer longer, stable runs while the sales units insist on more customized products. Further, organizational subunits differ not only in their interests but in their power.

Power has many sources, but the strategic contingency approach emphasizes that a primary source is the uncertainty posed by the environment. Following Crozier's (1964) observation that mechanics in tobacco manufacturing plants were unexpectedly powerful because they confronted one of the few sources of uncertainty in the plant—machine breakdown—Hickson and colleagues (1971) argued more generally that subgroups in organizations obtain power vis-à-vis one another depending on the amount and significance of the uncertainty to which they relate—and on the extent of their success in coping with it and thereby reducing uncertainty for their co-workers. Those able to control—successfully cope with—more, and more important, strategic contingencies garner power within the organization.

The larger implication of this argument is that "organizational structures are the outcomes of political contests within organizations" (Pfeffer, 1978: 38). Different groups of participants come together, and because some are able to make greater contributions to the stability and survival of the organization than others, these advantaged groups achieve power. And power is not only the outcome but also a determinant in later contests, providing "participants further advantages in the political struggle because of their structural position" (Pfeffer, 1981: 266).

Thus, strategic contingency theorists such as Hickson and Pfeffer have proposed a framework for the political explanation of organizational structure. In Chapter 9 we will consider in more detail this important alternative to the rational system "efficiency" arguments.

Finally, four quite different approaches to analyzing organizations have developed at the ecological level of analysis.

---

[6]This general approach to the "design" of natural systems has been more influential and more often emulated in Europe than in the U.S. Related research has been carried on, for example, by Thorsrud in Norway and Sweden (Emery and Thorsrud, 1969; 1976). In the U.S., some socio-technical themes are to be found in research on the quality of working life (see O'Toole, 1972), and socio-technical action research strategies have been adopted by the organizational development (OD) group.

Population ecology   The population ecology or natural selection model of organizations originated in biology with the work of Darwin. Although the application of these ideas to social systems has a long and
checkered history (see Hofstadter, 1945), more recent and promising efforts have been stimulated by the work of Hawley (1950) and Campbell
(1969). Applications of these general ideas to organizations by Hannan
and Freeman (1977) and by Aldrich (1979) have led to a rapidly growing
body of research and theory.

The population ecology model differs from other approaches to
organizations in that it applies primarily to *populations* of organizations
rather than to individual units.[7] It is designed to explain why certain
forms or types (or species) of organizations survive and multiply whereas
other types languish and die. For example, the model might be employed
to examine the decline of teacher's colleges and the growth in the numbers of general colleges over recent decades in the U.S.

It is central to the natural selection thesis that environments differentially select organizations for survival on the basis of fit between organizational forms and environmental characteristics. Three processes
are emphasized in evolutionary analysis: the creation of variety, the selection of some forms over others, and the retention of those forms
(Campbell, 1969). In the first stage, variety is created by some process,
planned or unplanned. In the second, a process occurs by which some
forms of organization are differentially selected for survival. And in
stage three, the selected forms are preserved in some fashion, by repro-
duction or duplication. Positively selected variations survive and reproduce similar others, which then form the starting point for a new round
of selection as mutants appear (Aldrich and Pfeffer, 1976). Emphasis is
placed on *selection* as the prime process by which change occurs in organizations. Hannan and Freeman (1977) have given primary attention to
organizational morality as the major force driving natural selection, but
as Carroll (1984: 75) points out, natural selection is also determined by
birth rates. That is, "population ecology predicts net mortality (deaths
over births)."

This approach has created much interest among students of organizations. This is partly because it employs a well-known and highly regarded intellectual framework and has been able to adapt for use quite
sophisticated concepts and measures from the work of population biolo-
gists. Also, by emphasizing the population level of analysis, it has focused
on a new set of issues largely ignored by earlier theorists.

This conception is firmly grounded in an open system model: the
importance of the environment can hardly be more strongly underlined
than in the population ecology framework. The conception is also clearly
a natural system approach. The bottom line is survival. And although
based on an evolutionary framework, in its contemporary usage, "evolution is no longer equated with progress, but simply with change over
time" (Carroll, 1984: 72). The ability to perpetuate one's form is the
hallmark of successful adaptation.

---

[7]Carroll (1984) argues that the underlying evolutionary arguments can be applied to
individual organizations and to organizational communities as well as to populations of
organizations. (See also, Aldrich, 1979) We discuss these other applications in Chapter 8.

Resource dependency   Whereas the population ecology approach stresses selection—attributing observed patterns in the distribution of organizational forms to the action of environmental selection, both in terms of what kinds of organizations are created and which survive—the resource dependence model emphasizes *adaptation.* It is assumed that individual organizations can act to improve their chances of survival.

The resource dependency approach shares many features with the strategic contingency perspective, but has as its primary focus the organization itself—its behavior and its relations with other organizations—rather than its component units. The approach has been developed by a number of investigators and has received a variety of labels. Zald and his colleagues refer to their version as a political economy model (Zald, 1970; Wamsley and Zald, 1973). Thompson (1967), some of whose work employs this model, describes the approach as an exchange, or as a power-dependency model. The most comprehensive development to date of the resource dependence approach is found in the work of Pfeffer and Salancik (1978).

This perspective is strongly rooted in an open system framework: it is argued that one cannot understand the structure or behavior of an organization without understanding the context within which it operates. No organization is self-sufficient; all must engage in exchanges with the environment as a condition of their survival. The need to acquire resources creates dependences between organizations and outside units. How important and how scarce these resources are determine the nature and the extent of organizational dependency. Dependency is the obverse of power. (Emerson, 1962) Economic dependencies give rise to political problems and may succumb to political solutions.

Much more so than in the population ecology approach, organizations are viewed as active, not passive, in determining their own fate. Organizational participants, particularly managers, scan the relevant environment, searching for opportunities and threats, attempting to strike favorable bargains and to avoid costly entanglements. All organizations are dependent on suppliers of inputs and consumers of outputs, but which specific suppliers and consumers are selected as exchange partners and what the terms of exchange are are partly determined by the organization itself. Astute managers are those who not only acquire the necessary resources but do so without creating crippling dependencies. Thus, the resource dependence model views organizations as

> capable of changing, as well as responding to, the environment. Administrators manage their environments as well as their organizations, and the former activity may be as important, or even more important, than the latter. (Aldrich and Pfeffer, 1976: 83)

One of the major contributions of the resource dependency perspective is to discern and describe the strategies—ranging from buffering to diversification and merger—employed by organizations to change and adapt to the environment. We review these strategies in Chapter 8.

Marxist theory   Of the influence of the two giants of German, or rather, European social thought, that of Max Weber was apparent from the beginning—indeed, constituted the beginning. The effect of the second, Karl Marx, though widely felt in many areas of inquiry, did not seriously begin to make waves in work on organizations until the 1970s. That decade witnessed a resurgence of interest in Marxist approaches among social scientists in the U.S. (see Burawoy, 1982), although European scholars had long been strongly influenced by this tradition. There is a tortuous trail of social thought leading from Marx's later writings (e.g., 1954 trans.: 1973 trans.) through the contributions of Lukacs (1971 trans.) and Gramsci (1971 trans.) to the contemporary work of Habermas (1971 trans.) and Althusser (1969 trans.).[8] We relate only the more recent developments of particular relevance to organizations.

Consistent with the origins of the natural system perspective, the Marxist approach began essentially as a critique of the dominant rationalist views, and of the earlier natural system models as well, particularly those developed by Barnard and the human relations school. Marxists argue that organizational structures are not rational systems for performing work in the most efficient manner; they are power systems designed to maximize control and profits more than they are technical systems designed to insure effectiveness. Work is divided and subdivided not to improve efficiency but to "deskill" workers, to displace discretion from workers to managers, and to create artificial divisions among the work force. (Braverman, 1974) Hierarchy develops not as a rational means of coordination but as an instrument of control and a means of accumulating capital through the appropriation of surplus value (Edwards, 1979; Marglin, 1974). Human relations and cooperative systems reforms are inadequate because they do not challenge the fundamental exploitative nature of organizations; indeed, they help to shore it up by assuming a congruence of goals and by providing managers with new psychological and social tools for controlling workers and with new arguments justifying this control (Bendix, 1956; Braverman, 1974).

To assume that organizations are rational instruments for the pursuit of goals ignores the question of whose goals are being served. It assumes that there is consensus rather than conflict over goals. From the Marxist perspective, rationality is an ideology—the use of ideas to legitimate existing arrangements and to deflect criticism of those with excessive power by depersonalizing the system of relations. (See Zey-Ferrell and Aiken, 1981.)

In addition to challenging these rational system assumptions,[9] the

---

[8]For a lucid review of the work of these and other theorists who link Marx's writings to contemporary Marxist approaches to organizations, see Burrell and Morgan (1979: 279–392). These two analysts distinguish the early writings of Marx, which inspired the more humanistic approaches of Lukacs, Gransci, Habermas, and others, from the more materialist later writings, which led to the work of Althusser, Dahrendorf, and Miliband. It is the latter emphasis that has stimulated the most interest among contemporary students of organizations.

[9]In his alternative schema for classifying theories of organization, Pfeffer (1982: 13, 162–70) categorizes Marxist theory as a "purposive" or "rational" approach to organizational analysis. This conclusion rests on Pfeffer's belief that to the extent that managers seek control and not efficiency, then the structures they design are effective means to these ends. Although this is a logically defensible position, we prefer to see Marxist approaches as more similar to natural system models with their emphasis on goal complexity conflict, hidden agendas and shifting interests, and more organic, historically shaped, evolutionary structures.

Marxist approach strongly eschews a closed system conception of organizations. Not only do Marxist theorists insist that organizations are strongly affected by their wider political and economic context, they vigorously urge organizational analysts to embrace a more historical perspective. As Benson (1982: 139) comments, Marxists call for "a contextualizing theory that locates observations within a comprehensive mapping of the social world and along an historical trajectory of social change."

Because of their sensitivity to the close interdependence of economic and political structures, Marxist theorists were among the first to call attention to the central role of the state in both public and private organizations (Burrell and Morgan, 1979: 371–77; Burawoy, 1982). Theorists such as Miliband (1969) and O'Connor (1973) emphasize the strong connections between the structure and functions of the modern state and those of the large corporations (the monopoly-capital sectors). These claims have prompted much disputation and have led to a flurry of empirical studies probing the relations between corporate elites and state structures. We review some of this work in Chapter 8.

With their strong emphasis on historical context, Marxist theorists have turned the attention of organizational theorists back to the more neglected aspects of Weber's legacy. As noted in Chapter 2, much of Weber's attention was devoted to describing the characteristics of prebureaucratic forms and the conditions giving rise to the new administrative systems. Marxists have newly underscored the value of a historical perspective for sociological analysis:

> By taking the particular experiences of capitalist society and shaping them into universal experiences, sociology becomes incapable of conceiving of a fundamentally different type of society in the future. . . . In order to conceive of, to anticipate, something "new," one must begin with different premises, which regard history as discontinuous and capitalist societies as fundamentally different from precapitalist and postcapitalist societies. (Burawoy, 1979; 13)

Finally, like the socio-technical school, Marxist theorists stress the importance of *praxis:* combining ideas and action (Benson, 1977). However, the Marxist conception is broader than the socio-technical version. Marxist theorists insist that investigators cannot choose whether to be involved with their subjects: they are inevitably involved. Theories grow out of existing social structures and either serve to "reproduce" them— legitimate and support them—or to transform them. Needless to say, Marxists view the great bulk of theory and research on organizations as, perhaps unconsciously but nevertheless effectively, serving to maintain existing organizational forms.

Institutional theory   The last group of ideas to be introduced, like Marxist theories, has developed quite rapidly during the 1970s and up to the present. While sharing the same label as Selznick's early work, discussed in Chapter 3, and having some features in common with it, contemporary versions of institutional theory are more directly related to work originating in the area of the sociology of knowledge. Based on philosophical underpinnings established by German idealists and phenomenologists such as Dilthey and Husserl, and strongly shaped by the work of Alfred Schutz (1962 trans.), most current efforts rest on the foundation built by sociologist Peter Berger.[10]

The most complete and influential statement of Berger's ideas on institutionalization is to be found in his work with Luckmann (Berger and Luckmann, 1967). They argue that social reality is a human construction, being created in social interaction. The process by which actions are repeated and given similar meaning by self and others is defined as *institutionalization*.

These ideas concerning the social construction of reality were first introduced into organizational analysis at the micro or social psychology level by researchers working in the symbolic interactionist and ethnomethodological traditions. Earlier in this chapter we reviewed the former as an attempt to negotiate social order. The latter may be viewed as an attempt to negotiate social reality:

> The ethnomethodologists are interested in the way in which actors make evident and persuade each other that the events and activities in which they are involved are coherent and consistent (Burrell and Morgan, 1979: 250).

In reviewing the empirical work of this group, one is struck by how much of it has been conducted within organizational settings (see, for example, Bittner, 1967; Cicourel, 1968; Zimmerman, 1970).[11]

At a more macro level, Berger and colleagues (Berger, Berger, and Kellner, 1973: 41–62) have argued that the very conception of bureaucracy is a meta-institution, which depicts in a generalized manner a portrait of orderliness, predictability, and, in its emphasis on formalization of relations, "moralized anonymity." Zucker (1983: 1) has pursued and elaborated this theme, arguing that "organizations are the preeminent institutional form in modern society."

Perhaps the most influential application of institutional ideas to the analysis of organizations is that of Meyer and Rowan (1977), who argue that modern societies contain many complexes of institutionalized rules and patterns—products of professional groups, the state, public opinion. These social realities provide a framework for the creation and elaboration of formal organizations. According to Meyer and Rowan, in modern societies, these institutions are likely to take the form of *rationalized myths*. They are *myths* because they are widely held beliefs that cannot be objectively tested: they are true because they are believed. They are *rationalized* because they take the form of rules specifying procedures necessary to accomplish a given end. Law provides a good example. How can property legitimately change hands? How can an organization become a corporation? Legal systems—as complexes of rationalized myths—provide solutions to such problems. Meyer and Rowan (1977: 343) argue that these institutional belief systems powerfully shape organizational forms:

---

[10]A useful summary of Berger's views will be found in Wuthnow et al. (1984: 21–76).

[11]Burrell and Morgan (1979: 225–78) provide a thorough review of the philosophical origins of the ethnomethodological approach as well as the more recent empirical applications to organizations.

Many of the positions, policies, programs, and procedures of modern organizations are enforced by public opinion, by the views of important constituents, by knowledge legitimated through the educational system, by social prestige, by the laws, and by the definitions of negligence and prudence used by the courts. Such elements of formal structure are manifestations of powerful institutional rules which function as highly rationalized myths that are binding on particular organizations.

Institutional theory emphasizes that organizations are open systems—strongly influenced by their environments—but that many of the most fateful forces are the result not of rational pressures for more effective performance but of social and cultural pressures to conform to conventional beliefs.

SUMMARY

The rational, natural, and open system perspectives for analyzing organizations provide contrasting paradigms. Because of the differing assumptions underlying these paradigms, one may replace another but cannot disprove it.

Nevertheless, several analysts have attempted to reconcile the three perspectives by combining them into more complex models of organizations. Etzioni suggests that the rational and natural system models are complementary, focusing on conflicting tendencies present in all organizations. Lawrence and Lorsch propose that all organizations are open systems, and that rational and natural forms emerge as varying adaptive structures in response to different environmental forces. And Thompson suggests that the three perspectives are differentially applicable to various levels of an organization's structure, the open system being most suited to analyzing the institutional level, the natural system applying best to the managerial level, and the rational system, to the technical level.

An alternative basis for combining the perspectives is to suggest that they have appeared in varying combinations over time and that they are applicable to differing levels of analysis. This framework suggests that the earliest models, dominant between 1900 and 1930, were closed rational system models. Some of these were developed at the social psychological level—for example, Taylor's scientific management approach—while others were advanced at the structural level—for instance, Weber's model of bureaucracy and Fayol's administrative theory. From the 1930s through the 1950s, a new set of perspectives developed that combined closed with natural system assumptions. Again, some of these approaches were developed primarily at the social psychological level—such as the human relations models of Roy and Katz—and others at the structural level—for example, Barnard's theory of cooperative systems and Mayo's version of human relations.

Beginning in the early 1960s, open system models largely replaced closed system assumptions, and analyses at the ecological level began to appear. At the same time, rational and natural system models persisted, providing competing theoretical explanations for organizational structure and behavior. During the 1960s, open rational system models were dominant, represented by the work of March and Simon at the social psychological level and by contingency theory and comparative analyses at the structural level. To these approaches was added, in the 1970s, the transactions costs framework. The open rational system models were joined and challenged by the open natural system models that became dominant in the 1970s and continue into the 1980s. These rapidly proliferating approaches range from the work of Weick and Strauss and March at the social psychological level, through the socio-technical and strategic contingencies models developed at the structural level, to the population ecology, resource dependence, Marxist, and institutional theories at the ecological level.

Our classification emphasizes the historical evolution of organization theory. The types of theories guiding work today differ from those in use ten or forty years ago. A question to be pondered is why this is the case. Does it represent changes in the nature of organizations or changes in the interest of theorists or both?

A great many new and competing theories concerning organizations now occupy the landscape. We have reviewed some of the most influential of these, and will consider them in more detail in later chapters.[12]

---

[12]See Burrell and Morgan (1979) and Pfeffer (1982) for alternative schemas for classifying organization theories; and see Scott (1986) for a discussion and comparison of the three systems.

ENVIRONMENTS, STRATEGIES, AND STRUCTURES

PART THREE

Three general perspectives on the nature of organizations have been described, along with several attempts to combine or integrate them. If these perspectives are as useful as we have claimed, they will enable us not simply to comprehend past efforts to dissect organizations but to better fathom current work and perhaps even to discern future analytic directions.

Part Three combines topics that are often separated in contemporary treatments of organizations. It deals both with the ways in which organizations relate to their environments as well as with the determinants of organizational structure. With the help of the open systems perspective, we see these topics as inseparable: how an organization relates to its environment—indeed, what its environment is—is generally influenced by the organization's structural features, and the characteristics of the organization's structure are strongly affected by the organization's environment. External forces shape internal arrangements, and vice versa.

We learn from the open systems perspective that organizations are not fortresses, impervious to the buffeting or the blessing of their environments. On the other hand, we learn from the rational and natural system perspectives that organizations are not wind tunnels, completely open and responsive to every perturbation of their context. Organizations construct and reconstruct boundaries across which they relate to the outside world. Between the organization and those outside there is not one barrier but many, and for most kinds of organizatons these barriers become higher and more impenetrable as we come closer to the organization's technical core.

Part Three begins with an examination of organizational environments. Having been persuaded that the open system perspective is critically important, we attempt to distinguish among various levels at which environments may be analyzed and to differentiate their technical from their institutional elements. The multiple ways in which organizations interact with their environments are stressed in Chapter 6.

Chapter 7 addresses the fundamental but difficult questions of why organizations exist and how they are created. These questions are pursued from both a historical and a comparative perspective. Rational system explanations stressing efficiency and reduction in transactions costs are contrasted with natural system accounts emphasizing power and conformity to external rules.

118

Organizations must both distinguish their systems from and connect themselves with their environment. Boundary-defining mechanisms as well as the strategies used by organizations to buffer their technical core and to build bridges to other organizations—both competitors and exchange partners—are examined in Chapter 8. Connections to both technical and institutional environments are considered.

Chapters 9 and 10 describe sources of structural complexity, Chapter 9 focusing on complexity within the technical core and Chapter 10 examining influences on the form of the pheripheral sectors: the wider, encompassing structures. Characteristics of the type of work being performed—the technology—and of the technical and institutional environment pose opportunities and challenges to which organizations respond. These responses have significant consequences for the structure of the organization. The extent to which organizations change by adaptation—the modification of an existing organization—or by selection—the elimination of one form of organization and the generation of new forms—is currently under debate.

Environmental factors are also argued, in Chapter 11, to be critical in determining the size and composition of the dominant coalition: that set of an organization's participants who have sufficient power to set the goals to be pursued by the organization.

Environments shape organizations, but organizations also shape environments. Organizations in part choose which environments to enter and to exit, and they seek, individually and in coalition with others, to influence the contexts within which they function. Organizations relate strategically to environments.

In all of these ways, we challenge the sharp dichotomy between inside and outside, between organization and environment. The structures and processes of organizations and environments penetrate one another in interesting and unexpected ways that are revealed when we combine the open system perspective with the rational and natural system viewpoints.

6 conceptions of environments

For a given system, the environment is the set of all objects a change in whose attributes affect the system and also those objects whose attributes are changed by the behavior of the system.

The statement above invites the natural question of when an object belongs to a system and when it belongs to the environment; for if an object reacts with a system in the way described above should it not be considered a part of the system? The answer is by no means definite. In a sense, a system together with its environment makes up the universe of all things of interest in a given context. Subdivision of this universe into two sets, system and environment, can be done in many ways which are in fact quite arbitrary. Ultimately it depends on the intentions of the one who is studying the particular universe as to which of the possible configurations of objects is to be taken as the system.

A. D. Hall and R. E. Fagen, (1956)

Since the emergence and increasing prominence of open systems models, investigators are no longer able to comfortably ignore the effects of environments on organizations. To examine these causal connections, it is necessary to develop some working conceptions of environments themselves: ideas as to how to circumscribe them and how to identify and assess their relevant features. This chapter describes the major conceptions that have arisen and that currently guide investigations in this area.

THE ANALYSIS OF ENVIRONMENTS

Levels of Environments

A basic source of variation among conceptions of environments stems from the level of analysis selected. In Chapter 1 we identified the social psychological, structural, and ecological levels, and we have made ample use of these distinctions in our examination of various theories of organizations. Since our current concern is with conceptions of organizational environments—the ecological level—all of the analyses to be developed in this chapter are within this level.[1] It is helpful to identify four sublevels within the ecological level.

Organizational sets   The first level of analysis is that of the organization *set* (see Blau and Scott, 1962: 195–99; Evan, 1966). Both Blau and I and Evan acknowledge that the concept of organization set was developed by analogy from Merton's (1957: 368–80) concept of role-set. Merton noted that a single social position such as "mother" is associated with not one but a cluster of different roles depending on the identity of the counterpositions. Thus, a mother has a number of specific role obligations toward her children; other obligations toward the father; still other obligations toward the child's teachers; and so on. Similarly, a given organization participates in a variety of relations depending on the identity of its specific partners. For example, a small grocery store will relate in one manner with its suppliers, another with its customers, yet another with its neighbors, and so on. The fundamental idea is a simple one, but its implications are quite rich. One is led to ask questions about the relative size of the organization set, the extent to which one group of role partners is aware of the demands made by another, the extent to which expectations held by partners coincide, and so on.

One of the more useful concepts to emerge at the analytical level of the organization set is that of organizational *domain* (Levine and White, 1961; Thompson, 1967). An organization's domain consists of the claims it makes with respect to products or services provided and populations served. These claims immediately relate it to a number of other organizations—suppliers, customers, competitors—that affect its behavior and outcomes. An important consideration for any organization is the degree of consensus among members of its set regarding its proper domain.

A crucial, defining characteristic of the concept of organization set is that it views the environment from the standpoint of a specific (*focal*) organization. Relations or connections between other (*counter*) members of the set are of no concern unless they affect the activities or interests of the focal organization. Analysts employing the resource dependence approach, as described in Chapter 5, typically work at the level of the organization set. It is from this level that the interests, the resources, the dependencies of a given organization are best examined and its survival tactics probed. It is also at this level that most discussions of strategic decision making occur (Porter, 1980). Indeed, the great majority of studies of organization-environment connections have been conducted at the organization-set level of analysis.

While the organization-set level of analysis has proved extremely

---

[1]This does not mean the other levels of analysis are not relevant to examining the relation between organizations and environments. Thus, when boundary roles are considered (see Chapter 8) the level of analysis often employed is the social psychological, and when organizational strategies and structural modifications are examined as modes of organizational adaptation to environments (see Chapters 9 and 10), the level of analysis is the structural. The concern at this point, however, is to determine variations in the way in which environments of organizations are circumscribed. In this sense, the four approaches we consider here are at the ecological level.

useful in directing attention to the impact of information and resource flows and relations on a select organization, it does so at the expense of detracting attention from the nature of the larger system of relations in which the focal organization is but one prarticipant among many.

Organizational populations   A second level identified by analysts is that of the *population* of organizations. This concept is used to identify aggregates of organizations that are alike in some respects—for example, institutions of higher education or newspapers. This is the level at which most natural selection theories have been applied, such as the population ecology model, introduced in Chapter 5.

Those concerned with studying populations have had to wrestle with the question of what it means to be "alike in some respects." How are populations identified? When one studies "colleges," for example, what organizations are included—private as well as public schools? Universities? Community or junior colleges? Technical institutes? Organizational ecologists borrow or adapt biological language and ideas in working on this problem. Hannan and Freeman (1977: 935) remind us that biologic species are defined in terms of genetic structure and propose that the appropriate analogue for organizations might be to define them in terms of their "blueprint for organizational action, for transforming inputs into outputs." McKelvey (1982) adopts a similar stance, suggesting that all organizations in the same population contain "elements of dominant competence," or *comps,* drawn from the same *compool,* or collection of elements. By *dominant competence* McKelvey means essentially the technical core of the organization—that is, the activities—both technical and managerial, that transform "inputs into those outputs critical to a population's survival" (p. 174). Both of these definition of the boundaries of populations are conceptually clear, but neither is easy to apply. Blueprints and comps are hard to measure.

Population ecologists do not agree on the value of devising general classifications of organizations.[2] Some, such as McKelvey and Aldrich (1983: 125), argue that they are of great value:

> A theoretically grounded empirical taxonomy would provide a conceptual framework for describing and understanding the diversity of organizational populations, and would identify populations useful for research of other substantive concerns about organizations.

McKelvey and Aldrich also note that a classification would help prevent overly enthusiastic researchers from recklessly generalizing their findings in one class of organization to classes they have not yet studied. But other ecologists, such as Hannan and Freeman, suggest that a more fruitful approach is to allow the defining criteria to change depending on the analyst's focus. For some studies, universities and research institutes would be considered members of the same population while colleges would be excluded. For other purposes, universities and colleges would be regarded as similar and research institutes excluded. Up to now, most

---

[2]For an extended discussion of typologies of organizations, their uses and limitations, see the first edition of this text. (Scott, 1981: 27–54)

of the empirical studies of organizational populations have relied on fairly common sense definitions of the population and have employed geographical criteria for bounding it. For example, Freeman and Brittain (1977) have studied mergers among national labor unions in the U.S., and Carroll and Delacroix (1982) have studied mortality rates of Irish and Argentine newspapers.

In a population ecology approach, primary attention is given to the analysis of competing forms, to varying strategies of competition, and to the selective effects of changes in environments. Although this level of analysis clearly identifies an important set of questions and has attracted great interest, its emphases direct attention away from connections among organizations, in particular those organizations whose relations are more symbiotic and cooperative than commensalistic and competitive. To examine these connections, we need other models that perhaps change not so much the level as the focus of analysis.

Areal organization fields   This level of analysis is employed when the investigator focuses on the relations among a collection of organizations (and perhaps other types of social units) within a geographical area. Also labeled the *ecological community* model (Hawley, 1950), the *interorganizational field* model (Warren, 1967), and the *collective-action* model (Astley and Van de Ven, 1983), this approach emphasizes not the individual organizational units or even their characteristics as an aggregate, but rather the network of relations among them.

Of course, the extent of such networks among organizations varies from time to time and place to place. In a highly theoretical fashion, the influential paper by Emery and Trist (1965) attempts to classify environments by the extent to which organizations sharing the same field have developed such interlocking relations. They distinguish among four types of fields:

> *placid, randomized environments*, in which resources required by organizations in the field are unchanging and randomly distributed over the area;
>
> *placid, clustered environments*, in which resources are unchanging but clustered, so that field location becomes an important factor in survival;
>
> *disturbed, reactive environments*, in which the availability of resources is partially determined by the actions of the organizations themselves, so that a given organization's survival is dependent on the use of strategies that take into account the behavior of competitors;
>
> *turbulent environments*, in which all organizational actors are interconnected, so that the organizational field or network itself becomes a force that each organization must attempt to take into account.

A related but more concrete typology based on the extent to which an "inclusive decision making structure" has come into existence has been proposed by Warren (1967). Four types of organizational fields are identified:

> *Social-choice context:* no formal or informal inclusive structure exists within which the participating organizations make their decisions. All decisions are made at the level of the individual units. An example is the relations among

diverse organizations that happen to reside in the same community.

Coalitional context: each organizational unit has its own decision-making apparatus and set of goals but collaborates informally and on an ad hoc basis when some of its goals are similar to those of other member units. An example is a group of independent child-care agencies collaborating to obtain a federal grant.

Federative context: Organizational units have individual goals but also participate in a structure in order to set more inclusive goals, which must be ratified by member units. An example is social agencies participating in a community council of agencies that has only delegated powers.

Unitary context: Decision making on policies and programs takes place at the top of a hierarchy of organizations, where final authority rests. An example is a center for emergency services established by a collection of community hospitals that coordinates and controls a decentralized network of emergency-service units.

The central message of both typologies—Emery and Trist's and Warren's—is that organizational fields vary greatly in the extent and nature of the relational and normative structures that develop among organizations. It is argued that these structures are important systems in their own right, and it is implied that they will have strong effects on their constituent organizations.

Organizational fields also vary in longevity. Aldrich and Whetten (1981: 387) have identified as an *action-set* a group of organizations "that have formed a temporary alliance for a limited purpose." Action-sets contrast with more permanent and stable organizational fields, although all fields are expected to evolve over time.

The most commonly employed areal unit within which organizational fields have been investigated is the community. There has been a regular and growing stream of research on the nature of the linkages that develop among similar or diverse organizations located within the same community or metropolitan area. (see Litwak and Hylton, 1962; Warren, 1963; Turk, 1977; Lincoln, 1979; Galaskiewicz, 1979; and Fennell, 1980).[2]

From an ecological perspective, the networks developing among organizations sharing the same field are adaptive mechanisms. As Astley and Van de Ven (1983: 250–51) point out,

> Rather than view organizations as pitched in a competitive battle for survival through a direct confrontation with the natural, or exogenous, environment, [areal field theorists] emphasize collective survival, which is achieved by collaboration between organizations through the construction of a regulated and controlled social environment that mediates the effects of the natural environment.

The areal organization field represents a significant shift in focus from that of the individual organization or the organization set. Organizations are treated as components of larger, overarching systems. However, two restrictions characterize this approach, one by definition and the other by usage. First and obviously, attention is restricted by definition to connections among organizations sharing the same territorial area. For many kinds of biological and social units, such a limitation would pose no problem, but for organizations, it is a serious and potentially biasing restriction. Modern transportation and communication systems are such that areal boundaries are for many purposes meaningless. A large number of types of organizations are influenced by distant as well as proximate connections, and for many organizations, the former are more fateful. Numerous organizations are linked to national and even international corporate systems, and many buy from and distribute to national and international markets. Second, by convention, most of the studies at this level give primary attention to "horizontal" relations among organizations—that is, to connections among competing or cooperating organizations lacking formal rights over one another. Neglected are the "vertical" connections that relate organizations in hierarchical systems—regulatory systems linking public and private organizations, formal authority connecting headquarters and branch offices, informal power channels relating dominant and subdominate organizations.

The fourth and final level of analysis to be considered was developed by theorists who wished to focus on the extralocal and vertical connections among organizations.[3]

Functional organization fields   A number of analysts have begun to isolate organizational systems for analysis on the basis of functional rather than geographic criteria.[4] As always, there are some differences in detail and terminology among the investigators working at this level. Thus, Hirsch (1972) employs the concept of *industry system* in his study of cultural production systems such as publishing houses, movie studios, and recording companies. (See also, Hirsch, 1985) He defines an industry system as

> all organizations engaged in the process of filtering new products and ideas as they flow from "creative" personnel in the technical subsystem to the managerial, institutional, and societal levels of organization (Parsons 1960). Each industry system is seen as a single, concrete, and stable network of identifiable and interacting components. (1972: 642)

Meyer and I have proposed the related concept of a *societal sector* —a domain in which organizations provide similar or substitutable services. This concept is very similar to that of industries or industrial groups, as studied by economists, but also includes those support, funding, and regulatory groups whose operation affects the central set of providers. (See Scott and Meyer, 1983: 137–39.) And DiMaggio and Powell (1983: 148) have suggested the concept of *organizational field,* which they define as

> those organizations that, in the aggregate, constitute a recognized area of institutional life: key suppliers, resource and product consumers, regulatory agencies, and other organizations that produce similar services or products.

---

[3]A discussion of previous work leading to a more functional definition of organization fields will be found in Scott and Meyer (1983: 130–36).

[4]Sometimes, of course, areal and functional criteria coincide. It is useful to distinguish them, however, because often they do not.

A number of empirical studies of functional organization fields have been conducted. For example, there have been several studies of new federal programs that were initiated and funded in Washington but created an elaborate set of relations among layers of public and private organizations from the national to the local level. (See, for example, Derthick's [1972] study of the "new towns" program; Aldrich's [1976] study of the Comprehensive Employment and Training Act [CETA]; and Pressman and Wildavsky's [1973] study of the Economic Development Administration's effort to create jobs in Oakland.) Other studies have examined the emergence of self-regulation among organizations lacking formal authority over one another. For example, Stern (1979) has examined the origin and evolution of the National Collegiate Athletic Association, the "voluntary" control system devised to regulate athletic competition among colleges. And there have been a number of attempts to examine the informal connections among organizational elites and between organizations and state structures to determine whether there exists a dominant capitalist class structure in contemporary societies. (See, for example, Herman, 1981; Mizruchi, 1982; and Mintz and Schwartz, 1983.)

Studies at the functional organization field level have been directed primarily at testing hypotheses stemming from the resource dependence, institutionalist, and Marxist perspectives. In later chapters in this volume, we will review some of the findings from these studies.

Organization sets, populations, areal fields, and functional fields are systems that may themselves be the primary object of study. Recall from Chapter 1 that levels of analysis are defined in terms of the dependent variables on which they focus. Much of the research conducted during the past decade has centered on these new units of analysis, examining how sets or populations or fields of organizations come into existence, vary over time, grow, and decline. Viewed in another way, however, these same distinctions among levels can be used as ways of depicting the environment of organizations. The characteristics of the counterorganizations constitute an important environment for the focal organization. Similarly, the distribution of organizational forms in a population may be viewed as a salient aspect of the environment for any particular organization in that distribution, and the characteristics of organizational fields—their degree of centralization or formalization—are of obvious significance for their component organizations.[5] Thus, the levels of analysis just described serve to define both wider systems of organizations and alternative conceptions of environments, depending on how they are employed.

Characteristics of Environments: Technical and Institutional Aspects

Establishing the level at which organizations and systems of organizations are to be defined is an important step in determining how environments are to be conceived: the environment of a population of hospi-

---

[5]This is not to say that organizations and their interrelations are the only environmental element of importance, but we do insist that other organizations and systems of organizations are of great importance as environmental actors.

TABLE 6–1   Technical and Institutional Environments with Illustrative Organizations

| | | Institutional Environments | |
		Stronger	Weaker
Technical Environments	Stronger	utilities banks pharmaceuticals general hospitals	general manufacturing
	Weaker	mental health clinics schools; legal agencies churches	restaurants health clubs

tals is assuredly different from the environment of a single hospital and its set of related organizations. But once the level of analysis is established, many choices remain. Meyer and I (Meyer and Scott, 1983) have proposed that it is useful to distinguish broadly between two types of organizational environments: technical and institutional. *Technical environments* are those in which organizations produce a product or service that is exchanged in a market such that they are rewarded for effective and efficient performance. These are environments that foster the development of rationalized structures that efficiently coordinate technical work. In the purest case, such environments are identical to the competitive markets so dear to the hearts of classical economists. Most types of manufacturing and service organizations operate in technical environments. By contrast, *institutional environments* are characterized by the elaboration of rules and requirements to which individual organizations must conform in order to receive legitimacy and support. Again in the extreme case, in institutional environments organizations are rewarded for the institution of correct structures and processes, not for the quantity and quality of their outputs. Organizations operating in institutional environments include schools and mental hospitals, whose resources do not depend primarily on evaluations of their outputs in a competitive market. Note that both types of environments place pressures on organizations to which they must be responsive if they are to survive. But the types of pressures and the types of responses required vary between the two.

To make these distinctions more useful, it is better to treat them as dimensions along which environments vary, not as dichotomies. That is, some types of environments pose stronger technical demands than others, but most types of organizations are exposed to some extent to such pressures. Similarily, the extent to which organizations are confronted with rules and procedural requirements varies across environments and over time. Technical and institutional environments are negatively associated, but not strongly so, such that various combinations and mixed cases exist. Table 6–1 cross-classifies the two dimensions and illustrates the types of organizations found in each. Thus, organizations such as utilities and banks are viewed as being subject to strong institutional and technical pressures. On the one hand, there are requirements that utilities produce energy, water, and other basic commodities effectively and reliably; on the other, there are equally strong demands that they conform to regulations governing safety, distribution, pricing, pollution control, employment practices, and so on. In general, organizations in this cell carry out tasks that combine complex technical requirements with a strong "public good" component. Moving to the right, we see most manufacturing organizations operate in environments characterized by strong technical and weaker institutional pressures. The major exceptions are those firms whose operation raises serious issues of health and safety for its employees or the public—for example pharmaceutical firms.

Many types of organizations, particularly professional service organizations such as schools, churches and welfare agencies, law firms, and stockbrokerages, are subject to stronger institutional but weaker technical pressures. Finally, some types of organizations operate in environments in which there are neither strong technical nor institutional pressures. Examples include organizations providing many types of personal services, such as restaurants and health clubs.

In the 1970s, when open rational system models were dominant, the environment was viewed primarily in technical terms. In the 1980s, increasing attention is being given to the institutional aspects of environments. Both conceptions are necessarily abstract, since our attempt is to develop concepts and dimensions applicable to many kinds of organizations. However, it is possible to describe more specific variables or dimensions associated with each type of environment.

Technical environments. Perhaps the most commonly held conception of the environment of organizations is that of the *task environment* as first proposed by Dill (1958: 410). This concept is broadly defined as all aspects of the environment "potentially relevant to goal setting and goal attainment," but is typically narrowed in use to refer to sources of inputs, markets for outputs, competitors, and regulators. The conception of a task environment emphasizes that most organizations are created to achieve goals, to perform some type of work. It also emphasizes that no organization is self-sufficient; all must enter into exchanges with the environment. Managers are viewed as ensuring adequate supplies of resources and markets, designing efficient work arrangements, and coordinating and controlling technical activities. Organization structure is viewed as being closely linked to external technical requirements and to internal work systems.

Broadly speaking, there are two types of language for describing what organizations exchange with their environments: some formulations emphasize environments as stocks of resources while others view them as sources of information (Aldrich and Mindlin, 1978). Those stressing the former are apt to focus on the degree to which the organization becomes dependent on others for vital resources. Investigators emphasizing the informational aspects of environments focus primarily on the degree of uncertainty confronting the organization. Both uncertainty and dependency are viewed as problematic situations confronting organizations, and much attention has been devoted to examining the types of strategies and mechanisms organizations use to cope with them. But before turning to attempted "solutions," we need to inquire into the general conditions that give rise to these states.

Several general dimensions have been proposed by investigators as affecting either organizational uncertainty or dependence. Without attempting an exhaustive summary, we will present here the major variables and their expected effects.

DIMENSIONS AFFECTING UNCERTAINTY

1. *Degree of homogeneity–heterogeneity:* the extent to which the environmental entities to which the organization must relate are similar to one another—for example, the number of different types of clients of a service organization. Other labels: *complexity, diversity* (see Dill, 1958; Thompson, 1967).

2. *Degree of stability–variability:* the extent to which the entities are undergoing change—for example, the rate of product innovation within the industry category to which a given firm belongs. It is possible to differentiate between the rate of change and its evenness or fluctuation (see Lawrence and Lorsch, 1967; Thompson, 1967).

3. *Degree of threat–security:* the extent to which an organization is vulnerable to its environment, or the degree to which "inefficiencies and errors by an organization result in its demise" (McKelvey, 1982: 185). An example is the nuclear energy program, where one mistake can endanger the lives of many and threaten support and funding for the program.

4. *Degree of interconnectedness–isolation:* the extent to which the organization is linked to many other environmental entities whose actions may impinge on it—for example, the number of different suppliers from whom a manufacturing company must buy its inputs (see Pfeffer and Salancik, 1978).

5. *Degree of coordination–noncoordination:* the extent to which the organization confronts a set of environmental entities whose actions are orchestrated or structured. For example, does a seller face a set of independent grocery stores or a chain of supermarkets? (See Jurkovich, 1974.)

In general, we would expect that the greater the heterogeneity, the higher the rate of instability, the greater the threat, the greater the interconnectedness, and the lower the coordination within the environment, the higher the uncertainty facing the organization.

DIMENSIONS AFFECTING DEPENDENCE

1. *Degree of munificence–scarcity:* the extent to which the resources required by the organization are available in its environment—for example, the availability of petroleum to a chemical company. Other label: *environmental capacity* (See Pfeffer and Salancik, 1978; Aldrich, 1979).

2. *Degree of concentration–dispersion:* the extent to which the resources required are evenly spread throughout the environment. For example, economic concentration has been defined as the proportion of an industry's sales controlled by the largest four or eight firms (see Nutter, 1968; Pfeffer and Salancik, 1978).

3. *Degree of coordination–noncoordination:* the extent to which the organization confronts a set of environmental entities whose actions are orchestrated or structured. For example, does a seller face a set of independent grocery stores or a chain of supermarkets?

The scarcer the resources, the higher the concentration, and the greater the coordination exhibited by entities within the environment, the greater the dependence of the organization.

Note that the two dependent variables, uncertainty and dependence, do not necessarily co-vary in response to a given environmental state. Thus, a higher degree of environmental coordination is expected simultanteously to decrease the organization's uncertainty but to increase its dependence. A similar prediction might well be made for level of concentration.

We believe that the identification of a number of environmental dimensions at this level of generality represents a significant advance in organization theory, although much work continues to be done on determining which are the primary dimensions. (See Dess and Beard, 1984.) The application of the variables has proved to be a difficult and often frustrating business. This is due partly to the abstract nature of the concepts and to the great variability in the types of organizations and, hence, in the kinds of environments to which they relate. The task of application is rendered particularly difficult by the differentiated nature of organizations: different components or subunits of an organization may confront quite different environmental sectors. For example, Lawrence and Lorsch (1967) investigated variation in the characteristics of some of the environmental sectors confronted by different departments within plastics manufacturing organizations. Their measures revealed that the scientific environment to which the applied research departments related was more uncertain than the marketing environment the sales department confronted. Of course, other specialized units—departments—relate to still other environmental sectors. To state the problem as succinctly as possible: every organization relates to a number of different environments, and these environments may exhibit differing characteristics. And any attempt to determine *the* characteristics of *the* environment requires respondents or investigators to arrive at a summary judgment that may conceal a great deal of variance.

The dimensions of uncertainty and dependence just reviewed are the product of energetic theoretical work and have given rise to an extensive number of empirical investigations testing and elaborating propositions relating environmental conditions and organizational characteristics and actions. We review this work in later chapters. A number of these dimensions can also be used to assess the institutional aspects of organizations, which we consider next.

Institutional environments   To the economic and related political aspects emphasized by technical conceptions of environments, institutional analysts have added additional dimensions. The development of interest in institutional environments is more recent, and hence the ideas are less clearly formulated than in the case of technical environments. However, all efforts in this area tend to stress the larger arrangements—network, culture, and history—in which organizations are embedded. A central common message of the institutional view is that the environments of organizations are themselves organized, and increasingly so.

Briefly, network elements consist of the connections among organizations, whether expressed as flows or linkages, such as shared participants. Cultural elements comprise both cognitive and normative systems on which organizations or fields of organizations draw and to which they are subject. And historical elements call attention to the relevance of past conditions for understanding the present and future prospects of organizations. Each set of elements will now be described.[6]

The examination of organizational *networks* is now well under way, with mathematical and graph techniques often employed in depicting and analyzing these complex systems (Burt, 1980). Network approaches differ from conventional social-science methodologies in that they attend to relational and structural connections among units, such as organizations, rather than simply to the attributes of the units. Of course, a variety of types of connections are possible. Some involve flows or exchanges (of services, resources, information); others entail structural linkages. Indeed, an important attribute of a connection is whether it is *multiplex*—whether it has multiple rather than single content (Barnes, 1972). Approaches more relevant to institutional concerns focus on the form taken by a set of linkages; numerous analytic techniques have been developed to measure such network properties as *connectivity*—the degree to which units are linked directly or indirectly—the extent of *clustering* of ties among units the *density* of ties, and so on. (See Laumann, Galaskiewicz, and Marsden, 1978; and Lincoln, 1982.) And since we have argued that the linkages developing within organizational fields are themselves increasingly organized, we can add other, more conventional variables for assessing network structure, such as the extent to which the linkages are *centralized, formalized, loosely coupled,* and so on. (See Aldrich and Whetten, 1981.)

As Burt (1980) has noted, there are two varying approaches to assessing network properties. Most network analysts have measured the *relational* properties of a network—examining the extent and nature of the direct and indirect linkages that exist, using concepts similar to those just described. But White, Boorman, and Breiger (1976) have developed a *positional* approach that assesses the extent to which patterns of relations within a network are similar. Using these techniques, one can assess the degree to which two or more portions of a network (or two or more networks) are *structurally equivalent.* Two networks may be very similar in structure—for example, two systems of prisons in two different U.S. states—although they are not, or are only very indirectly, connected to each other.

Shifting from form to content of organizational networks, we can focus on what types of *resources* are exchanged—such as money, use of staff, clients, technical assistance, or goodwill (see Van de Ven and Ferry, 1980: 325)—or what types of *interpenetrations* are present. As Laumann and colleagues note, some of the important types of connections among organizations are based on "interpenetration of organizational boundaries"—for instance, common membership in a coalition or federation, the undertaking of joint programs, and interlocking directorates (Laumann, Galaskiewicz, and Marsden, 1978: 463–64). In research on organizational sectors, Meyer and I have distinguished among the types of *decisions*—funding, programmatic, instrumental—that are made by higher units in a field that constrain the behavior of subordinate units, and among the types of *interlevel controls*—structural, process, outcome—that are exercised (Scott and Meyer, 1983). Although form has to date received more attention than content in research on linkages, content seems of equal importance, and, indeed, the form that linkages take often varies by content.

[6]This discussion of networks, culture, and history draws on my 1983 paper.

Network analysis has become more popular as levels of analysis have shifted from sets to fields. Its imagery and methods are useful for analyzing both technical and institutional environments. Dimensions such as degree of interconnectedness and extent of coordination obviously lend themselves to network approaches. The connections themselves may involve not organizations or their subunits but various types of interpersonal associations. For example, Powell (1985: 193), in analyzing the organization of book publishing, underscores the importance of "trust, personal networks, norms of reciprocity, reputational effects, and tacit collusion" in relations between editors and authors.

While institutional conceptions of the environment include these more immediate environments, they also emphasize the importance of larger systems of interdependence. For example, organization theorists have not given as much attention as desirable to larger corporate systems—both national and international—that include many specific companies and establishments within a single complex framework. (See Evans, 1981.) And we have not attended as carefully as necessary to the varying structure of different industries or sectors, although economists have long noted the diversity of their concentration and degree of connectedness. We are just beginning to become aware of the importance of state structures and activities—not only as complex interorganizational systems in themselves but as powerful forces shaping the environment of all types of organizations, through tax and regulatory policies, labor and antitrust law, subsidies and contracts, and numerous other ways.

Emphasis on institutional environments also calls attention to the importance of more general *cultural* features shaping organizations and organizational fields, in particular cognitive and normative systems. Of course, major cultural differences exist across societies or nation-states, and there is growing interest in and attention to the ways in which general cultural differences may influence the shape and operation of organizations. (See Crozier, 1964; Landsberger, 1970; Dore, 1973; Lammers and Hickson, 1979*b*; and Child, 1981) For example, Lammers and Hickson (1979*a*), summarizing several studies aimed at detecting cross-cultural differences in organizational types, conclude that current evidence points to at least three distinctive cultural forms. A *Latin* type, exemplified by French, Italian, and Spanish organizations, is characterized by relatively high centralization, rigid stratification and sharp inequalities among levels, and conflicts around areas of uncertainty. An *Anglo-Saxon* type, exemplified by British, United States, and Scandinavian organization, is marked by more decentralization, less rigid stratification, and more flexible approaches to the application of rules. And a *traditional* type, found in third-world, developing countries, is characterized by paternalistic leadership patterns, implicit rather than explicit rules, and lack of clear boundaries separating organizational from nonorganizational roles. And of late there has been a great deal of attention focused on ascertaining the distinctive cultural features that characterize Japanese society and organizations (Cole, 1979; Ouchi, 1981). However, the complexity of wider cultures and their multiple connections with other societal elements—demographic, economic, political—makes interpretations of these associations hazardous.

An ambitious attempt to systematically assess variations across societies in value patterns relevant to the functioning of organizations has been carried out by Hofstede (1984). He identifies four value dimensions—power distance, uncertainty avoidance, individualism, and masculinity—that in combination constitute a generalized framework that can be used to compare and contrast the varying cultural profiles of different societies. Using as data survey responses from over 120,000 respondents in the marketing and service departments of a multinational corporation, Hofstede gathered information in forty societies and at two time periods, 1968 and 1972. Hofstede finds substantial differences among societies on the four value dimensions. A society's position on most of the value profiles can be predicted with considerable accuracy from its geographical latitude, population size, and per capita wealth. And the value differences are strongly associated with the characteristics of organizational structures and practices. For example, cultures with larger power differences (inequalities in power) are likely to contain organizations that are more highly centralized, have higher ratios of supervisory and managerial personnel, and have larger disparities in qualifications and wages among personnel.

Hofstede suggests that not only organizaiton practice but organization theory is culturally based. Thus, Weber, the German, stresses authority of office; Fayol, the Frenchman, power of persons; and Follett, the American, the situational nature of power. More generally, Hofstede (1984: 218) points out that

> what is available as organization theory today is mostly written by Americans, and as such reflects the cultural context of one specific society. A collection of 15 contributions by leading Europeans (Hofstede and Kassem, 1976) shows remarkable differences in focus by culture area. Authors from Latin Europe focus on power; from Central Europe, including Germany, on truth; from Eastern Europe, on efficiency; from Northern Europe, on change; while the Western Europeans, in this case British and Dutch, have a bit of all of these but show more than the others a concern with data collection which we also find in the United States.

Of course, cultural beliefs vary not only between but within societies, and a highly developed and differentiated society such as that of the United States contains multiple, diverse value and meaning systems—cultures associated with regions, ethnic groups, classes, occupational communities, and generations. Similarly, cultural beliefs vary among organizational fields and sectors, both in content and in degree of consensus. Particularly important are those belief systems that define the collective goals or values governing the field, values that provide the basis for domain definition. In some arenas, such as the postal or domestic airlines services, the goals may be relatively noncontroversial; in others, such as criminal justice, there may be deep-seated controversies as to the nature of the mission. Also important are conceptions of the means available to pursue objectives. Theories of practice, as well as actual instrumentalities, are involved. In some fields, we observe the presence of technically defined procedures; in others, actions are based on and guided by rational myths, as noted by Meyer and Rowan (1977).

Closely related to these cognitive aspects of cultures, are the normative structures—collective norms governing behavior in organizational fields. Laumann and colleagues describe the normative contexts of these fields as varying from *competitive* to *cooperative* modalities (Laumann, Galaskiewicz, and Marsden, 1978). They further distinguish cooperation that is *contingent*—in that "organizations are expected to balance their commitments to collective purposes with their more specialized goals"—from cooperation that is *mandated*—a mode that "implies the existence of a centralized control agency, which has the power to structure and restructure the total network" (pp. 466, 468). Clearly, types of behavior that are encouraged in some fields would be condemned in others. For example, mutual cooperation and coordination of services is encouraged among community service agencies but condemned as "collusion" among computer software companies.

Finally, emphasis on institutional environments stresses the importance of a *historical* perspective in examining organizations and organizational fields. We accept Tilly's (1981: 6) straightforward definition that "an analysis is historical to the extent that the place and time of the action enter into its explanations." To call for a historical perspective is not to insist on longitudinal studies—studies collecting data over more than a single time period—although more such studies are needed, but to recognize that even when we observe an organization or a system of organizations at one point in time, we are seeing a cross-section of elements that are the residues of diverse past processes.

Each organization and organization field has its own history, its own sequence of development. Social systems tend to progress through certain developmental phases, a "life cycle" that, while not as definite in its stages or progression as biological systems, nevertheless exhibits a recognizable pattern. (See Kimberly, Miles, et al., 1980.) And where a system is in its own developmental sequence will influence its characteristics and its responses.

Just as significant as a system's own history is the larger historical frame within which it develops and operates. Many of these larger contexts are themselves structured and may be usefully viewed as systems with their own developmental history. Thus Marxist theorists call attention to the capitalist economic system and the relevance for present organizations of operating within the framework of "late capitalism" (Benson, 1982; Burawoy, 1985).

All system elements—units, relations, beliefs—should be thought of as having a time subscript. And knowing *when* some element developed may provide important clues as to its characteristics and behavior. Obviously, technologies and belief systems change over time. For example, our ideas about military defense or about mental illness and how to manage it are quite different today than they were 50 to 100 years ago. Because of differences in technologies, beliefs, and other founding conditions, we would expect the organizations that develop at a given time to differ from those that develop earlier or later. (See Stinchcombe, 1965.)

Also, various system elements may be expected to change at differing rates. Some aspects of organizations, such as technical features, are more easily and quickly changed than others, such as participant's skills or work routines. Both because different organizations and fields are founded at differing times and under varying circumstances and because they may change in differing ways and at varying rates, it is important to attend to time dimensions in examining the structure and composition of organizations and the fields in which they operate.

Both technical and institutional environments shape organizational forms and influence organizational behavior. To this point, we have attempted to review some of the more important environmental dimensions and distinctions used by analysts who are attempting to capture salient features of organizational environments. In later chapters, we review specific predictions and empirical studies attempting to explain how these features of the environment influence organizational structure and performance.

THE INTERDEPENDENCE OF ORGANIZATIONS AND ENVIRONMENTS

Enactment, Attention, and Outcomes

In research on organizational environments, a healthy controversy has developed about the relative merits of employing subjective or perceptual versus objective measures of environmental characteristics. This is not simply a measurement issue, but raises important theoretical issues concerning how organizations relate to their environments. A number of analysts (Dill, 1958; Lawrence and Lorsch, 1967; Duncan, 1972) argue that it makes sense to measure the environment in terms of the perceptions of participants, since only factors that they perceive can enter into their decision-making behavior. Weick's formulation is even stronger. He argues, as discussed in Chapter 4, that participants do not merely perceive and react but actively construct, "enact" their environments. Weick (1979: 164) insists that "the concept of an *enacted environment* is not synonymous with the concept of a *perceived environment*." Rather, the label *enactment* is meant "to emphasize that managers construct, rearrange, single out, and demolish many 'objective' features of their surroundings." Whereas symbolic interactionists emphasize the extent to which reality is interpersonally negotiated, Weick stresses the individual, cognitive aspects of the process by which "people, often alone, actively *put* things out there that they then perceive and negotiate about perceiving" (1979: 165).

March and colleagues build on this work by introducing the concept of *attention structure* to describe the distribution of connections among people, the types of information they send and receive, the distribution of problems, and the rules concerning who is entitled to make choices about what is known (Cohen and March, 1974; March and Olsen, 1976). This concept reminds us that although individuals may be the agents who enact their environment, they do so within an organizational structure that influences what types of stimuli reach them and sets some constraints on their decisions and actions. Much of the empirical research on the structuring of attention involves case studies of particular decisions (see for example, March and Olsen, 1976), but Sproull (1981) points out that studies of time allocation by managers are also quite germane. For example, in a very influential study, Mintzberg (1971; 1973) observed and systematically recorded the activities and interactions of the chief executive officer in five diverse organizations for one week each in order to answer the question "What do managers do?" Among the relevant findings, which have been replicated in similar studies, were that managers engage in multiple activities characterized by brevity, such that the manager "is forced to treat issues in an abrupt and superficial way" (1971: B100). Managers were also observed to rely primarily on verbal rather than written communications. Meetings, scheduled and unscheduled, consumed most of their time. Such findings reinforce the importance of attention structures in understanding how organizational participants enact their environments.

Pfeffer and Salancik (1978: 74) embrace these arguments regarding the importance of organizational arrangements for structuring attention and extend them by stressing the significance of the development of specialized units and routines for collecting and processing information.

> The *information system* is conceptualized as the reports, statistics, facts, or information that are regularly collected and their pattern of transmission through the organization. The fact that certain information is regularly collected focuses the organization's attention on it. The collection of certain information occupies the time and attention of the organization, which necessarily restricts the time and attention devoted elsewhere.

Some information is important because it is collected and, hence, available as an input to decision making. In this manner, information systems help to determine attention structures.

We must take care not to overstate the subtlety and complexity of the information systems devised by organizations. Recall in this connection Boulding's (1956) typology of system levels described in Chapter 4 of this volume. Organizations and their participants are capable of responding to their environments at levels 7 and 8 by creating complex consensual images of environmental processes as a basis for doing so. At the other end of the spectrum, organizations also devise and employ simple, tightly coupled mechanisms to track specific environmental variables.

Ashby (1952) stresses the adaptive behavior of which simple systems are capable as they monitor one or a few particular variables linked to one or a few response rules: witness the "intelligence" of the thermostat. Simon (1962) suggests two terms to distinguish between these lower- and higher-level responses. He proposes that a cybernetic response works on the principle of the *recipe:* feedback variables trigger the performance of a specified sequence of activities. Steinbruner (1974: 57) amplifies:

> The simplest cybernetic mechanisms do not confront the issue of variety at all, for they make no calculations of the environment. The mechanisms merely track a few feedback variables and beyond that are perfectly blind to the environment.

Organizational systems relying on recipes can perform effectively as long as the signals they track are reliable indicators of the true state of the variables of concern. However, such is often not the case, because of random error, changed circumstances, or deception. Under any of these circumstances, "smart" systems suddenly act quite stupidly. By contrast, higher-level responses entail the construction of what Simon terms a *blueprint*—an image of the environment that attempts to capture and reflect its salient complexity. Thus, some information systems create vastly simplified pictures of environments whereas others attempt to more fully capture and codify its complexity.

But whether the system is relying on recipes or blueprints, these theorists conclude that the environment of an organization is as much as, if not more then, a function of the organization, the cognitive work of its participants and their structure of attention, and its information system as it is of the external situation.

It is not necessary to embrace fully these phenomenological arguments to accept a related, but different point. Even if we prefer objective measures of an organization's environment, we must still take into account the characteristics and goals of the organization in order to evaluate what aspects of the external world are likely to be salient. If a church replaces a factory on the corner lot of a small town, the environments of the two types of organizations will not be very similar: each defines and functions in a different *domain*. The demands a specific organization makes on its environment, as well as the demands made by the environment on the organization, will vary with each type of organization. Hence, one cannot describe "objectively" the environment of an organization without knowledge of the organization and the domain in which it functions.

Still, we do not want to conclude that all is perception and enactment. The environment of a given organization does vary in its stability, its complexity, its threat—and such matters can be assessed apart from ascertaining what participants believe to be the case. For example, one can examine the density of competing organizations, or count the number of hostile takeovers in an industry, or examine fluctuations in profit margins over time. Participants may or may not attend to these matters, but this does not mean that what they don't know can't hurt (or help) them. Pfeffer and Salancik (1978: 62–63) correctly observe that although environments must be perceived in order to influence actions taken by organizational participants, they can influence organizational *outcomes* whether or not they have been perceived. Outcomes are results. Organizations produce *outputs*—goods and services—but *outcomes* represent the joint product of organizational performance and environment response. The surgeon may perform flawlessly, but the patient may die; the automobile may be well built but fail to sell. In this sense, environments directly influence outcomes. (See Chapter 13.)

Thus, one's measurement strategy should depend on what is being predicted: perceptual measures are necessary if we hope to predict the choices of organizational participants, but they are not sufficient if we wish to predict the outcomes of these choices, since outcomes are a product of many forces, many of which are outside the control of the organization. For example, perceptions of the market held by recording-studio executives can better predict what types of artists are given contracts than how well their records sell.

In Figure 6–1 we collect some of the distinctions we have described and attempt to depict their relations to one another. The result is a cycle of interdependence of organizations and environments. Beginning, arbitrarily, with the organizational structure, we argue that its decision makers determine a domain of operation, selecting what goods and services are to be produced for what types of consumers. Domain selection will strongly affect what types of information will be required. An infor-

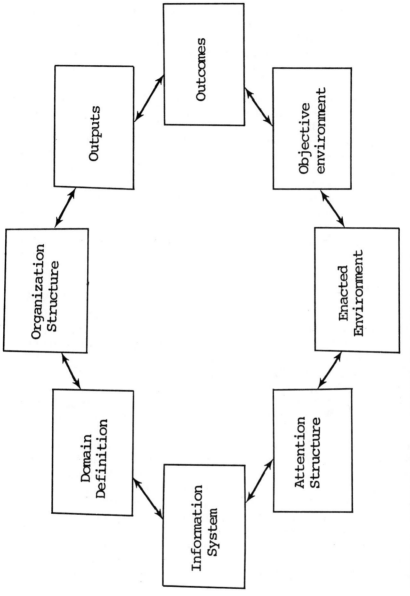

FIGURE 6–1 Organization-Environment Relations: A Cycle of Interdependence

137

mation system is designed that, in turn, gives rise to an attention structure that will help to determine what participants in varying locations attend to and what importance is assigned to their concerns. The attention structure contributes to the creation of the enacted environment—the constructed (and reconstructed) picture that participants have of the environment to which they relate.

But these organizational processes do not take place in a vacuum. Starting at the opposite point in the cycle, the "objective" environment directly influences the enacted environment. Environmental factors can also be expected to command attention, and will shape the information system of the organization. The objective environment will also affect the domain definition. An organization may claim to be a day-care center or an automobile-repair shop, but others—clients, distributors, regulators— must acknowledge and endorse these claims for them to have "reality."

Finally, as we have described, the environment can perform an "end run," influencing the structure of the organization indirection by affecting its outcomes. Outcomes are joint products of organizational performance and environmental response.

Influence

To this point we have suggested that organizations and environments are interdependent in terms of information systems and cognitive processes, and in terms of environmental effects on organizational outcomes. They are also interdependent in more direct ways: organizations attempt to directly influence environments, and vice versa. There is little doubt that environments profoundly shape organizations—their structures, their performances, their outcomes. How this occurs is subject to dispute. For example, resource dependency theorists argue that organizations take steps to adapt to their environment, changing their structural features as required to better match its requirements. By contrast, population ecologists emphasize the structural inertia of organizations; they assume that the more pervasive environmental effects occur through selection rather than adaptation. (See Chapter 8) Organizations are also recognized by many theorists to directly shape their environments. Such actions are obvious in the case of large and powerful organizations, such as monopolies, but they can be observed in other situations as well. Many of the strategies that organizations employ, to be discussed in detail in Chapter 8, involve direct attempts to alter the environment: to change demand by advertising, to absorb uncertainty by contracting, or to change environments by diversifying. Organizations can and do directly affect their environments. Influences are reciprocal.

Absorption and Interpenetration

We have previously noted the open system assertion that the boundary separating the organization from its environment is somewhat arbitrarily drawn and varies with the flows or activities being examined. For example, if we wish to examine the authority system regulating faculty members at a university, we will want to include professional colleagues from other universities who serve as significant evaluators, helping to determine promotion and tenure decisions for the host school. (See Hind, Dornbusch, and Scott, 1974.) Thus, elements that for some purposes are usefully analyzed as parts of a system's environment are for other purposes included within the system itself.

Also, even arbitrary boundaries change over time. What today is a functioning system operating outside the framework of a given organization may tomorrow be incorporated as a subsystem by the organization. As discussed in Chapter 8, one of the most effective strategies employed by organizations in relating to some aspect of their environment is to absorb it. With increasing frequency, organizations acquire—and disaffiliate from—other systems. In this sense, organizational executives, like researchers, take a pragmatic view of the boundary separating their organization and its environment.

Even without "official" redefinitions, organizations constantly incorporate environmental elements into their own structures. In a fully developed open system conception, all of the "materials" used to create organizations—resources and equipment, but also personnel and procedures—are obtained from the environment. If we add to this the institutionalist ingredients—beliefs, meanings, conceptual categories—then it is no longer possible to think of the environment as something "out there"; its elements are part of the organization, not absorbed by it so that they become separated from the environment but interpentrating it, infusing it with value, and connecting it with larger systems. Like most other ideas, however, these insights are better treated as variables: organizations are open systems, but some are more open than others. Similarly, organizations vary in the extent to which they relate to institutional environments.

The nested nature of organizational environments as well as the penetration of organizations by their environments raises serious problems for investigators who are trying to decide where to draw boundaries for analytical purposes. (See Chapter 8) In studying educational systems, for example, is the proper unit of analysis the individual classroom, the individual school, the school district, or the state educational system? Clearly, there is no way to answer this question without knowing what processes or relations within the system are to be examined. There is always the danger that we will select the wrong unit of analysis for a given topic. We may elect to study the influence of teachers on curriculum and select a sample of classrooms, only to discover that the major curriculum choices are made at the district or state office. Such *specification* errors become more likely when the boundaries of systems are indefinite. The boundaries of many organizations are diffuse with respect to many processes and are variable with respect to space and time. (See Freeman, 1978.)

THE EVOLUTION OF ENVIRONMENTS

After generating so many distinctions—dimensions, levels, types of measures—we are hesitant to conclude this chapter by commenting on the general direction of environmental change. Since commentators increasingly disagree on this subject, however, we feel somewhat protected from the dangers of overgeneralization.

The prevalent view is that first enunciated by Emery and Trist: "The environmental contexts in which organizations exist are themselves changing, at an increasing rate, and toward increasing complexity" (1965: 21). Except for noting that these conditions are occurring "under the impact of technological change" (p. 30), Emery and Trist are content to describe these developments rather than to explain them. Terreberry cites a considerable number of empirical studies on organizations that, in her opinion support Emery and Trist's thesis that

> these systems are increasingly finding themselves in environments where the complexity and rapidity of change in external interconnectedness gives rise to increasingly unpredictable change in their transactional interdependencies. This seems to be good evidence for the emergence of turbulence in the environments of many formal organizations. (Terreberry, 1968: 598)

However, Terreberry's major argument supporting Emery and Trist's thesis is a conceptual rather than an empirical one. Her reasoning is as follows: Organizations are, by definition, open systems. All open systems tend to evolve from less to more complex states. The environment of any given organization is increasingly composed of other organizations. Hence, it follows that organizational environments are evolving from less to more complex states. Two corollaries are developed: for any given focal organization (1) "these trends mean a gross increase in their area of relevant uncertainty" (Emery and Trist, 1965: 26); and (2) "the evolution of environments is characterized by an increase in the ratio of externally induced change over internally induced change" (Terreberry, 1968: 599).

We are not convinced by these arguments that all environments of organizations are moving toward greater turbulence—increased uncertainty and interdependency. Although Terreberry is correct that open systems evolve from more to less complex states, increased complexity need not be synonymous with increased uncertainty. Indeed, as Galbraith (1967) and others have noted, differentiation permits specialization of function, and specialization, in turn, permits the application of scientific or engineering knowledge to the problem at hand. Thus, differentiation contributes to rationalization and routinization of a field of action and, in this manner, to increased certainty. Similarly, the spread of organizations into more arenas of activity often results in increased standardization and predictability. Why trust the uncertainty of small-town cuisine when you can count on a Big Mac?

> On the modern McDonald's grills, winking lights tell countermen when to flip over the hamburger. . . . A small group of equipment makers furnished McDonald's with a stream of such continually updated gadgets designed to automate the serving and cooking of food to the ultimate degree: premeasured scoops, ketchup and mustard dispensers, computer-run fryers, infrared warning lights, instruments for testing the solidity of raw potatoes and the fluffiness of shakes. Nothing—as Hamburger Central proudly boasts—was left to chance. (Boas and Chain, 1977: 40–41)

An increase in the connections among organizations in the environment also does not always lead to increased uncertainty: it can lead to the creation of unitary or federative contexts (Warren, 1967), in which coordination and common goals supplant competition.

Not only are there important factors creating certainty among technical organizations, but organizations often confront relatively certain or predictable institutional environments. Thus, Meyer argues that "in post-industrial societies, rationalized states expand their dominance over more and more aspects of social life, increasing centralization and homogeneity in these domains." He insists that through the creation of rationalized myths, modern societies produce "vast new forms of certainty, which organizations may obtain by the mere process of conformity to environmental specifications" (1978: 361, 363).[7] Although Meyer stresses increased certainty in institutionalized environments, we will strike the opposing note. Although new laws, administrative agencies, and professional occupations are continually created, giving rise to new rationalized myths that provide a basis for organized action where none existed before, we should not overemphasize the amount of certainty that results. Laws are often ambiguous and variously interpreted; state and federal bureaus represent an increasingly vast and diverse collection of interests and programs that are often contradictory or competing; and professional occupations challenge one another's visions of truth.

While some arenas of organizational action are probably moving toward increasing certainty—whether because of the routinization of technical operations or the widespread acceptance of institutional rules—we also see evidence of increased uncertainty in many areas of social life. Given these contradictory processes—of standardization and rationalization on the one hand, and uncertainty and turbulence of the other—it seems inappropriate to make any assumption about the general direction of change in the environments within which organizations function. Empirical investigations, not *a priori* assumptions, should determine the rate and direction of environmental change.

SUMMARY

Determining how the environments of organizations can be usefully characterized and circumscribed is an issue that confronts, analysts embracing the open system perspective. Conceptions of environments vary by level of analysis as well as by substantive focus. Analysis levels—include the organizational set, organizational population, areal organizational field, and functional organizational field. Each focuses on a somewhat different aspect of organization-environment relations, and each is associated with varying theoretical perspectives.

[7]It is of interest to note that Emery and Trist, the authors who see the future of organizations as increasingly turbulent, simultaneously espouse a different view that, although little recognized, bears a striking resemblance to Meyer's conception. They argue that a possible solution for organizations in turbulent fields is represented by "the emergence of values that have overriding significance for all members of the field." These values "can be rational as well as irrational" and are likely to become more rational as "the scientific ethos takes greater hold in a society." The emergence of these commonly accepted values creates a field "which is no longer richly joined and turbulent but simplified and relatively static." (Emery and Trist, 1965: 28) In short, their vision of future organizational fields includes some circumstances—including the emergence of rationalized values—that result in more rather than less certainty for organizations.

Analysts examining environments also vary in substantive interests. A great deal of research has been devoted to the technical aspects of environments—the ways in which stocks of resources and sources of information are distributed and arranged. More recently, investigators have pursued institutional features of environments, studying how relational networks and cultural and historical contexts shape organizational structure and activities.

Organizations are viewed as interdependent with environments in a number of senses. Participants' perceptions of their environments together with the attention structures of organizations result in enacted environments that are products of both environmental features and organizational information systems. Environments directly affect organizational outcomes, which in turn affect subsequent perceptions and decisions. Environments influence organizations, but organizations also modify and select their environments. And environments supply the materials and ingredients of which organizations are composed.

Most observers argue that the environments of organizations are becoming more complex and uncertain over time. The increasing differentiation and interconnectedness of organizations cause increased uncertainty and interdependency for them. But other processes—routinization, standardization, the creation of rationalized myths—create new islands of certainty. We conclude that the extent and the direction of change in the environments of organizations is a matter to be settled not by assumption but by empirical investigation. a

7 creating organizations

The distinctive features of modern life derive from the fact that a large share of social activity is governed by bodies of systematic abstract doctrine. . . . The government of activities by doctrines is the primary function of bureaucracy. The foundation of the dominance of professions in modern society is competence in a specialized body of abstract knowledge, systematized and taught by scholars in professional schools. Science, education, bureaucratic administration, the professions—these distinctive features of modern life are primarily concerned with developing, transmitting, and governing activities by bodies of systematized intelligence. The study of modernization is, therefore, in large measure the study of the social role of systematized intelligence and its application to daily affairs.

Arthur L. Stinchcombe (1974)

In this chapter we attempt to explain how and why organizations come into existence. It is helpful to separate this broad question into two categories of more specific questions. The first deals with the emergence of organizations as a distinctive type of collectivity. This category subsumes such questions as these: Have organizations always existed? If not, when did they first emerge? What are the social conditions under which organizations develop? What alternatives to organizations exist for carrying out complex tasks? It will quickly become apparent that "authorities differ" in the answers they give to these and related questions. In particular, we contrast the views of rational system with natural system theorists.

The second set of questions assumes the existence of organizations as one general type of social arrangement and asks how specific organizations obtain resources that support their structures and activities. Questions include the following: What means do organizations use to induce participants to contribute resources to them? What effects are associated with the use of particular types of incentives or with the recruitment of particular types of participants? How do the resource needs of organizations vary by type of organization and by time and place? Although all such questions cannot be definitively answered, they serve to focus the discussion and point to areas of needed work.

THE EMERGENCE OF ORGANIZATIONS

It is only in modern, industrialized societies that organizations dominate the landscape. Their emergence, proliferation, and consolidation as a ubiquitous and significant building block of society is one of the great social transformations that distinguishes the modern from the premodern world. In a quite literal sense, the history of the development of modern society is also a history of the development of special purpose organizations: organizations were both created by and helped to produce these changes. We shall not attempt to recount here this vast and complex history but will only note some of the changes scholars have identified as among the most fateful for the development of organizations.

The Changing Relations of Individual and Corporate Actors

When we speak of the emergence of organizations, we are not implying that previous societal arrangements exhibited disorganization. Indeed, in important ways some of the preexisting social systems exhibited higher degrees of order! The correct contrast, then, is between different types of ordered social arrangements. The principal ways in which modern social structures differ from earlier, traditional forms are (1) in the relation of individual actors to corporate actors, and (2) in the relation of corporate actors to one another.

Coleman's (1974) analysis of these differences is most illuminating. Examining the corporate bodies of the Middle Ages, he observes that the basic units—the manor, the guild, the village—wholly contained their members and possessed full authority over them. What rights and interests individuals possessed, they acquired from their membership in these units. (Note that these bodies are the patrimonial systems dissected by Weber, as described in Chapter 2.) Moreover, the corporate actors were themselves organized in a strict hierarchicy, the subordinate units being responsible to and contained within superordinate systems in a concentric pattern (see Simmel, 1955 trans.).

Gradually and fitfully, over several centuries, these relations were altered. Individuals were able to acquire rights and were recognized to have interests, and corporate actors were allowed to acquire rights and to pursue interests that were not simply aggregates of the interests of their members. Coleman summarizes these developments:

> Two things happened. First, men themselves began to break out of their fixed estates, began to have rights to appear before the king's court, rights to make contracts on their own; became, in effect, persons before the law with a certain set of rights (elevated by seventeenth-century philosophers to the status of "natural rights") to engage in a variety of activities at their own pleasure. But second, and as a direct consequence of this fragmentation of

the feudal structure, a different kind of intermediate organization arose in society: a corporate actor which had, under charter from the king, a variety of rights to free and expansive action. This new corporate actor became the instrument through which men could jointly exercise their new-found rights. (Coleman, 1974: 28)

Under these altered conditions, corporate actors no longer contained their individual members but only the specific resources invested in them by persons acting as owners or investors; and they no longer fully controlled their members but only the specific behaviors contracted for by persons who agreed to function as their participants or agents. Individuals were only partially involved in these new organizations. Also, these organizations were no longer arranged in a concentric, hierarchical pattern, but were allowed to function somewhat independently of one another, competing for the loyalties and resources of individuals.

Coleman emphasizes the impact of individualism on the development of special-purpose organizations. Simmel (1955 trans.) in his brilliant essay "The Web of Group-Affiliations" stresses the reverse effect. When social arrangements consist of layers of concentrically related systems, the social spaces created tend to produce homogeneous individuals: batches of individuals are likely to share the same social location and perceive themselves as holding the same social identity. However, as social arrangements shift to contain overlapping and intersecting systems, a vastly increased variety of social spaces is created, and no two individuals are as likely to share the same social location or to hold the same social identity. As Simmel explains,

The groups with which the individual is affiliated constitute a system of coordinates, as it were, such that each new group with which he becomes affiliated circumscribes him more exactly and more unambiguously. To belong to any one of these groups leaves the individual considerable leeway. But the larger the number of groups to which an individual belongs, the more improbable is it that other persons will exhibit the same combination of group-affiliations, that these particular groups will "intersect" once again in a second individual.

. . . As individuals, we form the personality out of particular elements of life, each of which has arisen from, or is interwoven with, society. This personality is subjectivity par excellence in the sense that it combines the elements of culture in an individual manner. . . . As the person becomes affiliated with a social group, he surrenders himself to it. A synthesis of such subjective affiliations creates a group in an objective sense. But the person also regains his individuality, because his pattern of participation is unique; hence the fact of multiple group-participation creates in turn a new subjective element. (Simmel, 1955 trans.: 140–41)

Combining the insights of Coleman and Simmel, we conclude that there was an intimate, reciprocal, supportive relation between the emergence of individualism and the development of special-purpose organizations. Given this historical association, it is somewhat ironic that numerous commentators in our own time perceive organizations as the enemy of individualism. (We will explore this paradox in Chapter 12.)

Societal Conditions Favoring the Development
of Organizations

Thus far we have described some quite basic changes in societal arrangements without attempting to determine what brought these changes about. Drawing on the insights of Weber, Durkheim (1949 trans.), and other social theorists, Stinchcombe (1965) suggests that the capacity of a population to develop and support special-purpose organizations is determined by such general factors as widespread literacy and specialized advanced schooling, urbanization, a money economy, and political revolution. To these primarily economic and political factors, theorists such as Eisenstadt (1958) and Parsons (1966) add institutional and normative variables such as increased role and institutional differentiation, allocation of roles by universalistic and achievement rather than particularistic and ascriptive criteria, and increased dissensus among societal groups concerning the priority of goals, together with competition among them for resources. Eisenstadt concludes, "The most important characteristics of the environment conducive to the development of bureaucracies are first, the availability of various 'free-floating' resources, and second, the development of several centres of power which compete over such resources" (1958: 111). To these characteristics, Parsons (1960: 20–21) adds that societal environments support the emergence of organizations by legitimating their specialized functions and independent existence.

These arguments are all at a very general level: most of them describe conditions that are conducive to rationalization of the social structure in general and do not point specifically to conditions favoring the creation of organizations. Stinchcombe (1965: 146–50) recognizes this problem and has attempted to construct more specific arguments that relate these general conditions to the creation of organizations through intermediate variables. He suggests that such general societal factors influence the development of organizations (1) by motivating individuals to form and join such social units, and (2) by improving the chances that these units, once formed, will survive. Thus, individuals are motivated to join organizations by increased literacy, which facilitates the learning of new roles and the keeping of rules and records; by urbanization, which increases social differentiation and encourages the formation of mechanisms for regularizing relations among strangers; by a money economy, which liberates resources, depersonalizes economic relations, and simplifies the calculation of benefits and future conditions; and by political revolutions, which dislodge vested interests and loosen resources for new uses. These same social conditions also improve the likelihood of survival of newly formed organizations. Stinchcombe asserts that organizations suffer the *liability of newness:* new organizations and in particular new forms of organization are likely to fail. New organizations require the creation and learning of new roles, reliance on strangers, and the generation of new markets and customer ties. The same general factors—literacy, urbanization, monetarized exchange, and political upheavals—contribute to the creation of these conditions.

Although somewhat more specific, these arguments can still be sharpened. However, in doing so, we encounter once again the contrasting assumptions and arguments associated with the rational and the natural system views of the nature of organizations.

Rational System Explanations of the Origin of Organizations

Division of labor   Certainly the most widely accepted and one of the most compelling arguments concerning the origins of organizations ties their emergence to the division of labor. The classic statement of this argument was provided by Adam Smith in 1776 in his celebrated account of the manufacture of pins. Smith observed that whereas an untrained worker without the proper machinery could "scarce, perhaps, with his utmost industry, make one pin in a day," vastly different results obtain when the work is properly divided into a number of branches.

> One man draws out the wire, another straights it, a third cuts it, a fourth points it, a fifth grinds it at the top for receiving the head; to make the head requires two or three distinct operations; to put it on is a peculiar business, to whiten the pins is another; it is even a trade by itself to put them into the paper; and the important business of making a pin is, in this manner, divided into about eighteen distinct operations. . . (Smith, 1957 ed.: 2).

So arranged, ten persons "could make among them upwards of forty-eight thousand pins a day."

This miracle of productivity is accomplished primarily by the application of technology to the work process. As Galbraith explains, "technology means the systematic application of scientific or other organized knowledge to practical tasks." This is possible only when the tasks are divided into their components in such a manner that they become "coterminous with some established area of scientific or engineering knowledge." (1967: 24) In addition to this prime benefit, specialization within the work force allows the organization to take advantage of particular skills possessed by a member and also fosters the development of such skills through repetition and learning. And to the extent that the various skills required are of differential complexity, variable pay scales may be introduced, so that further economies are realized through task subdivision. (Braverman, 1974: 79)

The division of labor also tends to encourage its concentration in specified work settings. In order to minimize costs of handling and storage, to take advantage of central energy sources, and to improve surveillance and control, workers are often gathered into a common location.

These types of changes—the division of labor, advances in technology, concentration of the work force in factories—are all associated with the general process of industrialization. In an influential volume, Kerr and his colleagues (1964) attempt to identify a set of developments that are generic to the process of industrialization as well as to examine specific variants of the process that occur under differing societal and cultural conditions. Among the universal consequences, they include the creation of organizations. "The technology and specialization of the industrial society," they assert, "are necessarily and distinctively associated with large-scale organizations." (p. 21).

However, it is not only production organizations that are associated with work division and specialization. As we already know, Weber advanced similar arguments for systems of political administration. His ideal-type conception of bureaucracy places great emphasis on technical expertise and a fixed division of labor among officials. And he was quite explicit that this form replaced earlier, more traditional social structures because of its greater efficiency.

> Experience tends universally to show that the purely bureaucratic type of administrative organization . . . is, from a purely technical point of view, capable of attaining the highest degree of efficiency and is in this sense formally the most rational known means of exercising authority over human beings. It is superior to any other form in precision, in stability, in the stringency of its discipline, and in its reliability. (Weber, 1947 trans.: 337)

Giddens (1983: 202) correctly notes the extent to which Weber's conception draws on technical and mechanical imagery:

> Weber's talk of "precision," "stability" and "reliability" points to the direct connection between bureaucracy and mechanisation that he sometimes makes quite explicit. Bureaucracy, he says, is a "human machine": the formal rationality of technique applies with equal relevance to human social organisation as to the control of the material world.

On the other hand, work division entails overhead costs. Someone must design the work segments and someone must control and coordinate the divided work. A horizontal division of labor is usually accompanied by a vertical hierarchy providing oversight—over those engaged in either tasks of production or administration.

According to these well-known arguments, the division of labor supports the application of technology or rationalized procedures to work, increases the scale of work organizations, and gives rise to a managerial hierarchy. These developments occur because they are associated with increasing productivity and with heightened efficiency of operations. Rational system analysts assume that they are fundamental to the appearance and growth of organizations. As the administrative theorist Luther Gulick concludes, "work division is the foundation of organization; indeed, the reason for organization" (Gulick and Urwick, 1937: 3).

Transactions costs   As noted in Chapter 5, a newer rational (and open) system perspective, provides an alternative explanation for the emergence of organizations. This approach, developed by Williamson (1975) and others, shifts attention from technology and the production of commodities to *transactions*—the exchange of goods and services between persons or across boundaries. The typical neoclassical economic model conceived of firms as systems for managing production functions, with the primary decisions focused on the optimal mix of production factors—resources, labor, capital. In this model, variations in organizational structure are largely irrelevant. By contrast, the transactions costs perspective assumes that not the production but the exchange of goods and services is critical, and it emphasizes the importance of the structures that govern these exchanges. Two broad types of governance regimes are contrasted: the market and the organization (hierarchy).

In a market system, exchanges occur between buyers and sellers based on negotiated contractual agreements. These transactions are governed by the price system, which, in aggregate, provides a set of signals concerning what goods and services in what quantity are desired and hence will be profitable to produce. It is presumed that all parties are governed by self-interest. Several advantages are associated with a market arrangement as a basis for organizing transactions. Adam Smith (1957 ed.) was among the first to note that relatively little knowledge is required of the participants in such transactions. Assuming that individuals know their own preferences, price signals provide a comparatively simple basis on which to make decisions. And, as symbolized by Smith's famous simile of the invisible hand, market and pricing mechanisms do provide an overall basis for coordinating individual actions. Hence, it is not necessary to expend resources specifically to achieve coordination; no administrative overhead is required for planning, collective decision making, or control.

Recent analyses suggest that market transactions work well as a framework for *spot contracts*—contracts in which all obligations are fulfilled on the spot, such as the exchange of money for a commodity in hand. They fare less well when the transactions involve future values. When goods or services are not to be delivered on the spot, but at some future time, it is often possible to draw up a *contingent claims contract*. Such a document specifies the obligations of each party to the exchange, contingent upon possible future developments. For example, a farmer may agree to sell his grain to a warehouse if the price does not drop below a specified amount per ton. But as the future becomes more complex or uncertain, it becomes increasingly difficult and costly to draw up contracts that take into account all possible contingencies. In such circumstances, organizations are likely to be viewed as attractive alternatives to market-mediated transactions.

Arrow asserts that "organizations are a means of achieving the benefits of collective action in situations in which the price system fails" (1974: 33). The price system, viewed as a mechanism for the efficient allocation of personnel and resources to production tasks, fails when confronted with very complex relations among these factors or with uncertainty concerning future conditions. As such complexity and uncertainty increases, more information needs to be processed in order for contracts to be negotiated and transactions conducted. Both Arrow and Williamson conclude that the specific way in which organizations are superior to markets in managing complex and uncertain economic transactions is that organizations reduce the costs of such transactions.

Williamson (1975) elaborates the argument by developing an elegant and simple model of the conditions under which markets tend to give way to organizations.[1] The basic elements of the model appear in Figure 7–1.

[1]Williamson's terminology differs from our own and can cause confusion on first reading. He employs the term *organization* to refer to any social arrangement within which transactions are conducted. Thus, markets as well as organizations in our sense are regarded as organizations. This is why Williamson's discussion of the limitations of markets is presented in terms of an *organizational failures framework*. Williamson's terms for organizations in our sense are, variously, *internal organizations*, *hierarchies*, and *firms*.

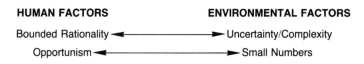

HUMAN FACTORS   **ENVIRONMENTAL FACTORS**

Bounded Rationality ◄───────────► Uncertainty/Complexity

Opportunism ◄───────────► Small Numbers

FIGURE 7–1   The Market Failures Framework. *Source:* Williamson (1975), Figure 3, p. 40.

Williamson uses the concept of bounded rationality simply to refer to the limitations of individuals as information processors. The cognitive limitations of individuals are emphasized by Simon (1957) and have already been described in Chapter 2. As environments become more complex or uncertain, these limitations are quickly reached. Hence, it is only when individuals are confronted with excessive environmental demands that their information-processing capacities become insufficient and alternative arrangements are required. Incorporating individual decision makers into organizational arrangements is one such alternative.

We have already described, in Chapter 2, how organizational structures facilitate and support individual decision making. The rational system perspective is the relevant one: the organization permits problem subdivision, simplifies choices, channels information, and restricts alternatives. Goal specificity and formalization overcome the cognitive limitations of individual actors. As Simon (1979: 501) asserts,

> it is now clear that the elaborate organizations that human beings have constructed in the modern world to carry out the work of production and government can only be understood as machinery for coping with the limits of man's abilities to comprehend and compute in the face of complexity and uncertainty.

Williamson uses the second pair of concepts in Figure 7–1—opportunism and small numbers—to develop a different argument regarding the relative advantages of markets and organizations. Opportunism is revealed in individual actors who are capable of "self-interest seeking with guile" and of making "self-disbelieved threats and promises" (Williamson, 1975: 26). In short, some people lie, cheat, and steal! Those of us who are honest will try to avoid entering into transactions with these disreputable types, but we may have no choice if we are faced with a small-numbers condition—that is, few alternative partners. Williamson cogently notes that many situations not characterized in the beginning by a small number of alternative partners may become so as transactions progress, because early exchange partners ("first-movers") gain decided advantages over their competitors.

The creation of organizations helps to solve the problem of opportunism among exchange partners. By bringing economic exchanges under a hierarchical structure, organizations can construct better auditing and surveillance systems. Also, incentive systems within an organization can be arranged so that individual participants are discouraged from behaving opportunistically. Further, arrangements by which individual performance can be more closely monitored are especially helpful when the work involves *nonseparabilities*—products of highly interdependent teams such that it is difficult to determine who has made what contributions. When outputs involve nonseparabilities it is useful to be able to inspect inputs (see Alchian and Demsetz, 1972).

Yet another difference between the market and the organization is the nature of the transactions that take place between exchange partners. In the case of organizations, a new type of contract comes into existence: the employment contract. The institutional economist John Commons first called attention to the special nature of this contract, noting that what the worker sells "when he sells his labor is his willingness to use his faculties according to a purpose that has been pointed out to him. He sells his promise to obey commands." (1924: 284) Under conditions of uncertainty, the advantages of this open-ended or "incomplete" contract are obvious: obedience is promised to a general range of commands,[2] the specific command being determined by the variable and unpredictable requirements of the changing situation.

The transactions costs framework provides a general explanation for the origins of organizations as mechanisms for supporting decisions under conditions of uncertainty and suppressing opportunism under conditions of restricted exchange. It is also useful for explaining how specific organizations determine their boundaries and design their governance systems, but these matters are reserved for later chapters. The transactions costs approach, like other economic explanations, focuses primarily on efficiency. Governance structures, among which organizations and markets are the leading alternatives, are compared and assessed "in terms of their capacities to economize on transaction costs" (Williamson, 1981: 549). Such arguments are well within the rational system perspective.[3]

Information processing   Yet another explanation for the emergence of the organization is its superior capacity to manage flows of information. A hierarchical structure incorporates several features—including status distinctions and power differences among positions—but among its most significant components is a centralized communications system. What, if any, are the advantages of carrying on work within a hierarchical structure—specifically, a centralized communications structure—compared with a more informal and equalitarian arrangement? Experiments on communication structures conducted during the 1950s and 1960s examined the effects of centralized versus decentralized communication

---

[2]The range of commands that will be obeyed automatically in any organizational situation is, of course, restricted. Ordinarily a supervisor does not have the right to tell an employee to perform personal services or to carry out activities beyond those specified in the job description. These boundaries are also influenced by generalized social beliefs. For example, some contemporary secretaries have decided that making coffee is outside their appropriate job definition. Barnard refers to the arena within which employees will unquestioningly comply with directives as the *zone of indifference* (1938: 168–69); Simon refers to the same concept as the *zone of acceptance* (1957: 12).

[3]Williamson's arguments are also functionalist in that they attempt to explain the origins of a structure in terms of its consequences (functions) rather than in terms of the processes or mechanisms that bring it about. (See Granovetter, 1985.)

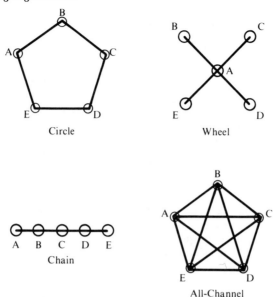

FIGURE 7-2   Examples of Communication Networks (five-person groups)

networks on the task performance of groups.[4] In a technique developed by Bavelas (1951), a small number of individuals are placed in cubicles and allowed to communicate only by means of written messages passed through slots in the cubicle walls. The slots connecting each cubicle can be opened or closed by the experimenter, so that differing communication patterns can be imposed on the interacting subjects. The most frequently studied communication networks are diagramed in Figure 7-2. The circle and all-channel networks are relatively decentralized communication structures; the chain and particularly the wheel are more highly centralized. A typical task presented to groups placed in these networks is to provide each individual with a card containing several symbols, only one of which is present on the cards of all subjects, and ask all participants to identify the common symbol. Most researchers using this type of task have reported that groups working in the more centralized structures are more efficient in their performance, as measured by the speed of attaining a solution or the number of messages transmitted to arrive at a solution, than groups in more decentralized structures (see Leavitt, 1951; Guetzkow and Simon, 1955).

Vroom accounts for these findings as follows:

[4]Some analysts are reluctant to generalize from findings based on "artificial" experiments to behavior in real-world organizations. However, we believe that, interpreted with caution, results from experimental studies can aid our understanding of natural phenomena. The great advantage of experimental settings is that they permit investigators to isolate certain variables from others whose presence may influence the effects being observed (see Zelditch, 1969). We just noted that hierarchies in organizations contain a number of elements only one of which defines the formal structuring of communication flows. Experiments allow us to examine the effects of these structured flows independently of those produced by formal status and power differences.

The centralized structures more rapidly organize to solve the problems. Participants in peripheral positions send information to the center of the network, where a decision is made and sent out to the periphery. Furthermore, this pattern of organization tends to be highly stable once developed. In less centralized structures the organization problem is more difficult and observed interaction patterns are less stable, as well as less efficient. (Vroom, 1969: 242)

Vroom stresses the functions of formalization, as discussed in Chapter 2. Arrow embraces the same conclusion, but his arguments concerning the superiority of centralized networks are based on efficiency of information processing:

> since transmission of information is costly, in the sense of using resources, especially the time of individuals, it is cheaper and more efficient to transmit all the pieces of information once to a central place than to disseminate each of them to everyone. (Arrow, 1974: 68)

Noting that the gathering of information is also essential to arriving at a decision, Arrow applies the same arguments to this process, concluding, "Thus, authority, the centralization of decision-making, serves to economize on the transmission and handling of information" (Arrow, 1974: 69).

Williamson (1975: 41–54) agrees that hierarchies are superior to peer groups or other types of decentralized communication networks in the economies of information flows effected. In addition, he asserts that the use of hierarchies reduces the likelihood of opportunistic behavior by improving surveillance of individual performance.

It would be incorrect, however, to conclude that hierarchies are superior to more decentralized or equalitarian arrangements under all conditions. Other studies employing the Bavelas networks have introduced more complex tasks—for example, mathematical problems—or provided subjects with more ambiguous information to process—for example, asking them to identify similar colors when the samples provided include unusual colors for which there are no common names (Shaw, 1954; Christie, Luce, and Macy, 1952). Such studies show that as tasks become more complex or ambiguous, decentralized nets are usually superior to centralized structures (Shaw, 1964).

Reviewing these communication-network studies, Blau and I (Blau and Scott, 1962: 116–28) concluded that formal hierarchies aid the performance of tasks requiring the efficient coordination of information and routine decision making, but they interfere with tasks presenting very complex or ambiguous problems. Specifically, we argued that hierarchies impede work on the latter by stifling free interactions that can result in error correction, by undermining the social support necessary to encourage *all* participants to propose solutions, and by reducing incentives for participants to search for solutions.

More generally, there appears to be a curvilinear relation between information-processing requirements and the utility of hierarchy. When little information is to be processed, there are no particular advantages to hierarchy and some clear disadvantages (for example, the administrative overhead). As information-processing needs increase up to a certain point, hierarchies can be of benefit, reducing transmission costs and ensuring coordination. But as information-processing needs continue to increase, hierarchies become overloaded and the intellectual resources of peripheral participants underutilized. Such increased demands do not require a return to informal systems, but they do encourage the creation of more decentralized structures. (Specific types of decentralization strategies are described in Chapter 9.)

The same type of argument can be made with respect to the relation between surveillance requirements and hierarchies. The creation of hierarchies can result in improved surveillance and control of participants up to a point, but if extraordinary demands are required for secrecy or loyalty, formal hierarchical surveillance may have to be supplemented or replaced by clan systems relying on more diffuse, internalized controls (see Ouchi, 1980). For example, organizations confronting hostile environments, such as the FBI or the Mafia, are likely to rely heavily on procedures that induce a strong personal commitment (see Wilson, 1978) or on the creation of diffuse interpersonal ties (see Ianni, 1972) to effect tight controls (see Chapter 11).

But we must return to the main theme. To summarize, from Smith and Weber to Arrow and Williamson, there is general agreement that organizations are called into existence by the increasing need to coordinate and control complex administrative and technical tasks and transactions. Enlarged political states, expanding markets, and improved technologies both require and are made possible by the development of organizations that can manage complex exchanges and coordinate diverse, interrelated activities.

Natural System Explanations of the Origins of Organizations

Institutional explanations   As described in Chapter 5, institutional theorists emphasize the extent to which the world is a product of our ideas and conceptions—the socially created and validated meanings that define reality. Associated with the rise of the modern world is not only a set of production technologies and administrative structures for coordinating complex activities but also the growth of certain beliefs and cognitions about the nature of the world and the way in which things happen (Ellul, 1964 trans.). Technology and bureaucracy are more than hardware and filing cabinets filled with papers: they are new states of consciousness. The concomitants of technological production at the level of consciousness include the belief that the work process has a machinelike functionality, that all actions within the process are reproducible, that productive activity entails participation in a large organization and in a sequence of production, that the work being performed is measurable, and so on. Similarly, bureaucracy connotes distinctive spheres of competence, the importance of proper procedures, orderliness, predictability, and an attitude of "moralized anonymity" (Berger, Berger, and Kellner, 1973: 23–62).

It is important to emphasize that such beliefs are widely held by people in modern society and are continually being created and reinforced by a wide range of corporate actors and forces: universities, professional groups, public opinion, the mass media, the state, law. Thus, these beliefs do not exist merely as general values that support organizations, but take on very specific and powerful forms in a variety of guises—as professional expertise, as procedural rules, and as legal requirements.

In short, as we argued in the previous chapter, the environments of organizations are not only technical, providing resources and information in support of the production of goods and services and rewarding efficient performance; they are also increasingly institutional, specifying rules and procedures and containing rationalized myths and roles that organizations are rewarded for incorporating.

> Thus organizational success depends on factors other than efficient coordination and control of productive activities. Independent of their productive efficiency, organizations that exist in highly elaborated institutional environments and succeed in becoming isomorphic with these environments gain the legitimacy and resources needed to survive. (Meyer and Rowan, 1977: 352)

DiMaggio and Powell (1983) have distinguished three mechanisms that are conducive to *isomorphism*—increasing structural homogeneity—among organizations in institutional environments. First of all, *coercive* isomorphism results from formal or informal pressures exerted by one organization on another as a condition for its support or approval. In modern societies, the nation-state, as a vital source of resources and as a major locus of coercive power, imposes uniform structures and/or procedures on many types of organizations. For example, DiMaggio (1983) reports how the National Endowment for the Arts, a federal program established to support artistic endeavors, followed a grants policy that encouraged states and then individual communities to establish arts councils that played a substantial role in determining what groups would receive funds. In this manner, a relatively disorganized organizational field has become rather highly structured around "the creation of a vertical network of public and private arts agencies from Washington to local communities" (p. 151).

The second mechanism identified by DiMaggio and Powell is *mimetic* or imitative isomorphism. They argue that this mode of isomorphism is especially prevalent among organizations confronting uncertainty.

> When organizational technologies are poorly understood, when goals are ambiguous, or when the environment creates symbolic uncertainty, organizations may model themselves on other organizations (DiMaggio and Powell, 1983: 151).

Organizations are quick to embrace "modern" management devices such as MBO (management by objective) or to adopt a multi-divisional structure so as to appear up to date. (See Chapter 10.) A study of the adoption of municipal reforms by the 267 largest American cities during the period 1900–1942 by Knoke (1982) found that the best basis for predicting the adoption, prior to the First World War, of the commission form of government or, prior to the Second World War, of the city manager form was the percentage of other municipalities in the same region that had adopted each administrative reform.

A third source of isomorphic pressure is *normative* isomorphism, which is carried primarily by professionals. The authority of professionals rests primarily on their claims to specialized knowledge and skills. This competence is based in university centers and spread through professional networks that span organizations. (See Clark, 1983.) Professionals seek to impose their own normative standards on the organizations in which they operate—encouraging them to embrace their definitions of the problems, their standards, and their solutions. It is no accident that most colleges contain the same assortment of disciplines or that most hospitals contain the same set of services.

Meyer and Rowan and DiMaggio and Powell emphasize the extent to which rationalized elements in the modern social environments encourage the development of organizations:

> The growth of rationalized institutional structures in society makes formal organizations more common and more elaborate. Such institutions are myths which make formal organizations both easier to create and more necessary. After all, the building blocks for organizations come to be littered around the societal landscape; it takes only a little entrepreneurial energy to assemble them into a structure. (Meyer and Rowan, 1977: 345)

Zucker (1983) argues that the increase in organizations is due to more than just the profusion of rationalized institutional elements that, like prefabricated forms, can be assembled into new structures. In addition, the organizational form itself has become "the focal defining institution in modern society." (p. 13) In order to demonstrate that we are serious about achieving some goal or protecting some value, we must create an organization to symbolize our commitment.

Both Zucker and DiMaggio and Powell suggest that whereas the early impetus for creating organizations was their technical benefits, their more recent growth largely reflects an institutional process. Zucker (1983: 13) argues that

> the rush to create organizations cannot be explained either by the need to counterbalance the power of existing organizations *or* by any distinct advantage inherent in organizational form (such as increased production efficiency). Rather, the rapid rise and continued spread of the organizational form is best interpreted as an instance of institutionalization: early in the process of diffusion, the organizational form is adopted because it has unequivocal effects on productivity, while later it becomes seen as legitimate to organize formally, regardless of any net benefit.

In a similar vein, DiMaggio and Powell (1983: 147) assert that "the causes of bureaucratization and rationalization have changed," in that "structural change in organizations seems less and less driven by competition or by the need for efficiency" and is more likely to reflect institutional processes.

Although we agree that both technical and institutional processes give rise to organizations, it does not seem obvious that technical forces were dominant in earlier periods and have now given way to institutional forces. New technologies are constantly being created, and institutional forms that were once strong—such as religion—are no longer as robust. Moreover, professions such as medicine that earlier could make few supportable claims to a scientific base are in a far stronger position to do so today. Technical and institutional systems both compete with and complement each other. Both appear vigorous across varying contemporary organizational environments.

Marxist explanations   We have already discussed, in Chapter 5, the crux of the Marxist explanation for the origin and growth of organizations: they exist to exercise control. While recognizing that all social structures involve role differentiation, most Marxists argue that the minute division of labor that developed in the early days of industrialization was aimed more at maximizing managerial control than at achieving productive efficiency. In their famous tract, Marx and Engels (1955 trans.: 65) described how in the factories of capitalist systems, the worker "becomes an appendage of the machine, and it is only the most simple, most monotonous and most easily acquired knack, that is required of him." Marx argued that the type of work division developed in these organizations destroyed the craft skills of workers:

> Hence, in the place of the hierarchy of specialized workmen that characterizes manufacture, there steps, in the automatic factory, a tendency to equalise and reduce to one and the same level every kind of work that has to be done by the minders of the machines (Marx, 1954 trans.: 420).

Braverman and Marglin have amplified Marx's position. The dissection of work separates workers from their products; deskills workers, turning artisans into operatives; increases the potential pool of workers, thereby weakening the job security of each; and segments workers, fragmenting their common experience and undermining their class consciousness (Braverman, 1974).

Not only does the division of labor reduce the power of workers, it increases and legitimates the power of managers. Returning to Adam Smith's pin factory, Marglin (1974: 38) insists that

> without specialization, the capitalist had no essential role to play in the production process. . . . Separating the tasks assigned to each workman was the sole means by which the capitalist could, in the days preceding costly machinery, ensure that he would remain essential to the production process as integrator of these separate operations into a product for which a wide market existed.

Indeed, dividing work provides many managerial and technical roles: not only that of integrator but those of designer of the work process, hirer, trainer, inspector, troubleshooter, procurer of supplies, securer of markets, and so forth.

In addition to arguing that discretion was removed from workers and transferred to managers (and their growing technical staff), Marx insisted that the surplus value created by productive labor was stripped from workers and grasped by manager-capitalists. Although Marx and many other social analysts have condemned this practice, Marglin (1974: 34) acknowledges that this form of "enforced savings" created the surplus capital that led to the subsequent technological revolution. He argues that "the social function of hierarchical work organization is not technical efficiency, but accumulation."

Both Stark and Burawoy suggest that Marx and Braverman have overstated the cohesion and unity of managers under capitalism and understated those of workers. Stark emphasizes the resourcefulness of workers who have found ways to counteract and undermine the effectiveness of the new control systems. Some changes introduced to improve managerial control have actually increased the power of workers:

> Assembly line production, for example, decreases the degree of direct cooperation among workers, but the objective interdependence of workers also increases their ability to disrupt production either through individual acts of sabotage, collective activity, or the more passive form of simply not showing up for work (Stark, 1980: 93).

And, as we noted in our introductory discussion of scientific management in Chapter 2, these attempts to rationalize the work process were resisted not only by workers but also by managers, who did not want to see their powers usurped by engineers. As Burawoy (1985: 46) notes, control over the labor process emerges as a result, "not only of struggle between capital and labour, but also of struggle among the different agents of capital. . . . one cannot *assume* the existence of a cohesive managerial and capitalist class that automatically recognizes its true interests."

Power contests are not restricted to factories. In his illuminating history of the rise of the Prussian bureaucracy, Rosenberg (1958) argues that many of the Prussian bureaucratic reforms were imposed by the newly emerging administrative elite on the Crown, restricting his arbitrary powers of appointment and promotion, rather than the reverse. (See also Chs. 10 and 11.)

In short, while it is important to recognize the power aspects of changes in the division of labor or in the structuring of work processes, it is an oversimplification to view all of the power advantages as being on any one side, or to presume that there are only two sides. The work setting is indeed a "contested terrain," as Edwards (1979) has argued, with various parties vying for control and for a greater share of the value created there; the outcomes to date do not support the conclusion that any single party has been either omniscient or all-powerful.

But, as might be expected, there is even disagreement about what outcomes have occurred. Marx predicted that the forces inherent in capitalist systems, unchecked, would lead inevitably to the proletarianization of the work force. Kerr and his colleagues insist that Marx's dark descriptions and dire predictions have not been borne out by the actual course of industrialization. They note that

> industrialization in fact develops and depends upon a concentrated, disciplined industrial work force—a work force with new skills, and a wide variety of skills, with high skill levels and constantly changing skill requirements. . . . The industrialization process utilizes a level of technology far in

advance of that of earlier societies. . . . The industrial system requires a wide range of skills and professional competency broadly distributed throughout the work force. (Kerr et al., 1964: 17)

But Braverman (1974) challenges this picture as misleading, insisting that the net effect of industrialization as it has progressed in the twentieth century has been the deskilling of a large segment of the population. He reviews considerable data bearing on job requirements at varying levels and concludes,

> Clearly the "average" scientific, technical, and in that sense "skill" content of these labor processes is much greater than in the past. But . . . the question is precisely whether the scientific and "educated" content of labor tends toward *averaging*, or, on the contrary, toward *polarization*. . . . The mass of workers gain nothing from the fact that the decline in their command over the labor process is more than compensated for by the increasing command on the part of managers and engineers. (Braverman, 1974: 425)

Moreover, Braverman argues that much of the upgrading of occupational groups does not reflect real changes in skill level but is an artifact of distinctions made by census categories that, for example, label workers who have any type of contact with a machine as *operatives* or *semiskilled* workers and that regard any type of office or clerical employment as superior to blue-collar work. Braverman also observes that the fastest-growing occupational sectors are those involved in service work, sales, and clerical positions. These positions are less affected by industrialization, require lower skills, and are generally associated with lower pay. And these are the positions into which women—a vast new labor pool—are primarily drawn.

Thus, the controversy over both the causes and the consequences of industrialization continues. All parties, however, seem to agree that an important by-product of the process has been the rapid growth of large-scale organizations.

We have reviewed a variety of rational and natural open system explanations for the emergence of organizations as distinctive forms of social structure. Accounting for the origins of organizational forms is, however, not the same as explaining how any particular organization is created and maintained. We view the latter process as a matter of mobilizing resources.

THE MOBILIZATION OF RESOURCES

Oberschall provides a useful definition of *mobilization*—"the process of forming crowds, groups, associations, and organizations for the pursuit of collective goals" (1973: 102). Organizations do not spontaneously emerge but require the gathering and harnessing of resources—materials, energy, information, and personnel. The availability of such resources varies from place to place and from time to time. In traditional societies, material resources are locked into landholdings and individuals into caste and kinship systems; in modern societies, to repeat the observation of Eisenstadt (1958), resources are more "free-floating" and easier to mobilize into the service of specialized goals. We have already reviewed, in the first section of this chapter, the general societal factors that facilitate the creation of these conditions.

Many factors affect the mobilization process, as we will see. The conditions present at the time of the founding of the organization have significant and enduring effects on an organization; what types of incentives are employed to induce contributions will affect the structure of the organization as will the characteristics of the members recruited; and the competitive environment confronting an organization will help to shape its distinctive strategies and structures.

Initial Resource Mix

Each specific type of organization presents a particular combination of resource requirements—economic and technical as well as social. The technological base on which the organization rests must be in place; labor, trained and movable, must be available; capital is required from individuals willing to risk it; and an appropriate organizational form must have been invented. Larger cultural norms must support the venture: the goals of the enterprise together with the means employed in their pursuit must be regarded as legitimate.[5] A given combination of requirements cannot always be met. Appropriate conditions come together at certain periods, creating new possibilities for the support of organizations that could not exist under different circumstances. This accounts for the pattern of organizational founding noted by Stinchcombe (1965: 154), who points out that

> an examination of the history of almost any type of organization shows that there are great spurts of foundation of organizations of the type, followed by periods of relatively slower growth, perhaps to be followed by new spurts, generally of a fundamentally different kind of organization in the same field.

Stinchcombe cites numerous United States examples: the founding of savings banks and the first factory industry, textiles, in the 1830s; the development of railroads and steel companies in the 1850s and 1870s; the founding of universities and labor unions from the 1870s to the 1900s; the development of department stores in the 1850s and mail-order houses in the 1870s; the growth of the oil, rubber, and automobile industries in the 1920s; the emergence of the airline manufacturing and transportation companies during and after World War II; and the development of data-processing and electronic equipment since the 1960s (1965: 154–55).

Given the similar resource requirements confronting each of these types of organizations, it should come as no surprise that each cohort of organizations of the same type is quite similar in its occupational composition and structural features. As Stinchcombe observes, "organizations

---

[5]Weber's (1958 trans.) most famous essay, "The Protestant Ethic and the Spirit of Capitalism," deals with the role of religious values and belief systems, particularly Christian asceticism such as Calvinism, in legitimating the accumulation and investment of capital and effort in economic enterprise.

which are founded at a particular time must construct their social systems with the social resources available (1965: 168). What is remarkable is that once established, an organization of a given type tends to retain the basic characteristics present at its founding. Organizational forms are *imprinted:* they are likely to retain the features acquired at their origin. Stinchcombe (pp. 155–69) cites a variety of evidence to support this conclusion: for example, industries composed of small firms at the outset tend to retain this characteristic; industries relying heavily on unpaid family workers tend to continue to do so. And only those firms established during the last few decades use professional staffs extensively.

Both rational and natural system explanations may account for this association between organizational characteristics and time of founding. The characteristics may provide a competitive advantage over alternative arrangements (a rational system argument); they may be preserved by a set of "traditionalizing forces," including vested interests; or the organizations that exhibit the characteristics may not be confronted by competitive forces and may therefore live on without major changes or technical improvements (a natural system explanation). Whatever the case, it is instructive to realize that the form organizations acquire at their founding are likely to affect the structure they retain over their life. The mix of initial resources out of which an organizational structure is created has lasting effects on the attributes of that structure.

Balance of Contributions and Inducements

Of all the many resources required by organizations, the most vital are the contributions of its human participants. Not only are these contributions themselves of infinite variety, they are also the ultimate means by which all other resources are acquired. More than other early theorists, Barnard (1938) stressed the importance of an organization's ability to motivate participants to continue to make contributions—of time, resources, effort—to it rather than to some competing system. Barnard's concerns were pursued by Simon (1957), the result being the Barnard-Simon theory of *organizational equilibrium.*[6] *Equilibrium* refers to the organization's ability to attract sufficient contributions to ensure its survival. The basic postulates of the theory are as follows:

1. An organization is a system of interrelated social behaviors of a number of persons whom we shall call *participants* in the organization.
2. Each participant and each group of participants receives *from* the organization *inducements* in return for which he makes to the organization *contributions.*
3. Each participant will continue his participation in an organization only so long as the inducements offered him are as great or greater (measured in terms of *his* values and in terms of the alternatives open to him) than the contributions he is asked to make.
4. The contributions provided by the various groups of participants are

[6]Recall from Chapter 2 that Barnard and Simon distinguish between the decisions a participant makes to join and continue to participate in an organization and those that he or she makes *as* a participant in the organization. The current discussion deals with the first category of decisions.

the source from which the organization manufactures the inducements offered to participants.

5. Hence, an organization is "solvent"—and will continue in existence—only so long as the contributions are sufficient to provide inducements in large enough measure to draw forth these contributions. (Simon, Smithberg, and Thompson, 1950: 381–82)

Although it points to an essential truth about the survival of organizations, the theory "verges on the tautological," as Simon himself observes (March and Simon, 1958: 84). It is difficult to measure the balance of inducements and contributions independently of the individual's decision to stay with or leave the organization. Also, as noted by Krupp, since the concept of organizational inducement includes techniques for changing an individual's values or needs, it is difficult to distinguish between inducements that "win participation because they create satisfactions at a given level of willingness and inducements that shift the level of willingness" (1961: 107). Further, it is difficult to determine what utilities or values are attached by individual participants to the contributions they are asked to make and the inducements they are offered. Indeed, one of the major contributions of the human relations school in attempting to counteract the myth of the economic person is its demonstration of the diversity of factors to which individuals attach importance—working conditions, tools, skills, personal relations, office furnishings, and raw materials—for example—whether they are processing fish or preparing desserts in a restaurant (see Whyte, 1948; Whyte et al., 1955). And related work emphasizes that level of satisfaction is not assessed on an absolute scale but depends on choice of reference of comparison group. That is, how one worker assesses his or her own benefits depends on those received by others regarded as comparable (see Adams, 1965; Homans, 1961; Patchen, 1961; Martin, 1981).

One of the most useful approaches to understanding how organizations attract and reward participants for their contributions is based on a simple typology developed by Clark and Wilson (1961: 134–36; see also Wilson, 1973). Clark and Wilson differentiate among three types of incentives:

material incentives: tangible rewards; rewards with a monetary value—for example, wages, interest, fringe benefits, patronage;

solidary incentives: intangible rewards derived from the act of association—for example, sociability, status, identification;

purposive incentives: intangible rewards related to the goals of the organization—for example, satisfaction obtained from working on the election of a candidate whose position on issues is similar to one's own, or the rewards perceived by a pacifist who contributes money and time to antiwar groups.

Like Etzioni (1961), whose similar typology was developed at the same time, Clark and Wilson (1961: 137–49) suggest that although all organizations use all three types of incentives, it is usually possible to identify a predominant type for each. And associated with each type are important structural and operational differences.

Organizations that rely primarily on material incentives are labeled *utilitarian organizations;* examples are business firms, trade unions, and political machines. Clark and Wilson predict that such organizations will explicitly seek material rewards for their members and develop fairly precise cost-accounting machinery. Executives will devote their energies first and foremost to obtaining the material resources needed to provide incentives; central conflicts within the organization will center on their equitable distribution. The substantive goals pursued by the organization will be of only secondary importance. Such organizations can be flexible about their goal-related activities: these "activities may change without disrupting member participation as long as material incentives continue to be available" (Clark and Wilson, 1961: 140).

Solidary organizations include most service-oriented voluntary associations and social clubs. Members make contributions in return for sociability and status. Executive efforts must therefore be devoted to obtaining additional organizational prestige, publicity, or good fellowship. The goals of such organizations need to be noncontroversial and socially desirable. Solidary organizations are tactically less flexible than utilitarian organizations: the means utilized must be acceptable to powerful participants, and projects must often be carried on publicly to stimulate the flow of approvals and publicity.

In many ways, *purposive organizations* represent the most interesting case. These organizations "rely almost exclusively on their stated purposes as incentives to attract and hold contributors" (Clark and Wilson, 1961: 146). This would appear to be the ideal organizational arrangement: members join because they wish to help achieve the goals espoused by the organization, and the organization, in achieving its goals, supplies inducements to its members to secure their continuing contributions. Wilson's (1962: 1973) analyses, however, suggest that this "ideal" is very difficult to realize. Executives in these organizations—like their counterparts in other organizations—must secure a continuing flow of inducements to sustain the interests of members, but many of the types of goals sought by purposive organizations are difficult to achieve. Political parties do not always succeed in electing their candidates; religious organizations do not always succeed in transforming the world or converting the heathen; and social movements may not succeed in achieving their specific goals—which range from achieving equality for minority racial groups to banning nuclear warheads. Sometimes the goals of such organizations may be only vaguely stated—so that the organization can appeal to a large number of potential adherents—but when the time comes for action and goals are more specifically defined, many participants may feel betrayed or at least sense that their interests are not being served. Alternatively, specific goals can serve as a guide to action but may only appeal to a narrow minority and prevent the organization from growing by attracting new recruits. Most purposive organizations are forced to set up intermediate objectives—for example, political clubs hold meetings in which their members debate and "endorse" specific positions in order to "manufacture" inducements for participants. Such contrived inducements can undermine the attainment of the organization's original goals. Thus, the club's endorsements of controversial political positions often embarrass, unduly constrain, or help to defeat candidates in the general election (Wilson, 1962).

Olson (1965) suggests yet another reason why purposive organizations are difficult to sustain. Under the classical economic assumption that individuals attempt to behave rationally and to pursue their self-interest, Olson points out that no individual should be expected to join an organization in order to achieve common or public interests. Rational persons will realize that their own act of joining, except under very special conditions, will not appreciably affect the chances of the organization to succeed in its mission. These individuals will also observe that because the goals served represent a collective good—one that cannot be unequally distributed but is available to all—they will share in the benefits of the organization's success whether or not they have contributed to its attainment.

Thus, both the analysis by Clark and Wilson and that by Olson conclude that purposive organizations—those attempting to equate organizational goals with individual motives—are difficult to manage and to maintain. Except for the most ideologically pure or the most extreme redemptive varieties (see Wilson, 1973: 45–51), purposive organizations typically supplement their primary incentives with material inducements—to retain a core staff—and solidary incentives—to help sustain the rank and file through the dry spells.

Membership Demographics

We have seen that there are a variety of ways in which organizations induce participants to contribute their time and resources to them, and that the mix of inducements employed has important consequences for the organization. The mix of participants also has important consequences. Considering only those participants who are identified as members of the organization, who are recruited and how long they stay has a wide range of implications for the structure and performance of the organization. The *demography* of the organization—the aggregated characteristics of its members, including their age, sex, education, ethnicity, and length of service—is increasingly recognized as a major determinant of organizational structure and performance. (See McNeil and Thompson, 1971; Pfeffer, 1983.)

The demographic composition of organizations is determined by such factors as the growth rate of the organization and the industry in which it is located, the rapidity with which the organization's technology is changing (the more rapid, the more likely the organization will be hiring new and better-educated workers), the personnel practices that are followed (for example, some types of organizations promote only from within their own ranks), and unionization (which is likely to promote longer tenure for workers) (Pfeffer, 1983).

The effects of demographic composition are wide-ranging and have yet to be fully explored. Their variety can be indicated by a few illustrations. Kanter (1977a) has examined the consequences of widely varying proportions of group members having one or another attribute—for example, the ratio of men to women, whites to blacks, or younger to older participants—on the attitudes and performance of the group. Focusing on a collection of women who occupied less than 10 percent of the exempt (salaried) jobs in a corporation, Kanter observed that the few women reaching the upper levels of management were treated as tokens: because they were "different" they were highly visible, the ways in which they varied from the majority took on exaggerated importance, and performance pressures were heightened by their "life in the limelight." Kanter (1977*a*: 241–42) explains how tokenism can shape the behavior and expectations of those involved:

> Tokens of Type O who are successful in their professional roles face pressures and inducements to dissociate themselves from other O's, and thus they may fail to promote, or even actively block, the entry of more O's. At the same time, tokens who are less than successful and appear less than fully competent confirm the organization's decision not to recruit more O's, unless they are extraordinarily competent and not like most O's. And since just a few O's can make the X-majority people feel uncomfortable, X's will certainly not go out of their way to include more O's.

In this manner, tokenism can become a self-perpetuating system.

Another example of the importance of membership composition is provided by Reed's (1978) analysis of the effects of cohort composition on the operation of the American Foreign Service bureaucracy. A *cohort* is simply a population of individuals who have experienced the same events at the same periods of their life. Thus an organizational cohort would be composed of those individuals who are recruited at the same time and whose careers develop in a parallel manner. Cohorts can significantly influence individual careers. Obviously, an individual's chances for promotion are going to be greatly affected by the size of one's own and preceding cohorts, especially in a system like that of the Foreign Service, where all promotions are made from within and few persons voluntarily transfer into some other system. But Reed also suggests that cohort composition can have organization-level effects. He argues that the slowness with which the Foreign Service adapted to its rapidly changing environment during the period surrounding World War II was significantly influenced by the characteristics of the cohort in charge—a collection of officers recruited many years earlier and under very different political and social conditions. A closed-career service bureaucracy is not well suited to changed demands that require rapid response.

A final example of the import of demography is suggested by the work of Ouchi (1980; 1981) on varying systems of organizational control. Ouchi argues that the Japanese-style model of the employment relation, which is based on the presumption of a lifetime commitment of organization to employee and vice versa, provides the basis for the creation of much more diffuse and informal control systems that rely greatly on the socialization of employees and their internalization of company norms and values than can be developed when there is a more rapid turnover of personnel. More generally, Pfeffer (1983) argues that the fewer the average years of service of the employees of an organization, the larger and more elaborate the bureaucratic control apparatus.

Thus, it is not only the initial resource mix and the assortment of incentives that shape the structure and performance of organizations. The creation of an organization is not a one-time event but a continuing process, and particularly fateful for the later stages of this process are the numbers and types of participants recruited earlier.

Acquisition of Resources

How difficult it is to garner the necessary resources to support an organization depends greatly on the nature of the organization and its goals. Much recent work has been devoted to describing protest or social-movement organizations that pursue controversial or change-oriented programs. Such organizations face a decidedly uphill struggle in their search for resources—including adherents and constitutents—and, more often than not, fail to survive (see Oberschall, 1973; Gamson, 1975).

Earlier theory and research on collective behavior—studies of crowds, mobs, riots, rebellions—stressed the importance of a common sense of grievance and discontent in motivating individuals to take collective action in behalf of their interests. More recent views emphasize that collective action is more a function of resource availability and mobilization, including organizational skills and connections, than of shared discontent (Zald and Ash, 1966; Tilly, 1978). Jenkins (1979: 224) summarizes this approach:

> The main thrust of "resource mobilization" theory has been to argue that discontent is at best secondary in accounting for the emergence of insurgency, that organizational resources and the changing power position of the aggrieved, not sudden increases in their grievances, are the major factors leading to the outbreak of disorders.

Thus, research by Snyder and Tilly (1972) demonstrates that industrial strikes in France were not associated with fluctuations in the discontent of workers but were affected by the size and strength of union organization. Such studies underline the significance of resource availability and acquisition in the creation of organizations.

Research also shows that some types of resources exact costs on their acquiring organizations. If the interests undergoing mobilization are resource-deprived and disorganized—as was the case with the National Welfare Rights Organization, an organization representing black welfare mothers that emerged in the 1960s—they may become dependent on more mainstream groups, such as foundations, for support. The latter are unlikely to subsidize radical attempts to change the system, so that in the case of the NWRO its goals were turned in more conservative and less activist directions. (Piven and Cloward, 1977)

All organizations must compete for resources, but various types of organizations face quite different circumstances affecting their survival. An important determinant of the competitive environment of any organization is the type of industry structure in which it is located. Porter (1980) has classified the many factors influencing industry competition into five major categories: rivalry among existing firms, the bargaining power of suppliers and of buyers, the threat of new entrants, and the threat of substitute products or services.

Population ecologists have reminded us of the difficult time faced by many types of organizations in acquiring sufficient resources to survive. While the birth rate of new organizations in a developed society such as the United States is high, so is the failure rate. Although data on organizational births and deaths are difficult to acquire and are limited largely to the business sectors, Aldrich (1979: 36) cites data from a discontinued census on the numbers of new businesses, businesses transferred to a new owner, and businesses discontinued for nine selected years between 1940 and 1962. During these years, roughly 3.4 million new businesses were started, 3.1 million were transferred, and 2.5 million ceased to exist. As would be expected, the likelihood of failure is considerably higher among newer and smaller organizations. Records collected by Dun and Bradstreet reveal that over half (54 percent) of the businesses that failed in the United States during 1980 were five years old or less (see Bedeian, 1984: 333). The "liability of newness" is often lethal. But it is not only the newer and smaller firms that fail or cease to exist as independent entities. If longer periods are used, then there is a surprising amount of turnover in the populations of all types of organizations. (See Carroll, 1984.)

If we shift the level of analysis from the population of organizations to that of the individual organization, it is useful to think of each organization as undergoing an evolutionary process from birth to maturity to old age and death. Although the organizational *life cycle* is not as distinct and regular as the life cycle of plants or animals or humans, it is nevertheless instructive to identify general phases of development and decline. (See Kimberly, Miles, et al., 1980.) Theorists have developed a variety of schemata for distinguishing stages of development (see Bedeian, 1984, for a review).

As an example of one such model, after examining a number of case studies of corporate development, Greiner (1972) identified five general evolutionary stages. He proposed that each stage ends in a predictable crisis calling for some type of appropriate adjustment by managment if the organization is to survive and proceed to the next stage. For example, the first crisis typically encountered is that of leadership: the founding members of the organization—often technical experts or entrepreneurial types—give way to managers who are more skilled at consolidation and routine administration. The next crisis occurs because controls become too centralized; the solution is more delegation, decentralizing of decision making. But decentralization in turn raises problems of integration that call for additional coordinating devices—planning procedures, reports, formal reviews. But these mechanisms multiply, causing a crisis of red tape, which in turn is solved by greater emphasis on trust and informal collaboration. And so development is accompanied by a series of more or less predictable crises.

Greiner's model is instructive in that each solution at one stage becomes the problem at the next. A leadership style or a structural arrangement that is adaptive at one level of size and complexity is unsuitable for another. Similarly, one would expect to observe changes over time in the relevance and utility of different types of personnel and resources. The problems encountered and hence the types of resources required vary with the stage of development. Obtaining sufficient capital resources to expand operations may be critical at the earlier stages of growth—and may represent a much greater challenge, since the risks to investors are higher—but less important in later stages, when capital will be easier to raise and may be available through internalized savings mechanisms. Resource acquisition is a necessary, but variable, process that continues throughout the life of the organization.

The ecologists in particular stress the difficulties confronting all organizations as they attempt to acquire and maintain a flow of resources adequate to perpetuate themselves. By contrast, institutional theorists such as Meyer and Rowan emphasize the ease with which some types of resources can be assembled to constitute an organization. To repeat their summary of the situation: in developed societies, "the building blocks for organizations come to be littered around the societal landscape; it takes only a little entrepreneurial energy to assemble them into a structure" (Meyer and Rowan, 1977: 345). That is, the more institutionalized the environment—the more it contains rules, accepted procedures, licensed actors, and taken-for-granted frameworks for carrying out specified actions—the less difficult it is to create and sustain organizations. However, although organizations in these circumstances may be able to more readily assemble various elements and actors, whether these resources can be fully mobilized by their managers is open to question. We will pursue these matters in Chapter 10.

SUMMARY

Organizations, as we know them, have not always existed. They evolved during the past few centuries as part of a dual-level process. The same social changes that brought about the development of individualism—the freeing of resources (including the individual) from all-absorbing social structures—are responsible for the growth of organizations. Both developments celebrate the legitimation of specialized, particularized goals and the freedom to own and mobilize resources in their pursuit.

From a rational system perspective, organizations arise to take advantage of the production economies offered by an elaborate division of labor and to meet the cognitive and control challenges posed by a complex and uncertain environment. From a natural system perspective, institutionalists propose that organizations emerge as an embodiment of rationalized belief systems that proliferate in the wider social structure; Marxists argue that organizations arise as structures created by capitalists to expropriate surplus value from productive labor. All of these explanations can be correct, but for different times and places and types of organizations.

The costs and benefits of creating organizations are more easily evaluated if organizations are compared with alternative social forms for carrying on complex work. Organizations are viewed as having advantages over market mechanisms when the tasks to be carried out are sufficiently complex and uncertain as to exceed the information-processing capacities of individuals, and when so few potential buyers or sellers exist that they may attempt to take advantage of one another. Under these conditions, organizations offer mechanisms for reducing transactions costs and for constraining opportunistic behavior. Organizations are viewed as superior to informal peer groups as mechanisms for overseeing and coordinating complex work. However, conventional hierarchies in organizations may function poorly on ambiguous or highly complex tasks that require the exercise of individual discretion and the exchange of large amounts of information.

All organizations must secure a continuing supply of resources—including participants—from their environment. The initial mix of resources that are mobilized at the creation of a particular organization are critical in that they constitute a structural pattern that tends to persist—imprinting the organization with characteristics that are preserved across succeeding generations of it. The types of incentives for participants to contribute and the mix of participants have important consequences for the structural features and flexibility of the organization. All organizations compete for resources, but the consequences and costs of obtaining them vary with the type of organization and environment as well as with the stage of development an organization has reached.

8

boundary setting and boundary spanning

The organizational world bubbles and seethes. Observed for a lengthy interval, the configuration of organizations within it changes like the patterns of a kaleidoscope. Organizations expand, contract, break up, fuse. Some surfaces become thick and opaque, reducing exchanges between their interior contents and the external environment, while others etherealize and permit heavier traffic in one or both directions. Shapes are altered. Some processes are depressed, some intensified. Levels of activity rise and fall. Organizations disintegrate and vanish as others form in droves, and the birth and death rates vary over time and space. Nothing stays constant.*

Herbert Kaufman (1975)

The central insight emerging from the open system model is that all organizations are incomplete: all depend on exchanges with other systems. All are open to environmental influences as a condition of their survival. By contrast, both the rational and natural system perspectives insist that organizatons, as a condition of their existence, must maintain boundaries that separate them from their environments. In the absence of distinguishable boundaries, there can be no organizations as we understand that term. In this chapter we explore the interdependence and the independence of organizations, and we examine the types of mechanisms used to set (and reset) and to span their boundaries.

THE SOCIAL BOUNDARIES OF ORGANIZATIONS

The problems confronting organizations in setting and policing their boundaries are complex and subtle. Given the essence of organizations as open systems, their boundaries must necessarily be sieves, not shells, ad-

*Excerpt from The natural history of human organizations, by Herbert Kaufman is reprinted from *Administration and Society* Vol. 7, No. 2 (August 1975) p. 143 by permission of the Publisher, Sage Publications, Inc.

mitting the desirable flows and excluding the inappropriate or deleterious elements. Determining what is desirable or harmful can be a difficult decision, in part because the criteria can vary from time to time and from location to location in the organization. To explicate these issues, we will first concentrate on the social boundaries of organizations, examining the various indicators used to mark those boundaries and the criteria employed by organizations in determining whom to admit or reject.

For the sake of simplicity, we focus on the organization as the principal unit of analysis. Other units—including individuals, groups, and coalitions within organizations; occupations and labor markets that crosscut organizations; and industries, sectors and fields incorporating organizations—provide important alternative systems around which to frame organizational analyses.

Determining Organizational Boundaries

Early in Chapter 1, after laboring over the concepts of normative and behavioral structure, we quietly slipped in the concept of *collectivity*. This concept serves to bring together the two components of structure but also adds a new element: the notion of boundary. A collectivity is a specific instance of social organization—an indentifiable "chunk" of the social order. As noted, the criteria for the existence of a collectivity are (1) a *delimited* social structure—that is, a *bounded* network of social relations—and (2) a normative order *applicable to the participants* linked by the network. All collectivities—including informal groups, communities, organizations, and entire societies—possess, by definition, boundaries that distinguish them from other systems.

Accepting the view that organizations, as a type of collectivity, possess boundaries is one thing, but deciding what and where they are is another. Establishing the boundaries of an organization is a difficult business, raising both theoretical and empirical problems.

To embrace the notion of organizations as open systems is to acknowledge that organizations are penetrated by their environments in ways that blur and confound any simple criterion for distinguishing the one from the other. How are we to regard customers? Clients? Stockholders? A second difficulty is the growing number of organizations that are subsumed under broader structures—for example, schools within districts, local banks that are branches of larger financial enterprises, and firms or establishments that are parts of multi-divisional corporations. Such connections may strongly influence many aspects of the structure and performance of the local units, so that treating them as independent units may create serious errors. Third, because more of our studies are including measures at more than one point in time, we need to realize that organizational boundaries are very likely to change. (See Freeman, 1978.)

Laumann, Marsden, and Prensky (1983) have noted that two approaches and, within each, three substantive focuses are used in attempts to define boundaries. The two approaches are the realist and the nominalist. In the *realist* approach, the investigator adopts the "vantage point of the actors themselves in defining the boundaries" of the system, assuming that this view will importantly influence their behavior. Under the *nominalist* strategy, the "analyst self-consciously imposes a conceptual framework constructed to serve his own analytic purposes." (p. 21) Regardless of the approach selected, the investigator must also determine what features of the situation to examine. Laumann and associates distinguish among three alternatives—the characteristics of the actors (or nodes), their relations, and their activities. Many investigators define the boundaries of an organization by focusing on its actors—for example, attempting to determine who is and who is not regarded as a member.

A second approach—favored by network analysts—is to establish the boundaries of the system by noting which actors are involved in social relations of a specified type. A widely used behavioral indicator of relatedness is frequency of interaction. Although no social unit is completely separated from its environment on the basis of this criterion, Homans (1950: 85) suggests that it is possible to locate the system boundaries where the web of interaction shows "certain thin places."[1]

The third possibility is to focus on the nature of the activities. We would expect to observe a change in the activities performed by individuals as they cross a system boundary.[2] Pfeffer and Salancik (1978: 32) favor this criterion, arguing that organizational boundaries are coterminous with activity control:

> When it is recognized that it is behaviors, rather than individuals, that are included in structures of coordinated behavior, then it is possible to define the extent to which any given person is or is not a member of the organization.... The organization is the total set of interstructured activities in which it is engaged at any one time and over which it has discretion to initiate, maintain, or end behaviors.... The organization ends where its discretion ends and another's begins.

A focus on relationships or activities emphasizes behavioral criteria for defining the limits of organizations. Since both interactions and activities require time and space, two useful indicators of significant boundaries are an organization's spatial barriers and their guardians (for example, fences, walls, doors, guards, receptionists) and the temporal systems (for example, working hours and activity schedules) it creates to contain them. By contrast, a focus on the characteristics of actors emphasizes normative criteria for defining the significant characteristics of membership.

Most groups, and particularly organizations, carefully differentiate members and nonmembers, developing explicit normative criteria for determining who is to participate in them. Why is this true? What is the importance of membership boundaries for the functioning of organizations?

---

[1]It is not only social scientists who wrestle with the question of how to bound a system under study. Other social analysts, such as novelists, confront a similar problem. The strategy proposed by Henry James (1907: vii) is not dissimilar to that adopted by scientific investigators:

> Really, universally, relations stop nowhere, and the exquisite problem of the artist is eternally but to draw, by a geometry of his own, the circle within which they shall happily *appear* to do so.

[2]Barnard (1938) took the position that activities, not participants, are the basis elements of organizations. Thus, he defined an organization as "a *system of coöperative activities* of two or more persons." (p. 75)

Recruitment Criteria

Rational system theorists are quite certain that they understand the functions of organizational boundaries: boundaries contribute to organizational rationality. Several of the characteristics Weber (1947 trans.: 334–35) identified as defining rational-legal systems may be viewed as bounding or insulating the organization from its social context. For example, his stipulation that officials be appointed by free contract according to their technical qualifications is intended to ensure that selection criteria are organizationally relevant and that the selection process will be relatively free from the influence of other social affiliations, whether religious, economic, political, or familial.

Udy's (1962) study of thirty-four production organizations in thirty-four different nonindustrialized societies lends strong credence to Weber's concerns. Udy sought to determine how the internal features of an organization's structure are related to the type of recruitment criteria used by the organization. His measures of structure are rather crude because the data are drawn from a systematic file of secondary data sources—the Human Relations Area File—based primarily on anthropological field studies. However, because the sample of organizations is drawn from nonindustrialized societies, it contains much greater variation in environmental and organizational characteristics than would be present in a comparable sample of organizations in industrialized societies. Udy differentiated five types of recruitment, ranging from participation in a production organization because of "voluntary self-commitment and self-defined interest" (high *social insulation*) to participation that was "required by compulsory political ascription" (high *social involvement*). To assess the structural characteristics of the thirty-four organizations, Udy developed a scale that measured the extent to which they reflected rational principles of organization. The presence or absence of seven indicators—including the organizational pursuit of limited objectives, rewards based on performance criteria, specialization, and rewards controlled by superiors—determined the degree of structural rationality within each organization. Analysis of the data revealed that the higher the degree of social insulation the organization achieved, the more likely it was to exhibit a rational structure.

Udy's findings do not seem surprising. Consider the case of a family that decides to run a retail store. The father might feel obliged to pay the older son a higher wage, in recognition of his superior status in the family structure, even if he does not contribute as much as others toward achieving the goals of the organization. The more an organization is insulated from its social environment—in this case an externally defined kinship structure—the more it can select, deploy, and reward its participants according to organizationally relevant criteria.

Organizationally controlled recruitment criteria are but one important mechanism fostering insulation of the organization from its social environment; Weber (1947 trans.) pointed to the need for others. His insistence that officials, once recruited, should regard their office as their sole, or at least their primary, occupation indicates his recognition that other occupational affiliations of members may affect their performance within organizations. And it is not only other occupational demands that may create claims on participants that may conflict with those of the focal organization. As the kinship example emphasizes, any social identity may become the basis of conflicting expectations and behavior patterns. Externally reinforced status characteristics such as age, sex, ethnicity, and social class are one important source of these expectations and obligations (see Hughes, 1958: 102–15; Dalton, 1959; Kanter, 1977a). And as the number and variety of other special-purpose organizations grow, membership in them supplies new identities and sources of power that may impinge on the participant's role performance in the organization. Salient identities can also develop as the result of interactions and exchange processes among participants in the organization, and these give rise to informal status distinctions (see Homans, 1961; Blau, 1964).

The external identities of individual participants play a relatively small role in rational system views of organization: they are viewed primarily as a problem to be managed by appropriate recruitment criteria and control mechanisms. By contrast, the many faces of participants are of great interest to natural system analysts. To begin, from a natural system perspective, it is impossible for any organization to eliminate completely these sources of "disturbance": social identities—externally validated roles, qualities, interests—are among the most portable of baggage. Some extreme types of organizations do attempt to eliminate the external status connections of a subset of their participants. This is the case for such "total institutions" as prisons, mental hospitals, monasteries, and army barracks. As Goffman (1961: 14) explains,

> the barrier that total institutions place between the inmate and the wider world marks the first curtailment of self. In civil life, the sequential scheduling of the individual's roles, both in the life cycle and in the repeated daily round, ensures that no one role he plays will block his performance and ties in another. In total institutions, in contrast, membership automatically disrupts role scheduling, since the inmate's separation from the wider world lasts around the clock and may continue for years. Role dispossession therefore occurs.

In addition to imposing these time and physical barriers, many such institutions forbid all contact with outsiders, strip the inmate of personal possessions, segregate sex or age groups, issue institutional garb, and restrict interaction among inmates. (see McEwen, 1980.) It is possible to view these measures as a set of mechanisms for ensuring that organizations will be buffered from the disturbing effects of the external roles occupied by participants. However, in our view they are sufficiently rare and extreme that they serve better to remind us how difficult it is for any organization to eliminate the influence on its participants of their nonorganizational roles and relationships. Total institutions are best viewed as a limiting case—as defining one extreme on a continuum. Most organizations do not erect excessive barriers or engage in elaborate stripping tactics; hence, we should expect most organizations to be composed of participants who possess multiple identities and behave accordingly. Certainly, natural system analysts embrace this view. We have already noted (in Chapter 3) the interest of human relations investigators in the effects of sex, class, and ethnicity on the allocation of workers to roles and on worker behavior.

And Selznick's analysis of individual "commitments" and the constraints they place on the rational deployment of personnel (also reviewed in Chapter 3) is highly germane to these issues.

Most natural system theorists do not emphasize the disruptive and constraining effects of participants' other roles; indeed, they insist that these characteristics are a vital resource for the organization. Even within a rational-system, performance-oriented context, natural system analysts point out that most organizations do not themselves train their members to talk, to think, or to use specialized tools: these fundamental skills are typically acquired in different settings and imported into the organization. But, from the natural system perspective, goal-attainment considerations are secondary to survival, and many participants are recruited precisely because they possess extraorganizational characteristics viewed as valuable to this end. For most organizations—and especially for those operating in more institutionalized environments—it is important to recruit the "right" participants, for symbolic as well as for technical considerations. Schools need to hire certificated instructors; nursing homes, licensed administrators; universities, instructing staffs with Ph.D.'s; and financial organizations, certified public accountants. Such environmental connections insure legitimacy and increased confidence in the organization.

Organizations also conform to the expectations of their social environments by maintaining some consistency between their own status systems and the stratification criteria used in the larger society (Anderson et al., 1966). For example, until recently women were not often promoted to high managerial positions in most United States corporations, partly because their special social identities were viewed by their male colleagues as introducing additional sources of uncertainty into transactions requiring high trust (Kanter, 1977a), but also because organizations wish to inspire confidence in outsiders with whom they conduct business, and so try not to violate widely shared community norms. Further, for certain types of boundary-spanning roles, such as being a member of a board of directors, an individual's selection may depend entirely on his or her external roles and connections. Thus, a banker may be asked to serve on the board of directors of a hospital because of ties with the financial community. The general point is that the external identities and connections of participants—far from being disruptive and restrictive—are, under many conditions, a primary resource for the organization, providing skills, legitimacy, and valued connections with the larger social environment.

Social Insulation and Social Engulfment

The strategic question facing all organizations is how to recruit participants and harness their roles and resources in the service of organizational goals (whether goal attainment or survival), while avoiding or minimizing the danger of becoming captive to participants' external interests or personal agendas. Once pipelines are established, resources may flow in either direction! Katz and Eisenstadt (1960) discuss this issue from a less organization-centered point of view. They note that problems can occur from either of two types of imbalance—when an organization imposes too many or too few restrictions on the types (and imputed relevance) of other roles held by its participants. When nonorganizational roles impinge on organization roles inappropriately, then we have the problem of *de-bureaucratization*. The simplest examples are those of nepotism or corruption. The reverse problem occurs when organizational roles improperly assume priority over nonorganizational roles, leading to *overbureaucratization*. Examples of this process are provided by Whyte's (1956) best seller, *The Organization Man*, which describes the unreasonable requirements placed by some corporations on the personal lives of upwardly mobile managers and their wives. It is by no means always a simple or noncontroversial matter to determine when external roles are or are not properly impinging on organizational roles, and vice versa. Clearly, value judgments are involved, and depending on which normative system provides the standard, different judgments are likely to be made. Courts of law and regulatory agencies often are asked to resolve these controversies. (Other problems associated with overbureaucratization are discussed in Chapter 12.)

The extreme case of de-bureaucratization involves the disappearance of the organization. An organization no longer exists when it does not maintain a delimited network of social relations to which a distinctive normative order is applicable. Diamond (1958) provides an interesting case study of a disappearing organization: the famous Virginia Company associated with the founding of the Jamestown colony.[3] This company was established in 1607 to exploit the riches of a new continent and the labors of its native peoples. Virginia proved to be different from previous English colonial sites in that native labor refused to be mobilized and mineral wealth was not to be found. It became necessary to establish an agricultural community based on voluntary labor imported from England. Over time, the company was forced to supply more and more inducements to its colonists: land became easier to acquire, women were recruited to become the wives of settlers, and company discipline was limited as representatives of the settlers acquired some voice in government. Diamond (1958: 471) summarizes these changes:

> At one time in Virginia, the single relationship that existed between persons rested upon the position they occupied in the Company's table of organization. As a result of the efforts made by the Company to get persons to accept that relationship, however, each person in Virginia had become the occupant of several statuses, for now there were rich and poor in Virginia, landowners and renters, masters and servants, old residents and newcomers, married and single, men and women; and the simultaneous possession of these statuses involved the holder in a network of relationships, some congruent and some incompatible, with his organizational relationship.

Gradually, settlers came to regard their roles outside the company as more important and were no longer willing to accept their organizational position as the primary basis of legitimate order. Thus, a society emerged where before there had been only an organization.

Note that we have now located both ends of the continuum of organizational control over the relevant properties of participants. At one

---

[3]This account is paraphrased from an earlier summary written with Blau (see Blau and Scott, 1962: 234).

end of this continuum of *social involvement,* to use Udy's phrase, the organization is highly insulated from its social environment, the limiting case being that of the *total institution* as defined by Goffman. At the other end, the organization is highly involved in its social environment, the extreme case being the *engulfed organization,* exemplified by the Virginia Company as described by Diamond.[4] Of course, the majority of organizations are somewhere between these two extremes, able to exert some control over the multiple roles participants bring into the organization or informally develop within its confines, but rarely in a position to eradicate or dominate them. In most cases organizations do not wish to eliminate these external roles but to mobilize them in their service.

Labor Markets
and Organizational Boundaries

The emergence of internal labor markets provides an especially pertinent example of how modern organizations manage their social boundaries. The classical economic assumption that workers move freely from job to job and firm to firm, governed by pressures to maximize the fit between their skills and the requirements of their job, and hence between their productivity and their earnings, has been severely challenged by labor and institutional economists such as Kerr (1954) and Doeringer and Piore (1971). The latter analysts have emphasized the extent to which information, opportunities, mobility, and rewards are differentially structured and shaped by varying occupational, industry, and organizational arrangements. Among the more important distinctions they introduce is that between internal and external labor markets. Doeringer and Piore (1971: 1) define *internal labor markets* as those within "an administrative unit, such as a manufacturing plant, within which the pricing and allocation of labor is governed by a set of administrative rules and procedures." The key features of internal labor markets are (1) a cluster of jobs that (2) are hierarchically structured into one or more job ladders representing a progression in knowledge or skills, and that (3) include a few "entry ports" at the lower levels connecting them with wider, external labor markets (Althauser and Kalleberg, 1981). The more internal labor markets that exist, the more that mobility processes within a society are shaped by organizational job structures and their hiring and promotional processes rather than by market processes, and the more control organizations have over their membership boundaries.[5]

And what are the factors that lead to the creation of internal labor markets? As might be expected, rational and natural system theorists have posed alternative explanations. Working within the transactions costs

---

[4]Note that Katz and Eisenstadt have in mind a different continuum. One end point, de-bureaucratization, is the same as Udy's high social involvement, but the other end point, over-bureaucratization, extends beyond the point where the organization insulates itself from the environment (as a total institution) to include situations in which the organization imposes its normative system on formerly autonomous systems.

[5]Althauser and Kalleberg (1981) also point out that internal labor markets can exist within and under the control of occupations. Occupations provide an alternative to organizations in the structuring of jobs and work activities, as discussed in the first edition of this text. (See Scott, 1981: 153–156)

framework—a rational open system model—Williamson (1981) argues that the most important influence on what type of labor market is created is the specificity of the human assets. The human assets of an organization are, of course, the skills and knowledge of its personnel. Specificity refers not simply to the extent of specialization of knowledge and skills, but to the degree to which these skills are transferable across employers. The deeper and more specialized one's skills are in the view of a specific employer, the more dependent is that employer on that employee, and vice versa, so that it is in the interests of both to create a "protective governance structure, lest productive values be sacrificed if the employment relation is unwittingly severed" (1981: 563). An internal labor market serves the employee's interests by providing the prospects of upward mobility through a regularized career of advancement, with increased earnings accompanying progression in skills. And the employer's interests are served because valuable workers in whom investments in training have been made are less likely to desert to a competitor.

In a related discussion, Williamson and Ouchi (1981: 361) distinguish between *hard* and *soft* contracting.

> Under hard contracting, the parties remain relatively autonomous, each is expected to press his or her interests vigorously, and contracting is relatively complete. Soft contracting, by contrast, presumes much closer identity of interests between the parties, and formal contracts are much less complete.

Soft contracting is characteristic of internal labor markets. It assumes a more elaborate governance structure (job ladders, grievance procedures, pay scales) and a higher level of investment and trust on the part of both employers and employees. In this sense, internal labor markets may be viewed as mechanisms for bringing employees more fully and firmly within the boundaries of an organization than is the case with external labor markets, in which the "hard" bargaining between employers and employees more closely resembles that occurring between two independent contractors.

The existence of internal labor markets is explained in a rather different manner by natural open system theorists. Marxist theorists such as Edwards (1979) argue that internal labor markets are more likely to arise in "core" segments of the economy—in large and powerful firms that have obtained an oligopoly, or near monopoly, in their industries. (See Averitt, 1968.) As these firms grow in size and complexity, they shift from simple hierarchical to technical to bureaucratic control systems. Edwards (1979: 131) explains:

> *Bureaucratic* control, like technical control, differs from the simple forms of control in that it grows out of the formal structure of the firm, rather than simply emanating from the personal relationships between workers and bosses. But while *technical* control is embedded in the physical and technological aspects of production and is built into the design of machines and the industrial architecture of the plant, *bureaucratic* control is embedded in the social and organizational structure of the firm and is built into job categories, work rules, promotion procedures, discipline, wage scales, definitions of responsibilities, and the like. Bureaucratic control establishes the impersonal force of "company rules" or "company policy" as the basis for control. (Emphasis added)

Because they rely on social definitions rather than technical distinctions, bureaucratic control structures can be elaborated with ease: the number of offices, levels, titles, and salary levels can be multiplied without limit. Moreover, incentives can be added to reward not simply effort and productivity but also such qualities as dependability, loyalty, and commitment to the organization.

Labor economists such as Averitt (1968) and Doeringer and Piore (1971) distinguish between core and peripheral economic sectors, arguing that large, highly differentiated, technically advanced firms are clustered in key manufacturing industries and provide employment for workers who are likely to be male, white, highly skilled, and educated; smaller, simpler organizations are to be found in more competitive, marginal industries, and employ workers who are likely to be female or minority, semiskilled, and less educated. However, empirical research by a number of sociologists has found only limited and mixed support for these generalizations linking economic sectors, organizational features, and labor market characteristics. (See, for example, Berg, 1971; Tolbert, Horan, and Beck, 1980; Zucker and Rosenstein, 1981.) Baron and Bielby (1984) point out that these economic theories imply—but do not explicate or empirically test—the proposition, familiar to organization theorists, "that organizational forms and environments cohere, yielding groups of enterprises with distinctive structures of work and opportunity" (p. 445) or, more specifically, that "key industries are the most complex organizational environments and accordingly are composed of firms that are the most internally complex" (p. 456). Although environmental location and organizational form are surely related, they are not the same. Baron and Bielby separated these two dimensions, developing a measure of environmental locus—occupation of a crucial location within key segments of the economy—and a measure of organizational form—size and technical complexity. Based on a study of 415 companies in California during the period 1959–1979, these analysts reported a correlation of .67 between their measures of location and form, suggesting that external location and internal features are associated, but not identical. Internal labor market features were more likely to be found in firms that were both centrally located and organizationally complex.

Jobs are locations within organizational structures, and so if we wish to understand how individuals are matched with jobs, we need to know what positions exist, how they are connected, and what rules are employed for sorting workers among them. This kind of research can be conducted only at the organizational level. (Baron and Bielby, 1980; Baron, 1984; Hodson and Kaufman, 1982) Not only are workers with differing characteristics employed, but workers with similar characteristics are treated differently depending on the organizational setting. For example, Stolzenberg (1978), using data from a national employment survey, has shown that size of the employer strongly affects the relation between a worker's education and his or her occupational status. Specifically, the larger the organization, the stronger the impact of education on position and earnings.

Talbert and Bose (1977), examining survey data on retail clerks in a single metropolitan area, observed that in addition to the characteristics of individual workers, such organizational features as the degree of work routinization, type of clientele served, and status of merchandise handled affect employees' wages. Since women and men are differentially located in organizations, much of the disparity in their earnings is attributable to sex segregation among store types, departments within stores, and jobs within departments. Although state and federal rules prohibit overt job discrimination by race or gender, we know far too little about the intraorganizational processes by which employees, once hired, are routed to different organizational locations that, independent of individuals' abilities, have a major impact on potential earnings and career opportunities. Kanter's (1977*a*) description of the maze of traps, dead ends, escalators, and fast tracks associated with different positions and departments in the large corporation she studied suggests how intricate and subtle are the mobility processes at work in contemporary organizations. Much detailed research remains to be done on how job structuring and mobility rules within specific organizations affect the returns to employees for their efforts.

Let us return to the more specific matter of internal labor markets. Marxists see the benefits to workers associated with these structures as reflecting their greater power vis-à-vis their employers, but they also view the structures as

> graded hierarchies that foster a docile "status" orientation and dissuade workers from utilizing the power implicit in their skills. Internal labor markets also institutionalize cleavages among workers along racial, sexual, and ethnic lines, thereby reducing the likelihood of working-class cohesion. (Baron, 1984: 40)

Pfeffer and Cohen (1984) employed data from a sample of about 300 large organizations in the San Francisco Bay area to test alternative explanations of internal labor markets. Degree of specificity of skills, as measured by extensiveness of employer training, somewhat predicted internal markets, providing support for the transactions cost arguments. But so did extent of unionization and being located in the core industries, providing support for a Marxist interpretation. In addition, Pfeffer and Cohen report that the development of internal labor markets was associated with the existence of a personnel department, a finding that supports an institutional interpretation of the spread of this structural form. Once such structures have been created in the more advanced organizations, they are apt to be picked up and promoted by professional personnel officers as being consistent with the principles of modern human-resources management. (See Dobbin et. al., in press.)

Although there remain differences in the explanations of internal labor markets, there is agreement that their existence within an organization constitutes a significant social boundary: would-be participants encounter barriers to entry and are restricted to a limited number of low-level positions from which they must work their way up; current employees enjoy job security and anticipate future advancement, reducing the probability of turnover and increasing their commitment to the organization.

From a broader historical perspective, there is no doubt that organizations have helped to bring about basic changes in societal stratification systems. (See Eisenstadt, 1981.) In our simple example of the family-run retail store, to the extent that the father does not honor the expectations generated by the kinship system in his distribution of rewards among family members, the kinship structure has lost power over the economic system. One of the "great transformations" of the last few centuries has been the increasing autonomy enjoyed by economic organizations in relation to other institutional sectors (Polanyi, 1944). Many excellent historical accounts describe the gradual, halting process by which ascriptive, hereditary stratification systems have given way to more competitive, open-class systems, and this change is attributable partially to the increasing use of organizationally relevant recruitment criteria (see Tout, 1916; Barker, 1944; Rosenberg, 1958). Individually, and in the short run, most organizations adapt to the demands of their social environments; collectively, and in a longer view, organizations gradually transform their environments.

MANAGING TASK ENVIRONMENTS

In Chapter 6, following Dill (1958), we defined the task environment as those features of the environment relevant to the organization viewed as a production system—in particular, the sources of inputs, markets for outputs, competitors, and regulators. Since no organization generates all the resources necessary for its goal attainment or survival, organizations are forced to enter into exchanges, becoming interdependent with other environmental groups, typically other organizations. Unequal exchange relations can generate power and dependency differences among organizations, which are therefore expected to enter into exchange relations cautiously and to pursue strategies that will enhance their own bargaining position. This general perspective, labeled the resource dependence approach (see Chapter 5), has given rise to considerable theoretical and empirical work since the early 1970's on these strategies. The level of analysis most often associated with this approach is that of the organization set: the environment is viewed as it relates to and impinges on some particular organization, which serves as the primary focus of the analysis. Using a different set of assumptions, transactions costs theorists and population ecologists have also examined the relation of task environments to organizational forms.

As discussed in Chapter 6, determining the nature and scope of its domain is a critical concern for any organization. We noted that in arriving at their domain definition, organizations must negotiate and bargain with members of their organization set so that their claims to be in a given business are recognized as legitimate by others to whom they must relate. The higher the consensus on an organization's domain, the easier it will be for its members to conduct routine transactions.

Domain definition concerns not simply the general arena of activity, but what particular roles or functions the organization will perform. The manufacturer decides not simply to produce toys, but particular types or lines of toys targeted to particular types of customers—distributors and consumers. Porter (1980) regards decisions concerning product differentiation—the creation of relatively distinctive products and services—and focus—the identification of a selected buyer group or segment of a product line—to be among the most significant made by organizations in determining their competitive strategies. Among other effects, these decisions determine the identity of the organization's most significant competitors and partners—its strategic location within the broader industry or sector.

In addition, organizations must determine what subset of all the stages involved in producing a particular product or service they are going to embrace. The toy company does not ordinarily produce its own steel or plastic, but purchases these inputs, in varying stages of completion, from other firms. All organizations are confronted by basic decisions concerning which items or services they will make and which they will purchase from others. As Williamson (1975; 1981) points out, these "make or buy" decisions are tantamount to defining the technical boundaries of the organization. To "make" goods or services is to bring these activities within your own boundaries; to "buy" them is to relinquish them to the environment. As we would expect, Williamson predicts that firms will set their boundaries in such a manner as to minimize their transactions costs. Even if we do not accept this account as the only or even the most important basis for setting boundaries, it is clear that these are critical boundary-defining decisions. And it is important to see that organizations can and do regularly review and revise these decisions, eliminating former departments (for example, by contracting out the services they handle) and adding new units (for example, through vertical integration). They can also decide to change domains (for example, by merging with a company in a different business.)

We continue our discussion of managing task environments by reviewing the main concerns and contributions of the resource dependency theorists. In general, two lines of argument may be distinguished. The first focuses on the central work processes of the organization and asks how they may be protected from disturbances arising from the task environment. The strategies considered are those designed to *buffer* the organization's technical core—to amplify its protective boundaries. This argument emphasizes the need to close the system artificially to enhance the possibilities of rational action.[6] The second line of argument recognizes that among the most important actions organizations can take is the modification of their boundaries, more or less drastically and more or less formally. These actions include boundary-spanning and boundary-shifting strategies that *bridge* organizations and their exchange partners, competitors, or regulators.

Buffering Strategies

Organizations may be viewed as technological systems—as mechanisms for transforming inputs into outputs. It is almost always possible to identify one or more central sets of tasks around which the organization is built. Teaching in schools, surgery and patient care in hospitals, laboratory work in research organizations, line work in assembly plants, legislating in Congress—these are examples of central tasks in varying types of organizations. Following Thompson (1967), we will refer to the arrangements developed to perform these central tasks—including the skills of personnel employed to carry them out—as the *core technology* of the organization.

---

[6]Some kinds of task demands make it impossible to exclude uncertainty from the technical core. Structural accommodations for dealing with these situations are examined in Chapter 9.

A key proposition formulated by Thompson is that "under norms of rationality, organizations seek to seal off their core technologies from environmental influences" (1967: 19). This proposition follows from Thompson's attempt to reconcile the rational, natural, and open system perspectives, as described in Chapter 5. He argues that the rational system perspective is most applicable at the technical level of the organization. Here, if anywhere, there is expected to be a concern with the careful selection of means to pursue ends and an attempt to reduce to a minimum the extraneous forces that can upset these connections. The purest example of these tendencies, which are expected to be present to some degree in all organizations, is the organization that is able to develop a *long-linked technology,* a series of sequential, interdependent production activities, exemplified by the assembly line in a manufacturing company (Thompson, 1967: 15–16).

Long-linked technologies can be created only when certain conditions are met. They require (1) a clear understanding of the cause-effect relations linking inputs with outputs, so that by carrying out the proper activities it is possible to produce the desired effect regularly; (2) a stable supply of appropriate inputs; and (3) a continuing demand for the standardized outputs. The last two conditions require the organization to deal with its environment. The long-linked technology, while effective and efficient for achieving limited objectives, is quite inflexible and, hence, vulnerable to change or uncertainty.

All organizations, but especially those with long-linked technologies, are highly motivated to secure enough stability, determinateness, and certainty to be able to function efficiently and effectively in environments that contain unknowns and uncertainties. Organizations seeking to buffer their technical flows from environmental perturbations may pursue a number of strategies.

Buffering strategies come in many forms and guises, but they all may be regarded as intraorganizational techniques aimed at reducing uncertainty for the technical core. As with all strategies, there are potential costs as well as gains for the organization, and in our brief review we will touch on both.

Coding Organizations can classify inputs before inserting them into the technical core. Preprocessing of inputs aids their proper routing and, if necessary, their exclusion. If inappropriate or inadequately processed inputs inadvertently gain entry, they can cause delays, create machinery problems, or require special attention, often from supervisory personnel. For example, on an automobile assembly line, the parts are carefully inspected and rejects are culled before they are placed on the conveyor belt. Coding is not restricted to long-linked technologies or even to industrial concerns; for example, human-service agencies classify clients as a means of determining their eligibility for service and facilitating their routing to the appropriate service units.

The costs of coding should not be overlooked. The coding process itself consumes resources and is always imperfect. No set of codes can capture all of the relevant properties of the raw materials; codes always simplify, sometimes in useful, but sometimes in distorting or biasing ways. Also, we should recall Weick's (1979) admonition: organizations need to reduce equivocality (by coding) in order to ensure some stability, but they also need to retain some equivocality in order to learn how their environment is changing and to retain flexibility (see Chapter 4).

Stockpiling Organizations can stockpile raw materials or products and thereby control the rate at which inputs are inserted into the technical core or outputs released to the environment. Organizations are likely to stockpile critical resources, those whose supply is uncertain or whose price fluctuates greatly over time. The hope is that regardless of vicissitudes on the supply side, the organization will be assured of a continuous flow of resources. Similarly, on the output side, products may be held in warehouses in order to be released on the market at the most propitious time. But the capital tied up in reserves is not productive, and the costs of stockpiling include storage costs and possible loss through spoilage, damage, deterioration, or obsolescence. The problem confronting all organizations is to ensure that inventories are sufficient to meet all needs—both on the supply and demand sides—while defending against the possibility of obsolescence as production needs or customer demands change.

Leveling Leveling, or smoothing, is an attempt by the organization to reduce fluctuations in its input or output environments. Whereas stockpiling is a relatively passive technique, leveling entails a more active attempt to reach out into the environment to motivate suppliers of inputs or to stimulate demand for outputs. Organizations may use advertising to stimulate demand for their products; retail stores may schedule sales during slack periods, utilities may stimulate or discourage use of their power supplies by variable time-of-day rates, and colleges may hold conferences in the summer to use idle facilities. Even hospitals may smooth their work flow by scheduling elective surgery during slack periods. The costs associated with such efforts are self-evident: seeking out suppliers or customers consumes energy and resources, and many of the techniques used, such as advertising, tend to combine high costs and high risks.

Forecasting If environmental fluctuations cannot be handled by stockpiling or by leveling, organizations may have to settle for forecasting: anticipating changes in supply or demand conditions and attempting to adapt to them. Environmental changes are often patterned, exhibiting a weekly or a seasonal trend. Organizations taking account of such regularities can often accommodate them. For example, taxi companies can anticipate changes in demand for their services over a twenty-four-hour period and arrange drivers' schedules accordingly; beaches or amusement parks can make educated guesses about crowd size based on school and holiday schedules. Costs associated with forecasting, in addition to those entailed in guessing wrong, include the difficulties of expanding and contracting capacity, in particular the problems and inefficiencies of using part-time or short-term help.

Growth One of the most general strategies employed by organizations is to change the scale of operations, to expand the technical core. (We postpone to the following section a discussion of growth by merger with other organizations.) Technological factors may encourage growth:

there are favorable economies of scale for virtually every kind of technical process, and Thompson argues that organizations will tend to expand "until the least-reducible component is approximately fully occupied" (1967: 46). Other, probably more compelling factors encourage growth as well. Distinct advantages accrue to the firm that is large, particularly in relation to its market. Large organizations are better able to engage in *planning,* in Galbraith's sense of that term: "much of what the firm regards as planning consists in minimizing or getting rid of market influences" (1967: 25). Thus, large firms are better able to set prices, control how much they produce, and influence the decisions of related organizations. Pfeffer and Salancik (1978: 139) summarize the advantages of size:

> Organizations that are large have more power and leverage over their environments. They are more able to resist immediate pressures for change and, moreover, have more time in which to recognize external threats and adapt to meet them. Growth enhances the organization's survival value, then, by providing a cushion, or slack, against organizational failure.

We have argued that buffering strategies are employed to help seal off or cushion the technical core from disturbances in the environment. The strategies described are particularly useful for organizations employing long-linked technologies, but as we have noted, other organizations often use some variant of them. Organizations also use bridging strategies, some of which buffer the technical core. More often, however, bridging strategies are oriented toward enhancing the security of the organization in relation to its environment. Safety, survival, and an improved bargaining position are the prizes that motivate bridge building, rather than simply increased certainty for the organization's technical operations.

Bridging Strategies

Virtually all of the formulations of power and exchange relations among organizations build on the conception of power developed by Emerson (1962). Emerson emphasizes that one actor's power over another is rooted in the latter's dependency on resources controlled by the former. As expressed by Emerson, "the power of A over B is equal to, and based upon, the dependence of B upon A" (1962: 33). Further, the dependence of one actor on another varies as a function of two factors: B's dependence on A (1) is directly proportional to the importance B places on the goals mediated by A, and (2) is inversely proportional to the availability of these goals to B outside the A–B relationship. Obviously, the actors involved may be individuals, groups, or organizations. (See also Chapter 11.)

Emerson's formulation is useful for several reasons when applied to a given organization and the set of organizations to which it relates (see Thompson, 1967). Power is not viewed as some generalized capacity but as a function of specific needs and resources that can vary from one exchange partner to another. Thus, it is possible for an organization to have relatively little power in relation to its suppliers, but considerable power in relation to its buyers. Further, we would expect each supplier's power to vary with the importance of the resources it supplies and the extent to which alternative suppliers are available. This approach avoids a *zero-sum* view of power, in which it is assumed that when one actor gains power another must lose it. Rather, it becomes possible for two actors to both gain in power over each other—through an increase in the extent of their interdependence.

Bridging strategies may be viewed as a response to increasing organizational interdependence. Interdependence can occur when two or more organizations that are differentiated from one another exchange resources. This is known as *symbiotic* interdependence and can give rise, as noted, to power differences if the resources exchanged are not of equal importance. Interdependence also occurs when two or more similar organizations compete for the resources of another party. This is known as *competitive* or commensalistic interdependence. Competitive interdependence is often resolved by differentiation, former competitors becoming exchange partners (Blau and Scott, 1962: 217–21). For example, an automobile manufacturer may be unable to compete successfully by selling automobiles but may survive by supplying parts to other automobile companies.

The most complete analysis of bridging strategies to date is that provided by Pfeffer and Salancik (1978: 43); our summary draws heavily on their work. Their general thesis is simply stated: "The typical solution to problems of interdependence and uncertainty involves increasing coordination, which means increasing the mutual control over each other's activities. . . ." Although all bridging strategies share this feature, they are quite varied in the strength and the nature of the connections forged. We shall discuss some of the more common types of bridging strategies.

Bargaining   We use the term *bargaining* to refer not to one but to a large family of strategies by which the focal organization attempts to ward off dependence. To be compulsively precise, bargaining is not really a bridging but a prebridging strategy: it consists of things to do before calling in the bridge builders or while waiting for them to arrive. Much of the bargaining to be done, of course, is concerned with the defining and defending of the organization's domain. Other types of bargaining are aimed at helping the organization increase its independence. Examples of bargaining strategies include (1) attempts by the focal organization to develop alternative suppliers of critical resources, and (2) selective disclosure of conflicting demands by two or more members of the organization set—for example, a company may call the attention of its regulators to a union's wage demands in the hope of enlisting their support in resisting the union. Pfeffer and Salancik (1978: 92–111) provide an excellent guide to these types of bargaining strategies, including such subtle tactics as organizations "helping" the various members of their set to define their demands on the focal organization and gaining control over the determination of when a demand made on them has been met.

Contracting   According to Thompson (1967: 35), contracting is "the negotiation of an agreement for the exchange of performances in the future." For present purposes, contracts may be more or less formally drawn up and more or less legally binding. The critical point is that they represent attempts by organizations to reduce uncertainty by coordinating their future behavior, in limited and specific ways, with other units. As we have learned from Williamson (1975), there is a limit to how much uncertainty can be hedged or handled by contracts (see Chapter 7), but Williamson himself notes (pp. 90–95) that contracts can be modified to handle considerable uncertainty; contingent claims contracts, incomplete long-term contracts, and sequential spot contracts are examples. The negotiation of contracts with labor unions and principal suppliers and buyers is one of the chief ways in which organizations assure themselves of some degree of certainty in a changing future.

Stinchcombe (1985) has observed, apparently in contradiction to the predictions of transactions costs theory, that contracts are sometimes employed as the principal control mechanism, even under conditions of extraordinary complexity and uncertainty—for example, in relations between defense agencies and supplier firms, or between nation-states and oil-construction and -production companies. We would ordinarily expect such transactions to be brought inside an organizational framework, where "softer" bargaining and greater controls are possible. But Stinchcombe usefully suggests that it is important to see "hierarchies" (organizations) and markets not as dichotomies but as a continuum, and that it is possible to build many hierarchical features into contracts. For example, defense contracts often allow the purchaser to inspect compliance to requirements and progress toward objectives as necessary; to change requirements or specifications as the work proceeds; and to renegotiate the allocation of costs and benefits depending on what outcomes occur. Such hierarchical rights undermine the autonomy of the independent contractors and constitute a step in the direction of creating a joint venture between the contracting parties—except that the "venture" is a specific project rather than a continuing organization. Such admittedly complex contracting arrangements seem to be widely employed in high-cost-high-gain (high-risk) situations, such as large-scale construction and defense and space technology.

Co-optation   As defined in Chapter 3, co-optation is the incorporation of representatives of external groups into the decision-making or advisory structure of an organization. The significance of this practice in linking organizations with their environments was first described by Selznick (1949), who also noted its possible costs. Selznick argued that by co-opting representatives of external groups, organizations are, in effect, trading sovereignty for support.

Most studies of co-optation have focused on boards of directors, investigating the extent of interlocking ties among various types of organizations.[7] It is argued that allowing representatives of other orga-

[7]There are two different, but related, perspectives from which interlocking directorates have been examined. The first is an interorganizational approach that assumes organizations are entities pursuing interests, during which they establish connections with other organizations. The resource dependence approach embraces this perspective. The second is an intraclass approach that assumes that individual actors, such as members of the business elite, have interests and that organizations are the agents they use to establish relations with other individuals sharing their class interests. (See Palmer, 1983; Mizruchi, 1982.) These two perspectives take basically similar views of the functions of interlocks—they secure resources, information, and support, for example—but differ as to what set of interests is being promoted—organizational versus class.

nizations to participate in decision making in the focal organization is an important indication of interdependence and an effort by all the organizations to coordinate their activities. Such representatives may range from strong, controlling directors imposed by one organization on another to common messengers transmitting information of mutual interest. (Pennings, 1981) Not all board members are environmental representatives: some are there to provide specialized expertise, to oversee and augment the administrative skills of management.

To the extent that directorate ties function as a co-optative strategy for dealing with the interdependence of organizations, we would expect board appointments to vary with the amount and type of resource needs and flows confronting the focal organization. Although it is often difficult to measure needs and flows, and although co-optation is only one possible means of managing interdependence, there is considerable evidence to support this interpretation. For example, studies by Pfeffer of eighty randomly selected nonfinancial corporations (1972a) and fifty-seven hospitals in Illinois (1973) provide empirical support for the expectation that board appointments are used by organizations to establish linkages with important segments of the environment on which they are dependent. Thus, the corporations that exhibited a high debt/equity ratio were observed to have a higher proportion of representatives from financial institutions on their boards. And hospitals having larger budgets, and those receiving a higher proportion of their capital budgets from private donations and lacking federal or religious affiliations, were more likely to stress fund-raising ability as a criterion for selecting board members.

More convincing evidence is provided by Burt and his colleagues (Burt, Christman, and Kilburn, 1980; Burt, 1983), who examined the extent of interlocking directorates among a sample of the largest manufacturing firms from each of twenty industries in the United States for 1967. In their approach, the economy is viewed as a network of industrial sectors, differing in degree of concentration and extent of interconnections as measured by empirical studies of interindustry sales (input-output ratios). The analysts propose that firms in more highly concentrated sectors that buy and sell to many other sectors that are less highly concentrated are likely to be more profitable and to have less need to establish interlocks. Interlocks are more common among firms in less highly concentrated industries and among firms having to deal with buyers and sellers in more highly concentrated sectors. These predictions were confirmed for profitability and for three types of directorate ties: firms owned by the same corporation (and thus having the same directors); firms owned by two corporations sharing one or more directors; and firms owned by two corporations sharing a director with the same financial institution. Burt and associates (1980: 821) conclude that

> each of the three types of directorate ties tends to occur where there is market constraint and tends not to occur in the absence of constraint. Further, the three types of ties are coordinated as multiplex directorate ties. Where establishments in one sector constrain those in another, there is a strong tendency for all three types of directorate ties to exist between the two sectors. . . . Whatever the cooptive intent of the directorate ties described, they are patterned as if they were intended to coopt market constraints on corporate pricing discretion.

Finally, Burt and associates note that the use of interlocks to manage dependence is much more common between firms in different industries than between firms in the same industry, probably because of antitrust regulations that prohibit such visible techniques of cooperation (collusion?) among competitors. High interdependence within industries is more likely to be resolved by merger.

Co-optation is also widely employed as a coordinating strategy among public agencies and nonprofit associations. From the mid 1960s, the era of the Great Society programs, to the late 1970s, a great many federally sponsored organizations were created whose hallmark was decentralized decision making combined with mandated participation of representatives from the areas affected. Such programs included community action agencies, model cities programs, community mental health programs, area agencies for the aged, and health systems agencies (See Piven and Cloward, 1971; Sundquist, 1969.) There is considerable controversy concerning the merits of this federal strategy and its outcomes, in part because the programs themselves were diverse and the effects of any single program were not uniform across sites. Some studies suggest that federal bureaucrats and reformers used the local participation ideology as a smoke screen simply to legitimate federal intervention (see Krause, 1968). Others suggest that influence ran in the reverse direction: local interests captured and subverted the reform-oriented goals of the designers of the programs (see Moynihan, 1970). The truth of the matter is probably that both processes were occurring: each of the parties was to some extent using the others to achieve its own objectives, and all were somewhat constrained by the need to take into account the interests of others. Co-optation as a bridging mechanism provides a two-way street, with both influence and support flowing sometimes in one direction, sometimes in the other, but more often in both.

With the coming of more conservative policies in the 1980s, including the reduction in the federal role and in funding for community services, co-optation has shifted from being a primarily vertical strategy to being a horizontal strategy. Community agencies employ numerous co-optation mechanisms—joint board memberships, liaison roles, interorganizational brokers—as a way to increase resources, reduce uncertainty, and increase legitimacy. (See Galaskiewicz, 1985.) Indeed, federal and state programs currently place great emphasis on coordination among community agencies, often as a condition of being eligible for funding. Whereas federal regulations proscribe co-optation among competing organizations in the for-profit sector, they mandate it as a means of coordination among public and nonprofit agencies.

Joint ventures   A joint venture occurs when two or more firms create a new organization to pursue some common purpose. Joint ventures differ from mergers, to be discussed next, in that they entail only a limited pooling of resources by the participating organizations. For example, several wholesale companies may combine resources to purchase a trucking operation, or a wholesale company may combine assets with a farmers' cooperative to build a canning company. As these examples suggest, joint ventures may occur among either competitors or exchange partners. Testing the hypothesis that joint ventures tend to reflect resource interdependencies, Pfeffer and Nowak (1976) examined data from 166 joint ventures occurring over a decade. In support of the hypothesis, they found that the more exchanges there were between different industry groups, as measured by interindustry sales figures, the more likely firms from these industries were to enter into joint ventures. Pfeffer and Nowak also tested the prediction that firms within industry groups facing higher competition would be more likely to develop joint ventures as a means of reducing competitive pressures. Again, the data supported the prediction: joint ventures were found to be more frequent within industries exhibiting an intermediate level of concentration, a situation of maximum competitive pressure.[8]

Mergers   One of the most drastic strategies used by organizations in relating to critical units of their environment is to absorb these units: two or more independent organizations become a single collective actor. Three major types of mergers have been identified.

1. *Vertical integration,* in which organizations engaged in related functions but at different stages in the production process merge, backward or forward, with one another. Vertical integration, of course, takes place between exchange partners, organizations that are symbiotically related. For example, furniture manufacturers may merge (backward) with lumber companies or (forward) with furniture distributors or showrooms.
2. *Horizontal merger,* in which organizations performing similar functions merge to increase the scale of their operation. For example, two car dealerships that formerly handled only one line of automobiles may merge into one dealership handling two or more brands.
3. *Diversification,* in which one organization acquires one or more other organizations that are neither exchange partners nor similar organizations competing with each other, but organizations operating in different domains. For example, in the 1960s International Telegraph and Telephone, an electronics-manufacturing company, acquired a rent-a-car company, a major hotel chain, a home-building company, a baking company, a producer of glass and sand, a consumer-lending firm, and a data-processing organization. The extreme form of diversification is the *conglomerate.*

This country has experienced several waves of mergers, each of a differing type. Drucker (1970) argues that most mergers at the turn of the century involved horizontal or vertical integration as a dominant industrialist or financier attempted to gain control within a single industry. Mergers occurring in the 1920s represented a "defensive" reaction to these earlier developments as smaller companies jockeyed for position in the second tier. Most recent mergers involve the creation of conglomerates, either as a result of organizations attempting to diversify or as a result of their being "taken over" by aggressive asset managers who promise stockholders a better return on capital.

---

[8]Industry groups with high concentration ratios are those dominated by a relatively small group of firms. These firms are likely to have developed an "understanding" with one another, and together they control the conditions of survival for the smaller firms within the industry. On the other hand, industry groups with low concentration ratios are, by definition, composed of a great many small firms, no one of which is able to generate great competitive pressures on its neighbors.

Research by Pfeffer (1972*b*) supports the expectation that mergers involving vertical integration are more likely to occur among companies in industries engaged in frequent transactions. His study of 854 large mergers of companies in manufacturing and mining shows that mergers tended to occur more often among types of firms highly interdependent in their resource flows. Further, his findings on the effects of competitive interdependence replicated those reported for joint ventures: horizontal mergers were more likely to occur among firms located in industries exhibiting intermediate levels of concentration—situations of maximum intraindustry competition. Finally, Pfeffer and Salancik argue that mergers involving diversification are most likely to occur "when exchanges are very concentrated and when capital or statutory constraints" limit the use of other options for managing interorganizational interdependence (1978: 127).

As we have seen, the resource dependence approach emphasizes the extent of interorganizational resource flows and the degree of market concentration as the basis for generating predictions about mergers in general and vertical integration in particular. And as noted earlier, Williamson (1975; 1981) suggests that decisions concerning vertical integration can also be explained as attempts to reduce transactions costs. It is expected that as the assets required by an organization become more specific, firms will elect to produce them internally to avoid becoming overly dependent on a small number of external suppliers. This prediction was tested by Monteverde and Teece (1982) in a study of decisions made by General Motors and by Ford for a list of 133 automotive components. Measuring asset specificity by the amount of development effort required to produce a given component, they reported that, as expected, specificity was positively associated with the decision to integrate-in the manufacture of the component. Walker and Weber (1984) studied sixty decisions made in a component division of a large U.S. automobile manufacturer, decisions both to integrate (make rather than buy) and to de-integrate (buy rather than make) components. Consistent with transactions costs predictions, the division was more likely to manufacture components itself if there were few competing suppliers and if the volume of parts needed was uncertain. Unexpectedly, however, the strongest predictors were comparative manufacturing costs. Production costs appeared to be more significant in this situation than transactions costs.

Resource dependency and transactions costs explanations of mergers are not necessarily in conflict, although the former place greater stress on the organization's interest in reducing uncertainty and dependence while the latter stress its interest in increasing economic efficiency.

Associations Associations are arrangements that allow similar (and sometimes diverse) organizations to work in concert to pursue mutually desired objectives. They operate under many names, including trade associations, cartels, coordinating councils, and coalitions.

Both similar and dissimilar organizations enter into associations at the community or local level. We find many associations of similar organizations—for example, hospital councils and associations of retail merchants—as well as examples of associations of diverse organizations—the community chest and chambers of commerce. Individual organizations join associations in order, variously, to garner resources, secure information, exercise influence, or obtain legitimacy and acceptance. The structure and strength of associations vary greatly: some are informal and weak, others are formally structured and exercise great power over their members. (See Warren, 1967.) Although these structures have been increasingly examined as areal organizational fields, they have received little help from resource dependency theorists, since, as Laumann, Galaskiewicz, and Marsden (1978: 470) comment,

> little insight into how the totality of interorganizational linkages is organized can be attained using a perspective centered on atomistically conceived, bilateral transactions.

The trade association is an important type of association operating at a national and even international level. It is "a coalition of firms or businesspersons who come together in a formal organization to cope with forces and demands to which they are similarly exposed" (Staber and Aldrich, 1983: 163; see also, Staber, 1985). There is some evidence that trade associations are more likely to form in less highly concentrated sectors where too many firms are present to permit more tacit coordination (Pfeffer and Salancik, 1978: 179).

The power of trade associations varies markedly from society to society. Trade associations in the United States are more numerous, more specialized, and much less influential than those in most Western European countries, Japan, and Korea. Trade associations in the United States are not sufficiently strong or organized to serve as vehicles for centralizing and representing the interests of industries, as do trade associations in the more corporatist states. (See Berger, 1981; Okimoto, 1984. Corporatism is discussed later in this chapter.) By the same token, only relatively recently has the United States government been sufficiently strong and active in economic matters to serve as a target for associations' influence attempts. Since not only associations but individual organizations can try to influence governmental policies, we treat these efforts as a separate bridging strategy.

Government connections   Governments at all levels—local, state, and national—affect the resource transactions of organizations in two general capacities: (1) as sources of authority specifying what types of negotiations and exchanges can legally occur among organizations, and (2) as parties that directly engage in transactions with organizations, exacting resources from some and providing them to others.

The first function is, broadly speaking, an institutional one: governments help to shape and play a central role in enforcing the general rules under which technical environments operate. However, because the rules concern the exchange of resources, we describe them here rather than in the following section on institutional environments.

Lindblom (1977: 21) has pointed out that "an easy way to acknowledge the special character of government as an organization is simply to say that governments exercise authority over other organizations." Although Lindblom goes on to caution that governmental authority is sometimes contested, it is nevertheless essential to take account of governments' special powers and of the unique role a government plays as an organization among organizations. Some requirements apply to all types of organizations—for example, those specifying general property rights, rules of fair trade, and employee benefits such as workmen's compensation and social security. Although the overall policies are generally applicable, their impact is determined by the specific wording of the statues, regulations, and court interpretations by which they are implemented. Individual organizations and associations of organizations are therefore motivated to influence these policies. Thus, when laws are being formulated or revised, organizations will see to it that their concerns and interests are expressed in testimony before legislative committees, in lobbying efforts directed at individual legislators, and in commentaries on the "feasibility" and fairness of proposed administrative regulations; when the laws are being enforced, organizations will court the favor of administrative officials and seek expert legal counsel to help themselves define and defend their interests through litigation.

Governments also place special constraints on the transactions conducted by certain categories of organizations. Many types of organizations confront governmental regulatory bodies that monitor closely the quality of their products or services or their transactions with exchange partners or competitors. Utilities, railroads, banks, and pharmaceutical companies, for example, have long operated under the close scrutiny of public regulatory bodies. Numerous observers have pointed out that although such surveillance may, as intended, help to protect the public interest, it also has had the unintended effect of protecting the interests of the organizations being regulated—by restraining competitive pressures, restricting the entry of new firms, and managing prices. (See Stigler, 1971; Wilson 1980; Noll, 1985). Thus, government regulation of economic transactions often reduces uncertainties in the environments of organizations and so is likely to be cultivated by them.

In addition to regulating economic transactions, public organizations also participate in them. Governments are able to impose both general and specific taxes on organizations, and for many organizations they are a major provider of resources. Some resource flows are indirect, coming in the form of tax breaks or exemptions; others are more direct, involving outright transfers of funds in the form of subsidies or grants; and still others involve the government's acting not as an interested third party but as a direct participant in the transaction—as a buyer of products or a client of services. Some departments of the federal government, such as the Pentagon, are the primary purchasers of the products of a vast complex of organizations—in its case, defense-oriented manufacturers. And some families of organizations—for example, applied research organizations such as RAND and SRI—exist largely on contracts to conduct studies and provide services for a large range of governmental agencies. Although it is often argued that organizations selling services to government are part of a highly concentrated market, in fact the operations of the government are becoming increasingly differentiated, so that sellers often find several governmental units of the same kind bidding for their services.[9]

---

[9]Competition among governmental units has long existed at the level of state and local governments, as individual jurisdictions compete with one another—using tax incentives, land grants, tax-exempt bonds, and labor policies—to attract business to their area. In recent years, as indicated above, the federal government has become large and fragmented enough so that a similar competition has developed among its several branches and departments.

The tactics organizations employ to influence governmental organizations are not the same ones they use with private organizations. In particular, as Pfeffer and Salancik (1978: 192) have noted, private organizations requesting special treatment from governmental agencies must justify their private claims on the grounds that they serve the public interest. Thus, universities seek to preserve academic freedom not primarily because professors and university administrators prefer unconstrained decision making but because academic freedom must be preserved "for society's good." And the Chrysler Corporation's successful pursuit of $1.5 billion in loan guarantees from the federal government was justified in the name of preserving competition in the automobile industry and safeguarding the jobs of American workers.

MANAGING INSTITUTIONAL ENVIRONMENTS

As discussed in earlier chapters, our ideas concerning institutional environments are more recent and less developed than those concerning technical environments, and we know less about how organizations relate to them. But there are at least two clear differences between organizational responses to technical and institutional aspects of their environments. First, most connections with technical environments involve flows or exchanges—of information, resources, personnel. Although some connections with institutional environments also involve flows—particularly of information—a more important linkage process is absorption or incorporation. Whereas organizations *exchange* elements with their technical environments, they are *constituted* by elements drawn from their institutional environments. Technical elements are secured, combined, and transformed by organizational processes so that they commonly are no longer visible in their original state. By contrast, institutional elements are secured and utilized without being transformed. Great efforts are made to insure their visibility to outsiders, and it is essential that their distinctive features remain intact.

Second, although organizations necessarily will attempt to screen out undesirable or inappropriate elements from their institutional environments, and in this sense engage in buffering processes, most of the arguments to date stress that bridging processes are central to these connections. Both Meyer and Rowan (1977) and DiMaggio and Powell (1983) propose that institutional *isomorphism* is the master bridging process pursued by organizations in their institutional environments: by incorporating institutional rules within their own structures, organizations become more homogeneous, more similar in structure, over time. It is important to emphasize, however, that the processes producing isomorphism are assumed to operate within a given institutional sphere or sector, so that to the extent that sectors vary in their rules, organizational forms would also be expected to diverge. (See Scott, 1983: 61.) While recognizing that it is not easy to develop a precise typology of isomorphic strategies, we can identify four somewhat distinctive institutional bridging mechanisms.

Institutional Bridging Strategies

Categorical conformity   This is the broadest and most general strategy, and can easily be extended to include as special cases the other three types. Categorical conformity is the process whereby institutional rules in the form of typifications, or taken-for-granted distinctions, provide guidelines to organizations on the basis of which they can pattern their structures. These distinctions are the aspects of institutionalization emphasized by Berger and Luckmann (1967) and by Meyer and Rowan (1977) (see Chapter 5). General distinctions such as those between research and development, production and distribution functions, blue- and white-collar workers, or professionals and administrators are widely accepted and often become the basis of structural differentiation within organizations. Organizations also incorporate and build their structures around widely institutionalized general roles such as students and teachers, managers, stockholders, and board members.

These types of distinctions are fundamental examples of more or less widely shared cognitive structures. They are built into our language. Meyer and Rowan (1977: 349) refer to them as "vocabularies of structure." All of them are aspects of a reality that is socially constructed but widely believed, so that, as Zucker (1983: 2) notes, "certain social relationships and actions come to be taken for granted, that is, part of the 'objective situation.' " Zucker also emphasizes that categorical conformity is not produced or reinforced by sanctions, but occurs because it seems the natural or "obvious" way to proceed.

Organizations incorporate these cognitive belief systems because doing so enhances their legitimacy and hence increases their resources and survival capacities. As Meyer and Rowan (1977: 349) argue,

> vocabularies of structure that are isomorphic with institutional rules provide prudent, rational, and legitimate accounts. Organizations described in legitimated vocabularies are assumed to be oriented to collectively defined, and often collectively mandated, ends. . . . On the other hand, organizations that omit environmentally legitimated elements of structure or create unique structures lack acceptable legitimated accounts of their activities. Such organizations are more vulnerable to claims that they are negligent, irrational, or unnecessary.

Structural conformity   Sometimes environmental actors impose very specific structural requirements on organizations as a condition for acceptance and support. Organizations are required to adopt specific structural elements—tables of organization, departments, roles—in order to merit approval. DiMaggio and Powell (1983: 152) point out that organizations confronting high levels of uncertainty often borrow structural forms, sometimes by consciously modeling a successful form, sometimes by bringing in personnel from other organizations who are known to be capable of importing innovative forms, and sometimes by seeking assistance from consulting firms, "which, like Johnny Appleseeds, spread a few organizational forms throughout the land."

The nation-state is an important source of structural isomorphism, creating fields of organizations with virtually identical forms or requiring existing organizations to adopt particular structural units as a condition of eligibility for funding. During the past three decades, the federal government has imposed considerable structural unity on many types of regional, state, and local agencies. In arenas ranging from mental health and community cancer control to museums and arts councils, many federal programs specify in considerable detail the structures and components to be established. (See Foley and Sharfstein, 1983; DiMaggio, 1983.) Also, governmental statutes frequently require that particular offices or units be added to existing structures—for example affirmative-action officers or safety units.

But it is not only governmental organizations that impose structural uniformity on numerous other types of organizations. Many quasi-public bodies, such as foundations and professional associations, have similar effects. Thus, the Joint Commission on Hospital Accreditation—a "private" joint venture involving the American College of Physicians and Surgeons and the American Hospital Association—requires as a condition of accreditation that hospitals have specific structural features, such as a medical staff organization with specific subcommittees to review staff admissions, quality assurance, medical records, and so forth. Although no hospital is compelled to conform to these requirements, there are strong normative pressures to do so, which are reinforced by financial policies that often restrict reimbursement to care received in accredited institutions.

Thus, both by choice and by coercion, organizations frequently exhibit structural isomorphism as a mechanism for adapting to their institutional environment.

Procedural conformity   Organizations are often placed under pressure from their institutional environments to carry out activities in specified ways. As with structural conformity, such pressures are sometimes the result of uncertainty—the procedures being adopted or copied by organizational choice—and sometimes the result of explicit normative or coercive pressures that require their adoption under threat of informal or formal sanctions.

Many of the rational myths described by Meyer and Rowan (1977) define procedures, spelling out in greater or lesser specificity the steps to be followed in carrying out certain types of activities. In a sense, rational myths are institutionally defined technologies specifying means—ends chains an organization is to follow in order to realize desired objectives. A vast range of procedural rules—from committing mental patients, to incorporating organizations, to baptizing new church members, to implementing PERT (planning, evaluation, and review techniques)—are devised in institutional environments and incorporated into organizations as part of their standard operating procedures.

In modern societies, the two major types of collective actors generating procedural requirements are governmental units and professional groups. DiMaggio and Powell (1983: 147) assert that

> bureaucratization and other forms of homogenization [are] effected largely by the state and the professions, which have become the great rationalizers of the second half of the twentieth century.

In some situations, particularly when professional groups are strong, the nation-state will collaborate with professionals in attempting to rationalize an arena of activity. For example, in the quality-assurance programs mandated by the federal government in the 1970s, such as the Professional Standard Review Organizations, dominant decision-making roles were reserved for physicians. (See Goran et al., 1975; Scott, 1982.) In other areas, such as social welfare, recent legislation has reduced the discretion of social workers, lowered the qualifications they must meet for employment, and in general substantially deprofessionalized the public welfare program in the United States (Simon, 1983). Rationalization can take many forms and can locate discretion at more or less centralized nodes in the organizational structures created. The state is more likely to prefer more centralized structures, and the professions, more decentralized systems of procedures.

Lawyers, particularly in the United States, operate under the mantle of both state power and professional authority. They occupy most of the positions in our legislative bodies and our courts, as well as a large proportion of the positions in public administrative agencies. They are the acknowledged experts in devising procedural approaches to dispute resolution and problem solving. Even when the demands being enforced are primarily technical, the requirements are often couched in procedural language—the language of lawyers—rather than in language that attempts to specify outcomes. (See Majone, 1980.) Regulatory units as varied as the Health Systems Agencies, the Food and Drug Administration, and the Environmental Protection Agency operate primarily by specifying elaborate procedures—certificates of need, clinical trials, environmental impact reports—to be followed in justifying the introduction of new products or constructions. Critics have noted that these procedures readily become disconnected from outcomes, creating legalistic mazes and bureaucratic rituals rather than providing a framework to support rational decision making (see Bardach and Kagan, 1982). But institutionalists would emphasize that adherence to procedural specifications is one way in which stable organizational forms can be created and legitimated to work in conflict-ridden arenas. That the decisions are technical is irrelevant in these arenas since the decisions involve value conflicts: how or in whose interests is the technology to be used? Since any outcome will be controversial, the resolution of the matter must rest on the legitimacy of the decision process.

Personnel conformity   One of the primary building blocks of complex, differentiated, formal organizations is the large number of educated, often certified workers who assume specialized roles within them. As Meyer (1978: 354; 1985) points out, cultures vary considerably in where in the social structure rationality is institutionalized, but in contemporary Western societies, there is heavy emphasis on the individual as the prime locus. The Western cultural conception is one of

> the competent, achieving individual, whose productive action brings rewards to the self and corresponding gains to the collectivity (in such conceptions as the gross national product). This individual is institutionally located and managed primarily in the system of education. . . . (Meyer, 1985: 593)

Institutional environments often specify what types of actors—in terms of their (primarily educational) qualifications—are to be allocated to particular functions or roles. Conformity to institutional rules often entails the hiring of specific types of personnel. The most obvious examples involve certification and licensure. To be licensed as a "skilled nursing facility" an institution must include on its staff a specified proportion of registered nurses; governmentally mandated audits must be performed by certified public accountants; and accreditation bodies require that university faculties contain sufficient numbers of Ph.D's. In a great many arenas, organizational designers and managers have no or little control over the definition of jobs or the types of personnel recruited to fill them: these decisions have been made by external certification, licensure, and accreditation agencies. For example, once a hospital decides to offer a particular service, it is highly constrained by licensing rules in its decisions on what types of personnel are to be hired and how work is to be allocated among them. (See Somers, 1969; Freidson, 1970*a*.) Even when licensure is not required as a condition of operation or of funding, it is often used by occupations and organizations as a means of assuring the public that employees are qualified to perform their duties. From aerobics instructors and bartenders to tree surgeons and television repairmen, certification is looked to as an important source of legitimation.

More generally, a number of analysts have argued that education provides an important base for most personnel systems within organizations. Modern employment and promotion structures are heavily interlaced with educational requirements, which are justified in terms of technical skills and specialized knowledge required by the job. Yet, a number of other analysts have assembled evidence that challenges the presumed association between education and job qualifications or between education and productivity. (See Berg, 1971; Collins, 1979.) It has been proposed that the connection between education and occupational attainment is better viewed as having an institutional rather (or more) than a technical basis. Hiring certified or educated employees signals to the environment that the employer is a modern, responsible firm employing rational criteria of personnel selection and promotion. Without insisting that education and certification have no relation to performance, it is possible to embrace the institutional insight that, independent of performance, the hiring of individuals with appropriate educational credentials enhances the legitimacy of the employing organization and secures for it additional support and resources.

COMBINING INSTITUTIONAL AND TECHNICAL ARGUMENTS

Zucker and Tolbert have argued that there is an important temporal dimension to environmental effects: earlier developments are dominated by technical processes but later phases are better explained by institutional processes. Tolbert has also suggested that once institutional linkages are in place, the kinds of adaptive linkages predicted by resource dependency theory may not be necessary. These arguments have been pursued both as a broad historical account of the growth of organizational forms and the variable timing of their penetration of differing sectors, and as an explanation of the diffusion of particular structural patterns in a delimited organizational field.

As discussed in Chapter 7, Zucker (1983: 13) formulates the broader version, suggesting that although the creation of organizational forms may have been encouraged by their superior production efficiency, "the rapid rise and continued spread of the organizational form is best interpreted as an instance of institutionalization: . . . it becomes seen as legitimate to organize formally, regardless of any net benefit." Emerging first in the manufacturing sector, organizations spread over time to become the dominant form for structuring local government, social services, and even social movements. Zucker (1983: 20) concludes,

> Initially, organizational form was adopted rationally to handle large-scale production and to create predictable conditions of work. . . . However, as the organizational form gained legitimacy and diffused outward to organize most economic, political, and (later) collective activities, it became a taken-for-granted element, so that it was unthinkable for a new business or political activity to take place *not* located in an organizational structure.

As discussed, we do not find these arguments convincing. Zucker's data are too sparse to support this broad a conclusion, and one can cite many instances of political and even religious systems being formally structured long before large-scale production systems developed. Nevertheless, it is apparent that organizational forms have spread over time into rather unlikely social arenas, with, for example, romantic pairings increasingly arranged by dating services and child care provided by licensed facilities.

The narrower arguments are better supported. Tolbert and Zucker (1983) examined the introduction of civil service procedures into a sample of ninety-three American municipal governments in states that did not mandate adoption of the reform, during the period 1880 to 1935. They report that early in this period, adoption of the reforms was associated with city characteristics such as number of immigrants, proportion of white-collar versus blue-collar inhabitants, and size. These are the types of associations that would be predicted by resource dependency theory: local governments were adopting changes that would buffer them from "undesirable elements" and link them to better segments of the community. However, after 1885 municipal characteristics no longer predicted adoption. The explanation offered is that the reforms had become institutionalized: after being adopted by a sufficient number of cities, they came to signify a modern community with a "rational" city administration, and so their adoption became widespread. (See also, Knoke, 1982)

Tolbert (1985) elaborates this argument in her study of administrative structures in a random sample of public and private colleges and universities. Resource dependency theory would predict that organizations depending on particular financial resources would be likely to develop offices that manage and protect those sources. Thus, private colleges were more likely to report the presence of a development officer and a director of admissions, whereas public colleges were more likely to have positions for managing sources of public funding, such as directors of planning and information. However, contrary to the predictions of resource dependency, among those institutions that were more heavily dependent on public funding, only the private and not the public schools showed a more differentiated structure; the reverse was true for institutions that were more heavily dependent on private gifts: only the public institutions added new officials to manage these flows. To account for these findings, Tolbert argues that specialized roles for managing interorganizational exchanges are necessary only when these exchanges are not institutionalized.

> Thus, increasing dependence does not necessarily produce administrative differentiation. It is only when dependency relations are not institutionalized that increasing dependency is strongly associated with the development of separate administrative offices to manage them. (1985: 11)

These studies are of interest because they are among the first to seek to determine how competing explanations of organizational structure can be combined. It is apparent that although some of these explanations are inconsistent, others may not be once we have better specified the conditions under which they are applicable. Also, it is likely that under some conditions the operation of some types of structures or relations will obviate the need for others.

ADAPTATION VERSUS SELECTION

Change in Organizations

Our discussion of the buffering and bridging strategies employed by organizations has been conducted primarily within the frameworks of resource dependence and institutional theory. We have emphasized that this approach works at the level of the organization set: we examined how the world appears from the windows of a specific focal organization and asked what strategies are available to that organization as it seeks at least to survive and, if possible, to thrive in its environment. Thus far we have not emphasized a second important characteristic of this approach: it assumes that organizational structures can be modified, that they are subject to manipulation by participants who are attempting to improve their adaptation. The strategies we have reviewed presume the presence of decision makers who survey the situation, confront alternatives as well as constraints, and select a course of action. They presume, in short, that organizational structures can be changed by modifications of existing structures.

This assumption is challenged by ecologists studying organizations at the population level of analysis. They argue that much of the variation in structural forms is due to environmental *selection* rather than adaptation (see Aldrich and Pfeffer, 1976). It is not necessary to insist that organizations do not exhibit structural change as a means of adapting to their environments, but only that many organizations do not learn about their environments and fail to modify their structures as quickly as their environments change (Hannan and Freeman, 1984).

In an earlier discussion, Hannan and Freeman (1977: 931–32) cite a large number of constraints upon change in organizations. Their list includes such internal limitations as the organization's investment in capital equipment and trained personnel, constraints on the transfer and processing of information, the costs of upsetting the internal political equilibrium, and the conservative forces of history and tradition. Equally important are the external constraints, including legal and fiscal barriers to entry and exit from markets, environmental limitations on the flow of information, and the difficulty of securing the external political and social support needed to legitimate any change. Evidence regarding the stability of organizational structures over time is provided by Stinchcombe's (1965) analysis, described in Chapter 7, of the link between time of founding and current structural characteristics of organizations. Stinchcombe's thesis of organizational imprinting is consistent with the view that organizations do not easily or quickly change their structural features. Thus, structural *inertia* is an important cause of environmental selection: structural forms are unable to keep pace with environmental change.

More recently, Hannan and Freeman (1984: 149) have suggested that the inertial properties of organizations may also be a *consequence* of selection: "high levels of structural inertia in organizational populations can be explained as an outcome of an ecological-evolutionary process." Both technical and institutional explanations are utilized. On the technical side, organizations are seen as being highly valued for their *reliability*— their capacity to "produce collective products of a given quality repeatedly." Such reliable performances are possible only in relatively stable structures. On the institutional side, organizations are prized for their *accountability*—their adherence "to norms of procedural rationality." (1984: 153) Organizations that exhibit either high reliability and/or high accountability are more likely to survive, given a reasonable degree of environmental stability. However, under conditions of higher environmental uncertainty, inertia becomes a liability rather than an asset, preventing the organization from changing enough, or quickly enough, to survive.

In the research to date, much attention has been devoted to states of the environment that give rise to particular adaptive forms. An environmental dimension of considerable importance is that of environmental *variability*—the extent of change observed (in resources, the level of competition, and so on) over a specific period. A related dimension is that of *grain*—the frequency with which changes occur over the period. An environment characterized by very rapid changes is said to be *fine-grained* and one with less frequent changes, *coarse-grained*. Following general ecological arguments, Freeman and Hannan (1983) predicted that generalist organizations—those organizations performing a greater diversity of tasks and having higher levels of excess or "slack" resources—would be more likely to survive in coarse-grained environments. Specialist organizations were expected to flourish in stable environments but also in those with rapid change—fine-grained environments. Specialist firms were expected to be able to ride out environmental changes in which a given state was rapidly replaced by an alternative state. But only the generalists were expected to survive wide fluctuations of longer duration.

These predictions were tested and generally confirmed in a study of restaurants in eighteen California cities (Freeman and Hannan, 1983). The variability of the environment was measured in terms of the variation in gross restaurant sales over the three-year period of the study; frequency of change, or grain, was based on the extent of seasonal variation experienced by each restaurant. Generalists were distinguished from specialist restaurants by the range of items on the menu, the differentiation of staff, and whether or not seating was provided to customers. During the three years, 13 percent of the 788 restaurants studied "died" and another 13 percent were sold. Modest and mixed empirical support was obtained for the prediction that specialist firms were more likely to survive in stable, and in fine-grained environments. The prediction that generalists survive better in coarse-grained environments received strong support. The results were observed only for restaurant deaths; sale rates were not responsive to these measures of environmental variation. Finally, as in most studies of organizational populations (see Carroll, 1984), newer restaurants exhibited a much higher death rate than older restaurants, a finding consistent with the alleged liability of newness.

The adaptation arguments of the resource dependence school and the selection arguments of the population ecologists are not completely incompatible and in fact can be viewed as complementary. Specifically, the population ecology approach seems to us to be particularly useful in focusing on the core features of organizations, explaining the life chances of smaller and more numerous organizations, and accounting for changes in organizational forms over longer periods. By contrast, the resource dependency approach emphasizes the more peripheral features of organizations, is better applied to larger and more powerful organizations, and stresses changes occurring over shorter periods. Let us briefly amplify each of these sources of divergence.

The population ecology approach usefully emphasizes that there are important constraints on the variability and adaptability of organizational structures. This argument applies particularly to those characteristics that are closely associated with the core technology:[10] it is here that we find the major investments in capital equipment and skilled personnel, investments not readily changed. On the other hand, the resource dependency advocates are correct in pointing out the many possibilities open to organizations in modifying their peripheral structures—their buffers and bridges. To label these structures as *peripheral* is not to regard them as superficial or of little adaptive consequence. As we have tried to argue throughout this chapter, the strategies employed by organizations to buffer and bridge can have profound effects on their chances for survival and their level of functioning. (See Chapter 10.)

The population ecology approach is more readily applied to relatively small and numerous organizations that are not individually in a position to exert much effect on their environments. (But such organizations can and do exert collective pressures through associations.) The approach has been usefully applied to the study of such organizations as newspapers, restaurants,[11] and semiconductor firms (see, for example, Carroll and Delacroix, 1982; Brittain and Freeman, 1980). Larger and more powerful organizations can be studied—for example, labor unions and trade associations (see Freeman and Brittain, 1977; Staber and Aldrich, 1983)—but this requires longer periods so that enough of the events of interest—births and deaths—can be observed. Further, the larger and more powerful the class of organizations under investigation,

---

[10]The emphasis placed by natural selection models on the core production processes of organizations is discussed in Chapter 6.

[11]Freeman and Hannan (1983) regard restaurants as the "fruit flies" of the organizational world. Since their expected life span is so brief, it is easier to observe changes in this species of organization over several "generations."

the more likely it is that they will be able to alter their environments significantly, and hence the more difficult it will be to sustain and test the argument that environments select organizational forms.

Finally, the population ecology approach is best suited to explain changes in the distribution of organizational forms over the long run—over a period of decades or centuries. For example, it is better used for explaining changes over time in the number of junior colleges in relation to other organizational forms in higher education than for explaining structural changes made by one college in reaction to some environmental challenge. The resource dependence approach is best employed to account for adaptive responses of specific organizations over a relatively short period.

Thus, we regard both points of view as valuable. However, we do take sides in the controversy to this extent: we believe that a single organization is capable of extensive structural change and elaboration over both shorter and longer periods. In our opinion, some population ecologists have overemphasized the structural rigidity or inertia of organizations. Perhaps this is because many of their general ideas and models are adapted from the work of biological ecologists. Although there are important analogies between biological and social forms, we side with the open system theorists in insisting that an important hallmark of the latter is their unusual capacity for structural modification and elaboration. Substantial portions of Chapters 9 and 10 are devoted to these significant and distinctive organizational processes.

Adaptation of Organizational Fields

Adaptation is not the exclusive province of the individual organization, but also occurs in important ways at the level of the organizational field. Biological ecologists observe that adaptation processes may involve the behavior of isolated organisms, the behavior of populations, or more elaborate, interspecies communal responses. Similarly, human ecologists have long insisted that human communities are usefully analyzed as collective adaptative responses of differing but interdependent populations to the constraints and opportunities posed by specific environments. (See Hawley, 1950.) Ecological perspectives emphasize the more "natural" and unwitting aspects of such adaptive behavior, but network theory and related approaches stress that such collective mechanisms are also created by purposeful actors joining forces to improve the circumstances for all their constituents. Although resource dependence ideas are typically applied at the organization-set level in examinations of the adaptive capabilities of individual organizations, many of the specific strategies employed—for example, contracts, co-optation, joint ventures, and associations—involve the creation of interorganizational systems that are themselves vehicles of collective action and adaptation operating at a different level of analysis. (See Astley and Van de Ven, 1983; Astley, 1985.)

These conceptions of communal or collective adaptation have been applied most frequently to examinations of the adaptive functions of interorganizational systems in areal organizational fields, but they are also applicable to the analysis of functional organizational fields. Applications at each of these levels can be briefly reviewed.

Areal fields   As noted in Chapter 6, a large literature has developed on community structures as interorganizational systems. (See Laumann, Galaskiewicz, and Marsden, 1978, for a review.) An important axis around which community interests may turn is local versus extralocal dependence. Some organizational interests—local businesses, financial institutions, local media, realtors, and lawyers—are highly dependent on and greatly advantaged by community growth and have strong incentives to combine forces to forge their community into a "growth machine." (Molotch, 1976) These are the groups that are most likely to be active in and centrally connected with local interorganizational networks. (Galaskiewicz, 1979) By contrast, local plants or branch offices of national corporations headquartered elsewhere are less likely to be involved in such communal systems.

Even though non-local organizations are not strongly connected to areal systems, they can exercise great influence when and if their interests are affected. (Freidland, 1980) The power of such organizations is based not only on their economic dominance, but also on their capacity to "exit": to move out of a specific community. While "dominant and mobile actors participate less than nondominant, immobile ones" (Friedland and Palmer, 1984: 410), their influence may be exerted in less direct ways. They can apply, informal pressure on political leaders or their business associates, and they influence what is put on the agenda for decision making more than they determine what decisions are made on those matters that do reach the agenda.[12] (See Chapter 11.)

Thus, which collective interests are mobilized in areal fields such as communities will be greatly influenced by how those interests are affected by a given decision matter. Moreover, some interests may be sufficiently powerful that little or no visible mobilization or active participation is required for their influence to be felt by the other parties to the decision.

Functional fields   One of the most complete and persuasive studies conducted to date at this level of analysis is that of Miles (1982), who studied the response of the "Big Six" corporations in the United States tobacco industry to the threat posed by the demonstration of a causal link between smoking and impaired health. Although there was some early warning, the publication of the surgeon general's report linking smoking and cancer and subsequent actions taken by various federal agencies constituted a major environmental crisis for these organizations. Although each corporation adopted a variety of strategies ranging from product innovation to diversification, they also engaged in collective action. For example, during the first signs of trouble, they created the Tobacco Industry Research Committee to conduct their own studies of the effects of tobacco use. Following the surgeon general's report, they collectively engaged in a wide variety of lobbying efforts, providing cancer-research grants to the American Medical Association and various universities and

---

[12]Preventing issues or questions from being raised and shaping the agenda of decision making have been identified as important, albeit difficult-to-investigate, modes of power. These types of power have been variously labeled *structural* and *systemic*, and this area of inquiry has been termed the study of *nondecisions*. (See Bachrach and Baratz, 1962; Alford and Friedland, 1975.)

monitoring closely and attempting to influence legislative and administrative actions affecting their interests.

Numerous studies have been conducted of the extent to which organizational fields within particular industries or societal sectors have developed networks or structures to support collective action. For example, Hirsch (1975) has contrasted the relatively successful efforts of companies within the pharmaceutical industry to organize to protect their interests with the much less successful activities of firms within the record industry. Although the two industries are somewhat similar in their level of technical development, reliance on batch processing, and dependence on external gatekeepers (physicians and disc jockeys) to mediate between themselves and their customers, pharmaceutical firms have been much more successful in obtaining legislation protecting brand-name drugs, in securing patent protections, and in co-opting physician groups in support of their interests. By contrast, record companies have been unable to obtain much collective control over pricing or distribution, have not secured exclusive copyright protections, and have not been able to co-opt disc jockeys to represent their interests. (The payola scandals of the 1950s and mid 1980s—attempts by record companies to bribe the staffs of radio stations—represent a notably crass and unsuccessful attempt to secure disc jockeys' loyalties.) It is not clear why pharmaceutical firms have been more successful in their collective efforts than record companies, but it is obvious that the degree of success associated with collective action by organizations within the same field can greatly affect the environment confronting each firm.

Although the results remain inconclusive, there have been a large number of studies of the extent to which private organizations are linked into networks of collective assistance that span industries or sectors. As we have already noted many of these connections are intraorganizational, involving the acquisition of many formerly independent firms and/or merger with these firms into vertically integrated or functionally diversified corporations. (We will consider these connections further in Chapter 10.) But other connections entail varying types of bridges among formally independent units that join forces to secure mutual benefits. There is disagreement over what interests are being served by such arrangements. Marxist theorists tend to emphasize class-based interests, focusing on connections among the elite families controlling major corporations, who utilize a variety of social networks—connections developed in elite colleges, corporate boards, and social clubs—to orchestrate and facilitate the safeguarding of their class advantages. (See Domhoff, 1983; Useem, 1980.) Other analysts point out that with the increasing separation of ownership from control rights in corporations, managerial interests—which emphasize the importance of organizational growth and security, rather than profits—are more likely to serve as the criteria by which interorganizational alliances are formed. Whether ownership has effectively been disconnected from control is, however, much in dispute (see Zeitlin, 1974), and whether managers pursue interests different from those of owners has not been established (see Pfeffer, 1982).

Although there is little doubt that complex adaptive patterns that connect corporate organizations into complex networks or systems have developed in more advanced economic systems—Marxists would describe these patterns as being characteristic of "late," or monopoly capitalist, systems—the specific features and functions of these arrangements remain in dispute. For example, whereas Scott (1979) has emphasized the ways in which interlocking directorates support information exchanges necessary for coordinating action, Palmer (1983) has noted that a high proportion (85 percent) of interlocks that accidentally broke—due to the death, retirement, or transfer of the incumbent—were not reconstituted, suggesting that such ties were not crucial to the corporation so linked. And there is controversy over whether banks and other financial institutions play a special role in connecting and controlling other types of organizations. Although the ownership by these institutions of large blocks of corporate stock is patent, their exercise of control over the firms whose stock they purchase has not been established. (See Mintz and Schwartz, 1983.) In this area, the hypotheses and questions seem to multiply more rapidly than the facts and findings. (See Glasberg and Schwartz, 1983; Mizruchi and Schwartz, 1986.)

Other analysts have examined the changing nature of functional fields in public service arenas. A number of observers have argued that there has been a growing trend toward "sectoralization," with services being defined in limited, functionally differentiated terms—for example, housing, employment, child care, and mental health (see Wildavsky, 1979). Employing network-analysis techniques, Laumann and colleagues (Knoke and Laumann, 1982; Laumann, Knoke, and Kim, 1985) have examined the ways in which shifting populations of public and private organizations become active in the setting of national policy in the sectors of health and energy. The boundaries of such interorganizational policy-making systems are vague, with participation being determined by interest in the issue (domain), capacity to mobilize relevant resources—such as staff, funds, and expertise—and centrality of location in the system.

Once policies are formulated, a different network of organizations—again spanning both the public and private sectors—is often constructed to link federal, state, and local agencies into a complex decision-making and implementation system. Meyer and I (Meyer and Scott, 1983) have argued that such networks in this country are likely to exhibit relatively high centralization of financial or funding decisions combined with more decentralized programmatic decision making. This is particularly the case for the more professionalized service sectors, such as health care and education. In such organizational fields, vertical controls among organizations are likely to be exercised primarily by financial officers and accountants.

> Rather than the development of a centralized hierarchical structure stretching from local delivery systems through regional and state agencies to a central federal agency, we have the burgeoning of accounting departments and fiscal units responsible for mediating the funding and reporting relations between delivery systems and funding sources. The controls exercised are indirect rather than direct, specifying what services will be reimbursed—not what services will be offered. (Meyer and Scott, 1983: 104)

Sectoral structuring of organizational services represents an attempt to create a coherent, rational system for implementing public policies in a specialized arena. In the case of the United States, two problems in the operation of these organizational fields have received considerable attention. First, it is argued that the interorganizational systems that are created for the purposes of policy making and implementation operate too independently from one another—that although policies are devised as though they will be implemented in insulated areas, there are inevitably important interdependencies in outcomes. Programs devised to subsidize rapid transit in cities interact with programs for renewing neighborhoods and improving housing. The current call by governmental reformers is for greater attention to the coordination of programs across sectors. (See Sundquist, 1969; Rogers and Whetten, 1982.) Although this may be partly a matter of simply designing better incentives for interagency cooperation and developing better mechanisms to bridge organizations, it is also partly an issue of how to reconcile the two somewhat competing bases of structuring organizational fields that we have identified. Some actors are attempting to rationalize a functional field, to design an interorganizational system that will support the implementation of a specific program in many different areas; other actors are struggling to articulate many different functional programs that converge in complex and unexpected ways to affect a single territory. The two attempts at rationalization may conflict, since what is viewed as rational will depend on how the boundaries of the system are defined. (See Scott, 1985a.) On the other hand, we should not be too quick to assume that rational design is the name of the game.

Benson (1982: 170) suggests that a different game is being played. He regards the problem of inadequate coordination as signifying the more general problem of "interorganizational feudalism" and suggests that its basis is to be found in the historic weakness of central governmental structures in the United States, which are largely incapable of overcoming the vested private interests that tend to dominate outcomes in most societal sectors. This is the second major criticism leveled at organizational systems created to implement public programs. Benson argues that these organizational fields are shaped by existing structures of interest and power that importantly influence and constrain policy goals and programs. Similar to the analyses of Lowi (1969), Lindblom (1977), and Wolfe (1977), Benson asserts that in a large number of arenas in this country, public authorities have been willing to collaborate with private interests, not only by giving them access to public resources and allowing them to exert influence on public decision makers but also by bestowing on them varying degrees of public authority. Private interests are alleged to dominate and undermine attention to the public good.

The examination of the bases around which organizational fields or sectors are organized thus leads us directly to the organization of the nation-state. One does not have to be a Marxist—although Marxist theorists have been at the forefront of this work—to recognize the important role played by the nation-state. (See Bright and Harding, 1984; Krasner, 1984; Skowronek, 1982.) While the power of the state is general and affects the structure of all organizational fields, its influence varies from sector to sector, and differing societies vary in their capacity to exercise influence in one or another domain.

A number of modern nation-states have moved far in the direction

of articulating the connections between public agencies and private interests into a relatively tight and consciously directed system known as
corporatism.

> Corporatism can be defined as a system of interest representation in which
> the constituent units are organized into a limited number of singular, com-
> pulsory, noncompetitive, hierarchically ordered and functionally differenti-
> ated categories, recognized or licensed (if not created) by the state and
> granted a deliberate representational monopoly within their respective cate-
> gories in exchange for observing certain controls on their selection of
> leaders and articulation of demands and supports (Schmitter, 1974: 93–94).

Two types are identified. The first, *societal* corporatism, is one in which
private interests in a given sector have gradually become more singular,
noncompetitive, and hierarchically organized so that specific, centrally
located organizations gain the legitimacy to represent the interests of their
"constituency" in negotiations with the state. Trade associations often perform this function. (See Staber, 1985) The societal type of corporatism is
best exemplified in Sweden, Switzerland, the Netherlands, Norway and
Denmark, and, to a lesser extent, Great Britain, West Germany, France,
Canada, and the United States. (See Berger, 1981.) The second type, *state*
corporatism, involves a much more active role on the part of the state:
sectors are defined and representatives created or selected by state decree. This pattern is currently to be found primarily in "Iberian" countries such as Portugal, Spain, Brazil, Chile, Peru, Mexico, and Greece,
and, in the past, in such totalitarian regimes as fascist Italy and Nazi
Germany. (Schmitter, 1974: 102–4)

Although the U.S. state is widely acknowledged to be relatively
"weak" as a formal, administrative system of rights and powers (see Huntington, 1966), it is important to insist that this weak state resides within a
strong and active *polity.* There has long existed a larger set of political and
cultural institutions that locates a substantial portion of legitimate public
authority in bodies formally outside of the state. The weakness of the
state is offset by the strength of the society. (See Thomas and Meyer,
1984.) And it is this rich institutional environment that has given rise to
much of the variety and complexity of the organizational fields that have
arisen in United States society.

Thus, a rapid and fruitful convergence is occurring between the
long-standing but recently reinvigorated interests of political scientists in
the structure of the nation-state and the interests of organizational theorists in the structure of organizational fields. (See DiMaggio and Powell,
1983; Meyer and Scott, 1983; Olsen, 1983; Evans, Rueschemeyer, and
Skocpol, 1986.) While from one point of the view the two subjects are
causally interdependent, from another they are but two sides of the same
complex societal system.

SUMMARY

At one and the same time, organizations must be open to their environments and attentive to their boundaries. This poses an intricate problem

with respect to the recruitment of participants. Organizations require some control over the criteria by which individuals are admitted and rewarded, and in some extreme cases organizations hold sufficient power to eliminate participant characteristics or identities that are based on their involvement in other social systems. In the more usual case, however, an organization has neither the power nor the desire to eliminate such identities, which can be put to use by the organization. How to mobilize these characteristics in the service of organizational goals while preventing participants from using organizational resources in the service of other goals is a continuing challenge for managers of all organizations.

To varying degrees, organizations try to internalize labor market processes exerting a major effect on individuals' mobility chances—determining what positions are to be filled, what positions are open to entry from outside, what linkages exist among positions, and how individuals are selected or positions.

Two broad classes of strategies have been identified by which organizations relate to their task environments. Organizations employ buffering techniques—coding, stockpiling, leveling, forecasting, and growth—to seal off their technical core from environmental disturbances. They use bridging techniques—bargaining, contracting, co-optation, joint ventures, mergers, associations, and governmental connections—to increase the number and variety of their linkages with competitors and exchange partners and thereby enhance their security in technical environments. Other types of bridging strategies—categorical, structural, procedural, and personnel conformity—are employed in securing legitimacy and support in institutional environments. Analysis of such strategies is most readily conducted at the level of the organization set and presumes that the managers of an organization can fashion its activities so as to enhance its security or effectiveness. This assumption is challenged by analysts working at the population level, who emphasize the inertia of organizational behavior and insist that most change occurs because of natural selection—the differential survival of different organizational types—rather than rational selection—conscious design by organizational managers.

Adaptation occurs not only at the level of the individual organization but also at the communal level: within areal and functional fields. Both adaptation and selection approaches—which are addressed to different levels, time periods, and types of organizations—appear useful for examining organization-environment interdependencies.

9

sources of structural complexity: the technical core

Every organized human activity—from the making of pots to the placing of a man on the moon—gives rise to two fundamental and opposing requirements: the *division of labor* into various tasks to be performed, and the *coordination* of these tasks to accomplish the activity. The structure of an organization can be defined simply as the sum total of the ways in which it divides its labor into distinct tasks and then achieves coordination among them.

Henry Mintzberg (1979)

Whether by natural or rational selection—by evolution or learning—organizations tend to move toward higher levels of complexity. This thesis will be amplified at two levels. First, in this chapter we examine the sources of structural complexity that develop within the technical core of an organization. The prime source of core complexity is the nature of the work being carried out—the demands made by the technology on the structure. Second, in Chapter 10 we consider the sources of structural complexity that occur outside the technical core, in the peripheral sectors of the organization, including the managerial and institutional levels. These structures respond in particular to demands posed by the size or scale of the organization and to the task and institutional environments. At the conclusion of Chapter 10 we examine the relation between the core and peripheral structures.

The structural features of organizations that are of primary interest are those defining the division of labor—structural differentiation, including occupational and role specialization, departmentalization, and multi–divisional forms—and those relating to coordination and control of work—formalization, hierarchy, centralization, and various structures for facilitating lateral information flows.

Contingency theory provides the primary orienting framework for the topics addressed in this chapter. As described in Chapter 4, this approach insists that there is no single best way in which to design the structure of an organization. Rather, what is the best or most appropriate structure depends—is contingent—on what type of work is being performed and on what environmental demands or conditions confront the organization. Lawrence and Lorsch and Jay Galbraith utilize a rational open perspective and stress formalized responses to task complexity. Other theorists, such as the Tavistock group, Burns and Stalker, Cole, and Ouchi, assume a natural open system perspective and emphasize the value of more diffuse and informal control systems. Both groups will inform our attempts to account for the complexity of the technical core.

To the extent possible, organizations attempt to seal off their technical core from environmental disturbances. This central proposition developed by Thompson (1967) helps to account for the defensive behavior of many types of organizations. The specific strategies devised by organizations to buffer their technical core were reviewed in the previous chapter. But what if the buffers are inadequate and uncertainty penetrates the technical core? As organizations take on more complex and unpredictable tasks, we cannot assume that all traces of uncertainty will be buffered out of the core. How can the structure of the technical core be modified so as to accommodate more demanding tasks? To address this question, we need to develop a clearer conception of how to define and measure the work performed in the technical core.

DEFINING AND MEASURING TECHNOLOGY

As we pointed out in Chapter 1, *technology* is the term that has come to refer to the work performed by an organization.[1] This concept is broadly defined by organization theorists and includes not only the hardware used in performing work but also the skills and knowledge of workers, and even the characteristics of the objects on which work is performed. We must acknowledge at the outset that there is considerable overlap between *technology, task environment,* and *environment* as these terms are employed by organizational analysts. *Environment* is the more inclusive term and incorporates political, technological, and institutional aspects of the organizational context. *Task environment* emphasizes those features of the environment relevant to its supply of inputs and its disposition of outputs but also includes the power-dependence relations within which the organization must make its exchanges. *Technology,* as defined above, is the more restricted term. However, it is important to emphasize the extent to which an organization's technology—although an "internal" element—links the organization to its environment: the environment not only is the source of inputs and the recipient of outputs but also is the major source of the work techniques and tools employed by the organization. Most organizations do not themselves invent their technologies but import them from the environment. Also, given the degree of overlap between the concepts of technology and environment, it should not surprise us to find many of the same analytical dimensions being used by analysts to identify their relevant features.

Earlier students of industrial and organizational sociology have noted the impact of technical and production features of the work process on worker behavior and work group structure (for example, Sayles, 1958;

[1]The following discussion draws on my description (Scott, 1975) of the characteristics of technology and the relation between technology and structure.

Trist and Bamforth, 1951; Walker and Guest, 1952; Whyte, 1948). But it was the empirical research of Woodward (1958; 1965) and a theoretical article by Thompson and Bates (1957) that first called attention to technology as a general determinant of organizational structure. Woodward's conception of technology as applied to industrial organizations was broadened and generalized by Thompson (Thompson and Bates, 1957; Thompson, 1967), by Litwak (1961), and by Perrow (1967; 1970) so as to be applicable to all types of organizations.

An examination of the many recent attempts to define and measure technology indicates that the concept has been viewed very broadly to include (1) the characteristics of the *inputs* utilized by the organization; (2) the characteristics of the *transformation processes* employed by the organization; and (3) the characteristics of the *outputs* of the organization.[2] Alongside this view of technologies varying by stage of processing, Hickson, Pugh, and Pheysey (1969) point out that approaches to technology vary by whether analysts emphasize (1) the *materials* on which work is performed, (2) the *operations* or techniques used to perform the work, or (3) the state of *knowledge* that underlies the transformation process. If these two sets of distinctions are cross-classified, they allow us to both categorize and summarize many of the specific measures that have been employed to assess organizational technologies. The classification together with illustrative measures appears in Table 9–1.

Although a great many specific measures of technology have been generated, we believe that it is possible to identify three general underlying dimensions that encompass most of the more specific measures and, more to the point, isolate the most critical variables needed to predict structural features of organizations.[3] These three dimensions are complexity or diversity, uncertainty or unpredictability, and interdependence. We will discuss each briefly.

Complexity or diversity   This dimension refers to the number of different items or elements that must be dealt with simultaneously by the organization. Specific measures such as multiplicity and customization of outputs and variety of inputs tap this dimension.

Uncertainty or unpredictability   This dimension refers to the variability of the items or elements upon which work is performed or to the extent to which it is possible to predict their behavior in advance. Some of the general factors affecting the degree of uncertainty of the organiza-

---

[2]A large number of output measures have been developed by the Aston group—a team of researchers working at the University of Aston in Birmingham, England (see Pugh et al., 1969: 99–102). These researchers regard their measures as relating to the concept of *charter*—the social function or goals of an organization—rather than to an organization's technology. In fact, though, many of the measures relate to the characteristics of outputs—for example, multiplicity of products and degree of customization—and so from our point of view are appropriate measures of technology.

[3]The stage-of-processing distinction illustrated in Table 9–1 is also useful for predicting structural features since it indicates *where* in the technical core work-processing demands are likely to be heavier. Input units that must deal with a large amount of uncertainty will be structured differently than input units that handle only a small amount of uncertainty.

TABLE 9–1. Classification of Technology Measures. *Source:* Scott (1975), pp. 5–6.

FACETS OF TECHNOLOGY	STAGE OF PROCESSING		
	Inputs	*Throughputs*	*Outputs*
Materials	Uniformity of inputs (Litwak, 1961) Hardness of materials (Rushing, 1968) Variability of stimuli (Perrow, 1970)	Number of exceptions (Perrow, 1970; Lynch, 1974) Interchangeability of components (Rackham and Woodward, 1970)	Major project changes (Harvey, 1968) Multiplicity of outputs (Pugh et al.1969) Customization of outputs (Pugh et al., 1969)
Operations	Preprocessing, coding, smoothing of inputs (Thompson, 1967)	Complexity of technical processes (Udy, 1959b; Woodward, 1965) Work-flow integration (Pugh et al., 1969) Routiness of work (Hage and Aiken, 1969) Automaticity of machinery (Amber and Amber, 1962) Interdependence of work units (Thompson, 1967; Lynch, 1974)	Control of outputs through stockpiling, rationing (Thompson, 1967) Value added in manufacture
Knowledge	Predictability (Dornbusch and Scott, 1975) Anticipation of fluctuations in supplies (Thompson, 1967)	Knowledge of cause-effect relations (Thompson, 1967) Analyzability of search processes (Perrow, 1970; Van de Ven and Delbecq, 1974) Information required to perform task compared with information possessed (Galbraith, 1973)	Time span of definitive feedback (Lawrence and Lorsch, 1967) Anticipation of fluctuations in demand (Thompson, 1967)

tion's task environment described in Chapter 6 are also relevant here. Specific measures of uncertainty include uniformity or variability of inputs, the number of exceptions encountered in the work process, and the number of major product changes experienced.

Interdependence   This dimension refers to the extent to which the items or elements upon which work is performed or the work processes themselves are interrelated so that changes in the state of one element affect the state of the others. Thompson (1967: 54–55) has proposed a useful typology for assessing degree of interdependence. Three levels are identified: (1) *pooled* interdependence, in which the work performed is interrelated only in that each element or process contributes to the overall goal (for example, selecting fabrics and color schemes for the inside decor of a jet airplane is related to the plane's aerodynamic design only in that both contribute to the overall objective or final product); (2) *sequential* interdependence, which exists when some activities must be performed before others (for example, component parts of a jet engine must be produced before they all can be assembled into a single functioning unit); and (3) *reciprocal* interdependence, which is present to the degree that elements or activities relate to each other as both inputs and outputs (for example, design decisions regarding the weight and thrust of a jet engine and the aerodynamic design of the fuselage and wings must take each other into account). Thompson points out that these three levels of interdependence form a Guttman-type scale, in that elements or processes that are reciprocally interdependent also exhibit sequential and pooled interdependence, and processes that are sequentially interdependent also exhibit pooled interdependence.

As indicated, these dimensions are of interest because they can be employed to predict the structural features of organizations.

TECHNOLOGY AND FORMAL STRUCTURE

Since matters can rapidly become complicated, we will state at the outset the major linkages that are expected to exist between an organization's technology and its structure. In noting these main effects, we recognize that the interaction effects—the effects produced by two or more of the variables in combination—are more powerful and frequently of greater interest. The predictions are as follows:

1. The greater the technical complexity, the greater the structural complexity. The structural response to technical diversity is organizational differentiation.

2. The greater the technical uncertainty, the less formalization and centralization.

3. The greater the technical interdependence, the more resources must be devoted to coordination. More specifically, Thompson (1967: 55–56) argues that pooled interdependence can be managed by *standardization*, the development of rules or routines; sequential interdependence requires the development of *plans* or *schedules*, which specify timing and order in the work processes; and reciprocal interdependence requires the use of *mutual adjust-*

ment or coordination by feedback, in which the interrelated parties must communicate their own requirements and respond to the needs of each other. Each coordination strategy is increasingly costly in terms of resources.

Coordination Mechanisms

Galbraith (1973; 1977) has usefully argued that one way in which the varying demands of technologies on structures can be summarized is to ask how much information must be processed during the execution of a task sequence. He argues that information requirements increase as a function of increasing diversity, uncertainty, and interdependence of work flows. Using this simple formula to gauge information-processing demands, Galbraith then outlines a series of structural modifications organizations can make in their technical core as a means of adapting to increased demands for the processing of information. The following formal structures, discussed in order of increasing complexity, may be employed to manage the work flow.

Rules and programs Organizations performing the simplest and most routine tasks rely primarily on rules and performance programs to secure acceptable outcomes. And, of course, organizations carrying on even the most complex types of work perform many activities that can be regulated by rules and programs. These structural devices represent agreements about how decisions are to be made or work is to be processed that predate the work performance itself. They can be made to handle considerable complexity and some uncertainty, particularly as regards the sequence of events. For example, it is possible to develop rules for carrying out specific task activities and to add "switching rules" that signal which of several clusters of activities is to be performed or the order of their performance (see March and Simon, 1958: 142–50).

Schedules Schedules are necessary when different kinds of activities are to be carried on in the same location or when sequential interdependence is present. To information concerning the what and how of task performance, schedules add the dimension of when. Schedules also specify the period they are in force, and so are subject to modification. Galbraith suggests that increasing uncertainty can be handled by shortening the *plan-replan cycle*—that is, the period during which a given set of rules and schedules is in force.

Departmentalization One of the most difficult and critical of all decisions facing organization is how work is to be divided: what tasks are to be assigned to what roles and what roles to departments. As described in Chapter 2, early administrative theorists suggested that homogeneous activities be placed in the same organizational units, but critics noted that there are often several, competing bases for determining homogeneity (see March and Simon, 1958: 22–32). Thompson (1967: 57) has proposed that organizations will seek to group tasks according to their degree of interdependence, with reciprocally related tasks placed in the same or closely adjacent units, sequentially related tasks placed in less closely adjacent units, and tasks exhibiting pooled interdependence placed in the least closely adjacent units. Organizations are expected to behave in this manner because the type of coordination mechanism needed to cope with reciprocal tasks—mutual adjustment—is the most costly in terms of organizational resources; schedules, which are used to cope with sequential tasks, are the next most costly; and rules are the least costly. In short, Thompson argues that organizations attempt to group tasks so as to minimize coordination costs. It is instructive to note that Thompson's principle of minimizing coordination costs as an explanation for the location of departmental boundaries can be viewed as a special case of Williamson's (1975) principle of minimizing transactions costs as an explanation for the location of organizational boundaries (see Chapter 7).[4]

Hierarchy   Hierarchy can be used to respond to increased information flows in two ways. First, as Fayol and other administrative theorists emphasized early in this century (see Chapter 2), officials can be used to deal with unexpected or irregular occurrences on an "exception" basis. Of course, this practice can provide a satisfactory solution only if the exceptions do not arise too frequently. Second, as suggested by open system theorists (see Chapter 4), hierarchies can be used to group tasks (Simon, 1962). According to Thompson (1967: 59);

> it is unfortunate that [hierarchy] has come to stand almost exclusively for degrees of highness or lowness, for this tends to hide the basic significance of hierarchy for complex organizations. Each level is not simply higher than the one below, but is a more inclusive clustering, or combination of interdependent groups, to handle those aspects of coordination which are beyond the scope of any of its components.

As the amount of interdependence among organizational tasks increases, it becomes more difficult to handle it by departmentalization—to contain, for example, all of the instances of reciprocal interdependence within an organizational unit. As interdependence overflows departmental units, a heavier burden of information processing is placed on hierarchical officers who are expected to provide links across units. For example, consider a manufacturing firm that begins to perform more customized work, fitting the product to the customer's particular requirements. We would expect the interdependence between the sales and the production departments to increase and to be reflected in higher levels of information to be processed during task performance: for example, specifications of desired products, information about cost and feasibility, and requirements for and predictions concerning delivery date. Under these circumstances, we would expect the sales and production units to be clustered under a common superior, who would facilitate the flow of information between the two as a means of coordinating their work.

---

[4]Williamson's concept of transactions costs is broader than Thompson's concept of coordination costs because it includes the costs of negotiations between prospective exchange partners as well as the negotiations needed to coordinate exchanges once an agreement has been established. Within most organizations the former negotiations do not occur: one department is not allowed to determine whether or not to enter into exchanges with another unit in the same organization. However, in some very large organizations an attempt is made to simulate a market situation, and departments are allowed to decide whether to enter into exchange agreements with other internal units or to seek more favorable exchange rates externally.

Delegation Rather than attempting to program and regulate closely the work of all participants and requiring that all decisions be made above the level of the performers, organizations confronting increased complexity and uncertainty can delegate some autonomy to workers. Galbraith (1973) refers to this arrangement as *targeting* or *goal setting*, indicating that coordination is secured not by minute descriptions of work procedures but by specification of the desired outcomes. In the example of the manufacturing firm performing more customized work, a manager could provide the production department with a detailed specification of the desired product together with cost and time constraints but allow participants to exercise their own judgment and skills in arriving at a product that would satisfy these requirements. Delegation is present to some extent and for some positions in most organizations. However, it reaches its most highly developed form in professional organizations, a form to be discussed more fully later in this chapter.

Reducing Information versus Increasing Capacity

Rules and programs, schedules, departmentalization, hierarchy, and some delegation: these are the ubiquitous features of complex formal organizations. By means of these conventional structural mechanisms, organizations are able to respond to task demands posing moderate information-processing requirements. But what if the levels of diversity, uncertainty, and interdependence are higher still so that conventional solutions prove inadequate? Galbraith argues that an organization confronting excessive levels of task complexity and uncertainty can choose one of two general responses: it may elect to (1) "reduce the amount of information that is processed," or (2) "increase its capacity to handle more information" (1973: 15). Although these two responses push in different directions, they are not necessarily incompatible. Moreover, each response may be made through one of several strategies, and an organization may pursue more than one strategy at the same time. Strategies designed to reduce information processing are described first.

Slack resources An organization can reduce its information-processing demands simply by reducing the required level of performance (see Galbraith, 1973). Higher performance standards increase the need for coordination; lowered standards create slack—unused resources—which provides some ease in the system. For example, if delivery deadlines are not set so as to challenge the production units, then the need for information processing is reduced. If there are few constraints on inventory levels, then rapid response to changes in supply and demand messages is less essential. And, to use a nonmanufacturing example, if every third-grade teacher uses the first several weeks to reteach the basic lessons and skills of the second grade, then the sequential interdependence between second- and third-grade teachers is reduced, and there is less need for coordination of their efforts.

In addition to storing extra components and introducing redundancy into task performances, an organization can store surplus task or work-flow information. In his study of the complex structures that supply repair services for the electronic equipment required to support the

U.S. Naval Air Systems Command, Kmetz (1984: 272) details the use of *information buffers*—"pools or collections of information formed to support decision making or monitoring of workflow variables." At critical junctures in the repair process, varying types of information—samples of data, knowledge of legitimate and unsanctioned routines, backup guides and records—develop as alternatives to or supports for the official communications and data packages. For example, "a relatively formalized buffer, such as a workaround notebook, supports repair of a WRA [weapon replaceable assembly] independently of the accuracy of the test program" (1984: 273). Such slack resources allow looser coupling of interdependent work systems.

Some slack in the handling of resources, including information, is not only inevitable but essential to smooth operations. All operations require a margin of error—an allowance for mistakes, waste, spoilage, and similar unavoidable accompaniments of work. The question is not whether there is to be slack but how much slack is to be permitted. Excessive slack resources increase costs for the organization that are likely to be passed on to the consumer. Since creating slack resources is a relatively easy and painless solution available to organizations, whether or not it is employed is likely to be determined by the amount of competition confronting the organization in its task environment.

Product versus process organization   We have noted that information-processing costs can be reduced by placing highly interdependent tasks in the same or adjacent work units. This principle underlies the creation of product-based departments. For example, a publishing organization may begin with a departmental structure based on function or process criteria: editorial, production, and marketing divisions. Suppose that two product lines develop: college texts and *trade* (commercial bookstore) publications. At some point, the costs of attempting to handle the information that must accompany these quite different types of products across the three divisions may become sufficiently high that the company decides to reorganize on a product basis. Now we have two divisions: text and trade, each with its own departments of design, production, and marketing. The diversity of information processing required by the former structure has been substantially reduced by a shift from process to product organization.

The costs accompanying the use of product departments are primarily those associated with the loss of economies of scale. The scale of each unit has been reduced, and this may prevent the use of specialized personnel or machinery that can be supported only by a large volume of work. Product-based organization also reduces the likelihood that the benefits of variety—stimulation, transfer of learning, overlap of domains—will be available to enrich the organization or its participants.

The remaining strategies are intended to increase the information-processing capacity of the organization. We describe here only the more formalized strategies—those that rely on the explicit design of new roles and relations to process heightened information flows.

Augmented hierarchies   Many analysts have observed that although hierarchies can assist the coordination of work by imposing patterns and constraints on the flow of information, if the messages sent become too numerous or the content too rich, a hierarchical system can quickly become overloaded (see Chapter 7; see also Guetzkow, 1965; Rogers and Agarwala-Rogers, 1976). The capacity of the hierarchical system can be increased in two ways. The first is to improve the methods by which information is gathered and transmitted to the decision-making centers. In earlier times, and at the present time for many functions, this is accomplished by adding specialized administrative and clerical personnel— inspectors, accountants, secretaries—charged with gathering and summarizing the information needed for decision making. More recently, some of these functions have been taken over by increasingly sophisticated electronic monitoring, transmission, and data-reduction systems. The design of systems that will permit the rapid transmission of relevant, "on-line" information through feedback loops to appropriate decision centers is one of the major aims and achievements of the modern systems-design movement (see Simon, 1960; Myers, 1967; House, 1971).

The second method for increasing a hierarchical system's capacity to process information is to work not on the receptors or the transmitters but on the decision centers, the nodes of the system. One of the earliest and most widely used structural modifications of the simple hierarchy—the creation of the staff-line distinction—may be viewed as a means of increasing the information-processing and problem-solving capacity of the system without formally decentralizing or sacrificing the unity-of-command principle. Staff "experts" give technical assistance and specialized advice to the generalist managers who are empowered to make the final decision. However, we know from a large number of studies that although the staff-line distinction may preserve the appearance of a unified command system, much actual power passes from the hands of line officers to staff associates (see Dalton, 1959; Goldner, 1970). In addition to these staff-line arrangements, the modern executive is likely to be supported not only by technical specialists but also by a variety of "assistants," "assistants-to," and "associates" who perform stable or shifting duties but always act on behalf of and subject to the approval of their superiors. All, however, contribute to the capacity of the system to process information.

The new generation of microcomputers can affect both the collection of information and the transmission, processing, and analysis of it. There are conflicting predictions and evidence regarding the impact of this new technology on the centralization of decision making and on participant skill levels. (See Whisler, 1970; Zimbalist, 1979; Giuliano, 1982)

Lateral connections Consider the following situation. An aircraft company has reorganized, grouping workers within divisions by product, and one of the divisions is responsible for the development and testing of new types of jet engines. The departments have been created on a functional basis: there is a department housing the scientists and engineers responsible for design, a production department composed of the mechanical engineers and technicians responsible for building prototype engines, and a department of scientists and engineers responsible for evaluating and testing the models. Clearly this situation involves high levels of task complexity, uncertainty, and interdependence and will require the exchange of large amounts of information as the work is carried on. In a normal hierarchical structure, the communications required to coordinate performance among departments would be expected to flow up the chain of command from workers through supervisors to departmental managers. The managers would be expected to exchange information among themselves and with the division manager, arrive at a comon definition of how the work was to proceed, and then communicate detailed instructions back down the hierarchies within each department. Given the extent of interdependence and the amount of information to be processed, such a process would entail long delays and great inefficiencies.

In situations of such heavy information flow, the development of more direct, lateral connections across work groups and departments is an obvious response. That is, lateral connections allow information to flow more directly among participants in interdependent departments or work groups, rather than up and over through hierarchical channels. Although the opening of such channels may seem both simple and obvious, it represents an organizational revolution! Informal communications and arrangements among interdependent workers exist in virtually all organizations and undoubtedly often save them from floundering because of inadequacies of the vertical channels. But we are dealing here not with informal but formal structures: we are discussing the official legitimation of connections among workers across departmental boundaries. To permit such developments is to undermine the hierarchical structure: department heads are no longer fully in control of, and so cannot be held fully accountable for, the behavior of their subordinates. This is why organizations—even organizations facing fairly high degrees of uncertainty and interdependence—are reluctant to develop formal lateral connections. But if they decide to do so, they may choose among several mechanisms (see Galbraith, 1973; 1977), including the following.

•LIAISON ROLES

Liaison roles are specialized positions or units created to facilitate interchange between two or more interdependent departments. The responsibilities of such integrating roles may include troubleshooting, conflict resolution, and anticipation of problems. These positions are similar to staff roles except that they relate to two or more managers rather than to one. Lawrence and Lorsch (1967) examine the functions of such positions in organizations and discuss the characteristics of those individuals who fill them successfully. Their work is discussed more fully in Chapter 10. Note that the creation of liaison roles makes for a more complex management structure but does not undermine the hierarchical principle.

•TASK FORCES

A task force is by definition a temporary group that is given a delimited problem to solve. The expectation is that the group will be dissolved once its work is completed. The task force may involve its members full or part time. Participants are drawn from several departments, and frequently from several levels, and are selected not only because of their interest or ability with respect to the work of the task force but also because of their stature in their own departments. In the case of the jet engine division, a task force involving representatives from all three departments might be created to codify the technical terms and symbols used by members of that division. The strength of the task force is that it allows multiple representatives to interact intensively over a short period to achieve a specific objective. Status distinctions that hinder free interaction are typically suspended during the group's existence. That such distinctions are present but ignored contributes to the special atmosphere of a task force (see Miles, 1964).[5] Because the task force is defined as temporary, its existence is compatible with the maintenance of the hierarchy. Indeed, task forces may function as safety valves, reducing tensions and solving problems generated by the continuation of the hierarchy.

•PROJECT TEAMS

Whereas task forces are temporary systems created to solve nonrecurring problems, project teams are groupings of personnel across departmental lines that carry on some portion of the regular work of the organization. In the jet engine example, a team comprising several members from each department could be built around the design and testing of a highly experimental prototype engine. Members would be released from their regular duties over an extended period in order to better contribute to this effort. The typical project team would have a leader or manager responsible for planning and coordinating the work of the team as long as it performed as a unit. Departmental officers would, in effect, delegate authority to the project manager to act on their behalf during the project but would see to it that their own personnel were being used and treated appropriately.

•MATRIX STRUCTURES

The hallmark of the matrix is its multiple command structure: vertical and lateral channels of information and authority operate simultaneously. The ancient and sacred principle of unity of command is set aside, and competing bases of authority are allowed to jointly govern the work flow. The vertical lines are typically those of functional departments that operate as "home bases" for all participants; the lateral lines represent project groups or geographical arenas where managers combine and coordinate the services of the functional specialists around particular projects or areas. (See Davis and Lawrence, 1977; Hill and White, 1979.) This type of structure is illustrated in Figure 9–1, which depicts the formal structure of the rocket division of a space agency.

[5]A particularly interesting and dramatic example is provided by President Kennedy's creation of a task force—the Excom, composed of trusted advisers and associates—to make recommendations to him on the course of action to be pursued during the Cuban missile crisis of 1962. The best account of this group's structure and deliberations is provided by the president's brother, Robert Kennedy (1969).

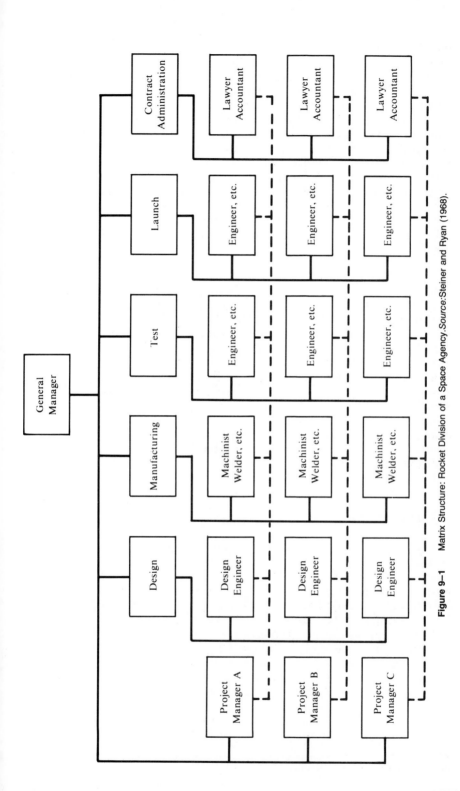

Figure 9–1   Matrix Structure: Rocket Division of a Space Agency. *Source:* Steiner and Ryan (1968).

The constituent units of matrix structures may be relatively permanent or shifting (Sayles, 1976). The permanent matrix structure is illustrated by a multi-location department store that organizes functionally around merchandise lines but also geographically around stores. Examples of organizations employing a shifting matrix structure are those who carry on most of their work within various project teams. These organizations also rely on a functionally based structure, often focused on occupational or disciplinary specialization, for one side of the matrix, but allocate varying combinations of specialists to a shifting set of project teams as the second basis of control. Such organizations include aerospace firms and research centers. All participants are responsible both to their functional superior and to one or more project leaders.

The conflicts between function and product that exist in at least a latent form in most organizations are elevated by the matrix organization into two competing structural principles. Although such institutionalization of conflict does not resolve it, it does ensure that both the functional and the product (or areal) interests are viewed as legitimate and have managerial representatives who will continually define and defend them. Moreover, assigning specific roles the responsibility for defending particular values gives them higher visibility and makes trade-offs or compromises more evident: conflicts between decision makers are more visible than conflicts within a single decision maker.

Some of the overt interrole conflicts built into the matrix structure are managed by sequential attention to one or another set of priorities. In what has been called the *matrix swing,* functional priorities may receive more attention at the beginning and ending of a project cycle as personnel are hired or released and as budgets are negotiated, but once a project is under way, attention and authority swing to the project leader. Still, much ambiguity must be tolerated and competing claims accommodated for the matrix to function. For many participants, matrix structures are high-demand, high-stress work environments. (See Davis and Lawrence, 1977.)

Matrix structures suffer some of the same diseconomies of scale as other types of product-based systems. For one, each project group tends to duplicate some of the capacities of the others. Also, these structures presume enormous flexibility of resources and personnel, for project teams are continually being initiated, discontinued, and reconstituted.

PROBLEMS IN RELATING
TECHNOLOGY AND STRUCTURE

In the previous sections, we argued that characteristics of the work being performed—in particular, its complexity, uncertainty, and interdependence—are associated with the characteristics of the structure devised to organize the work—for example, the extent of its differentiation, decentralization, and modes of coordination. With the help of Thompson, Galbraith, and others, we attempted to illustrate ways in which formal structural arrangements can be adjusted to accommodate differences in task demands. But although we have argued and illustrated, we have presented little in the way of evidence. When we turn to the empirical studies relating technology and structure, we find that the evidence is, at best, mixed. Although some studies do support the arguments (for example, Woodward, 1965; Hage and Aiken, 1969; Khandwalla, 1974; Van de Ven, Delbecq, and Koenig, 1976), others report at best weak and often conflicting evidence (for example, Hickson, Pugh, and Pheysey, 1969; Mohr, 1971; Child and Mansfield, 1972).

Measurement Problems

Some of the confusion in research findings is due to the variety of measures employed for assessing both technology (see Table 9–1) and structure: there is not much consensus on what variables to measure or how to measure them. Another source of difficulty is differences in the types of data gathered and in the level at which information is collected (see Scott, 1977*b*). The data employed may be obtained from documents and records, informant reports, or individual responses to surveys, and, in Lazarsfeld and Menzel's (1961) terms, defined in Chapter 1, the measures developed on the basis of these data may be analytical, structural, or global. Substantial problems of reliability and validity attend each of these data sources, and in the case of collective measures based on the aggregated response of individual participants, it is difficult to determine how weights should be assigned to each response.[6] Moreover, there is sometimes little agreement among different types of measures of the same variables. For example, Pennings (1973) used a variety of types of measures of structural variables, such as centralization and formalization, in a study of ten organizations. When measures of these variables based on the judgments of officials acting as informants were compared with measures of the same variables based on aggregated survey data from rank-and-file participants, correlations among them proved to be very low, and in some cases were negative, indicating their low convergent validity.

Theoretical Issues

In addition to these important methodological problems, several unresolved theoretical issues generate disagreement among investigators and militate against the cumulation of consistent empirical findings. We will review three of these issues: inconsistencies in the organizational levels at which the predictions relating technology to structure are formulated and tested; disagreements over the conception of technology; and differences in hidden or implicit assumptions that underlie research on the relation between technology and structure.

Varying organizational levels   The relation between technology and structure has been studied at differing organizational levels, including

---

[6]For example, as an indicator of centralization, participants may be asked to describe where decisions of various types are made in the organization. A common procedure in organizational studies is to combine all responses to the question and calculate a mean, which in effect gives the same weight to each response. However, as I note elsewhere,

> equal weighting flies in the face of everything we know about social structure—both formal and informal—the most important characteristic of which is differentiation: differentiation of knowledge, of competence, of influence, of commitment, of power, etc. (Scott, 1972: 141).

those of (1) the organization as a whole (for example, Woodward, 1965; Hickson, Pugh, and Pheysey, 1969; Khandwalla, 1974); (2) the work group or department (Bell, 1967; Lawrence and Lorsch, 1967; Grimes and Klein, 1973; Hrebiniak, 1974; Van de Ven and Delbecq, 1974); and (3) the individual participant (Hrebiniak, 1974; Dornbusch and Scott, 1975).

Efforts to relate technical and structural measures at the organizational level are extremely hazardous because organizations tend to employ a variety of technologies and to be structurally complex. Some analysts have attempted to resolve the difficulty by what might be termed a "mix-master" method: data on technology and structure are gathered from various participants and work units and then combined to produce overall scores for the two subsystems. Thus, the Aston group (Hickson, Pugh, and Pheysey, 1969) aggregated data gathered by interviews with chief executives and a number of department heads into a single measure, work-flow integration, to characterize the technology of the organization as a whole. And Hage and Aiken (1969), while careful to give greater weighting to the reports of the supervisory staff, combined worker and supervisor responses across departments to arrive at a single measure of routineness of work for each organization in a sample of health and welfare agencies. Similarly, structures that are likely to exhibit considerable diversity in centralization or in formalization, for example, are characterized by an average score reported for the organization. A different approach to the problem of technical and structural heterogeneity is exemplified by the work of Woodward (1965) and Khandwalla (1974), who restricted their studies to the "production systems" of the organizations they surveyed. But the structure of one department or division is not likely to be representative of the entire organization.

Analysts studying technology and structure at the departmental level confront less severe, but similar, problems caused by technical and structural heterogeneity. Many work groups and most departments include different types of work, particularly in the case of product-based organizational structures. Further, studies (for example, Bell, 1967; Mohr, 1971) that measure the characteristics of tasks performed by individual workers and aggregate them to form measures of some modal task characteristics may not only cause the analyst to overlook variance across individual workers but fail to capture those characteristics of technology that are distinctive to the group level, such as work variety or complexity at the departmental level (see Comstock and Scott, 1977).

Dornbusch and I (Dornbusch and Scott, 1975), in collaboration with a large number of graduate student colleagues, conducted a series of studies on the relation between technology and structure at the level of the individual participant. We focused on the participants' conception of the nature of the work performed and their perception of the work arrangements governing them. Studies of diverse types of workers in varied settings, including school teachers in public and alternative schools, university faculty members, football players, assembly bench workers, Catholic priests, and members of a hospital house staff, convinced us that most workers perform a variety of tasks and work under a number of structural arrangements. How much uncertainty is confronted, how much interdependence is present, how complex are the demands posed—all vary depending on what tasks or aspects of a given participant's work are singled out.

In summary, given the great diversity and complexity of the types of work and the structures encompassed by most organizations, we should not be surprised to learn that many specific studies report varying and contradictory findings. When the subject of study is variable and complex, findings will be highly susceptible to differences in the variables and indicators employed, the sample drawn, the level of organization studied, and similar research decisions.

The choice of the level of organization at which to conduct a study is particularly critical because organizational levels often relate in a complementary fashion: that is, uncertainty may be relatively low at one level *because* it is high at another. Thus, it is quite possible for individual workers to be confronted by complex and uncertain tasks within a relatively simple administrative system—for example the work of physicians in a small group-practice clinic. Conversely, individual workers may carry out a few simple tasks as part of a technology that is highly complex when viewed at the departmental level, as is the case with workers on an assembly line (see Mohr, 1971). The level of complexity and uncertainty at two adjacent organizational levels may vary dramatically. Indeed, an important aspect of organizational design is to decide where to locate such demands.

Given these conditions, in our opinion, if progress is to be made, researchers must exhibit greater sensitivities to the complexities of organizational systems. Our measures and predictions should allow for differences in the relation between technology and structure at the individual, work-group, and organizational level. Thus, Comstock and I (Comstock and Scott, 1977), in a study of the organization of 142 patient-care wards in a sample of sixteen hospitals showed that the predictability of the tasks confronting individual nurses was more closely associated with the characteristics of the nursing personnel in that unit (for example, level of qualifications and professionalism) than with the characteristics of the control system of the ward itself (for example, degree of formalization and centralization). The latter were more closely associated with measures of complexity and uncertainty at the *ward* level—for example, ward size, the extent of staff differentiation, and the level of work-flow predictability. By analogy, the same type of argument applies when one attempts to characterize the structure of the organization as a whole. Rather than treating the wider organizational structure as some kind of average of the characteristics of its work activities and work units, it would seem more appropriate to treat it as an overarching framework of relations linking subunits of considerable diversity, and to develop measures that capture the distinctive characteristics of this suprastructure.

Varying task conceptions   Most investigators assume that organizational participants agree on the characteristics of the technology in use: on the nature of the materials, the operations, and the state of knowledge. Presumably such consensus exists because these technological traits are real and objective, determined by the state of the environment. It appears, though, that the characteristics of technologies are much less solid than they seem at first, that they are often socially determined and can vary from participant to participant or from one set of participants to another. Thus, given the same set of task objects, it is possible for participants to emphasize their uniformity or their diversity, their unpredictability and complexity or their certainty and simplicity. (See Scott, 1972; Dornbusch and Scott, 1975: 76–91.) For example, historical and comparative accounts of treatment of the mentally ill demonstrate that conceptions of the raw materials—in this case, mental patients—have varied enormously over time and place. Under such circumstances, Perrow (1965) has suggested that ideology substitutes for technology. Similarly, conceptions of students' characteristics vary somewhat from one teacher to another, but even more from one type of school to another—for example, traditional public schools versus alternative schools (see Swidler, 1979). In like manner, participants may disagree on the characteristics of the operations performed. Where one sees repetitive activities another sees ingenuity and artful adaptation. Thus, Freidson (1970*b*) has pointed out that physicians are likely to insist on the problematic and unpredictable nature of many aspects of their work that others regard as relatively straightforward and routine. And although the differences might not be as large, we would expect similar disagreements in task conceptions among individuals working with physical or material objects and techniques.[7]

Differing task conceptions may also develop between performers and administrators within a given type of organization. The conceptions of performers are relevant inasmuch as performers must relate directly to the task objects and perform the task operations; the conceptions of administrators are of interest because administrators are responsible for designing the structure within which the work is to be carried out. We would expect that, in general, participants more closely associated with the actual conduct of task activities will be more likely to emphasize the uncertainty and the complexity of the task performed. And as we move from the work location to administrative levels, perceived variability tends to diminish. In addition to variation in task conceptions rooted in distance from the work, performers and administrators often differ in their views of the scope of the task. Performers are more apt to concentrate on individual cases, but administrators will be more concerned with classes of objects or events. For example, a classroom teacher may view the task of teaching as reacting appropriately to the differing needs and problems of individual students. School administrators, however, are more likely to be concerned that all students perform sufficiently well to move smoothly from one class or grade to another.

Variations in conceptions of work are expected to be associated with variations in *preferred* work structures. Performers who view their work as more uncertain and complex will desire more discretion and work autonomy; administrators who view the work of performers under their control as more predictable and routine will prefer work arrangements that are more formalized and centralized. How are these discrepancies between the conceptions of work held by performers and administrators to be resolved?

---

[7]We had presumed that the task of making beds in a hospital was relatively simple and certain, but many nurse's aides informed us that this job was highly variable and often very difficult, depending on the location of the bed in the room, the attitude and the weight of the patient, the quality of the sheets, and so on.

Hidden assumptions To answer this and related questions regarding the relation between technology and structure, it is necessary to expose some hidden or implicit assumptions underlying much of the work in this area. Certainly, one of the most pervasive assumptions made by investigators in this area is that of rationality of decision making. We have already noted that Thompson prefaces all of his propositions relating technology and structure with the phrase "Under norms of rationality." Theorists such as Galbraith presume that structures are designed to match information-processing needs of the tasks performed. And even Perrow, whose work is grounded primarily in the natural system perspective, embraces a rationalist orientation when he focuses on this topic: "We must assume here that, in the interest of efficiency, organizations wittingly or unwittingly attempt to maximize the congruence between their technology and their structure" (1970: 80).

Precisely what is meant by congruence or fit is seldom specified. Schoonhoven (1981) notes that although contingency arguments implicitly assume an interaction effect between two variables—for example, complexity and coordination—and a third, such as effectiveness, the shape or form of the relation—whether it is a simple monotonic relation, a multiplicative relation, or a threshold effect—is rarely considered. Contingency theorists, to their credit, explicitly argue that organizations devise specific structural arrangements in order to be efficient and effective.[8] This suggests that the predicted relations between technology and structure will be observed only, or most strongly, within a subset of organizations—those that are functioning effectively. But only a portion of the empirical studies in this area include measures of organizational effectiveness and employ them as intervening variables to test contingent hypotheses. Among this portion of studies again the evidence is mixed, but findings consistent with the contingency argument are reported in the original Lawrence and Lorsch (1967) investigation and in later studies by Khandwalla (1974), Tushman (1979), and Argote (1982). Contradictory findings or inconsistent support are reported in studies by Mohr (1971) and Pennings (1975).

The assumption of rationality not only implies that those who attempt to design organizational structures will be correct in their analysis of what is required, given the tasks to be performed, and will be effective in implementing these structures; it also assumes that managers and others in a position to design structures are attempting to serve performance goals. As we know, a number of theoretical perspectives challenge this assumption. Marxist theorists assert that the structures devised by managers are primarily designed not to maximize efficiency but to insure control. It is not necessary to review but only to note the relevance of these arguments here (see Chapter 7). It should be pointed out that most of the empirical support for this approach to date consists primarily of detailed, qualitative historical and contemporary case studies of the organization of work (the labor process) in particular situations (see Burawoy, 1985; Zimbalist, 1979).

---

[8]In Chapter 13 we discuss problems and complexities in defining and measuring efficiency and effectiveness.

Another perspective that emphasizes the role of power in shaping organizational structure is the *strategic contingency* approach. As described in Chapter 5, this perspective can be viewed as combining the contingency assumptions about the need of the organization to adust its structural configuration to the demands of its environments with the resource dependence arguments concerning the varying threats and opportunities posed by different segments of the environment. The organization becomes differentiated to deal with these varying environmental contingencies. But whereas the resource dependence approach emphasizes the implications of these processes for boundary setting and spanning, focusing on the use of buffering and bridging strategies, the strategic contingency approach stresses their consequences for the organization's internal structure.

Like interorganizational relations, intraorganizational relations are significantly shaped by power-dependence processes both internal and external to the organization. Complex environments not only give rise to complex, differentiated organizational structures; they also generate varying interests within organizations as well as new sources of power that can be used to pursue these interests. (Hickson et al., 1971) The recognition of multiple interests within organizations has led to the coalitional model of organizations: many organizations are in no sense unified actors but are instead shifting combinations of varying interest groups moving in and out of the organization and up and down in relative power. If a particular group has a corner on some valued resource, such as legal expertise or scientific creativity, and there is no readily available alternative, it is likely to acquire power *within* the organization. And one of the uses to which power is put is to shape the structure of the organization.[9] More powerful actors are likely to attempt to locate more discretion in the positions they occupy and to attempt to reduce that located in other positions. Thus, physicians and hospital administrators are regularly engaged in a contest—both in nationwide forums and in local hospital organizations—over what decisions should be controlled by physicians and which by administrators. Such arguments are invariably accompanied by claims that the nature of the work performed—its complexity, its value—justifies one's own need for discretion.

Thus, it appears that task conceptions are not neutral descriptions of work demands but value-laden claims concerning the "appropriate" conditions of work. If people desire greater autonomy and discretion over their work, they are likely to emphasize the complex and uncertain nature of the tasks for which they are responsible. Alternatively, if managers prefer to retain control over the workplace by centralizing decisions and promulgating rules, they will attempt to define the work as predictable and will respond to complexity with increased differentiation—which reduces the skill level of individual workers. Whose task conceptions prevail will be determined, at least in part, by the power position of the participants. As Benson (1977: 7) argues,

---

[9]A related use to which power is put is shaping the goals of the organization (see Chapter 11).

the ideas which guide the construction of the organization depend upon the power of various participants, that is, their capacity to control the direction of events. Some parties are in dominant positions permitting the imposition and enforcement of their conceptions of reality. Others are in positions of relative weakness and must act in conformity with the definitions of others.

Power no less than technology is a major determinant of structure.[10]

Conflicts over task definitions occur in all organizations, but are particularly visible in organizations employing professional workers (see Scott, 1972). Such occupational groups are more likely to develop divergent task conceptions, these notions being transmitted by external socializing organizations and reinforced by peer-group processes (see Chapter 7). Because specific alternative task conceptions are collectively held by performers, these shared conceptions and expectations concerning appropriate work arrangements become important unifying forces for occupational groups across varying settings (see Reeves, 1980; Clark, 1983; DiMaggio and Powell, 1983). In addition, a more or less tight monopoly over the performance of some aspects of the work, plus in some cases the ability to regulate the supply of perfomers, ensures that professional groups will be in a relatively powerful position vis-à-vis organizational managers.

These arguments concerning power also challenge a second major assumption underlying the conventional arguments relating technology and structure: that technology causes structure rather than the reverse. If conceptions of technology are socially determined, then it is clear that one of the most powerful influences on task conceptions are the structural arrangements within which the work is performed. Whoever controls the structure can have a powerful effect on performers' task definitions. Thus as noted in Chapter 8, the combined efforts of administrators and lawyers have succeeded in transforming the definition of the work of the case-worker administering the Aid to Families with Dependent Children (AFDC) public-assistance program. In less than two decades, there have been extensive reductions in worker discretion: the number and detail of the rules governing decisions has increased; the extent and type of hierarchical controls have been intensified; and the professional and educational qualifications for workers have been reduced. The organized power of social workers has not proved sufficient to successfully resist the deprofessionalization of work that had once been defined as requiring considerable expertise and the discretion necessary to apply generalized norms and standards to specific cases. (Simon, 1983)

Structures affect the nature of work in even more direct ways. How uncertain or complex work is at a given point in the system is, in large measure, a question of how the structure is designed. Through differentiation, complex tasks can be divided and made simple; alternatively, through professionalization, complex tasks can be retained and delegated to individual performers. Similarly, how much interdependence is present in a given system is, in part, a matter of structural design. The interdependence of work groups can be reduced by a product-based division of

---

[10]These arguments concerning both the sources and the consequences of power are developed at length in Pfeffer (1981) and Mintzberg (1983).

labor and increased by a functional structure. So does technology determine structure or does structure determine technology? The answer must be that the relation is reciprocal but variable. Presumably technology always exerts some general constraints on the shape of the structure, but within these limits market conditions and power processes may be expected to play an important role (see Chapter 7).

A third assumption that guides studies of technology and structure is that the relation between the two is determined primarily by intraorganizational forces. This assumption is challenged by much of the previous discussion, which argues that market forces and occupational systems external to the organization help to shape both the participants' conceptions of work as well as the outcomes of struggles between performers and administrators for control over work structures. It is also called into question by examples such as the following. The major incentive for many organizations to develop a project-management structure came not from within as a rational response to information processing demands but from outside the organization. The Department of Defense required its contractors to use this structural arrangement in the 1950s as a condition for obtaining financial support! (Wieland and Ullrich, 1976: 39). Government contract officers were tired of getting the runaround from functional department heads, each of whom had only partial control over any given project. The development of a project management format gave these officers someone they could more easily relate to and hold responsible for the successful and timely completion of the project. We should never overlook or underestimate the effect of environmental forces on "internal" structures and processes.

A fourth and final assumption that underlies the structural models described to this point for dealing with technical complexity, uncertainty, and interdependence is that they all embrace the rational system view of the benefits of formalization. The rational system response to increasing task demands is to shorten and strengthen the leash: provide superiors with more and faster information so they can more rapidly change the instructions to performers; increase the ratio of superiors to performers so that more information can be processed more quickly and revised guidelines supplied to performers. Some of these modifications move in the direction of decentralization: power and authority are more widely dispersed as hierarchies are augmented and, particularly, as lateral connections are added. But formalization is, if anything, increased in these systems.[11] New types of roles are created and new linkages specified that increase the complexity, flexibility, and capacity for change in the structure. But the flexibility involved is designed, not spontaneous, and the changes reflect capacity to shift rapidly from one set of formal rules and roles to another.

We know, of course, that this central assumption is challenged by natural system theorists, who stress the advantages of informal structures, particularly as strategies for dealing with task uncertainty. These alternative approaches, which have received much recent attention, rely primarily on enlarged roles, internalized control, and informal structures to confront high levels of uncertainty and complexity. Rather than augment-

---

[11]The relation between formalization and decentralization is discussed in Chapter 10.

ing hierarchies, they minimize vertical distinctions, and rather than creating new, specialized lateral roles and relations, they encourage more direct, face-to-face communications among any or all participants as required. Decision making and the exercise of control become more decentralized, and organizational roles less formalized. In the next section, we review some of the major models stemming from the natural system perspective for dealing with complex technologies.

TECHNOLOGY AND INFORMAL STRUCTURE

Several discussions of natural open system responses to task complexity and uncertainty will be briefly reviewed. All are alike in stressing the value of informal structures, but each contains somewhat varying emphases, including differences in the level of analysis.

Socio-Technical Systems and Work Redesign

We have briefly described the socio-technical system approach developed at the Tavistock Institute in London following World War II (see Chapter 5.) One of the guiding premises of this approach is that work involves a combination of social and technical requisites and that the object of design is to "jointly optimize" both components—not sacrifice one for the other. By contrast, rational system approaches are more likely to focus on the demands of the technical system, ignoring the psychological and social needs of workers. Technical systems are designed; then human workers are "fitted in" to their requirements. And to fit human behavior into a prespecified technical system requires that it be highly programmed, that the activities and interactions be specified and predictable—in a word, formalized.

If human as well as technical requirements are to be served, then it is necessary to determine what kinds of work situations motivate and satisfy workers. The Tavistock group emphasizes both individual task features as well as social organizational, particularly work-group, features. At the task level, repetitive, undemanding, isolated jobs undermine commitment and performance motivation. And at the work-group level, competition and close supervision foments stress, petty deceptions, scapegoating, and low morale. These effects were observed when more highly mechanized approaches were introduced in British coal mines—technical approaches that disrupted worker autonomy and work-group cohesion. (Trist and Bamforth, 1951) The solution was to restructure the situation so as to give more attention to its social components. In the restructured situation,

> groups of men are responsible for the whole task, allocate themselves to shifts and to jobs within the shift, and are paid on a group bonus. Thus the problems of overspecialized work roles, segregation of tasks across shifts with consequent scapegoating and lack of group cohesion were overcome. (Pugh, Hickson, and Hinings, 1985: 86)

The rational system assumption that worker performance is enhanced when work demands are routinized and standardized—when complexity is factored into simple tasks and when uncertainty is removed—is strongly challenged by this approach. Organizations may thrive on certainty, but individuals do not! This counterassumption originating in the socio-technical school has given rise to a large body of theory and research pursued primarily at the social psychological level of the individual worker. The most influential of these are *job characteristics* theory and its elaboration in *work design and individual needs* approaches.

Briefly, research on job characteristics pursues the assumption that specific attributes of the job, such as variety, autonomy, and required interaction, are associated with worker motivation and work performance. Turner and Lawrence (1965) developed and tested these predictions by measuring the characteristics of forty-seven industrial jobs, but found the expected relations held only for workers in rural areas, who were presumed to have different needs or expectations for work than urban workers. Later research has pursued this "contingent" assumption that the relation between job characteristics and worker responses is mediated by worker expectations or needs (see Hackman and Oldman, 1980.) The same types of job characteristics—variety, task identity, autonomy—are identified as important, as having "high motivating potential," but whether the potential is recognized depends on the psychological needs of the particular worker. Although a number of empirical tests of this more complex model of task characteristics and performance have been conducted (see, for example, Brief and Aldag, 1975; Stone, Mowday, and Porter, 1977; Steers and Spencer, 1977), the support is at best weak, and the research has been criticized on both methodological and theoretical grounds (see Roberts and Glick, 1981; Salancik and Pfeffer, 1977; Staw, 1984).[12]

The socio-technical approach has placed greater emphasis on the social organization of work groups—together with the necessary support features at higher organizational levels—than on the narrower matter of the design of individual jobs. Work groups, properly structured, can provide workers with an ongoing source of incentives, error correction, assistance, and social support that no amount of attention to individual job design can hope to match. The restructured semiautonomous work groups developed for the British coal mines suggests the type of approach deemed suitable to mechanized organizations with moderate levels of uncertainty and interdependence. A similar solution was developed by Volvo of Sweden when it decided to replace the traditional conveyor line for assembling its automobiles with movable automobile carriers that would permit more task variety and worker discretion embedded within a system empowering work groups as the central work elements (see Gyllenhammar, 1977). And Cole (1979) has described how on the other side of the globe, Toyota Auto Body of Japan reorganized its work process to enrich worker

---

[12]As might be expected, the concerns raised are similar to the problems already discussed involving the relation of technology to structure, including the issues of task conceptions (subjective versus objective views of task characteristics), direction of causation, and levels of analysis. For more detailed, critical reviews of this research, see Pfeffer (1982: 54–63) and Staw (1984).

skills, enlarge worker discretion, and activate work-group incentives and controls in the now-famous "quality circles." These work groups are ordinarily organized around a particular type of job and are granted primary responsibility for such matters as safety and quality control. They become involved with "almost every other kind of problem, including improvement of productivity, the speed and way of stopping the conveyor belt, job procedures, job training, and human relations problems" (Cole, 1979: 161).

When the organizational environment becomes more turbulent and the work demands more uncertain, a socio-technical design suggests that redundancy of function is superior to redundancy of parts (Emery and Trist, 1965). Pugh, Hickson, and Hinings (1985: 89) summarize the critical difference between these two emphases:

> The traditional technocratic bureaucracy is based on *redundancy of parts.* The parts are broken down so that the ultimate elements are as simple as possible; thus an unskilled worker in a narrow job who is cheap to replace and who takes little time to train would be regarded as an ideal job design. But this approach also requires reliable control systems—often cumbersome and costly.
>
> An alternative design, based on the *redundancy of functions,* is appropriate to turbulent environments. In this approach individuals and units have wide repertoires of activities to cope with change, and they are self-regulating. For the individual they create roles rather than mere jobs; for the organization, they bring into being a *variety-increasing* system rather than the traditional control by variety reduction.... Autonomous working groups, collaboration rather than competition (between organizations as well as within them) and reduction of hierarchical emphasis, are some of the requirements for operating effectively in modern turbulence.

Organic Systems and Clans

During the early 1960s, Burns and Stalker studied a rather diverse group of about twenty industrial firms in Great Britain. Their sample included rather traditional textile companies, engineering firms, and a number of firms attempting to move into the rapidly growing market of electronics. Early in their field research, the investigators were struck by the presence of two quite distinct management styles—which they labeled the *mechanistic* and the *organic.* They noted that the two approaches tended to be associated with differing industries, or, more accurately, with differing types of industrial environments. The mechanistic firms were to be found in relatively stable environments, the organic in more rapidly changing environments. Burns and Stalker (1961: 5–6) describe these two organizational systems as follows:

> In mechanistic systems the problems and tasks facing the concern as a whole are broken down into specialisms. Each individual pursues his task as something distinct from the real tasks of the concern as a whole, as if it were the subject of a subcontract. "Somebody at the top" is responsible for seeing to its relevance. The technical methods, duties, and powers attached to each functional role are precisely designed. Interaction within management tends to be vertical ...
>
> Organic systems are adapted to unstable conditions, when problems and requirements for action arise which cannot be broken down and distributed

among specialist roles within a clearly defined hierarchy. Individuals have to perform their special tasks in the light of their knowledge of the tasks of the firm as a whole. Jobs lose much of their formal definition in terms of methods, duties and powers, which have to be redefined continually by interaction with others participating in a task. Interaction runs laterally as much as vertically. Communication between people of different ranks tends to resemble lateral consultation rather than vertical command.

More recent analyses have added to our understanding of this type of structure. Ouchi (1980; 1981) defines it as a *clan* or *type Z* structure. Building on the distinctions proposed by Williamson, he argues that just as hierarchies replace markets when transactions become moderately uncertain and complex, in a parallel fashion hierarchies fail and are replaced by clan structures when the transactions reach levels of extreme complexity and uncertainty.[13] Ouchi suggests that the costs of monitoring very complex exchanges by conventional or augmented authority systems is prohibitive and will increasingly give rise to "organizational failures" and the search for alternative structures. One viable alternative is the clan—a group that may or may not be linked by kinship ties but is based on common internalized goals and strong feelings of solidarity.[14]

Although clan structures are distinguished from formalized bureaucracies by a number of elements—including nonspecialized roles and career paths, implicit and internalized control mechanisms, holistic rather than segmented concerns, and slow and diffuse evaluation—Ouchi argues that their most important feature is the long-term, often lifetime, employment that they offer their participants. This characteristic was identified quite early as a distinctive feature of Japanese organizations (see Abegglen, 1958; Dore, 1973); Ouchi proposes it as a defining characteristic of all clan organizations—which include not only Japanese organizations but many others including some of the most "modern" and progressive U.S. firms, including Hewlett-Packard, IBM, and Eastman Kodak (see Ouchi, 1981).

The expectation of long-term employment creates the conditions for a different type of control system. The employee sees his or her career prospects as being directly linked to the company's success. And the long-term commitment provides both incentive and opportunity for the organization to "invest" in its employees, not only increasing their specific work skills and knowledge by providing extensive training and varied job experience, but also developing their general understanding of organizational needs and programs and increasing their commitment to its goals and values. In short, we have the conditions for the development of elaborated internal labor markets. (See Chapter 8.)

These discussions that emphasize internalized controls and more

---

[13]Note that whereas the structural mechanism—informal, diffuse ties among participants—is one associated with the natural system perspective, the argument—reduction in transactions costs—is one stemming from the rational system perspective.

[14]Granovetter (1985) argues that Williamson greatly exaggerates the effectiveness of hierarchies in combating opportunism and underestimates the importance of informal, interpersonal controls in building trust and discouraging malfeasance. Thus, from this perspective, Ouchi's concept of clan is only a more highly developed instance of the control processes operating in all organizations.

diffuse, long-term attachments have been supplemented by analyses that stress the importance of creating and sharing a common corporate culture. Cultural symbols and meanings are held to be an important alternative to structural forms. (See Deal and Kennedy, 1982; Peters and Waterman, 1982.) We discuss and evaluate these arguments in Chapter 11.

PROFESSIONAL ORGANIZATIONS

Certainly the most elaborate and intricate organizational arrangements yet devised for coping with high orders of complexity and uncertainty in production systems are to be found in the *professional organization*. We began the discussion of technology and structure by stating three general principles relating characteristics of technology and of structure: greater technical complexity is associated with greater structural complexity, greater technical uncertainty is related to lower formalization and centralization, and greater interdependence is associated with more elaborate coordination structures. We now call attention to an important exception to the first principle. Technical complexity does not invariably give rise to greater complexity of structure; it may give rise instead to greater "complexity" of the performer. That is, one way to manage greater task complexity is not to divide the work and parcel it out among differentiated work groups or departments, but to confront the complexity with more highly qualified and flexible performers—with professionals. This response is particularly effective when (1) the work is also uncertain, a condition that militates against preplanning and subdivision, and (2) the work does not involve high levels of interdependence among workers. As an example of the latter, the teaching by faculty members in universities, the work of lawyers in law firms, and the work of physicians in clinics as customarily performed tend to involve relatively little interdependence. Whether complexity and uncertainty of work give rise to complex organizations or to complex performers is determined partly by the characteristics of the work itself but is also influenced by the political and social power of the performer group. (See Chapter 9; and Larson, 1977.)

As complexity, uncertainty, and interdependence increase, professionals are more likely to move their work into organizational structures and take advantage of a more explicit division of labor and more formalized coordination mechanisms. Thus, complex performers enter into and are supported by complex organizational structures.

Professionals perform the core tasks of the organization under two general types of arrangements. The first, which we have labeled the *autonomous* professional organization, exists to the extent that "organizational officials delegate to the group of professional employees considerable responsibility for defining and implementing the goals, for setting performance standards, and for seeing to it that standards are maintained" (Scott, 1965*b*: 66). The professional performers organize themselves—as a "staff" in hospitals, as an "academic council" in universities—to assume these responsibilities. A fairly well demarcated boundary is established between those tasks for which the professional group assumes responsibility and those over which the administrative officials have jurisdiction. Even when professionals occupy the administrative positions, as is often the case, the boundaries tend to remain intact, so that the professional officials exercise authority over administrative procedures but are not granted direct control over professional tasks (see Goss, 1961). Rather, considerable discretion and autonomy are delegated to individual professionals, and they are subject only to collegial review and control systems, some formally mandated but others operating only informally. Examples of types of professional organizations likely to conform to the autonomous pattern include general hospitals, therapeutic psychiatric hospitals, medical clinics, elite colleges and universities, and scientific institutes oriented to basic research (see Stanton and Schwartz, 1954; Clark, 1963; Smigel, 1964; Freidson, 1975).

We have labeled the second type the *heteronomous* professional organization because in this arrangement "professional employees are clearly subordinated to an administrative framework," and the amount of autonomy granted them is relatively small (Scott, 1965b: 67). Employees in these settings are subject to administrative controls, and their discretion is clearly circumscribed. Unlike their autonomous counterparts, they are subject to routine supervision. This type of professional organization is exemplified by many public agencies—libraries, secondary schools, social welfare agencies—as well as some private organizations, such as small religious colleges, engineering companies, applied research firms, and public accounting firms (see Bidwell, 1965; Etzioni, 1969; Kornhauser, 1962; Montagna, 1968). Also, as Hall (1968) has pointed out, the distinction between autonomous and heteronomous structures can be applied to organizational departments as well as to entire organizations. Thus, the research and development department of a manufacturing company is likely to be organized as a heteronomous structure.

. The structure of heteronomous professional organizations is in many respects similar to the arrangements already described in which organizations handle somewhat complex and uncertain tasks by *delegation.* The work of the professionals takes place within a structure of general rules and hierarchical supervision, but individual performers are given considerable discretion over task decisions, particularly those concerning means or techniques. Thus, individual teachers make choices regarding instructional techniques, and individual engineers make decisions concerning design or construction strategies.

Given that performers are expected to exercise more autonomy, we might expect to observe savings in supervisory costs: lower ratios of managers to performers or larger spans of control for supervisors. Several empirical studies, however, report just the opposite. In a study of 30 departments within a community hospital, Bell (1967) found that the greater the complexity of work performed by departmental participants, the smaller the spans of supervisory control—the fewer workers a supervisor could manage. Similarly, in a study of 252 public personnel agencies, Blau, Heydebrand, and Stauffer (1966) found that the higher the qualifications of staff members, the higher the manager-worker ratio. (See also Pugh, Hickson, and Hinings, 1969: 118–19). Blau and colleagues interpret these unexpected findings in terms that are now familiar to us: more managers are needed to handle the larger amount of information that must be communicated upward. Blau (1968) also points out that having more supervisors or managers reduces the centralization of decision making.

These analyses suggest that the more complex work carried on in heteronomous professional organizations is managed by both delegation and *augmentation of the hierarchy.* The hierarchy is augmented by the simple expedient of hiring more managers and reducing the span of control. Note, however, that the terms *manager* and *span of control* are misleading in this context, because the managers are themselves professionals and the proportional increase in their numbers signifies not increased closeness of supervision but an attempt to improve the transmission of information and the decision-making capacity of the organization.

The organization of autonomous professionals takes many forms, depending in particular on the degree of interdependence among the individual performers and performer groups. One of the primary strengths of the full-fledged professional is that he or she is deemed capable of independent decision making and performance, and this includes coordinating work with others as required by the situation. Thus, in many kinds of autonomous professional organizations we would expect to see coordination, through *direct contacts,* of the formal organization of the professional staff with its elaborate committee structures—the whole functioning much in the manner of Burns and Stalker's (1961) *organic system.* However, more explicit structural forms for coordinating work are required as professionals themselves become more highly specialized and are expected to coordinate not only their own work but the work of a growing number of paraprofessional workers, and as interdependence among work groups and departments increases. In many cases *project teams* are used. In hospitals such teams may be built around a particular type of surgical procedure—open-heart surgery is a dramatic example— or around the care of a particular group of patients—for example, children with cancer (see Fox, 1959; Beckhard, 1972). And faculty members in universities conduct an increasing amount of their research in project teams, each of which has a coordinator or leader, often designated the principal investigator. These arrangements support collaborative effort across disciplinary or departmental lines. *Matix designs* are common in research organizations such as RAND (Smith, 1966) and are used in some hospital departments (Neuhauser, 1972). In many of these organizations professional participants and administrators exercise roughly equivalent power—an arrangement we have termed the *conjoint* professional organization (see Scott, 1982). Such arrangements attempt to combine the advantages of both professional and bureaucratic forms.

Organizations that in one way or another utilize lateral relationships as legitimate avenues of information and influence flows constitute the new generation of organizational forms. As we have attempted to illustrate, a number of different lateral structural arrangements are in use—including project teams, matrix structures, organic or clan systems, and professional organizations. All move us away from unitary hierarchical arrangements, "beyond bureaucracy," or "from bureaucracy to adhocracy." Futurists and social commentators such as Bennis and Slater (1968), Bell (1973), Toffler (1970; 1980) and Naisbitt (1982) agree that these new organizational forms offer new opportunities and challenges to participants but at the same time impose greater pressures and requirements on them.

SUMMARY

Most efforts to explain the structural complexity within the technical core of an organization focus on the characteristics of the work being performed—on the technology. A great many specific measures of technology have been proposed, some emphasizing different phases of the work process—inputs, throughputs, or outputs—and some focusing on different facets of the process—materials, operations, or knowledge. Most important for explaining differences in structural characteristics of organizations are three dimensions of technology: complexity, uncertainty, and interdependence. In general, we expect technical complexity to be associated with structural complexity or performer complexity (professionalization); technical uncertainty with lower formalization and decentralization of decision making; and interdependence with higher levels of coordination. Complexity, uncertainty, and interdependence are alike in at least one respect: each increases the amount of information that must be processed during the course of a task performance. Thus, as complexity, uncertainty, and interdependence increase, structural modifications need to be made that will either (1) reduce the need for information processing—for example, by lowering the level of interdependence or by lowering performance standards—or (2) increase the capacity of the information-processing system, by increasing the channel and node capacity of the hierarchy or by legitimating lateral connections among participants.

Empirical studies of the relation between technology and structure show mixed and often conflicting results. Among the factors contributing to this confusion are methodological problems, such as lack of consensus on measures or on measurement strategies, and theoretical problems, including misspecifications of the level of analysis at which the measures apply, disagreements among participants about the nature of the technology employed, and lack of clarity about the causal connections between technology and structure.

Although significant attention has been devoted to the relation between technology and formal structures such as rules, schedules, hierarchies, and coordinating roles, much recent work emphasizes the importance of informal structures, particularly when high levels of uncertainty are confronted. Organic systems or clan structures are viewed as simultaneously fostering reliability and flexibility and as increasing worker motivation and commitment.

Professional organizations combine elements from both formal and informal approaches, stressing internalization of controls and worker autonomy and at the same time utilizing more formalized control systems such as project teams and matrix structures.

10 sources of structural complexity: the peripheral sectors

The device by which an organism maintains itself stationary at a fairly high level of orderliness . . . really consists in continually sucking orderliness from its environment.

Erwin Schrödinger (1945)

The division between the technical core and the peripheral sectors of an organization is admittedly somewhat arbitrary. It is intended to emphasize that organizations are composed of different units that respond to different forces. The previous chapter emphasized those portions of the organization—labeled the technical core—that carry on its primary work. We argued that the characteristics of the work performed are related to the characteristics of the structures created to contain the work. (Whether work characteristics produce structural characteristics or the reverse was discussed but not fully resolved.) Attention was limited to the characteristics of those structures that contain, control, or are close to the organization's central work flow.

In this chapter the focus broadens to include structures less directly tied to the technical core. They are peripheral in this sense and only in this sense: *peripheral* is not synonymous with *marginal*. The peripheral structures, for present purposes, encompass many aspects of the managerial and the institutional levels as defined by Parsons (see Chapter 3). We will examine, in particular, the structural changes at these levels that accompany the organization's attempt to buffer its technical core and construct bridges to other social units. These changes accompany the organization's efforts to adapt to and modify its task environment. We also will examine structural features associated with the size of the organization. As we will learn, the meaning of size is far from clear, but its importance as a determinant of structural characteristics is well established. In the final section, relations between the core and peripheral structures are discussed.

A brief methodological note: Examinations of the structural features of organizations, their determinants, and their interrelations require the collection of data from a large sample of organizations. In these studies, the organizations are themselves the units of analysis. Ideally, what is required is a large sample of organizations randomly drawn from a population of independent organizations. The two major series of comparative studies to date—the research by Blau and his associates and the studies in England conducted by the Aston group—only partially meet these requirements, as will be discussed. Nevertheless, these pioneer projects constitute an important beginning to the systematic comparative study of organizational structure.

SIZE AND STRUCTURE

Defining and Measuring Size

What is size? Some analysts treat it as a dimension of organizational structure like formalization or centralization—one of several structural properties of an organization that may be seen to co-vary (see, for example, Hall and Tittle, 1966). Others treat size more as a contextual variable that measures the demand for an organization's services or products and thereby provides opportunities for and imposes constraints on its structure (see, for example, Blau and Schoenherr, 1971; Pugh et al., 1969). Like technology, size appears to be a variable that is on the interface between the organization and its environment: both variables are, on the one hand, internal features interacting with other structural properties and, on the other hand, features strongly shaped by external conditions. And, because it is externally driven like technology, size is more likely to be treated as an independent variable that shapes and determines other structural variables. If technology assesses what type of work is performed by the organization, size measures how much of that work the organization carries on— the scale on which the work is conducted.[1]

As Kimberly (1976) notes, several different indicators of organizational size have been employed by researchers, each measuring a somewhat different aspect of size. Thus, some indicators, such as square footage of floor space in a factory or number of beds in a hospital, measure the physical capacity of an organization to perform work. Others, such as the sales volume or number of clients served during a given period, focus less on potential capacity and more on current scale of performance. And indicators such as net assets provide a measure of discretionary resources available to the organization.

Most studies of the relation between organizational size and structure have used the number of participants (usually employees) as an indicator of size. The advantages of this measure are that it tends to reflect both the capacity of the organization for performing work as well as the current scale of actual performance. Also, most of the dependent variables of interest—formalization, centralization, bureaucratization—are measures of methods for controlling and coordinating people, so that numbers of individuals are of more relevance than other possible indicators of size. However, using the number of participants as an indicator of

[1]Size can also be given an institutional interpretation. Size, particularly relative size, is closely associated with visibility. Larger organizations are more likely to be the targets of institutional actors (for example, state regulatory bodies) and are also more likely to provide the models imitated by other organizations.

size poses some problems. As previously discussed, it is often difficult to determine how to set the boundary between participants and nonparticipants. Also, comparisons of numbers of participants across different types of organizations can be misleading, since some types of organizations are much more labor-intensive than others.[2]

We turn now to consider the major predicted and empirical relations between size and structure.

Size, Bureaucracy, and Differentiation

Early interest in the effects of size focused on its relation to the degree of bureaucratization, defined as the relative size of the administrative component of an organization. A number of critics—for example, Parkinson (1957)—have asserted that large organizations are overbureaucratized, devoting a disproportionate amount of their staff resources to administration. Empirical investigations of the relation between organization size and bureaucratization conducted during the 1950s reported contradictory results: some researchers found that the administration was disproportionally large in larger organizations (for example, Terrien and Mills, 1955); some, that the proportion of administrators was smaller in large organizations (for example, Melman, 1951; Bendix, 1956); and some, that there was no association (for example, Baker and Davis, 1954). One important reason for the absence of any clear results is noted by Rushing (1966*b*). He points out that the administrative component of an organization is not a unitary structural element but rather, in his words, a "heterogeneous category" composed of varying participants performing quite different functional roles. Numerous studies have shown that if the administrative component is separated into its occupational categories—for example, managerial, professional and technical, and clerical—then these categories relate differently to size. In general, the proportion of managers tends to decline with increases in size, but the proportion of technical and clerical personnel is positively associated with size (see Rushing, 1966*b*: Blau and Schoenherr, 1971; Kasarda, 1974). The general point, however, is that the administrative component comprises various occupational groups that may relate differently to size.

A second basic reason for the absence of consistent associations between organizational size and administrative size is that size produces two different effects, which have opposing consequences for the size of the administrative component. On the one hand, organizational size is positively associated with structural differentiation. Studies of a wide variety of organizations show reasonably consistent and positive associations between size of organization and various measures of structural differentiation, including number of occupational categories, number of hierarchical levels, and spatial dispersion of the organization—for example, the number of branch offices (see Blau, 1973; Blau and Schoenherr 1971; Hall, Haas, and Johnson, 1967; Meyer, 1972; 1979*b*; and Pugh et al., 1969). Larger organizations tend to be structurally more complex. On the other

---

[2]For an extended discussion of conceptual and empirical difficulties associated with current definitions and measures of size, see Kimberly (1976).

hand, size is positively associated with the presence of more activities of the same general type. Size involves an increase in the *scale* of operations, which means not necessarily more kinds of operations (that is, differentiation) but more operations of the same kind.

As noted, these two effects of size have opposing consequences for the size of the administrative component. In a remarkable series of propositions, Blau (1970) attempts to summarize and resolve these conflicts, as follows. Large size is associated with structural differentiation, and differentiation, in turn, creates pressures to increase the size of the administrative component. This occurs because differentiation increases the heterogeneity of work among the various subunits and individuals, creating problems of coordination and integration. The administrative component expands to assume these responsibilities. On the other hand, organizational size is associated with increases in the average size of units, within which the work performed is relatively homogeneous. The larger the number of persons engaged in similar work, the smaller the number of administrative personnel needed to supervise them. In sum, larger organizational size, by increasing structural differentiation—that is, by increasing the number of different types of organizational subunits—increases the size of the administrative component, which must coordinate the work of these units; at the same time, larger organizational size, by increasing the volume of homogenous work within organizational subunits, reduces the size of the administrative component, which must supervise work within these units.

In their analysis of the fifty-three state employment security agencies, Blau and Schoenherr conclude that

> large size, by promoting differentiation, has the indirect effect of enlarging the managerial component, but the savings in managerial manpower resulting from a large scale of operations outweigh these indirect effects, so that the overall effect of large size is a reduction in the managerial component (1971:91).

Such a conclusion may well hold for the type of organization studied, but in our opinion should not be generalized to other types of organizations. Whether the administrative component is, on balance, affected positively or negatively by size would seem to depend primarily on what type of differentiation, is involved. For example, differentiation that merely creates new units of the same type (segmentation) would be expected to have a less positive effect on the administrative component than functional differentiation which creates new types of units. And how much functional differentiation occurs would be determined primarily by the type of work the organization is performing—that is, by its technology—and by the type of environment—both technical and institutional—in which it is operating. We amplify these comments later in this chapter.

Size, Formalization, and Centralization

We have defined formalization as the extent to which roles and relationships are specified independently of the personal characteristics of the occupants of positions. Most empirical studies of formalization emphasize the extent to which rules such as formal job definitions and procedural specifications govern activities within the organizations. A Weberian model of structure would lead us to expect that the larger the size of the organization, the more formalized its structure would be, and indeed, most empirical studies support this prediction. Hall, Haas, and Johnson (1967) report only moderate but fairly consistent positive correlations between size and six indicators of formalization, including "concreteness" of positional descriptions and formalization of the authority structure. Blau and Schoenherr's (1971) study of state employment security agencies reports a positive association between organizational size and the extent of written personnel regulations in the state's civil service system.[3] And the Aston group (Pugh et al., 1969), in their study of forty-six work organizations, reports a strong positive correlation between size and scales measuring formalization and standardization of procedures for selection and advancement.

The conventional view of the bureaucratic model of organizational structure would also lead to the prediction that large organizations will have more highly centralized systems of decision making (see Hage, 1965). However, the studies by Blau and Schoenherr and the Aston group do not support this expectation. Rather, both research groups found that organization size was negatively correlated with several indicators of centralization. (For example, Blau and Schoenherr used measures of the decentralization of influence to division heads and the delegation of responsibility to local office managers, and Pugh and his colleagues developed scales for determining the level in the hierarchy where executive action could be taken subject only to pro forma review.) Consistent with the positive association between size and formalization, centralization was negatively associated with most of the measures of formalization. This pattern of results was also reported by Child (1972), who applied the scales developed by the Aston group to a national sample of eighty-two business organizations in Britain. And Mansfield (1973) reanalyzes these data to show that although the relationships are not very strong, the negative association between measures of centralization and standardization or formalization persist when the effects of size are controlled.

Blau and Schoenherr explain this unexpected pattern of results by suggesting that centralization and formalization may be viewed as alternative control mechanisms: more formalized arrangements permit more decentralized decision making. They argue that

> formalized standards that restrict the scope of discretion make decentralized decisions less precarious for effective management and coordination, which diminishes the reluctance of executives to delegate responsibilities way down the line to local managers far removed in space as well as in social distance from top managment at the headquarters (1971: 121).

Mansfield, perhaps with the aid of hindsight, scolds his colleagues for expecting a positive relation between formalization and centralization in the first place, arguing that Weber has been misread:

[3]Noting that this relation might better be tested at the state rather than the agency level, Blau and Schoenherr (1971: 58–59) also report a strong positive correlation between the total number of all state employees, as an indicator of the size of the state government, and the extent of formalized personnel regulations in the state's civil service system.

It can be argued, paradoxically, that the only method by which the director-ate in large organizations can retain overall control of the organization's functioning is by decentralizing much of the decision making within the framework of bureaucratic rules. It is reasonable to interpret Weber as implying a moderate negative relationship between the bureaucratic vari-ables and the centralization of decision making. This proposition, however, runs counter to everyday notions of bureaucracy. (1973: 478)

Mansfield's interpretation of Weber's view is supported by our conclusion (in Chapter 2) that Weber's model of rational-legal authority provides a structure of roles that supports the exercise of relatively greater independence and discretion, within specified constraints, than are found in earlier administrative arrangements. The extent of bureaucratization and centralization is also affected by the organization's technology and, especially, by the degree of staff professionalization; we will discuss these relations after we briefly comment on some problems in determining the effects of size on structure.

Problems in Relating Size and Structure

A number of problems attend studies of the relation between size and structure. Kimberly (1976) has addressed many of the more important issues. In addition to the fundamental question of the theoretical status of size—what does size measure?—the causal status of this variable is problematic. One reason we know little about the causal relation between size and structure is that virtually all of the studies conducted have relied on cross-sectional data. Several longitudinal studies suggest that inferences based on cross-sectional studies of organizations regarding the effects of organizational growth or decline on structure may prove quite misleading.

Holdaway and Blowers (1971), using data from 41 urban school systems in western Canada, report that when the data are examined cross-sectionally, the relation between organization size and administrative ratio exhibits the expected negative relation, but when they are viewed longitudinally, administrative ratios do not decline as a function of increasing size in most of the districts examined over a five-year period. And a study by Freeman and Hannan (1975) based on data from 769 California school districts suggests that different relations obtain between size of organization and the administrative component, depending on whether the organization is in a period of growth or decline. Their analysis reveals that the size of the administrative component increases along with the size of the organization during periods of growth, but that during periods of decline the size of the administration does not decrease at the same rate as the rest of the organization. This disparity in rates leads Freeman and Hannan to be skeptical about attempts to develop generalizations relating organization size and administration from cross-sectional studies, since these studies will inevitably combine data from both growing and declining organizations.

Meyer (1979*b*) examined changes in the structure of 240 finance agencies located within the public bureaucracy of larger urban communities (greater than 50,000 residents), larger counties (greater than 100,000 residents), and the fifty states. Some data on change were collected as part of a panel study, with surveys being conducted in 1966 and again in 1972, but other change measures involved reports by agency officials describing when specified events occurred. Although Meyer's findings are complex and not easily summarized, they underline the importance of time of founding on structure: agencies established prior to 1900 exhibited lower levels of formalization than those founded between 1900 and 1939, and the latter class of firms was less formalized than those founded after 1940. Unlike the previous studies reported, Meyer found no association between formalization and decentralization, but he did find positive correlations between formalization and number of levels in the hierarchy and between levels and decentralization. Meyer (1979*b*: 179) suggests that his longitudinal data support the conclusion that "hierarchy follows from extensive personnel procedures [formalization] and decentralized decision making from hierarchical differentiation."

Even these few studies make it clear that our present understanding of the interrelations among various structural characteristics of organizations is likely to be improved if not entirely transformed by the inclusion of longitudinal and historical data and analyses.

TECHNOLOGY, SIZE, AND STRUCTURE

Professionals and Structure

In Chapter 9 we discussed the relation between the presence of professionals and the structural features of the technical core. We also noted that the presence of professional workers can affect the characteristics of more remote administrative structures. We cited findings from a study of public personnel agencies that those with a greater proportion of highly educated workers were characterized by higher manager-worker ratios (Blau, Heydebrand, and Stauffer, 1966). Similar results are reported in a study of United States hospitals (Heydebrand, 1973). Data from a study of finance departments also indicate that decision making is more decentralized in organizations having more highly qualified workers (Blau, 1968).

Hall's (1968) study of varying occupational groups in twenty-seven different organizations provides more complete information on the relation between professional employees and organizational structure. Hall assessed six structural features of these organizations: hierarchy of authority (defined as the extent to which the locus of decision making is prestructured); the division of labor (extent of functional specialization); presence of rules; extent of procedural specification; impersonality (degree of formalization); and technical competence (extent to which universalistic standards such as qualifications and education are used in selection and promotion). Reasonably strong, positive correlations were found among all of these dimensions with the exception of technical competence. This variable was negatively correlated with all of the other structural attributes! Moreover, dividing the sample of organizations according to our distinction between autonomous and heteronomous types revealed that, as expected, the former organizations were much lower than the latter in their levels of each of the structural variables, with the exception of level of technical competence. The more highly qualified professionals were found in those organizations that exhibited fewer "bureaucratic" attributes, as Weber defined the term: that is, those organizations with lower levels of task specialization, formalization, and standardization.

These results suggest that whether work is simplified and divided among less highly skilled participants or assigned to workers with higher skills who are granted more autonomy of action has implications not only for the immediate structure of the technical core but for the more re- mote, general structural characteristics of organizations. They also should remind us of the criticisms by Parsons, Gouldner, and others that Weber's model of bureaucracy tends to overlook the difference between authority based on office and that based on expertise or technical qualifications (see Chapter 2). Further, the results suggest that Udy (1959a) was correct to insist that Weber's ideal-type model of bureaucratic structure should be subjected to empirical validation. Udy's early study, based on a sample of 150 production organizations in 150 different nonindustrial societies dis- tinguished a highly intercorrelated set of bureaucratic (hierarchical) char- acteristics from a second set of intercorrelated characteristics that mea- sured the presence of limited objectives and a performance emphasis—a cluster of "rational" characteristics. These results suggest that rational organizations may or may not assume a hierarchical form (see Chapter 2; Blau and Scott, 1962: 206–9; and Blau, 1968).

We conclude that one of the great watersheds in the design of or- ganizations is the decision concerning whether work is to be divided and hierarchically coordinated or left intact and delegated to a professional- ized work force. Both are instances of rational organization. But each is associated with a different overall structural form.

Technology versus Size

With two externally driven factors affecting the structural character- istics of organizations, the question naturally arises as to which is the more powerful. Both Blau and his colleagues and the Aston group argue for the overriding importance of size. Thus, early in the presentation of their findings on the employment security agencies, Blau and Schoenherr sum- marize the conclusion to which their data point: "Size is the most impor- tant condition affecting the structure of organizations" (1971: 57). It is difficult to accept this sweeping generalization because of the design of this and other studies carried out in Blau's program of comparative studies. In each of several studies—of employment security agencies, pub- lic finance departments, colleges and universities, industrial firms—a single type of organization was selected for study. This has the effect of not allowing technology to vary meaningfully across organizations, since organizations of the same type all perform basically the same tasks or functions, while permitting size to vary freely, since both large and small organizations of the same type were included within the sample. Focusing on a single type of organization also reduces variation in other important environmental factors, such as the organization's political and economic context. (The effects of these environmental factors on organizational structure are examined in the following section.) It is not appropriate to make comparative assertions as to the relative power of classes of variables under circumstances in which certain of them—in this case, technology and environment—are arbitrarily restricted in variation or excluded from consideration. (See Beyer and Trice, 1979)

The studies conducted by the Aston group seem better designed in this respect (Pugh et al., 1963; 1968; 1969; Pugh and Hickson, 1976.) Concerned with the limitations of focusing on one or a few selected variables, they defined and measured a large number of structural and contextual variables. These measures were then applied to a heterogeneous, random sample of forty-six organizations in the Birmingham area in the original study and to a similar national sample of eighty-two British organizations in Child's (1972) replication. However, the Aston studies are difficult to interpret and, in particular, to compare with other studies because of the way in which the measures of structure and technology were treated. After carefully developing complex scales and subscales for measuring a number of widely recognized structural dimensions, including specialization, standardization, formalization, centralization, and configuration (the shape of the hierarchy), the analysts examined the interrelations of all of the scales. Rather than retaining the original theoretically based dimensions, they performed a factor analysis to determine what scales were sufficiently highly correlated to suggest the presence of a common underlying dimension or factor. Three major factors emerged from this empirical procedure: the first, labeled *structuring of activities*, emphasized the covariation of those scales measuring specialization, standardization, and formalization; the second, *concentration of authority*, emphasized measures of centralization; and the third, *line of control of work flow*, emphasized control over work by line officials rather than by impersonal mechanisms. The factor analysis used was such that the resulting factors are orthogonal—relatively independent of one another. These factors were then related to such "contextual" variables as size and technology. And, as noted in Chapter 9, technology itself was measured by a complex series of scales combined to measure what the analysts termed *work-flow integration*.

As reported, size was found to exhibit strong and positive associations with the factor structuring of activities but was not correlated with the other two factors (Pugh et al., 1969). Technology, as measured by work-flow integration, showed "modest but distinct" correlations with all three factors, positive with structuring of activities and line control of work-flow, negative with concentration of authority. But after a more detailed analysis of these data, including multiple correlations in which technology was combined with other variables, Hickson, Pugh, and Pheysey (1969: 388–89) conclude,

> Operations technology as defined here is accounting for but a small proportion of the total variance in structural features. Other variables contribute more. On this sample, the broad "technological imperative" hypothesis that operations technology is of primary importance to structure is not sup-

ported. . . . The present data suggest that operations technology has only a limited specific effect compared with size.[4]

Although the Aston group's design appears better suited to comparing the relative effects of size and technology, a number of problems reduce confidence in their conclusions. The use of factor scores disrupts the connection between theoretically defined variables and empirical measures, so that it is often difficult to interpret measures of relations. Also, the measure of technology, work-flow integration, seems both to be narrow and to combine measures of work and work-flow inappropriately across levels, so that it also is difficult to interpret or accept. In addition, there are problems with the samples developed. The first sample was drawn exclusively from the Birmingham area and so can hardly be regarded as a representative sample of independent—that is, unrelated—organizations.[5] Further, as Child (1972) has noted, the sample contained a large number of branches, in contrast with independent companies, and this may have resulted in an inflated score for centralization and affected the observed relation between structuring of activities and centralization. The second sample used in the replication study was drawn from a broader sampling frame—all of Britain—but was restricted by type to business organizations. It seems clear that if investigators hope to conduct convincing studies of the relative impact of varying factors on the structural features of organizations, more care and attention must be devoted to adequacy of measurement and to sample design (see McKelvey and Aldrich, 1983).

Finally, the problems with this research are not only methodological but theoretical. Aldrich (1972) has shown that the specific empirical findings reported by the Aston group may be used to support quite varying interpretations of the relations among size, technology, and structure. The correlational data are consistent with models in which technology is presumed to influence structure directly as well as indirectly through size as well as with models in which size is assumed to have causal priority. Therefore, empirical results from cross-sectional studies alone cannot resolve the issue of the relative importance of size and technology as determinants of organization structure.

[4]Hickson and his colleagues intend this generalization to apply only to the relation between technology and peripheral organizational structure. They did find associations between technology and some aspects of the technical core structures and suggest that the pervasiveness of these effects is a function of organizational size. They argue that

> structural variables will be associated with operations technology only where they are centered on the workflow. The smaller the organization the more its structure will be pervaded by such technological effects: the larger the organization, the more these effects will be confined to variables such as job-counts of employees on activities linked with the workflow itself, and will not be detectable in variables of the more remote administrative and hierarchical structure. (Hickson, Pugh, and Pheysey, 1969: 394–95)

[5]The same criticism can be made of Woodward's (1965) sample of industrial firms, all of which were drawn from the same region of South Essex, and of Hage and Aiken's (1969) sample of sixteen health and welfare organizations, all of which were located in the same metropolitan area (see Scott, 1977b). Thus, each of these studies was limited to a sample of organizations within the same areal field.

ENVIRONMENT AND STRUCTURE

Buffering, Bridging, and Structural Complexity

Chapter 8 was devoted in part to describing some of the specific mechanisms used by organizations to buffer their technical cores from disturbing environmental influences and to build bridges to essential exchange partners and allies. Such organizational responses to the technical environment are not a simple matter of utilizing selected techniques or mechanisms. Associated with their use are fundamental changes in the structure of the organization.

Mapping environmental complexity   What changes may be expected when organizations employ one or more of the several buffering techniques we have described: coding, stockpiling, leveling, or forecasting? Such activities will require the development or recruitment of personnel with new and different skills from those employed in the technical core itself. These participants will require additional space and special equipment. In short, as the need for such buffering techniques grows, we would expect to observe the development and growth of new specialized roles and departments at either end of the technical core—in other words, buffering units that interface with the input and output environments of the organization.

Consider also the use of the simpler bridging techniques, such as bargaining, contracting, and co-optation. As the task environment becomes more differentiated and active with the development of segmented labor markets, rapid technical and scientific developments, multiple types of buyers and sellers, subcontractors to oversee, and competitors to watch and attempt to outmaneuver, the organization responds by adding new types of occupational groups and specialists to deal with each of these environmental sectors. Organizations hire personnel officers and labor relations experts to deal with more complex labor markets; scientists, engineers, research administrators, and patent lawyers to participate in and keep pace with scientific developments; purchasing agents and marketing specialists to relate to the input and output environments; contract specialists and auditors to negotiate with and police contractors, market analysts, and sometimes even industrial spies to look after competitors. Most of these additions to the organizational structure involve the creation of new staff or support departments attached to the managerial level of the organization.

Structural elaboration may also occur at the institutional level as the size of boards of directors is increased to allow for the addition of new types of board members, who will connect the organization with sectors or units of importance in their environment. Or it may occur as advisory structures are created to broaden the linkage of the organization to its task environment. Thus, the increasing complexity of the task environment is adapted to by increased structural complexity—differentiation—on the part of the organization.

This adaptation occurs not only in response to technical environments but also as a reaction to institutional environments. Organizations in such environments enhance their own chances for survival and resource acquisition by adhering closely to the institutionally defined patterns, by incorporating them in their own structures, by becoming structurally isomorphic with them. (Meyer and Rowan, 1977; DiMaggio and Powell, 1983)

As might be expected, organizations are very sensitive to the nuances of the normative climate in their institutional environments: they take account of the amount of support for and conflict over particular reforms and proposed changes. Rowan (1982) has examined changes in the staffing of a sample of California school districts between 1930 and 1970. He reports that the hiring of district specialists in the areas of health, psychology, and curricular matters was highly responsive to the level of support and attention to these domains that was reflected in broader educational movements and national and state political acts. The higher the consensus—or, in Rowan's words, the more "balanced" the institutional environment—the more widely diffused were officials identified with these movements; the more unbalanced the domain, the more irregular were the patterns traced by the districts in hiring and retaining appropriate specialists.

Whereas the career lines of specialists are subject to disruption because of changing levels of consensus and variations in the power and influence of groups shaping institutional norms, administrative officials in general appear to thrive on conflict. A widely accepted proposition in open systems theory is that organizations located in more complex and uncertain environments will exhibit more complex internal structures. When the environmental units take the form of varied public funding and regulatory bodies whose actions are not coordinated but fragmented—a relatively common pattern in the United States (see Meyer and Scott, 1983)—organizational complexity is likely to develop particularly at the administrative levels where boundary-spanning activities are centered. Thus, Rowan (1981) reports that, controlling for size and internal technical complexity, school districts in California receiving larger amounts of federal and state funding for special programs had a larger complement of administrators than districts not engaged in such programs. Similar results were found in a study of public districts and schools and private schools in the San Francisco Bay area (Scott and Meyer, 1986). Meyer and I found, for both public and private schools, that the larger the number of special state and federal programs in which the schools were participating, the greater the proportion of administrators at both the district and the school level. Administrative structures above the school level—district and state structures—are particularly affected in the public system.

> It is exactly these organizational levels that expanding environmental controls from state and national levels have acted to foster in recent decades: the complex fundings, programs, and requirements in which public schooling is immersed create pressures that generate much administrative expansion (Scott and Meyer, 1984: 39).

Whether differentiation of organizational structure occurs as a rational system response designed to support the buffering and bridging activities of organizations attempting to regulate critical resource flows, or as a natural system response designed to coalign the structure with its institutional environment to ensure its survival, the more general processes at work here are best depicted by the open systems perspective. This approach insists that an organization, as an open system, adapts to more complex environments by itself becoming more complex: it is a type of system "whose persistence and elaboration to higher levels depend upon a successful mapping of some of the environmental variety and constraints into its own organization on at least a semipermanent basis" (Buckley, 1967: 63).

It is important to stress that the organization's "mapping," or incorporating, of portions of the "environmental variety" into its own structure introduces new and different, and sometimes alien and hostile, elements into its own system. For example, the hiring of a labor relations specialist by a personnel department presumably introduces a person with expertise in, and experience with, labor unions. Such persons are hired because of their ability to understand, communicate, and negotiate with unions and their representatives. They may be more similar in background and training and attitudes to their counterparts in the unions than to their colleagues in the personnel department (see Goldner, 1970). The same is true for hundreds of other types of occupational groups whose services are required by the organization but whose value depends on their marginality to the system and on their connections with similar groups in other organizations. These associations among persons in similar occupational groups—accountants, computer specialists, labor lawyers, public relations experts, advertising managers—across different organizations are among the most important bridges linking contemporary organizations. The flow of individuals back and forth across these bridges sometimes creates problems for the larger society (see Chapter 12) but always creates problems for the host organization, which must attempt to control and integrate their activities and resolve their conflicts.[6]

Integration and loose coupling The study by Lawrence and Lorsch (1967) of plastics manufacturing companies, which has been referred to several times in this volume, illustrates many of the major points we wish to emphasize.[7] As will be recalled (see Chapter 4), their research showed that (1) the task environments confronting the plastics manufacturing companies were highly varied, differing for research, production, and marketing functions; (2) this environmental variety was mapped into the structure of the organization, resulting in the creation of separate departments to confront these diverse environments; (3) the more closely aligned were the structural characteristics of each of these departments with the characteristics of the task environments they confronted, the

[6]The effect of these connections among similar occupational groups across organizations on the generation of power differences is discussed in Chapter 11.

[7]The results of interest in the present context are based on a study by Lawrence and Lorsch of only six plastics companies. Since the organizations themselves were the units of analysis, this is a very small sample on which to base any firm conclusions. We prefer to treat their research as a stimulating exploratory study valuable chiefly for the ideas generated, not for the hypotheses confirmed.

more effective was the organization;[8] (4) hence, the more differentiated the organization's departments—the more unlike their structural characteristics—the more effective the organization; (5) however, the more differentiated the departments within each organization, the more likely were disagreements and conflicts to develop and the more difficult the problems of coordinating and integrating their work; and (6) therefore, the more differentiated the departments *and* the more successful the organization in integrating their efforts, the more effective the organization.

The primary integrating mechanism used in the plastics companies studies was that of liaison roles: special roles were created to help to integrate the work of the three basic departments and resolve conflicts among them. Lawrence and Lorsch (1967: 54–83) report that the more successful integrators possessed attributes and orientations intermediate to those of the units they bridged, exercised influence based on technical competence, were oriented to the performance of the system as a whole, and enjoyed high influence throughout the organization. Walton and his colleagues (Walton, Dutton, and Fitch, 1966; Walton and Dutton, 1969) have also studied interdepartmental conflict in organizations and strategies for resolving it. They note that such conflicts often develop out of mutual task dependence, task-related asymmetries, conflicting performance criteria, dependence on common resources, communication obstacles, and ambiguity of goals as well as organizational differentiation. Such conflicts can be met with varying responses, from structural redesign to third-party consultation and attempts at reeducation of participants (see Blake, Shephard, and Mouton, 1964; Likert and Likert, 1976; Walton, 1969).

Note, however, that it is a rational system perspective that underlies most of these concerns with the integration of structurally differentiated departments. It is assumed that the organization is primarily a production system and that when conflicts occur among subunits, they must be resolved. Conflict interferes with goal attainment, and its resolution is associated with greater effectiveness of performance. A quite different view of conflict and conflict resolution processes is associated with the natural system perspective, which presumes that interdepartmental conflict is not primarily a product of error, ambiguity, and ignorance but results from quite fundamental divergences in group interests, and that the struggles are concerned not simply with means but with the goals to be served by the organization. These matters will be discussed in Chapter 11.

The assumption that integration is required because differentiation is present is also consistent with the rational system assumption that the various parts of the organization should be tightly coupled, each harnessed in the service of unified objectives. By contrast, the open systems model of organizations envisages a system of more or less loosely coupled elements, each capable of autonomous action (see Chapter 4). Weick (1976) notes a number of ways in which loose coupling of these structural elements may be highly adaptive for the organization, particularly when it

---

[8]To arrive at a composite rating of effectiveness Lawrence and Lorsch (1967: 40) combined objective measures of change in profits, sales volume, and number of new products with subjective ratings by managers of how well their companies were performing. We will examine these and other measures of effectiveness in Chapter 13.

confronts a diverse, segmented environment. To the extent that department units are free to vary independently, they may provide a more sensitive mechanism for detecting environmental variation. Loose coupling also encourages opportunistic adaptation to local circumstances, and it allows simultaneous adaptation to conflicting demands. Should problems develop with one department, it can be more easily sealed off or severed from the rest of the system. Moreover, adjustment by individual departments to environmental perturbation allows the rest of the system to function with greater stability. Finally, allowing local units to adapt to local conditions without requiring changes in the larger system reduces coordination costs for the system as a whole.

Obviously some organizations effect tighter coupling among their department than others, and within a given organization we will see variation in the degree of coupling. In general, we would expect to observe tighter coupling between units within a technical core linked by serial or reciprocal interdependence than between core units and those operating on the boundaries. Nevertheless, two words of caution merit emphasis. First, the extent of the interdependence, coordination, or coupling between any two organizational subunits is a matter for empirical determination, not assumption. Second, whether looser or tighter coordination or coupling is adaptive for the organization depends on the specific circumstances confronted, and is also a matter for investigation, not prejudgment.

From unitary to multi-divisional structures   Before we conclude our discussion of the structural consequences of buffering and bridging strategies, two techniques remain to be considered: growth and merger. Both represent changes in the scale of the organization, and, based on our discussion in the previous section, we would expect increased size to be associated with increased structural differentiation. But we can be more specific than this. Chandler (1962; 1977) and Williamson (1975; 1985) argue that when firms grow beyond a certain point, not just further differentiation but a structural reorganization is likely to take place. This shift is described as a change from a unitary to a multi-divisional structure. The *unitary* structure is the conventional organizational form composed of a central office and several functionally organized departments. The *multi-divisional* structure is depicted in Figure 10–1. It consists of a general office and several product-based or regional divisions, each of which contains functionally differentiated departments. These departmental units are subdivided into work units (establishments) that are distributed on a geographical or product basis.

In his classic account of the history of American business enterprise, Chandler (1962) points out that the multi-divisional form first appeared in this country shortly after World War I, and that it apparently was independently developed at about the same time by a number of major companies, including du Pont, General Motors, Standard Oil of New Jersey, and Sears, Roebuck. Chandler's arguments are complex and varied, but in brief, he identifies four phases of growth for American industrial enterprise. The first period, just after the Civil War, was a time of rapid expansion and resource accumulation. This was the age of the larger-than-life entrepreneurs who expanded their organizations, most often through vertical integration. In the second phase, a new generation

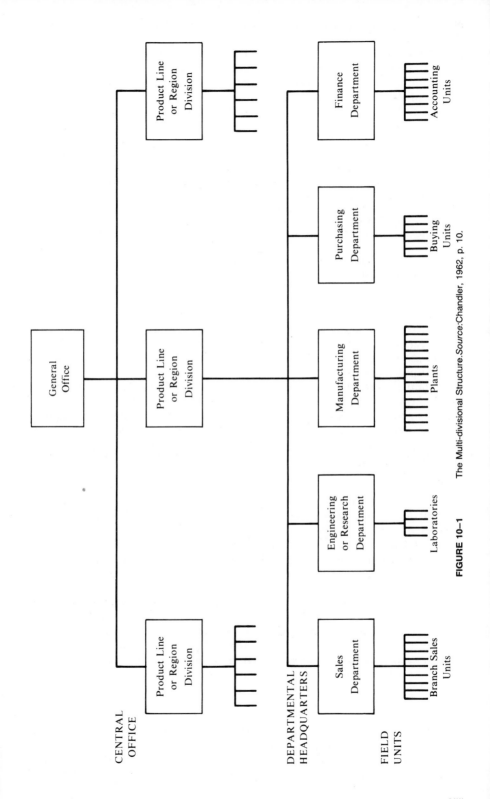

FIGURE 10-1 The Multi-divisional Structure. *Source:* Chandler, 1962, p. 10.

255

of professional managers developed "methods for managing rationally the larger agglomerations of men, money, and materials" (1962: 388). Attention was concentrated on the reduction of unit costs and the coordination of diverse functional activities. The first two phases are best represented in the United States by the development of the railroads. Chandler (1977: 87) points out that

> the safe, reliable movement of goods and passengers, as well as the continuing maintenance and repair of locomotives, rolling stock, and track, roadbed, stations, roundhouses, and other equipment, required the creation of a sizable administrative organization. It meant the employment of a set of managers to supervise these functional activities over an extensive geographical area; and the appointment of an administrative command of middle and top executives to monitor, evaluate, and coordinate the work of the managers, resonsible for the day-to-day operations. It meant, too, the formulation of brand new types of internal administrative procedures and accounting and statistical controls. Hence, the operational requirements of the railroads demanded the creation of the first administrative hierarchies in American business.

Of course, the expansion of the railroads had a significant impact on the development of all types of businesses, the availability of reliable and inexpensive transportation enabling them to vastly expand their input and output markets.

Thus, phase three, lasting from the turn of the century to the First World War, witnessed the filling out of existing product lines as firms continued to expand. And, in order to ensure the continuing and efficient use of their resources, firms began to diversify, moving into related fields that would capitalize on their technical skills and marketing contacts.

In the fourth phase, following World War I, a few major companies that had diversified and were attempting to manage several related product lines found it necessary to reorganize in order to ensure the efficient employment of their resources. The new form that emerged was the "decentralized" or multi-divisional (M-form) structure, whose chief advantage was that it suported the clear separation of entrepreneurial or strategic from operational decision making. Day-to-day operational and tactical decisions were delegated to managers at the divisional level; longer-range entrepreneurial or strategic decisions were located at the general-office level. (See Figure 10–1.)

Firms can undertake horizontal mergers in order to increase the size of their markets, or vertical mergers in order to incorporate more phases of the production or distribution process and still fit comfortably into a unitary structure. However, as the firm begins to diversify its products and attempts to enter markets related or unrelated to those presently served, it will benefit from moving into a multi-divisional form. This is the sense in which Chandler insists that a firm's structure should be suited to its strategy. He argues that

> unless structure follows strategy, inefficiency results. This certainly appears to be the lesson to be learned from the experience of our four companies [du Pont, General Motors, Standard Oil, and Sears, Roebuck]. Volume expansion, geographical dispersion, vertical integration, product diversification,

and continued growth by any of these basic strategies laid an increasingly heavy load of entrepreneurial decision making on the senior executives. If they failed to reform the lines of authority and communication and to develop information necessary for administration, the executives throughout the organization were drawn deeper and deeper into operational activities and often were working at cross purposes to and in conflict with one another. (Chandler, 1962: 314–15)

Chandler argues that, given a diversified strategy, the new multi-divisional form is superior to the unitary form because it frees some officials from the tyranny of daily operational decisions and allows them to concentrate on positioning the organization in its environment and determining the proper mix of product lines and markets and thereby the allocation of resources among divisions. The M-form is also particularly well suited to supporting a multinational strategy, in which numerous divisions offering the same general product lines are situated to take advantage of multiple national markets (see Vaupel and Curhan, 1969; Tsurumi, 1977).

Williamson (1975: 132–54) points out that Chandler's historical account of the problems accompanying diversification and the structural solution to these problems is consistent with predictions generated by the transactions cost framework. He argues that the principal problem created by diversification is that it creates increasing complexity and uncertainty— this time *within* the organization rather than in the environment—up to a level that exceeds the information-processing and decision-making capacity of the managers. The structural development that occurs is one that simplifies the informational and decision situations by clearly differentiating between the long-range policy decisions to be handled by the general office and the short-run operational decisions to be determined at the divisional level. Also, since companies within a diversified structure may be expected to buy from each other where possible, a small-numbers situation prevails that may motivate opportunistic behavior at the divisional or departmental levels. To curb these natural tendencies, an elite staff is attached to the general office to perform both advisory and auditing functions and in this manner to secure greater control over the behavior of the operating divisions. Williamson (1985: 283–84) amplifies the advantages of the multi-divisional structure in controlling opportunism:

> The M-form structure removes the general office executives from partisan involvement in the functional parts and assigns operating responsibilities to the divisions. The general office, moreover, is supported by an elite staff and has the capacity to evaluate divisional performance. Not only, therefore, is the goal structure altered in favor of enterprise-wide considerations, but an improved information base permits rewards and penalties to be assigned to divisions on a more discriminating basis, and resources can be reallocated within the firm from less to more productive uses. A concept of the firm as an internal capital market thus emerges.

Viewing the M-form as an "internal capital market" introduces a fifth phase—one that carries the historical progression beyond the development charted by Chandler. In important respects, the emergence of the *conglomerate* firm represents a further extension of M-form logic. Conglomerate firms are those containing divisions engaged in unrelated businesses: the diversification spans industry groups, not simply product lines. But, as Williamson (1985: 288) notes, its development builds logically on the M-form structure:

> once the merits of the M-form structure for managing separate, albeit re-lated, lines of buiness (e.g., a series of automobile or a series of chemical divisions) were recognized and digested, its extension to manage less closely related activities was natural.

In such firms, divisions are treated primarily as profit centers: the prime criteria for their continuation and support is their current or future prof-itability, and the general office functions as an (internal) capital market, by which cash flows are directed to high-yield uses. Although capital requests and allocations are formally internalized—a division approaches its own headquarters with its financial requests—in some of the more extreme cases the allocation decisions appear to rest primarily on almost pure market criteria. More often, however, other types of organizational criteria enter into decisions regarding the fate of the divisions. Thus, in important respects, as Eccles and White (1983) have pointed out, markets and hierarchies—come together within the modern corporation, each of these types of control systems helping to determine the disposition of the divisional profit centers.

Several empirical studies have attempted to test the explanations proposed by Chandler and by Williamson, and in general the findings are supportive. For example, Armour and Teece (1978) studied a sample of firms in the petroleum industry and concluded that those adopting the M-form exhibited higher performance, as measured by profitability, than those failing to do so. And in a study based on data from 125 of the largest 500 U.S. corporations in 1964, Palmer and colleagues (Palmer et al., 1986) developed a causal model to test the argument that firms that are industrially diversified and operating in geographically dispersed areas are more likely to adopt the M-form structure. The empirical evidence confirmed both predictions. The analysis also shows that although size contributes to both diversification and dispersion, it does not have a direct effect on structure, confirming Chandler's assertion that large size does not, in itself, cause firms to adopt the M-form structure. Finally, Fligstein (1985a) has assembled a data file containing information on 216 large U.S. firms spanning the period 1919 to 1979. His sample contains the 100 largest nonfinancial corporations in existence during each of three periods: 1919–1939, 1939–1959, and 1959–1979. This data set reveals that whereas less than 2 percent of these major corporations had adopted the multi-divisional structure before 1929, over 84 percent had done so by 1979. And again, Chandler's central predictions are confirmed:

> Industries where product-related strategies dominated, like machine, chemi-cal and transportation industries, adopted the MDF [M-form] in large num-bers relatively early; while industries that were more likely to be vertically integrated, like mining, metalmaking, lumber and paper, and petroleum, adopted the MDF later and to a lesser extent (Fligstein, 1985a: 386).

Although these results support Chandler's and Williamson's efficiency-based explanations, other evidence suggests that institutional pressures have also influenced both the extent and timing as well as the specific strategies involved in the adoption of the multi-divisional form. Applying DiMaggio and Powell's (1983) notions of the role of mimetic processes in producing structural isomorphism in organizational fields, Fligstein (1985a: 387) reports that by 1939 and thereafter a mimetic effect is observed "whereby firms in industries with other firms who have already changed to the MDF are more likely to do so," independent of strategy. Giant corporations were observed to embrace the multidivisional structure not as a solution to internal problems but as a signal to external constituencies. Fligstein also calls attention to the role of the state—a major actor in the institutional environment of large corporations—which responded to increasing concentration in product lines within industries by passage in 1950 of the Celler-Kefauver Act. This act together with subsequent court decisions curtailed corporate efforts to increase market share within the same industry, and in effect forced corporate expansion to occur in product-unrelated areas—that is, through conglomerate strategies. Thus, Fligstein (1985*a*; 1985*b*) suggests that what we have characterized above as a fifth phase of corporate development—the shift to conglomerates—was the adaptive response of expansionist-oriented firms to governmental restrictions imposed on earlier, successful product-related strategies.

Assumptions involved in Explanations of Structure

Just as we did in our examination of the relation between technology and the core structures of the organization, we need to make explicit the assumptions underlying attempts to account for the characteristics of the organization's peripheral structures. Most analysts who have examined the relation between technology and structure, size and structure, or task environment and structure attempt to account for these associations by using rational open system arguments. Blau, Galbraith, Lawrence and Lorsch, Thompson, Chandler, Williamson—all explain their empirical findings or justify their predictions on the basis of improved performance or reduced costs or other language that implies that organizations are fundamentally goal-attainment systems seeking to maximize effectiveness and efficiency. Thus, Thompson argues that to a large extent the variation in organizational structure "can be accounted for as attempts to solve the problems of concerted action under different conditions, especially conditions of technological and environmental constraints and contingencies" (1967: 74). Structure is viewed as a "joint result" of adaptations to technology and environment.

Child criticizes much of the research relating technology, environment, and structure on the grounds that it allows insufficiently for the exercise of choice on the part of those who design the organization. He points out that these studies

attempt to explain organizational structure at one remove. They draw attention to possible constraints upon the choice of effective structures, but fail to consider the process of choice itself in which economic and administrative exigencies are weighed by the actors concerned against the opportunities to operate a structure of their own and/or other organizational members' preferences. (Child, 1972: 16)

Certainly, Chandler (1962) insists on the importance of choice. His study, summarized above, of the development of multi-divisional forms by selected United States firms stresses the role of strategy—the setting of goals and objectives—and the uncertain relation between "strategy and structure"—the design of a satisfactory organizational form. He notes that even in the four innovative organizations he studied—du Pont, General Motors, Standard Oil, and Sears, Roebuck—

there was a time lag between the appearance of the administrative needs and their satisfaction. A primary reason for delay was the very fact that responsible executives had become too enmeshed in operational activities. (Chandler, 1962: 315)

His survey of seventy other large industrial companies, some of which adopted the structural changes and others of which did not, revealed that although "expansion did cause administrative problems which led, in time, to organizational change and readjustment," any fundamental "reshaping of administrative structure nearly always had to wait for a change in the top command" (1962: 380). Such comments remind us of the importance of organizational inertia, a feature stressed by the populational ecologists (see Chapter 8). Child and Chandler stress that organizations change—and fail to change—because of choices made by organizational participants.

Contingency theory—which predicts a relation between structure-environment match and performance—is consistent with either the rational selection view that successful managers design their structures to fit environmental contingencies or with the natural selection view that environments select organizations so that only those best matched to their environments survive.

If organizational change or its absence reflects not only external constraints but also internal choices, we may still ask what determines the choices made by organizational participants. Most analysts would embrace the assumption of, at least, intended rationality: members may not always behave rationally, because of misinformation or ignorance or a lapse of attention, but they are believed to be motivated to serve the goals of the organization. However, natural systems analysts, as we already know, would challenge this view.

Early natural system researchers have devoted their efforts to accounting for the departure of behavior from the dictates of formal structure or describing the emergence of the informal structure (see Chapter 3). However, since the early 1960s they have concerned themselves with the determinants of the formal structure itself. As we know, some of these theorists, following Cyert and March (1963), view the organization as a coalition of groups, each pursuing its own interests. Pfeffer (1978: 36) has attempted to spell out the possible implications of this view for explaining organizational structure:

> If we take seriously the conceptualization of organizations as coalitions, then a critical issue is not just what the consequences of various structural arrangements are, but who gains and who loses from such consequences. Structure, it would appear, is not just the outcome of a managerial process in which designs are selected to ensure higher profit. Structure, rather, is itself the outcome of a process in which conflicting interests are mediated so that decisions emerge as to what criteria the organization will seek to satisfy. Organizational structures can be viewed as the outcome of a contest for control and influence occurring within organizations.

Similar to our own discussion in the previous chapter, Pfeffer points out that the relation between technology and structure may result from power processes rather than from rational design decisions: powerful participants defend the definitions of their work as uncertain and hence prevent its routinization. He also suggests that the relation between environmental diversity and structural differentiation may be explained simply by the organization's tendency to incorporate external interest groups into its own structure as a means of co-opting or placating them. And the same argument is used to explain the relation between organizational size and differentiation: size is associated with diversity of interests encountered by the organization, and differentiation is its response to this diversity. While these and related arguments require further refinement and verification, they appear sufficiently plausible to suggest that many features of organizational structure can be explained by nonrational power or conflict models as well as, if not better than, by rational models.

CONNECTING THE CORE AND PERIPHERAL STRUCTURES

Tight and Loose Coupling

Much of what passes for organizational structure consists of varying types of mechanisms for controlling the behavior of participants. Hierarchy, formalization, centralization, modes of coordination—are all devices to help ensure that the organizational managers can shape and influence the behavior of other participants charged with carrying on the production activities of the organization. Indeed, a primary justification for the existence of managers is the impact of their ideas and decisions and designs and plans on the behavior of other participants. Many accounts of organizational structure—or, alternatively, many types of organizational structure—emphasize the tight coupling of managers and performers' behavior. Managers decide, performers implement; managers command, performers obey; managers coordinate, performers carry out specialized tasks. Organizations or segments of organizations of this type certainly exist, particularly in situations in which work activities have been divided and routinized. Rational system analysts emphasize this view of organizational structure.

By contrast, early natural system analysts, with their interest in behavioral rather than normative structures, looked more carefully at the operation of these supposedly tightly coupled systems and failed to observe the presence of the taut command systems described by the textbooks in administrative science. Rather, their studies revealed that workers were reluctant to accept close supervision and likely to develop protective work-group mechanisms or understandings with their supervisors that allowed them some leeway and breathing space in defining and meeting require-ments (see Roethlisberger and Dickson, 1939; Roy, 1952; Gouldner, 1954; Rushing, 1966a). The control systems were less tightly coupled in operation than in theory.

All formal structural devices, however, do not connote tight cou-pling of activities. Decentralization, delegation, professionalization, even the creation of the staff-line distinction—these are mechanisms for ensur-ing *some* coordination and control but also for legitimating and supporting the exercise of discretion. They build in flexibility and encourage initia-tive in the technical core of the organization and so reduce its dependence on and its responsiveness to hierarchical directives. Moreover, as Parsons (1960: 65–66) pointed out when he distinguished among the technical, managerial, and institutional levels of organization, a qualitative break in the line-authority relation exits at the points where the three levels con-nect (see Chapter 3). Parsons argues that only within a level can a supe-rior directly supervise the work of subordinates and assume responsibility for it, since differences in the nature of the work performed at each level are too great to permit direction of the lower by the higher levels. Thus, board members functioning at the institutional level would not be ex-pected to exercise direct, routine line authority over managers but to grant them considerable freedom in exercising their managerial responsi-bilities; managers, in turn, would not ordinarily exercise direct line au-thority over the technical functions of workers. In short, the functions performed at each level are seen to be relatively distinct and not readily linked to one another. Thus, even the relatively conventional views of rational and natural system theorists recognize the presence of consider-able loose coupling as an important structural and operational feature of most organizational systems.

Meyer and Rowan (1977) take a more extreme view of the possibili-ties of loose coupling in organizations. They suggest that organizations in institutional environments will be inclined to selectively *decouple* their for-mal structures from the activities carried on in their technical core. The rationalized myths that provide meaning and legitimacy to the formal structures often do not provide clear and consistent guidelines for techni-cal activities. The result is that the organization conforms closely to the ritually defined meanings and categories supplied by the environment but does not attempt seriously to implement them at the operational level. For example, Meyer and Rowan argue that educational organizations adhere closely to the ritual categories of education: "There seem to be centralized and enforced agreements about exactly what teachers, students, and top-ics of instruction constitute a particular school" (1978: 84). But at the operational level, there is little organizational coordination or control over instructional activities. These activities are delegated to teachers, and there is little or no attempt to evaluate and control their performance— either hierarchically or collegially—or to collect and use data on outputs, such as student-performance scores, as a means of improving their performance.[9] The solution of decoupling is particularly effective where environmental rules impose conflicting requirements on organizations. Thus, schools may be simultaneously required to give special treatment to educationally handicapped children but at the same time to *mainstream* them, not segregate them from their fellow students. Organizations can adapt to conflicting demands by creating appropriate programs and offices at the administrative level that can create the required reports, but then decoupling these offices from the operational level.

In a closely related discussion, Marshall Meyer (1979*a*) argues that changes in organizational structure can serve as an important signaling mechanism to the organization's constituencies. For example, the creation of an office for affirmative action can signal to interested parties an organization's commitment to the goals of this program independently of whether or not affirmative action policies are pursued. Meyer points out that such signals are taken seriously by outsiders because changes in structure are highly observable and do cost money (unlike pronouncements of goals or policy statements, which are relatively inexpensive and hence discounted), but are still much less costly than actual changes in rules together with the imposition of inspection and sanctioning procedures to ensure conformity with the new program.

The arguments of these institutional theorists are novel because they suggest that the formal structures of organizations have meaning and importance *regardless of whether they affect the behavior of performers in the technical core.* Formal structures can symbolize meaning and order. And, as Meyer and Rowan (1977: 352) have emphasized, organizations that devise structures that conform closely to institutional requirements "maximize their legitimacy and increase their resources and survival capabilities."

It is important to stress, however, that organizations in both technical and institutional environments engage simultaneously in tight and loose coupling activities, but in different directions. Meyer, Deal, and I (Meyer, Scott, and Deal, 1981: 152–53) summarize the contrasting strategies:

> Organizations arising in connection with technical flows closely control and manage them. Their structures act to regulate the flows, to buffer them from uncertainty, and thus to insulate them in some measure from external forces.... The intent is to decouple technical work from environmental conditions so that it can be more tightly managed by the organization.

[9]As Meyer and Rowan note, the problem is not typically the absence of data on student outputs:

> Schools use elaborate tests to evaluate pupils and to shape the course of their present and future lives. But the same data are almost never aggregated and used to evaluate the performance of teachers, schools, or school systems. (Some data of this kind are made available for school and district evaluation in California, but only under the pressure of the state legislature, not the local school system.) (1978: 88–89)

Meyer and Rowan cite numerous benefits associated with these practices, including increased commitments of school participants, both teachers and students; the shielding of ritual classifications from uncertainties arising in the technical core; and the provision of mechanisms allowing schools to adapt to inconsistent and conflicting institutionalized rules.

By contrast, institutionalized organizations closely integrate their own structural arrangements with the frameworks established by the larger institutional structures. In doing so they tend to buffer their structures from the actual technical work activities performed within the organizations. . . .

Thus the technical organization faces in toward its technical core and turns its back on the environment, while the institutional organization turns its back on its technical core in order to concentrate on conforming to its institutional environment.

Managing Up and Down

It is certainly obvious that over the course of this century, organizational forms have become more and more top-heavy. As Bendix (1956) and others have pointed out, the proportion of administrators to production workers has grown continuously throughout this period (see Chapter 1). A number of factors contributing to this result have been described in previous portions of this volume: the augmentation of the hierarchy to increase the information-processing capacity of the organization as the tasks performed become more complex and uncertain; the elaboration of managerial and staff positions in response to the need to buffer core departments and build connections with other units in the task environment; the incorporation of representatives from external units at the managerial or institutional level in order to relate more adequately to these interests, either as exchange partners or symbolically.[10] All of these developments imply the growth of peripheral roles and structures in relation to the technical core. However, only some of them orient the managerial level in and down toward the activities of the technical core. Many direct their attention up and out to the larger social and political environment. Managers of today's organizations must devote as much time and energy to "managing" their environments as to managing their production system.

Marxist theorists point out the close, interdependent connections between control arrangements within organizations and political systems in the wider society. Economic enterprises always rests on a political base. Whereas the prevailing rhetoric in capitalist societies stresses that enterprise is free and independent from state interference, Burawoy (1985) argues that political regimes within firms and in the wider polity are always linked. Capitalist systems differ from state socialism not in the absence of connections but the directness and visibility of those connections that do exist.

When the environment is heavily institutionalized, managers have their work cut out for them. Although, as we have already noted, Meyer and Rowan (1977: 345) suggest that "it takes only a little entrepreneurial energy to assemble" the relevant components—roles, rules, rituals—which are "littered around the societal landscape," to assemble these components is one thing and to fully mobilize them is another. (See Chapter 7.) Tilly (1978: 69) has proposed that the level of mobilization is a function of

---

[10]In addition to these changes in the "numerator," important changes in the "denominator" have also transpired. The number of production workers has continuously declined in many industries because of technological developments substituting capital equipment for labor.

the product of two factors: the value of the resources acquired and the probability of "delivering" them when needed. He further suggests that the variables affecting delivery include "the extent of competing claims on the resources involved, the nature of the action to which the resources are to be committed, and how organized the mobilizing group is" (p. 71). It is apparent that many of the resources managers acquire in order to adapt to institutional requirements incorporate elements—whether professional roles or legal rules—that are subject to many competing claims, and are not likely to be readily assimilated or mobilized in the service of organizational objectives.

These conditions help to account for Meyer's (1983) assertion that as the larger societal structures become more "rationalized," individual organizations attempting to operate within them become less "rational."

> Modern rationality has a vastly expanded jurisdiction, and many fewer aspects of society are organized in other ways. All these rationalized perspectives enter into the life of typical formal organizations, which contain and must legitimate the rationalistic perspectives of citizen-members, representatives of various occupational perspectives, carriers of bodies of authoritative knowledge, and organized representatives of a variety of external perspectives that penetrate the organizations and have some sovereign standing. It is exactly this rationalization of so many aspects of society that limits the rationality of formal organizational structure: modern formalized organizations are built up around the acknowledgment of the external legitimation, definition, and control of their internal processes. (Meyer, 1983: 269)

In this fashion, modern organizations "look less like rational organizations than holding companies incorporating various institutionally defined packages" (p. 262). The packages can be acquired and exhibited, but not mobilized in the service of specific goals. The increasingly rationalized institutional structures to be found in modern societies constitute a normative exoskeleton that both supports and constrains its constituent organizations.

SUMMARY

This chapter has examined some of the factors affecting the larger structure of the organization: the extent of its bureaucratization, centralization, formalization, and differentiation. Although the characteristics of the organization's core technology influence its peripheral features, the latter also respond to other forces, in particular the organization's size and its task environment. A number of empirical studies show that larger organizations are more highly differentiated and more formalized than smaller organizations. However, these studies also reveal that larger organizations tend to be less bureaucratized and centralized in their decision-making structures. It is suggested that reductions in bureaucratization occur because of administrative economies resulting from the managing of more of the same type of work, although these savings are counteracted and may be offset by increased administrative costs associated with greater differentiation—the costs of managing more different kinds of work. Decentralization is both necessary, because of information overload at the top caused by increased size and differentiation, and possible, because formalization promotes consistency of decision making. Technology also affects the characteristics of peripheral structures; in particular, the division and routinization of work are associated with higher levels of differentiation, formalization, and bureaucratization, but the delegation of work to professional personnel is associated with the opposite structural effects. Whether the effects of size or of technology dominate in determining structural features of organizations cannot be determined from existing studies: longitudinal studies designed to test explicit casual models based on better samples of organizations are required.

The peripheral structures of organizations are also affected by the buffering and bridging strategies employed by organizations in relating to their task environment. Associated with all of these specific techniques are structural modifications—additions of new roles and departments and representatives of external interests. Open systems map critical features of their environments into their own structures as a major adaptive strategy. Structural reorganization is also associated with organizational growth. A prime example of such reorganization is the shift during the first half of this century in many major corporations from a unitary to a multi-divisional structure.

The extent to which managerial units control and coordinate work in the technical core varies by type of organization but has probably been overstated. Considerable looseness of coupling has not only been observed in most organizations in the behavior of supervisors and workers but is legitimated by many types of formal arrangements. Recent analysts have called attention to some of the adaptive features of loosely coupled systems—whether the coupling involves boundary units relating to specific environmental segments, connections among boundary units, or connections between boundary and core units. The symbolic importance of structure has also been noted. Changes in structure at the institutional or managerial level are important whether or not they are associated with changes in procedures or behaviors within the technical core.

Managers must expend as much time and energy in relating to environmental demands as in directing the internal affairs of the organization. Balancing and reconciling—as well as buffering and segregating—are the primary administrative tasks in contemporary organizations.

11 goals, power, and control

Group decision-making extends deeply into the business enterprise. Effective participation is not closely related to rank in the formal hierarchy of the organization. This takes an effort of mind to grasp. Everyone is influenced by the stereotyped organization chart of the business enterprise. . . . Power is assumed to pass down from the pinnacle. Those at the top give orders; those below relay them on or respond.

This happens, but only in very simple organizations—the peacetime drill of the National Guard or a troop of Boy Scouts moving out on Saturday maneuvers. Elsewhere the decision will require information. Some power will then pass on to the person or persons who have this information. If this knowledge is highly particular to themselves then their power becomes very great.

John Kenneth Galbraith (1967)

The subjects of goals, power, and control have recurred frequently enough throughout the preceding chapters of this volume that their importance must now be established. Although we have touched on these topics in many places—and have skirted them in others—we have not yet confronted them directly. We begin by discussing the concept of organizational goals, indicating some of the reasons it has proved so obstreperous. We will find that it is helpful to change the questions What are goals: and Do organizations have goals? to the question Who set the goals in organizations? It is here that the questions of goals and power come together. It is also instructive to ask whether there are organizations that lack goals and, if so, what effect this has on their structure and functioning.

We also examine control systems in organizations. What are the sources of power, and how does power become authority? Some organizations substitute internal for external control systems, relying heavily on shared cultural beliefs. These types of controls are also described.

GOAL SETTING IN ORGANIZATIONS

Problems in Conceptualizing
Organizational Goals

The varying uses of goals   The concept of organizational goals is among the most slippery and treacherous of all those employed by organizational analysts. Many factors contribute to the confusion in this area. A brief description of some of these factors may not resolve all of the questions but at least will clarify some of them. One source of difficulty is that statements of organizational goals are used in a number of ways by organizations. Thus, rational system analysts emphasize that goals provide criteria for generating and selecting among alternative courses of action (Simon, 1957; 1964). These analysts stress the *cognitive* functions of goals: goals provide directions for and constraints on decision making and action. Natural system analysts, such as Barnard (1938) and Clark and Wilson (1961), emphasize that goals serve as a source of identification and motivation for participants. And Selznick (1949) notes that goals may be employed as ideological weapons with which to overcome opposition and garner resources from the environment. These analysts all emphasize the *cathectic* (emotional) properties of goals: goals serve as bases of attachment for both organizational participants and external publics. Note that a goal statement that is satisfactory for analysts concerned with the cathectic properties of goals may be unsatisfactory for analysts intersted in their cognitive contributions. Vague and general descriptions of goals may suffice for motivational purposes—indeed, they may be especially suited to this function—but be unsatisfactory for cognitive guidance. For example, colleges may be able to attract students or funds with the claim that they are "preparing tomorrow's leaders," but such goal statements will provide little help in designing the curriculum or hiring the faculty.

Institutional analysts stress the *symbolic* functions of goals. Whereas the cognitive and cathectic properties of goals emphasize their effects on organizational participants, the symbolic aspect of goals points to their significance for organizational audiences: publics, clients, taxpayers, regulators. The goals an organization espouses, the goals it appears to be serving, the goals it embodies and is perceived to represent—these symbolic goals have important effects on the organization's ability to acquire legitimacy, allies, resources, and personnel.

Still other analysts have challenged the conventional view of behavior in which goals precede actions. Weick has insisted on the relevance of dissonance theory as formulated by Festinger (1957) and others to decision making in organizations. Weick argues that

> rationality seems better understood as a postdecision rather than a predecision occurrence. Rationality makes sense of what has been, not what will be. It is a process of justification in which past deeds are made to appear sensible to the actor himself and to those other persons to whom he feels accountable. (Weick, 1969: 38)

In short, behavior sometimes precedes goals, and goal statements can serve as a *justification* for the actions taken (Staw, 1980).

Goal statements also serve as a basis for *evaluating* the behavior of participants or of entire organizations (see Scott, 1977a). They provide criteria for identifying and appraising selected aspects of organizational functioning. We will examine goals used as evaluation criteria applied to organizational performance in Chapter 13. The criteria used to evaluate performance may or may not be the same as those employed to direct it.

More generally, the various types of goal statements—that goals are used to guide behavior, to motivate it, to symbolize it, to justify it, or to evaluate it—may not coincide closely not only because they serve different functions but because they emanate from different sources. Symbolic goals are likely to be promulgaged at the institutional level of the organization, which seeks to legitimate organizational purposes by stressing their larger social functions. The top managers of a company are likely to stress cathectic goals as a way of developing commitment among their participants. From Barnard (1938) to Selznick (1957) to Peters and Waterman (1982) the "functions of the executive" are said to be articulate and inculcate commitment to corporate values. Middle-level managers, in concert with their technical staff, are expected to translate general aspirations into specific products and services, and so may be expected to emphasize the cognitive aspects of goals. Evaluators at all levels employ goals as a source of criteria for evaluating participants as they carry on the work of the organization, and participants at all levels employ goal statements to help them justify their past actions when asked to give an accounting. In Chapter 13, we pursue further how goals enter into the evaluation of organizational performance.

Individual and organizational goals   Simon (1957; 1964) has most forcefully urged the distinction between individual goals that govern the decision to join or remain in an organization, and organizational goals that are expected to govern the decision of individuals as participants (see Chapters 2 and 7). Simon proposes that for the sake of clarity such individual goals be labeled *motives*. This rational system conception of a relatively clear distinction between individual motives and organizational goals is challenged by the natural system perspective, which insists that individuals are not completely contained within their roles but may be expected to impose their own preferences on the choice of opportunities that confront them as participants. Simon (1964) does not deny the operation of such processes but insists that the distinction retains value. He notes, for example, that many requirements organizations impose on their participants are orthogonal to their motives—for example, it is a matter of indifference to individuals who have accepted employment as secretaries whether they type one letter rather than another. More generally, one would need to deny the existence of social roles and their impact on individual behavior in order to maintain that organizational goals are indistinguishable from individual motives. The separation of these concepts is also aided by Clark and Wilson's (1961) discussion of incentive systems (see Chapter 7). Their typology reminds us that in only a limited set of organizations—which they label *purposive*—do individual motives and organizational goals coincide. In most organizations the goals toward which participants direct their behavior are different from the goals that motivate them to participate in the organization.

One implication of these considerations is that we will not want to survey individual participants and then aggregate their individual objectives to arrive at a description of the organization's goals. In escaping from this reductionist fallacy, however, we must be careful not to go to the opposite extreme and posit the existence of some type of metaphysical corporate mind in which collective goals are formulated. To do so is inappropriately to reify the organization, granting it anthropomorphic properties it does not possess. We can avoid both reductionism and reification by reformulating our question. Instead of asking, Do organizations have goals? we will ask, Who sets organizational goals, and How are organizational goals set?

The Dominant Coalition

The most satisfactory answer to date to the question of who sets organizational goals is provided by Cyert and March (1963). They note that the classic economist's response to this question is to point to the goals of the entrepreneur and to equate the organization's goals with this person's objectives: the firm is seen as the shadow of one powerful actor. A second proposed solution is to presume that goals are consensually defined: all participants share in goal setting. Both of these models of goal setting are rejected as exceptional patterns found only rarely in nature. Cyert and March ((1963: 27–32) propose the alternative conception of organizational goals being set by a negotiation process that occurs among memers of *dominant coalitions*. We will briefly summarize this important conception.

Organizations are viewed as being composed of coalitions—groups of individuals pursuing certain interests. Each group will attempt to impose its preferences (goals) on the larger system, but in the typical case, no single group will be able to determine completely what goals are to be pursued. Group members seek out as allies other groups whose interests are similar, and they negotiate with those groups whose interests are divergent but whose participation is necessary. One group will make a *side payment* to another to secure its cooperation; that is, will accede to that group's demands. For example, a management group, to secure its goal of continued growth, will agree to provide a given level of return on investment to its stockholders and will agree to pay a specified level of wages to its employees. Note, however, that what is a goal for one group is viewed as a side payment by another group, and vice versa. Each group whose interests must be taken into account helps to define the goals of the organization.

All such groups are, by definition, members of the dominant coalition. Each negotiated agreement provides guidance to the organization and places constraints on what may be regarded as an acceptable course of action. And the goals themselves are complex preference statements that summarize the multiple conditions any acceptable choice must satisfy. Simon (1964:7) amplifies this latter point:

> In the decision-making situations of real life, a course of action, to be acceptable, must satisfy a whole set of requirements, or constraints. Sometimes one of these requirements is singled out and referred to as the goal of the

action. But the choice of one of the constraints, from many, is to a large extent arbitrary. For many purposes it is more meaningful to refer to the whole set of requirements as the (complex) goal of the action.

Simon points out that the complexity of these goal statements provides yet another reason why there is often disagreement over whether organizations may be said to have goals. He argues that

> If we use the phrase organization goals broadly to denote the constraint sets, we will conclude that organizations do, indeed, have goals (widely shared constraint sets). If we use the phrase organization goals narrowly to denote the generators [preferences held by individual coalition participants that are proposed as satisfactory alternatives], we will conclude that there is little communality of goals among the several parts of large organizations. (1964: 9)

The conception of the dominant coalition, though certainly not the last word on the subject of who sets organizational goals, does help to avoid many of the problems that have plagued earlier explanations. We embrace this conception because it offers the following features:

•The problem of reification is avoided: individuals and groups have interests, and the process by which these preferences come to be imposed on the organization is specified.

•It is recognized that although individuals and groups are allowed to specify the goals of the organization, there is no presumption that they do so on an equal footing, nor is it assumed that they hold common objectives.

•It is recognized that although individuals and groups impose goals on the organization, in most cases no single individual or group is powerful enough to determine completely the organization's goals; hence, the organization's goals are distinct from those of any of its participants.

•Allowance is made for differences in interests among participants. Some, but not all, of these differences may be resolved by negotiation, so at any time, conflicting goals may be present.

•It is recognized that the size and composition of the dominant coalition may vary from one organization to another and within the same organization from time to time.

Coleman (1975) points out that another advantage to this general approach to goal setting in organizations is that it easily permits the analyst to shift the level of analysis from, for example, the individual groups and their interests to the organization as a unit comprising these interests. He asserts that

> if we conceive of this system [the organization] as an actor in the next level (which I shall call a "corporate actor"), then its interests are given by the values of events at the lower level. In such an integrated system, the organization acts as if it were a single actor, and the directions in which it acts are given by the values of events generated at the lower level. . . .
> Thus the shift between levels in this theory is accomplished by conceiving of organizations as continuing systems of action, subject to internal analysis, and also as corporate actors, with interests derivable from that internal analysis. (Coleman, 1975: 86)

Coleman's explication helps to clarify the model, but in so doing calls attention to a major weakness.

With all of its advantages over previous conceptions, the coalition model of goal setting remains basically an aggregative model. Individual actors and even groups are allowed to have genuine interests, but organizations are not: they are viewed simply as collections of interests or, in Pfeffer and Salancik's words, "as settings in which groups and individuals with varying interests and preferences come together and engage in exchanges" (1978: 26). Such a conception may suffice for a coalitional or open systems theorist but cannot be expected to be acceptable to a rational or natural system analyst. Wallace voices the latter's concerns in his critique of Coleman's view that " 'interests' are fixed in individuals" and that "causal dominance" is located at the bottom rather than the top of the hierarchy.

> . . . Coleman appears to deny or ignore the reverse possibility that the values of events at the higher level may "give" the interest of the individual actor; he also appears to overlook the possibility that genuinely new interests may emerge from a new arrangement (especially a hierarchical arrangement) of individual actors.
>
> Coleman's rejection of corporate determination of individual interest and his apparent choice of interest-aggregation over interest-emergence between the individual and the corporate levels seem clearly to constitute psychological reductionism. (Wallace, 1975: 127)

Although interests are certainly brought to the organization and imposed on it by some powerful participant groups, it seems entirely plausible that interests also are generated within the organization. Managers who stand to profit from economies realized by increased scale or technical innovation may be expected to coalesce around these "new" interests, and others whose power is closely associated with the condition and survival prospects of the larger enterprise may be expected to champion the interests of the organization as a whole.

The natural system theorists are correct in assuming that in most cases a set of participants will perceive that their interests are served by the survival and strengthening of the organization. Thus, we need to allow for the possibility that new interests and new coalitions will emerge over time in response to the opportunities and dangers created by the existence of the organization itself. The dominant coalition model can thereby be modified and interpreted so as to avoid the reductionist fallacy.

As noted, all organizations are not expected to look alike in the size and composition of their dominant coalitions. We need to examine what factors account for these differences.

Factors Affecting
the Dominant Coalition

There are many potential sources of power in modern organizations. Those who own property, whether in the form of capital, land, machinery, or disposable goods, have "a socially defensible right to make a decision on how to use" these resources (Stinchcombe, 1983:131). *Ownership* is an important basis of power in most economic systems. However, usually the person or group that has a socially and legally defensible right to make a decision on the use of the resource does not do so directly. . . . Instead, the fund of resources is entrusted to an administrative apparatus, of which the property-owning group (the board of directors) is the formal head. . . . the property rights are . . . used to make the activities of an administrative apparatus controlling the resources legitimate. (Stinchcombe, 1983: 135–36)

Owners delegate control over resources to *managers,* who are expected to act on their behalf—to serve as their agents. But, as numerous analysts from Berle and Means (1932) to Galbraith (1967) to economic agency theorists (such as Alchian and Demsetz, 1972; Jensen and Meckling, 1976; Fama, 1980) have noted, the interests of owners—whether capitalists or widely dispersed middle-class stockholders—and managers may diverge; managers develop their own power base as owners become dependent on their expertise and detailed knowledge of the administration of the enterprise.[1]

Organizations also depend on the energies and skills of workers or *labor* who carry out the work of transforming resources. Although as individuals they may exercise relatively little power, collectively workers are often able to acquire considerable power by engaging in or threatening strikes, slowdowns, or sabotage and expressing their demands through collective bargaining or other forms of negotiation. And, as noted in Chapter 8, the higher the specificity of worker skills in a particular organization, the more power workers will enjoy.

Finally, power accrues to those who occupy critical *boundary roles* in the organization. Individuals and work groups that connect with important resource suppliers, mediate the demands of critical regulatory agencies, or embody the concerns of institutional actors obtain power within the organizations they serve.

Hickson and colleagues (1971) have proposed a useful set of dimensions for explaining power in organizations. Like the resource dependency theorists, they build on Emerson's (1962) formulation of power-dependency relations, but rather than applying these ideas to interorganizational relations, they focus on explaining the distribution of power within organizations a strategic contingency approach.

Hickson and associates offer three general propositions relating to the acquisition of intraorganizational power. First, building on the insights of Crozier, they propose that subunits that cope more effectively with uncertainty are more likely to acquire power. The source of uncertainty may vary from technical to environmental disturbances. Crozier (1964), in an intensive case study of the French tobacco manufacturing industry, observed that mechanics held considerable power—much more than their formal position in the organization would suggest—because they were capable of dealing with machine breakdowns, the major source of uncertainty in the highly mechanized plants. The importance of environmental uncertainty for internal power is further illustrated by Goldner's study of the industrial relations (IR) unit in a manufacturing organization. Goldner writes that

---

[1]See Chapter 12 for a discussion of the same process in public bureaucracies: the power of administrative officials grows to challenge that of the political rulers.

the major source of IR's power over specific plant-level issues was . . . the use of the union as an outside threat. Recognition that their nominal antagonists were the source of their internal power was even made explicit by one IR manager: "As I told one of the (other IR) guys who was damning the unions—Don't bite the hand that feeds you." (Goldner, 1970: 104–5)

Uncertainty is not a constant but is subject to change over time. For example, improvements in technology can lead to increased routinization of work and hence, to reductions in uncertainty. Thus, in the corporation studies by Goldner,

> the dominant theme in the recent history of the operations unit has been its steady loss of power, which had accompanied the increased rationalization of the organization. Those in operations were subject to the effect or more extensive decision-making by others on matters that directly affected operations. They had lost autonomy and resented it. (1970: 109)

However, the main contribution of this first proposition by Hickson and colleagues is its insistence that it is not the presence of uncertainty alone but the *successful coping with uncertainty* that produces power for the subunit. Only if the subunit can effectively manage the uncertainty confronted, and in doing so protect the other units from its disturbing effects, can the subunit parlay uncertainty into power. In Goldner's example, for the IR unit to profit from the threat posed by the union, it had to be able to cope with that threat, thereby reducing uncertainty for the rest of the organization.

The second proposition is "the lower the *substitutability* of the activities of a subunit, the greater its power within the organization" (Hickson et al., 1971: 221). This prediction is a direct application of Emerson's principle that power is inversely affected by alternative sources. In operational terms, this variable can be measured by the extent to which an organization can obtain alternative services to those provided by the unit or by the extent to which the personnel within the unit are replaceable.

The third proposition relates to the *centrality* of the subunit, which is defined as having two components: pervasiveness—"the degree to which the workflows of a subunit connect with the workflows of other units"—and immediacy—"the speed and severity with which the workflows of a subunit affect the final outputs of the organization" (1971: 221–22). Hickson and colleagues predict that the higher the centrality—pervasiveness and immediacy—of the subunit, the greater its power.[2]

These researchers have tested these propositions in a study of four principal subunits—the engineering, marketing, production, and accounting departments—in each of seven small manufacturing organizations, or twenty-eight subunits in all (Hinings et al., 1974). A sample of organizations was selected so as to vary the uncertainty faced by the subunits, in particular, marketing. Independent variables were measured by scales

---

[2]Those interested in designing more egalitarian organizations must not only be attentive to the design of the formal authority system but must also guard against these sources of differential power. Among the techniques employed are task and worker rotation, demystification of expertise, and de-differentiation of work roles—attempts to insure that coping skills are shared, work is substitutable, and centrality is shared and thus neutralized. (See Rothschild-Whitt, 1979; Rothschild-Whitt and Whitt, 1986.)

based on both questionnaire and interview responses. The dependent variable, power, was measured in several ways: perceived influence attributed to the subunits over a variety of task areas; perceived formal authority over the same task areas; and reported participation in decision making. The several power indicators showed, in general, high and positive intercorrelations. Generally speaking, the data provided support for the three propositions. In terms of relative importance, coping with uncertainty was observed to have the greatest impact on power, followed, in order, by immediacy, nonsubstitutability, and pervasiveness.

But alongside these technical arguments, we need to add the institutionalist perspective. As Meyer (1978: 357) points out,

> organizations and their internal units derive legitimacy, power, and authority from their status in social environments. . . . the social validity of a given unit—a professional group, a technical procedure, or a departmentalized function—is often defined more importantly in the environment than by internal technical efficacy.

Such units have power—based on their external connections and supports—that is *independent* of their contributions to internal operations.

These various arguments suggest that as environmental conditions vary, we may expect power to shift within an organization from one group to another. Thus, Perrow's (1961) case study of a community hospital documents the gradual transition of power from the owners and trustees to the physicians, as a result of the increasing ability of the latter group to effectively cope with medical uncertainties presented by patients, and the more recent shift of power from the physicians to the professional administrators, as a result of the importance of internal coordination and external boundary mangement and the administrators' capacity to deal with these problems. Similarly, Fligstein (1986) has shown that as the environments confronting major corporations have changed over this century, the composition of the dominant coalition has also varied. Using as an indicator of power shifts the type of department from which the CEO is selected, Fligstein examined the departmental background of the top executive in his sample of 216 major corporations and observed how this background changed between 1919 and 1979. He reports that whereas entrepreneurs—the founders and builders of corporations—dominated during the period 1880–1920, CEOs tended to be selected from manufacturing departments between 1920 and 1940, from sales departments between 1940 to 1960, and from finance departments from 1960 into the 1980s. He argues that these shifts mirror the changing challenges confronting corporations: production problems dominated in the 1920s and 1930s, distributional problems in the 1940s and 1950s, and capital problems from the 1960s to the present.

The number of potential power holders and the various sources of power help to explain why the size of the dominant coalition has increased in most organizations in recent years. Rather than highly centralized hierarchies in which one or a few persons exercise most of the power and make most of the decisions, most contemporary organizations exhibit power and decision-making structures that include a substantial number of individuals. Galbraith (1967) argues that one of the most fundamental changes in the organization of the modern corporation is a shift from an entrepreneurial mode in which a single powerful person dominates the enterprise to a *technostructure* in which power is widely diffused. According to Galbraith (1967: 58), the technostructure consists of

> men of diverse technical knowledge, experience or other talent which modern industrial technology and planning require. It extends from the leadership of the modern industrial enterprise down to just short of the labor force and embraces a large number of people and a large variety of talent. [It constitutes the] new locus of power in the business enterprise and in the society.

More so that Galbraith, Thompson (1967: 127–36) makes clear the reason for the increasing size of the organization's power structure. Consistent with the views of Crozier and Hickson, Thompson argues that the number of positions of power within the organization and hence the size of the dominant coalition, is affected both by the nature of the organization's technology and by its task and institutional environments. The more uncertain the technology and the greater the number of sources of uncertainty in the organization's environment, the more bases for power there are within the organization and the larger will be the dominant coalition. When organizations embrace more uncertain technologies, as in the case of professional organizations, and when the sources of uncertainty increase in the environment of the organization, we may expect those who cope with these problems to demand and receive a place in the decision-making councils of the organization.

What difference, if any, does it make when power shifts from one group to another or is shared with a larger proportion of the participants? The difference should be reflected, of course, in the goals pursued by the organization. Admission to the dominant coalition is an empty victory if the new partners cannot affect the definition of the goals to be served. And, on the basis of his case study of the community hospital, Perrow (1961) asserts that as doctors replaced trustees, hospital goals shifted from community welfare concerns to business-professional objectives, including research; and as the administrators gained dominance over the physicians, the hospital's goals shifted to emphasize the role of the hospital as the medical center for the community. And in the case of the coalitions of interests present in the modern corporation, Galbraith argues that although the stockholders must receive their side payment of a satisfactory return on their investment, the maximization of profits associated with the entrepreneurial regime has given way to a new goal prefered by the now-dominant coalition of technical and managerial specialists: "the greatest possible rate of corporate growth as measured in sales." This goal is valued by the technostructure because "expansion of output means expansion of the technosctucture itself . . . including more jobs with more responsibility and hence more promotion and more compensation" (1967: 171).

Similarly, Fligstein (1985a; 1985b) asserts that associated with changes in the origins of the types of persons assuming command within the corporations are basic changes in the goals of these organizations—the types of strategies being pursued. Founding entrepreneurs pursued strategies of horizontal merger in attempting to control the market. As the scale of production increased, coordination and resource problems came to the fore and manufacturing officials became dominant, pursuing strategies of vertical integration. Functional (unitary) forms were constructed to support these strategies.

> Once production is routinized, power shifts to sales and marketing personnel as the key issue for the organization becomes growth.... A sales and marketing strategy focuses on attempting to broaden the firm's markets by expanding across regions and countries. (Fligstein, 1985a: 380)

This strategy is supported by the creation of multi-divisional forms to support production and product-related distribution systems. Finally, governmental actions in the 1950s designed to prevent further concentration forced the development of alternate strategies: corporations were forced to abandon their attempt to increase their market share and began to pursue growth through multiple, unrelated product lines. Financial experts were in the best position to devise these strategies, and the conglomerate form was best suited to their support.

Environmental changes, shifting power-dependency relations, changing goals and strategies, and new structural forms—while the temporal sequence and the causal ordering of these elements are not clear, and will often be difficult to establish, it does appear that there are strong interdependencies among them.

In more differentiated and loosely coupled systems such as universities, power differences among subunits may be reflected not so much in direct attempts to redefine the goals of the larger system but in efforts to lay claim to a disproportionate share of the organization's resources. This process is well illustrated in a study by Pfeffer and Salanick (1974) of the allocation of general university resources among twenty-nine academic departments examined over a thirteen-year period. These researchers convincingly show that the greater power of individual departments, as measured by indicators such as perceived influence and representation on powerful university committees, the greater the proportion of general university funds they received. Although such budgetary decisions may appear remote from the general goals of the university, they are in reality highly relevant: the allocation of scarce resources among diverse university programs is one of the clearest indicators available of the "real" goals of the institution.

Anarchies and Adhocracies

Both the bureaucratic-administrative model of the rational system perspective and the coalitional-bargaining model of the natural and open system perspectives provide for the development of a set of goals by which organizational decisions can be made. Both allow for the construction of relatively clear criteria or preference orderings in terms of which priorities can be set and selections made among alternative courses of action. But there are classes of organizations—and, more important, classes of decision situations within many organizations—in which no clear preference orderings have been determined. Such organizations are on the fringe if not beyond the pale of those collectivities included within the conventional definitions and theories of organizations (see Chapter 1). Yet they present both interesting and instructive cases.

Thompson and Tuden (1959) focus on these situations by constructing a typology that combines two dimensions: (1) how much agreement there is among participants of the organization about the goals or preferred outcomes of the system, and (2) how much agreement there is about the means or the casual processes by which these outcomes can be realized. The cross-classification of this simple ends-and-means distinction produces four types of decision contexts, each of which is argued to be associated with a different decision strategy:

BELIEFS ABOUT CAUSATION	PREFERENCES ABOUT OUTCOMES	
	Agreement	Disagreement
Agreement	*Computation*	*Compromise*
Disagreement	*Judgment*	*Inspiration*

We are most interested in the right-hand column—situations in which participants lack consensus on goals—but let us briefly comment on the simpler and more familiar situations in which such agreement is present. Thompson and Tuden use the term *computation* to denote those decisions most suited to the typical bureaucratic decision-making structure, which, as we have often noted, is most appropriate in situations in which goals are clearly defined and the technology relatively certain. The term *judgment* is employed to refer to the strategies required when agreement on goals exists but the means of achieving them is uncertain. This situation is best confronted with a collegium and is well illustrated, in our opinion, by the structure of professional organizations previously described.

As for the column of interest, Thompson and Tuden argue that there are sometimes situations in which participants agree about how to accomplish some objective or about what the expected consequences of available alternatives are, but disagree over which alternative is preferable. A mild version of this situation is provided by the coalitional view of decision making—which, as we have described, is resolved by negotiation, bargaining, and sequential attention to goals. More extreme instances of disagreement and conflict can sometimes be resolved through the creation of representative bodies that allow for the expression of differences and the engineering of compromises. Most such forums—for example, the United Nations and the United States Congress—presume the existence of substantive differences in preferences but rely on procedural agreements—such as Robert's Rules of Order—for resolving them.

The fourth and final decision situation is characterized by the absence of agreement about either ends or means. Thompson and Tuden suggest that these anomic situations are more commonly found among organizations than conventional theories suggest. They propose that such circumstances, if they are not to be followed by complete system disintegration, call for *inspiration,* perhaps of the type suggested by Weber's (1947 trans.) description of the charismatic leader. This is not inconsistent with Weber's own views, described in Chapter 2, in which charismatic leaders are viewed as more likely to emerge in crisis situations—times when conventional goals are being challenged and established procedures are not working. And, like Weber, Thompson and Tuden expect such leadership to give rise over time to a computational (bureaucratic) structure based on a new definition of goals and accepted procedures, as charisma is routinized.

March and his colleagues (March and Olsen, 1976; Cohen, March, and Olsen, 1972, 1976; Cohen and March, 1976; March, 1978) have also examined decision making under conditions of "inconsistent and ill-defined preferences," "unclear technologies," and "fluid participation"— the shifting involvement of members in decision situations (Cohen, March, and Olsen, 1972: 1). They label these conditions *organized anarchies*. But unlike Thompson and Tuden, March and associates do not view these circumstances as crises or as transitory states. Rather, they insist that they have been "identified often in studies of organizations," "are characteristic of any organization in part," and "are particularly conspicuous in public, educational, and illegitimate organizations" (Cohen, March, and Olsen, 1976: 25).

The portrait of organized anarchies is set within a more general framework that stresses the ambiguity in decision making. (See Chapter 5) March and Olsen comment on their approach:

> We remain in the tradition of viewing organizational participants as problem-solvers and decision-makers. However, we assume that individuals find themselves in a more complex, less stable, and less understood world than that described by standard theories of organizational choice; they are placed in a world over which they often have only modest control. (March and Olsen, 1976: 21)

The organizational world depicted here is similar to that described by Weick (1969; see also Chapter 4): individual decision makers have cognitive and attention limits; external conditions constrain alternatives and affect outcomes but often go unnoticed; and choices by individuals in decision-making positions may not eventuate in organizational action. Under such conditions, all choices are somewhat ambiguous.

> Although organizations can often be viewed conveniently as vehicles for solving well-defined problems or structures within which conflict is resolved through bargaining, they also provide sets of procedures through which participants arrive at an interpretation of what they are doing and what they have done while in the process of doing it. From this point of view, an organization is a collection of choices looking for problems, issues and feelings looking for decision situations in which they might be aired, solutions looking for issues to which they might be the answer, and decision makers looking for work. (Cohen, March, and Olsen, 1972: 2)

Under conditions of organized anarchy, the ambiguity of choice present in all decision-making situations reaches its apex. Here problems, solutions, participants, and choice opportunities are viewed as flows that more relatively independently into and out of the decision arena—metaphorically labeled a "garbage can." Which solutions get attached to which problems is largely determined by chance—by what participants with what goals happened to be on the scene, by when the solutions or the problems entered, and so on. Although the system described seems bizarre and even pathological when compared with the conventional model of rational decision making, it does produce decisions under conditions of high uncertainty: that is, some solutions do get attached by some participants to some problems.

Cohen, March, and Olsen (1972) have developed and examined some of the implications of their garbage-can model under varying assumptions by using computer-simulation techniques. However, this model of decision making was originally suggested to them on the basis of observations of decision-making processes in colleges and universities:

> Opportunities for choice in higher education can easily become complex "garbage cans" into which a striking variety of problems, solutions, and participants may be dumped. Debate over the hiring of a football coach can become connected to concerns about the essence of a liberal education, the relations of the school to ethnic minorities, or the philosophy of talent. (Cohen and March, 1976: 175)

Perhaps it is due specifically to the characteristics of universities, or perhaps they intend their comments to apply more generally to all organized anarchies, but unlike Thompson and Tuden, Cohen and March (1974: 1976) do not look for a charismatic leader to ride in on horseback bringing inspiration for new goals. They perceive the role of leaders—for example, university presidents—in such situations in much more problematic and pessimistic terms. They do suggest that leaders can improve their performance if they take into account the unusual nature of decision-making situations in these organizations. By carefully timing issue creation, by being sensitive to shifting interests and involvement of participants, by recognizing the status and power implications of choice situations, by abandoning initiatives that have become hopelessly entangled with other, originally unrelated problems, by realizing that the planning function is largely symbolic and chiefly provides excuses for interaction, leaders in organized anarchies can maintain their sanity and, sometimes, make a difference in the decision made.

One major factor often accounting for the absence of clearly specified goals is the unstable nature of some organizational environments. If environments are turbulent, then it is difficult to establish clear and specific objectives around which to design a structure and orient participant activities. Under unsettled conditions, tents may be preferable to palaces:

> In constant surroundings, one could confidently assemble an intricate, rigid structure combining elegant and refined components—an organizational palace. . . .
> However, systematic procedures offer weak protection against unpredictability, just as increased rigidity does not effectively prepare a building for earthquakes. Some flaws of systematic procedures are inherent in the concept of strategic planning: drafting plans, dismantling an old structure, and erecting a new structure take so long that designers need to forecast how the environment will shift. Since forecasts are only conjectures derived from past experiences, greater reliance on forecasts induces greater design errors. Systematic procedures also sap an organization's flexibility by strengthening its rationality.

... Residents of changing environments need a tent. An organizational tent placed greater emphasis on flexibility, creativity, immediacy, and initiative than on authority, clarity, decisiveness, or responsiveness; and an organizational tent neither asks for harmony between the activities of different organizational components, nor asks that today's behavior resemble yesterday's or tomorrow's. Why behave more consistently than one's world does? (Hedberg, Nystrom, and Starbuck, 1976: 44–45)

Unstable environments undermine clear and consistent goals, just as they unsettle rigid formalized structures. (See Chapter 9.)

Still, some elements of consistency can be found in the goal structures of organizations operating under unstable conditions. If, following Mintzberg and McHugh (1985), strategies are defined as "a pattern in a stream of decisions or actions," then it may be possible to retrospectively identify underlying motifs. Not all intended strategies are realized, and those that are realized may be emergent rather than deliberate. In their case study of the National Film Board (NFB) of Canada from its inception in 1939, Mintzberg and McHugh were able to discern a number of patterns in its products and approach that although unplanned, nevertheless provided a fabric with discernible designs. The film makers provided the warp, but the environment furnished the woof.

... the NFB had an ironic relationship with its environment. In one sense, it was highly responsive—to social trends, new fashions, new media, social turmoil. Ultimately, the NFB found its purpose—when it did—in the world around it, not in itself: it truly was a mirror for its society. ... Yet in another sense, this was truly an organization that "did its own thing." Except during the war years, the NFB as a whole catered largely to its own needs, for the most part selecting those parts of the environment to which it cared to respond. ...

The essence of adhocracy, in contrast to machine bureaucracies that seek to control their environments in order to support their standardized systems of mass production, would seem to be rapid and continuous responsiveness to the environment, with minimal organizational momentum. (Mintzberg and McHugh, 1985: 191)

Organizations such as the NFB that rely less on long-term strategic planning and more on ad hoc, emergent strategies may also be said to replace coventional rational decision-making techniques with *experiential learning*. (See Hedberg, 1981; March, 1981.) Whereas rational system models assume that goals are stable, learning modes assume that they are subject to change, that many choices are not guided by preestablished intentions but result in the discovery of new purposes. And whereas rational systems models propose that technologies are known, learning models stress that they must be continuously invented, shaped, and modified in the light of feedback from the environment. Learning approaches embrace the open system conception of organizations:

Learning in open, cognitive systems takes the form of positive feedback which changes the systems or their knowledge, whereas learning in closed, natural systems is the function of negative feedback which aims at maintaining the genotype unchanged (Hedberg, 1981: 5).

Learning that "changes the system," that results not simply in new decisions but in new rules and methods for deciding, is what Argyris and

Schon (1978) term *double-loop learning*. It requires the "unlearning" of the old ways as well as the acquisition of new ones.

It should be clear, however, that we should not underestimate how difficult it is for organizational systems to learn anything useful, given a rapidly changing environment, selective attention and inattention processes, enactment processes, inertia, cognitive limits, and ambiguity of feedback.

CONTROL SYSTEMS

It is one thing to set goals; it is another to see that energies are directed toward their accomplishment. To this end, control must be exercised. Of course, all collectivities control their members. As we have previously argued in defining them, if collectivities do not show evidence of a distinctive normative structure and some regular patterns of participant behavior, we cannot even establish their existence. But, as Etzioni has argued, the problems of control in organizations are especially acute:

> The artificial quality of organizations, their high concern with performance, their tendency to be far more complex than natural units, all make informal control inadequate and reliance on identification with the job impossible. Most organizations most of the time cannot rely on most of their participants to internalize their obligations to carry out their assignments voluntarily, without additional incentives. Hence, organizations require formally structured distribution of rewards and sanctions to support compliance with their norms, regulations, and orders. (Etzioni, 1964: 59)

Perhaps this explains why so many of the topics discussed in connection with organizations relate more or less directly to the subject of control. Consider the following list: administration, authority, automation, boundaries, bureaucratization, centralization, contracts, coordination, decision premises, discipline, evaluation, formalization, hierarchy, incentives, integration, internalization, performance programs, power, procedures, routinization, rules, sanctions, socialization, supervision—these are some of the specific manifestations and instruments of control.

We begin this section by discussing the interpersonal control system— the structure of power and authority in organizations. Then we consider how these arrangements are supplemented and, in some measure, replaced by various impersonal control mechanisms. Finally, we discuss culture as a mode of control prevalent in some types of organizations.

Power

A great many pages have been filled with discussions of power, and many definitions of this important concept have been proposed (see Cartwright, 1965; Schopler, 1965). One of the simplest and most satisfactory approaches to this topic is that of Emerson (1962: 32):

> It would appear that the power to control or influence the other resides in control over the things he values, which may range all the way from oil

resources to ego-support, depending upon the relation in question. In short, power resides implicitly in the other's dependency.[3]

Emerson views power as relational, situational, and at least potentially reciprocal. Thus, his approach emphasizes that power is to be viewed not as a characteristic of an individual but rather as a property of a social relation. To say that a given person has power is meaningless unless we specify over whom he or she has power. We must take into account the characteristics of both the superordinate and the subordinate individual in describing a power relation. The power of superordinates is based on their ability and willingness to sanction others—to provide or withhold rewards and penalties—but we must recognize that what constitutes a reward or a penalty is ultimately determined by the goals or values of subordinates in the relation. To use two extreme examples, a gunman has no power over the individual who does not value his or her life, nor does a person with money have power over another who does not value money or the things it will buy. Emerson's formulation also provides a means of determining the degree of power in a relation: recall his suggestion that A's power over B is (1) directly proportional to the importance B places on the goals mediated by A, and (2) inversely proportional to the availability of these goals to B outside the A–B relation (1962: 32).

It is consistent with this approach that power can have many bases. An individual's power is based on all the resources—money, skills, knowledge, strength, sex appeal—that he or she can employ to help or hinder another in the attainment of desired goals. What types of resources will function as sanctions will vary from one individual to another and from situation to situation. Thus, if workers in an office value the quality of their technical decisions, then expertise becomes an important resource that can be used as a sanction by them (see Blau, 1955); if boys at a camp prefer to avoid black eyes and to be on winning teams, then such characteristics as strength and athletic prowess will become important bases of power for them (see Lippitt et al., 1953).

Emerson's formulation also allows for the possibility of mutual dependency. Power relations can be reciprocal: one individual may hold resources of importance to another in one area but be dependent on the same person because of resources held by the latter in a different area. And just as the degree of individual dependence may vary by situation, so may the degree of mutual dependence, or interdependence.

We will define interpersonal *power* as the potential for influence that is based on one person's ability and willingness to sanction another person by manipulating rewards and punishments important to the other person. That is, power has its origin in the dependency of one person on resources controlled by another, but power itself is best defined as a potential for influence. We turn now to discuss briefly the emergence of power structures in informal and formal systems.

---

[3]An important advantage to this approach is that it is applicable to relations among varying types of units: individuals, groups, organizations. Here we apply the conception to relations among individuals; in Chapter 8, we used it to examine power relations among organizations.

Power in informal groups   During the late 1950s a large number of studies examined the operation of power in informal groups and, in particular, the emergence of power differences in previously undifferentiated task groups. The emergence of power was examined in field studies (Lippitt et al., 1953; Sherif and Sherif, 1953) as well as in the laboratory (Bales, 1952; Bales and Slater, 1955). These studies describe the way in which certain personal qualities that differ among members become the basis for differences in sanctioning ability. As analyzed by Homans (1961) and Blau (1964), the process of differentiation occurs through a series of exchanges among group participants. Over time, some members emerge who are both more willing and more able to make important contributions to goal attainment, whether to the goals of individual members of to those of the group as a whole: they can manipulate sanctions of importance to others. As Blau notes, "a person who commands services others need, and who is independent of any at their command, attains power over others by making the satisfaction of their need contingent on their compliance" (1964: 22). Both Blau and Homans see the origin of power structures as a product of unequal exchange relations that occur when some individuals become increasingly dependent on others for services required in reaching their objectives. A person lacking resources to repay the other for these services, who is unwilling to forgo them and unable to find them in other relations, has but one alternative: "he must subordinate himself to the other and comply with his wishes, thereby rewarding the other with power over himself as an inducement for furnishing the needed help" (Blau, 1964: 21–22). In this manner, exchange processes that involve asymmetries give rise to a differentiated power structure.

Power in formal organizations   Power in informal groups is based on the characteristics of individuals—individual differences that can function as resources allowing some to reward and punish others. It is the differential distribution and use of such characteristics or resources that give rise in informal groups to a power structure. By contrast, power in formal organizations is determined at least in part by design. Most organizations are designed in such a manner that a hierarchy of positions is created: one position is defined as controlling another. A supervisory position, for example, is defined as being more powerful than that of a worker, and in accordance with this definition, sanctioning powers are attached to the position. Thus, supervisors may be allowed to evaluate the work of their subordinates, determining by these evaluations who receives what rate of pay and who is to be recommended for promotion. Such powers are attached to the position: they are available to any individual who occupies it, regardless of his or her personal qualities.

Rational system theorists emphasize the importance of formal power structures in the functioning of organizations. They argue that it is possible to design power structures in such a manner that sanctioning power may be made commensurate with responsibilities and distributed so as to facilitate the organization's requirements for coordination and control of participants' contributions. They also note that although the theoretical range of subordinates' values and, hence, of power bases is quite broad, the actual range is quite narrow: certain values are widely shared, so that it is possible to identify resources, such as money and status, that will function as sanctions for most participants most of the time. They further note the quite palpable advantages associated with the formalization process itself, which results in the "domestication" of power. Thus, tensions associated with the generation of power differences are avoided; the organization is freed from the necessity of finding "superior" individuals to fill superior positions; and power is more readily transferred from one person to another as position occupants come and go (see Chapter 2). Formalization is one of the important ways in which the "personal" element is removed from interpersonal control systems.

Natural systems theorists insist, on the other hand, that no organization ever succeeds in completely controlling all sources of power or in rationally allocating power among its positions. There are two reasons for this. First, we come again to the chief thesis of the natural system perspective: positions are filled by persons, and persons possess diverse and variable characteristics, some of which may become the basis for informal power differences in formal organizations. Differences among individuals in intelligence, motivation, training, skills, attractiveness, and other respects can serve as resources that sometimes supplement and sometimes contradict and erode the formal distribution of power. Second, in the organization's allocation of resources to positions, some participants inevitably obtain access to resources that can be used in ways not intended by the organizational designers. For example, access to information is an important resource that can become the basis for sanctioning and controlling others. A position such as secretary can make its occupants privy to sensitive information that they can use to enhance their own power and influence (see Mechanic, 1962). And, as we have learned from Hickson and associates (1971), a strategic location in the structure—a high degree of uncertainty confronted or the centrality of the work performed—can be an important, unanticipated source of sanctioning ability and hence of influence.

Research by Tannenbaum and associates (Tannenbaum, 1968; Tannenbaum et al., 1974) supplies evidence for the general expectation that amount of control or influence is positively associated with position in the formal hierarchy. If individuals are asked to describe how much influence is associated with each type of position in the organization, then it is possible to construct a "control graph" that depicts how centralized or decentralized is the distribution of power in the organization. The centralization of power varies from organization to organization, largely as a function of differences in ideology or goals that directly affect the formal definitions of how power is to be distributed: for example, power was more evenly distributed in the League of Women Voters, a voluntary agency emphasizing member participation, and in Yugoslavian companies emphasizing worker participation than in more traditional United States business and industrial concerns. (However, as Tannenbaum emphasizes, power was somewhat centralized in all of these organizations, ideology and preferences notwithstanding.) Of more interest is Tannenbaum's demonstration that aside from its distribution, the *total amount* of control exercised varies from one organization to another. That is, in some organizations none of the positions is perceived as exercising very much influence over others, whereas in other organizations all of the positions are seen to exercise considerable power. This finding underlines our earlier point that organizations may be expected to vary in the amount of mutual dependence or interdependence they display.

Authority

Weber has pointed out that in his experience no organization

> voluntarily limits itself to the appeal to material or affectual motives as a basis for guaranteeing its continuance. In addition, every such system attempts to establish and to cultivate the belief in its "legitimacy" (Weber, 1947 trans.: 325)

In other words, no organization is likely to be content with establishing a power structure; in addition, it will attempt to create an authority structure. Most social scientists define authority as legitimate power. *Legitimacy* is the property of a situation or behavior that is defined by a set of social norms as correct or appropriate. Thus, to speak of legitimate power is to indicate (1) a set of persons or positions linked by power relations and (2) a set of norms or rules governing the distribution and exercise of power and the response to it.

In the case of informal groups, we refer to the exercise of power as legitimate to the extent that there emerges a set of norms and beliefs among the members subordinate to the power wielder that the distribution and exercise of power is acceptable to them and is regarded as appropriate. The emergence of such norms significantly alters the control structure, as Blau and I have argued:

> Given the development of social norms that certain orders of superiors ought to be obeyed, the members of the group will enforce compliance with these orders as part of their enforcement of conformity to group norms. The group's demand that orders of the superior be obeyed makes obedience partly independent of his coercive power or persuasive influence over individual subordinates and thus transforms these other kinds of social control into authority. (Blau and Scott, 1962: 29)

In sum, a set of dyadic power relations between the superior and each subordinate is transformed by the emergence of legitimacy norms into a multiperson control structure in which each subordinate now participates in the control of each of his or her colleagues. Peer-group controls are harnessed in the support of the power structure. Another way of describing these important developments is to say that a stable role structure has emerged that guides the expectations of participants, making it possible for a leader to lead and for followers to follow without the generation of disruptive emotional responses. Further, the emergence of legitimacy norms helps to render power relations more impersonal and reduces the tensions associated with the exercise of interpersonal power. As Thibaut and Kelley (1959: 129) suggest, in an authority structure, in contrast with a power structure,

> nonadherence is met with the use of power to attempt to produce conformity, but the influence appeal is to a supra-individual value ("Do it for the group" or "Do it because it's good") rather than to personal interests ("Do it for me" or "Do it and I'll do something for you").

For all of these reasons—involvement of subordinate participants in the control system, development of differentiated expectations among participants, depersonalization of power processes with consequent reduction of interpersonal tensions—authority structures tend to be much more stable and effective control systems than power structures. Like formalization, authority helps to clothe personal power in impersonal garb.

There is, however, another equally important consequence of the legitimation process. The emergence of social norms not only allows a greater measure of control of subordinates by the power wielder but also regulates and circumscribes his or her exercise of power. Emerson (1962) points out that the emergence of legitimacy norms among subordinates allows them to act as a coalition vis-à-vis the power wielder, defining the arena within which he or she can appropriately exercise power. Subordinates are individually weaker but collectively stronger than the superior, allowing them to place some limits on his or her power. Legitimacy norms specify the orders to which subordinates are expected to comply—and hence support the exercise of power—but also identify demands that the power wielder cannot appropriately make of subordinates—and hence limit the exercise of power. In sum, legitimacy norms cut both ways: they permit greater and more reliable control of subordinates within certain limits defined as appropriate areas of control—Barnard (1938) referred to these areas as the "zone of indifference"—and they restrict the exercise of power to these areas. We conclude that *authority is legitimate power* and that *legitimate power is normatively regulated power*.

Two types of authority: endorsed and authorized power   Dornbusch and I (Dornusch and Scott, 1975) have raised a question that has not been explicitly asked by previous students of authority. Having determined that social norms that regulate power relations provide the basis for legitimate control structures, we sought to determine who—what group of participants—defines and enforces these norms. In most informal groups, there is only one possible source: the set of participants who are subject to the exercise of power and hence are subordinates of the power wielder. We have noted how, by acting as a coalition, this subordinate group can limit and regulate the exercise of power over them by a superordinate. We label this type of situation *endorsed power*, or authority by endorsement. A number of theorists—in particular, Barnard (1938)—view the enforcement of norms by subordinates, or endorsement, as the basic mechanism underlying authority in formal organizations. While we do not deny this process operates in organizations, in our opinion it is secondary to another process.

An important characteristic of formal organizations is the presence of persons superordinate to as well as persons subordinate to a given power wielder. Most hierarchies are multi-level, so that norms may be developed and enforced by persons superior to the power wielder. Indeed, this is one of the primary features of hierarchy of offices. As Weber states,

> the principles of office hierarchy and of levels of graded authority mean a firmly ordered system of super- and subordination in which there is a supervision of the lower offices by the higher ones (Weber, 1946 trans.: 197).

A familiar safeguard built into most hierarchies is the principle of appeal, by which subordinates who feel that their immediate superior is making unfair or unreasonable demands on them, may turn to their superior's boss with the expectation that he or she will enforce authority norms that curb the superior's power. We label a situation in which power is regulated by those superior to the power wielder *authorized power,* or authority by authorization.[4]

For authorization to operate as a source of normative control, there must be a level of the hierarchy above that of the person or position whose exercise of power is at issue. What happens at the very top of the hierarchy, where there is no superordinate level to regulate the exercise of power? In the usual case, as Parsons (1960) has pointed out, the managerial hierarchy ends with its top position being responsible to a different type of office: the institutional level, exemplified by the board of directors or board of trustees. These offices are defined as being legitimated by—normatively regulated by—some different, nonhierarchical principle. Often, they are legitimated by some type of electoral process (for example, election of officers by stockholders), or officers are appointed to represent the interests of the ultimate beneficiaries—for example, the owners or the citizenry.

It is important to emphasize that a principle function of the institutional level—one noted serveral times throughout this volume—is to secure the legitimation of the organization's hierarchy. This is accomplished by linking the norms and values supporting the hierarchy to broader institutionalized normative systems, demonstrating their congruence and consistency. Weber's famous typology of authority systems, described in Chapter 2, is based on differences in the types of norms that legitimate power systems. Recall that he distinguished between traditional, charismatic, and bureaucratic systems, each of which justifies and regulates an existing structure of power on a different basis. Both Weber (1947 trans.) and Bendix (1956) have examined how these broadly accepted normative beliefs change over time, causing and reflecting changes in power arrangements within specific administrative systems. For example, the legitimacy of the nation-state is no longer likely to be justified by the doctrine of the divine right of kings, but is instead supported by beliefs in its consistency with constitutional documents or the "people's will." Similarly, the authority systems of more limited organizations are justified by beliefs in property rights, or procedural correctness, or the legitimacy of specialized expertise.

Returning to our basic distinction, it is possible for some control attempts to be authorized—that is, supported by superiors of the power wielder—but not endorsed—that is, not supported by subordinates of the power wielder—or vice versa. It is also possible for control attempts to be both authorized and endorsed. An instance of the first type would be the authority exercised by a police officer in an urban neighborhood whose residents are suspicious or hostile toward police activities; the second type is illustrated by the authority exercised by an informal leader in a work

---

[4]Another possible source of the creation and enforcement of norms in organizations is the colleagues or equals of the power wielder—those occupying the same formal position in the organization. This source may be expected to be of particular importance in professional organizations, and is labeled *collegial power.*

group. The third type—authority that is both authorized and endorsed—is represented by an individual serving as a supervisor who is also a natural leader. Authority that is both authorized and endorsed may be said to enjoy greater legitimacy and may be expected to be more effective and more stable than that which receives support from only one source (Dornbusch and Scott, 1975: 56–64).[5]

We do not equate formal with authorized and informal with endorsed power systems: these pairs of concepts are analytically distinct. However, we would expect them to be empirically associated. Consider the relation between authorized and formal power. Managers attempting to regulate the control attempts of the supervisors under their charge are more likely to attempt to treat them equally—to emphasize the power of position rather than the power of person—partly because of equity and precedent and partly because the possibility of turnover in personnel is always present. By contrast, subordinates typically relate to only a single superior and are likely to have some difficulty in separating personal from official characteristics. If comparisons are made, they are more likely to focus on those features that differentiate their own supervisor from others of whom they have knowledge. For these reasons, informal power is likely to be associated with endorsed power. It is striking that virtually all of the empirical studies of supervision and control in organizations tend to focus on informal and endorsed power, often termed *leadership,* to the neglect of formal and authorized systems of control.[6]

Structural Control

Authority and power are usually regarded as personal or interpersonal control systems, but as we have noted, in moving from informal to formalized power and from power to authority, we introduce more impersonal supports. Formal power is attached to positions rather than persons, and authority is power justified—authorized or endorsed—by normative beliefs.

As Edwards (1979) has pointed out, simple and more personal power systems tend to give way over time to more complex and impersonal forms—to technical and bureaucratic structures. (See Chapter 8.) Controls are built into technical production systems in the form of machine pacing or, in the case of continuous-flow systems, in the layout and speed of the assembly line. These "built-in" controls reduce the need for personal direction and in this manner change the role of supervisors from overseer to troubleshooter. (See Walker and Guest, 1952; Blau and Scott, 1962: 176–83.) Similar functions are performed by statistical records of performance and increased automation for white-collar work. (See Blau, 1955; Whisler, 1970.) Even more elaborate and less visible controls are embedded in the organization structure itself—in the layout of offices,

[5]The distinction between authorization and endorsement and their contribution to stabilizing authority systems have been pursued in experimental research. (See Zelditch and Walker, 1984.)

[6]The manner in which authority rights are linked to evaluation processes to provide a basis for the control of task performances in organizations is described at length in Dornbusch and Scott (1975) and is summarized in the first edition of this text. (See Scott, 1981: 283–86)

functions, rules, and policies. Edwards (1979: 145–46) emphasizes that the force of these bureaucratic arrangements resides in their seemingly impersonal character.

> Above all else, bureaucratic control institutionalized the exercise of capitalist power, making power appear to emanate from the formal organization itself. Hierarchical relations were transformed from relations between (unequally powerful) people to relations between jobholders or relations between jobs themselves, abstracted from the specific people or the concrete work tasks involved. "Rule of law"—the firm's law—replaced rule by supervisor command. And indeed, the replacement was not illusory. To the extent that firms were successful in imposing bureaucratic control, the method, extent, and intensity of sanctions imposed on recalcitrant workers were specified by organizational rules. . . .
>
> By establishing the overall structure, management retained control of the enterprise's operations. Once the goals and structure had been established, the system could operate under its own steam. . . . the ability to establish rules provided the capitalist with the power to determine the terrain, to set the basic conditions around which the struggle [with workers] was to be fought. . . . The capitalist's power was effectively embedded in the firm's organization.

Technical and bureaucratic control structures thus represent important instances of *structural controls*. Differences in power are built into the definition of relations among positions, and these power differences are normatively justified. There are two major advantages to power wielders in gaining structural control. The first is that one's power advantages are partially concealed: all participants—both those with greater power and those with lesser power—appear to be commonly subordinated to a normative framework exercising control over all. The second advantage is that those with structural power do not need to mobilize in order to have their interests taken into account. It is automatically assumed that they are "entitled" to be represented in any matter affecting their interests. By contrast, interests that are not structured have to become mobilized if they are to be heard. (See Alford, 1975.) It is in this sense that power can function less as a "wild card" and more like a "trump suit" in the game of politics within organizations. (See Heilbroner, 1980: 146.)

But it is not only capitalists whose power is coded into structural arrangements. As labor's power has increased and as unions have been organized and recognized as legitimate bargaining agents, worker interests have received structural support. More generally, as Selznick (1969) has argued, participants in organizations increasingly enjoy generalized legal supports as "citizenship" rights are coded into the unwritten constitutions of "private governments"—that is, private organizations and associations. As organizations become larger and more powerful, and as their effects on individual participants—on their security, income, and life chances—becomes more potent, the protection of individual rights becomes a matter of public concern. Various due-process protections— the right to a review of decisions, to access to records, to hearings and appeals—are increasingly made available to individual participants of organizations, and are supported by the power of larger political and legal institutions. Such structural protections have spread widely across many types of organizations in recent decades. (See Dobbin et al., in press.)

Culture

Some types of organizations, as described in Chapter 9, rely primarily on internalized controls. Although a formal control structure is in place and there are expectations that rewards will be distributed according to performance, the organization relies primarily on an informal structure and on individual participants' embracing of common norms and values that can orient and govern their contributions. These types of controls are described as denoting an organizational culture. Pointing to culture as the basis of control should come as no surprise, since anthropologists have long believed most of the orderliness and patterning found in social life is accounted for by cultural systems, but such views have only recently been widely employed by students of organizations.

Smircich (1983: 339) points out that the concept of culture is used in two quite different ways by organizational analysts: "as a critical variable and as a root metaphor." In the first usage, culture is something that an organization *has*. Employed in this manner,

> the term "culture" describes an attribute or quality internal to a group. We refer to an organizational culture or subculture. In this sense culture is a possession—a fairly stable set of taken-for-granted assumptions, shared beliefs, meanings, and values that form a kind of backdrop for action. (Smircich, 1985: 58)

Culture so defined may be employed either as an external independent variable that may affect the organization—for example, organizations in France are molded by a distinctive set of cultural beliefs unique to that society (Crozier, 1964)—or as an internal variable that characterizes the values or style of one or more organizations: organizations possess a culture just as they possess a distinctive technology.

Employed in the second sense, as a root metaphor, culture is something an organization *is*. To view organizations as cultures is to shift from a mechanical or organic to a cognitive or symbolic model. "Organizations are understood and analyzed not mainly in economic or material terms, but in terms of their expressive, ideational and symbolic aspects" (Smircich, 1983: 347–48). Clearly this second perspective embraces a more subjectivist or phenomenological view (see Burrell and Morgan, 1979) and has much in common with the open system conception as developed by Boulding, Pondy and Mitroff, and Weick; with Strauss's conception of organizations as negotiated orders; and with the views of the institutional theorists.

Both conceptions of culture contribute to the analyses of the ways in which culture functions as a control system. Every organization necessarily has a culture, but some create *strong* cultures—belief systems that define a general mission sustaining commitment to something larger than self; that provide guidelines by which participants can choose appropriate activities; that create sources of meaning and identification such that participants not only know what they are to do for the good of the organization but want to do it. Such beliefs are inculcated and reinforced by rituals and ceremonies that provide collective occasions for expressing solidarity and commitment; by the raising up of heroes that personify common goals; and by the creation of slogans and symbols that signify shared values. (Deal and Kennedy, 1982; Peters and Waterman, 1982) Precisely how such strong cultures are created and maintained is the subject of much current study. (See Jelinek, Smircich, and Hirsch, 1983; Frost et al., 1985.)

Culture as a control mechanism closely resembles what Lindblom (1977) has termed a *preceptoral system*. He argues that there are three basic types of control systems: markets based on exchange, authority based on legitimated power, and preceptoral systems based on persuasion and indoctrination. As in a strong culture,

> in a preceptoral system rationality rests on an ideology which once taught to the individual gives him both a "correct" understanding of the social world and guidelines for his own decisions. Although a preceptoral system depends on simple moral and emotional appeals to supplement the rational, the core element in the creation of the new man is his idological education, a genuine attempt to raise the level of his conscious, thoughtful, deliberated understanding. (Lindblom, 1977: 59)

Lindblom also comments on the creation of cultural heroes:

> In social organization great feats can be accomplished in either of two ways. By a finely tuned coordination of individual efforts, which is an accomplishment prized both in market theory and administrative theory. Or by somehow inducing each only loosely coordinated participating individual to rise to unusual levels of individual accomplishment and innovation. (p. 60)

Preceptoral systems stress the latter approach to excellence, and in so doing—like those who emphasize the virtures of strong cultures—they are highly critical of overly formalist, bureaucratic approaches.

Lindblom's central illustration of the full-blown preceptoral system is the Chinese political regime under Mao. This example suggests a major concern raised by the cultural control model: its potential development into an authoritarian system that is subject to abuse precisely because its controls are internalized and individual participants are unconstrained in the demands that they place on themselves. Peters and Waterman (1982: 77) describe this darker side of cultural controls,in the corporate setting:

> So strong is the need for meaning, . . . that most people will yield a fair degree of latitude or freedom to institutions that give it to them. The excellent companies are marked by very strong cultures, so strong that you either buy into their norms or get out.

This high level of commitment to special-purpose organizations is of concern in a society based on pluralism and committed to democratic institutions. We regard this kind of commitment as a potential source of pathology and comment further on its implications in the next chapter.

SUMMARY

Goals are put to many uses by organizational participants. They serve cognitive functions, guiding the selection of alternative courses of action; they have cathectic properties, serving as a source of identification and commitment for participants and as symbolic properties appealing to external constituencies; they provide present justifications for actions taken in the past; they provide criteria for the evaluation of performances, participants, and programs of action; and under some conditions they provide ideological guidance for the contributions of participants. Moreover, individual participants bring their own private goals or motives with them into the organization, and these rarely coincide with those of the organization.

The concept of a dominant coalition that determines goals in organizations solves some of the mysteries of goal setting. It helps to avoid reification of the organization as a single purposeful actor but at the same time allows the organization's goals or preference structures to differ from those of all its human agents. The concept allows for the possibility that groups and individual participants have different interests and agendas and indicates how, through negotiation and the making of side payments, bargains are struck and a basis for common action developed. The concept of dominant coalitions also reminds us that individual participants do not have equal power in decision making and that the preferences and interests of some will receive more attention than those of others. Although individuals and groups bring preferences and interests with them into the organization, organizations are more than a setting where existing interests come together: they are places where new interests are created.

The size and shape of the dominant coalition changes over time in response to the changing external conditions to which the organization must adapt. As new sources of uncertainty and challenge develop in its environment, the organization creates offices to deal with them. Officers who can successfully cope with such problems may be expected to acquire power within the organization, since others are dependent on them for critical services. As environments become more complex and turbulent, the dominant coalition grows and its shape changes to incorporate more and different specialists capable of managing one or another boundary problem. And as the composition of the membership of the dominant coalition changes, the goals of the organization also change, reflecting these shifts in power.

Some organizations lack clear goals or efficacious technologies. Such conditions are not very hospitable to the formation and maintenance of organizations, but when they exist several alternative strategies are possible. Organizations may suffer and hope for the millennium, awaiting the appearance of a charismatic leader who will clarify ends and supply means. They may attune themselves to high ambiguity, recognizing that almost-random connections among streams of problems, participants, and solutions will produce some decisions. Some will seek to institutionalize themselves such that meaning and matter are supplied by rationalized myths. And still others may rely on experiential learning, reading environmental cues in order to improvise changing strategies.

All collectivities control their members, but some distinctive control arrangements are to be found in organizations. Power is the potential for influence based on sanctioning ability, and authority is normatively regulated power. In informal groups authority tends to exist as endorsed power—power constrained by norms enforced by subordinates—but in formal organizations authority exists primarily as authorized power—power circumscribed and supported by norms enforced by officers superior to the power wielder. Most organizations attempt to regulate the contributions of participants by developing evaluation systems that link performances to organizational sanctions. Although such control systems are ubiquitous, they are often cumbersome and complex, and many are flawed. This is particularly so as the goals pursued by organizations and the tasks allocated to participants become increasingly difficult in definition and uncertain in performance. In some types of organizations, control may reside more in organizational cultures—that is, in shared, internalized beliefs and norms that provide meaning and guidance to individual members engaged in collective action.

ORGANIZATIONS

PART FOUR

AND
SOCIETY

We have emphasized throughout this volume that organizations are only subsystems of larger social systems and are connected in numerous and vital ways to them. What differentiates the focus of the next two chapters from previous ones is not a concern with these connecting links but a shift in reference. Thus far, the organization itself has served as the primary point of reference. We have explored goals, structures, technologies, and participants from the standpoint of what they can reveal about the system of which they are parts. Now we adopt a different benchmark: that of the host society. We ask in these two concluding chapters what organizatins can do to and for the societies that support them. We examine unintended as well as intended effects.

Chapter 12 explores some of the problems and dangers associated with the operation and growth of organizations. In particular, we focus on power and its potential misuse. Organizations generate power as a consequence of their functioning. Previous chapters have examined how power can be employed in the service of organizational goals—whether those goals be certain outputs or the survival of the organization. Chapter 12 investigates the side effects of the power that is generated—its unanticipated consequences for both internal participants and external publics. As might be imagined, these are issues raised primarily by the natural system perspective on the functioning of organizations.

From the rational system perspective, organizations are instruments for the attainment of goals. We have asked numerous questions about the implications of this view for the organization. However, a crucial question for the larger society within which organizations operate is how effective and efficient they are in meeting their goals. Are they sufficiently adept in their functions—in achieving their respective goals—that they merit social support in spite of problems they raise? Although the question of effectiveness is most readily addressed from the rational system perspective, we shall quickly discover that different questions regarding organizational effectiveness are raised by natural and open systems points of view. These queries and issues are addressed in Chapter 13.

12 organizational pathologies

Bureaucracy has been and is a power instrument of the first order. . . . The individual bureaucrat cannot squirm out of the apparatus in which he is harnessed. . . . In the great majority of cases, he is only a single cog in an ever-moving mechanism which prescribes to him an essentially fixed route of march. . . .

The ruled, for their part, cannot dispense with or replace the bureaucratic apparatus of authority once it exists. For this bureaucracy rests upon expert training, a functional specialization of work, and an attitude set for habitual and virtuoso-like mastery of single, yet methodically integrated functions. . . . This holds for public administration as well as for private economic management. More and more the material fate of the masses depends upon the steady and correct functioning of the increasingly bureaucratic organizations of private capitalism. The idea of eliminating these organizations becomes more and more utopian.

Max Weber (1947 trans.)

Weber was aware of the use and the possible misuse of power in modern organizations. Inappropriate applications can occur both internally, when participants are exploited or stunted or in other ways damaged by their involvement, and externally, when publics who rely on organizations for goods and services find that organizations are unresponsive to their needs or interests. Internal problems may appear to be an issue only for the individuals involved, but a moment's reflection will convince us that damage done to organizational participants is a social, and not simply a personal, problem. As has been noted, individuals are only partially involved in any given organization: injury inflicted on participants in one setting may be expected to affect their performance in others. Two types of problems for individual participants are frequently cited: the problem of alienation and that of overconformity or ritualism. Both are examined in the first section of this chapter.

Turning to problems involving publics, we will first examine the issue of responsiveness. What can be done to ensure that organizations are attentive to the needs and interests of external constituencies? This is a particularly acute problem for public organizations, which are expected to be oriented primarily to public interests, but is by no means restricted to them. We also examine the broader issue of corporate versus individual interests, which raises more general questions about the distribution and use of power in contemporary society.

Throughout this chapter, we endeavor to show that it is not necessary to develop new concepts or arguments to explain organizatonal pathologies. There is a close correspondence between many of the best and the worst features of organizations. In some cases, similar processes, with slight variations, produce both an organization's strengths and its weaknesses. In other cases, the organization's strengths *are* its weaknesses, when viewed from a different perspective.

PROBLEMS FOR PARTICIPANTS

Alienation

Much time and attention has been devoted over the years to the impact of organizations on the personal characteristics of their participants. There are many claims and considerable evidence regarding these effects—and most of them are conflicting! At least since the time of Adam Smith and down to the present, observers have pointed to the debilitating consequences of organizational involvement, and in particular, employment, for individual participants. These destructive processes are often summarized under the concept of alienation—a concept with enough facets and varied interpretations to serve as an adequate umbrella under which to gather a quite varied set of criticisms.

Even Marx, who more than any other theorist called attention to the importance of alienation of workers, identified several possible forms of alienation (see Marx, 1963 trans.; Faunce, 1968). Workers may be alienated from the *product* of their labor. Labor gives value to the objects it creates, but as a worker loses control over his product, it comes to exist "independently, outside himself, and alien to him and . . . stands opposed to him as an autonomous power" (Marx, 1963 trans.: 122–23). Workers can also be alienated from the *process* of production. This occurs to the extent that

> the work is external to the worker, that it is not part of his nature, and that, consequently, he does not fulfil himself in his work but denies himself, has a feeling of misery rather than well-being, does not develop freely his mental and physical energies but is physically exhausted and mentally debased. . . . His work is not voluntary but imposed, forced labor. (Marx, 1963 trans.: 124–25)

As a consequence of the first two processes, workers become alienated from others in the work setting. Marx explains:

> The alien being to whom labour and the product of labour belong, to whose service labour is devoted, and to whose enjoyment the product of labour

goes, can only be man himself. If the product of labour does not belong to the worker, but confronts him as an alien power, this can only be because it belongs to a man other than the worker. (1963 trans.: 130)

Enter the capitalist. And enter the argument that it is not work that alienates, but exploitation of workers by the misuse of power.

Before turning to some evidence regarding the pervasiveness and distribution of alienation, a second influential formulation deserves mention. Like Marx, Seeman (1959; 1975) views alienation as a multi-faceted concept; he identifies six varieties: (1) powerlessness—the sense of little control over events; (2) meaninglessness—the sense of incomprehensibility of personal and social affairs; (3) normlessness—commitment to socially unapproved means for the achievement of goals; (4) cultural estrangement—rejection of commonly held values and standards; (5) self-estrangement—engagement in activities that are not intrinsically rewarding; and (6) social isolation—the sense of exclusion or rejection. Seeman has argued that powerlessness and self-estrangement are the two types of alienation that have most meaning in the workplace, and these seem most consistent with Marx's distinctions. A great many measures, including several multiple-item scales, have been developed to assess one or the other of these dimensions (see Seeman, 1975); most of them treat these conditions as internal, social psychological states. Israel (1971) has taken strong exception to this practice, insisting that alienation is more accurately and usefully viewed as an objective condition of the social structure, not a subjective attitude or disposition. Individuals may not be able to recognize that they are alienated: sentiments may not accurately reflect circumstances.

In spite of Israel's concerns, most empirical studies on alienation are based on data obtained from individual respondents who report their feelings or attitudes—for example, work satisfaction and dissatisfaction, levels of interest or commitment—or their behavior—for example, turnover, absenteeism, physical and mental health symptoms. Most surveys conducted in this country over the past half century report (1) generally high levels of worker satisfaction and morale but (2) large variation in satisfaction and symptoms across differing occupational strata and work situations. These surveys also show that higher satisfaction tends to be associated with such factors as intrinsic interest of the work, level of control, level of pay and economic security, and opportunities for social interaction (see Blauner, 1960; Sheppard and Herrick, 1972; Special Task Force, 1973).

Such clear and expected results do not hold up very well in more detailed and limited investigations of the relation between job characteristics and worker attitudes. As discussed in Chapter 9, research on such job characteristics as variety, autonomy, interaction, and level of skills required have not found strong or consistent associations with worker satisfaction or absenteeism. And efforts to introduce measures of worker "needs" or other assessments of personality have not clarified the situation, indeed have raised more questions than they have resolved. (See Cummings, 1982; Staw, 1984.)

A number of analysts have claimed that the impact of organizations on their participants extends far beyond the walls of the organization itself. Argyris (1957; 1973) summarizes several studies that indicate that workers who experience "constraint and isolation" on the job carry these attitudes into their free time: such workers are less involved in organized leisure, community, or political activities. Kanter (1977*b*) reviews a number of studies that suggest that both men's and women's occupational experiences have important implications for their family roles. She asserts that these studies contradict the "myth of separate worlds" perpetuated by companies that do not wish to assume responsibility for the effects of their policies and practices on the "personal" lives of their employees (and also by social scientists who tend to specialize in studying organizations or families but not their interdependence). Similarly, Ouchi (1979: 36–37) argues that organizations have a vested interest in failing to recognize their psychological casualties:

> The costs of psychological failure are not borne entirely by the firm, but rather are externalized to the society generally. That is, employees who reach the point of emotional disability, who become unsatisfactory workers, are the first to be laid off during depressions or, in extreme cases, are fired. The firm which has "used up" people emotionally does not have to face the cost of restoring them. In much the same manner that firms were able until recently to pollute the air and the water without paying the costs of using up these resources, they continue to be able to pollute our mental health with impunity.

And Kanter concludes that "a major social welfare issue of the decades to come" is likely to be focused on the question "Can organizations more fully and responsibly take into account their inevitable interface with the personal lives of their participants?" (1977*b*: 89). Our own view is much closer to that of Seeman (1975: 108), whose survey of research on alienation leads him to conclude,

> Given the tendency to assume that work is of primary importance in defining the self and in connecting the individual with the larger society, and given the centrality of work in the Marxian sources on alienation, it seems surprising how limited the demonstration has actually been concerning this purported generalization (from the job proper to the extra-job milieu) of alienated labor.

That is, we do not question the importance of the issues raised, but only the quality of the evidence produced thus far.

We are most concerned, however, with one of the proposed solutions for dealing with the problem of alienation. This solution, endorsed by a long and distinguished list of social analysts, is that organizations should absorb more aspects of the personalities of their participants; that they should become the primary focus of social integration, personal identity, and meaning; that they should function as the new communities, or *Gemeinschaften*, of modern society. From Saint-Simon (1952 trans.) and Durkheim (1949 trans.) through Barnard (1938), and Mayo (1945), and Selznick (1957) to Ouchi (1981) and Peters and Waterman (1982), organization theorists have looked to production organizations as a primary source of social integration in a social structure that is judged to be increasingly anomic and disorganized. Wolin calls attention to the underlying conservative and elitist stance that nurtures this point of view:

The fondness for large scale organization displayed by contemporary writers largely stems from anxieties provoked by the emergence of the mass. They see organizations as mediating institutions, shaping disoriented individuals to socially useful behavior and endowing them with a desperately needed sense of values. These large entities supply the stabilizing centers, which not only integrate and structure the amorphous masses, but control them as well. (Wolin, 1960: 427)

That organizations have some impact on the personal characteristics and the mental health of their participants we do not dispute. That these effects often are detrimental to participants and, hence, to the larger society is a hypothesis that calls for more investigation. But that organizations should be viewed as the principal centers of moral and social integration in modern society we cannot accept.

As indicated in Chapter 7, we see the emergence of organizations as special-purpose systems as being closely associated with the emergence of the ideology of individualism, including the doctrine of natural rights and the value of individual freedom. The development of the rational-legal out of the traditional forms, to use Weber's terms, signals the emergence of norms and structures that place restrictions on the hierarchy of the organization and reduce the leverage of the organization in relation to the individual. We endorse these developments and view with alarm proposals to expand the power and influence of organizations over individuals. This argument will be amplified at the end of this chapter.

Overconformity

In his justly famous essay "Bureaucratic Structure and Personality," Merton calls attention to a set of processes by which "the very elements which conduce toward efficiency in general produce inefficiency in specific instances" (1957: 200). He argues that structural devices established to ensure reliability and adequacy of performance—rules, discipline, a graded career—can "also lead to an over-concern with strict adherence to regulations which induces timidity, conservatism, and technicism" (1957: 201). Merton also argues that

adherence to the rules, originally conceived as a means, becomes transformed into an end-in-itself; there occurs the familiar process of *displacement of goals* whereby an instrumental value becomes a terminal value (1957: 199).

Other possible sources of goal displacement are described by natural system analysts, such as Selznick (1949) and Dalton (1959), who emphasize the commitments individuals develop to their tools, working arrangements, procedures, and work groups (see Chapter 3). Rational system analysts March and Simon (1958: 150–58) examine the manner in which means-ends chains designed to support rationality of decision making (see Chapters 2 and 4) also foster goal displacement, which they refer to as *sub-goal formation.* They point out that cognitive processes operating at the individual, group, and organizational levels all contribute to such developments, supplementing the cathectic process emphasized by Merton, Selznick, and Dalton. Since goals are divided and factored among individuals and groups, goal displacement is encouraged by selective perception and attention processes among individuals, the selective content of in-group communication, and the selective exposure to information occasioned by the division of labor within the larger organization. Goals assigned to individuals and groups as means are viewed as ends in themselves. Scientists in research and development units emphasize creativity without regard to feasibility: manufacturing units emphasize producibility without attention to marketability; and so on.

If we take a somewhat larger view, however, we will see that goal displacement is not confined to organizations but is quite widespread in modern societies. Indeed, we would argue that it is synonymous with differentiation of the social structure and elaboration of the cultural system. As societies and cultures develop, activities formerly regarded as means become ends in themselves: eating becomes dining; buildings and garments needed for protection from the elements take on symbolic importance and give rise to architecture and fashion; sexual relations intended "by Nature" as a means to the survival of the species become a terminal value, elaborated in romantic love and sex as play. The myriad occupations that emerge in modern societies may be viewed as instances of means transformed into ends: scientists pursue truth for its own sake; physicians prolong life as an ultimate value; and teachers devote their lives to socialization of the young. And we have noted, time and again, that the goals of organizations can be viewed as specialized functions or means from the perspective of the larger society.

Once we realize that goal displacement is the hallmark of any advanced civilization, it seems unfair and somewhat disingenuous to single out bureaucrats and accuse them of unique vices. They are involved in a process in which we all participate.

It appears to us that the basis for concern is not the displacement of ends by means but the continued pursuit of means that have somehow become disconnected from, or are at odds with, the ends they were designed to serve. In times of rapid change, we can easily imagine such dislocations becoming more common: ultimate goals change, but it is difficult to rapidly design and implement necessary adjustments down the chains of means-ends connections. Efforts to modify organizational structures to enable them to process information more rapidly—augmenting the hierarchy and developing lateral connections (see Chapter 9)—may be interpreted as attempts to shorten and improve the consistency of these chains. Similarly, emphasizing the overriding importance of collectively valued goals as a basis for decision making and action provides another approach to counteracting the disassociation of subgoals and goals (see Chapter 11).

To return to the narrower topic of rigidity or overconformity, results from two large surveys suggest that rather than increasing rigidity, participation in organizations encourages individual flexibility and openness to new ideas. The first study, conducted by Inkeles (1969), reports the results of a cross-national survey of 1000 men from each of six developing societies. The study identified a series of interrelated attitudes labeled *modernity*, which included such specific attitudes as openness to new experiences, assertion of increasing independence from the authority of traditional figures, abandonment of passivity and fatalism, interest in planning and punctuality, and interest in political issues and in keeping abreast of the news. The two most important influences on individuals' development of "modern" attitudes were school attendance and work in a factory. On the role of schools, Inkeles (1969: 213) comments,

> These effects of the school, I believe, reside not mainly in its formal, explicit, self-conscious pedagogic activity, but rather are inherent in the school as an *organization*. . . . It teaches ways of orienting oneself toward others, and of conducting oneself, which could have important bearings on the performance of one's adult roles in the structure of modern society.

And as for the factory experience:

> Just as we view the school as communicating lessons beyond reading and arithmetic, so we thought of the factory as training men in more than the minimal lessons of technology and skills necessary to industrial production. We conceived of the factory as an organization serving as a general school in attitudes, values, and ways of behaving which are more adaptive for life in a modern society. (1969: 213)

Inkeles found organizational participation to be a liberating, consciousness-expanding experience for individuals in developing societies.

Kohn (1971) used survey data from a sample of over 3000 men employed in a variety of civilian occupations to examine the effect of bureaucratic employment on individuals' attitudes. Characteristics of employment settings were measured simply in terms of the number of levels of supervision and the size of the organization; individual attitudes were assessed in terms of three dimensions: (1) emphasis placed on conformity or respectability, (2) intolerance or rigid conformity and resistance to change, and (3) intellectual rigidity. The resulting associations were not particularly strong but were consistent. Kohn found that

> men who work in bureaucratic firms or organizations tend to value, not conformity, but self-direction. They are more open-minded, have more personally responsible standards of morality, and are more receptive to change than are men who work in nonbureaucratic organizations. They show greater flexibility in dealing both with perceptual and with ideological problems. (Kohn, 1971: 465)

Controlling for educational differences reduced but did not eliminate the positive relation between organizational employment and individual flexibility. The data also suggest that such "bureaucratic" factors as greater job security, somewhat higher levels of income, and substantively more complex work contributed to these attitudinal differences.[1] Like Inkeles, Kohn emphasizes the liberalizing effects of organizational involvement on individual participants.

Lest we begin to feel overly sanguine at this point, we need only

---

[1]The argument relating complexity of work to psychological functioning is pursued in Kohn and Schooler (1973), who show that although there is a reciprocal relation between substantive complexity of work and intellectual flexibility of the performer, the job characteristics have a stronger effect on the person's psychological functioning than the reverse.

confront Milgram's (1973: 1974) series of experiments on conformity. Milgram's design called for a three-person situation in which a scientist-teacher is assisted by a second person in attempting to teach a student a series of word pairs. The experiment is described as examining the effects of punishment on learning, and it is the task of the assistant to administer punishments—electrical shocks—to the student when he or she gives an incorrect answer. Intensity of the shocks administered increased systematically throughout the experiment, from a low of 15 volts to a maximum of 450 volts: the upper end of the scale on the generator is labeled "Extreme Intensity/Shock; Danger, Severe Shock," and the final position, "XXX." In reality, the assistant is the true subject of the experiment; both the teacher and the student are actors, and no real shocks are administered. The true purpose of the study is to determine how much (apparent) pain one individual will inflict on another when ordered to do so.

The results are unsettling, to say the least. Across a wide variety of types of subjects—from Yale undergraduates to adult professionals and blue-collar workers to individuals from many different countries—approximately 60 percent of the subjects conformed to the demands of the scientist and administered shock at the highest levels possible to the student. The possibility that all these subjects were sadists was ruled out: left to their own devices, with no instruction from the scientist as to "appropriate" shock levels, the great majority of subjects administered very low, apparently painless shocks.

On examination, the experimental setting is a powerful one: many factors induce conformity. The scientist-teacher enjoys the authority of office as well as of expertise. The setting—a university laboratory—exudes propriety and legitimacy. The subject is a temporary, short-term assistant—not ostensibly the focus of the study but only a supportive or auxiliary figure. To disrupt the experiment by refusing to carry out orders is, apparently, a difficult thing to do. In authority structures, the orientation tends to be directed upward. As Milgram (1973: 77) notes,

> the person feels responsible *to* the authority directing him but feels no responsibility *for* the content of the actions that the authority prescribes. Morality does not disappear—it acquires a radically different focus: the subordinate person feels shame or pride depending on how adequately he has performed the actions called for by authority.

Other experimental variations suggest factors that affect the level of conformity observed. Distance from the punitive action affected conformity: assistants who were asked to force the subject's hand down on an electric plate were less likely to conform than those who simply selected the shock level and pulled a switch; assistants who were asked only to read the word list were more likely to conform than those who were more directly involved in administering the punishment. Pertaining to this latter group, Milgram (1973: 77) observes,

> Predictably, they excused their behavior by saying that the responsibility belonged to the man who actually pulled the switch. This may illustrate a dangerously typically arrangement in a complex society: it is easy to ignore responsibility when one is only an intermediate link in a chain of action.

The terrible consequences that may be associated with "simply following orders" are graphically illustrated by the behavior of officials in Hitler's death camps. It is to stress such simple bases for these heinous crimes that Arendt (1963) subtitles her analysis of the actions of Adolf Eichmann, chief executor of Hitler's "final solution," "A Report on the Banality of Evil."

Although we would not presume to entirely account for the complex problem of overconformity in organizations, one variable of apparent importance can be singled out: insecurity, or uncertainty. Recall that Kohn reported that greater job security of workers was associated with higher flexibility and less resistance to change. We would argue that Milgram's experimental subjects were highly insecure, recognizing that they were amateur, temporary contributors to a professional, ongoing, scientific study. And numerous analysts (Arendt, 1951; Neumann, 1942) have emphasized that totalitarian states such as Nazi Germany are characterized by duplications of office, divisions of power between state and party, and arbitrary acts by charismatic leaders, so that the entire system creates great anxiety and insecurity among its officeholders. Two case studies of organizations—Blau's (1955) study of a law-enforcement agency and Kanter's (1977a) study of a large industrial corporation—lend support to this thesis. Blau reports that the least secure agents were the most resistant to change and the most susceptible to ritualistic adherence to existing procedures. And Kanter asserts that most of the pressures for conformity in business corporations can be attributed to uncertainty. Writing of managers, for example, Kanter asserts,

> It is the uncertainty quotient in managerial work, as it has come to be defined in the large modern corporation, that causes management to become so socially restricting: to develop tight inner circles excluding social strangers; to keep control in the hands of socially homogenous peers; to stress conformity and insist upon a diffuse, unbounded loyalty; and to prefer ease of communication and thus social certainty over the strains of dealing with people who are "different." (Kanter, 1977a: 49)

Finally, Fox and Staw (1979) report that subjects in an experiment who were told that their assignment to an office was temporary and dependent on the quality of their performance were more likely to rigidly adhere to an earlier poor decision than were subjects told that they had permanent assignments. Similarly, the more resistance a decision encountered, the more likely subjects were to reaffirm it. Fox and Staw (1979: 465) summarize and generalize from their series of experiments:

> The results demonstrate the effect of political vulnerability upon commitment to a course of action. When an administrator is worried about keeping his job or fending off critics within an organization, he is less likely to be flexible in his decision making. Thus, the trapped administrator can be thought of as one who is most likely to increase rather than decrease his commitment to a previously chosen policy and most likely to become inflexible in his defense of such positions.

Insecurity and uncertainty appear to produce overconformity and rigidity.

Uncertainty, Alienation
and Overconformity

Uncertainty again! We have asked this concept to bear a heavy burden for us throughout this volume. Uncertainty is the source of variety and power, and it is the enemy of rationality and planning. Too much uncertainty can cause individuals to seek protection in ritualism and oversimplification of alternatives; too little uncertainty can cause individuals to wither in boredom and alienation.

Organizations and individuals are forever seeking to reduce uncertainty. Organizations attempt to buffer it out, and individuals are always programming themselves and others "out of a challenging and novel situation, and then losing interest" (Leavitt, 1964: 546). Fortunately for both, however, they never completely succeed. Uncertainty floods the barriers, bringing variety and challenge. And, as Goldner (1970: 97–98) observes,

> what starts out as a search for ways to reduce problems and uncertainties in organizations leads . . . to the increase of other uncertainties. Rationalization sows the seeds of increased complexity and hence of pressures for yet new forms of rationalization.

How to avoid levels of uncertainty that are too high or too low and to seek out levels that are "just right" in their mix of security and stimulation—this search for the "Goldilocks" standard is a central challenge to all organizations and all participants within them.

PROBLEMS FOR PUBLICS

Unresponsiveness

All organizations must provide benefits to external publics—customers, clients, citizens—as a condition for their continued existence. The contributions required from these publics vary according to the nature of the organization but may involve direct payments for products or services received, indirect support in the form of taxes, and normative support in the form of goodwill and legitimacy. A concern with organizational responsiveness to the demands of external publics is most often raised in connection with public organizations, since the public is expected to be the primary beneficiary of their activities. However, problems can also develop in the relations between publics and organizations in the private sector. We will examine both situations.

Public sector organizations Weber, in company with many other past and present political analysts, believed that the most serious challenge facing contemporary societies was to maintain control over the expanding state bureaucracies. Numerous observers before Weber, including Mill, Bagehot, Le Play, and Mosca, noted the growth in numbers and power of paid government officials, but Weber's analyses provide the most complete and systematic conceptualization of this major change in governmental systems (see Albrow, 1970). Unlike some of the previous critics, Weber insisted that the primary problem with the growth of bureaucracy was not that of inefficiency or mismanagement. Indeed, Weber cogently argued that in comparison with earlier administrative forms, the bureaucratic structures were highly efficient and reliable (see Chapter 2). But for Weber, these characteristics—the administrative virtues—also constituted bureaucracies' most serious threat.[2] Accompanying increased bureaucratization was the strong likelihood of growth in the power of public officials. Weber (1946 trans.: 232–33) argued,

> Under normal conditions, the power position of a fully developed bureaucracy is always overpowering. The "political master" finds himself in the position of the "dilettante" who stands opposite the "expert," facing the trained official who stands within the management of administration. This holds whether the "master" whom the bureaucracy serves is a "people" . . . or a parliament. . . . It holds whether the master is an aristocratic, collegiate body, legally or actually based on self-recruitment, or whether he is a popularly elected president, a hereditary and "absolute" or a "constitutional" monarch.

Weber's explanation for this development was quite straightforward: "More and more the specialized knowledge of the expert became the foundation for the power position of the officeholder" (1946 trans.: 235). Recall in this connection Weber's description of the transition from patrimonial to bureaucratic administrative forms (see Chapter 2). As a ruler's territory increased, it would increasingly become necessary to decentralize operations and delegate authority to members of the administrative staff. The division of labor among the staff members becomes more fixed; specialized competence of officers increases, and, at the same time, the ruler's ability to oversee each operation is reduced. Relative to the ruler, each staff member becomes more knowledgeable in each specific area of operation. The staff also becomes more aware of itself as a distinct social group with common interests. We have, in brief, a classic instance of a shift in power-dependence relations: each subordinate is individually less powerful than the ruler, but collectively the subordinates have become more powerful, and by acting in concert they can impose conditions on the ruler's exercise of power (see Chapter 11). These constraints on the ruler's power, which developed slowly and haltingly over long periods, include such bureaucratic "safeguards" as civil service commissions and elaborate codes of conduct. Rosenberg (1958: 180) has described the effects of these developments in his analysis of the evolution of the Prussian state:

> The raising of standardized prerequisites for admission had a profound effect upon the bureaucracy as a social elite and as a political group. Whatever the motives and ostensible objectives of the ministerial sponsors of the

---

[2]Weber was not alone in admitting the likely efficiency of the bureaucracy but expressing reservations about the use of this instrument. Thus, in one of his celebrated essays on bureaucracy, the poet Ezra Pound responds to the claim that bureaucrats are active and attentive to their duty by noting that "the idea of activity as a merit is, when applied to bureaucrats, as deadly as the idea of activity among tuberculous bacillae" (1973: 219).

reformed merit system, the new service tests turned out to be, in the hands of the bureaucratic nobility, a wonderful device for consolidating its control over personnel recruitment and for gaining greater freedom from royal molestations in this crucial area.

The increasing dependence of the dilettante on the expert goes a long way toward accounting for the shift of power "down" from titular rulers to the nominal subordinates—the administrative officials.[3]

In the case of democratic systems, where power is expected to reside in the hands of the governed, other factors operate to shift power "up" from the people to administrative elites. The most influential analysis of these processes is that provided by Michels (1949 trans.) Rather than focusing exclusively on state bureaucracies, Michels insists that processes that withdraw power from the people and place it in the hands of bureaucrats can be studies equally well in organizations such as political parties that are expected to serve the interests of their rank and file.[4] Michels's (1949 trans.) major work is based on a case study of the Social Democratic Party in pre–World War I Germany (see Chapter 3). His famous aphorism "Who says organization, says oligarchy" summarizes his central argument that oligarchic tendencies to shift power from the majority and place it in the hands of an elite minority are built into the very structure of organization. They are an unintended consequence of organization. He points to the division of functions, which creates specialized knowledge; to the hierarchy of offices, which fosters and legitimates the uneven distribution of information and decision-making privileges; and to the structure of incentives, which encourages officials to remain in office but discourages rank-and-file members from involvement in the day-to-day business of the party. Michels's theoretical formulation emphasizes the internal factors giving rise to oligarchical processes; his descriptive account of the development of the Social Democratic party, however, places equal importance on the organization's relation with its environment. Throughout the period from 1890 to 1910, this party, the first of the strong working-class parties, was fighting for its existence. Leaders emphasized the need to present a unified front; internal disagreement and dissent were viewed as a luxury to be forgone until the party came to power; and leaders were reluctant to engage in any activities that weakened the strength of the organization in relation to its external environment.

Michels thus poses the following dilemma: a party or a union must build a strong organization and ensure its survival to achieve its objectives, yet preoccupation with such organizational problems leads to the surrender of these very objectives. "Thus, from a means, organization becomes an end" (1949 trans.: 390). Experience since Michels's time tends to

---

[3]Note that the same arguments were used in Chapter 11 to account for the increasing shift of power in individual organizations—both governmental and nongovernmental—from the owners and general managers to the technical experts and specialist managers. This process results, as noted, in increases in the size of the dominant coalition within organizations.

[4]Lipset (1960: 357) refers to such organizations as *private governments*. Blau and I (Blau and Scott, 1962: 45) refer to them as *mutual benefit associations*. They include such organizations as political parties, unions, and professional associations. Since they are formed to serve the interests of their members, most such organizations develop ideologies and procedures that support the participation of the majority in setting organizational goals.

confirm his thesis. Most unions, most professional associations and other types of voluntary associations, and most political parties exhibit oligarchical leadership structures; the democratic machinery established to prevent such arrangements functions primarily as a feeble device allowing rank-and-file participants to rubber-stamp executive decisions and "elect" slates of nominees running in uncontested elections (see Barber, 1950; Editors of the Yale Law Journal, 1954; Wilson, 1973). Even the well-known study by Lipset, Trow, and Coleman (1956) of a "deviant case," a democratically run union, suggests that although such processes are not inevitable, the conditions—both internal and external—causing the drift of power from the rank-and-file to the upper levels of the organization are sufficiently widespread to vindicate Michels's pessimistic generalization.

Lest we forget, the focus of the present discussion is on representativeness: the degree to which administrative and political bodies reflect the interests of those whom they are presumed to serve. Michels insists that the leaders of the German Social Democratic party forsook the values and interests of its membership, betraying socialist values and working-class interests for bourgeois values and selfish interests. Although it is true that the party's goals shifted over time, it is not obvious that this process was resisted by the members or was contrary to their interests. Thus, Coser (1951) has argued that the shift to the right in the party's program may not have resulted primarily from the bureaucratic conservatism of the leaders but from the rapid improvement in the social and economic situation of the working class during this period. Gouldner (1955) endorses this general line of argument by insisting that there is as much evidence to support an "iron law of democracy" as an "iron law of oligarchy." Gouldner's law asserts that political and administrative elites in both nations and organizations cannot endure for long without some support from the governed. Gouldner (1955: 506) also counters on logical grounds:

> Even as Michels himself saw, if oligarchical waves repeatedly wash away the bridges of democracy, this eternal recurrence can happen only because men doggedly rebuild them after each inundation.

Before leaving the topic of democratic processes within organizations, we wish to make one additional point. We have consciously shifted the level of analysis from the larger society and its bureaucratic apparatus to the individual organization and its administrative staff. In so doing, we agreed with Michels that processes operating at the organizational level may be applicable to the societal level, and vice versa. However, we need to be aware of Lipset's (1960: 395) conclusion regarding the relation between the two levels:

> Institutionalized democracy within private governments is not a necessary condition for democracy in the large society, and may in fact at times weaken the democratic process of civil society.

Specifically, Lipset notes that processes that act to incorporate members more fully in the life of their association and hence activate them in its political processes may also serve to isolate them from the larger community and make them more rigid and single-minded in their commitments. Lipset (1960: 396) summarizes the dilemma:

> Integration of members within a trade-union, a political party, a farm organization, a professional society, may increase the chances that members of such organizations will be active in the group and have more control over its policies. But extending the functions of such organizations so as to integrate their members may threaten the larger political system because it reduces the forces making for compromise and understanding among conflicting groups.

Arguments such as these support our earlier conclusions concerning the dangers of treating individual organizations as if they were the primary centers of moral and social—and political—integration.

With respect to the problem of ensuring responsiveness of governmental officials in the larger society, political analysts generally agree that formal safeguards such as constitutions and legal codes are not in themselves sufficient to curb the power of officeholders. Additional mechanisms are needed to ensure responsiveness. In an instructive historical survey of governmental institutions in the United States, Kaufman (1956; 1969) has identified several "principles" for securing responsiveness that have come to the fore during differing periods of this nation's history. He argues that the public first puts its faith in the principle of *representativeness*, placing great confidence in electoral institutions and granting broad powers to the legislatures, both state and federal. However, as ballots grew longer, voters were unable to choose intelligently and legislatures proved highly vulnerable to the corrupting pressures of special interests. During the second, post–Civil War period, the public endorsed the principle of *neutral competence:* a host of independent boards and commissions were created, the Civil Service Commission was created (in 1883), and the watchword became "take administration out of politics" (Kaufman, 1956: 1060). The major drawback to this approach was, and continues to be, that it led to the fragmentation of government, to the creation of "highly independent islands of decision-making." Further, because administration was protected from politics, the impact of elections on the conduct of government was minimized.

Concerned with this new source of recalcitrance, the public suported, beginning during the 1930s and 1940s, the principle of *executive leadership*. The specific mechanisms utilized during this third phase have been the introduction of the executive budget as a tool of centralized planning and control; the frequent use of administrative reorganization, as executives struggled to reduce the number of independent agencies and centralize them in some meaningful pattern; and the growth of the executive staff.[5] At first glance the last of these mechanisms appears to reflect simply the need for increased information processing on the part of governmental executives: it is a case of the augmentation of hierarchies in political systems (see Chapter 9). Such needs are involved, but they are

---

[5]Not only has there been a large increase in recent decades in the president's own executive staff at the national level. In addition, the number of "supergrade" political appointees to positions of authority over civil service bureaucrats has also increased dramatically. (See Heclo, 1977.)

subordinate to other requirements. The central function of the enlarged executive staffs is to increase political control over the *line* administrators—the civil servants. To do this, the executive must recruit staff members possessing two qualities: in order of importance, loyalty and specialized expertise. Expertise is required to defend the "dilettante" (executive) from the specialized knowledge of public officials; loyalty is essential to ensure that the expertise will be harnessed in the service of the executive's goals. In many ways this development may be seen as an attempt to repoliticize administration, in belated recognition of the truth that expertise may be neutral, but experts never can be.[6]

Kaufman (1969) argues that the late 1960s witnessed a return to the principle of representation, with the introduction of different mechanisms to breathe new life into this old value. Electoral reforms extended the franchise to new groups of voters and, more important, attempted to reform the systems by which elected officials were nominated and their campaigns financially supported. And for the first time, there were attempts to allow public representatives to participate not only in the creation but in the administration of federal programs. As noted in Chapter 8, a new generation of federal agencies, which stressed decentralized decision making and the inclusion of representation from the affected groups, developed between 1960 and 1980. It is characteristic of all these programs that broad discretionary powers are delegated to the administrative units: the language of the statutes sets overall policy directions but does not provide precise legal guidelines for administrative action. As Lowi notes, "broad discretion makes a politician out of a bureaucrat" (1969; 300–301). And since administrators help to set policy, the public is legitimately concerned about the influences to which they are subject. "The further down the line one delegates power, the further into the administrative process one is forced to provide representation" (1969: 233).

From the earliest days of the Republic, our forefathers were wary of the abuse of power by public servants and took pains to limit and divide power—among the three traditional branches of government as well as within each branch among various offices, commissions, bureaus, and agencies. Executive offices forge political alliances with congressional committees, and commissions and bureaus became linked to special interests both inside and outside the government. Although there are many diagnoses of our current plight, the most prevalent complaints heard from contemporary students of bureaucratic politics are (1) that public power is so fragmented that elected officials cannot ordinarily count on individual agencies to support and implement their policy initiatives (see Pressman and Wildavsky, 1973), and (2) that private special interests have so penetrated public agencies that officials are incapable of acting to support the larger public interest (see Lowi, 1969; Weiss and Barton, 1980). In sum, it is alleged that today's bureaucrats are insufficiently responsive to their political superiors and overly responsive to special interests.

---

[6]It is of some interest to observe that the fullest development of this structural arrangement is to be found in totalitarian systems such as Nazi Germany and the communist regimes. The so-called parallel structures in which the state bureaucracy is duplicated (and penetrated) by a party bureaucracy is a widely recognized feature of such politican systems (see Friedrich and Brzezinski, 1956).

This overly cozy relation between political bureaus and private interests has already been discussed in a different context. In Chapter 8, considerable attention was devoted to describing bridging strategies as an important means of increasing the security of organizations in their task environments. As we noted, the increasing scale and scope of governmental activity encourages organizations of all types to view public agencies as salient features of ther environments and as targets of co-optation. Government officials, for their part, are vulnerable to influences from such groups for many reasons: they must relate to these organized interests on a regular basis, and they may become dependent on them for information, cooperation, political support, and even future employment (See Heclo, 1977). Thus, contemporary governmental bureaus appear to have insufficient social insulation from specific sources of power in their environment; they are often unresponsive to the public interest because they are overly responsive to the interests of special publics.

Private sector organizations   Much more briefly, we must note that recent analysts are increasingly concerned with the responsiveness of private organizations to the interests of their clients and the larger public. In an important and influential essay, *Exit, Voice, and Loyalty,* Hirschman (1970) distinguishes between two general options open to disgruntled publics wishing to express dissatisfaction with the types and quality of services received. The first, *exit,* involves the withdrawal of patronage. Dissatisfied customers simply withdraw from a relation with one firm and seek another that is expected to serve their interests more adequately. Exit is the typical economic response; it is typified in the relations between private firms and their customers and presumes the existence of alternatives. The second option, *voice,* is broadly defined as "any attempt at all to change, rather than to escape from, an objectionable state of affairs" (Hirschman, 1970: 30). Voice is the typical political option—expressed through elections, petitions, complaints, protests, and riots—because it is more likely to be exercised in situations in which a monopoly exists. Voice is a more costly option than exit, demanding at a minimum the investment of time and energy; in extreme cases, its exercise can entail personal risk and sacrifice.

Hirschman argues that private firms can greatly benefit from publics who take the trouble to exercise the option of voice rather than exit. He notes that the quality of services provided by firms can deteriorate when alternative suppliers are available to some, since the more discerning customers withdraw their business, leaving those who are less quality-conscious—or who have no alternatives—to endure substandard service. Such problems are especially characteristic of "lazy monopolies," such as subsidized railroads or public educational systems. Hirschman argues that publics would benefit from the use of mixed options. Incentives need to be provided to encourage quality-conscious customers to exercise voice before resorting to exit—this is one of the major functions of *loyalty;* and public organizations should be encouraged to develop exit options—for example, the use of educational vouchers enabling students to seek alternative suppliers of educational services.

Lindblom (1977) enlarges Hirschman's comparisons of the varying controls available to publics in regulating public and private organizations. He points out that the most frequently employed voice options—elections—are relatively blunt control devices: the selection of a decision maker, especially one who will be placed in a complex political and organizational arena and subjected to varying cross-pressures on numerous issues, may provide little real control to the voter. By contrast, the exit options of buying or refusing to buy an organization's products or services can be exercised frequently and provide a direct signal to producers about what customers think of their products. On closer examination, however, it turns out that the public's control over private companies is "limited to saying yes or no on what is to be produced and in what quantities" (Lindblom, 1977: 154). On a broad range of other decisions, which Lindblom refers to as *delegated decisions*, private corporations exercise broad discretion:

> The delegated decisions are all the other decisions instrumental to production: among others, on technology, organization of the work force, plant location, and executive prerogatives. Even in an idealized market system, consumer control over them ranges from weak to nonexistent. (1977: 154)

A moment's reflection will suggest that these decisions can be of profound significance for the public interest:

> The discretionary decision of a single large corporation (to move in or out) can create or destroy a town, pollute the air for an entire city, upset the balance of payments between countries, and wipe out the livelihood of thousands of employees. (1977: 155).

Some observers have been content to rely on the development of a sense of "social responsibility" among corporate executives (see Berle, 1963; Cheit, 1964). Others, such as Lindblom, insist that market (exit) incentives must be supplemented with political (voice) controls if social responsibility is to become a reality.

Inefficiency

In Chapter 7 we encountered Olson's (1965) analysis of the perverse incentives associated with organizing to produce some public good. Because the benefits produced are available to all regardless of their contributions, "rational" actors will not contribute to their production unless compelled to do so—the solution for most public agencies—or unless more selective incentives are developed.

More recently, Olson (1982) has suggested a somewhat parallel and equally problematic dilemma operating at an organizational level in the incentive structure of associations that have been created to produce benefits for their members—associations such as labor unions, professional societies, farmers' organizations, manufacturers' and trade associations, and special interest lobbies. Generally speaking, such associations can provide benefits for their members in one of two ways. First, they can enable members to operate more efficiently and effectively, thus expanding the economic resources of the society as a whole and hence their own welfare as constituent groups within the society. Second, they can facilitate the

efforts of their members to secure a larger share for themselves of existing economic resources, by restricting the supply or raising the price of
the goods and services they offer or by obtaining special protections or
subsidies. Olson argues that "rational" associations will always pursue the
second of these two options. For an association to pursue the first alternative is not in the best interests of its membership, since the benefits produced are public—available to and enjoyed by all—but the costs are borne
by the membership alone. By contrast, the second alternative provides
benefits for association members only; although there are costs created
because overall efficiency of the economy has been reduced, these costs
do not rest on the association's members alone but are spread across all
sectors of the society. In short, the structure of incentives operating in
associations created to advance the interests of their membership penal-
izes efforts to increase their overall productive efficiency and rewards
attempts to use their power and influence to secure special privileges for
themselves, even at the expense of others. Olson (1982: 47) labels these
associations *distributive coalitions* because their primary focus is on influencing the distribution of resources to their members, not on the production of resources by their members. He concludes that "the great majority
of special-interest organizations redistribute income rather than create it,
and in ways that reduce social efficiency and output."

Olson asserts that these associations do not serve simply to reduce
efficiency in the sector involved, but create additional disturbances—for
example, drawing capital from other sectors because investors wish to
share in the special benefits created, or reducing incentives to adopt new
technologies to increase productivity—that magnify the dysfunctional
consequences for the society as a whole. As special interests proliferate,
tax laws and regulatory structures become more complex, and over time
many actors—politicians, lawyers, consultants—gain a vested interest in
maintaining if not magnifying this nonproductive machinery.

Olson proceeds to combine the two levels of his argument in order
to provide a general explanation for the "rise and decline of nations."
According to his 1965 thesis, collective organizations producing indivisible
goods are difficult to create. Smaller groups can be more easily organized
than larger ones because they can more readily detect beneficiaries who
are not contributors—that is, opportunists—and they have at their disposal a wider range of sanctions. Larger groups are more difficult to
organize and usually require the creation of some selective incentives. (Of
course, once established, such associations are quite resilient, since they
almost always provide "selective incentives" (salaries) to an administrative
staff, which thereby acquires a vested interest in the survival of the association.) Other things being equal, over time, more and more interests
finally succeed in becoming organized into associations, so that older,
politically stable societies gradually tend to accumulate more collective
associations. The growing numbers of these associations, each attempting
to maximize its own share of the wealth by securing special advantages for
its members even at the expense of the general welfare, is proposed as a
central cause of economic stagnation among developed societies.

Thus, Olson suggests, the democratic stability that has characterized
Great Britain since the early eighteenth century is a prime cause of its
economic decline. And the economic miracles enjoyed by Germany and

Japan during the past three decades are attributed to the destruction of the congeries of special interests in these societies in the aftermath of World War II. Olsen suggests that his general arguments also help to account for the more rapid recent growth of the southern and western states in the United States in comparison with the more settled, over-organized Northeast and Midwest.

Although there is undoubtedly no satisfactory single-factor theory of economic growth and decline, Olson provides persuasive support for this thesis with examples drawn from many societies and over broad periods of history. The collective organization of special interests is shown to have important effects on the economic well-being of a society.

On the other hand, like many economists, Olsen takes a relatively narrow view of the political process. He tends to see political organizations only as vehicles for expressing existing economic interests; a broader view would recognize that such organizations also shape the ends of their participants. As Reich (1983: 28) argues,

> it is precisely through broadly political activities—within local trade unions, civic groups, grass-roots political movements, town meetings, professional associations, chambers of commerce, shop floor organizations, charitable organizations, and election campaigns—that individuals discover the subtler dimensions of their own needs and learn about the needs of others. They begin to understand the relationship between self and society; the encounter itself shapes their social values. If political organization is understood as a source of social values as well as conduit for political demands, there is no inherent conflict between interest-group politics and economic growth.

While recognizing the power of Olson's argument, Reich emphasizes the need to preserve special-interest groups as an important component of—and contributor to—democratic political institutions.

Relentlessness

A final concern to be raised about the functioning of organizations in relation to publics is the relentlessness of their behavior. This problem, though neglected by most critics and analysts, is in our view the most serious one raised by the existence of organizations. It consists not in a malfunction of the organization but in the pathological aspects of "normal" organizational activities.

Coleman's (1974) analysis is most compelling. As noted earlier (see Chapter 7), Coleman distinguishes between natural persons, like you and me, and corporate actors—organizations. Organizations are composed not of persons but of positions, and persons are not completely contained within organizations. Persons contribute to and invest in organizations specific resources over which they lose full control. (The corporate actor is empowered to make decisions concerning the use of the resources available to it, and except in the rare and debilitating case in which an individual retains veto power over the use of his or her resources, individuals must be willing to give up a measure of control over their resources as the price for collective action.) With the creation of a corporate actor, a new set of interests comes into existence.

From the perspective of the natural actor, organizations are agencies for achieving desired objectives. However, from the point of view of the corporate actor, individuals are agents hired to pursue the goals of the collective actor. Individual actors are means for attaining corporate ends. Coleman (1974: 49) clearly spells out the implications of this view:

> It is the corporate actors, the organizations that draw their power from persons and employ that power to corporate ends, that are the primary actors in the social structure of modern society.
>
> What does this mean in practice? It means a peculiar bias in the direction that social and economic activities take. It means that among the variety of interests that men have, those interests that have been successfully collected to create corporate actors are the interests that dominate society.

Unorganized interests of persons are neglected in a society dominated by corporate actors. Further, corporate interests differ from those of natural persons in being more narrow, more intense, more refined, and more single-minded.

> ...decisions about the employment of resources are more and more removed from the multiplicity of dampening and modifying interests of which a real person is composed—more and more the resultant of a balance of narrow intense interests of which corporate actors are composed (1974: 29).

Individual administrators are constrained by organizational goals and the definitions of their roles. They are expected to act as agents of the organization and as stewards of its resources. University trustees cannot in good conscience use the resources of their institution to relieve poverty or to build low-cost housing for members of the surrounding community. Pentagon officials are expected to build our armaments and strengthen our defenses regardless of the deleterious effects of such activities on the national economy or on the long-range prospects for survival of the human race. Organizations do not speak with one voice, as we have seen, and they are frequently loosely coupled coalitions of interests, but compared with natural persons, they are relatively specialized in their purposes and organized so as to pursue them relentlessly.

Ashby, the noted general system theorist, has pointed out that all "synthetic" organisms, including organizations, exhibit this tendency toward specialization of a sort likely to be dysfunctional for those who create them:

> There is no difficulty, in principle, in developing synthetic organisms as complex, and as intelligent as we please. But we must notice two fundamental qualifications: first, their intelligence will be an adaptation to, and a specialization toward, their first particular environment, with no implication of validity for any other environment such as ours; and secondly, their intelligence will be directed toward keeping their own essential variables within limits. They will be fundamentally selfish. (Ashby, 1968: 116)

Given the expectation that organizations will take a relatively narrow band of interests and pursue them unremittingly, our reluctance to enshrine organizations as the social and moral centers of the new society may seem more intelligible. This reluctance is shared. For example, Hart and W. G. Scott express alarm at the growing acceptance of a new set of values they label "the organizational imperative," which presumes that "whatever is good for man can only be achieved through modern organization" and "therefore, all behavior must enhance the health of such modern organizations" (1975: 261; see also Scott and Hart, 1979).

In a more extreme form, corporate pressures may not only cause participants to pursue a limited set of goals without regard to their effect on other values; they may induce participants to engage in actions that are illegal or immoral. Corporate crime is a matter of growing concern. And much of the deviant behavior identified is encouraged by such "normal" organizational conditions as limitations on information, circumscribed responsibilities, and strong performance pressures. (See Clinard and Yeager, 1980; Ermann and Lundman, 1982)

In our introduction to Part Four, we commented that all of the pathologies of organizations to be identified relate in some manner to the problem of power. This statement applies to the current topic. Coleman (1974) points out that in a social structure containing both natural persons and corporate actors, it is possible for one natural person to lose power without a corresponding gain on the part of another person. Persons can lose power to corporate actors. Coleman argues that this loss or transfer is currently going on at a rapid rate, a situation giving rise to a widespread feeling of powerlessness among individuals. And Coleman (1974: 39) points out that as a result of this transfer

> the outcome of events is only partly determined by the interests of the natural persons, giving a society that functions less than fully in the interests of the persons who make it up.

This seems to us to represent the ultimate form of alienation. In Marx's simpler world, power stripped from one person (the worker) belonged to another (the capitalist). In today's more complex world, power lost by one person may not be gained by any similar person but absorbed by a corporate actor and employed in pursuit of its specialized purposes.

SUMMARY

Pathologies in the operation of contemporary organizations afflict both individual participants and external publics. We emphasize those that are based on the abuse of power.

Problems affecting individual participants include alienation and overconformity. Alienation can be defined either subjectively as a sense of powerlessness and self-estrangement or objectively as a condition under which workers lose control over the products of their labor or the value created by it. Most empirical studies are based on the subjective conception and reveal that the level of alienation among workers in this country is not high but that it varies greatly by the type of occupation, and that similar objective positions are experienced and reacted to differently by individuals. Although it is suspected that worker alienation will affect nonwork situations such as family life, there are few convincing studies establishing such relationships. We criticize the proposal that work organizations should function as the primary center of social and moral integration for individuals.

Organizational participants are frequently castigated for ritualism in the sense that they convert means into ends. Such transformations are, however, widespread throughout highly differentiated societies and do not become problematic unless there is a disjunction between means and ends. Studies reveal that organizational participation can be a source of flexibility and liberation as well as of timidity and overconformity. Job insecurity and uncertainty appear to be powerful factors governing conformity. Designers of organizational positions should seek to set uncertainty levels such that a proper mix of security and stimulation is achieved.

The responsiveness of organizations to the needs of external publics is of concern for all types of organizations, but especially those in which the public is designated as the prime beneficiary. The central problem with the growth of public organizations is that of maintaining their responsiveness to public interests. Responsiveness may be curtailed by the specialization and increasing expertise of administrative officials, the developing class interests of the administrative cadre, the uneven distribution of information and incentives for participation, and pressures for unity in the face of external threats. Responsiveness is sought through such mechanisms as securing representativeness, promoting neutral competence, and stressing executive leadership. It is suggested that some of the difficulties that beset public organizations are also created by their *over*responsiveness to public interests—the interests of *special* publics.

Private sector organizations are expected to be responsive to economic signals—for example, the withdrawal of business by customers searching for better quality or lower prices. Such options are not available to customers lacking alternatives, who must attempt through political means to change organizations from which they cannot escape. It is increasingly suggested that both private and public organizations should be made susceptible to both economic and political signals.

The structure of economic incentives can be an important source of pathology if there is a lack of incentives to motivate individuals to contribute to the production of public goods and a surplus of incentives to reward associations for pursuing their special interests. It has been proposed that the increasing inefficiency and economic stagnation that characterizes the more stable, advanced societies may be the result of the gradual accumulation of more and more associations representing special interests that may be expected to pursue advantages for their own members even at the expense of damaging those of the larger socioeconomic structure in which they participate.

Thus, even when organizations perform effectively and efficiently, they may nevertheless cause difficulties for the larger society because of their tendency to embody and mobilize support for relatively narrow goals. Individual interests that happen to coincide with organizational domains are well served; those that do not are liable to be seriously neglected. Our interests as individuals may be alienated not only by the actions of powerful others who strip us of our rights and resources but also by the normal functioning of impersonal organizations to whom we bequeath our resources and over which we lose control.

13 organizational effectiveness

There is no such thing as "good organization" in any absolute sense. Always it is relative; and an organization that is good in one context or under one criterion may be bad under another.

W. Ross Ashby (1968)

In recent years organizational analysts have become increasingly interested in the topic of organizational effectiveness. During the 1950s and early 1960s, the topic was generally neglected, in part because of the belief that considerations of effectiveness represented only an applied or practical, not a theoretical, concern.[1] Gradually, however, analysts began to perceive that there could be as much theoretical justification in examining the consequences of varying structural arrangements as in probing their determinants. And an important boost to the topic occurred when contingency theorists began to argue that some types of structures were better suited than others to certain tasks or environments. The question was raised, Better suited in what sense? and the answer given was often couched in terms of effectiveness. In this sense, effectiveness is argued by some theorists to be a determinant as well as a consequence of organizational structure.

The topic of organizational effectiveness is eschewed by some analysts on the ground that it necessarily deals with values and preferences that cannot be determined objectively. Such criticisms, however, apply not to the general topic but only to certain formulations of it. We will not seek to determine, for example, whether a given organization is or is not effective in some general sense. Rather, we shall attempt to learn what types of criteria of effectiveness are suggested by what constituencies and what types of indicators of effectiveness are proposed with what implications for organizational assessment. In sum, as was the case in our discussions of such value-loaded topics as decision making, goal setting, and power, we will attempt to remain descriptive and analytic in our approach rather than normative and perspective. (We confess that some of our comments in the previous chapter on pathologies were prescriptive.)

[1]This belief has been reaffirmed by Hannan and Freeman, who regard effectiveness as "a concept of applications and engineering but not of abstract theory and research." (See Goodman and Pennings, 1977: 108.)

Three major questions are addressed in the following discussion: What are the major criteria that have been proposed to define effectiveness? What are the approaches to assessing effectiveness? and What types of explanations are given to account for differences in effectiveness? As we will see, each of these topics is affected by the type of organization examined, and in particular by whether the organization is or is not responsive to market mechanisms.

DETERMINING CRITERIA OF EFFECTIVENESS[2]

To the novice, defining and determining the effectiveness of an organization must seem a relatively straightforward affair: to inquire into effectiveness is to ask how well an organization is doing, relative to some set of standards. This is not wrong, but by this time, we experts in organizational analysis know that the pursuit of this simple question will lead us into some complex and controversial issues. There are many possible bases for generating criteria of effectiveness, and as we would expect, many different constituencies have an interest in the effectiveness of any organization and will want to propose criteria that reflect this interest.

Multiple Criteria

Price (1968), Steers (1975; 1977), Campbell (1977), and Cameron and Whetten (1982) as well as others have assembled lengthy lists of criteria that have been used by one or more analysts in measuring effectiveness. Campbell, for example, lists thirty different criteria, ranging from productivity and profits to growth, turnover, stability, and cohesion. Steers (1975) limited his attention to seventeen studies of organizational effectiveness in which multiple criteria of effectiveness were devised. Noting that many differing criteria of effectiveness were used in these studies, Steers (1975: 547, 549) points out,

> One of the most apparent conclusions emerging from a comparison of these multivariate models is the lack of consensus as to what constitutes a useful and valid set of effectiveness measures. While each model sets forth its three or four defining characteristics for success, there is surprisingly little overlap across the various approaches.

In attempting to understand why so many and such varied criteria of effectiveness have been proposed, we do not need to search very far beyond the thesis of this volume; quite diverse conceptions of organizations are held by various analysts, and associated with each of these conceptions will be a somewhat distinctive set of criteria for evaluating the effectiveness of organizations. Although several schemata for differentiating among these conceptions have been proposed, we will argue that our

---

[2]Some of the discussion in this section draws on my papers on organizational effectiveness (Scott, 1977a; Scott et al., 1978).

old friends—the rational, natural, and open systems perspectives—account for much of the variance in measures of effectiveness.

Under a rational system model, since organizations are viewed as instruments for the attainment of goals (see Chapter 2), the criteria emphasized focus on the number and quality of outputs and the economies realized in transforming inputs into outputs. General criteria include measures of total output and of quality, productivity, and efficiency. More so than for the other two models, measures of effectiveness from a rational system perspective take the specific goals of the organization as the basis for generating effectiveness criteria. Thus, automobile companies focus on how many cars are manufactured during a given period in absolute numbers or in relation to cost measures; employment bureaus emphasize how many clients are placed in positions, perhaps in relation to the number of persons processed.[3]

As we know, the natural system model views organizations as collectivities that are capable of achieving specified goals but are engaged in other activities required to maintain themselves as a social unit. Thus, natural system analysts insist on adding a set of support goals to the output goals emphasized by the rational system model. Further, these support goals are expected to dominate output goals if the two do not coincide: organizations are governed by the overriding goal of survival (see Chapter 3). The criteria generated by this conception include measures of participant satisfaction and morale (indicators of whether the organization's inducements are sufficient to evoke contributions from participants adequate to ensure survival), the interpersonal skills of managers, and survival itself.

The open systems perspective views organizations as being highly interdependent with their environments and engaged in system-elaborating as well as system-maintaining activities. Information acquisition and processing is viewed as an especially critical activity, since an organization's long-term well-being is dependent on its ability to detect and respond to subtle changes in its task environment (see Chapter 4). Yuchtman and Seashore specify one criterion that they argue is most appropriate for assessing the effectiveness of organizations from the open systems perspective: "bargaining position, as reflected in the ability of the organization, in either absolute or relative terms, to exploit its environment in the acquisition of scarce and valued resources" (1967: 898). Criteria such as profitability, which may be viewed as the excess of returns over expenditures, are also emphasized by open systems analysts. And a great many theorists stress the importance of adaptability and flexibility as criteria of effectiveness. Weick (1977) emphasizes these dimensions when he insists that effective organizations are characterized by a diversity of linguistic forms, techniques for breaking out of normal cognitive and normative constraints, means of simultaneously crediting and discrediting information received,

---

[3]Because of its focus on goals, the rational system is virtually synonymous with the *goals model* described by Etzioni (1960). Several critics have pointed out that because of the emphasis placed by the rational system or goals model on the specific types of goals pursued, these models do not provide an adequate basis for comparing the effectiveness of differing types of organizations (see Yuchtman and Seashore, 1967).

and structural units that are loosely articulated so as to maximize sensitivity to the environment and diversity of response.[4]

Analysts' diverse conceptions of organizations are not the only source of variation in effectiveness criteria. Other important bases of diversity include time perspective and level of analysis. Time considerations enter into the generation and application of effectiveness criteria in two senses. First, the criteria employed may vary depending on whether a relatively shorter or longer time frame is adopted. Steers (1975: 553) provides an example of this distinction:

> If current production, a short-run effectiveness criterion, is maximized at the expense of research and development investments in future products, an organization may ultimately find itself with an outmoded product and threatened for its very survival, a long-run criterion.

How critical a time frame is may depend on how rapidly the environment is changing. Hannan and Freeman (1977: 116), working from an ecological perspective, point out that highly specialized organizations well adapted to their environment may outperform generalist organizations at a given point in time, but may fare much less well over a longer period to the extent that the environment has changed. Second, organizations are necessarily at different stages of their life cycles, and criteria appropriate for assessing effectiveness at one stage may be less so for another. As Seashore has noted, "the meaning of growth for the health, survival, and overall effectiveness of the organization was very different at different stages of the organizational life cycle" (1962). And Cameron and Whetten (1981), in a study of eighteen simulated organizations, found that participants were more apt to stress the effectiveness of acquiring inputs at earlier stages in the history of their organization and the effectiveness of producing outputs at later stages.

We have stressed the importance of level of analysis throughout this volume, and it is a critical factor in accounting for variations in effectiveness criteria. Our conclusions concerning the relative effectiveness of organizations will vary greatly depending on whether we emphasize their impact on individual participants, on the organization itself, or on broader, external societal systems. Cummings argues for the first, social psychological–level criteria for assessing organizational effectiveness. He proposes that

> an effective organization is one in which the greatest percentage of participants perceive themselves as free to use the organization and its subsystems as instruments for their own ends (Cummings, 1977: 60).

Most analysts take the organization itself as the appropriate level of analysis for assessing effectiveness. Yuchtman and Seashore (1967: 896) explicitly adopt this posture, suggesting that a relevant view of effectiveness answers the question How well is the organization doing for itself? Still other investigators adopt a more ecological framework and propose that

---

[4]In his inimitable fashion, Weick summarizes his criteria as follows: "Specifically, I would suggest that the effective organization is (1) garrulous, (2) clumsy, (3) superstitious, (4) hypocritical, (5) monstrous, (6) octopoid, (7) wandering, and (8) grouchy" (1977: 193–94).

organizations should be evaluated in terms of their contributions to other, more general systems. Parsons's (1960) approach to the study of organizations exemplifies this functionalist type of criteria.

Variations in theoretical perspectives on organizations, in time horizons and developmental stage, and in level of analysis—these help to account for the diversity of criteria proposed in analyzing effectiveness. Yet another source of diversity is to be found in the varying sets of participants and constituents associated with organizations. (See Zammuto, 1982.)

Participants, Constituents, and Criteria

Whether organizations are viewed as rational, natural, or open systems, our conceptions of their goals, participants, and constituencies have become progressively more complex. We have been instructed by Simon to view even "simple" output goals as complex and multi-faceted (see Chapters 2 and 11), and we have learned from Etzioni and Perrow to add support or maintenance goals to output goals (see Chapter 3). This more complex conception of goals is reinforced by viewing organizations as collections of subgroups of participants who possess various social characteristics, are in different social locations, and exhibit divergent views and interests regarding what the organization is and what it should be doing (see Chapters 4 and 11). This conception of the organization as a political system can be expanded to include outside constituencies who hold goals "for" the organization (Thompson, 1967: 127), and who attempt to impose these goals on the organization.

It is important to emphasize that when we speak of goals in relation to ascertaining the effectiveness of organizations, we are focusing on the use of goals to supply evaluation criteria. As argued in Chapter 11, goals are used to evaluate organizational activities as well as to motivate and direct them. In a rational world, we would expect the criteria that are developed to direct organizational activities to be the same as those employed to evaluate them, but as we have emphasized, events in organizations are not always as rational and tightly coupled as some theorists would have us believe. Instead, we must be prepared to observe different criteria employed by those who assign tasks and those who evaluate performance (see Dornbusch and Scott, 1975). Discrepancies are more likely to occur when the control system becomes differentiatied and these functions are assigned to different actors, but they can occur when the same persons or groups perform both directing and evaluating activities. An oft-cited problem in organizations develops when vague and broad criteria are used to direct task activities but very explicit criteria are employed to evaluate them, with the consequence that evaluation criteria deflect attention and effort from the original stated objectives to a different or narrower set of goals embodied in the evaluation system. Evaluation criteria often focus on the more easily measured task attributes and ignore others less readily assessed. Thus, social workers may be directed by their supervisors to provide therapeutic casework services but be evaluated primarily on the basis of the number and timeliness of their visits to clients and the correctness of their calculation of budgets (see Scott, 1969). Such discrepancies are likely to result in a displacement of goals as participants come to realize what criteria are used to determine evaluations and to dispense rewards (see also Blau, 1955; Dalton, 1959; Dornbusch and Scott, 1975).

Varying goals—viewed both as directive and as evaluative criteria—will be held by different participant groups and constituencies in organizations. The managers of organizations may not speak with one voice but with many, since they may be composed of a shifting coalition of interests. Similarly, top managers' goals for directing and evaluating activities may not coincide with or be completely reflected in the criteria used by middle-level personnel such as supervisors or technical specialists. Performers vary in the extent to which their own conceptions of their work coincide with those of their superiors, and also in their capacity to enforce their preferences. Finally, many "external" constituencies—stockholders, clients, suppliers and buyers, regulators, community leaders, and news media—have genuine interests in the functioning of an organization and may be expected to attempt to advocate and, if possible, impose their own effectiveness criteria on the organization. In general, the number of persons and groups who propose criteria for evaluating the performance of an organization will be much larger than the number who explicitly seek to direct its activities. "A cat may look at a king," and a reporter for the hometown newspaper may scrutinize the performance of the town's leading industry.

According to this conception of organizations, we would expect little commonality in the criteria employed by the various parties who assess organizational effectiveness. This expectation is shared by Friedlander and Pickle (1968), who impute appropriate interests to such groups as owners, employees, creditors, suppliers, customers, governmental regulators, and the host community. Their data on a sample of small business organizations show that performance assessed by these varying criteria results in a pattern of low and often negative correlation coefficients: to do well on a criterion preferred by one constituency is to do poorly on a criterion favored by another. Friedlander and Pickle conclude that "organizations find it difficult to fulfill simultaneously the variety of demands made upon them" (1968: 302–3).

Another consideration complicating the examination of effectiveness is the recent challenges to the assumption that organizations necessarily exhibit a unified or consistent set of performances. The political models just reviewed allow for divergence and conflict of interests among participants but presume their resolution through negotiation and power processes. In the end, the organization is presumed to pursue a single program. Alternative models that we have explored in earlier chapters suggest the utility of viewing some organizations as "organized anarchies" or as loosely coupled systems containing subunits that exhibit a high degree of autonomy and are capable of pursuing inconsistent objectives. This conception admits the possibility that, with respect to any specific criterion of effectiveness, an organization can be both effective and ineffective depending on what components are being evaluated!

Given the wide variety of participants groups and constituencies that can attempt to set criteria for organizational effectiveness, what generalizations, if any, can be suggested to guide investigations in this area? We offer three predictions. First, the criteria proposed by each group will be self-interested ones. Customers will desire higher quality at lower cost, supplier will wish to sell more dearly and wholesalers to buy more cheaply, workers will prefer higher wages and greater fringe benefits, and managers will seek higher profits and lower costs. We should not look for heroes or villians but for parties with varying interests. And all parties will evaluate the performance of the organization in terms of criteria that benefit themselves. Second, although no criteria are disinterested—each will benefit some groups more than others—all will be stated so as to appear universalistic and objective. This generalization receives support from Pfeffer and Salancik's (1974) study of the allocation of resources among university departments. They report that the stronger departments succeed in budget allocation contests not by imposing particularistic criteria on decisions but by ensuring that the universalistic criteria selected favor their own position. For example, strong departments that have larger graduate-student enrollments will favor this criterion in allocating resources while departments with larger numbers of undergraduate majors will seek to impose this criterion as a distribution rule. Third, given multiple sets of actors pursuing their own interests and a situation of scarce resources, we would expect little commonality or convergence and some conflicts in the criteria employed by the various parties to assess organizational effectiveness, a prediction supported by the study conducted by Friedlander and Pickle (1968).

One final constituency remains to be considered. Researchers who attempt to assess the effectiveness of organizations are not immune to these political processes. Which, and whose, criteria we choose to emphasize in our studies of organizations will depend on our own interests in undertaking the study. We must be willing to state clearly what criteria we propose to employ, recognizing that whatever they are and whoever espouses them, they are always normative conceptions, serving some interests more than others, and likely to be both limited and controversial.

Market and Nonmarket Organizations

The distinction between market-based and nonmarket organizations is especially salient when the question of effectiveness is raised. When properly functioning, the market provides a mechanism for linking the interests of organizational participants and external constituencies in such a manner that the former do not prosper unless they serve the interests of the latter. The effectiveness of market-controlled organizations is directly determined by their customers: if their interests are satisfied, then they will continue to supply the inputs required by the organization; if not, then they can withhold their contributions, causing the organization to suffer and perhaps ultimately to fail. Under ideal market conditions an organization's output goals and system-maintenance goals are tightly linked. However, for reasons explored in Part Three, many organizations have bargained or bridged their way out of competitive market situations and are increasingly the target of governmental regulation.[5]

[5]As noted in Chapter 8, although instituted as a mechanism to protect the interests of the public, regulatory agencies are often "captured" by the organizations they were empowered to control, and operate in the latter's interests (see Stigler, 1971; Pfeffer and Salancik, 1978; Noll, 1985).

Other organizations, primarily government agencies, operate from the outset in nonmarket environments. Thus, Downs employs as his major criterion for defining a bureau the condition that "the major portion of its output is not directly or indirectly evaluated in any markets external to the organization by means of voluntary *quid pro quo* transactions" (1967: 25). As Downs emphasizes, an important implication of this condition is that "there is no direct relationship between the services a bureau provides and the income it receives for providing them" (1967: 30). As governments have come under pressure from hard-pressed taxpayers to make every tax dollar count, new techniques have been developed to ascertain the effectiveness of governmental agencies and, more specifically, government-funded programs. The emergence of evaluation research, both as a set of developing methodologies and as a collection of new professional service organizations, may be viewed as a response to this demand. Evaluation research attempts to provide a basis for assessing the effectiveness and efficiency of governmental programs and thus helps to inform decisions concerning what programs are to be closed, continued, or expanded. Although these efforts began with quite naive assumptions regarding techniques for assessing program and agency effectiveness, they have rapidly become more sophisticated, both technically and politically (see Suchman, 1967; Weiss, 1972; Cronbach et al., 1980).

Evaluation research has proved to be no panacea, however, and general discontent with the effectiveness of public organizations has continued to mount.

> Just as the widespread perception of the failures of private enterprise and the market system in the 1930s generated the political impetus for the creation of the welfare state, which reached its climax in the Great Society programs of the 1960s, so have the recent critiques of federal efforts gradually generated a new reaction back toward belief in the magic of the marketplace and the virtues of private sector dynamism and local initiative (Brooks, 1984: 5).

The drive toward "privatization" of the public sector has taken several routes. Increasingly, publicly owned and operated services are expected at least in part to "pay their own way"—to take in enough revenue to cover most if not all the services provided. Indeed, the variety of organizational forms allowing some degree of governmental ownership or sponsorship combined with some degree of reliance on the marketplace is quite remarkable. These forms range from fully owned governmental corporations (such as the U.S. Postal Service) to a wide variety of government-sponsored enterprises (for example, COMSAT— the Communications Satellite Corporation—and the Corporation for Public Broadcasting). (See Seidman, 1975.) Alternatively, many organizations supplying public services are supported by public funds but are privately owned. This is the case, for example, with defense contractors. A large and increasing proportion of public services—health care, education, police and fire protection—are contracted to private agencies. (See Brooks, Liebman, and Schelling, 1984; Hanrahan, 1983) It is argued that contracting out goods and services fosters competition and hence greater efficiency and effectiveness, but small number of suppliers and the widespread use of sole-source bidding greatly reduce the utility of such safeguards, as has been demonstrated by recurrent overpricing and mismanagement scandals involving weapons procurement by the Pentagon. Reliance on the market also presumes that consumers can evaluate the quality of products and services being purchased. But such an assumption is not tenable for many types of services; indeed, this is one of the major reasons why nonmarket organizations came into existence!

Nonmarket organizations are particularly likely to lack clear output measures. When the goals are to provide for an adequate defense, to negotiate advantagious treaties with other countries, or to fight poverty, it is difficult to determine how effective performances are. Of course, other types of organizations also pursue goals that are vague and difficult to assess. Two problems are involved: how to select indicators—the evidence to employ in evaluating performances—and how to set standards—the criteria to be used in judging whether a given performance is good or poor. Issues of standard setting and indicator selection are discussed in the following section.

ASSESSING EFFECTIVENESS

In order for an evaluation of a performance to occur, criteria must be selected, including the identification of properties or dimensions and the setting of standards; work must be sampled, with decisions made concerning the types of indicators to be employed and the nature of the sample to be drawn; and sampled values must be compared with the selected standards (see Dornbusch and Scott, 1975). In our view, the same components are applicable whether the intent is to evaluate an individual performer or an entire organization. To this point, we have discussed only the problems encountered in determining the properties or dimensions of the organizational performance to be evaluated. In the current section, we discuss the setting of standards and the selection of indicators for assessing organization effectiveness and briefly comment on decisions regarding selection of the sample.

Setting Standards

The setting of standards is a central component in establishing criteria for evaluating the effectiveness of an organization. By definition, standards are normative and not descriptive statements. The problem of how standards for assessing organizations are set is an interesting one but has received relatively little attention from social scientists. Cyert and March have attempted to adapt the psychological concept of aspiration level to explain how organizations establish goals for use as evaluative standards. They argue that

> organizational goals in a particular time period are a function of (1) organizational goals of the previous time period, (2) organizational experience with respect to that goal in the previous time period, and (3) experience of comparable organizations with respect to the goal dimension in the previous time period (Cyert and March, 1963: 123).

Thompson (1967: 84–87) proposes a somewhat more complex model in which types of assessment are viewed as a function of a combination of two factors: (1) whether the standards of desirability are relatively clearly formulated or ambiguous, and (2) whether the beliefs about cause-effect relations are relatively complete or are incomplete.[6] He argues that when standards are clear and cause-effect relations are known, then *efficiency* tests are appropriate. Such tests assess not simply whether a desired effect was produced but whether it was done so efficiently—that is, with a minimum of inputs. If standards are clear but cause-effect relations are uncertain, then *instrumental* tests are suitable. These tests ascertain only whether the desired state was achieved and do not demand conservation of resources. When standards of desirability are themselves ambiguous, then the organization must resort to *social* tests. Social tests are those validated by consensus or by authority. Their validity depends on how many or on who endorses them. Organizations operating in institutionalized environments are likely to depend on social tests for assessing their effectiveness. Such organizations

> become sensitive to, and employ, external criteria of worth. Such criteria include, for instance, such ceremonial awards as the Nobel Prize, endorsements by important people, the standard prices of professionals and consultants, or the prestige of programs or personnel in external social circles. (Meyer and Rowan, 1977: 350)

Thompson's typology is far from definitive, but it calls attention not only to the diversity of standards employed in assessing organizations but also to factors that help to account for these differences.

Selecting Indicators

Among the most critical decisions to be made in attempting to assess organizational effectiveness is the choice of the measures or indicators to be employed. Three general types of indicators have been identified: those based on outcomes, those based on processes, and those based on structures (see Donabedian, 1966; Suchman, 1967; Scott, 1977a). The advantages and disadvantages of each type will be reviewed.

Outcomes   Outcome indicators focus on specific characteristics of materials or objects on which the organization has performed some operation. Examples of outcome indicators are changes in the knowledge or attitudes of students in educational organizations, or changes in the health status of patients in medical institutions. Outcomes are often regarded as the quintessential indicators of effectiveness, but they also may present serious problems of interpretation. Outcomes are never pure indicators of quality of performance, since they reflect not only the care and accuracy with which work activities are carried out but also the current state of the technology and the characteristics of the organization's input and output environments. These matters are of little import when cause-

[6]This second factor is a measure of knowledge of the technology utilized during the throughput process; it is similar to the dimension of predictability (see Chapter 9).

effect knowledge is relatively complete and when organizations are able to exercise adequate controls over their input and output sectors—that is, when the organization is well buffered from its environment. In such situations, represented by the manufacture of standardized equipment in competitive markets, outcomes serve as safe indexes of quality and quantity of organizational performance. However, many types of organizations lack such controls over their work processes and task environments. For example, a patient's medical condition following surgery will reflect not only the quality of care rendered by the surgical staff and the hospital personnel but also the development of medical science with respect to the particular condition treated, as well as the patient's general physical condition and extent of surgical disease at the time of the operation. Such problems are too much for some analysts, who dismiss the attempt to use outcome measures to assess effectiveness under these circumstances. Thus, Mann and Yett (1968: 196–97) reason,

> There are those who argue that the output of a health facility should be specified in terms of its effect on the patient. . . . We reject this definition of hospital output for the same reason that we do not regard the output of a beauty salon as beauty.

In our view, the use of outcome measures presents difficult, but not unsolvable, problems in assessing effectiveness of organizations such as hospitals and schools. The problem of inadequate knowledge of cause-effect relations can be handled by the use of relative rather than absolute performance standards, so that the performance of an organization is compared against others carrying on similar work. This approach presumes that the organizations assessed can—or should—participate in the same cultural system and have access to the same general knowledge pool. A particular organization possessing more relevant knowledge—for example, having better-trained personnel—would be expected to perform better than one possessing less knowledge, but the use of relative standards ensures that an organization is not penalized for lacking knowledge that no one has.

The problem posed by the contribution of variations among input characteristics to variations in outcomes experienced is less easily resolved. Although we can safely assume that organizations have access to the same knowledge, we cannot assume that they have access to the same client pool or supply sources. Indeed, one of the principal ways in which organizations vary is in the amount and quality of inputs they are able to garner. The pattern of inputs characterizing various types of organizations is not as simple as might appear on superficial examination. For example, as might be expected, prestigious universities recruit highly intelligent students, as indicated by scores on standard entrance examinations or past performance in academic settings, whereas less highly regarded institutions accept higher proportions of less qualified students. By contrast, highly regarded teaching hospitals focus primarily on the care of the very sick or on those whose problems pose the greatest challenge to medical science. In these organizations, there is an inverse relation between presumed quality of institution and patient condition. We would expect organizations to seek to take credit for acquiring inputs that enhance their outcomes—a widely used indicator of quality for universities is the characteristics of the student body they are able to attract—but to resist being held accountable for inputs that negatively affect outcomes. Thus, teaching hospitals insist that if patient outcome measures are employed as indicators of performance quality, they be standardized to take account of differences in patient mix. Statistical techniques are available that allow analysts to adjust outcome measures to take into account differences in characteristics of inputs.[7]

Outcome measures may also be affected by the characteristics of output environments. For example, indicators of outcomes relating to sales for products, or to placement or rehabilitation for prisoners or mental patients, will reflect not simply organizational performance but also market conditions or the receptivity of community groups external to the organization. As with inputs, we would expect organizations to prefer to take credit for conditions enhancing outcomes but insist that conditions having a negative effect be taken into account if outcomes are evaluated.

More generally, the decision as to how to treat input characteristics and output environments is not primarily a methodological but a theoretical issue. Do we wish to adjust for differences in student intelligence among universities in assessing student performance, or do we wish to regard student recruitment as an important aspect of a university's performance? Do we wish to adjust for market conditions in assessing a firm's retail sales, or do we wish to consider ability to build a solid market niche an important component of the firm's performance? Answers to these and similar questions depend on whether we seek to concentrate simply on the organization's throughput processes—its technical-core activities—or to include in our assessment the performance of the organization's bridging units—its input and output components.

Still other issues are involved in the use of outcome measures to assess organizational effectiveness. Briefly, it is difficult to determine the appropriate timing of such measures. Some organizations insist that their full effects may not be apparent for long period following their performance. For example, some educators claim that relevant academic outcomes can only be assessed long after the students have left school and have attempted to apply their knowledge in the "real world." And when is the appropriate time to assess a hospital's effect on a patient's health—immediately following a major therapeutic intervention such as surgery, at discharge, or following a post-hospitalization recovery period? Another problem in employing outcome indicators is the lack of relevant information. Many types of organizations have little or no data on outcomes achieved: they quickly lose contact with their "products"—whether these be human graduates or manufactured commodities. The collection of relevant outcome data can become very costly indeed if it entails tracking down such products after they are distributed throughout the environment.

Partly because of these quite formidable difficulties in assessing and interpreting outcome measures, other types of indicators of organiza-

---

[7]My colleagues and I have developed methods for adjusting patient outcome measures in order to assess the relative effectiveness of hospitals in providing surgical services. (See Scott et al., 1978; Flood and Scott, 1987).

tional effectiveness are often preferred. These measures—of processes and structures—can be more briefly described.

Processes Process measures focus on the quantity or quality of activities carried on by the organization. As Suchman (1967: 61) notes, this type of indicator

> represents an assessment of input or energy regardless of output. It is intended to answer the questions, "What did you do?" and "How well did you do it?"

Process measures assess effort rather than effect. Some process measures assess work quantity—for example, staying with our hospital illustration, we may ask how many laboratory tests were conducted during a given period or how many patients were seen in the emergency room. Others assess work quality—for example, hospitals might be rated by the frequency with which medication errors occur or by the proportion of healthy tissue removed from patients during surgery. Still other measures assess the extent of quality-control efforts—for instance, the autopsy rate in hospitals or the proportion of X rays reviewed by radiologists.

In some respects, process measures are more valid measures of the characteristics of organizational performance. Rather than requiring inferences from outcomes to performance characteristics, process measures directly assess performance values. On the other hand, it is important to emphasize that all process measures evaluate efforts rather than achievements, and when the focus is on quality of performance rather than quantity, they assess conformity to a given standard but not the adequacy or correctness of the standards themselves. Process measures are based on the assumption that it is known what activities are required to ensure effectiveness. Students of medical care are currently challenging the assumption that there is a strong correlation between conformity to current standards of medical practice and improvements in patient outcomes (see Brook, 1973), as well as the assumption that higher levels of medical care result in improved health status (see Fuchs, 1974). More generally, social critics such as Illich (1972; 1976) claim that the substitution of process for outcome is one of the great shell games perpetrated by modern institutions against individuals. Illich (1972: 1) argues that contemporary individuals are trained

> to confuse process and substance. Once these become blurred, a new logic is assumed: the more treatment there is, the better are the results; or, escalation leads to success. The pupil is thereby "schooled" to confuse teaching with learning, grade advancement with education, a diploma with competence, and fluency with the ability to say something new. His imagination is "schooled" to accept service in place of value. Medical treatment is mistaken for health care, social work for the improvement of community life, police protection for safety, military poise for national security, the rat race for productive work. Health, learning, dignity, independence, and creative endeavor are deigned as little more than the performance of the institutions that claim to serve these ends, and their improvement is made to depend on allocating more resources to the management of hospitals, schools, and other agencies in question.

Recognizing that Illich's broad accusations have some merit, we would, however, express two sorts of reservations. The first relates to an argument we made in Chapter 12. Focusing on processes rather than outcomes represents a type of goal displacement. However, as noted earlier, goal displacement is a very widespread phenomenon and need not be regarded as pathological. Only when means and ends become disconnected is there cause for distress. Our second demurring relates to the case of organizations in institutionalized environments, in which, to a large extent, process *is* substance. In these organizations, conformity to ritually defined procedures produces a successful outcome, by definition. Ceremony is substance in many contemporary organizations, including religious bodies, legal firms, and many professionally staffed organizations.

Organizations are more likely to compile data on work processes than on outcomes. Performance quality and quantity are often regularly monitored. Gathering information on work processes, however, can still be problematic. Inspections based on observation of ongoing performances are both expensive and reactive—that is, likely to influence the behavior observed. In most work situations there are numerous barriers to work visibility, and workers often resist attempts to directly observe their work in process. Many kinds of work occur under circumstances that render routine inspection impossible, and other kinds, such as those emphasizing mental activities, are by their nature difficult to observe. Because of such difficulties, organizations may rely on self-reports of activities performed. However, such data are likely to be both biased and incomplete representations of work processes (see Dornbusch and Scott, 1975: 145–62). Because of these and related difficulties in obtaining process measures, many organizations rely on structural indicators of effectiveness.

Structures   Structural indicators assess the capacity of the organization for effective performance. Included within this category are all measures based on organizational features or participant characteristics presumed to have an impact on organizational effectiveness. Manufacturing organizations can be assessed by the value and age of their machine tools; hospitals are assessed by the adequacy of their facilities and equipment and by the qualifications of the medical staff as reflected in past training and certification; and schools are assessed by the qualities of their faculties measured in terms of types of degrees acquired, and by such features as the number of volumes in their libraries. These types of measures form the basis of accreditation reviews and organizational certification systems.

If process measures are once removed from outcomes, then structure indicators are twice remote, for these measures index not the work performed by structures but their *capacity* to perform work—not the activities carried out by organizational participants but their qualifications to perform the work. Structural indicators focus on organizational inputs as surrogate measures for outputs. Economists warn us that quality of outputs should not be confused with quality (or cost) of inputs, but Yuchtman and Seashore (1967) are close to embracing this position in their influential paper on organizational effectiveness. As noted above, they suggest that the effectiveness of an organization can be defined in terms of its ability to acquire scarce and valued resources—for example, expensive facilities and highly qualified personnel. They make the explicit assumption that an organization's bargaining position in its input environment is "a function of all the three phases of organizational behavior—the importation of resources, their use (including allocating and processing), and their exportation in some output form that aids further input" (Yuchtman and Seashore, 1967: 898).

As was the case with measures of organizational process, a number of observers have suggested that an emphasis on structural measures may have detrimental consequences for quality of outcomes. For example, numerous observers have argued that personnel licensure requirements have become a major obstacle to innovation in work procedures and to the optimal deployment of workers (see Somers, 1969; Tancredi and Woods, 1972). Thus, we have the interesting situation in which some measures of organizational effectiveness based on the assessment of process or of structure are argued to adversely affect other measures of effectiveness based on outcomes.

Selecting Samples

Once indicators have been selected, decisions must still be made regarding the gathering of information relevant to these measures. We leave aside here discussion of specific techniques of data gathering as well as decisions pertaining to sample size, ensuring of representativeness, and other technical considerations, in order to emphasize the critical importance of the definition of the universe from which the sample is to be drawn. A basic decision confronting the analyst who assesses the effectiveness of any organization is whether to focus on the actual work performed by the organization or instead to ask whether the organization is attending to the appropriate work. The first option takes as given the current program of the organization—its structures, processess, or outcomes—and seeks to ascertain its quality or effectiveness. The second option assumes a broader perspective, asking whether the organization is engaged in the right program. Never mind whether the organization is doing things right; is it doing the right things? Reinhardt (1973) labels the first criterion *microquality* and the second, *macroquality*. If this distinction were applied to a service organization, an assessment of microquality would focus on the quality of structures, processes, or outcomes actually experienced by clients who were the recipients of the organization's services. By contrast, an assessment of macroquality would seek to determine whether the appropriate services were being provided or, more critically, whether the proper clients were receiving services. The effectiveness of a medical care organization might be assessed in terms of the health status of the clients who had received services (microqualitiy) or by the health status of the population residing within the organization's service area (macroquality).

Participants, Constituents, and Measures

Just as with evaluation criteria, we would expect differing participant and constituency groups to prefer some types of measures over others. Generally, we expect organizational managers to emphasize struc-

334 Organizational Effectiveness

tural measures of effectiveness, in part because these reflect factors that are more under their control than other types of indicators. Thus, organizational administrators are likely to have considerable influence over the types of facilities provided or the standards used in hiring personnel. By contrast, we would expect performers or rank-and-file participants to emphasize process measures of effectiveness. Skilled and semiskilled workers, who have little or no discretion in the selection of their activities, will prefer to be evaluated on the basis of their conformity to their performance programs rather than on the basis of the efficacy of these programs. And professional personnel, who are granted discretion in their choice of activities, will also usually prefer to be evaluated on the basis of process measures—their conformity to "standards of good practice"— since inadequacies in the knowledge base mean that they lack full control over outcomes.

Clients who use the products or receive the services are likely to focus primarily on outcome measures of effectiveness. They will evaluate the organization's product in terms of the extent to which it has met their own needs and expectations. Did the motor run? Was something of interest or use learned? Was pain relieved or functioning improved? In addition, clients who receive personal services are likely to place considerable value on process measures having to do with promptness, courtesy, and sensitivity of treatment. In circumstances where outcomes are difficult to evaluate, process measures will receive more weight from clients than outcome indicators. The most extreme cases involve institutionalized environments in which no outcomes at all can be demonstrated to occur regularly—although they are alleged to occur—so that both performers and recipients devote attention to evaluating conformity to established norms of practice.

All of the interest groups considered to this point—organizational managers, performers, and consumers—are likely to focus on microquality indicators of effectiveness. They will prefer to focus on the structures, processes, and outcomes associated with the work that the organization is actually performing. But another interest group consisting of the public at large, including some public regulatory bodies, will be more likely to emphasize measures of macroquality. Is the organization concentrating its attention and resources on the proper products or problems? Do eligible clients have access to its services? Is the community as a whole benefiting from its operation?

Our final constituency are the researchers dedicated to the objective, scientific analysis of organizational effectiveness. We would hope to find this group busily engaged in analyzing *all* types of indicators of effectiveness, exploring their interrelation, and employing criteria variously drawn from all of the interested parties. Although we have not conducted the type of systematic survey of the literature required to support such a conclusion, it appears that we analysts have emphasized the structural and process measures of effectiveness—those measures preferred by organizational managers and performers—to the neglect of outcome measures— those preferred by clients and the larger public. Both ideological and economic factors help to produce this bias in orientation. It is our belief that organizational analysts are more likely to identify with organizational managers and professional performers than with client and public interests. Indeed, most of the research on organizations is conducted by persons who train future managers while consulting for present ones. Also, most of the data available to us for analysis are collected by the organizations for their own purposes or are based on information supplied by organizational managers. Organizations, as noted above, are much less likely to collect data on outcomes than data based on their structural features and processes. If we want data on outcomes—and especially on outcomes that represent measures of macroquality—we will have to collect them for ourselves, or persuade governmental agencies to collect them for us. We should not minimize the cost or the value of such data in correcting the bias that currently exists in indicators of organizational effectiveness.

EXPLAINING EFFECTIVENESS

Given the multiple possible meanings and measures of effectiveness that have been proposed, our comments on explanations of effectiveness can be brief since they are mostly by way of warning. When effectiveness can be viewed as comprising such varied criteria as flexibility, low turnover, and growth, we must seek explanatory variables as varied as what they are asked to account for. Given that many of the proposed measures of effectiveness are uncorrelated or even negatively correlated, we should not expect to find general explanations that will distinguish effective from ineffective organizations. We must agree to settle for modest and limited measures of specific aspects of organizational structures, processes, and outcomes.

Also given the complexity and openness of organizations as detailed in this volume, we would not expect any single set of factors to account for organizational effectiveness. This is the major defect, in our opinion, of some recent best sellers in the organizational literature. For example, such studies as Ouchi's *Theory Z* and Peters and Waterman's *In Search of Excellence,* while they provide valuable insights into new managerial techniques, convey the message that organizational performance is primarily a matter of management effectiveness—of management's capacity to create the right culture and motivational structure. Overlooked or underemphasized are such factors as industrial location, positioning in various markets—resource, labor, capital, sales—critical alliances and connections, information systems, and institutional supports. Effective organizations require more than enthusiastic managers and motivated workers.

Since the appearance of the open systems perspective, a popular approach to explaining variations in effectiveness has involved the use of contingency models: organizations whose internal features best match the demands of their technologies or task environments are expected to be most effective (see Chapter 4). The adequacy of such models depends, among other things, on the quality of our ideas about the appropriate relation (match) between task or environmental demands and organizational arrangements. We have attempted to summarize some of these evolving principles in Chapters 8 through 10, and while we do not apologize for the state of our knowledge, we readily admit that there is much room for improvement. The principles developed are generally vague and need to be carefully adapted for application to specific settings. That this is not a straightforward task is illustrated by Perrow's critique of Neuhauser's attempt to apply these ideas to the organization of doctors' work in hospitals. Neuhauser (1971) embraces the widely accepted design principle that when work is complex and uncertain, attempts to control performance with the use of highly specified procedures—high formalization—will lower work quality. Perrow would certainly subscribe to this general principle, but he takes issue with Neuhauser's specific application of it to the hospital setting:

> Tasks are complex on the medical side of the hospitals, so when dealing with doctors, specification of procedures should be low. But the specifications of what kind of procedures? Any, it seems. For example, he includes the number of tests required at admissions . . . and the number of limitations placed upon the surgery that people can perform (a general practitioner cannot do heart surgery). Using knee-jerk theorizing, he says that if there are a lot of specifications of these kinds, quality should be low. Presumably he could have included scrubbing before surgery as a specification of procedures that would lower quality when tasks are complex. (Perrow, 1972: 420)

Perrow's tone is overly caustic, but his point is well taken, and the problem illustrated is all too common in organizational analysis. We are too often in thralldom before a general principle, applying it mindlessly to situations whose complexity swamps whatever truth might have been revealed by a more thoughtful approach. Let us not be misunderstood. We need the guidance of general principles. But we also require sufficiently detailed knowledge of the organizations and their technologies and environments to be able to select valid indicators of the variables to be assessed. Surgeons do need to be able to exercise discretion in some critical areas of their work, but this requirement need not be inconsistent with the precise specification of other aspects of their performance. If we wish to explain effects, there is no substitute for a knowledge of the specific causal processes linking them with relevant inputs, technologies, and work arrangements.

Contingency models often overlook the open systems concept of equifinality: that many different causal paths can lead to the same effect. In particular, it is often presumed that an organization's ability to maximize its productivity or its profits is due to the superior design of its production structures and the resulting technical efficiency. However, we should know by this time that organizations are technical systems but not simply technical systems. As Katz and Kahn (1978: 249) remind us,

> the textbook path to organizational survival is internal efficiency: build the better mousetrap or build the old trap less expensively. There is, however, a whole class of alternative or supplementary solutions—the political devices that maximize organizational return at some cost to other organizations or individuals.

Pfeffer and Salancik stress the importance of these political solutions throughout their analysis of organizational functioning, concluding: that "the effectiveness of an organization is a sociopolitical question" (1978:

11). Consumers and (some) regulators seek ways to link an organization's effectiveness in goal attainment to its effectiveness in resource acquisition and survival. Sometimes they succeed but often they fail: an organization's resource acquisition and survival are not always tightly linked with the quality of its services to the publics it claims to benefit.

SUMMARY

Criteria for evaluating organizational effectiveness cannot be produced by some objective, apolitical process. They are always normative and often controversial, and they are as varied as the theoretical models used to describe organizations and the constituencies that have some interest in their functioning. Similarly, the indicators to be used in assessing organizational effectiveness must also be chosen from among several possible types, and data gathered from several possible sampling frames. Measures based on outcomes, processes, and structural features of organizations are likely to produce inconsistent conclusions and are differently favored by various constituencies. We should not seek explanations for organizational effectiveness in general, since such general criteria are not available, and we must be cautious in celebrating the truism that organizations that are better adapted to their environments are more likely to survive. Adaptation can be achieved in numerous ways, many of which contribute to the survival of the organization but fail to serve the interests of external constituencies.

references

ABEGGLEN, JAMES C. (1958). *The Japanese Factory: Aspects of Its Social Organization*. Glencoe, Ill.: Free Press.

ADAMS, J. STACEY (1965). "Inequity in Social Exchange," in *Advances in Experimental Social Psychology*, vol. 2, pp. 267–300, ed. Leonard Berkowitz. New York: Academic Press.

AIKEN, MICHAEL, and JERALD HAGE (1968). "Organizational Interdependence and Intraorganizational Structure," *American Sociological Review*, 33 (December), 912–29.

ALBROW, MARTIN (1970). *Bureaucracy*. New York: Praeger.

ALCHIAN, A. A., and H. DEMSETZ (1972) "Production, Information Costs, and Economic Organization," *American Economic Review*, 62 (December), 777–95.

ALDRICH, HOWARD E. (1972). "Technology and Organizational Structure: A Reexamination of the Findings of the Aston Group," *Administrative Science Quarterly*, 17 (March), 26–43.

————— (1976). "Resource Dependence and Interorganizational Relations: Local Employment Service Offices and Social Services Sector Organizations," *Administration and Society*, 7 (February), 419–54.

————— (1979). *Organizations and Environments*. Englewood Cliffs, N.J.: Prentice-Hall.

ALDRICH, HOWARD E., and SERGIO MINDLIN (1978). "Uncertainty and Dependence: Two Perspectives on Environment," in *Organization and Environment*, pp. 149–70, ed. Lucien Karpit, Beverly Hills, Calif.: Sage Publications, Inc.

ALDRICH, HOWARD E., and JEFFREY PFEFFER (1976). "Environments of Organizations," *Annual Review of Sociology*, 2, 79–105.

ALDRICH, HOWARD E., and DAVID A. WHETTEN (1981). "Organization-Sets, Action-Sets, and Networks: Making the Most of Simplicity," in *Handbook of Organizational Design*, vol. 1, pp. 385–408, ed. Paul C. Nystrom and William H. Starbuck. New York: Oxford University Press.

ALFORD, ROBERT R. (1975). *Health Care Politics*. Chicago: University of Chicago Press.

ALFORD, ROBERT R. and ROGER FRIEDLAND (1975). "Political Participation and Public Policy," *Annual Review of Sociology*, 1, 429–79.

ALLISON, GRAHAM T. (1971). *Essence of Decision: Explaining the Cuban Missile Crisis*, Boston: Little, Brown.

ALTHAUSER, ROBERT P., and ARNE L. KALLEBERG (1981). "Firms, Occupations, and the Structure of Labor Markets: A Conceptual Analysis and Research Agenda," in *Sociological Perspectives on Labor Markets*, pp. 119–49, ed. Ivan Berg. New York: Academic Press.

ALTHUSSER, LOUISE (1969 trans.). *For Marx*. Harmondsworth, England: Penguin.

AMBER, G. H., and P. S. AMBER (1962). *Anatomy of Automation*. Englewood Cliffs, N.J.: Prentice-Hall.

ANDERSON, BO, JOSEPH BERGER, BERNARD P. COHEN, and MORRIS ZELDITCH, JR. (1966). "Status Classes in Organizations," *Administrative Science Quarterly*, 11 (September) 264–83.

ARENDT, HANNAH (1951). *The Origins of Totalitarianism*. New York: Harcourt, Brace.

————— (1963). *Eichmann in Jerusalem*. New York: Viking.

ARGOTE, LINDA (1982). "Input Uncertainty and Organizational Coordination in Hospital Emergency Units," *Administrative Science Quarterly*, 27 (September), 420–34.

ARGYRIS, CHRIS (1957). *Personality and Organization*. New York: Harper.

————— (1962). *Interpersonal Competence and Organizational Effectiveness*. Homewood, Ill.: Richard D. Irwin.

————— (1973). "Personality and Organization Theory Revisited," *Administrative Science Quarterly*, 18 (June), 141–67.

ARGYRIS, CHRIS, and DONALD A. SCHON (1978). *Organization Learning*. Reading, Mass.: Addison-Wesley.

ARMOUR, HENRY O., and DAVID J. TEECE (1978)."Organization Structure and Economic Performance: A Test of the Multidivisional Hypothesis," *Bell Journal of Economics*, 9 (Spring), 106–22.

ARROW, KENNETH J. (1974). *The Limits of Organization*. New York: W. W. Norton & Co., Inc.

ASHBY, W. ROSS (1952). *A Design for a Brain*. New York: John Wiley.

————— (1956). "The Effect of Experience on a Determinant System," *Behavioral Science*, 1 (January), 35–42.

————— (1968) "Principles of the Self-Organizing System," in *Modern Systems Research for the Behavioral Scientist*, pp. 108–18, ed. Walter Buckley. Chicago: Aldine.

ASTLEY, W. GRAHAM (1985). "The Two Ecologies: Population and Community Perspectives on Organizational Evolution," *Administrative Science Quarterly*, 30 (June), 224–41.

ASTLEY, W. GRAHAM, and ANDREW H. VAN DE VEN (1983). "Central Perspectives and Debates in Organization Theory," *Administrative Science Quarterly*, 28 (June), 245–73.
AVERITT, RICHARD T. (1968). *The Dual Economy: The Dynamics of American Industry Structure*. New York: W. W. Norton & Co., Inc.

BABER, WALTER F. (1983). *Organizing the Future: Martix Models for the Postindustrial Polity*. Birmingham: University of Alabama Press.
BACHRACH, PETER, and MORTON S. BARATZ (1962). "The Two Faces of Power," *American Political Science Review*, 56 (December), 947–52.
BAKER, ALTON W., and RALPH C. DAVIS (1954). *Ratios of Staff to Line Employees and Stages of Differentiation of Staff Functions*. Columbus: Bureau of Business Research, Ohio State University.
BALES, ROBERT F. (1952). "Some Uniformities of Behavior in Small Social Systems," in *Readings in Social Psychology* (2nd ed.), pp. 146–59, ed. Guy E. Swanson, Theodor M. Newcomb, and Eugene L. Hartley. New York: Holt, Rinehart & Winston.
—— (1953). "The Equilibrium Problem in Small Groups," in *Working Papers in the Theory of Action*, pp. 111–61 by Talcott Parsons, Robert F. Bales, and Edward A. Shils. Glencoe, Ill.: Free Press.
BALES, ROBERT F., and PHILIP E. SLATER (1955). "Role Differentiation in Small Decision-Making Groups,: in *Family, Socialization and Interaction Process*, pp. 259–306, ed. Talcott Parsons and Robert F. Bales. New York: Free Press.
BARBER, BERNARD (1950). "Participation and Mass Apathy in Associations," in *Studies in Leadership*, pp. 477–504, ed. Alvin W. Gouldner. New York: Harper.
BARDACH, EUGENE, and ROBERT A. KAGAN (1982). *Going by the Book: The Problem of Regulatory Unreasonableness*. Philadelphia: Temple University Press.
BARKER, E. (1944). *The Development of Public Services in Western Europe, 1660–1930*. New York: Oxford University Press.
BARNARD, CHESTER I. (1938). *The Functions of the Executive*. Cambridge, Mass.: Harvard University Press.
—— (1948). *Organization and Management*. Cambridge, Mass.: Harvard University Press.
BARNES, JOHN A. (1972). *Social Networks*. Reading, Mass.: Addison-Wesley.
BARON, JAMES N. (1984). "Organizational Perspectives on Stratification," *Annual Review of Sociology*, 10, 37–69.
BARON, JAMES N., and WILLIAM T. BIELBY (1980). "Bringing the Firms Back In: Stratification, Segmentation, and the Organization of Work," *American Sociological Review*, 45 (October), 737–65
—— (1984). "The Organization of Work in a Segmented Economy," *American Sociological Review* 49 (August), 454–73.
BATESON, GREGORY (1972). *Steps to an Ecology of Mind*. New York: Ballantine.
BAVELAS, ALEX (1951). "Communication Patterns in Task-Oriented Groups," in *The Policy Sciences*, pp. 193–202, ed. Daniel Lerner and Harold D. Lasswell. Stanford, Calif.: Stanford University Press.
BECKHARD, RICHARD (1972) "Organizational Issues in the Team Delivery of Comprehensive Health Care, *Milbank Memorial Fund Quarterly* 50 (July) part 1, 287–316.
BEDEIAN, ARTHUR G. (1984). *Organizations: Theory and Analysis* (2nd ed.) Chicago: Dryden Press.
BEER, STAFFORD (1964). *Cybernetics and Management*. New York: John Wiley.
BELKNAP, IVAN (1956). *The Human Problems of a State Mental Hospital*. New York: McGraw-Hill.
BELL, DANIEL (1960). Work and Its Discontents: The Cult of Efficiency in America," in *The End of Ideology*, pp. 222–62, by Daniel Bell. Glencoe, Ill.: Free Press.
—— (1973). *The Coming of Post-Industrial Society*. New York: Basic Books.
BELL, GERALD D. (1967). "Determinants of Span of Control," *American Journal of Sociology*, 73 (July), 100–109.
BEN-DAVID, JOSEPH (1963). "Professions in the Class System of Present-Day Societies," *Current Sociology*, 12, 247–330.
BENDIX, REINHARD (1956). *Work and Authority in Industry*. New York: John Wiley.
—— (1960). *Max Weber: An Intellectual Portrait*. Garden City, N.Y.: Doubleday, 1960.
BENDIX, REINHARD, and LLOYD H. FISHER (1949). "The Perspectives of Elton Mayo," *Review of Economics and Statistics*, 31 (November), 312–19.
BENDIX, REINHARD, and SEYMOUR MARTIN LIPSET (1966). "Karl Marx's Theory of Social Classes," in *Class, Status and Power* (rev. ed.) pp. 6–11, ed. Reinhard Bendix and Seymour Martin Lipset. New York: Free Press.
BENNIS, WARREN G. (1959). "Leadership Theory and Administrative Behavior," *Administrative Science Quarterly*, 4 (December), 259–301.
—— (1966). *Changing Organizations*. New York: McGraw-Hill.
BENNIS, WARREN G., and PHILIP E. SLATER (1968). *The Temporary Society*. New York: Harper & Row, Pub.
BENSON, J. KENNETH (1977). "Organizations: A Dialectical View," *Administrative Science Quarterly*, 22 (March), 1–21.
—— (1982). "A Framework for Policy Analysis," in *Interorganizational Coordination*, pp. 137–76, ed. David L. Rogers and David A. Whetten. Ames: Iowa State University Press.
BERG, IVAR (1971). *Education and Jobs: The Great Training Robbery*. New York: Praeger.
BERGER, PETER L., BRIGITTE BERGER, and HANSFRIED KELLNER (1973). *The Homeless Mind: Modernization and Consciousness*. New York: Random House, Vintage Books.
BERGER, PETER L., and THOMAS LUCKMANN (1967). *The Social Construction of Reality*. New York: Doubleday.

BERGER, SUZANNE, ed. (1981). *Organizing Interests in Western Europe: Pluralism, Corporatism and the Transformation of Politics.* New York: Cambridge University Press.

BERLE, A. A. (1963). *The American Economic Republic.* New York: Harcourt, Brace & World.

BERLE, A. A., and GARDINER C. MEANS (1932). *The Modern Corporation and Private Property.* New York: Macmillan.

BERTALANFFY, LUDWIG VON (1956). "General System Theory," in *General Systems: Yearbook of the Society for the Advancement of General Systems Theory,* ed. Ludwig von Bertalanffy and Anatol Rapoport, 1, 1–10.

——— (1962). "General System Theory: A Critical Review," in *General Systems: Yearbook of the Society for General Systems Research,* ed. Ludwig von Bertalanffy and Anatol Rapoport, 7, 1–20.

BEYER, JANICE M., and HARRISON M. TRICE (1979). "A Reexamination of the Relations between Size and Various Components of Organizational Complexity," *Administrative Science Quarterly,* 24 (March), 48–64.

BIDWELL, CHARLES E. (1965). "The School as a Formal Organization," in *Handbook of Organizations,* pp. 972–1022, ed. James G. March. Chicago: Rand McNally.

BITTNER, EGON (1967). "The Police on Skid Row: A Study of Peace Keeping," *American Sociological Review,* 32 (October), 699–715.

BLAKE, R. R., and J. S. MOUTON (1964). *The Managerial Grid.* Houston: Gulf.

BLAKE, R. R., H. A. SHEPHARD, and J. S. MOUTON (1964). *Intergroup Conflict in Organizations.* Ann Arbor, Mich.: Foundation for Research on Human Behavior.

BLAU, PETER M. (1955). *The Dynamics of Bureaucracy.* Chicago: University of Chicago Press (rev. 1963).

——— (1956). *Bureaucracy in Modern Society.* New York: Random House.

——— (1957). "Formal Organization: Dimensions of Analysis," *American Journal of Sociology,* 63 (July), 58–69.

——— (1960). "Structural Effects," *American Sociological Review,* 25 (April) 178–93.

——— (1964). *Exchange and Power in Social Life.* New York: John Wiley.

——— (1968). "The Hierarchy of Authority in Organizations," *American Journal of Sociology,* 73 (January), 453–67.

——— (1970). "A Formal Theory of Differentiation in Organizations," *American Sociological Review,* 35 (April), 201–18.

——— (1973). *The Organization of Academic Work.* New York: John Wiley.

BLAU, PETER M., and OTIS DUDLEY DUNCAN, *The American Occupational Structure.* New York: John Wiley. (1967).

BLAU, PETER M. CECILIA McHUGH FALBE, WILLIAM McKINLEY, and PHELPS K. TRACY (1976). "Technology and Organization in Manufacturing," *Administrative Science Quarterly,* 21 (March) 20–40.

BLAU, PETER M., WOLF V. HEYDEBRAND, and ROBERT E. STAUFFER (1966). "The Structure of Small Bureaucracies," *American Sociological Review,* 31 (April), 179–91.

BLAU, PETER M., and RICHARD A. SCHOENHERR (1971). *The Structure of Organizations.* New York: Basic Books.

BLAU, PETER M., and W. RICHARD SCOTT (1962). *Formal Organizations.* San Francisco: Chandler.

BLAUNER, ROBERT (1960). "Work Satisfaction and Industrial Trends in Modern Society," in *Labor and Trade Unionism,* pp. 339–60 ed. Walter Galenson and Seymour Martin Lipset. New York: John Wiley.

BLUMBERG, PAUL (1968). *Industrial Democracy: The Sociology of Participation.* New York: Schocken Books.

BOAS, MAX, and STEVE CHAIN (1977). *Big Mac: The Unauthorized Story of McDonald's.* New York: New American Library.

BOGUSLAW, ROBERT (1965). *The New Utopians: A Study of System Design and Social Change.* Englewood Cliffs, N.J.: Prentice-Hall.

BOORMAN, SCOTT, and HARRISON C. WHITE (1976). "Social Structures from Multiple Networks: II. Role Structures," *American Journal of Sociology,* 81 (May) 1384–446.

BOULDING, KENNETH E. (1953). *The Organizational Revolution.* New York: Harper & Brothers.

——— (1956). "General Systems Theory: The Skeleton of Science," *Management Science,* 2 (April), 197–208.

BRAVERMAN, HARRY (1974). *Labor and Monopoly Capital: The Degradation of Work in the Twentieth Century.* New York: Monthly Review Press.

BRAYFIELD, ARTHUR H., and WALTER H. CROCKETT (1955). "Employee Attitudes and Employee Performance," *Psychological Bulletin,* 52 (September), 396–424.

BRIEF, ARTHUR P., and RAMON J. ALDAG (1975). "Employee Reactions to Job Characteristics: A Constructive Replication," *Journal of Applied Psychology,* 60 (April), 182–86.

BRIGHT, CHARLES, and SUSAN HARDING, eds. (1984). *Statemaking and Social Movements.* Ann Arbor: University of Michigan Press.

BRITTAIN, JACK, and JOHN FREEMAN (1980). "Organizational Proliferation and Density-Dependent Selection," in *Organizational Life Cycles,* pp. 291–338, ed. John Kimberly and Robert Miles. San Francisco: Jossey-Bass.

BROOK, ROBERT H. (1973). *Quality of Care Assessment: A Comparison of Five Methods of Peer Review.* Washington, D.C.: Bureau of Health Services Research and Evaluation.

BROOKS, HARVEY (1984). "Seeking Equity and Efficiency: Public and Private Roles," in *Public-Private Partnership: New Opportunities for Meeting Social Needs.* pp. 3–29, ed. Harvey Brooks, Lance Liebman, and Corinne S. Schelling. Cambridge, Mass.: Ballinger.

BROOKS, HARVEY, LANCE LIEBMAN, and CORINNE S. SCHELLING, eds. (1984). *Public-Private Partnership: New Opportunities for Meeting Social Needs.* Cambridge, Mass.: Ballinger.

Brown, Richard Harvey (1978). "Bureaucracy as Praxis: Toward a Political Phenomenology of Formal Organizations," *Administrative Science Quarterly*, 23 (September), 365–82.

Brunsson, Nils (1985). *The Irrational Organization*. New York: John Wiley.

Bucher, Rue, and Anselm Strauss (1961). "Professions in Process," *American Journal of Socioogy*, 66 (January), 325–34.

Buckley, Walter (1967). *Sociology and Modern Systems Theory*. Englewood Cliffs, N.J.: Prentice-Hall.

Burawoy, Michael (1979). *Manufacturing Consent: Changes in the Labor Process under Monopoly Capitalism*. Chicago: University of Chicago Press.

——— (1982). "Introduction: The resurgence of Marxism in American Sociology," in *Marxist Inquiries: Studies of Labor, Class, and States*. Supplement to *American Journal of Sociology*, 88, S1–S30, ed. Michael Burawoy and Theda Skocpol. Chicago: University of Chicago Press.

——— (1985). *The Politics of Production*. London: Verso.

Burns, Tom, and George M. Stalker (1961). *The Management of Innovation*. London: Tavistock.

Burrell, Gibson, and Gareth Morgan (1979). *Sociological Paradigms and Organizational Analysis*. London: Heinemann.

Burt, Ronald S. (1980). "Models of Network Structure," *Annual Review of Sociology*, 6, 79–141.

——— (1983). *Corporate Profits and Cooptation*. New York: Academic Press.

Burt, Ronald S., Kenneth P. Christman, and Harold C. Kilburn, Jr. (1980). "Testing a Structural Theory of Corporate Cooptation: Interorganizational Directorate Ties as a Strategy for Avoiding Market Constraints on Profits," *American Sociological Review*, 45 (October), 821–41.

Cameron, Kim S., and David A. Whetten (1981). "Perceptions of Organizational Effectiveness over Organizational Life Cycles," *Administrative Science Quarterly*, 26 (December), 525–44.

——— eds. (1982). *Organizational Effectiveness: A Comparison of Multiple Models*. New York: Academic Press.

Campbell, Donald (1969). "Variation and Selective Retention in Socio-Cultural Evolution," *General Systems: Yearbook of the Society for General Systems Research*, 16, 69–85.

Campbell, John P. (1977). "On the Nature of Organizational Effectiveness," in *New Perspectives on Organizational Effectiveness*, pp. 13–55, ed. Paul S. Goodman and Johannes M. Pennings. San Francisco: Jossey-Bass.

Carey, Alex (1967). "The Hawthorne Studies: A Radical Criticism," *American Sociological Review*, 32 (June), 403–16.

Carroll, Glen R. (1984). "Organizational Ecology," *Annual Review of Sociology*, 10, 71–93.

Carroll, Glen R., and Jacques Delacroix (1982). "Organizational Mortality in the Newspaper Industries of Argentina and Ireland: An Ecological Approach," *Administrative Science Quarterly*, 27 (June), 169–98.

Carter, Launor, William Haythorn, Beatrice Shriver, and John Lanzetta (1953). "The Behavior of Leaders and Other Group Members," in *Group Dynamics*, pp. 551–60, ed. Dorwin Cartwright and Alvin Zander. Evanston, Ill.: Row, Peterson.

Cartwright, Dorwin (1965). "Influence, Leadership, Control," in *Handbook of Organizations*, pp. 1–47, ed. James G. March. Chicago: Rand McNally.

Carzo, Rocco, Jr., and John N. Yanouzas (1967). *Formal Organization: A Systems Approach*. Homewood, Ill.: Richard D. Irwin, Dorsey.

Chandler, Alfred D., Jr. (1962) *Strategy and Structure: Chapters in the History of the American Industrial Enterprise*. Cambridge, Mass.: M.I.T. Press.

——— (1977). *The Visible Hand: The Managerial Revolution in American Business*. Cambridge, Mass.: Harvard University Press, Belknap Press.

Cheit, Earl F. (1964). "The New Place of Business: Why Managers Cultivate Social Responsibility," in *The Business Establishment*, pp. 152–92, ed. Earl F. Cheit. New York: John Wiley.

Child, John (1972). "Organizational Structure, Environment and Performance: The Role of Strategic Choice," *Sociology*, 6 (January), 1–22.

——— (1981). "Culture, contingency and capitalism in the cross-national study of organizations," in *Research in Organizational Behavior*, vol. 3, pp. 303–56, ed. L. L. Cummings and Barry M. Staw. Greenwich, Conn.: JAI Press.

Child, John, and Roger Mansfield (1972). "Technology, Size and Organization Structure," *Sociology*, 6 (September), 369–93.

Christie, L. S., R. S. Luce, and J. Macy, Jr. (1952). "Communication and Learning in Task-Oriented Groups," Technical Report No. 231. Cambridge: Research Laboratory of Electronics, Massachusetts Institute of Technology.

Cicourel, Aaron (1968). *The Social Organization of Juvenile Justice*. New York: John Wiley.

Clark, Burton R. (1956). *Adult Education in Transition*. Berkeley: University of California Press.

——— (1963). "Faculty Organization and Authority," in *The Study of Academic Administration*, pp. 37–51, ed. Terry F. Lunsford. Boulder, Colo.: Western Interstate Commission for Higher Education.

——— (1965) "Interorganizational Patterns in Education," *Administrative Science Quarterly*, 10 (September), 224–37.

——— (1970). *The Distinctive College: Antioch, Reed and Swarthmore*. Chicago: Aldine.

——— (1972). "The Organizational Saga in Higher Education," *Administrative Science Quarterly*, 17 (June), 178–183.

——— (1983). *The Higher Education System*. Berkeley: University of California Press.

CLARK, PETER M., and JAMES Q. WILSON (1961). "Incentive Systems: A Theory of Organizations," *Administrative Science Quarterly*, 6 (September), 129–66.

CLEMMER, DONALD (1940). *The Prison Community*. Boston: Christopher.

CLINARD, MARSHALL B. and PETER C. YEAGER (1980). *Corporate Crime*. New York: Free Press.

CLOUGH, DONALD J. (1963). *Concepts in Management Science*. Englewood Cliffs, N.J.: Pentice-Hall.

COASE, R. H. (1937). "The Nature of the Firm," *Economica*, N.S., 4 (November), 386–405.

COCH, L., and J. R. P. FRENCH, JR. (1948). "Overcoming Resistance to Change," *Human Relations*, 1:4, 512–32.

COHEN, BERNARD P. (1972). "On the Construction of Sociological Explanations," *Synthese*, 24 (December), 401–9.

COHEN, MICHAEL D., and JAMES G. MARCH (1974). *Leadership and Ambiguity: The American College President*. New York: McGraw-Hill.

——— (1976). "Decisions, Presidents, and Status," in *Ambiguity and Choice in Organizations*, pp. 174–205, ed. James G. March and Johan P. Olsen. Bergen, Norway: Universitetsforlaget.

COHEN, MICHAEL D., JAMES G. MARCH, and JOHAN P. OLSEN (1972). "A Garbage Can Model of Organizational Choice," *Administrative Science Quarterly*, 17 (March), 1–25.

——— (1976). "People, Problems, Solutions and the Ambiguity of Relevance," in *Ambiguity and Choice in Organizations*, pp. 24–37, ed. James G. March and Johan P. Olsen. Bergen, Norway: Universitetsforlaget.

COLE, ROBERT E. (1979). *Work, Mobility, and Participation*. Berkeley: University of California Press.

COLEMAN, JAMES S. (1974). *Power and the Structure of Society*. New York: W. W. Norton & Co., Inc.

——— (1975). "Social Structure and a Theory of Action," in *Approaches to the Study of Social Structure*, pp. 76–93, ed. Peter M. Blau. New York: Free Press.

COLLINS, ORVIS (1946). "Ethnic Behavior in Industry: Sponsorship and Rejection in a New England Factory," *American Journal of Sociology*, 21, 293–98.

COLLINS, RANDALL (1971). "Functional and Conflict Theories of Educational Stratification," *American Sociological Review*, 36 (December), 1002–19.

——— (1979). *The Credential Society*. New York: Academic Press.

COMMONS, JOHN R. (1924). *Legal Foundations of Capitalism*. New York: Macmillan.

COMSTOCK, DONALD E., and W. RICHARD SCOTT (1977). "Technology and the Structure of Subunits: Distinguishing Individual and Workgroup Effects," *Administrative Science Quarterly*, 22 (June), 177–202.

COSER, ROSE LAUB (1951). "An Analysis of the Early German Socialist Movement," Unpublished M.A. thesis, Department of Sociology, Columbia University.

CRONBACH, LEE J. and ASSOCIATES (1980). *Toward Reform of Program Evaluation*. San Francisco: Jossey-Bass.

CROZIER, MICHEL (1964). *The Bureaucratic Phenomenon*. Chicago: University of Chicago Press.

CUMMINGS, LARRY L. (1977). "Emergence of the Instrumental Organization," in *New Perspectives on Organizational Effectiveness*, pp. 56–62, ed. Paul S. Goodman and Johannes M. Pennings. San Francisco: Jossey-Bass.

——— (1982). "Organizational Behavior," *Annual Review of Psychology*, 33, 541–79.

CYERT, RICHARD M., and JAMES G. MARCH (1963). *A Behavioral Theory of the Firm*. Englewood Cliffs, N.J.: Prentice-Hall.

DAHL, ROBERT A. (1970). *After the Revolution?* New Haven: Yale University Press.

DAHRENDORF, RALF (1959 trans.). *Class and Class Conflict in Industrial Society*. Stanford, Calif.: Stanford University Press (first published in 1957).

DALTON, MELVILLE (1950). "Conflicts between Staff and Line Managerial Officers," *American Sociological Review*, 15 (June), 342–51.

——— (1959). *Men Who Manage*. New York: John Wiley.

DAVIS, KINGSLEY (1949). *Human Society*. New York: Macmillan.

DAVIS, STANLEY M., and PAUL R. LAWRENCE (1977). *Matrix*. Reading, Mass.: Addison-Wesley.

DEAL, TERRENCE E., and ALLAN A. KENNEDY (1982). *Corporate Cultures*. Reading, Mass.: Addison-Wesley.

DELANY, WILLIAM (1963). "The Development and Decline of Patrimonial and Bureaucratic Administrations," *Administrative Science Quarterly*, 7 (March), 458–501.

DERTHICK, MARTHA (1972). *New Towns In-Town*. Washington, D.C.: Urban Institute.

DESS, GREGORY G., and DONALD W. BEARD (1984). "Dimensions of Organizational Task Environments," *Administrative Science Quarterly*, 29 (March), 52–73.

DIAMOND, SIGMUND (1958). "From Organization to Society," *American Journal of Sociology*, 63 (March), 457–75.

DIBBLE, VERNON K. (1965). "The Organization of Traditional Authority: English County Government, 1558 to 1640," in *Handbook of Organizations*, pp. 879–909, ed. James G. March. Chicago: Rand McNally.

DILL, WILLIAM R. (1958). "Environment as an Influence on Managerial Autonomy," *Administrative Science Quarterly*, 2 (March), 409–43.

DIMAGGIO, PAUL (1983). "State Expansion and Organizational Fields," in *Organizational Theory and Public Policy*, pp. 147–61, ed. Richard H. Hall and Robert E. Quinn. Beverly Hills, Calif.: Sage Publications, Inc.

DIMAGGIO, PAUL J., and WALTER W. POWELL (1983). "The Iron Cage Revisited: Institutional Isomorphism and Collective Rationality in Organizational Fields," *American Sociological Review*, 48 (April), 147–60.

DOBBIN, FRANK, LAUREN EDELMAN, JOHN W. MEYER, W. RICHARD SCOTT, and ANN SWIDLER (in press). "Legalization in Organizations: The Expansion of Due Process Protections," in *Institutional Patterns and Organizations: Culture and Environment*, ed. Lynne G. Zucker. New York: Academic Press.

DOERINGER, PETER B., and MICHAEL J. PIORE (1971). *Internal Labor Markets and Manpower Analysis*. Lexington, Mass.: Heath.

DOMHOFF, G. WILLIAM (1983). *Who Rules America Now? A View for the 80s*. Englewood Cliffs, N.J.: Prentice-Hall.

DONABEDIAN, AVEDIS (1966). "Evaluating the Quality of Medical Care," *Milbank Memorial Fund Quarterly*, 44 (July), part 2, 166–206.

DORE, RONALD (1973). *British Factory–Japanese Factory*. Berkeley: University of California Press.

DORNBUSCH, SANFORD M., and W. RICHARD SCOTT, with the assistance of BRUCE C. BUSCHING and JAMES D. LAING (1975). *Evaluation and the Exercise of Authority*. San Francisco: Jossey-Bass.

DOWNS, ANTHONY (1967). *Inside Bureaucracy*. Boston: Little, Brown.

DRUCKER, PETER (1970). "The New Markets and the New Capitalism," *Public Interest*, 21 (Fall), 44–79.

—— (1976). "What Results Should You Expect? A User's Guide to MBO," *Public Administration Review*, 36 (January-February), 1–45

DUBIN, ROBERT, ed. (1968). *Human Relations in Administration* (3rd ed.). Englewood Cliffs, N.J.: Prentice-Hall.

DUNCAN, ROBERT B. (1972). "Characteristics of Organizational Environments and Perceived Environmental Uncertainty," *Administrative Science Quarterly*, 17 (September), 313–27.

DURKHEIM, EMILE (1949 trans.) *Division of Labor in Society*. Glencoe, Ill.: Free Press (first published in 1893).

ECCLES, ROBERT G., and HARRISON C. WHITE (1983). "Firm and Market Interfaces of Profit Center Control," unpublished paper, Harvard University.

EDITORS OF THE YALE LAW JOURNAL (1954). "The American Medical Association: Power, Purpose, and Politics in Organized Medicine," *Yale Law Journal*, 63 (May), 938–1022.

EWARDS, RICHARD (1979). *Contested Terrain: The Transformation of the Workplace in the Twentieth Century*. New York: Basic Books.

EISENSTADT, S. N. (1958). "Bureaucracy and Bureaucratization: A Trend Report and Bibliography," *Current Sociology*, 7:2, 99–164.

—— (1981). "Interactions between Organizations and Societal Stratification," in *Handbook of Organizational Design*, Vol. 1, pp. 309–22, ed. Paul C. Nystrom and William H. Starbuck. Oxford: Oxford University Press.

ELLUL, JACQUES (1964 trans.). *The Technological Society*. New York: Knopf (first published in 1954).

EMERSON, RICHARD M. (1962). "Power-Dependence Relations," *American Sociological Review*, 27 (February), 31–40.

EMERY, FRED E. (1959). *Characteristics of Socio-Technical Systems*. Tavistock Document 527. London: Tavistock.

EMERY, FRED E., and E. THORSRUD (1969 trans.) *Form and Content in Industrial Democracy*. London: Tavistock (first published in 1964).

—— (1976). *Democracy at Work*. Leiden: Martinus Nijhoff.

EMERY, FRED E., and E. L. TRIST (1965). "The Causal Texture of Organizational Environments," *Human Relations*, 18 (February), 21–32.

ERMANN, M. DAVID and RICHARD J. LUNDMAN (1982). *Corporate Deviance*. New York: Holt, Rinehart and Winston.

ETZIONI, AMITAI (1960). "Two Approaches to Organizational Analysis: A Critique and a Suggestion," *Administrative Science Quarterly*, 5 (September), 257–78.

—— (1961). *A Comparative Analysis of Complex Organizations*. New York: Free Press of Glencoe (rev. 1975).

—— (1964). *Modern Organizations*. Englewood Cliffs, N.J.: Prentice-Hall.

——, ed. (1969). *The Semi-Professions and Their Organization*. New York: Free Press.

EVAN, WILLIAM M. (1966). "The Organization Set: Toward a Theory of Interorganizational Relations," in *Approaches to Organizational Design*, pp. 173–88, ed. James D. Thompson. Pittsburgh: University of Pittsburgh Press, 1966.

EVANS, PETER B. (1981). "Recent Research on Multinational Corporations," *Annual Review of Sociology*, 7, 199–223.

EVANS, PETER B., DIETRICH RUESCHEMEYER and THEDA SKOCPOL, ed. (1986). Bringing the State Back In. Cambridge: Cambridge University Press.

FAMA, EUGENE F. (1980). "Agency Problems and the Theory of the Firm," *Journal of Political Economy*, 88 (April), 288–307.

FAUNCE, WILLIAM A. (1968). *Problems of an Industrial Society*. New York: McGraw-Hill.

FAYOL, HENRI (1949 trans.). *General and Industrial Management*, London: Pitman (first published in 1919).

FENNELL, MARY L. (1980). "The Effects of Environmental Characteristics on the Structure of Hospital Clusters," *Administrative Science Quarterly*, 25 (September), 485–510.

FERGUSON, KATHY E. (1984). *The Feminist Case against Bureaucracy*. Philadelphia: Temple University Press.

FESTINGER, LEON (1957). *A Theory of Cognitive Dissonance*. Evanston, Ill.: Row, Peterson.

FIEDLER, FRED E. (1964). "A Contingency Model of Leadership Effectiveness," in *Advances in Experimental Social Psychology*, ed. Leonard Berkowitz. New York: Academic Press.
—— (1971). "Validation and Extension of the Contingency Model of Leadership Effectiveness: A Review of Empirical Findings," *Psychological Bulletin*, 76 (August), 128–48.
FLIGSTEIN, NEIL (1985a). "The Spread of the Multidivisional Form among Large Firms, 1919–1979," *American Sociological Review*, 50 (June), 377–91.
—— (1985b). "The Intraorganizational Firm Power Struggle: The Rise of Finance Presidents in Large Firms, 1919–1979," presented at the annual meetings of the American Sociological Association, Washington, D.C.
FLOOD, ANN BARRY, and W. RICHARD SCOTT (1987). *Hospital Structure and Performance*. Balitmore: Johns Hopkins.
FOLEY, HENRY A., and STEVEN S. SHARFSTEIN (1983). *Madness and Government: Who Cares for the Mentally Ill?* Washington, D.C.: American Psychiatric Press.
FOLLETT, MARY PARKER (1942). *Dynamic Administration*. New York: Harper.
FOX, FREDERICK V., and BARRY M. STAW (1979). "The Trapped Administrator: Effects of Job Insecurity and Policy Resistance upon Commitment to a Course of Action," *Administrative Science Quarterly*, 24 (September), 449–71.
FOX, RENÉE (1959). *Experiment Perilous*. Glencoe, Ill.: Free Press.
FREEDMAN, MARCIA (1976). *Labor Markets: Segments and Shelters*. Montclair, N.J.: Allanheld, Osmun.
FREEMAN, JOHN H. (1978). "The Unit of Analysis in Organizational Research," in *Environments and Organizations*, pp. 335–51, ed. Marshall W. Meyer. San Francisco: Jossey-Bass.
FREEMAN, JOHN H., and JACK W. BRITTAIN (1977). "Union Merger Process and Industrial Environment," *Industrial Relations*, 16 (May), 173–85.
FREEMAN, JOHN H., and MICHAEL T. HANNAN (1975). "Growth and Decline Processes in Organizations," *American Sociological Review*, 40 (April), 215–28.
—— (1983). "Niche Width and the Dynamics of Organizational Populations," *American Journal of Sociology*, 88 (May), 1116–45.
FREIDSON, ELIOT (1970a). *Professional Dominance: The Social Structure of Medical Care*. Chicago: Aldine.
—— (1970b). *Profession of Medicine*. New York: Dodd, Mead.
—— (1975). *Doctoring Together: A Study of Professional Social Control*. New York: Elsevier.
FREIDSON, ELIOT, and BUFORD RHEA (1963). "Processes of Control in a Company of Equals," *Social Problems*, 11 (Fall), 119–31.
FRIEDLAND, ROGER (1980). "Corporate Power and Urban Growth: The Case of Urban Renewal," *Politics and Society*, 10:2, 203–24.
—— (1983). *Power and Crisis in the City: Corporations, Unions and Urban Policy*. New York: Schocken Books.
FRIEDLAND, ROGER, and DONALD PALMER (1984). "Park Place and Main Street: Business and the Urban Power Structure," *Annual Review of Sociology*, 10, 393–416.
FRIEDLANDER, FRANK, and HAL PICKLE (1968). "Components of Effectiveness in Small Organizations," *Administrative Science Quarterly*, 13 (September), 289–304.
FRIEDRICH, CARL J., and ZBIGNIEW K. BRZEZINSKI (1956). *Totalitarian Dictatorship and Autocracy*. Cambridge, Mass.: Harvard University Press.
FROST, PETER J., LARRY F. MOORE, MERYL REIS LOUIS, CRAIG C. LUNDBERG, and JOANNE MARTIN, eds. (1985). *Organizational Culture*. Beverly Hills, Calif.: Sage Publications, Inc.
FUCHS, VICTOR R. (1974). *Who Shall Live? Health, Economics, and Social Choice*. New York: Basic Books.

GALASKIEWICZ, JOSEPH (1979). "The Structure of Community Organizational Networks," *Social Forces*, 57 (June), 1346–64.
—— (1985). "Interorganizational Relations," *Annual Review of Sociology*, 11, 281–304.
GALBRAITH, JAY (1973). *Designing Complex Organizations*. Reading, Mass.: Addison-Wesley.
—— (1977). *Organization Design*. Reading, Mass.: Addison-Wesley.
GALBRAITH, JOHN KENNETH (1952). *American Capitalism*. Boston: Houghton Mifflin.
—— (1967). *The New Industrial State*. Boston: Houghton Mifflin.
GALL, JOHN (1978). *Systematics*. New York: Simon & Schuster, Pocket Books.
GAMSON, WILLIAM (1975). *The Strategy of Protest*. Homewood, Ill.: Dorsey.
GARFINKEL, HAROLD (1967). *Studies in Ethnomethodology*. Englewood Cliffs, N.J.: Prentice-Hall.
GEORGOPOULOS, BASIL S. (1972). "The Hospital as an Organization and Problem-Solving System," in *Organization Research on Health Institutions*, pp. 9–48, ed. Basil S. Georgopoulos. Ann Arbor: Institute for Social Research, University of Michigan.
GEORGOPOULOS, BASIL S., and ALEX MATEJKO (1967). "The American Hospital as a Complex Social System," *Health Services Research*, 2 (Summer), 76–112.
GIDDENS, ANTHONY (1983). *Profiles and Critiques in Social Theory*. Berkeley: University of California Press.
GILBRETH, F. B., and L. M. GILBRETH (1917). *Applied Motion Study*. New York.
GIULIANO, VINCENT (1982). "The Mechanization of Office Work," *Scientific American*, 247 (September), 148–65.
GLASBERG, DAVITA SILFEN, and MICHAEL SCHWARTZ (1983). "Ownership and Control of Corporations," *Annual Review of Sociology*, 9, 311–32.
GLASSMAN, ROBERT (1973). "Persistence and Loose Coupling in Living Systems," *Behavioral Science*, 18 (March), 83–98.

GLENNON, LYNDA M. *Women and Dualism.* New York: Longman, 1979.

GOFFMAN, ERVING (1961). *Asylums.* Garden City, N.Y.: Doubleday, Anchor Books.

——— (1974). *Frame Analysis.* Cambridge, Mass.: Harvard University Press.

GOLDMAN, PAUL, and DONALD R. VAN HOUTEN (1977). "Managerial Strategies and the Worker: A Marxist Analysis of Bureaucracy," *Sociological Quarterly*, 18 (Winter), 108–25.

GOLDNER, FRED H. (1970). "The Division of Labor: Process and Power," in *Power in Organizations*, pp.97–143, ed. Mayer N. Zald. Nashville, Tenn.: Vanderbilt University Press.

GONOS, GEORGE (1977). " 'Situation' versus 'Frame': The 'Interactionist' and the 'Structuralist' Analyses of Everyday Life," *American Sociological Review*, 42 (December), 854–67.

GOODMAN, PAUL (1968). *People or Personnel* and *Like a Conquered Providence.* New York: Random House, Vintage.

GOODMAN, PAUL S., and JOHANNES M. PENNINGS, eds. (1977). *New Perspectives on Organizational Effectiveness.* San Francisco: Jossey-Bass.

GORAN, M. J., J. S. ROBERTS, M. A. KELLOG, J. FIELDING, and W. JESSEE (1975). "The PSRO Hospital Review System," *Medical Care*, 13 (Supplement to April), 1–32.

GORDON, DAVID M., RICHARD EDWARDS, and MICHAEL REICH (1982). *Segmented Work, Divided Workers.* Cambridge: Cambridge University Press, 1982.

GOSNELL, HAROLD F. (1937). *Machine Politics: Chicago Model.* Chicago: University of Chicago Press.

GOSS, MARY E. W. (1961). "Influence and Authority among Physicians in an Outpatient Clinic," *American Sociological Review*, 26 (February), 39–50.

GOULDNER, ALVIN W. (1954). *Patterns of Industrial Bureaucracy.* Glencoe, Ill.: Free Press.

——— (1955). "Metaphysical Pathos and the Theory of Bureaucracy," *American Political Science Review*, 49 (June), 496–507.

——— (1959). "Organizational Analysis," in *Sociology Today*, pp. 400–428, ed. Robert K. Merton, Leonard Broom, and Leonard S. Cottrell, Jr. New York: Basic Books.

GRAMSCI, ANTONIO (1971 trans.). *Selections from the Prison Notebooks of Antonio Gramsci*, ed. Quinton Hoare and Geoffrey Nowell Smith. New York: International Publishers (first published 1948–1951).

GRANOVETTER, MARK (1985). "Economic Action and Social Structure: The Problem of Embeddedness," *American Journal of Sociology*, 91 (November), 481–510.

GREINER, LARRY E. (1972). "Evolution and Revolution as Organizations Grow," *Harvard Business Review*, 50 (July-August), 37–46.

GRIMES, A. J., and S. M. KLEIN (1973). "The Technological Imperative: The Relative Impact of Task Unit, Modal Technology, and Hierarchy on Structure," *Academy of Management Journal*, 16 (December), 583–97.

GROSS, EDWARD (1953). "Some Functional Consequences of Primary Controls in Formal Work Organizations," *American Sociological Review*, 18 (August), 368–73.

——— (1968). "Universities as Organizations: A Research Approach," *American Sociological Review*, 33 (August), 518–44.

GROSS, EDWARD, and AMITAI ETZIONI (1985). *Organizations in Society.* Englewood Cliffs, N. J.: Prentice-Hall.

GROSS, NEAL, WARD S. MASON, and ALEXANDER W. MCEACHERN (1958). *Explorations in Role Analysis.* New York: John Wiley.

GUETZKOW, HAROLD (1965). "Communications in Organizations," in *Handbook of Organizations*, pp. 534–73, ed. James G. March. Chicago: Rand McNally.

GUETZKOW, HAROLD, and HERBERT A. SIMON (1955). "The Impact of Certain Communication Nets upon Organization and Performance in Task-Oriented Groups," *Management Science*, 1 (April-July), 233–50.

GULICK, LUTHER, and L. URWICK, eds. (1937). *Papers on the Science of Administration.* New York: Institute of Public Administration, Columbia University.

GUSFIELD, JOSEPH R. (1968). "The Study of Social Movements," *International Encyclopedia of the Social Sciences*, vol. 14, pp. 445–52. New York: Macmillan.

GYLLENHAMMAR, P. G. (1977). *People at Work.* Reading, Mass.: Addison-Wesley.

HABERMAS, JURGEN (1971 trans.). *Toward A Rational Society.* London: Heinemann.

HABERSTROH, CHADWICK J. (1965). "Organization Design and Systems Analysis," in *Handbook of Organizations*, pp. 1171–211, ed. James G. March. Chicago: Rand McNally.

HACKMAN, J. RICHARD, and GREG R. OLDHAM (1980). *Work Redesign.* Reading, Mass.: Addison-Wesley.

HAGE, JERALD (1965). "An Axiomatic Theory of Organizations," *Administrative Science Quarterly*, 10 (December), 289–320.

HAGE, JERALD, and MICHAEL AIKEN (1969). "Routine Technology, Social Structure, and Organization Goals," *Administrative Science Quarterly*, 14 (September), 366–76.

HALL, A. D., and R. E. FAGEN (1956). "Definition of System," *General Systems: The Yearbook of the Society for the Advancement of General Systems Theory*, 1, 18–28.

HALL, RICHARD H. (1963). "The Concept of Bureaucracy: An Empirical Assessment," *American Journal of Sociology*, 69 (July), 32–40.

——— (1967). "Some Organizational Considerations in the Professional-Organizational Relationship," *Administrative Science Quarterly*, 12 (December), 461–78.

——— (1968). "Professionalization and Bureaucratization," *American Sociological Review*, 33 (February), 92–104.

HALL, RICHARD H., J. EUGENE, HAAS, and NORMAN J. JOHNSON (1967). "Organizational Size, Complexity, and Formalization," *American Sociological Review*, 32 (December), 903–12.

HALL, RICHARD H., and CHARLES R. TITTLE (1966). "Bureaucracy and Its Correlates," *American Journal of Sociology*, 72 (November), 267–72.

HANNAN, MICHAEL T., and JOHN FREEMAN (1977). "The Population Ecology of Organizations," *American Journal of Sociology*, 82 (March), 929–64.

—— (1984). "Structural Inertia and Organizational Change," *American Sociological Review*, 49 (April), 149–64.

HANRAHAN, JOHN D. (1983). *Government by Contract*. New York: W. W. Norton & Co., Inc.

HART, DAVID K., and WILLIAM G. SCOTT (1975). "The Organizational Imperative," *Administration and Society*, 7 (November), 259–85.

HARVEY, EDWARD (1968). "Technology and the Structure of Organizations," *American Sociological Review*, 33 (April), 247–59.

HAWLEY, AMOS (1950). *Human Ecology*. New York: Ronald Press.

HECLO, HUGH (1977). *A Government of Strangers: Executive Politics in Washington*. Washington D. C.: Brookings Institution.

HEDBERG, BO (1981). "How Organizations Learn and Unlearn," in *Handbook of Organizational Design*, vol. 1, pp. 3–27, ed. Paul C. Nystrom and William H. Starbuck. Oxford: Oxford University Press.

HEDBERG, BO L. T., PAUL C. NYSTROM, and WILLIAM H. STARBUCK (1976). "Camping on Seesaws: Prescriptions for a Self-Designing Organization," *Administrative Science Quarterly*, 21 (March), 41–65.

HEILBRONER, ROBERT L. (1980). *An Inquiry into the Human Prospect* (rev. ed.). New York: W. W. Norton and Co., Inc.

HEMPEL, C. (1959). "The Logic of Functional Analysis," in *Symposium on Sociological Theory*. pp. 271–307, ed. Llewellyn Gross, Evanston, Ill.: Row, Peterson.

HENDERSON, LAWRENCE J. (1935). *Pareto's General Sociology*. Cambridge, Mass.: Harvard University Press.

HERMAN, E. S. (1981). *Corporate Control, Corporate Power*. Cambridge: Cambridge University Press.

HERZBERG, FREDERICK (1966). *Work and the Nature of Man*. Cleveland: World Publishing.

HEYDEBRAND, WOLF V. (1973). "Autonomy, Complexity, and Non-Bureaucratic Coordination in Professional Organizations," pp. 158–189, in *Comparative Organizations*, ed. Wolf V. Heydebrand. Englewood Cliffs, N.J.: Prentice-Hall.

HICKSON, DAVID J., C. R. HININGS, C. A. LEE, R. E. SCHNECK, and J. M. PENNINGS (1971). "A Strategic Contingencies' Theory of Intraorganizational Power," *Administrative Science Quarterly*, 16 (June), 216–29.

HICKSON, DAVID J., D. S. PUGH, and DIANA C. PHEYSEY (1969). "Operations Technology and Organization Structure: An Empirical Reappraisal," *Administrative Science Quarterly*, 14 (September), 378–97.

HILL, RAYNARD E., and BERNARD J. WHITE (1979). *Matrix Organization and Project Management*. Ann Arbor: University of Michigan Press.

HILLERY, GEORGE A., JR. (1968). *Communal Organizations: A Study of Local Societies*. Chicago: University of Chicago Press.

HIND, ROBERT R., SANFORD M. DORNBUSCH, and W. RICHARD SCOTT (1974). "A Theory of Evaluation Applied to a University Faculty," *Sociology of Education*, 47 (Winter), 114–28.

HININGS, C. R., D. J. HICKSON, J. M. PENNINGS, and R. E. SCHNECK (1974). "Structural Conditions of Intraorganizational Power," *Administrative Science Quarterly*, 19 (March), 22–44.

HIRSCH, PAUL M. (1972). "Processing Fads and Fashions: An Organization-Set Analysis of Cultural Industry Systems," *American Journal of Sociology*, 77 (January), 639–59.

—— (1975). "Organizational Effectiveness and the Institutional Environment," *Administrative Science Quarterly*, 20 (September), 327–44.

—— (1985). "The Study of Industries," in *Research in the Sociology of Organizations*, vol. 4 pp. 271–309, ed. Samuel B. Bacharach and Stephen M. Mitchell. Greenwich, Conn.: JAI Press.

HIRSCHMAN, ALBERT O. (1970). *Exit, Voice, and Loyalty*. Cambridge, Mass.: Harvard University Press.

HOBSBAWM, ERIC, and TERENCE RANGER, eds. (1983). *The Invention of Tradition*. Cambridge: Cambridge University Press.

HODSON, RANDY D., and ROBERT L. KAUFMAN (1982). "Economic Dualism: A Critical Review," *American Sociology Review*, 47 (December) 727–39.

HOFSTADTER, RICHARD (1945). *Social Darwinism in American Thought, 1860–1915*. Philadelphia: University of Pennsylvania Press.

HOFSTEDE, GEERT (1984). *Culture's Consequences: International Differences in Work-Related Values* (abridged ed.). Beverly Hills, Calif.: Sage Publications, Inc.

HOFSTEDE, GEERT, and M. S. KASSEM, eds. (1976). *European Contributions to Organization Theory*. Assen, The Netherlands: Van Gorcum.

HOLDAWAY, EDWARD A., and THOMAS A. BLOWERS (1971). "Administrative Ratios and Organizational Size: A Longitudinal Examination," *American Sociological Review*, 36 (April), 278–86.

HOLLANDER, EDWIN P., and JAMES W. JULIAN (1969). "Contemporary Trends in the Analysis of Leadership Processes," *Psychological Bulletin*, 71 (May), 387–97.

HOMANS, GEORGE C. (1950). *The Human Group*. New York: Harcourt.

—— (1961). *Social Behavior: Its Elementary Forms*. New York: Harcourt, Brace & World.

HOPKINS, TERENCE K. (1961). "Bureaucratic Authority: The Convergence of Weber and Barnard," in *Complex Organizations: A Sociological Reader*, pp. 82–100, ed. Amitai Etzioni. New York: Holt, Rinehart & Winston.

HOUSE, WILLIAM C., ed. (1971). *The Impact of Information Technology on Management Operation.* Princeton, N.J.: Auerbach Publishers.

HREBINIAK, LAWRENCE G. (1974). "Job Technology, Supervision and Work Group Structure," *Administrative Science Quarterly,* 19 (September), 395–410.

HUGHES, EVERETT C. (1946). "The Knitting of Racial Groups in Industry," *American Sociological Review,* 11 (October), 512–19.

———— (1958). *Men and Their Work.* Glencoe, Ill.: Free Press.

HULIN, CHARLES L., and MILTON R. BLOOD (1968). "Job Enlargement, Individual Differences, and Worker Responses," *Psychological Bulletin,* 69 (January), 41–55.

HUNTINGTON, SAMUEL P. (1966). "Political Modernization: American vs. Europe," *World Politics,* 18 (April), 378–414.

IANNI, FRANCIS A. J. (1972). *A Family Business: Kinship and Social Control in Organized Crime.* New York: Russell Sage Foundation.

ILLICH, IVAN (1972). *Deschooling Society.* New York: Harper & Row, Pub., Harrow Books.

———— (1976). *Medical Nemesis.* New York: Random House.

INKELES, ALEX (1969). "Making Men Modern: On the Causes and Consequences of Individual Change in Six Developing Countries," *American Journal of Sociology,* 75 (September), 208–25.

ISRAEL, JOACHIM (1971). *Alienation: From Marx to Modern Sociology.* Boston: Allyn & Bacon.

JACOBS, DAVID (1974). "Dependency and Vulnerability: An Exchange Approach to the Control of Organizations," *Administrative Science Quarterly,* 19 (March), 45–59.

JACOBY, HENRY (1973). *The Bureaucratization of the World,* trans. Eveline L. Kanes. Berkeley: University of California Press.

JAMES, HENRY (1907). Preface to *Roderick Hudson.* New York: Scribner's.

JAQUES, ELLIOTT (1951). *The Changing Culture of a Factory.* London: Tavistock.

JELINEK, MARIANN, LINDA SMIRCICH, and PAUL HIRSCH eds. (1983). "Organizational Culture," *Administrative Science Quarterly,* 28 (September), entire issue.

JENKINS, J. CRAIG (1979). "What Is to Be Done: Movement or Organization?" *Contemporary Sociology,* 8 (March), 222–28.

JENSEN, MICHAEL C., and WILLIAM H. MECKLING (1976). "Theory of the Firm: Managerial Behavior, Agency Costs and Ownership Structure," *Journal of Financial Economics,* 3 (October) 305–60.

JURKOVICH, RAY (1974). "A Core Typology of Organizational Environments," *Administrative Science Quarterly,* 19 (September), 380–94.

KAHN, ROBERT L., D. M. WOLFE, R. P. QUINN, J. D. SNOEK, and ROBERT A. ROSENTHAL (1964). *Organizational Stress.* New York: John Wiley.

KAHNEMAN, DANIEL, P. SLOVIC, and AMOS TVERSKY (1982). *Judgment under Uncertainty: Heuristics and Biases.* Cambridge: Cambridge University Press.

KALLEK, SHIRLEY (1975). "Potential Applications of Census Bureau Economic Series in Microdata Analysis," *American Economic Review,* 65 (May), 257–62.

KANTER, ROSABETH MOSS (1972). *Commitment and Community: Communes and Utopias in Sociological Perspective.* Cambridge, Mass.: Harvard University Press.

———— (1977a). *Men and Women of the Corporation.* New York: Basic Books.

———— (1977b). *Work and Family in the United States: A Critical Review and Agenda for Research and Policy.* New York: Russell Sage Foundation.

KASARDA, JOHN D. (1974). "The Structural Implications of Social System Size: A Three-Level Analysis," *American Sociological Review,* 39 (February), 19–28.

KATZ, DANIEL, and ROBERT L. KAHN (1952). "Some Recent Findings in Human Relations Research in Industry," in *Readings in Social Psychology* (2nd ed.), pp. 650–65, ed. Guy E. Swanson, Theodor M. Newcomb, and Eugene L. Hartley. New York: Holt.

———— (1966). *The Social Psychology of Organizations.* New York: John Wiley (rev. 1978).

KATZ, DANIEL, N. MACCOBY, G. GURIN, and L. FLOOR (1951). *Productivity, Supervision and Morale among Railroad Workers.* Ann Arbor: Institute for Social Research, University of Michigan.

KATZ, DANIEL, N. MACCOBY, and N. MORSE (1950). *Productivity, Supervision and Morale in an Office Situation.* Ann Arbor: Institute for Social Research, University of Michigan.

KATZ, ELIHU, and S. N. EISENSTADT (1960). "Some Sociological Observations on the Response of Israeli Organizations to New Immigrants," *Administrative Science Quarterly,* 5 (June), 113–33.

KAUFMAN, HERBERT (1956). "Emerging Conflicts in the Doctrines of Public Administration," *American Political Science Review,* 50 (December), 1057–73.

———— (1969). "Administrative Decentralization and Political Power," *Public Administration Review,* 29 (January-February), 3–15.

———— (1975). "The Natural History of Human Organizations," *Administration and Society,* 7 (August), 131–49.

———— (1976). *Are Government Organizations Immortal?* Washington, D. C.: Brookings Institution.

KENDALL, PATRICIA L., and PAUL F. LAZARSFELD (1950). "Problems of Survey Analysis," in *Continuitites in Social Research: Studies in the Scope and Method of "The American Soldier,"* pp. 133–96, ed. Robert K. Merton and Paul F. Lazarsfeld. Glencoe, Ill.: Free Press.

KENNEDY, ROBERT F. (1969). *Thirteen Days: A Memoir of the Cuban Missile Crisis.* New York: W. W. Norton & Co., Inc.

KERR, CLARK (1954). "The Balkanization of Labor Markets," in *Labor Mobility and Economic Opportunity*, pp. 92–110, ed. E. Wight Bakke. Cambridge, Mass.: M.I.T. Press.

KERR, CLARK, JOHN T. DUNLOP, FREDERICK HARBISON, and CHARLES A. MYERS (1964). *Industrialism and Industrial Man (2nd ed.).* New York: Oxford University Press.

KHANDWALLA, PRADIP N. (1974). "Mass Output Orientation of Operations Technology and Organizational Structure," *Administrative Science Quarterly*, 19 (March), 74–97.

———— (1977). *The Design of Organizations.* New York: Harcourt Brace Jovanovich.

KIMBERLY, JOHN (1976). "Organizational Size and the Structuralist Perspective: A Review, Critique and Proposal," *Administrative Science Quarterly*, 21 (December) 571–97.

KIMBERLY, JOHN R., ROBERT H. MILES, and ASSOCIATES (1980). *The Organizational Life Cycle.* San Francisco: Jossey-Bass.

KING, NATHAN (1970). "Clarification and Evaluation of the Two-Factor Theory of Job Statisfaction," *Psychological Bulletin*, 74 (July), 18–31.

KMETZ, JOHN L. (1984). "An Information Processing Study of a Complex Workflow in Aircraft Electronics Repair," *Administrative Science Quarterly*, 29 (June), 255–80.

KNOKE, DAVID (1982). "The Spread of Municipal Reform: Temporal, Spatial, and Social Dynamics," *American Journal of Sociology*, 87 (May), 1314–39.

KNOKE, DAVID, and EDWARD O. LAUMANN (1982). "The Social Organization of National Policy Domains," in *Structure and Network Analysis*, pp. 255–70, ed. Peter V. Marsden and Nan Lin. Beverly Hills, Calif.: Sage Publications, Inc.

KOHN, MELVIN L. (1971). "Bureaucratic Man: A Portrait and an Interpretation," *American Sociological Review*, 36 (June), 461–74.

KOHN, MELVIN L., and CARMI SCHOOLER (1973). "Occupational Experience and Psychological Functioning: An Assessment of Reciprocal Effects," *American Sociological Review*, 38 (February), 97–118.

KORNHAUSER, WILLIAM (1962). *Scientists in Industry: Conflict and Accommodation.* Berkeley: University of California Press.

KRASNER, STEPHEN D. (1984). "Approaches to the State: Alternative Conceptions and Historical Dynamics," *Comparative Politics*, (January), 223–46.

KRAUSE, ELLIOTT A. (1968). "Functions of a Bureaucratic Ideology: 'Citizen Participation,' " *Social Problems*, 16 (Fall), 129–43.

KRUPP, SHERMAN (1961). *Pattern in Organization Analysis.* Philadelphia: Chilton.

KUHN, THOMAS S. (1962). *The Structure of Scientific Revolutions.* Chicago: University of Chicago Press.

LAMMERS, CORNELIS J., and DAVID J. HICKSON (1979a). "A Cross-National and Cross-Institutional Typology of Organizations," in *Organizations Alike and Unlike: International and Interinstitutional Studies in the Sociology of Organizations*. pp. 420–34, ed. Cornelis J. Lammers and David J. Hickson. London: Routledge & Kegan Paul.

————, eds. (1979b). *Organizations Alike and Unlike: International and Interinstitutional Studies in the Sociology of Organizations.* London: Routledge & Kegan Paul.

LANDSBERGER, HENRY A. (1958). *Hawthorne Revisited.* Ithaca, N.Y.: Cornell University Press.

———— (1961). "Parsons' Theory of Organizations," in *Social Theories of Talcott Parsons*, pp. 214–49, ed. Max Black. Englewood Cliffs, N.J.: Prentice-Hall.

———— (1970). *Comparative Perspectives on Formal Organizations.* Boston: Little, Brown.

LARSON, MAGALI SARFATTI (1977). *The Rise of Professionalism.* Berkeley: University of California Press.

LAUMANN, EWARD O., JOSEPH GALASKIEWICZ, and PETER V. MARSDEN (1978). "Community Structure as Interorganizational Linkages," *Annual Review of Sociology*, 4, 455–84.

LAUMANN, EDWARD O., DAVID KNOKE, and YONG-HAK KIM (1985). "An Organizational Approach to State Policy Formation," *American Sociological Review*, 50 (February), 1–19.

LAUMANN, EWARD O., PETER V. MARSDEN, and DAVID PRENSKY (1983). "The Boundary Specification Problem in Network Analysis," in *Applied Network Analysis*, pp. 18–34, ed. Ronald S. Burt and Michael J. Minor. Beverly Hills, Calif.: Sage Publications, Inc.

LAUMANN, EDWARD O., and FRANZ U. PAPPI (1976). *Networks of Collective Action.* New York: Academic Press.

LAWRENCE, PAUL R., and JAY W. LORSCH (1967). *Organization and Environment: Managing Differenciation and Integration.* Boston: Graduate School of Business Administration, Harvard University.

LAZARSFELD, PAUL F. (1959). "Problems in Methodology," in *Sociology Today*, pp. 39–78, ed. Robert K. Merton, Leonard Broom, and Leonard S. Cottrell, Jr. New York: Basic Books.

LAZARSFELD, PAUL F., and HERBERT MENZEL (1961). "On the Relation between Individual and Collective Properties," in *Complex Organizations: A Sociological Reader*, pp. 422–40, ed. Amitai Etzioni. New York: Holt, Rinehart & Winston.

LAZARSFELD, PAUL F., and WAGNER THIELENS, JR. (1958). *The Academic Mind.* Glencoe, Ill.: Free Press.

LEAVITT, HAROLD J. (1951). "Some Effects of Certain Communication Patterns on Group Performance," *Journal of Abnormal and Social Psychology*. 46, 38–50.

———— (1964). "Unhuman Organizations," in *Readings in Managerial Psychology*, pp. 542–56, ed. Harold J. Leavitt and Louis R. Pondy. Chicago: University of Chicago Press.

———— (1965). "Applied Organizational Change in Industry: Structural, Technological and Humanistic

Approaches," in *Handbook of Organizations,* pp. 1144–70, ed. James G. March. Chicago: Rand McNally.

LEAVITT, HAROLD J., WILLIAM R. DILL, and HENRY B. EYRING (1973). *The Organizational World.* New York: Harcourt Brace Jovanovich.

LEVENSON, BERNARD (1961). "Bureaucratic Succession," in *Complex Organizations: A Sociological Reader,* pp. 362–75, ed. Amitai Etzioni. New York: Holt, Rinehart & Winston.

LEVINE, SOL, and PAUL E. WHITE (1961). "Exchange as a Conceptual Framework for the Study of Interorganizational Relationships," *Administrative Science Quarterly,* 5 (March), 583–601.

LEWIN, KURT (1948). *Resolving Social Conflicts.* New York: Harper.

LIGHT, IVAN H. (1972). *Ethnic Enterprise in America.* Berkeley: University of California Press.

LIKERT, RENSIS (1961). *New Patterns of Management.* New York: McGraw-Hill.

LIKERT, RENSIS, and JANE C. LIKERT (1976). *New Ways of Managing Conflict.* New York: McGraw-Hill.

LILIENTHAL, DAVID E. (1944). *TVA: Democracy on the March.* New York: Harper & Brothers.

LINCOLN, JAMES R. (1979). "Organizational Differentiation in Urban Communities: A Study in Organizational Ecology," *Social Forces,* 57 (March), 915–29.

—— (1982). "Intra-(and Inter-) Organizational Networks," in *Research in the Sociology of Organizations,* vol. 1, pp. 1–38, ed. Samuel B. Bacharach. Greenwich, Conn.: JAI Press.

LINDBLOM, CHARLES E. (1959). "The 'Science' of Muddling Through," *Public Administration Review,* 19 (Spring), 79–88.

—— (1977). *Politics and Markets.* New York: Basic Books.

LIPPITT, RONALD, NORMAN POLANSKY, FRITZ REDL, and SIDNEY ROSEN (1953). "The Dynamics of Power," in *Group Dynamics,* pp. 462–82, ed. Dorwin Cartwright and Alvin Zander. Evanston, Ill.: Row, Peterson.

LIPSET, SEYMOUR MARTIN (1960). *Political Man.* New York: Doubleday.

LIPSET, SEYMOUR MARTIN, MARTIN A. TROW, and JAMES S. COLMAN (1956). *Union Democracy.* Glencoe, Ill.: Free Press.

LITTERER, JOSEPH A., ed (1963). *Organizations: Structure and Behavior.* New York: John Wiley.

LITWAK, EUGENE (1961). "Models of Bureaucracy Which Permit Conflict." *American Journal of Scoiology,* 67 (September), 177–84.

—— (1968). "Technological Innovation and Theoretical Functions of Primary Groups and Bureaucratic Structures," *American Journal of Sociology,* 73 (January), 468–81.

LITWAK, EUGENE, and LYDIA F. HYLTON (1962). "Interorganizational Analysis: A Hypothesis on Coordinating Agencies," *Administrative Science Quarterly,* 6 (March), 395–420.

LITWAK, EUGENE, and HENRY J. MEYER (1966). "A Balance Theory of Coordination between Bureaucratic Organizations and Community Primary Groups," *Administrative Science Quarterly,* 11 (June), 31–58.

LOWI, THEODORE J. (1969). *The End of Liberalism.* New York: W. W. Norton & Co., Inc.

LOWIN, AARON, and JAMES R. CRAIG (1968). "The Influence of Level of Performance on Managerial Style: An Experimental Object-Lesson in the Ambiguity of Correlational Data," *Organizational Behavior and Human Performance,* 3 (November), 440–58.

LUKACS, GEORG (1971 trans.). *History and Class Consciousness.* London: Merlin (first published in 1923).

LYDEN, F. J. (1975). "Using Parsons' Functional Analysis in the Study of Public Organizations," *Administrative Science Quarterly,* 20 (March), 59–70.

LYNCH, BEVERLY P. (1974). "An Empirical Assessment of Perrow's Technology Construct," *Administrative Science Quarterly,* 19 (September), 338–56.

McCARTHY, JOHN D., and MAYER N. ZALD (1973). *The Trends of Social Movements in America: Professionalization and Resource Mobilization.* Morristown, N.J.: General Learning Press.

—— (1977). "Resource Mobilization and Social Movements: A Partial Theory," *American Journal of Sociology,* 82 (May), 1212–41.

McEWEN, C. A. (1980). "Continuities in the Study of Total and Nontotal Institutions," *Annual Review of Sociology,* 6, 143–85.

McGREGOR, DOUGLAS (1960). *The Human Side of Enterprise.* New York: McGraw-Hill.

MacIVER, ROBERT M. (1947). *The Web of Government.* New York: Macmillan.

McKELVEY, BILL (1982). *Organizational Systematics.* Berkeley: University of California Press.

McKELVEY, BILL, and HOWARD ALDRICH (1983). "Populations, Natural Selection, and Applied Organizational Science," *Administrative Science Quarterly,* 28 (March), 101–28.

McLEAN, ALAN (1970). *Mental Health and Work Organizations.* Chicago: Rand McNally.

McLUHAN, MARSHALL (1964). *Understanding Media: The Extensions of Man.* New York: Signet.

McMILLAN, CHARLES J., DAVID J. HICKSON, CHRISTOPHER R. HININGS, and RODNEY E. SCHNECK (1973). "The Structure of Work Organizations across Societies," *Academy of Management Journal,* 16 (December), 555–69.

McNEIL, KENNETH, and JAMES D. THOMPSON (1971). "The Regeneration of Social Organizations," *American Sociological Review,* 36 (August), 624–37.

MAIER, NORMAN R. F. (1952). *Principles of Human Relations.* New York: John Wiley.

MAILER, NORMAN (1968). "The Steps of the Pentagon," *Harper's,* 236 (March), 47–142.

MAINES, DAVID R. (1977). "Social Organization and Social Structure in Symbolic Interactionist Thought," *Annual Review of Sociology,* 3, 235–59.

MAJONE, GIANDOMENICO (1980). "Process and Outcome in Regulatory Decision-Making," in *Making Bu-*

reaucracies Work, pp. 235–58, ed. Carol H. Weiss and Allen H. Barton. Beverly Hills, Calif.: Sage Publications, Inc.

MALINOWSKI, BRONISLAW (1939). "The Group and the Individual in Functional Analysis," *American Journal of Sociology*, 44, 938–64.

MANN, JUDITH K., and DONALD E. YETT (1968). "The Analysis of Hospital Costs: A Review Article," *Journal of Business*, 41 (April), 191–202.

MANNHEIM, KARL (1950 trans.) *Man and Society in an Age of Reconstruction*, trans. Edward Shils. New York: Harcourt Brace Jovanovich (first published 1935).

MANSFIELD, ROGER (1973). "Bureaucracy and Centralization: An Examination of Organizational Structure," *Administrative Science Quarterly*, 18 (December), 77–88.

MARCH, JAMES G., (1976). "The Technology of Foolishness," in *Ambiguity and Choice in Organizations*, pp. 69–81, ed. James G. March and Johan P. Olsen. Bergen, Norway: Universitetsforlaget.

——— (1978). "Bounded Rationality, Ambiguity, and the Engineering of Choice," *Bell Journal of Economics*, (Autumn), 587–608.

——— (1981). "Decisions in Organizations and Theories of Choice," in *Perspectives on Organization Design and Behavior*, pp. 205–44, ed. Andrew H. Van de Ven and William F. Joyce. New York: John Wiley, Wiley-Interscience.

——— ed. (1965). *Handbook of Organizations*. Chicago: Randy McNally.

MARCH, JAMES G., and JOHAN P. OLSEN (1976). *Ambiguity and Choice in Organizations*. Bergen, Norway: Universitetsforlaget.

MARCH, JAMES G., and HERBERT A. SIMON (1958). *Organizations*. New York: John Wiley.

MARGLIN, STEPHEN (1974). "What the Bosses Do: The Origins and Functions of Hierarchy in Capitalist Production," *Review of Radical Political Economics*, 6 (Summer), 60–112.

MARTIN, JOANNE (1981). "Relative Deprivation: a Theory of Distributive Injustice for an Era of Shrinking Resources," in *Research in Organizational Behavior*, vol. 3, pp. 53–107, ed. L. L. Cummings and Barry M. Staw. Greenwich, Conn.: JAI Press.

MARX, KARL (1954 trans.). *Capital*. Moscow: Foreign Languages Publishing House (first published in 1867).

——— (1963 trans.). *Karl Marx: Early Writings*. trans. and ed. T. B. Bottomore. London: C. A. Watts (first published as *Economic and Philosophical Manuscripts*, 1844).

——— (1972 trans.). "Economic and Philosophic Manuscripts of 1844: Selections," in *the Marx-Engels Reader*, ed. Robert C. Tucker. New York: W. W. Norton & Co., Inc.

——— (1973 trans.). *Grundrisse: Foundations of the Critique of Political Economy*. Harmondsworth, England: Penguin (first published in 1939–1941).

MARX, KARL, and FREDERICK ENGELS (1955 trans.). *Manifesto of the Communist Party*. Moscow: Foreign Languages Publishing House (first published in 1848).

MASLOW, ABRAHAM (1954). *Motivation and Personality*. New York: Harper.

MASSIE, JOSEPH L. (1965). "Management Theory," in *Handbook of Organizations*, pp. 387–422, ed. James G. March. Chicago: Rand McNally.

MAYO, ELTON (1945). *The Social Problems of an Industrial Civilization*. Boston: Graduate School of Business Administration, Harvard University.

MEAD, GEORGE HERBERT (1934). *Mind, Self and Society*. Chicago: University of Chicago Press.

MECHANIC, DAVID (1962). "Sources of Power of Lower Participants in Complex Organizations," *Administrative Science Quarterly*, 7 (December), 349–62.

MELMAN, SEYMOUR (1951). "The Rise of Administrative Overhead in the Manufacturing Industries of the United States, 1899–1947," *Oxford Economic Papers*, 3, 62–112.

MERTON, ROBERT K. (1957). *Social Theory and Social Structure* (2nd ed.). Glencoe, Ill.: Free Press.

MERTON, ROBERT K., AILSA P. GRAY, BARBARA HOCKEY, and HANAN C. SELVIN, eds. (1952). *Reader in Bureaucracy*. Glencoe, Ill.: Free Press.

MESSINGER, SHELDON L. (1955). "Organizational Transformation: A Case Study of a Declining Social Movement," *American Sociological Review*, 20 (February), 3–10.

MEYER, JOHN W. (1977). "The Effects of Education as an Institution," *American Journal of Sociology*, 83 (July), 55–77.

——— (1978). "Strategies for Further Research: Varieties of Environmental Variation," in *Environments and Organizations*, pp. 352–68, ed. Marshall W. Meyer. San Francisco: Jossey-Bass.

——— (1983). "Institutionalization and the Rationality of Formal Organizational Structure," in *Organizational Environments: Ritual and Rationality*, pp. 261–82, by John W. Meyer and W. Richard Scott. Beverly Hills, Calif.: Sage Publications, Inc.

——— (1985). "Institutional and Organizational Rationalization in the Mental Health System," *American Behavioral Scientist*, 28 (May/June), 587–600.

MEYER, JOHN W., and BRIAN ROWAN (1977). "Institutionalized Organizations: Formal Structure as Myth and Ceremony," *American Journal of Sociology*, 83 (September), 340–63.

——— (1978). "The Structure of Educational Organizations," in *Environments and Organizations*, pp. 78–109, ed. Marshall W. Meyer. San Francisco: Jossey-Bass.

MEYER, JOHN W., and W. RICHARD SCOTT, with the assistance of BRIAN ROWAN and TERRENCE E. DEAL (1983). *Organizational Environments: Ritual and Rationality*. Beverly Hills, Calif.: Sage Publications, Inc.

MEYER, JOHN W., W. RICHARD SCOTT, SALLY COLE, and JO-ANN K. INTILI (1978). "Instructional Dissensus and Institutional Consensus in Schools," in *Environments and Organizations*, pp. 233–63, ed. Marshall W. Meyer. San Francisco: Jossey-Bass.

MEYER, JOHN W., W. RICHARD SCOTT, and TERRENCE E. DEAL (1981). "Institutional and Technical Sources of Organizational Structure: Explaining the Structure of Educational Organizations," in *Organization and the Human Services: Cross-Disciplinary Reflections*, pp. 151–79, ed. Herman D. Stein. Philadelphia: Temple University Press.

MEYER, MARSHALL W. (1972). "Size and the Structure of Organizations: A Causal Analysis," *American Sociological Review*, 37 (August), 434–41.

—— (1979a). "Organizational Structure as Signaling," *Pacific Sociological Review*, 22 (October), 481–500.

—— (1979b). *Change in Public Bureaucracies*. Cambridge: Cambridge University Press.

MICHELS, ROBERT (1949 trans.). *Political Parties*, trans. Eden and Cedar Paul. Glencoe, Ill.: Free Press (first published in 1915).

MILES, MATTHEW B. (1964). "On Temporary Systems," in *Innovations in Education*, pp. 437–90, ed. Matthew B. Miles. New York: Teachers College, Columbia University.

MILES, ROBERT H. (1982). *Coffin Nails and Corporate Strategies*. Englewood Cliffs, N.J.: Prentice-Hall.

MILGRAM, STANLEY (1973). "The Perils of Obedience," *Harper's* (December), 62–66; 75–77.

—— (1974). *Obedience to Authority*. New York: Harper & Row, Pub.

MILIBAND, RALPH (1969). *The State in Capitalist Society*. New York: Basic Books; Harper Colophon Books.

MILLER, E. J., and A. K. RICE (1967). *Systems of Organization*. London: Tavistock.

MILLER GEORGE A. (1953). "What Is Information Measurement?" *American Psychologist*, 8, 3–12.

MILLER, JAMES GRIER (1978). *Living Systems*. New York: McGraw-Hill.

MILLS, C. WRIGHT (1956). *The Power Elite*. New York: Oxford University Press.

MINER, ANNE S. (1985). "The Strategy of Serendipity: Ambiguity, Uncertainty and Ideosyncratic Jobs." Unpublished Ph.D. dissertation, Graduate School of Business, Stanford University.

MINER, ANNE S., and SUZANNE E. ESTLER (1985). "Accrual Mobility: Job Mobility in Higher Education through Responsibility Accrual," *Journal of Higher Education*, 56 (March/April), 121–43.

MINTZ, BETH, and MICHAEL SCHWARTZ (1983). *Bank Hegemony, Corporate Networks and Intercorporate Power: A study of Interlocking Directorates in American Business*. Chicago: University of Chicago Press.

MINTZBERG, HENRY (1971). "Managerial Work: Analysis from Observation,: *Management Science*, 18 (October), B97–B110.

—— (1973). *The Nature of Managerial Work*. New York: Harper & Row, Pub.

—— (1979). *The Structure of Organizations*. Englewood Cliffs, N.J.: Prentice-Hall.

—— (1983). *Power in and around Organizations*. Englewood Cliffs, N.J.: Prentice-Hall.

MINTZBERG, HENRY, and ALEXANDRA MCHUGH (1985). "Strategy Formation in an Adhocracy," *Administrative Science Quarterly*, 30 (June), 160–97.

MISES, LUDWIG VON (1944). *Bureaucracy*. New Haven: Yale University Press.

MIZRUCHI, MARK (1982). *The American Corporate Network, 1904–1974*. Beverly Hills, Calif.: Sage Publications, Inc.

MIZRUCHI, MARK, and MICHAEL SCHWARTZ, eds. (1986). *The Structural Analysis of Business*. Cambridge: Cambridge University Press.

MOE, EDWARD O. (1959). "Consulting with a Community System: A Case Study," *Journal of Social Issues*, 15:2, 28–35.

MOHR, LAWRENCE B. (1971). "Organizational Technology and Organizational Structures," *Administrative Science Quarterly*, 16 (December), 444–59.

MOLOTCH, HARVEY (1976). "The City as a Growth Machine: Toward a Political Economy of Place," *American Journal of Sociology*, 82 (September), 309–32.

MONTAGNA, PAUL D. (1968). "Professionalization and Bureaucratization in Large Professional Organizations," *American Journal of Sociology*, 72 (September), 138–45.

MONTEVERDE, KIRK, and DAVID J. TEECE (1982). "Supplier Switching Costs and Vertical Integration in the Automobile Industry," *Bell Journal of Economics*, 12 (Spring), 206–13.

MOONEY, JAMES D. (1937). "The Principles of Organization," in *Papers on the Science of Administration*, pp. 89–98, ed. Luther Gulick and L. Urwick. New York: Institute of Public Administration, Columbia University.

MOONEY, JAMES D., and ALLAN C. REILEY (1939). *The Principles of Organization*. New York: Harper.

MORRISSEY, JOSEPH P., RICHARD H. HALL, and MICHAEL L. LINDSEY (1982). *Interorganizational Relations: A Sourcebook of Measures for Mental Health Programs*. National Institute of Mental Health, Series BN No. 2. DHHS Pub. No. (ADM) 82-1187. Washington, D. C.: Government Printing Office.

MORSE, CHANDLER (1961). "The Functional Imperatives," in *Social Theories of Talcott Parsons*, pp. 100–52, ed. Max Black. Englewood Cliffs, N.J.: Prentice-Hall.

MOUZELIS, NICOS P. (1968). *Organization and Bureaucracy: An Analysis of Modern Theories*. Chicago: Aldine.

MOYNIHAN, DANIEL P. (1970). *Maximum Feasible Misunderstanding*. New York: Free Press.

MYERS, CHARLES A., ed. (1967). *The Impact of Computers on Management*. Cambridge, Mass.: M.I.T. Press.

NAGEL, ERNEST (1961). *The Structure of Science*. New York: Harcourt, Brace & World.

NAISBITT, JOHN (1982). *Megatrends*. New York: Warner Books.

NATIONAL TRAINING LABORATORIES (1953). *Explorations in Human Relations Training*. Washington, D.C.: National Training Laboratories.

NEUHAUSER, DUNCAN (1971). *The Relationship between Administrative Activities and Hospital Performance*. Research Series 28. Chicago: Center for Health Administration Studies, University of Chicago.

—— (1972). "The Hospital as a Matrix Organization," *Hospital Administration*, 17 (Fall), 8–25.

NEUMANN, FRANZ (1942). *Behemoth.* London: Victor Follancz, 1942.
NEWMAN, KENNETH (1975). "Voluntary Associations in a British City," *Journal of Voluntary Action Research,* 4 (January-April), 43–62.
NISBETT, RICHARD, and LEE ROSS (1980). *Human Inference: Strategies and Shortcomings of Social Judgment.* Englewood Cliffs, N.J.: Prentice-Hall.
NOLL, ROGER G., ed. (1985). *Regulatory Policy and the Social Sciences.* Berkeley: University of California Press.
NUTTER, G. WARREN (1968). "Concentration," *International Encyclopedia of the Social Sciences,* vol. 3, pp. 218–22. New York: Crowell Collier and Macmillan.

OBERSCHALL, ANTHONY (1973). *Social Conflict and Social Movements.* Englewood Cliffs, N.J.: Prentice-Hall.
O'CONNOR, JAMES (1973). *The Fiscal Crisis of the State.* New York: St. Martin's Press.
ODIONE, GEORGE S. (1965). *Management by Objective.* New York: Pitman.
OKIMOTO, DANIEL I. (1984) *Competitive Edge: The Semiconductor Industry in the United States and Japan.* Stanford, Calif.: Stanford University Press.
OLSEN, JOHAN P. (1983). *Organized Democracy: Political Institutions in a Welfare State—The Case of Norway.* Bergen, Norway: Universitetsforlaget.
OLSON, MANCUR, JR. (1965). *The Logic of Collective Action.* Cambridge, Mass.: Harvard University Press.
——— (1982). *The Rise and Decline of Nations: Economic Growth, Stagflation, and Social Rigidities.* New Haven: Yale University Press.
O'TOOLE, J., ed. (1972). *Work in America: A Report to the Secretary of State for Health, Education and Welfare.* Cambridge, Mass.: M.I.T. Press.
OUCHI, WILLIAM G. (1979). "Markets, Bureaucracies and Clans." Unpublished paper, Graduate School of Management, University of California, Los Angeles.
——— (1980). "Markets, Bureaucracies and Clans," *Administrative Science Quarterly,* 25 (March), 129–41.
——— (1981). *Theory Z.* Reading, Mass.: Addison-Wesley.
OUCHI, WILLIAM G., and ALFRED M. JAEGER (1978). "Type Z Organization: Stability in the Midst of Mobility," *Academy of Management Review,* 3 (April), 305–14.

PALMER, DONALD (1983). "Broken Ties: Interlocking Directorates and Intercorporate Coordination," *Administrative Science Quarterly,* 28 (March), 40–55.
PALMER, DONALD, ROGERT FRIEDLAND, P. DEVEREAUX JENNINGS, and MELANIE E. POWERS (1985). "The Determinants of the Multidivisional Form in Large U.S. Corporations," presented at the annual meeting of the American Sociological Association, Washington, D.C.
PARKINSON, C. NORTHCOTE (1957). *Parkinson's Law and Other Studies in Administration.* Boston: Houghton Mifflin.
PARSONS, TALCOTT (1947). Introduction to *The Theory of Social and Economic Organization,* pp. 3–86, by Max Weber. Glencoe, Ill.: Free Press.
——— (1951). *The Social System.* Glencoe, Ill.: Free Press.
——— (1953). "A Revised Analytical Approach to the Theory of Social Stratification," in *Class, Status and Power: A Reader in Social Stratification,* pp. 92–129, ed. Reinhard Bendix and Seymour M. Lipset. Glencoe, Ill.: Free Press.
——— (1960). *Structure and Process in Modern Societies.* Glencoe, Ill.: Free Press.
——— (1966). *Societies: Evolutionary and Comparative Perspectives.* Englewood Cliffs, N.J.: Prentice-Hall.
PARSONS, TALCOTT, ROBERT F. BALES, and EDWARD A. SHILS (1953). *Working Papers in the Theory of Action.* Glencoe, Ill.: Free Press.
PATCHEN, MARTIN (1961). *The Choice of Wage Comparisons.* Englewood Cliffs, N.J.: Prentice-Hall.
PELZ, DONALD C. (1952). "Influence: A Key to Effective Leadership in the First-Line Supervisor," *Personnel,* 29, 209–17.
PENNINGS, J. (1973). "Measures of Organizational Structure: A Methodological Note," *American Journal of Sociology,* 79 (November), 686–704.
——— (1975). "The Relevance of the Structural-Contingency Model for Organizational Effectiveness," *Administrative Science Quarterly,* 20 (September), 393–410.
——— (1981). "Strategically Interdependent Organizations," in *Handbook of Organizational Design,* vol. 1, pp. 433–55, ed. Paul C. Nystrom and William H. Starbuck. Oxford: Oxford University Press.
PERROW, CHARLES (1961). "The Analysis of Goals in Complex Organizations," *American Sociological Review,* 26 (December), 854–66.
——— (1965). "Hospitals: Technology, Structure, and Goals," in *Handbook of Organizations,* pp. 910–71, ed. James G. March. Chicago: Rand McNally.
——— (1967). "A Framework for the Comparative Analysis of Organizations," *American Sociological Review,* 32 (April), 194–208.
——— (1970). *Organizational Analysis: A Sociological View.* Belmont, Calif.: Wadsworth.
——— (1972). "Review of Neuhauser, D.: *The Relationship between Administrative Activities and Hospital Performance,*" *Administrative Science Quarterly,* 17 (September), 419–21.
——— (1973). "The Short and Glorious History of Organizational Theory," *Organizational Dynamics,* 2 (Summer), 2–15.
——— (1979). *Complex Organizations: A Critical Essay* (2nd ed.). Glenview, Ill.: Scott, Foresman.
——— (1982). "Three Mile Island: A Normal Accident," in *The International Yearbook of Organizational Studies 1981,* pp. 1–25, ed. David Dunkerley and Graeme Salaman. London: Routledge & Kegan Paul.
——— (1984). *Normal Accidents: Living with High-Risk Technologies.* New York: Basic Books.

PETERS, THOMAS J., and ROBERT H. WATERMAN, JR. (1982). *In Search of Excellence.* New York: Harper & Row, Pub.

PFEFFER, JEFFREY (1972a). "Size and Composition of Corporate Boards of Directors: The Organization and Its Environment," *Administrative Science Quarterly*, 17 (June), 218–28.

—— (1972b). "Merger as a Response to Organizational Interdependence," *Administrative Science Quarterly*, 17 (September), 382–92.

—— (1973). "Size, Composition, and Function of Hospital Boards of Directors: A Study of Organization-Environment Linkage," *Administrative Science Quarterly*, 18 (September), 349–64.

—— (1978). "The Micropolitics of Organizations," in *Environments and Organizations*, pp. 29–50, ed. Marshall W. Meyer. San Francisco: Jossey-Bass.

—— (1981). *Power in Organizations.* Marshfield, Mass.: Pitman.

—— (1982). *Organizations and Organization Theory.* Boston: Pitman.

—— (1983). "Organizational Demography," in *Research in Organizational Behavior*, vol. 5, pp. 299–357, ed. L. L. Cummings and Barry M. Staw. Greenwich, Conn.: JAI Press.

PFEFFER, JEFFREY, and YINON COHEN (1984). "Determinants of Internal Labor Markets in Organizations," *Administrative Science Quarterly*, 29 (December), 550–72.

PFEFFER, JEFFREY, and PHILLIP NOWAK (1976). "Joint Ventures and Interorganizational Dependence," *Administrative Science Quarterly*, 21 (September), 398–418.

PFEFFER, JEFFREY, and GERALD R. SALANCIK. (1974). "Organizational Decision Making as a Political Process: The Case of a University Budget," *Administrative Science Quarterly*, 19 (June), 135–51.

—— (1978). *The External Control of Organizations.* New York: Harper & Row, Pub.

PIVEN, FRANCES FOX, and RICHARD A. CLOWARD. (1971). *Regulating the Poor.* New York: Pantheon.

—— (1977). *Poor People's Movements: Why They Succeed, How They Fail.* New York: Pantheon.

POLANYI, KARL (1944). *The Great Transformation.* New York: Holt.

PONDY, LOUIS R., and IAN I. MITROFF (1979). "Beyond Open System Models of Organization," in *Research in Organizational Behavior*, vol. 1, pp. 3–39, ed. Barry M. Staw. Greenwich, Conn.: JAI Press.

PORTER, LYMAN W., and EDWARD E. LAWLER, III (1968). *Managerial Attitudes and Performance.* Homewood, Ill.: Richard D. Irwin.

PORTER, LYMAN W., EDWARD E. LAWLER, and J. R. HACKMAN (1975). *Behavior in Organizations.* New York: McGraw-Hill.

PORTER, MICHAEL E. (1980). *Competitive Strategy.* New York: Free Press.

POUND, EZRA (1973). *Selected Prose, 1909–1965*, ed. William Cookson. New York: New Directions.

POWELL, WALTER W. (1985). *Getting into Print: The Decision-Making Process in Scholarly Publishing.* Chicago: University of Chicago Press.

PRESSMAN, JEFFREY L., and AARON WILDAVSKY (1973). *Implementation.* Berkeley: University of California Press.

PRICE, JAMES L. (1968). *Organizational Effectiveness.* Homewood, Ill.: Richard D. Irwin.

PUGH, D. S., and D. J. HICKSON (1976). *Organizational Structure in Its Context: The Aston Programme I.* Lexington, Mass.: Heath, Lexington Books.

PUGH, D. S., D. J. HICKSON, and C. R. HININGS (1969). "An Empirical Taxonomy of Structures of Work Organizations," *Administrative Science Quarterly*, 14 (March). 115–26.

—— (1985). *Writers on Organizations* (3rd ed.). Beverly Hills, Calif.: Sage Publications, Inc.

PUGH, D. S., D. J. HICKSON, C. R. HININGS, K. M. MACDONALD, C. TURNER, and T. LUPTON (1963). "A Conceptual Scheme for Organizational Analysis," *Administrative Science Quarterly*, 8 (December), 289–315.

PUGH, D. S., D. J. HICKSON, C. R. Hinings, and C. TURNER (1968). "Dimensions of Organization Structure," *Administrative Science Quarterly*, 13 (June), 65–91.

—— (1969). "The Context of Organization Structures," *Administrative Science Quarterly*, 14 (March), 91–114.

RACKHAM, JEFFREY, and JOAN WOODWARD (1970). "The Measurement of Technical Variables," in *Industrial Organization: Behaviour and Control*, pp. 19–36, ed. Joan Woodward. London: Oxford University Press.

RADCLIFFE-BROWN, A. R. (1952). *Structure and Function in Primitive Society.* Glencoe, Ill.: Free Press.

REED, THEODORE L. (1978). "Organizational Change in the American Foreign Service, 1925–1965: The Utility of Cohort Analysis," *American Sociological Review*, 43 (June), 404–21.

REEVES, WILLIAM JOSEPH (1980). *Librarians as Professionals.* Lexington. Mass.: Heath, Lexington Books.

REICH, ROBERT B. (1983). "Why Democracy Makes Economic Sense," *New Republic* (December 19), 25–32.

REINHARDT, UWE E. (1973). "Proposed Changes in the Organization of Health-Care Delivery: An Overview and a Critique," *Milbank Memorial Fund Quarterly*, 51 (Spring), 169–222.

RICE, A. K. (1958). *Productivity and Social Organization: The Ahmedabad Experiment.* London: Tavistock.

ROBERTS, KARLENE H., and WILLIAM GLICK (1981). "The Job Characteristics Approach to Task Design: A Critical Review," *Journal of Applied Psychology*, 66 (April), 193–217.

ROBOCK, STEFAN H., and KENNETH SIMMONDS (1973). *International Business and Multinational Enterprises.* Homewood, Ill.: Richard D. Irwin.

ROETHLISBERGER, F. J., and WILLIAM J. DICKSON (1939). *Management and the Worker.* Cambridge, Mass.: Harvard University Press.

ROGERS, DAVID L., and DAVID A. WHETTEN (1982). *Interorganizational Coordination: Theory, Research, and Implementation.* Ames: Iowa State University Press.

ROGERS, EVERETT M., and REKHA AGARWALA-ROGERS (1976) *Communication in Organizations.* New York: Free Press.

ROSENBERG, HANS (1958). *Bureaucracy, Aristocracy and Autocracy: The Prussian Experience 1660–1815.* Cambridge, Mass.: Harvard University Press.

ROSZAK, THEODORE (1969). *The Making of a Counter Culture.* Garden City, N.Y.: Doubleday, Anchor Books.

ROTHSCHILD-WHITT, JOYCE (1979). "The Collectivist Organization: An Alternative to Rational Bureaucratic Models," *American Sociological Review,* 44 (August), 509–27.

ROTHSCHILD-WHITT, JOYCE, and A. WHITT (1986). *Work without Bosses: Conditions and Dilemmas of Organizational Democracy in Grassroots Cooperatives.* New York: Cambridge University Press.

ROWAN, BRIAN (1981). "The Effects of Institutionalized Rules on Administrators," in *Organizational Behavior in Schools and School Districts,* pp. 47–55, ed. Samuel B. Bacharach. New York: Praeger.

—— (1982). "Organizational Structure and the Institutional Environment: The Case of Public Schools," *Administrative Science Quarterly,* 27 (June), 259–79.

ROY, DONALD (1952). "Quota Restriction and Goldbricking in a Machine Shop," *American Journal of Sociology,* 57 (March), 427–42.

RUSHING, WILLIAM A. (1966a). "Organizational Rules and Surveillance: Propositions in Comparative Organization Analysis," *Administrative Science Quarterly,* 10 (March), 423–43.

—— (1966b). "Organizational Size and Administration," *Pacific Sociological Review,* 9 (Fall), 100–108.

—— (1968) "Hardness of Material as an External Constraint on the Division of Labor in Manufacturing Industries," *Administrative Science Quarterly,* 13 (September), 229–45.

SAGE, ANDREW P. (1981). "Designs for Optimal Information Filters," in *Handbook of Organizational Design,* vol. 1, pp. 105–21, ed. Paul C. Nystrom and William H. Starbuck. London: Oxford University Press.

SAINT-SIMON, HENRI COMTE DE (1952 trans.). *Selected Writings,* trans. F. M. H. Markham. New York: Macmillan (first published in 1859).

SALAMAN, GRAEME, and KENNETH THOMPSON, eds. (1980). *Control and Ideology In Organizations.* Cambridge, Mass.: M.I.T. Press.

SALANCIK, GERALD R., and JEFFREY PFEFFER (1977). "An Examination of Need-Satisfaction Models of Job Attitudes," *Administrative Science Quarterly,* 22 (September), 427–56.

SATOW, ROBERTA LYNN (1975). "Value-Rational Authority and Professional Organizations: Weber's Missing Type," *Administrative Science Quarterly,* 20 (December), 526–31.

SAYLES, LEONARD R. (1958). *Behavior of Industrial Work Groups.* New York: John Wiley.

—— (1976). "Matrix Organization: The Structure with a Future," *Organizational Dynamics,* (Autumn), 2–17.

SCHMITTER, PHILIPPE C. (1974). "Still the Century of Corporatism?" in *The New Corporatism: Social-Political Structures in the Iberian World,* pp. 85–131, ed. Frederick B. Pike and Thomas Stritch. Notre Dame, Ind.: University of Notre Dame Press.

SCHOONHOVEN, CLAUDIA BIRD (1981). "Problems with Contingency Theory: Testing Assumptions Hidden within the Language of Contingency Theory," *Administrative Science Quarterly,* 26 (September), 349–77.

SCHOPLER, JOHN (1965). "Social Power," in *Advances in Experimental Social Psychology,* vol. 2, pp. 177–219, ed. Leonard Berkowitz. New York: Academic Press.

SCHRÖDINGER, ERWIN (1945). *What Is Life?* Cambridge: Cambridge University Press.

SCHUMPETER, JOSEPH A. (1947). *Capitalism, Socialism and Democracy* (2nd ed.). New York: Harper.

SCHUTZ, ALFRED (1962 trans.). *Collected Papers,* vols. 1 and 2. The Hague: Nijhoff.

SCHWAB, DONALD P., and LARRY L. CUMMINGS (1970). "Theories of Performance and Satisfaction: A Review," *Industrial Relations,* 9 (October), 408–30.

SCHWAB, J. J. (1960). "What Do Scientists Do?" *Behavioral Science,* 5 (January), 1–27.

SCOTT, JOHN (1979). *Corporations, Classes and Capitalism.* New York: St. Martins Press.

SCOTT, W. RICHARD (1964). "Theory of Organizations," in *Handbook of Modern Sociology,* pp. 485–529, ed. Robert E. L. Faris. Chicago: Rand McNally.

—— (1965a). "Field Methods in the Study of Organizations," in *Handbook of Organizations,* pp. 261–304, ed. James G. March. Chicago: Rand McNally.

—— (1965b). "Reactions to Supervision in a Heteronomous Professional Organization," *Administrative Science Quarterly,* 10 (June), 65–81.

—— (1969). "Professional Employees in a Bureaucratic Structure: Social Work," in *The Semi-Professions and Their Organization,* pp. 82–144, ed. Amitai Etzioni. New York: Free Press.

—— (1970). *Social Processes and Social Structures: An Introduction to Sociology.* New York: Holt, Rinehart & Winston.

—— "Professionals in Hospitals: Technology and the Organization of Work," in *Organization Research on Health Institutions,* pp. 139–58, discussion, pp. 173–89, ed. Basil S. Georgopoulos. Ann Arbor: Institute for Social Research, University of Michigan.

—— (1975). "Organizational Structure," *Annual Review of Sociology,* 1, 1–20.

—— (1977a). "Effectiveness of Organizational Effectiveness Studies," in *New Perspectives on Organizational Effectiveness,* pp. 63–95, ed. Paul S. Goodman and Johannes M. Pennings. San Francisco: Jossey-Bass.

—— (1977b). "Some Problems in the Study of Organization Structure," *Mid-American Review of Sociology,* 2 (Spring), 1–16.

—— (1978). "Theoretical Perspectives," in *Environments and Organizations,* pp. 21–28, ed. Marshall W. Meyer. San Francisco: Jossey-Bass.

—— (1981). *Organizations: Rational, Natural and Open Systems.* Englewood Cliffs, N.J.: Prentice-Hall. (First edition)

—— (1982). "Managing Professional Work: Three Models of Control for Health Organizations," *Health Services Research,* 17 (Fall), 213–40.

—— (1983). "The Organization of Environments: Network, Cultural, and Historical elements," in *Organizational Environments: Ritual and Rationality,* pp. 155–75, by John W. Meyer and W. Richard Scott. Beverly Hills, Calif.: Sage Publications, Inc.

—— (1985a). "Conflicting Levels of Rationality: Regulators, Managers, and Professionals in the Medical Care Sector," *Journal of Health Administration Education,* 3 (Spring), 113–31.

—— (1985b). "Systems within Systems: The Mental Health Sector," *American Behavioral Scientist,* 28 (May/June), 601–18.

—— (1986). "The Sociology of Organizations: Crisis or Continuum?" in *Sociology: The Aftermath of Crisis,* ed. Ulf Himmelstrand. Beverly Hills, Calif.: Sage Publications, Inc.

SCOTT, W. RICHARD, SANFORD M. DORNBUSCH, BRUCE C. BUSHING, and JAMES D. LAING (1967). "Organizational Evaluation and Authority," *Administrative Science Quarterly,* 12 (June), 93–117.

SCOTT, W. RICHARD, SANFORD M. DORNBUSCH, CONNIE J. EVASHWICK, LEONARD MAGNANI, and INGER SAGATUN (1971). "Task Conceptions and Work Arrangements." Technical Report 47, Laboratory for Social Research. Stanford, Calif.: Stanford University.

SCOTT, W. RICHARD, ANN BARRY FLOOD, WAYNE EWY, and WILLIAM H. FORREST, JR. (1978). "Organizational Effectiveness and the Quality of Surgical Care in Hospitals," in *Environments and Organizations,* pp. 290–305, ed. Marshall W. Meyer. San Francisco: Jossey-Bass.

SCOTT, W. RICHARD, and JOHN W. MEYER (1983). "The Organization of Societal Sectors," in *Organizational Environments: Ritual and Rationality,* pp. 129–54, by John W. Meyer and W. Richard Scott. Beverly Hills, Calif.: Sage Publications, Inc.

—— (1984). "Environmental Linkages and Organizational Complexity: Public and Private Schools," (Project Report no. 84-A16) Stanford, Calif.: Institute for Research on Educational Finance and Governance, Stanford University.

SCOTT, WILLIAM G., and DAVID K. HART. (1979) *Organizational America.* Boston: Houghton Mifflin.

SEASHORE, STANLEY E. (1954). *Group Cohesiveness in the Industrial Work Group.* Ann Arbor: Institute for Social Research, University of Michigan.

—— (1962). *The Assessment of Organizational Performance.* Ann Arbor: Survey Research Center, University of Michigan.

SEEMAN, MELVIN (1959). "On the Meaning of Alienation," *American Sociological Review,* 24 (December), 783–91.

—— (1975). "Alienation Studies," *Annual Review of Sociology,* 1, 91-123.

SEIDMAN, HAROLD (1975). "Government-Sponsored Enterprise in the United States," in *The New Political Economy: The Public Use of the Private Sector,* pp. 83–108, ed. Bruce L. R. Smith. New York: John Wiley.

SELZNICK, PHILIP (1948). "Foundations of the Theory of Organization," *American Sociological Review,* 13 (February), 25-35.

—— (1949). *TVA and the Grass Roots.* Berkeley: University of California Press.

—— (1957). *Leadership in Administration.* New York: Harper & Row, Pub.

—— (1969). *Law, Society, and Industrial Justice.* New York: Russell Sage Foundation.

SEWELL, WILLIAM H., and ROBERT M. HAUSER (1975). *Education, Occupation and Earnings: Achievement in the Early Career.* New York: Academic Press.

SHANNON, CLAUDE E., and WARREN WEAVER (1963). *The Mathematical Theory of Communication.* Urbana: University of Illinois Press.

SHAW, M. E. (1954). "Some Effects of Problem Complexity upon Problem Solution Efficiency in Various Communication Nets," *Journal of Experimental Psychology,* 48, 211–17.

—— (1964). "Communication Networks," in *Advances in Experimental Social Psychology,* vol. 1, pp. 111–47, ed. Leonard Berkowitz. New York: Academic Press.

SHEPPARD, HAROLD L., and NEAL HERRICK (1972). *Where Have All the Robots Gone?* New York: Free Press.

SHERIF, MUZAFER, and CAROLINE W. SHERIF (1953). *Groups in Harmony and Tension.* New York: Harper & Row, Pub.

SHILS, EDWARD E. (1960). *Political Development in the New States.* The Hague: Mouton.

SILVERMAN, DAVID (1971). *The Theory of Organizations.* New York: Basic Books.

SIMMEL, GEORG (1955 trans.). *Conflict and The Web of Group-Affiliations.* Glencoe, Ill.: Free Press. (The firs essay was first published in 1908, the second in 1922.)

SIMON, HERBERT A. (1957). *Administrative Behavior* (2nd ed.). New York: Macmillan (1st ed., 1945).

—— (1966). *The New Science of Management Decision.* New York: Harper.

—— "The Architecture of Complexity," *Proceedings of the American Philosophical Society,* 106 (December), 467–82.

—— (1964) "On the Concept of Organizational Goal," *Administrative Science Quarterly,* 9 (June), 1–22.

—— (1979). "Rational Decision Making in Business Organizations," *American Economic Review,* 69 (September), 493–513.

SIMON, HERBERT A., DONALD W. SMITHBERG, and VICTOR A. THOMPSON (1950). *Public Administration.* New York: Knopf.

SIMON, WILLIAM H. (1983). "Legality, Bureaucracy, and Class in the Welfare System," *Yale Law Journal*, 92 (June), 1198–1269.

SKOWRONEK, STEPHEN (1982). *Building a New American State: The Expansion of National Administrative Capacities.* New York: Cambridge University Press.

SLATER, PHILIP E. (1955). "Role Differentiation in Small Groups," *American Sociological Review*, 20 (June), 300–310.

SMIGEL, ERWIN O. (1964). *The Wall Street Lawyer: Professional Organization Man?* New York: Free Press.

SMIRCICH, LINDA (1983). "Concepts of Culture and Organizational Analysis," *Administrative Science Quarterly*, 28 (September), 339–58.

—— (1985). "Is the Concept of Culture a Paradigm for Understanding Organizations and Ourselves?" in *Organizational Culture*, pp. 55–72, ed. Peter J. Frost, Larry F. Moore, Meryl Reis Louis, Craig C. Lundberg, and Joanne Martin. Beverly Hills, Calif.: Sage Publications, Inc.

SMITH, ADAM (1957). *Selections from the Wealth of Nations*, ed. George J. Stigler. New York: Appleton Century Crofts (originally published in 1776).

SMITH, BRUCE L. R. (1966). *The Rand Corporation.* Cambridge, Mass.: Harvard University Press.

SMITH, THOMAS SPENCE, and R. DANFORTH ROSS (1978). "Cultural Controls on the Demography of Hierarchy: A Time-Series Analysis of Warfare and the Growth of the United States Army, 1960–68." Unpublished paper, University of Rochester.

SNYDER, DAVID, and CHARLES TILLY (1972). "Hardship and Collective Violence in France, 1830 to 1960," *American Sociological Review*, 37 (October), 520–32.

SOMERS, ANNE R. (1969). *Hospital Regulation: The Dilemma of Public Policy.* Princeton, N.J.: Industrial Relations Section, Princeton University.

SPECIAL TASK FORCE TO THE SECRETARY OF HEALTH, EDUCATION AND WELFARE (1973). *Work in America.* Cambridge, Mass.: M.I.T. Press.

SPROULL, LEE S. (1981). "Response to Regulation: An Organizational Process Framework," *Administration and Society*, 12 (February), 447–70.

STABER, UDO (1985). "A Population Perspective on Collective Action as an Organizational Form: The Case of Trade Associations," in *Research in the Sociology of Organizations*, vol. 4, pp. 181–220, ed. Samuel B. Bacharach and Stephen M. Mitchell. Greenwich, Conn.: JAI Press.

STABER, UDO, and HOWARD ALDRICH (1983). "Trade Association Stability and Public Policy," in *Organizational Theory and Public Policy*, pp. 163–78, ed. Richard H. Hall and Robert E. Quinn. Beverly Hills, Calif.: Sage Publications, Inc.

STANTON, ALFRED H., and MORRIS S. SCHWARTZ (1954). *The Mental Hospital.* New York: Basic Books.

STARK, DAVID (1980). "Class Struggle and the Transformation of the Labour Process: A Relational Approach," *Theory and Society*, 9 (January), 89–130.

STAW, BARRY M. (1980). "Rationality and Justification in Organizational Life," in *Research in Organizational Behavior*, vol. 2, pp. 45–80, ed. Barry M. Staw and Larry L. Cummings. Greenwich, Conn.: JAI Press.

—— (1984). "Organizational Behavior: A Review and Reformulation of the Field's Outcome Variables." *Annual Review of Psychology*, 35, 627–66.

STEERS, RICHARD M. (1975). "Problems in the Measurement of Organizational Effectiveness," *Administrative Science Quarterly*, 20 (December), 546–58.

—— (1977). *Organizational Effectiveness: A Behavioral View.* Pacific Palisades, Calif.: Goodyear.

STEERS, RICHARD M., and DANIEL G. SPENCER (1977). "The Role of Achievement Motivation in Job Design," *Journal of Applied Psychology*, 62 (August), 472–79.

STEINBRUNER, JOHN D. (1974). *The Cybernetic Theory of Decision.* Princeton, N.J.: Princeton University Press.

STEINER, GEORGE A., and WILLIAM G. RYAN (1968). *Industrial Project Management.* New York: Crowell-Collier and Macmillan.

STERN, ROBERT N. (1979). "The Development of an Interorganizational Control Network: The Case of Intercollegiate Athletics," *Administrative Science Quarterly*, 24 (June), 242–66.

STIGLER, GEORGE J. (1971). "The Theory of Economic Regulation," *Bell Journal of Economics and Management Science*, 2 (Spring), 3–21.

STINCHCOMBE, ARTHUR L. (1959). "Bureaucratic and Craft Administration of Production: A Comparative Study," *Administrative Science Quarterly*, 4 (September), 168–87.

—— (1965). "Social Structure and Organizations," in *Handbook of Organizations*, pp. 142–93, ed. James G. March. Chicago: Rand McNally.

—— (1974). *Creating Efficient Industrial Administrations.* New York: Academic Press.

—— (1983). *Economic Sociology.* New York: Academic Press.

—— (1985). "Contracts as Hierarchical Documents," in *Organization Theory and Project Management*, by Arthur Stinchcombe and Carol Heimer. Bergen, Norway: Universitetsforlaget.

STOGDILL, R. M., and A. E. COONS, eds. (1957). *Leader Behavior: Its Description and Measurement.* Research Monograph 88. Columbus, Ohio: Bureau of Business Research, Ohio State University.

STOLZENBERG, ROSS, M. (1978). "Bringing the Boss Back In: Employer Size, Employee Schooling, and Socioeconomic Achievement," *American Sociological Review*, 43 (December), 813–28.

STONE, EUGENE (1978). *Research Methods in Organizational Behavior.* Santa Monica, Calif.: Goodyear.

STONE, EUGENE F., RICHARD T. MOWDAY, and LYMAN W. PORTER (1977). "Higher Order Need Strengths as Moderators of the Job Scope–Job Satisfaction Relationship," *Journal of Applied Psychology*, 62 (August), 466–71.

STRAUSS, ANSELM, LEONARD SCHATZMAN, DANUTA EHRLICH, RUE BUCHER, and MELVIN SABSHIN (1963).

"The Hospital and Its Negotiated Order," in *The Hospital in Modern Society*, pp. 147–69, ed. Eliot Freidson. New York: Free Press of Glencoe.

STREET, DAVID, GEORGE T. MARTIN, JR., and LAURA KRAMER GORDON (1979). *The Welfare Industry: Functionaries and Recipients in Public Aid*. Beverly Hills, Calif.: Sage Publications, Inc.

STREET, DAVID, ROBERT VINTER, and CHARLES PERROW (1966). *Organization for Treatment*. New York: Free Press.

SUCHMAN, EDWARD A. (1967). *Evaluative Research*. New York: Russell Sage Foundation.

SUNDQUIST, JAMES L. (1969). *Making Federalism Work*. Washington, D.C.: Brookings Institution.

SWANSON, GUY E. (1976). "The Tasks of Sociology," *Science*, 192 (May), 665–67.

SWIDLER, ANN (1979). *Organization without Authority: Dilemmas of Social Control in Free Schools*. Cambridge, Mass.: Harvard University Press.

SWINTH, ROBERT L. (1974). *Organizational Systems for Management: Designing, Planning and Implementation*. Columbus, Ohio: Grid.

SYKES, A. J. M. (1965). "Economic Interests and the Hawthorne Researchers: A Comment," *Human Relations*, 18 (August), 253–63.

TALBERT, JOAN, and CHRISTINE E. BOSE. (1977). "Wage-Attainment Processes: The Retail Clerk Case," *American Journal of Sociology*, 83 (September), 403–24.

TANCREDI, LAURENCE R., and J. WOODS (1972). "The Social Control of Medical Practice: Licensure versus Output Monitoring," *Milbank Memorial Fund Quarterly*, 50 (January), part 1, 99–126.

TANNENBAUM, ARNOLD S. (1968). *Control in Organizations*. New York: McGraw-Hill.

TANNENBAUM, ARNOLD S., BOGDAN KAVCIC, MENACHEM ROSNER, MINO VIANELLO, and GEORG WIESER (1974). *Hierarchy in Organizations*. San Francisco: Jossey-Bass.

TAUSKY, CURT (1970). *Work Organizations: Major Theoretical Perspectives*. Itasca, Ill.: F. E. Peacock.

TAYLOR, DONALD W. (1965). "Decision Making and Problem Solving," in *Handbook of Organizations*, pp. 48–86, ed. James G. March. Chicago: Rand McNally.

TAYLOR, FREDERICK W. (1911). *The Principles of Scientific Management*. New York: Harper.

——— (1947). *Scientific Management*. New York: Harper & Brothers.

TERREBERRY, SHIRLEY (1968). "The Evolution of Organizational Environments," *Administrative Science Quarterly*, 12 (March), 590–613.

TERRIEN, FRED W., and DONALD L. MILLS (1955). "The Effect of Changing Size upon the Internal Structure of Organizations," *American Sociological Review*, 29 (February), 11–13.

THIBAUT, JOHN W., and HAROLD H. KELLEY (1959). *The Social Psychology of Groups*. New York: John Wiley.

THOMAS, GEORGE M., and JOHN W. MEYER (1984). "The Expansion of the State," *Annual Review of Sociology*, 10, 461–82.

THOMPSON, JAMES D. (1967). *Organizations in Action*. New York: McGraw-Hill.

THOMPSON, JAMES D., and FREDERICK L. BATES (1957). "Technology, Organization, and Administration," *Administrative Science Quarterly*, 2 (December), 325–42.

THOMPSON, JAMES D., and ARTHUR TUDEN (1959). "Strategies, Structures, and Processes of Organizational Decision," in *Comparative Studies in Administration*, pp. 195–216, ed. James D. Thompson et al. Pittsburgh: University of Pittsburgh Press.

THOMPSON, VICTOR A. (1961). *Modern Organization*. New York: Knopf.

TILLY, CHARLES (1978). *From Mobilization to Revolution*. Reading, Mass.: Addison-Wesley.

——— (1981). *As Sociology Meets History*. New York: Academic Press.

TOFFLER, ALVIN (1970). *Future Shock*. New York: Random House.

——— (1980). *The Third Wave*. New York: Morrow.

TOLBERT, CHARLES M., PATRICK M HORAN, and E. M. BECK (1980). "The Structure of Economic Segmentation: A Dual Economy Approach," *American Journal of Sociology*, 85 (March), 1095–116.

TOLBERT, PAMELA S. (1985). "Institutional Environments and Resource Dependence: Sources of Administrative Structure in Institutions of Higher Education," *Administrative Science Quarterly*, 30 (March), 1–13.

TOLBERT, PAMELA S., and LYNNE G. ZUCKER (1983). "Institutional Sources of Change in the Formal Structure of Organizations: The Diffusion of Civil Service Reform, 1880–1935," *Administrative Science Quarterly*, 28 (March), 22–39.

TOUT, T. F. (1916). *The English Civil Service in the Fourteenth Century*. Manchester, England: University Press.

TRIST, ERIC L. (1981). "The Evolution of Sociotechnical Systems as a Conceptual Framework and as an Action Research Program," in *Perspectives on Organization Design and Behavior*, pp. 19–75, ed. Andrew H. Van de Ven and William F. Joyce. New York: John Wiley, Wiley-Interscience.

TRIST, ERIC L., and K. W. BAMFORTH (1951). "Social and Psychological Consequences of the Longwall Method of Coal-Getting," *Human Relations*, 4 (February), 3–28.

TROW, D. B. (1957). "Autonomy and Job Satisfaction in Task-Oriented Groups," *Journal of Abnormal and Social Psychology*, 54, 204–9.

TSURUMI, Y. (1977). *Multinational Management*. Cambridge, Mass.: Ballinger.

TURK, HERMAN (1970). "Interorganizational Networks in Urban Society: Initial Perspectives and Comparative Research," *American Sociological Review*, 35 (February), 1–19.

——— (1977). *Organizations in Modern Life*. San Francisco: Jossey-Bass.

TURNER, ARTHUR N., and PAUL R. LAWRENCE (1965). *Industrial Jobs and the Worker*. Boston: Harvard Graduate School of Business Administration.

TUSHMAN, MICHAEL L. (1979). "Work Characteristics and Subunit Communication Structure: A Contingency Analysis," *Administrative Science Quarterly*, 24 (March), 82–97.
TVERSKY, AMOS, and DANIEL KAHNEMAN (1974). "Judgment under Uncertainty: Heuristics and Biases," *Science*, 185, (September), 1124–31.

UDY, STANLEY H., JR. (1959a). " 'Bureaucracy' and 'rationality' in Weber's Organization Theory," *American Sociological Review*, 24 (December), 791–95.
────── (1959b). *Organization of Work*. New Haven: Human Relations Area Files Press.
────── (1962). "Administrative Rationality, Social Setting, and Organizational Development," *American Journal of Sociology*, 68 (November), 299–308.
────── (1970). *Work in Traditional and Modern Society*. Englewood Cliffs, N.J.: Prentice-Hall.
USEEM, MICHAEL (1980). "Corporations and the Corporate Elite," *Annual Review of Sociology*, 6, 41–77.
U.S. BUREAU OF THE CENSUS (1984). *Statistical Abstracts of the United States 1985*. Washington, D.C.: Government Printing Office.
U.S. DEPARTMENT OF LABOR, BUREAU OF LABOR STATISTICS (1979). *Employment and Wages, 1976*. Springfield, Va.: National Technical Information Service.
U.S. OFFICE OF THE FEDERAL REGISTER, GENERAL SERVICE ADMINISTRATION (1984/85). *The United States Government Manual*. Washington, D.C.: Government Printing Office.

VAN DE VEN, ANDREW H., and ANDRE DELBECQ (1974). "A Task Contingent Model of Work-Unit Structure," *Administrative Science Quarterly*, 19 (June), 183–97.
VAN DE VEN, ANDREW H., ANDRE L. DELBECQ, and RICHARD KOENIG, JR. (1976). "Determinants of Coordination Modes within Organizations," *American Sociological Review*, 41 (April), 322–38.
VAN DE VEN, ANDREW H., and DIANE L. FERRY (1980). *Measuring and Assessing Organizations*. New York: John Wiley, Wiley-Interscience.
VAN DORN, JACQUES (1979). "Organizations and the Social Order: A Pluralist Approach," in *Organizations Alike and Unlike*, pp. 61–75, ed. Cornelis J. Lammers and David J. Hickson. London: Routledge & Kegan Paul.
VAUPEL, JAMES W., and JOAN P. CURHAN (1969). *The Making of Multinational Enterprise*. Cambridge, Mass.: Harvard University Press.
VEBLEN, THORSTEIN (1904). *The Theory of Business Enterprise*. New York: Scribner's.
VERBA, SIDNEY (1961). *Small Groups and Political Behavior*. Princeton, N.J.: Princeton University Press.
VERBA, SIDNEY, and NORMAN H. NIE (1972). *Participation in America: Political Democracy and Social Equality*. New York: Harper & Row, Pub.
VROOM, VICTOR H. (1969). "Industrial Social Psychology," in *The Handbook of Social Psychology* (2nd ed.), vol. 5, pp. 196–268, ed. Gardner Lindzey and Elliot Aronson. Reading, Mass.: Addison-Wesley.

WALKER, CHARLES R., and ROBERT H. GUEST. (1952). *The Man on the Assembly Line*. Cambridge, Mass.: Harvard University Press.
WALKER, GORDON, and DAVID WEBER (1984). "A Transaction Cost Approach to Make-or-Buy Decisions," *Administrative Science Quarterly*, 29 (September), 373–91.
WALLACE, WALTER L. (1975). "Structure and Action in the Theories of Coleman and Parsons," in *Approaches to the Study of Social Structure*, pp. 121–34, ed. Peter M. Blau. New York: Free Press.
WALTON, RICHARD E. (1969). *Interpersonal Peacemaking: Confrontations and Third Party Consultation*. Reading: Mass.: Addison-Wesley.
WALTON, RICHARD E., and JOHN M. DUTTON (1969). "The Management of Interdepartmental Conflict: A Model and Review," *Administrative Science Quarterly*, 14 (March), 73–84.
WALTON, RICHARD E., JOHN M. DUTTON, and H. GORDON FITCH (1966). "A Study of Conflict in the Process, Structure, and Attitudes of Lateral Relationships," in *Some Theories of Organization* (rev. ed.), pp. 444–65, ed. Chadwick J. Haberstroh and Albert H. Rubenstein. Homewood, Ill.: Richard D. Irwin; Dorsey.
WAMSLEY, GARY L., and MAYER N. ZALD (1973). *The Political Economy of Public Organizations*. Lexington, Mass.: Heath.
WARD, JOHN WILLIAM (1964). "The Ideal of Individualism and the Reality of Organization," in *The Business Establishment*, pp. 37–76, ed. Earl F. Cheit. New York: John Wiley.
WARNER, W. LLOYD, and J. O. LOW (1947). *The Social System of the Modern Factory*. New Haven: Yale University Press.
WARREN, ROLAND L. (1963). *The Community in America*. Chicago: Rand McNally (rev. ed., 1972).
────── (1967). "The Interorganizational Field as a Focus for Investigation," *Administrative Science Quarterly*, 12 (December), 396–419.
WEBER, MAX (1946 trans.). *From Max Weber: Essays in Sociology*, ed. Hans H. Gerth and C. Wright Mills. New York: Oxford University Press. (first published in 1906–24).
────── (1947 trans.). *The Theory of Social and Economic Organization*, ed. A. H. Henderson and Talcott Parsons, Glencoe, Ill.: Free Press (first published in 1924).
────── (1958 trans.). *The Protestant Ethic and the Spirit of Capitalism*. trans. Talcott Parsons. New York: Scribner's (first published in 1904–5).
WEICK, KARL E. (1969). *The Social Psychology of Organizing*. Reading, Mass.: Addison-Wesley (2nd ed., 1979).
────── (1974). "Middle Range Theories of Social Systems," *Behavioral Science*, 19 (November), 357–67.

—— (1976). "Educational Organizations as Loosely Coupled Systems," *Administrative Science Quarterly,* 21 (March), 1–19.

—— (1977). "Re-Punctuating the Problem," in *New Perspectives on Organizational Effectiveness,* pp. 193–225, ed. Paul S. Goodman and Johannes M. Pennings. San Francisco: Jossey-Bass.

WEISS, CAROL H. (1972). *Evaluation Research.* Englewood Cliffs, N.J.: Prentice-Hall.

WEISS, CAROL H., and ALLEN H. BARTON, eds. (1980). *Making Bureaucracies Work.* Beverly Hills, Calif.: Sage Publications, Inc.

WHISLER, THOMAS (1970). *The Impact of Computers on Organizations.* New York: Praeger.

WHITE, HARRISON C., SCOTT A. BOORMAN, and RONALD L. BREIGER (1976). "Social Structure from Multiple Networks: 1. Blockmodels of Roles and Positions," *American Journal of Sociology,* 81 (January) 730–80.

WHITE, RALPH, and RONALD LIPPITT (1953). "Leader Behavior and Member Reaction in Three 'Social Climates,' " in *Group Dynamics,* pp. 586–611, ed. Dorwin Cartwright and Alvin Zander. Evanston, Ill.: Row, Peterson.

WHITEHEAD, ALFRED NORTH (1929). *The Aims of Education.* New York: Macmillan.

WHYTE, MARTIN KING (1973). "Bureaucracy and Modernization in China: The Maoist Critique," *American Sociological Review,* 38 (April), 149–63.

WHYTE, WILLIAM FOOTE, ed. (1946). *Industry and Society.* New York: McGraw-Hill.

—— (1948). *Human Relations in the Restaurant Industry.* New York: McGraw-Hill.

—— (1951). "Small Groups and Large Organizations," in *Social Psychology at the Crossroads,* pp. 297–312, ed. John H. Rohrer and Muzafer Sherif. New York: Harper.

—— (1959). *Man and Organization.* Homewood, Ill.: Richard D. Irwin.

WHYTE, WILLIAM FOOTE, et al. (1955). *Money and Motivation: An Analysis of Incentives in Industry.* New York: Harper.

WHYTE, WILLIAM H., JR. (1956). *The Organization Man.* New York: Simon & Schuster.

WIELAND, GEORGE F., and ROBERT A. ULLRICH (1976). *Organizations: Behavior, Design, and Change.* Homewood, Ill.: Richard D. Irwin.

WIENER, NORBERT (1956). *I Am a Mathematician.* New York: Doubleday.

WILDAVSKY, AARON B. (1959). "A Methodological Critique of Duverger's *Political Parties," Journal of Politics,* 21, 303–18.

—— (1979). *Speaking Truth to Power: The Art and Craft of Policy Analysis.* Boston: Little, Brown.

WILLIAMS, LAWRENCE K., WILLIAM F. WHYTE, and CHARLES S. GREEN (1966). "Do Cultural Differences Affect Workers' Attitudes?" *Industrial Relations,* 5 (May), 105–17.

WILLIAMSON, OLIVER E. (1975) *Markets and Hierarchies: Analysis and Antitrust Implications.* New York: Free Press.

—— (1981). "The Economics of Organization: The Transaction Cost Approach," *American Journal of Sociology,* 87 (November) 548–77.

—— (1985). *The Economic Institutions of Capitalism.* New York. Free Press.

WILLIAMSON, OLIVER E., and WILLIAM G. OUCHI (1981). "The Markets and Hierarchies and Visible Hand Perspectives," in *Perspectives on Organization Design and Behavior,* pp. 347–70, ed. Andrew H. Van de Ven and William F. Joyce. New York: John Wiley.

WILSON, JAMES Q. (1962). *The Amateur Democrat.* Chicago: University of Chicago Press.

—— (1973). *Political Organizations.* New York: Basic Books.

—— (1978). *The Investigators: Managing FBI and Narcotics Agents.* New York: Basic Books.

——, ed. (1980). *The Politics of Regulation.* New York: Basic Books.

WOLFE, ALAN (1977). *The Limits of Legitimacy: Political Contradictions of Contemporary Capitalism.* New York: Free Press.

WOLIN, SHELDON S. (1960). *Politics and Vision: Continuity and Innovation in Western Political Thought.* Boston: Little, Brown.

WOODWARD, JOAN (1958). *Management and Technology.* London: H. M. S. O.

—— (1965). *Industrial Organization: Theory and Practice.* New York: Oxford University Press.

——, ed. (1970). *Industrial Organization: Behaviour and Control.* London: Oxford University Press.

WUTHNOW, ROBERT, JAMES DAVISON HUNTER, ALBERT BERGESEN, and EDITH KURZWEIL (1984). *Cultural Analysis.* Boston: Routledge & Kegan Paul.

YUCHTMAN, EPHRAIM, and STANLEY E. SEASHORE (1967). "A System Resource Approach to Organizational Effectiveness," *American Sociological Review,* 32 (December), 891–903.

ZALD, MAYER N (1970). "Political Economy: A Framework for Comparative Analysis," in *Power in Organizations,* pp. 221–61, ed. Mayer N. Zald. Nashville: Vanderbilt University Press.

ZALD, MAYER N., and ROBERTA ASH (1966). "Social Movement Organizations: Growth, Decay and Change," *Social Forces,* 44 (March), 327–40.

ZALD, MAYER N., and PATRICIA DENTON (1963). "From Evangelism to General Service: The Transformation of the YMCA," *Administrative Science Quarterly,* 8 (September), 214–34.

ZAMMUTO, RAYMOND F. (1982). *Assessing Organizational Effectiveness.* Albany: State University of New York Press.

ZEITLIN, MAURICE (1974). "Corporate Ownership and Control: The Large Corporation and the Capitalist Class," *American Journal of Sociology,* 79 (March), 1073–119.

ZELDITCH, MORRIS, JR. (1969). "Can You Really Study an Army in the Laboratory?" in *A Sociological*

Reader on Complex Organizations (2nd ed.), pp. 528–39, ed. Amitai Etzioni. New York: Holt, Rinehart & Winston.

ZELDITCH, MORRIS, JR., and HENRY A. WALKER (1984). "Legitimacy and the Stability of Authority," in *Advance in Group Processes: Theory and Research,* vol. 1, pp. 1–25, ed. Edward J. Lawler. Greenwich, Conn.: JAI Press.

ZEY-FERRELL, MARY, and MICHAEL AIKEN, eds. (1981). *Complex Organizations: Critical Perspectives.* Glenview, Ill.: Scott, Foresman.

ZIMBALIST, ANDREW, ed. (1979). *Case Studies in the Labor Process.* New York: Monthly Review Press.

ZIMMERMAN, DON H. (1970). "The Practialities of Rule Use," in *Understanding Everyday Life,* ed. J. D. Douglas. Chicago: Aldine.

ZIMMERMAN, DON H., and D. WIEDER (1970). "Ethnomethodology and the Problem of Order," in *Understanding Everyday Life,* pp. 287–95, ed. J. D. Douglas. Chicago: Aldine.

ZUCKER, LYNNE G. (1977). "The Role of Institutionalization in Cultural Persistance," *American Sociological Review,* 42 (October), 726–43.

—— (1983). "Organizations as Institutions," in *Research in the Sociology of Organizations,* vol. 2, pp. 1–47, ed. Samuel B. Bacharach. Greenwich, Conn.: JAI Press.

ZUCKER, LYNNE G., and CAROLYN ROSENSTEIN (1981). "Taxonomies of Institutional Structure: Dual Economy Reconsidered," *American Sociological Review,* 46 (December), 869–84.

Acknowledgments, continued

Fig. 7–1. Adapted from Oliver E. Williamson, *Markets and Hierarchies: Analysis and Antitrust Implications,* p. 40. New York, The Free Press, Copyright © 1975 by The Free Press; A Division of Macmillan Publishing Co., Inc. Reprinted by permission.

Fig. 9–1. From George A. Steiner and William G. Ryan, *Industrial Project Management,* p. 10. New York, The Trustees of Columbia University of the City of New York, 1968. Reprinted by permission.

Fig. 10–1. Reprinted from Alfred D. Chandler, Jr., *Strategy and Structure,* p. 10. by permission of the MIT Press, Cambridge, Massachusetts. Copyright © 1962 by Massachusetts Institute of Technology.

Table 5–1. Adapted from W. Richard Scott, Theoretical perspectives, in Marshall W. Meyer and Associates, *Environments and Organizations,* Table 1, p. 22, San Francisco, California, Jossey-Bass, Inc. 1978. Reprinted by permission.

Table 9–1. Adaptation reproduced, with permission, from W. Richard Scott, Organizational structure. *Annual Review of Sociology,* 1 (1975): 5–6. Copyright © 1975 by Annual Reviews Inc.

p. 3. From Guy E. Swanson, The tasks of sociology, *Science* 192 (May 1976): 666. Copyright © 1976 by the American Association for the Advancement of Science. Reprinted by permission.

p. 31. From John William Ward, The ideal of individualism and the reality of organization, in Earl F. Cheit (ed.) *The Business Establishment,* p. 62. New York: John Wiley & Sons, Inc., 1964. Reprinted by permission.

p. 51. From Peter M. Blau, *Bureaucracy in Modern Society,* p. 58. New York: Random House, 1956. Copyright © 1956 by Random House, Inc. Reprinted by permission.

p. 76. From Walter Buckley, *Sociology and Modern Systems Theory,* p. 50. Englewood Cliffs, New Jersey: Prentice-Hall, Inc., 1967. Copyright © 1967 by Prentice-Hall, Inc. Reprinted by permission.

p. 93. Reprinted from *The Structure of Scientific Revolutions* by Thomas S. Kuhn, by permission of the University of Chicago Press. Copyright © 1962 by The University of Chicago. All rights reserved.

p. 143. From Arthur L. Stinchcombe, *Creating Efficient Industrial Administrations,* p. 46. New York: Academic Press, 1974. Reprinted by permission.

p. 119. From A. D. Hall and R. E. Fagen, Definition of system, *General Systems: Yearbook of the Society for the Advancement of General Systems Theory* 1 (1956): 20. Washington, D.C.: Society for General Systems Research. Reprinted by permission.

p. 170. Excerpt from The natural history of human organizations by Herbert Kaufman is reprinted from *Administration and Society* Vol. 7, No. 2 (August 1975) p. 143 by permission of the Publisher, Sage Publications, Inc.

p. 210. From Henry Mintzberg, *The Structuring of Organizations,* p. 2. Englewood Cliffs, New Jersey: Prentice-Hall, Inc., 1979. Copyright © 1979 by Prentice-Hall, Inc. Reprinted by permission.

p. 240. From Erwin Schrödinger, *What Is Life?,* p. 75. New York: Cambridge University Press, 1945. Reprinted by permission.

p. 267. From John Kenneth Galbraith, *The New Industrial State,* 2nd edition, p. 65. Boston, Massachusetts: Houghton Mifflin Company. 1971 (rev.). Copyright © 1967, 1971 by John Kenneth Galbraith. Reprinted by permission of the publisher and Andre Deutsch, Ltd., England.

p. 297. From Max Weber, *From Max Weber: Essays in Sociology,* pp. 228–229, H. H. Gerth and C. Wright Mills, eds. New York: Oxford University Press, 1946. Reprinted by permission.

p. 319. From W. Ross Ashby, Principles of the self-organizing system, in Heinz von Foerster and George W. Zopf, eds. Oxford, England, Pergammon Press, 1962. Reprinted by permission.

Quotes reprinted from *Organizations in Action* by James D. Thompson with permission of the McGraw-Hill Book Company. Copyright © 1967 by McGraw-Hill Book Company. Reprinted by permission.

name index

subject index

Professions (*cont.*)
  and organizational form, 236–38, 246–47
  power, 230, 236–38
Public organizations, 4–5, 10, 24–26, 125, 237, 306–12, 325–27
  controls over, 306–12
Public policy, 189, 310–12
  implementation, 206–7
  sectoralization, 206

Quality
  circles, 234
  micro vs. macro, 333

Rationalism, 84–85
Rationality, 5, 7, 31
  bounded, 48–49, 102–3, 150–51
  defined, 31
  functional, 31
  as ideology, 111–12
  and social involvement, 173–74
Rational-legal authority, 40–41
Rational system
  combined with closed or open system, 99–115
  criteria of effectiveness, 321
  definition of organization, 20–22
  explanation of internal labor markets, 177–80
  explanation of organizations, 147–54
  explanation of structure, 214–23, 228, 231, 259
  perspective, 29–50
  views of boundaries, 173–74
  views of goals, 268
  views of participants, 74–75
  views of power, 94–95, 285
Recruitment criteria, 173–75
Regulation, 193
Research
  action, 106, 108
  basic vs. applied, 11–12
  methods, 13
Resource dependence theory, 111, 120, 181–82, 200–203
Resources, 127–29, 159–68
  concentration, 128
  free-floating, 144–46
  initial mix, 160–61
  mobilization, 159–68
  slack, 201, 217–18
Roles. *See also,* Job
  boundary, 120, 250–52, 273–75
  conflict, 223
  defined, 15
  family and organizations, 173, 299–301
  liaison, 220, 253
  multiple, 174–75
  set, 120–21
  sex, 164–65, 180
Rules, 215

Satisfaction, 60–61, 298–301
Schedules, 215
Scientific management, 36–37, 49–50, 57, 99
Sector, societal 124
  and public services, 206–7
Selection, natural, 110, 138, 200–203
Sex roles, and mobility, 164–65, 180
Simulation, 85–86
Size, 9–10, 241–49
  and bureaucratization, 242–44
  and centralization, 243–45
  definitions, 241–42
  and differentiation, 242–43
  of dominant coalition, 272–77
  and formalization, 243–45
  measures, 241–42
  and structure, 242–49
  vs. technology, 247–49
Slack, 201, 217–18
Social Democratic Party (German), 53, 308–9
Social-psychological level of analysis, 12, 14, 70, 89, 98, 105, 322
Social structure, 15, 17, 171
  comparative analyses, 44–45, 103–4
  defined, 16
  formal vs. informal, 17, 53–56
  normative vs. behavioral, 15–17
Sociometric structure, 16, 34
Socio-technical system, 108, 232–34
Specialization. *See* Differentiation
Staff-line, 38, 44, 218–19
State. *See* Nation state, Public organizations
Stockpiling, 184
Strategic contingency, 109, 229–31, 273–75
Strategy, 138, 181–209, 276–77, 281
  bridging, 185–98
  buffering, 182–85
  and structure, 250–61
Stratification, social, 175, 180–81
  and mobility, 179–81
Structural
  equivalence, 130
  inertia, 138, 200–203
  level of analysis, 13–15, 69, 98, 107–9
Structuralist approach, 94–95
Structure. *See also,* Social structure
  attention, 134–35
  matrix, 221–23, 238
  measures, 332–35
  vs. process, 89, 91
Survival, organization, 9, 23, 51–53, 56–57, 63, 67–68, 110, 166–68
System. *See also* Open system
  complexity, 77–78, 85–86
  cooperative, 61–63
  cybernetic, 78–82, 135
  design, 85–87, 233
  general, 76–78

institutional vs. managerial vs. technical,
71
loosely coupled, 77, 81–82
mechanical vs. organic, 75
open vs. closed, 82–84, 97
organic, 234–35
social, 68–72, 75
socio-technical, 108, 232–34

Task. *See* Technology
Task environment, 127–29, 181,82
defined, 127, 181
and structure, 250–52
Task force, 220–21
Team, project, 221
Technical system (level), 71, 96–97
Technology, 18–19, 147–48, 210–39
complexity, 212–14
conceptions, 226–28
core, 94, 121, 182–83, 211
buffering, 182–85, 211
vs. periphery, 118, 210,.240
dimensions, 212–14
long-linked, 183–85
measures, 211–14
vs. size, 247–49
and structure, 103–4, 210–39, 250–52
and uncertainty, 212–14
Technostructure, 276
Tennessee Valley Authority, 66
Tokenism, 164–65
Total institution, 19, 174–77

Traditional authority, 40–42
Training, supervisory, 60
Transaction costs, 104–5, 148–51, 177–
78, 216, 257–58
Typologies, 121
authority, 40–41
decisions, 70
environments, 122–23
incentives, 161–63
interdependence, 214
organizations, 69, 161–63
systems, 77–78
technologies, 212–1?

Uncertainty
and alienation, 306
in environment, 127–28, 139–41
and overconformity, 304–6
and power, 109, 229–31, 273–77, 335–
37
of technology, 212–14, 229–30
Unions, labor, 8, 122, 158, 202, 252, 273–
74, 308–10, 313

Value premises, 46
Values, 46, 319
cultural, 131–33
and leadership, 63, 66–68
defined, 15
Vertical integration, 190–91, 254–59
Virginia Company, 176–77